BEGINNING XML

BEGINNING

XML

BEGINNING
XML

Joe Fawcett
Liam R.E. Quin
Danny Ayers

John Wiley & Sons, Inc.

Beginning XML

Published by
John Wiley & Sons, Inc.
10475 Crosspoint Boulevard
Indianapolis, IN 46256
www.wiley.com

Published simultaneously in Canada

ISBN: 978-1-118-16213-2
ISBN: 978-1-118-22612-4 (ebk)
ISBN: 978-1-118-23948-3 (ebk)
ISBN: 978-1-118-26409-6 (ebk)

Manufactured in the United States of America

10 9 8 7 6 5 4 3 2

Library of Congress Control Number: 2012937910

I'd like to dedicate this book to my parents, especially to my mother Sheila who, unfortunately, will never be able to read this. I love you both.

—Joe Fawcett

Dedicated to Yuri Rubinsky, without whom there would be no XML.

—Liam Quin

Dedicated to my mother, Mary (because this will amuse her no end).

—Danny Ayers

ABOUT THE AUTHORS

JOE FAWCETT (`http://joe.fawcett.name`) has been writing software, on and off, for forty years. He was one of the first people to be awarded the accolade of Most Valuable Professional in XML by Microsoft. Joe is head of software development for Kaplan Financial UK in London, which specializes in training people in business and accountancy and has one of the leading accountancy e-learning systems in the UK. This is the third title for Wrox that he has written in addition to the previous editions of this book.

LIAM QUIN (`http://www.holoweb.net/~liam`) is in charge of the XML work at the World Wide Web Consortium (W3C). He has been involved with markup languages and text since the early 1980s, and was involved with XML from its inception. He has a background in computer science and digital typography, and also maintains a website dedicated to the love of books and illustrations at `www.fromoldbooks.org`. He lives on an old farm near Milford, in rural Ontario, Canada.

DANNY AYERS (`http://dannyayers.com`) is an independent researcher and developer of Web technologies, primarily those related to linked data. He has been an XML enthusiast since its early days. His background is in electronic music, although this interest has taken a back seat since the inception of the Web. Offline, he's also an amateur woodcarver. Originally from the UK, he now lives in rural Tuscany with two dogs and two cats.

ABOUT THE TECHNICAL EDITOR

KAREN TEGTMEYER is an independent consultant and software developer with more than 10 years of experience. She has worked in a variety of roles, including design, development, training, and architecture. She also is an Adjunct Computer Science Instructor at Des Moines Area Community College.

CREDITS

EXECUTIVE EDITOR
Carol Long

PROJECT EDITOR
Victoria Swider

TECHNICAL EDITOR
Karen Tegtmeyer

PRODUCTION EDITOR
Kathleen Wisor

COPY EDITOR
Kim Cofer

EDITORIAL MANAGER
Mary Beth Wakefield

FREELANCER EDITORIAL MANAGER
Rosemarie Graham

ASSOCIATE DIRECTOR OF MARKETING
David Mayhew

MARKETING MANAGER
Ashley Zurcher

BUSINESS MANAGER
Amy Knies

PRODUCTION MANAGER
Tim Tate

VICE PRESIDENT AND EXECUTIVE GROUP PUBLISHER
Richard Swadley

VICE PRESIDENT AND EXECUTIVE PUBLISHER
Neil Edde

ASSOCIATE PUBLISHER
Jim Minatel

PROJECT COORDINATOR, COVER
Katie Crocker

PROOFREADERS
James Saturnio, Word One
Sara Eddleman-Clute, Word One

INDEXER
Johnna VanHoose Dinse

COVER DESIGNER
Ryan Sneed

COVER IMAGE
© Marcello Bortolino

ACKNOWLEDGMENTS

I'D LIKE TO HEARTILY ACKNOWLEDGE the help of the editor Victoria Swider and the acquisitions editor Carol Long, who kept the project going when it looked as if it would never get finished. I'd like to thank the authors of the previous edition, especially Jeff Rafter and David Hunter, who let us build on their work when necessary. I'd also like to thank my wife Gillian and my children Persephone and Xavier for putting up with my absences and ill humor over the last year; I'll make it up to you, I promise.

—Joe Fawcett

THANKS are due to my partner and to the pets for tolerating long and erratic hours, and of course to Alexander Chalmers, for creating the Dictionary of Biography in 1810.

—Liam Quin

MANY THANKS to Victoria, Carol, and the team for making everything work. Thanks too to Joe for providing the momentum behind this project and to Liam for keeping it going.

—Danny Ayers

CONTENTS

PART II: VALIDATION

PART IV: DATABASES

INTRODUCTION

THIS IS THE FIFTH EDITION OF A BOOK that has proven popular with professional developers and academic institutions. It strives to impart knowledge on a subject that at first was seen by some as just another fad, but that instead has come to maturity and is now often just taken for granted. Almost six years have passed since the previous edition — a veritable lifetime in IT terms. In reviewing the fourth edition for what should be kept, what should be updated, and what new material was needed, the current authors found that about three-quarters of the material was substantially out of date. XML has far more uses than five years ago, and there is also much more reliance on it under the covers. It is now no longer essential to be able to handcraft esoteric configuration files to get a web service up and running. It has also been found that, in some places, XML is not always the best fit. These situations and others, along with a complete overhaul of the content, form the basis for this newer version.

So, what is XML? XML stands for eXtensible Markup Language, which is a language that can be used to describe data in a meaningful way. Virtually anywhere there is a need to store data, especially where it may need to be consumed by more than one application, XML is a good place to start. It has gained a reputation for being a candidate where interoperability is important, either between two applications in different businesses or simply those within a company. Hundreds of standardized XML formats now exist, known as *schemas*, which have been agreed on by businesses to represent different types of data, from medical records to financial transactions to GPS coordinates representing a journey.

WHO THIS BOOK IS FOR

This book aims to suit a fairly wide range of readers. Most developers have heard of XML but may have been a bit afraid of it. XML has a habit nowadays of being used behind the scenes, and it's only when things don't work as expected or when developers want to do something a little different, that users start to realize that they must *open the hood*. To those people we say: *fear no longer*. It should also suit the developer experienced in other fields who has never had a formal grounding in the subject. Finally, it can be used as reference when you need to try something out for the first time. Nearly all the technologies in the book have a Try It Out section associated with them that first gets you up and running with a simple example and then explains how to progress from there.

What you don't need for this book is any knowledge of markup languages in general. This is all covered in the first few chapters. It is expected that most of the readership will have some knowledge of and experience with web programming, but we've tried to spread our examples so that knowledge could include using the Microsoft stack, Java, or one of the other open source frameworks, such as PHP or Python.

And just in case you are worried about the *Beginning* part of the title, that's a Wrox conceit that applies more to the style of the book than to your level of experience. Many of the concepts covered, especially in later chapters, are from the real world and are far from the *Hello World* genre.

WHAT THIS BOOK COVERS

This book aims to teach you all you need to know about XML — what it is, how it works, what technologies accompany it, and how you can make it work for you, from simple data transfer to a way to provide multi-channeled content. The book sets out to answer these fundamental questions:

- What is XML?
- How do you use XML?
- How does it work?
- What can you use it for?

The basic concepts of XML have remained unchanged since their launch, but the surrounding technologies have changed dramatically. This book gives a basic overview of each technology and how it arose, but the majority of the examples use the latest version available. The examples are also drawn from more than one platform, with Java and .NET sharing most of the stage. XML products have also evolved; at one time there were many free and commercial Extensible Stylesheet Language Transformation (XSLT) processors; for example, XSLT is used to manipulate XML, changing it from one structure to another, and is covered in Chapter 8, but since version 2 appeared the number has reduced considerably as the work needed to develop and maintain the software has risen.

HOW THIS BOOK IS STRUCTURED

We've tried to arrange the subjects covered in this book to lead you along the path of novice to expert in as logical a manner as possible. The sections each cover a different area of expertise. Unless you're fairly knowledgeable about the basics, we suggest you read the introductory chapters in Part 1, although skimming through may well be enough for the savvier user. The other sections can then be read in order or can be targeted directly if they cover an area that you are particularly interested in. For example, when your boss suddenly tells you that your next release must offer an XQuery add-in, you can head straight to Chapter 9. A brief overview of the book is as follows:

- You begin by learning exactly what XML is and why people felt it was needed.
- We then take you through how to create XML and what rules need to be followed.
- Once you've mastered that, you move on to what a valid XML document is and how you can be sure that yours is one of them.
- Then you'll look at how you can manipulate XML documents to extract data and to transform them into other formats.
- Next you deal with storing XML in databases — the advantages and disadvantages and how to query them when they're there.
- You then look at other ways to extract data, especially those suitable to dealing with large documents.

- We then cover some uses of XML, how to publish data in an XML format, and how to create and consume XML-based web services. We explain how AJAX came about and how it works, alongside some alternatives to XML and when you should consider them.
- We follow up with a couple of chapters on how to use XML for web page and image display.
- Finally, there's a case study that ties a lot of the various XML-based technologies together into a real-world example.

We've tried to organize the book in a logical fashion, such that you are introduced to the basics and then led through the different technologies associated with XML. These technologies are grouped into six sections covering most of topics that you'll encounter with XML, from validation of the original data to processing, storage, and presentation.

Part I: Introduction

This is where most readers should start. The chapters in this part cover the goals of XML and the rules for constructing it. After reading this part you should understand the basic concepts and terminology. If you are already familiar with XML, you can probably just skim these chapters.

Chapter 1: What Is XML? — Chapter 1 covers the history of XML and why it is needed, as well as the basic rules for creating XML documents.

Chapter 2: Well-Formed XML — This chapter goes into more detail about what is and isn't allowed if a document is to be called XML. It also covers the modern naming system that is used to describe the different constituent parts of an XML document.

Chapter 3: XML Namespaces — Everyone's favorite, the dreaded topic of namespaces, is explained in a simple-to-understand fashion. After reading this chapter, you'll be the expert while everyone else is scratching their heads.

Part II: Validation

This part covers different techniques that help you verify that the XML you've created, or received, is in the correct format.

Chapter 4: Document Type Definitions — DTDs are the original validation mechanism for XML. This chapter shows how they are used to both constrain the document and to supply additional content.

Chapter 5: XML Schemas — XML Schemas are the more modern way of describing an XML document's format. This chapter examines how they work and discusses the advantages and disadvantages over DTDs.

Chapter 6: RELAX NG and Schematron — Sometimes neither DTDs nor schemas provide what you need. This chapter discusses two other methods by which you can check if your XML is valid, and also includes examples of mixing more than one validation technique.

Part III: Processing

This section covers retrieving data from an XML document and also transforming one format of XML to another. Included is a thorough grounding in XPath, one of the cornerstones of many XML technologies.

> **Chapter 7: Extracting Data from XML** — This chapter covers the document object model (DOM), one of the earliest ways devised to extract data from XML. It then goes on to describe XPath, one of the cornerstone XML technologies that can be used to pinpoint one or many items of interest.
>
> **Chapter 8: XSLT** — XSLT is a way to transform XML from one format to another, which is essential if you are receiving documents from external sources and need your own systems to be able to read them. It covers the basics of version 1, the more advanced features of the current version, and shows a little of what's scheduled in the next release.

Part IV: Databases

For many years there has been a disparity between data held in a database and that stored as XML. This part brings the two together and shows how you can have the best of both worlds.

> **Chapter 9: XQuery** — XQuery is a mechanism designed to query existing documents and create new XML documents. It works especially well with XML data that is stored in databases, and this chapter shows how that's done.
>
> **Chapter 10: XML and Databases** — Many database systems now have functionality designed especially for XML. This chapter examines three such products and shows how you can both query and update existing data as well as create new XML, should the need arise.

Part V: Programming

This part looks at two programming techniques for handling XML. Chapter 11 covers dealing with large documents, and Chapter 12 shows how Microsoft's latest universal data access strategy, LINQ, can be used with XML.

> **Chapter 11: Event-Driven Programming** — This chapter looks at two different ways of handling XML that are especially suited to processing large files. One is based on an open source API and the examples are implemented in Java. The second is a key part of Microsoft's .NET Framework and shows examples in C#.
>
> **Chapter 12: LINQ to XML** — This chapter shows Microsoft's latest way of handling XML, from creation to querying and transformation. It contains a host of examples that use both C# and VB.NET, which, for once, currently has more features than its .NET cousin.

Part VI: Communication

This part has five chapters that deal with using XML as a means of communication. It covers presenting data in a way that many different systems can utilize and then shows how web services can make data available to a variety of different clients. It concludes with a discussion on how complex data can be described in a standard way that's accessible to all.

Chapter 13: RSS, Atom, and Content Syndication — This chapter covers the two main ways in which content, such as news feeds, is presented in a platform-independent fashion. It also covers how the same XML format can be used to present structured data such as customer listings or sales results.

Chapter 14: Web Services — One of the biggest software success stories over the past ten years has been web services. This chapter examines how they work and where XML fits into the picture, which is essential knowledge, should things start to go wrong.

Chapter 15: SOAP and WSDL — This chapter burrows down further into web services and describes two major systems used within them: SOAP, which dictates how services are called, and Web Services Description Language (WSDL), which is used to describe what a web service has to offer.

Chapter 16: AJAX — The final chapter in this section deals with AJAX and how it can help your website provide up-to-the-minute information, yet remain responsive and use less bandwidth. Obviously XML is involved, but the chapter also examines the situations when you'd want to abandon XML and use an alternative technology.

Part VII: Display

This part shows two ways in which XML can help display information in a user-friendly form as well as in a format that can be read by a machine.

Chapter 17: XHTML and HTML 5 — This chapter covers how and where to use XHTML and why it is preferred over traditional HTML. It then goes on to show the newer features of HTML 5 and how it has removed some of these obstacles.

Chapter 18: Scalable Vector Graphics (SVG) — This chapter shows how images can be stored in an XML format and what the advantages are to this method. It then shows how this format can be combined with others, such as HTML, and why you would do this.

Part VIII: Case Study

This part contains a case study that ties in the many uses of XML and shows how they would interact in a real-world example.

Chapter 19: Case Study: XML in Publishing — The case study shows how a fictional publishing house goes from proprietary-based publishing software to an XML-based workflow and what benefits this brings to the business.

Appendices

The three appendices contain reference material and solutions to the end-of-chapter exercises.

Appendix A: Answers to Exercises — This appendix contains solutions and suggestions for the end-of-chapter exercises that have appeared throughout the book.

Appendix B: XPath Functions — This appendix contains information on the majority of XPath functions, their signatures, return values, and examples of how and where you would use them.

Appendix C: XML Schema Data Types — This appendix contains information on the numerous built-in data types defined by XML Schema. It shows how they are related and also how they can be constrained by different facets.

WHAT YOU NEED TO USE THIS BOOK

There's no need to purchase anything to run the examples in this book; all the examples can be written with and run on freely available software. You'll need a machine with a standard browser — Internet Explorer, Firefox, Chrome, or Safari should do as long it's one of the more recent editions. You'll need a basic text editor, but even Notepad will do if you want to create the examples rather than just download them from the Wrox site. You'll also need to run a web server for some of the code, either the free version of IIS for Windows or one of the many open source implementations such as Apache for other systems will do. For some of the coding examples you'll need Visual Studio. You can either use a commercial version or the free one available for download from Microsoft.

If you want to use the free version, Visual Studio Express 2010, then head to `www.microsoft.com/visualstudio/en-us/products/2010-editions/express`. Each edition of Visual Studio concentrates on a specific area such as C# or web development, so to try all the examples you'll need to download the C# edition, the VB.NET edition, and the Web edition. You should also install service pack 1 for Visual Studio 2010 which can be found at `www.microsoft.com/download/en/details.aspx?id=23691`. Once everything is installed you'll be able to open the sample solutions or, failing that, one of the sample projects within the solutions by Choosing File ➪ Open ➪ Project/Solution . . . and browsing to either the solution file or the specific project you want to run. As this book went to press Microsoft was preparing to release a new version, Visual Studio 2011. The examples in this book should all work with this newer version although the screenshots may differ slightly.

CONVENTIONS

To help you get the most from the text and keep track of what's happening, we've used a number of conventions throughout the book.

TRY IT OUT

The Try It Out is an exercise you should work through, following the text in the book.

1. They usually consist of a set of steps.
2. Each step has a number.
3. Follow the steps through with your copy of the database.

How It Works

After each Try It Out, the code you've typed will be explained in detail.

WARNING *Boxes with a warning icon like this one hold important, not-to-be forgotten information that is directly relevant to the surrounding text.*

NOTE *The pencil icon indicates notes, tips, hints, tricks, and asides to the current discussion.*

As for styles in the text:

- We *highlight* new terms and important words when we introduce them.
- We show keyboard strokes like this: Ctrl+A.
- We show filenames, URLs, and code within the text like so: `persistence.properties`.
- We present code in two different ways:

```
We use a monofont type with no highlighting for most code examples.
```

```
We use bold to emphasize code that's particularly important in the present context.
```

SOURCE CODE

As you work through the examples in this book, you may choose either to type in all the code manually, or to use the source code files that accompany the book. All the source code used in this book is available for download at `www.wrox.com`. When at the site, simply locate the book's title (use the Search box or one of the title lists) and click the Download Code link on the book's detail page to obtain all the source code for the book. Code that is included on the website is highlighted by the following icon:

Available for download on Wrox.com

Listings include the filename in the title. If it is just a code snippet, you'll find the filename in a code note such as this:

filename

NOTE *Because many books have similar titles, you may find it easiest to search by ISBN; this book's ISBN is 978-1-118-16213-2.*

Once you download the code, just decompress it with your favorite compression tool. Alternately, you can go to the main Wrox code download page at `www.wrox.com/dynamic/books/download.aspx` to see the code available for this book and all other Wrox books.

ERRATA

We make every effort to ensure that there are no errors in the text or in the code. However, no one is perfect, and mistakes do occur. If you find an error in one of our books, like a spelling mistake or faulty piece of code, we would be very grateful for your feedback. By sending in errata you may save another reader hours of frustration and at the same time you will be helping us provide even higher quality information.

To find the errata page for this book, go to `www.wrox.com` and locate the title using the Search box or one of the title lists. Then, on the book details page, click the Book Errata link. On this page you can view all errata that has been submitted for this book and posted by Wrox editors. A complete book list including links to each book's errata is also available at `www.wrox.com/misc-pages/booklist.shtml`.

If you don't spot "your" error on the Book Errata page, go to `www.wrox.com/contact/techsupport.shtml` and complete the form there to send us the error you have found. We'll check the information and, if appropriate, post a message to the book's errata page and fix the problem in subsequent editions of the book.

P2P.WROX.COM

For author and peer discussion, join the P2P forums at `p2p.wrox.com`. The forums are a web-based system for you to post messages relating to Wrox books and related technologies and interact with other readers and technology users. The forums offer a subscription feature to e-mail you topics of interest of your choosing when new posts are made to the forums. Wrox authors, editors, other industry experts, and your fellow readers are present on these forums.

At `http://p2p.wrox.com`, you will find a number of different forums that will help you not only as you read this book, but also as you develop your own applications. To join the forums, just follow these steps:

1. Go to `p2p.wrox.com` and click the Register link.
2. Read the terms of use and click Agree.
3. Complete the required information to join as well as any optional information you wish to provide and click Submit.
4. You will receive an e-mail with information describing how to verify your account and complete the joining process.

> ***NOTE*** *You can read messages in the forums without joining P2P but in order to post your own messages, you must join.*

Once you join, you can post new messages and respond to messages other users post. You can read messages at any time on the web. If you would like to have new messages from a particular forum e-mailed to you, click the Subscribe to this Forum icon by the forum name in the forum listing.

For more information about how to use the Wrox P2P, be sure to read the P2P FAQs for answers to questions about how the forum software works as well as many common questions specific to P2P and Wrox books. To read the FAQs, click the FAQ link on any P2P page.

PART I
Introducing XML

1

What Is XML?

WHAT YOU'LL WILL LEARN IN THIS CHAPTER:

- The story before XML
- How XML arrived
- The basic format of an XML document
- Areas where XML is useful
- A brief introduction to the technologies surrounding, and associated with, XML

XML stands for *Extensible Markup Language* (presumably the original authors thought that sounded more exciting than *EML*) and its development and usage have followed a common path in the software and IT world. It started out more than ten years ago and was originally used by very few; later it caught the public eye and began to pervade the world of data exchange. Subsequently, the tools available to process and manage XML became more sophisticated, to such an extent that many people began to use it without being really aware of its existence. Lately there has been a bit of a backlash in certain quarters over its perceived failings and weak points, which has led to various proposed alternatives and improvements. Nevertheless, XML now has a permanent place in IT systems and it's hard to imagine any non-trivial application that doesn't use XML for either its configuration or data to some degree. For this reason it's essential that modern software developers have a thorough understanding of its principles, what it is capable of, and how to use it to their best advantage. This book can give the reader all those things.

NOTE *Although this chapter presents some short examples of XML, you aren't expected to understand all that's going on just yet. The idea is simply to introduce the important concepts behind the language so that throughout the book you can see not only how to use XML, but also why it works the way it does.*

STEPS LEADING UP TO XML: DATA REPRESENTATION AND MARKUPS

There are two main uses for XML: One is a way to represent low-level data, for example configuration files. The second is a way to add metadata to documents; for example, you may want to stress a particular sentence in a report by putting it in *italics* or **bold**.

The first usage for XML is meant as a replacement for the more traditional ways this has been done before, usually by means of lists of name/value pairs as is seen in Windows' *INI* or Java's *Property* files. The second application of XML is similar to how HTML files work. The document text is contained in an overall container, the `<body>` element, with individual phrases surrounded by `<i>` or `<b>` tags. For both of these scenarios there has been a multiplicity of techniques devised over the years. The problem with these disparate approaches has been more apparent than ever, since the increased use of the Internet and extensive existence of distributed applications, particularly those that rely on components designed and managed by different parties. That problem is one of intercommunication. It's certainly possible to design a distributed system that has two components, one outputting data using a Windows INI file and the other which turns it into a Java Properties format. Unfortunately, it means a lot of development on both sides, which shouldn't really be necessary and detracts resources from the main objective, developing new functionality that delivers business value.

XML was conceived as a solution to this kind of problem; it is meant to make passing data between different components much easier and relieve the need to continually worry about different formats of input and output, freeing up developers to concentrate on the more important aspects of coding such as the business logic. XML is also seen as a solution to the question of whether files should be easily readable by software or by humans; XML's aim is to be both. You'll be examining the distinction between data-oriented and document-centric XML later in the book, but for now let's look a bit more deeply into what the choices were before XML when there was need to store or communicate data in an electronic format.

This section takes a mid-level look at data representation, without taking too much time to explain low-level details such as memory addresses and the like. For the purposes here you can store data in files two ways: as binary or as text.

Binary Files

A *binary file*, at its simplest, is just a stream of *bits* (1s and 0s). It's up to the application that created the binary file to understand what all of the bits mean. That's why binary files can only be read and produced by certain computer programs, which have been specifically written to understand them.

For example, when saving a document in Microsoft Word, using a version before 2003, the file created (which has a *doc* extension) is in a binary format. If you open the file in a text editor such as Notepad, you won't be able to see a picture of the original Word document; the best you'll be able to see is the occasional line of text surrounded by gibberish rather than the prose, which could be in a number of formats such as bold or italic. The characters in the document other than the actual text are metadata, literally information about information. Mixing data and metadata is both common and straightforward in a binary file. Metadata can specify things such as which words should be shown in bold, what text is to be displayed in a table, and so on. To interpret this file you the need the help of the application that created it. Without the help of a converter that has in-depth knowledge of the underlying binary format, you won't be able to open a document created in Word with another similar application such as WordPerfect. The main advantage of binary formats is that they are concise and can be expressed in a relatively small space. This means that more files can be stored (on a hard drive, for example) but, more importantly nowadays, less bandwidth is used when transporting these files across networks.

Text Files

The main difference between text and binary files is that text files are human and machine readable. Instead of a proprietary format that needs a specific application to decipher it, the data is such that each group of bits represents a character from a known set. This means that many different applications can read text files. On a standard Windows machine you have a choice of Notepad, WordPad, and others, including being able to use command-line–based utilities such as Edit. Non-Windows machines have a similar wide range insert of programs available, such as Emacs and Vim.

NOTE *The way that characters are represented by the underlying data stream is referred to as a file's* encoding. *The specific encoding used is often present as the first few bytes in the file; an application checks these bytes upon opening the file and then knows how to display and manipulate the data. There is also a default encoding if these first few bytes are not present. XML also has other ways of specifying how a file was encoded, and you'll see these later on.*

The ability to be read and understood by both humans and machines is not the only advantage of text files; they are also comparatively easier to parse than binary files. The main disadvantage however, is their size. In order for text files to contain metadata (for example, a stretch of text to be marked as important), the relevant words are usually surrounded by characters denoting this extra information, which are somehow differentiated from the actual text itself. The most common examples of this can be found in HTML, where angle brackets are special symbols used to convey the meaning that anything within them refers to how the text should be treated rather than the actual data. For example, if I want mark a phrase as important I can wrap it like so:

```
<strong>returns must include the item order number</strong>
```

Another disadvantage of text files is their lack of support for metadata. If you open a Word document that contains text in an array of fonts with different styles and save it as a text file, you'll just get a plain rendition; all of the metadata has been lost. What people were looking for was some way to have the best of both worlds — a human-readable file that could also be read by a wide range of applications, and could carry metadata along with its content. This brings us to the subject of markup.

A Brief History of Markup

The advantages of text files made it the preferred choice over binary files, yet the disadvantages were still cumbersome enough that people wanted to also standardize how metadata could be added. Most agreed that markup, the act of surrounding text that conveyed information about the text, was the way forward, but even with this agreed there was still much to be decided. The main two questions were:

- How can metadata be differentiated from the basic text?
- What metadata is allowed?

For example, some documents needed the ability to mark text as bold or italic whereas others were more concerned with who the original document author was, when was it created, and who had subsequently modified it. To cope with this problem a definition called *Standard Generalized Markup Language* was released, commonly shortened to *SGML*. SGML is a step removed from defining an actual markup language, such as the Hyper Text Markup Language, or HTML. Instead it relays how markup languages are to be defined. SGML allows you to create your own markup language and then define it using a standard syntax such that any SGML-aware application can consume documents written in that language and handle them accordingly. As previously noted, the most ubiquitous example of this is HTML. HTML uses angular brackets (< and >) to separate metadata from basic text and also defines a list of what can go into these brackets, such as `em` for emphasizing text, `tr` for table, and `td` for representing tabular data.

THE BIRTH OF XML

SGML, although well thought-out and capable of defining many different types of markup, suffered from one major failing: it was very complicated. All the flexibility came at a cost, and there were still relatively few applications that could read the SGML definition of a markup language and use it to correctly process documents. The concept was correct, but it needed to be simpler. With this goal in mind, a small working group and a larger number of interested parties began working in the mid-1990s on a subset of SGML known as Extensible Markup Language (XML). The first working draft was published in 1996 and two years later the W3C published a revised version as a recommendation on February 10, 1998.

NOTE The World Wide Web Consortium (W3C) *is the main international standards organization for the World Wide Web. It has a number of working groups targeting different aspects of the Web that discuss standardization and documentation of the different technologies used on the Internet. The standards documents go through various stages such as* Working Draft *and* Candidate Recommendation *before finally becoming a* Recommendation. *This process can take many years. The reason that the final agreement is called a recommendation rather than a standard is that you are still free to ignore what it says and use your own. All web developers know the problems in developing applications that work across all browsers, and many of these problems arise because the browser vendors did not follow a W3C recommendation or they did not implement features before the recommendation was finalized. Most of the XML technologies discussed in this book have a W3C recommendation associated with them, although some don't have a full recommendation because they are still in draft form. Additionally, some XML-related standards originate from outside the W3C, such as SAX which is discussed in Chapter 11, "Event Driven Programming." and therefore they also don't have official W3C recommendations.*

XML therefore derived as a subset of SGML, whereas HTML is an application of SGML. XML doesn't dictate the overall format of a file or what metadata can be added, it just specifies a few rules. That means it retains a lot of the flexibility of SGML without most of the complexity. For example, suppose you have a standard text file containing a list of application users:

```
Joe Fawcett
Danny Ayers
Catherine Middleton
```

This file has no metadata; the only reason you know it's a list of people is your own knowledge and experience of how names are typically represented in the western world. Now look at these names as they might appear in an XML document:

```
<applicationUsers>
  <user firstName="Joe" lastName="Fawcett" />
  <user firstName="Danny" lastName="Ayers" />
  <user firstName="Catherine" lastName="Middleton" />
</applicationUsers>
```

Immediately it's more apparent what the individual pieces of data are, although an application still wouldn't know just from that file how to treat a `user` or what `firstName` means. Using the XML format rather than the plain text version, it's much easier to map these data items within the application itself so they can be handled correctly.

The two common features of virtually all XML file are called *elements* and *attributes*. In the preceding example, the elements are `applicationUsers` and `user`, and the attributes are `firstName` and `lastName`.

A big disadvantage of this metadata, however, is the consequent increase in the size of the file. The metadata adds about 130 extra characters to the file's original 43 character size, an increase of more than 300 percent. The creators of XML decided that the power of metadata warranted this increase and, indeed, one of their maxims during the design was that *terseness is not an aim*, a decision that many would later come to regret.

> **NOTE** *Later on in the book you'll see a number of ways to minimize the size of an XML file if needed. However, all these methods are, to some extent, a trade-off against readability and ease of use.*

Following is a simple exercise to demonstrate the differences in how applications handle simple text files against how XML is treated. Even though the application, in this case a browser, is told nothing in advance of opening the two files, you'll see how much more metadata is available in the XML version compared to the text one.

TRY IT OUT Opening an XML File in a Browser

This example shows the differences in how XML files can be handled compared to plain text files.

1. Create a new text file in Notepad, or an equivalent simple text editor, and paste in the list of names first shown earlier.
2. Save this file at a convenient location as `appUsers.txt`.
3. Next, open a browser and paste the path to `appUsers.txt` into the address bar. You should see something like Figure 1-1. Notice how it's just a simple list:

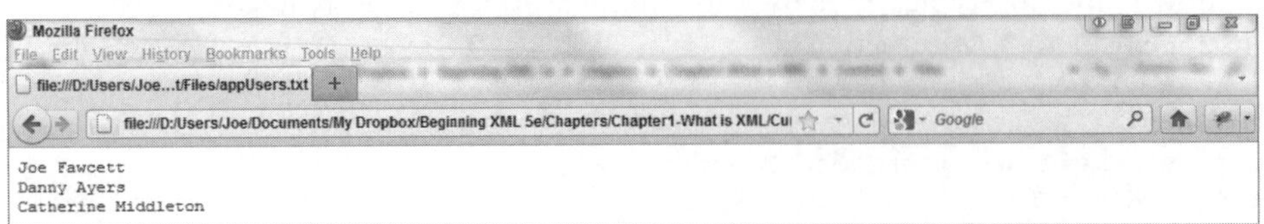

FIGURE 1-1

4. Now create another text file based on the XML version and save it as `appUsers.xml`. If you're doing this in Notepad make sure you put quotes around the full name before saving or otherwise you'll get an unwanted `.txt` extension added.
5. Open this file and you should see something like Figure 1-2.

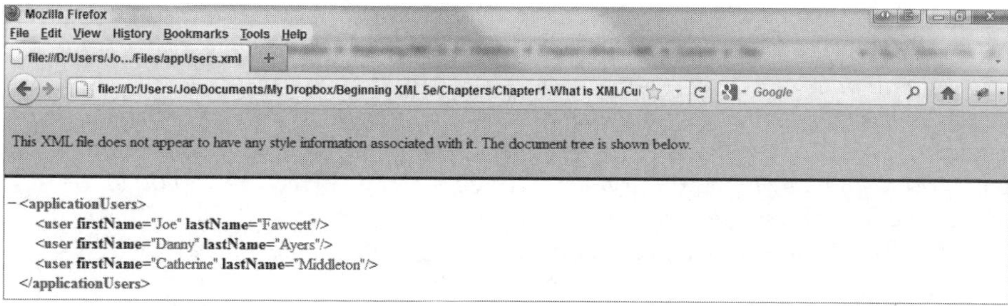

FIGURE 1-2

WARNING *If you are using Internet Explorer for this or other activities, you'll probably have to go to Tools ➪ Internet Options and choose the Advanced tab. Under the Security section, check the box in front of Allow Active Content to Run in Files on My Computer. This effectively allows script to work on local files.*

As you can see the XML file is treated very differently. The browser has shown the metadata in a different color than the base data, and also allows expansion and contraction of the `applicationUsers` section. Even though the browser has no idea that this file represents three different users, it knows that some of the content is to be handled differently from other parts and it is a relatively straightforward step to take this to the next level and start to process the file in a sensible fashion.

How It Works

Browsers use an XML stylesheet or transformation to display XML files. An XML stylesheet is a text-based file with an XML format that can transform one format into another. They are most commonly used to convert from a particular XML format to another or from XML to HTML, but they can also be used to process plain text. In this case the original XML is transformed into HTML, which permits the styling of elements to give the different colors as well as the ability to expand and contract sections using script. Transformations are covered in depth in Chapter 8, "XSLT."

NOTE *If you want to view the default style sheet that Firefox uses to display XML, type* **`chrome://global/content/xml/XMLPrettyPrint.xsl`** *into the Firefox address bar. IE has a similar built-in style sheet but it's not so easily viewable and it's written in an older, and now no longer used, version of XSLT that Microsoft brought out before the current version was standardized.*

NOTE *You'll be using a browser a few times in this chapter to view XML files. This has a number of advantages — they're easy, they give reasonable messages if the XML file has errors, and you'd be unlikely to find a machine that doesn't have one. However, for serious development they are not such a good idea, especially if you are trying to convert XML to HTML as you do in the next Try It Out. Because most browsers allow for poorly formed HTML you won't be able to see if what you've produced has errors, and you certainly won't be able to easily debug if something is wrong. For this reason we suggest you use a proper XML editor when developing. Chapter 2, "Well-Formed XML" covers a number of these.*

MORE ADVANTAGES OF XML

One of the aims of XML is to implement a clear separation between data and presentation. This means that the same underlying data can be used in multiple presentation scenarios. It also means that when moving data, across a network for example, bandwidth is not wasted by having to carry redundant information concerned only with the look and feel. This separation is simple with XML as there are no built-in presentational features such as exist in HTML, and is one of its main advantages.

XML Rules

In order to maintain this clear separation, the rules of XML have to be quite strict, but this also works to the user's advantage. For instance, in the `appUsers.xml` file you saw, values of the users' first and last names were within quotes; this is a prerequisite for XML files; therefore, the following would not be considered XML:

```
<applicationUsers>
  <user firstName=Joe lastName=Fawcett />
  <user firstName=Danny lastName=Ayers />
  <user firstName=Catherine lastName=Middleton />
</applicationUsers>
```

The need for quotes in turn makes it easy to tell when certain data is missing, for example here:

```
<applicationUsers>
  <user lastName="Fawcett" />
  <user lastName="Ayers" />
  <user lastName="Middleton" />
</applicationUsers>
```

None of the users has a first name. Now your application may find that acceptable or it may not, but either way it's easier to tell whether the file is legitimate, or *valid* as it's known in XML, when the data is in quotation marks. This means unsuitable files can be rejected at an early stage without causing application errors. Additional ways of validating XML files are covered in Part 2 of this book.

Another advantage is the easy extensibility of XML files. If you want to add more data, perhaps a middle name for example, to the application users' data, you can do that easily by creating a new attribute, middleName:

```
<applicationUsers>
  <user firstName="Joe" middleName="John" lastName="Fawcett" />
  <user firstName="Danny" middleName="John" lastName="Ayers" />
  <user firstName="Catherine" middleName="Elizabeth" lastName="Middleton" />
</applicationUsers>
```

Consider if you had an application that consumed the original version of the data, with just first name and last name stored in the file, and used it to present a list of application users on its main screen. Originally the software was designed to show just the first name and last name of each user but a new requirement demands that the middle name is displayed as well. The newer version of the XML adds the middleName attribute to satisfy this new requirement. Now the older version of the application can still consume this data and simply ignore the middle name information while the new versions can take advantage of it. This is more difficult to accomplish if the data is in the type of simple text file such as appUsers.txt:

```
Joe John Fawcett
Danny John Ayers
Catherine Elizabeth Middleton
```

If the extra data is added to the middle column, the existing application will probably misinterpret it, and even if the middle name becomes the third column it's likely to cause problems parsing the file. This occurs because there are no delimiters specifying where the individual data items begin and end, whereas with the XML version it's easy to separate the different components of a user's name.

Hierarchical Data Representation

Another area where XML-formatted data flourishes over simple text files is when representing a hierarchy; for instance a filesystem. This scenario needs a root with several folders and files; each folder then may have its own subfolders, which can also contain folders and files. This can go on indefinitely. If all you had was a text file, you could try something like this, which has a column representing the path and one to describe whether it's a folder or a file:

```
Path Type
C:\folder
C:\pagefile.sys file
C:\Program Files folder
C:\Program Files\desktop.ini file
C:\Program Files\Microsoft folder
C:\Program Files\Mozilla folder
C:\Windows folder
C:\Windows\System32 folder
```

```
C:\Temp folder
C:\Temp\~123.tmp file
C:\Temp\~345.tmp file
```

As you can see, this is not pretty and the information is hard for us humans to read and quickly assimilate. It would be quite difficult to write code that interprets this neatly. Comparatively, now look at one possible XML version of the same information:

```
<folder name="C:\">
  <folder name="Program Files">
    <folder name="Microsoft">
    </folder>
    <folder name="Mozilla">
    </folder>
  </folder>
  <folder name="Windows>
    <folder name="System32">
    </folder>
  </folder>
  <folder name="Temp">
    <files>
      <file name="~123.tmp"></file>
      <file name="~345.tmp"></file>
    </files>
  </folder>
  <files>
    <file name="pagefile.sys"></file>
  </files>
</folder>
```

This hierarchy is much easier to appreciate. There's less repetition of data and it would be fairly easy to parse.

Interoperability

The main advantage of XML is interoperability. It is much quicker to agree on or publish an XML format and use that to exchange data between different applications (with the associated metadata included in the file) than to have an arbitrary format that requires accompanying information for processing. Due to the high availability of cheap XML parsers and the pieces of software that read XML and enable interrogation of its data, anyone can now publish the format that their application deals with and others can then either consume it or recreate it. One of the best examples of this comes back to the binary files discussed at the beginning of this chapter. Before Microsoft Word 2003, Word used a binary format for its documents. However, creating an application that could read and create these files was a considerable chore and often led to converters that only partially worked. Since Word 2003, all versions of Word can save documents in an XML format with a documented structure. This has meant the ability to read these documents in other applications (OfficeLibre, for example), as well as the ability to create Word documents using even the most basic tools. It also means that corrupted documents, which would previously have been completely lost, can now often be fixed by opening them in a simple text editor and repairing them. With this and the previously discussed advantages, XML is truly the best choice.

NOTE *OfficeLibre is an open source application that mimics, to a large extent, other office work applications such as Microsoft Office. It was originally called OpenOffice but split off when OpenOffice was taken over by Oracle. You can obtain it at* `www.libreoffice.org`.

XML IN PRACTICE

Since its first appearance in the mid-'90s the actual XML specification has changed little; the main change being more freedom allowed for content. Some characters that were forbidden from earlier versions are now allowed. However, there have been many changes in how and where XML is used and a proliferation of associated technologies, most with their associated standards. There has also been a massive improvement in the tools available to manage XML in its various guises. This is especially true of the past several years, Five years ago any sort of manipulation of XML data in a browser meant reams of custom JavaScript, and even that often couldn't cope with the limited support in many browsers. Now many well-written script libraries exist that make sending, receiving, and processing XML a relatively simple process, as well as taking care of the gradually diminishing differences between the major makes of browser. Another recent change has been a more overall consensus of when *not* to use XML, although plenty of die-hards still offer it as the solution to every problem. Later chapters cover this scenario, as well as others. This section deals with some of the current uses of XML and also gives a foretaste of what is coming in the chapters ahead.

NOTE *You can find the latest W3C XML Recommendation at* `www.w3.org/TR/xml`.

NOTE *JSON stands for JavaScript Object Notation and is discussed more in Chapters 14 and 16 which relate to web services and Ajax. If you need more information in the meantime, head to* `www.json.org`.

Data Versus Document

So far the examples you've seen have concentrated on what are known as data-centric uses of XML. This is where raw data is combined with markup to help give it meaning, make it easier to use, and enable greater interoperability. There is a second major use of XML and markup in general, which is known as *document-centric*. This is where more loosely structured content (for example, a chapter from a book or a legal document) is annotated with metadata. HTML is usually considered to be a document-centric use of SGML (and XHTML, is similarly a document-oriented application of XML) because HTML is generally content that is designed to be read by humans rather than data that will be consumed by a piece of software. XML is designed to be read and understood by both humans and software but, as you will see later, the ways of processing the different styles of XML can vary considerably.

Document-centric XML is generally used to facilitate multiple publishing channels and provide ways of reusing content. This is useful for instances in which regular content changes need to be applied to multiple forms of media at once. For example, a few years ago I worked on a system that produced training materials for the financial sector. A database held a large number of articles, quizzes, and revision aids that could be collated into general training materials. These were all in an XML format very similar to XHTML, the XML version of HTML. Once an editor finalized the content in this database, it was transformed using XSLT (as described in Chapter 8) into media suitable for both the Web and a traditional printed output. When using document-centric XML in this sort of system, whenever content changes, it is only necessary to alter the underlying data for changes to be propagated to all forms of media in use. Additionally, when a different form of the content is needed, to support mobile web browsers for example, a new transformation is the only necessary action.

XML Scenarios

In addition to document-centric situations, XML is also frequently used as a means of representing and storing data. The main reasons for this use are XML's flexible nature and the relative ease with which these files can be read and edited by both humans and machines. This section presents some common, relevant scenarios in which XML is used in one way or another, along with some brief reasons why XML is appropriate for that situation.

Configuration Files

Nearly all modern configuration files use XML. Visual Studio project files and the build scripts used by Ant (a tool used to control the software build process in Java) are both examples of XML configuration files. The main reasons for using XML are that it's so much easier to parse than the traditional name/value pair style and it's easy to represent hierarchies.

Web Services

Both the more long-winded SOAP style and the usually terser RESTful web services use XML, although many now have the option to use JSON as well. XML is used both as a convenient way to serialize objects in a cross-platform manner and as a means of returning results in a universally accepted fashion. SOAP-style services (covered in depth in Chapters 15 and 16) are also described using an XML format called *WSDL*, which stands for *Web Services Description Language*. WSDL provides a complete description about a web service and its capabilities, including the format of the initial request, the ensuing response, and details of exactly how to call the service, its hostname, what port it runs on, and the format of the rest of the URL.

Web Content

Although many believe that XHTML (the XML version of HTML) has not really caught on and will be superseded by HTML 5, it's still used extensively on the Web. There's also a lot of content stored as plain XML, which is transformed either server-side or client-side when needed. The reason for storing it as XML can be content re-use as mentioned earlier, but also it can be a way to save on bandwidth and storage. Content that needs to be shown as an HTML table, for example, nearly always takes up less room as XML combined with code to transform it.

Document Management

In addition to XML being used to store the actual content that will be presented via the Web, XML is also used heavily in document-management systems to store and keep track of documents and manage metadata, usually in conjunction with a traditional relational database system. XML is used to store information such as a document's author, the date of creation, and any modifications. Keeping all this extra information together with the actual content means that everything about a document is in one place, making it easier to extract when needed as well as making sure that metadata isn't orphaned, or separated from the data it's describing.

Database Systems

Most modern high-end database systems, such as Oracle and SQL Server, can store XML documents. This is good news because many types of data don't fit nicely into the relational structure (tables and joins) that traditional databases implement. For example, a table of products may need to store some instructions that are in an XML format that will be turned into a web page or a printed manual when needed. This can't be reduced to a simpler form and only needs modifying very rarely, perhaps to insert a new section to support a different language. These modifications are easy and straightforward if the data being manipulated is stored in a database system that has a column designed specifically for XML. This XML should enable updates using the XQuery language, which is briefly covered later in this chapter. Both Oracle and SQL Server, as well as some open source applications such as MySQL, provide such a column type, designed specifically to store XML. These types have methods associated with them that allow for the extraction of particular sections of the XML or for its modification.

Image Representation

Vector images can be represented with XML, the SVG format being the most popular. The advantage of using an XML format over a traditional bitmap when portraying images is that the images can be manipulated far more easily. Scaling and other changes become transformations of the XML rather than complex intensive calculations.

Business Interoperability

Hundreds of industries now have standard XML formats to describe the different entities that are used in day-to-day transactions, which is one of the biggest uses of XML. A brief list includes:

- Medical data
- Financial transactions such as purchasing stocks and shares and exchanging currency

- Commercial and residential properties
- Legal and court records
- Mathematical and scientific formulas

XML Technologies

To enable the preceding scenarios you can use a number of associated technologies, standards, and patterns. The main ones, which are all covered throughout the book, are introduced here to give a broad overview of the world of XML.

XML Parsers

Before any work can be done with an XML document it needs to be parsed; that is, broken down into its constituent parts with some sort of internal model built up. Although XML files are simply text, it is not usually a good idea to extract information using traditional methods of string manipulation such as `Substring`, `Length`, and various uses of regular expressions. Because XML is so rich and flexible, for all but the most trivial processing, code using basic string manipulation will be unreliable.

Instead a number of XML parsers are available — some free, some as commercial products— that facilitate the breakdown and yield more reliable results. You will be using a variety of these parsers throughout this book. One of the reasons to justify using a handmade parser in the early days of XML was that pre-built ones were overkill for the job and had too large a footprint, both in actual size and in the amount of memory they used. Nowadays some very efficient and lightweight parsers are available; these mean developing your own is a waste of resources and not a task to be undertaken lightly.

Some of the more common parsers used today include the following:

- **MSXML (Microsoft Core XML Services):** This is Microsoft's standard set of XML tools including a parser. It is exposed as a number of COM objects so it can be accessed using older forms of Visual Basic (6 and below) as well as from C++ and script. The latest version is 6.0 and, as of this writing it is not being developed further, although service packs are still being released that address bugs and any other security issues. Although you probably wouldn't use this parser when writing your own application from scratch, this is the only option when you need to parse XML from within older versions of Internet Explorer (6 and below). In these browsers the MSXML parser is invoked using ActiveX technology, which can present problems in some secure environments. Fortunately versions 7 and later have a built-in parser and cross-browser libraries. Choose this one in preference if it's available.
- **System.Xml.XmlDocument:** This class is part of Microsoft's .NET library, which contains a number of different classes related to working with XML. It has all the standard *Document Object Model* (DOM, covered in the next section) features plus a few extra ones that, in theory, make life easier when reading, writing, and processing XML. However, since the world is trending away from using the DOM, Microsoft also has a number of other ways of tackling XML, which are discussed in later chapters.

- **Saxon:** Ask any group of XML cognoscenti what the leading XML product is and Saxon will likely be the majority verdict. Saxon's offerings contain tools for parsing, transforming, and querying XML, and it comes from the software house of Dr. Michael Kay, who has written a number of Wrox books on XML and related technologies. Although Saxon offers ways to interact using the document object model, it also has a number of more modern and user-friendly interfaces available. Saxon offers a version for Java and .NET; the basic edition is free to download and use.
- **Java built-in parser:** The Java library has its own parser. It has a reputation for being a bit basic but is suitable for many XML tasks such as parsing and validation of a document. The library is designed such that you can replace the built-in parser with an external implementation such as Xerces from Apache or Saxon.
- **Xerces:** Xerces is implemented in Java and is developed by the famous and open source Apache Software Foundation. It is used as the basis for many Java-based XML applications and is a more popular choice than the parser that comes with Java.

The Document Object Model

Once an XML parser has done its work, it produces an in-memory representation of the XML. This model exposes properties and methods that let you extract information from and also modify the XML. For example, you'll find methods such as `createElement` to manufacture new elements in the document and properties such as `documentElement` that bring back the root element in the document (`applicationUsers` in the example file).

One of the earliest models used was the *Document Object Model* (*DOM*). This model has an associated standard but it doesn't just apply to XML; it also works with HTML documents. At its heart, the DOM is a tree-like representation of an XML document. You can start at the tree's root and move to its different branches, extracting or inserting data as you go. Although the DOM was used for many years, it has a reputation for being a bit unwieldy and difficult to use. It also tends to take up a lot of memory. For example, opening an XML document that is 1MB on a disk can use about 5MB of RAM. This can obviously be a problem if you want to open very large documents. As a result of these problems, a number of other models have sprung up, especially because the DOM is typically only an intermediate step in processing XML; it's not a goal in itself. However, if you need to extract just a few pieces of information from XML or HTML the DOM is widely supported, especially across browsers, and is used a lot by many of the script libraries that are popular nowadays such as jQuery.

DTDs and XML Schemas

Both *document type definitions* (*DTDs*) and *XML Schemas* serve to describe the definition of an XML document, its structure, and what data is allowed where. They can then be used to test whether a document that has been received is consistent with the prescribed format, a process known as validation. DTDs are the older standard and have been around since SGML. They are gradually succumbing to XML Schemas but are still in widespread use particularly with (X)HTML. They also have a few features that XML lacks, such as the ability to create entity declarations (covered in Chapter 4, "Document Type Definitions") and the ability to add default attribute content.

In general, XML Schemas offer more functionality; they also have the advantage of being written in XML so the same tools can be used with both the data and its schema. DTDs on the other hand use a completely different format that is much harder to work with. In addition to assisting with validation, DTDs and XML Schema are also used to help authorship of XML documents. Most modern XML editors allow you to create an XML document based on a specified schema. They prompt you with valid choices from the schema as you're editing and also warn you if you've used an element or attribute in the wrong location. Although many have misgivings about how XML Schemas have developed it's probably true to say that most recently developed XML formats are described using schemas rather than DTDs.

There are also other ways of ensuring the documents you receive are in the correct format, ones that can cope with some scenarios that neither DTDs nor XML Schemas can handle. A selection of these alternatives are covered in Chapter 6, "RELAX NG and Schematron." DTDs and XML Schemas are covered in depth in Chapters 4 and 5, respectively.

NOTE *If you take a look at the source for an XHTML document you'll see the reference to the DTD at the top of the page. It will look something like this:*

```
<!DOCTYPE html PUBLIC "-//W3C//DTD XHTML 1.0 Transitional//EN"
"http://www.w3.org/TR/xhtml1/DTD/xhtml1-transitional.dtd">
```

XML Namespaces

XML Namespaces were added to the XML specification sometime after the initial recommendation. They have a reputation for being difficult to understand and also for being poorly implemented. Basically, namespaces serve as a way of grouping XML. For instance, if one or two different formats need to be used together, he element names can be grouped under a namespace; this ensures that there is no confusion about what the elements represent, especially if the authors of the different formats have chosen the same names for some of the elements. The same idea is used in software all the time; in both .NET and Java, for example, you may design a class that represents a type of XML document that you call `XmlDocument`. To prevent that class from conflicting with other classes that might exist with the same name, the class is placed in a namespace. (NET terminology) or a package (Java terminology). So your class may have a full name of `Wrox.Entities.XmlDocument`, which will differentiate it from Microsoft's `System.Xml.XmlDocument`. See Chapter 3 for the full story on namespaces.

XPath

XPath is used in many XML technologies. It enables you to target specific elements or attributes (or the other building blocks you'll meet in the next chapter). It works similar to how paths in a filesystem work, starting at the root and progressing through the various layers until the target is found. For example, with the `appUsers.xml` file, you may want to select all the users. The XPath for this would be:

```
/applicationUsers/user
```

The path starts at the root, represented by a forward slash (`/`), then selects the `applicationUsers` element, and then any `user` elements beneath there. XPaths can be very sophisticated and allow you to traverse the document in a number of different directions as well as target specific parts using predicates, which enable filtering of the results. In addition to being used in XSLT, XPath is also used in XQuery, XML Schemas, and many other XML-related technologies. XPath is dealt with in more detail in Chapter 7, "Extracting Data From XML."

XSLT

One of the main places you find XPath is XSLT. *Extensible Stylesheet Language Transformations (XSLT)* is powerful way to transform files from one format to another. Originally it could only operate on XML files, although the output could be any form of text file. Since version 2.0 however, it also has the capability to use any text file as an input. XSLT is a declarative language and uses templates to define the output that should result from processing different parts of the source files.

XSLT is often used to transform XML to (X)HTML, either server-side or in the browser. The advantages of doing a client-side transformation are that it offloads the presentational side of the process to the application layer that deals with the display. Additionally it frees resources on the server making it more responsive, and it tends to reduce the amount of data transmitted between the server and the browser. This is especially the case when the data consists of many rows of similar data that are to be shown in tabular form. HTML tables are very verbose and can easily double or triple the amount of bandwidth between client and server.

The following Try It Out shows how browsers have been specially designed to be able to accept an XML as an input and transform the data using a specified transformation. You won't be delving too deeply into the XSLT at this stage, (that's left for Chapter 8) but you'll get a good idea of how XML enables you to separate the intrinsic data being shown from the visual side of the presentation.

TRY IT OUT XSLT in the Browser

Use the `appUsers.xml` file created earlier to produce a demonstration of how a basic transformation can be achieved within a browser:

1. To start, create the following file using any text editor and save it as `appUsers.xslt` in the same folder as `appUsers.xml`:

```
<xsl:stylesheet version="1.0" xmlns:xsl="http://www.w3.org/1999/XSL/Transform">
    <xsl:template match="/">
      <html>
        <head>
          <title>Application Users</title>
        </head>
        <body>
          <table>
            <thead>
              <tr>
                <th>First Name</th>
```

```
                <th>Last Name</th>
              </tr>
            </thead>
            <tbody>
              <xsl:apply-templates select="applicationUsers/user" />
            </tbody>
          </table>
        </body>
      </html>
    </xsl:template>

  <xsl:template match="user">
    <tr>
      <td>
        <xsl:value-of select="@firstName"/>
      </td>
      <td>
        <xsl:value-of select="@lastName"/>
      </td>
    </tr>
  </xsl:template>
</xsl:stylesheet>
```

code snippet appUsers.xslt

2. Next make a small change to appUsers.xml so that, if it is opened in a browser, the browser will know to use the specified XSLT to transform the XML, rather than the built-in default transformation that was used in earlier examples. Save the modified file as appUsersWithXslt.xml.

Available for download on Wrox.com

```
<?xml-stylesheet type="text/xsl" href="appUsers.xslt" ?>
<applicationUsers>
  <user firstName="Joe" lastName="Fawcett" />
  <user firstName="Danny" lastName="Ayers" />
  <user firstName="Catherine" lastName="Middleton" />
</applicationUsers>
```

code snippet appUsersWithXslt.xml

3. Finally, open appUsersWithXslt.xml in a browser. The results will be similar to Figure 1-3.

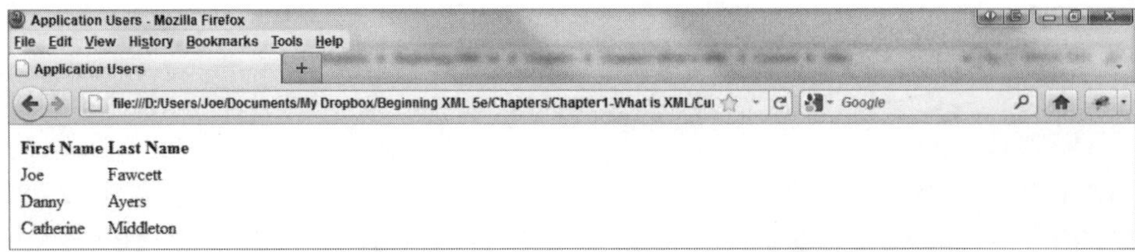

FIGURE 1-3

How It Works

When the browser sees the following line at the top of the XML:

```
<?xml-stylesheet type="text/xsl" href="appUsers.xslt" ?>
```

It knows that, instead of the default style sheet that produced the result shown in Figure 1-2, it should use `appUsers.xslt`.

`appUsers.xslt` has two `xsl:templates`. The first causes the basic structure of an HTML file to appear along with the outline of an HTML table. The second template acts on any `user` element that appears in the file and produces one row of data for each that is found. Once the transformation is complete the resultant code is treated as if it were a traditional HTML page. The actual code produced by the transformation is shown here:

```
<html>
  <head>
    <title>Application Users</title>
  </head>
  <body>
    <table>
      <thead>
        <tr>
          <th>First Name</th>
          <th>Last Name</th>
        </tr>
      </thead>
      <tbody>
        <tr>
          <td>Joe</td>
          <td>Fawcett</td>
        </tr>
        <tr>
          <td>Danny</td>
          <td>Ayers</td>
        </tr>
        <tr>
          <td>Catherine</td>
          <td>Middleton</td>
        </tr>
      </tbody>
    </table>
  </body>
</html>
```

XQuery

XQuery shares many features with XSLT and because of this, a common question on the XML development forums is, “Is this a job for XSLT or XQuery?” The answer is, “It depends.” Like XSLT, XQuery can operate against single documents, but it is also often used on large collections, especially those that are stored in a relational database. Say you want to use XQuery to process the appUsers.xml file from the previous examples and again produce an HTML page showing the users in a tabular form. The XQuery needed would look like this:

```
<html>
  <head>
    <title>Application Users</title>
  </head>
  <body>
    <table>
      <thead>
        <tr>
          <th>First Name</th>
          <th>Last Name</th>
        </tr>
      </thead>
      <tbody>
    {for $user in doc("appUsers.xml")/applicationUsers/user
    return <tr><td>{data($user/@firstName)}</td>
    <td>{data($user/@lastName)}</td></tr>}
      </tbody>
    </table>
  </body>
</html>
```

As you can see, a lot of the query mimics the XSLT used earlier. One major difference is that XQuery isn't itself an XML format. This means that it's less verbose to write, making it somewhat simpler to author than XSLT. On the other hand, being as it's not XML, it cannot be authored in standard XML editors nor processed by an XML parser, meaning it needs a specialized editor to write and custom built software to process.

NOTE *There is an XML-based version of XQuery called XQueryX. It has never gained much acceptance and nearly all examples of XQuery online use the simpler non-XML format.*

With regards to authoring XQuery, the main difference in syntax between it and XSLT is that XQuery uses braces ({}) to mark parts of the document that need processing by the engine; the rest of the document is simply output verbatim.

Therefore, in the example the actual code part is this section:

```
{for $user in doc("appUsers.xml")/applicationUsers/user
    return <tr><td>{data($user/@firstName)}</td>
    <td>{data($user/@lastName)}</td></tr>}
```

this uses the doc() function to read an external file, in this case the appUsers.xml file, and then creates one <tr> element for each user element found there. XQuery is covered in depth in Chapter 9.

There are many instances where the choice of XSLT or XQuery is simply a matter of which technology you're happier with. If you want a terser, more readable syntax or you need to process large numbers of documents, particularly those found in databases, then XQuery, with its plain text syntax and functions aimed at document collections, is probably a better choice. If you prefer an XML style syntax that can be easily read by standard XML software, or your goal is to rearrange existing XML into a different format rather than create a whole new structure, then XSLT will most likely be the better option.

XML Pipelines

XML pipelines are used when single atomic steps are insufficient to achieve the output you desire. For example, it may not be possible to design an XML transformation that copes with all the different types of documents your application accepts. You may need to perform a preliminary transform first, depending on the input, and follow with a generalized transformation. Another example might be that the initial input needs validating before being transformed. In the past, these pipelines or workflows have been created in a rather ad hoc manner. More recently, there have been calls for a recognized standard to define how pipelines are described. The W3C recommendation for these standards is called *XProc* and you can find the relevant documentation at `www.w3.org/TR/xproc`. Only a handful of implementations exist at the moment, but if you have the need for this type of workflow it's certainly worth taking a look at XProc rather than re-inventing the wheel.

SUMMARY

- The situation before XML and the problems with binary and plain text files
- How XML developed from SGML
- The basic building blocks of XML: elements and attributes
- Some of the advantages and disadvantages of XML
- The difference between data-centric and document-centric XML
- Some real-world uses of XML
- The associated technologies such as parsers, schemas, XPath, transformations with XSLT, and XQuery

The next chapter discusses the rules for constructing XML and what different constituent parts can make up a document.

EXERCISES

Answers to the exercises can be found in Appendix A.

1. Change the format of the `appUsers.xml` document to remove the attributes and use elements to store the data.

2. State the main disadvantage to having the file in the format you've just created. Bear in mind that data is often transmitted across networks rather than just being consumed where it is stored.

▶ WHAT YOU LEARNED IN THIS CHAPTER

TOPIC	KEY POINTS
Before XML	Most data formats were proprietary, capable of being read by a very small number of applications and not suitable for today's distributed systems.
XML's Goals	To make data more interchangeable, to use formats readable by both humans and machines, and to relieve developers from having to write low-level code every time they needed to read or write data.
Who's In Charge of Standardization?	No one, but many XML specifications are curated by the World Wide Web Consortium, the W3C. These documents are created after a lengthy process of design by committee followed by requests for comments from stakeholders.
Data-centric versus Document-centric	There are two main types of XML formats: those used to store pure data, such as configuration settings, and those used to add metadata to documents, for example XHTML.
What Technologies Rely On XML?	There are hundreds, but the main ones are XML Schemas, to validate that documents are in the correct format; XSLT which is mainly used to convert from one XML format to another; XQuery, which is used to query large document collections such as those held in databases; and SOAP which uses XML to represent the data that is passed to, and returned from, a web service.

2

Well-Formed XML

WHAT YOU WILL LEARN IN THIS CHAPTER:

- The meaning of well-formed XML
- The constituent parts of an XML document
- How these parts are put together

So far you've looked at the history before XML, why it came about, and some of its advantages and disadvantages. You've also taken a whirlwind tour of some of the technologies associated with XML that are featured in this book.

In this chapter you'll be examining the rules that apply to a document that decide whether or not it *is* XML. This knowledge is needed in two main situations: first, when you're designing an XML format for your own data so that you can be sure that any standard XML parser can handle your document; second, when you are designing a system that will accept XML input from an external source so you'll be sure that the data you receive is legitimate XML. There are, unfortunately, a number of systems that purport to export data as XML but break some of the rules, meaning that unless you can get the problem fixed at source, you have to resort to handling the input using non-XML tools. This makes for a lot of unnecessary development and defeats the object of having a universally recognized method of data representation.

Additionally, you'll take a look at the basic and more advanced building blocks of XML starting with the most common, *elements* and *attributes*, and see how these are used to construct a complete document. You'll also be introduced to the modern terminology that describes these constituent parts; this is one of the major changes from earlier editions of this book as great efforts have been made in the XML world to have a vocabulary that is independent of the technology used to handle XML, yet is precise and extensive enough to enable the XML standards to be clearly written and form the basis for technological development.

WHAT DOES WELL-FORMED MEAN?

To the purist there is no such thing as well-formed XML; a document is either XML and therefore, by definition, well-formed, or it's just text. But in common parlance well-formed XML means a document that follows the W3C's XML Recommendation with all its rules governing the following:

- How the content is separated from the metadata (markup)
- What is used to identify the markup
- What the constituent parts are
- In what order and where these parts can appear

VARYING XML TERMINOLOGY

One small problem that exists when talking about XML is that its constituent parts can be described in many different ways. These varying descriptions have arisen for two reasons:

- The many different technologies associated with XML each have their own jargon; only a few terms are common to all of them. For instance the Document Object Model (covered in Chapter 7) and XSLT (covered in Chapter 8) have very different vocabularies for the same concepts
- The official W3C XML recommendations were finalized long after XML had been in use. The terms used in these documents often differ from the vernacular.

This chapter tries to stick with the terminology used by the W3C in two Recommendations: the first, simply called Extensible Markup Language (`www.w3.org/TR/xml`), describes the lexical representation or, in simpler terms, how XML is created in a text editor. The second, called Infoset Recommendation (`www.w3.org/TR/xml-infoset/`), describes an idealized abstract representation of an XML document.

CREATING XML IN A TEXT EDITOR

Creating XML in a text editor, something as simple as Notepad in Windows or Vim in Linux, is the first place to start when discussing the elements of XML. Throughout the process of creating XML, you gradually build up an example document and, at each stage, identify the constituent parts and what rules need to be followed in their construction.

Forbidden Characters

The first thing to know before writing XML is that a few restrictions exist on what characters are permitted in an XML document. These rules vary slightly depending on whether you're using version 1.0 or 1.1, the latter being a bit more permissive. Both versions forbid the use of *null* in a document; this is the character represented by 0x0 in hexadecimal. In version 1.0 you are also forbidden to use the characters represented by the hexadecimal codes between 0x01 and 0x19, except for three: the tab (0x9), the newline (0xA), and the carriage return (0xD).

NOTE *These three characters, and a fourth, the standard space character (0x20), are collectively known as whitespace and have special rules governing their treatment in XML. These rules are covered later in the chapter.*

For example, you cannot use the character 0x7, known as the bell character, because it sounds a bell or a beep on some systems. In version 1.1 you can use all these control characters although their use is a little unusual. You see how to specify which version you are using in the next section. A few characters in the Unicode specification also can't be used but you're unlikely to come across these. You can find the full list in the W3C's XML Recommendation.

XML Prolog

The first part of a document is the *prolog*. It is optional so you won't see it every time, but if it does exist it must come first. The prolog begins with an XML *declaration* which, in its simplest form, looks like the following:

```
<?xml version="1.0"?>
```

This declaration contains only one piece of information, the version number, and currently this will always be either 1.0 or 1.1. Sometimes the declaration may also contain information about the encoding used in the document:

```
<?xml version="1.0" encoding="UTF-8"?>
```

Here the encoding is specified as UTF-8, a variety of Unicode.

Encoding with Unicode

Encoding is the process of turning characters into their equivalent binary representation. Some encodings use only a single byte, or eight bits; others use more. The disadvantage of using only one byte is that you are limited to how many characters can be encoded without recourse; this can go to such means as having a special sequence of bits to indicate that the next two bytes refer to one character or other similar workarounds. When an XML processor reads a document, it has to know which encoding was used; but, it's a chicken-and-egg situation — if it doesn't know the encoding how can it read what you've put in the declaration? The simple answer to this lies in the fact that the first few bytes of a file can contain a *byte order mark*, or *BOM*. This helps the parser enough to be able to read the encoding specified in the declaration. Once it knows this it can decode the rest of the document. If, for some reason, the encoding specified is not the actual encoding used you'll most likely get an error, or mistakes will be made interpreting the content. If you want to see the full workings about how encodings are decided the URL is `www.w3.org/TR/2008/REC-xml-20081126/#sec-guessing.`

Unicode is a text encoding specification designed from scratch with internationalization in mind. It tries to define every possible character by giving it a name and a *code point*, which is a number that can be used to represent it. It also assigns various categories to each character such as whether it's a letter, a numeral, or a punctuation mark. You will see how to use these code points when you look at character references later in the chapter.

Two main encoding systems use Unicode: UTF-8 and UTF-16. *UTF* stands for *UCS Transformation Format*, and *UCS* itself means *Universal Character Set*. The number refers to how many bits are used to represent a simple character, either 8 or 16 (one or two bytes, respectively). The reason UTF-8 manages with only one byte whereas UTF-16 needs two is because UTF-8 uses a single byte to represent the more commonly used characters and two or three bytes for the less common ones. UTF-16 uses two bytes for the majority of characters and three bytes for the rest. It's a bit like your keyboard — the lowercase letters and digits require only one key press but by using the Shift key you have access to the uppercase letters and other symbols. The advantage of UTF-16 is that it's easier to decode because of its fixed size of two bytes per character (very few need three); the disadvantage is that file sizes are typically larger than UTF-8 if you are only using the Latin alphabet plus the standard numerals and punctuation marks

All XML processors are mandated to understand UTF-8 and UTF-16 even if those are the only encodings they can read. UTF-8 is the default for documents without encoding information. Despite the advantages of Unicode, many documents use other encodings such as ISO-8859-1, Windows-1252, or EBCDIC (an encoding found on many mainframes). You will also come across files written using ASCII — a basic set of characters that at one time was used for almost all files created. ASCII is a subset of Unicode though so it can be read by any application that understands Unicode.

NOTE *You will often see the side effects of files being encoded in one system and then decoded using another when browsing the Web — seemingly meaningless characters appear interspersed with otherwise readable text. This is a byproduct of the files often being created on one machine, uploaded to a second, the web server, and then read by a third, the one running the browser. If the encoding is not correctly interpreted by all three machines in the chain then you'll get some characters misinterpreted. You'll notice how the gibberish characters are usually those not found in ASCII and hence have different code points in different systems.*

In practical terms the UTF-8 encoding is probably best because it has a wide range of characters and is supported by all XML parsers. UTF-8 encoding is also the default assumed if no specific encoding is declared. If you do run into the problem of creating or reading files encoded with characters UTF-8 doesn't recognize, you should still manage without many problems by just creating these character yourself. You'll learn how to do this later in the "Entity and Character References" section. Additionally, the Unicode specification grows in time as more characters are added. You can find the current version at `http://unicode.org`.

Completing the Declaration

Now that you have specified the type of encoding you are using, you can finish the declaration. The final part of the declaration is determining whether the document is considered to be *standalone*:

Available for download on Wrox.com

```
<?xml version="1.0" encoding="UTF-8" standalone="yes"?>
```

Example.xml

Standalone applies only to documents that specify a DTD and then only when that DTD is used to add or change content. `Example.xml` isn't using a DTD (remember that most modern XML formats rely on schemas instead), therefore you can set the standalone declaration to yes or leave it out altogether.

> ***NOTE*** *DTD stands for document type definition and is a way to specify the format the XML should take as well as describing any default content that should appear and how references within the XML should be interpreted. Chapter 4 is devoted to DTDs.*

If you were to ever use a DTD, an example for an XHTML document would look something like this: `<!DOCTYPE html PUBLIC "-//W3C//DTD XHTML 1.0 Transitional//EN" "www.w3.org/TR/xhtml1/DTD/xhtml1-transitional.dtd">`. Chapter 4 goes into more detail on DTD declarations.

Sometimes there are a few additional, elements to the XML prolog. These optional parts include *comments* and *processing instructions*. Processing instructions are discussed later this chapter. Comments are usually meant for human consumption and are not supposed to be part of the actual data in a document. They are initiated by the sequence `<!--` and terminated by `-->`. Following is `example.xml` with a comment added:

```
<?xml version="1.0" encoding="UTF-8" standalone="yes"?>
<!-- This is a comment that follows the XML declaration -->
```

In general, comments are solely for the benefit of humans; you might want to include the date you created the file, your name, and other author details. However, if you think that the file will only be processed by a software application there's little point inserting them.

Once the XML prolog is finished you need to create the *root element* of the document. The following section details elements and how to create them.

Creating Elements

Elements are the basic building blocks of XML and all documents will have at least one. All elements are defined in one of two ways. At its simplest, an element with content consists of a start tag, which is a left angle bracket (<) followed by the name of the element, such as `myElement`, and then a right angle bracket (>). So a full start tag might be `<myElement>`. To close the element the end tag starts with a left angle bracket, a forward slash, and then the name of the element and a right angle bracket. So the end tag for `<myElement>` would be `</myElement>`. You can add spaces after the name in a start tag, such as `<myElement >`, but not before the name as in `< myElement>`. You can add this to `Example.xml`:

```
<?xml version="1.0" encoding="UTF-8" standalone="yes"?>
<!-- This is a comment that follows the XML declaration -->
  <myElement></myElement>
```

Example.xml

There is an alternative syntax used to define an element, and this can only be used for elements with no content:

```
<?xml version="1.0" encoding="UTF-8" standalone="yes"?>
<!-- This is a comment that follows the XML declaration -->
  <myElement />
```

This sort of element is known as *self-closing*.

Naming Styles

In addition to the two ways to define an element, there are a few different naming styles for elements and, as in many things IT-related, people can get quite evangelical about them. The one thing almost everyone agrees on is to be consistent; choose a style for the document and stick with it. Following are the main contenders for how you should name your elements — the main idea is how you distinguish separate words in an element name:

- **Pascal-casing:** This capitalizes separate words including the first: `<MyElement />`.
- **Camel-casing:** Similar to Pascal except that the first letter is lowercase: `<myElement />`.
- **Underscored names:** Use an underscore to separate words: `<my_element />`.
- **Hyphenated names:** Separate words with a hyphen: `<my-element />`.

While there are many other styles to use, these four seem to work the best.

Naming Specifications

Along with naming styles come a few specific rules used when naming elements that you must follow. These main rules include the following:

- An element name can begin with either an underscore or an uppercase or lowercase letter from the Unicode character set. This means you can use the Roman alphabet used by English and many other Western languages, the Cyrillic one used by Russian and its language relatives, characters from Greek, or any of the other numerous scripts, such as Thai or Arabic, that are defined in the Unicode standard.

- Subsequent characters can also be a dash (-) or a digit.
- Names are case-sensitive, so the start and end tags must match exactly.
- Names cannot contain spaces
- Names beginning with the letters XML, either in uppercase- or lowercase, are reserved, and shouldn't be used (although many parsers allow them in practice).

***NOTE** Just because names are case-sensitive doesn't mean it's sensible to have two elements that differ only by case, such as `<myElement />` and `<MyElement />`. Just as this would be poor practice for variable names in a case-sensitive programming language such as C#, you should not have elements with such similar names in XML.*

In theory you can also use a colon (`:`) as part of a name but this conflicts with the way XML Namespaces (covered in the next chapter) are handled, so in practice you should avoid using it. If you want to see the full range of element naming specifications, visit `www.w3.org/TR/2008/REC-xml-20081126/#NT-Name`.

Formatting your elements correctly is critical to creating well-formed XML. Table 2-1 provides some examples of correctly and incorrectly formed elements:

TABLE 2-1: Legal and illegal elements

LEGAL ELEMENT	REASON	ILLEGAL ELEMENT	REASON
`<myElement> </myElement>`	Spaces are allowed after a name.	`<my Element />`	Names cannot contain spaces.
`<my1stElement/>`	Digits can appear within a name.	`<1stName />`	Names cannot begin with a digit.
`<myElement />`	Spaces can appear between the name and the forward slash in a self-closing element.	`< myElement />`	Initial spaces are forbidden.
`<my-Element />`	A hyphen is allowed within a name.	`<-myElement/>`	A hyphen is not allowed as the first character.
`<όνομα />`	Non-roman characters are allowed if they are classified as letters by the Unicode specification. In this case the element name is *forename* in Greek.	`<myElement> </MyElement>`	Start and end tags must match case-sensitively.

Root Element

The next step after writing the prolog is creating the *root element*. All documents must have one and only one root element. Everything else in the document lies under this element to form a hierarchical tree. The rule stating that there can only be one root element is one of the keystones of XML, yet it has led to many complaints and a lot of people have put forward cases where having more than one "root" would be advantageous. One example is when using XML as a logging format. A typical log file might look like this:

```
<entry date="2012-03-03T10:09:53" type="audit">Failed logon attempt
 with username jfawcett</entry>
<entry date="2012-03-03T10:11:01" type="audit">Successful
 logon attempt with username jfawcett</entry>
<entry date="2012-03-03T10:12:11" type="information">Successful folder
 synchronisation for use jfawcett</entry>
```

This is an easy format to manage. Each time the machine wants to add a log entry it opens the relevant file and writes one line to the end of it, a standard task for any system. The problem with this format, though, is that there isn't a unique root element; you have to add one to make it well-formed:

```
<log>
  <entry date="2012-03-03T10:09:53" type="audit">Failed logon attempt
   with username jfawcett</entry>
  <entry date="2012-03-03T10:11:01" type="audit">Successful
   logon attempt with username jfawcett</entry>
  <entry date="2012-03-03T10:12:11" type="information">
  Successful folder synchronisation for use jfawcett</entry>
</log>
```

But now, with only one root element, it's difficult to add new entries. A simple file writer would have to open the file, find the closing log tag (`</log>`), and then add a line. Alternatively, the file could be opened by a parser, the root element (`<log>`) found, and a new child `<entry>` added at the end of all the other `<entry>` children. This task is much more process-heavy, and might prove to be a problem if dozens of entries need to be created every minute.

However the XML standards committees have stuck to their guns, deciding that the advantages of having a single, all-encompassing element, (the main one being easier parsing) outweigh the issues, such as the difficulty creating log files. They have, however, agreed that there is a need for such a construct and it is known as a *document fragment*. Document fragments do not need a single root element but they cannot be processed in isolation; they need to be nested inside a document that does have a single root. There are a number of ways that this can be done and some are covered in the "Entity Declarations" section of Chapter 4.

Other Elements

Underneath the root element can lie other elements that follow the same rules for naming and attributes and, as you saw earlier, there can also be free text. These nested elements can be used to show individual or repetitive items of data depending on what you are trying to represent. For example, your root element could be `<person>` and the elements underneath could show the person's characteristics, such as <biography>and <address>. Alternatively, your main element could be <people> and underneath that you could have one or more <person> elements, each with its own children. You can add more elements and comments to the example document like so:

```
<?xml version="1.0" encoding="UTF-8"?>
<!-- This is a comment that follows the XML declaration -->
<!DOCTYPE myElement [
  <!ENTITY nbsp  " ">
]>
<myElement myFirstAttribute="One"mySecondAttribute="Two">
Here is some text with a non-breaking space in it.
  <anotherElement>
    <aNestedElement anotherAttribute="Some data here">
Some more text</aNestedElement>
    <!-- a second comment -->
  </anotherElement>
</myElement>
```

Remember that all elements must be nested underneath the root element, so the following sort of markup, which you may have gotten away with in HTML, is not allowed:

```
<myElement>
  <elementA><elementB></elementA></elementB>
</myElement>
```

You can't have the end tag of an element before the end tag of one nested below it.

Attributes

Elements are one of the two main building blocks of XML — the other one is *attributes*. Attributes are name-value pairs associated with an element. You can add a couple of attributes to the example document like so:

```
<?xml version="1.0" encoding="UTF-8" standalone="yes"?>
<!-- This is a comment that follows the XML declaration -->
  <myElement myFirstAttribute="One" mySecondAttribute="Two"></myElement>
```

The way you style your attribute names should be consistent with the one chosen for elements, so don't mix and match like this: `<applicationUser first-name="Joe" />`, where you have camel-casing for the element names and hyphenated attributes.

A number of rules also govern attributes exist:

- Attributes consist of a name and a value separated by an equals sign. The name, for example, `myFirstAttribute`, follows the same rules as element names.
- The attribute value must be in quotes. You can use either single or double quotes, the choice is entirely yours. You can use single on some attributes and double on others, but you can't mix them in a single attribute.
- There must be a value part, even if it's just empty quotes. You can't have something like `<option selected>` as you might in HTML.

- Attribute names must be unique per element.
- If you use double quotes as the delimiter you can't also use them as part of the value. The same applies for single quotes.

Table 2-2 provides some examples of correct and incorrect usage:

TABLE 2-2: Legal and illegal attributes

LEGAL ATTRIBUTE	REASON	ILLEGAL ATTRIBUTE	REASON
<myElement value="Joe's attribute" />	Single quote inside double quote delimiters.	<myElement 1stAttribute= "value" />	Attribute names cannot begin with a digit.
<myElement value='"a quoted value"' />	Double quotes inside single quote delimiters.	<myElement value= 'Joe's attribute' />	Single quote inside single quote delimiters.
		<myElement name="Joe" name="Fawcett" />	Two attributes with the same name is not allowed.
		<myElement name='Joe" />	Mismatching delimiters.

Element and Attribute Content

Attribute values and elements can both contain character data (called *text* in normal parlance). You've already seen examples of attributes in earlier code snippets. A similar example for an element would be:

```
<myElement>Here is some character content</myElement>
```

In addition to the rules described previously, there are only two more restrictions to follow regarding character content. Two characters cannot appear in attribute values or direct element content: the ampersand (&) and the left angle bracket (<). You cannot use the latter because it's used to delimit elements and it can confuse the parser. You cannot use the former because it's used to begin entity and character references.

Entity and Character References

There are two ways of inserting characters into a document that cannot be used directly, either because they are forbidden by the specification or because they don't exist in the encoding you have chosen. The first is *entity references*. There are five entity references in XML, shown in the Table 2-3.

TABLE 2-3: Entity References

CHARACTER	REFERENCE
&	&
<	<
>	>
"	"
'	'

References start with an ampersand and finish with a semicolon. The actual reference appears as the middle part and is an abbreviation of the character; for instance, lt stands for less than. So instead of using & or < as characters for instance, you must use the reference instead. References ' and " are especially useful if you need an attribute value to contain both types of quote marks.

The references in Table 2-3 are the only built-in entity references. You can declare your own if you want using a DTD — an example of this is shown shortly.

Character references take a similar form. They begin with &# and end with a semicolon, but instead of an abbreviation as the middle part they have a number representing the character's Unicode code point. The number can be in hexadecimal or decimal. For example, if you wanted to represent the Greek letter omega (Ω) as a reference it would be Ω in hexadecimal or &937#; in decimal.

A common question in XML forums is how to represent the non-breaking space—the character that has no visible output but prevents two words joined by it from breaking across a line. It's commonly used in web pages for formatting purposes where it's represented by the reference . You have four ways to insert this into an XML document. The first is to simply insert it as a character; there's often no need to use a reference at all. For example, in Microsoft Word you can type the omega character by first typing 3A9 and then hitting Alt+X. Various other methods exist for different editors. The Unicode code point of the non-breaking space is xA0 so the same technique can be used. The second and third ways use the character reference   in hexadecimal and   in decimal. The fourth method requires that you create a DTD at the start of the document and declare the entity. You might want to do this if the character is used many times in the XML and you want the reader to recognize it more easily. In HTML, the reference   is used to insert a non-breaking space, so to mimic this in an XML document you'd do this:

```
<?xml version="1.0" encoding="UTF-8"?>
<!-- This is a comment that follows the XML declaration -->
<!DOCTYPE myElement [
  <!ENTITY nbsp " ">
]>
<myElement myFirstAttribute="One" mySecondAttribute="Two">
Here is some text with a non-breaking space in it.
</myElement>
```

The DTD (covered in more detail in Chapter 4) declares that the root element is named `myElement`, and then there's one entity declaration; wherever ` ` appears in the document the parser will read it as the Unicode character A0, a non-breaking space.

You could also use this method to add references that refer to more than one character. For instance, you may want a reference named copyright that outputs © *Wrox 2012* wherever you put `©right`, that way you can just update the DTD in one place if you want to change all your references to read © *Wrox 2013*. This is achieved in exactly the same way as the preceding example, using the following:

```
<!DOCTYPE myElement [
  <!ENTITY copyright "© Wrox 2012">
]>
```

See Chapter 4 for more on these types of references.

WARNING *It's important to remember that you can't add the forbidden characters, such as null, to your document using either entity or character references.*

Elements Versus Attributes

On many occasions you will have a choice whether to represent data as an element or an attribute. For example, take the `appUsers.xml` file from Chapter 1 (shown in Listing 2-1):

Available for download on Wrox.com

LISTING 2-1: appUsers.xml

```
<applicationUsers>
  <user firstName="Joe" lastName="Fawcett" />
  <user firstName="Danny" lastName="Ayers" />
  <user firstName="Catherine" lastName="Middleton" />
</applicationUsers>
```

You could choose to represent the users' first names and last names as elements instead as shown in Listing 2-2:

Available for download on Wrox.com

LISTING 2-2: appUsers-elementCentric.xml

```
<applicationUsers>
  <user>
    <firstName>Joe</firstName>
    <lastName>Fawcett</lastName>
  </user>
  <user>
```

```
    <firstName>Danny</firstName>
    <lastName>Ayers</lastName>
  </user>
  <user>
    <firstName>Catherine</firstName>
    <lastName>Middleton</lastName>
  </user>
</applicationUsers>
```

There are no fixed rules regarding whether you should use one form or the other, but the following are some things to consider when making your decision.

When to Use Attributes

Attributes are usually a good choice when there is only one piece of data to be shown. In Listing 2-1 a person can have only one first name so an attribute is the best choice. Attribute names cannot be repeated, though; putting a list into an attribute, perhaps by separating role names with a comma, makes the file difficult to work with when you want to extract and manipulate this data later. Therefore, if you need to show something like role names for a user multiple times, you would have to use elements.

Using attributes also results in a smaller file size because each element containing data needs an end tag as well as the small overhead of the angle brackets, which means more characters are being used to show the same amount of data. This might be a consideration if you know your files will often be sent across a network where bandwidth is an issue.

Typically, veering toward using attributes is a good idea unless there is a firm reason not to.

When to Use Elements

Elements are useful when the data is not a simple type—that is, some text or a date that can be easily represented as a string in an attribute value. So something like an address would be better split into its constituent parts and represented via elements rather than be represented as a delimited string and squashed into an attribute.

Therefore use this:

```
<person firstName="Joe" lastName="Fawcett">
  <address>
    <line1>Chapter House</line1>
    <line2>Crucifix Lane</line2>
    <city>London</city>
    <postCode>SE1 3JW</postCode>
    <country>England</country>
  </address>
</person>
```

Rather than this:

```
<person
   firstName="Joe"
   lastName="Fawcett"
   address="Chapter House, Crucifix Lane, London, SE1 3JW, England" />
```

Elements are also better when items may need to be repeated. To associate role names with a user in the file previously shown, a structure like this one would work best:

```
<applicationUsers>
  <user firstName="Joe" lastName="Fawcett">
    <roles>
      <role name="administrators" />
      <role name="general" />
    </roles
  <!-- other users here -->
</applicationUsers>
```

Notice how each `role` can have only one name, so an attribute rather than an element represents that portion.

Another plus for elements is that they can be ordered. Attributes are, by definition, unordered. You can place attributes in a special order in your document but the XML parser may ignore this order for processing purposes. If you need data items in a specific sequence, elements are the way to go.

The other major case for using an element is when you have a large amount of content that is just text. Technically, you could use an attribute in this instance, but that would mean you could get a file that looks like this:

```
<longDocument data="In here is a very long piece of text that goes on for many,
many,
many,
many,
lines" />
```

This can look very unusual. A file with a lot of text is normally easier to read if the content is within an element and possibly uses a CDATA section to avoid having to escape special characters.

Processing Instructions

Another common building block of an XML document is the *processing instruction*. You already saw one of these in Chapter 1 when you tried a browser-based XSL transformation. The processing instruction, or PI, is used to communicate with the application that is consuming the XML. It is not used directly by the XML parser at all.

A PI takes the form of a target that identifies which application should be carrying out the instruction and some data that is fed to the application. A common PI is the one that tells a browser to perform a transformation on the XML and looks like this:

```
<?xml-stylesheet type="text/xsl" href="appUsers.xslt" ?>
```

The target in this example is `xml-stylesheet`, followed by two pseudo attributes: `type="text/xsl"` and `href="appUsers.xslt"`. They are not true attributes because they don't have to follow the rules of having a name and value and using quotes; they're just data that the target application will use. In this case a browser will recognize the target as saying that the XML should be transformed before being shown; the first attribute states that the type of the transform is XSL and the second attribute points to its location. This particular processing instruction works only for a limited number of applications, mostly browsers; if you open the file in a standard text editor the PI will be ignored.

NOTE *Processing instructions and XML declarations look quite similar, but the declaration is not technically a processing instruction and therefore is not handled as such.*

CDATA Sections

One further construct you may need to use in a document is known as a *CDATA section* (*CDATA* stands for *character data* and means that no markup is present). These are used as a way to avoid repetitive escaping of characters. For example, suppose you have a simple document that contains information that makes use of the less than sign (<). Normally this is taken as part of the markup so it must be escaped using the entity reference `<`. So your document may look like this:

```
<conversionData>
  1 kilometer &lt; 1 mile
  1 pint &lt; 1 liter
  1 pound &lt; 1 kilogram
</conversionData>
```

If you'd prefer the text to use the readily recognizable < sign, which makes it easier for humans to read and write, you can mark the element's contents as a CDATA section:

```
<conversionData><![CDATA[
  1 kilometer < 1 mile
  1 pint < 1 liter
  1 pound < 1 kilogram
]]></conversionData>
```

The CDATA section starts with `<![CDATA[` and ends with `]]>`. Anything inside is considered text, not markup, and you can use any characters that normally need escaping such as the less than sign and the ampersand. If you need to represent the combination `]]>`, which marks the end of a section, you'll have to escape the final character of the sequence as so: `]]>`.

A common use of CDATA is in XHTML, the XML version of HTML. When you need to embed some JavaScript in an XHTML page, many of the characters often need escaping. Rather than doing this, which often then confuses the JavaScript parser, you can wrap the whole script section in a CDATA section such as the following example. This example tests whether a customer is trying to transfer more money from his account than he actually has:

```
<script type=text/javascript>
//<![CDATA[
function validateTransfer(currentBalance, transferAmount)
{
  if (currentBalance > 0 && transferAmount < currentBalance)
  {
    return true;
  }
  alert("Insufficient funds to transfer the requested amount.");
  return false;
}
//]]>
</script>
```

Because the text has been wrapped in a CDATA section, the JavaScript can be written in its standard form; otherwise, if the test for the transfer amount is less than the current balance you would have to escape the `&&` and the `<` sign as shown in the following code:

```
if (currentBalance > 0 &amp;&amp; transferAmount &lt; currentBalance)
```

This leaves a line that's difficult for both a human and a script parser to interpret.

Another noteworthy item is the JavaScript comments (`//`) before the CDATA section start and end markers. This is meant to help older browsers that don't know how to handle the construct.

Remember that a CDATA section is only a visual aid for human readers. The XML parser won't treat the two preceding examples differently, so once the XML has been parsed you won't be able to tell whether the character data was escaped using references or marked as CDATA. Some people use CDATA sections as a way to embed one XML document inside another, like this:

```
<myDocument>
  <someData>
    <myNestedDocument><![CDATA[
      <anotherDocument>This is bad practice</anotherDocument>
    ]]></myNestedDocument>
  </someData>
</myDocument>
```

This sort of XML is difficult to work with and should be avoided. The correct way to handle multiple documents—without mixing up what belongs where—is with namespaces, which are covered in the following chapter.

ADVANCED XML PARSING

You've now covered all the common building blocks of an XML document and can move on to more advanced matters. The next three major areas of discussion relating to advanced XML parsing include the following:

- **XML equivalence:** How documents that are written differently can still be treated as identical by the XML parser.

- **Whitespace handling:** How characters such as spaces and tabs receive special treatment.
- **Error handling:** What happens if your document contains an error.

XML Equivalence

XML equivalence refers to the idea that many documents, though having a different lexical representation, are considered equal by the XML parser. Once the document has been parsed it is impossible to tell if a particular style was used to create the XML. For example, the following two documents, Listing 2-3 and Listing 2-4, differ in three places:

Available for download on Wrox.com

LISTING 2-3: Document 1

```
<exampleData source="web">
  <section><![CDATA This is some example data ]]></section>
  <section>Here's some more data</section>
</exampleData>
```

Available for download on Wrox.com

LISTING 2-4: Document 2

```
<exampleData source='web'>
  <section>This is some example data</section>
  <section>Here&apos;s some more data</section>
</exampleData>
```

The three lexical differences are as follows:

- In the first file the attribute values are enclosed in double quotes whereas the second uses single quotes.
- The first file has a CDATA section for the first `<section>` element whereas the second doesn't.
- Finally, the second file uses an entity reference for the apostrophe in the second `<section>` element and the first does not.

There is nothing wrong with either of these two representations, it's purely a matter of personal preference but once either of these files is parsed it will be impossible to tell which one was the source. To the parser, how attribute values have been quoted and other differences have no bearing on the internal representation of the XML. Therefore, these documents have achieved XML equivalence.

The fact that more than one lexical version of an XML document can lead to the same in-memory representation has some negative effects. For example, if you are going to transform the file and want to treat data in a CDATA section differently than text that isn't in a CDATA section, you're out of luck and will need a different approach. You can handle variations like these differently if you prefer though, perhaps by preprocessing the file using a non-XML tool to add some markup identifying which elements need to be treated differently.

Similarly, a common request in the XML forums is that people want to create XML with various characters represented by references rather than the characters themselves, similar to Listing 2-4 where the apostrophe was shown as `'`. The reason for this is that the software that processes the XML "needs" this particular format. The fact that these two forms are XML equivalent indicates that the receiving application is not XML-compliant, otherwise it would accept either variation, and the best thing to do with this request is to throw it back and fix the relevant application. Obviously this isn't always going to be possible, but again there's no way to insist on how an apostrophe is represented. You'd have to find a non–XML-based workaround in order to fulfill this particular need if you couldn't get the problem fixed at source.

Whitespace Handling

Whitespace is text that is composed of a space, a tab, a newline, or a carriage return (the characters defined in Unicode as 0x20, 0x9, 0xA, and 0xD, respectively). Whitespace does not include the non-breaking space you saw earlier in the chapter that is in common use in web pages. Although the non-breaking space cannot be seen it is treated as though it can be, just like any other letter or punctuation mark:

Whitespace doesn't sound like it would cause problems; any human reading a document can usually cope with blank lines or occasionally two spaces together. But in XML it has to be treated carefully for the following two main reasons:

- First, some whitespace is significant. Take a standard English sentence; each word is separated by a space, and without these spaces the text would be difficult to read. On the other hand, some whitespace is insignificant — many books have blank pages at the front or back that wouldn't be missed and don't add to the content. In XML there is a similar situation; you will see a few examples shortly.
- The second reason whitespace is important in XML is that different operating systems use different conventions regarding such things as the line endings in a file which are constructed using the newline and carriage return whitespace characters. For example, a Windows-produced text file would normally have line endings that mimic the old typewriter action: a carriage return and a newline. On the contrary, files created on a UNIX environment will just have the newline character.

Therefore, whitespace handling rules exist to provide a consistent experience, and so that XML files can be portable data formats. For example, when an XML file is processed, the line endings (whether they started as a carriage return and newline, just newline, or just carriage return) will all be transformed into a single newline character.

Significant and Insignificant Whitespace

There is a big difference between how whitespace in XML documents is handled by XML parsers and how HTML is treated by browsers. If you are used to developing HTML you know that multiple consecutive whitespace characters are merged and that newlines and carriage returns are typically ignored. For example, the following HTML markup has lots of whitespace between the letters and two newlines in the middle.

```
<p>Here is some text     with    lots of   whitespace

          That won't show in a browser</p>
```

Figure 2-1 shows what you'll see in a browser.

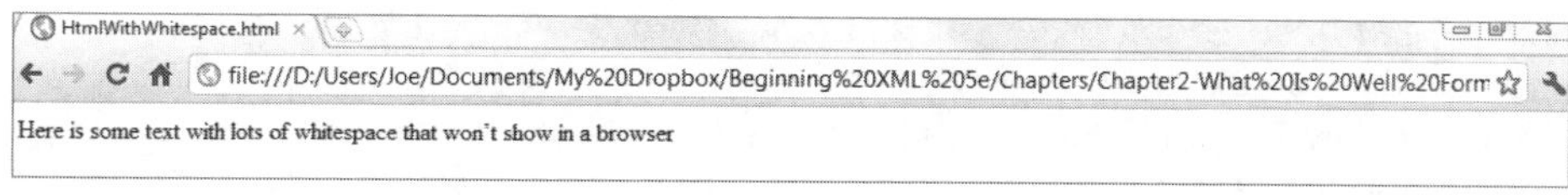

FIGURE 2-1

You can see that neither the long spaces nor the newline characters are shown. This is because HTML browsers normalize space by merging multiple spaces into one single space and ignoring newlines. If you do want a newline character to appear in HTML you need to use markup, specifically the `<br />` element.

XML isn't as strict as HTML; the parser preserves whitespace that's not part of markup. Take, for example, the following snippet:

```
<chapter   title="What is XML? ">
  <para> XML stands for Extensible Markup Language (presumably the original authors
 thought that sounded more exciting than EML) and has followed a path similar to
others in the software and IT world.</para>
</chapter>
```

This design is such that there will never be any text directly inside the `<chapter>` element, but it will just contain `<para>` elements. Due to this design, the whitespace at the end of the start tag and the general indentation are just there to make it easier for a human to read and see the document's structure. There are also some extra spaces between the `<chapter>` element's name and its attribute, `title`. All this whitespace is deemed insignificant. Any whitespace that appears inside the `<para>` element is known as significant.

An XML parser can choose to ignore insignificant whitespace — but how does it know that the element has no direct text content? It can only know the content type of an element if there is an XML schema or DTD associated with the document. Schemas and DTDs are not fully covered until Chapters 4 and 5; suffice it to say that insignificant whitespace does not have to be preserved by the parser. If you do want all of your document's whitespace to remain, there is a special attribute that you can add to either the root element or one lower down: `xml:space="preserve"`. This informs the parser to leave your document completely intact. So for the preceding example you'd add this to the `<chapter>` element:

```
<chapter xml:space="preserve"  title="What is XML? ">
  <para> XML stands for Extensible Markup Language (presumably the original authors
 thought that sounded more exciting than EML) and has followed a path similar to
others in the software and IT world.</para>
</chapter>
```

There is also an `xml:space="default"` if you need to reset whitespace handling back to its default.

WARNING *As stated previously, XML parsers are obliged to preserve whitespace unless they categorically know it to be insignificant. Unfortunately Microsoft's COM-based parser, known as MSXML Core Services, falls from grace here and ignores the standards by stripping what it considers to be insignificant space. This has caused many problems in the past for developers who were forced to use this parser (for example, when working inside Internet Explorer). You can overcome the problem in some scenarios by setting the* `preserveWhitespace` *property of the parser to* `true`*.*

Error Handling

As you've seen you have a few hurdles to overcome to make sure your document is classified as XML — matching tags, quoted attribute values, and escaped characters when necessary, to name a few. If an XML parser finds that one of the rules has been broken it has two main options, which depend on whether the specification states that it's an *error* or a *fatal error.*

You can recover from an error and continue document parsing if possible. A fatal error, as its name suggests, cannot be recovered from and the processor's only option is to report it. It can also report other errors if necessary, but it can't produce a parsed document at the end of the procedure. Any errors that are to do with well-formedness are considered fatal.

This strict view was deliberately taken after seeing how allowing HTML writers to be lax with their syntax has adversely affected the Web. Because browsers accept incorrect HTML and try to second guess the author's intention, there is inconsistency on how such pages are displayed — each browser has a different set of rules on how to cope with badly formed content. It also means that web pages cannot easily be processed by machines to extract meaningful information without first putting the content through a number of different algorithms. This was one of the problems that an XML-based version of HTML, namely XHTML, was meant to solve. Unfortunately it didn't work in practice because it was too difficult to learn for many. Additionally there was not enough toolset support and many browsers, Internet Explorer in particular, couldn't handle it properly.

At the end of the day you can compare XML strict error checking to standard programming languages. Some enforce strict type checking at compile time whereas others only fail at runtime. The XML view is that it's better to find errors earlier even if that means having the document rejected for only minor glitches.

Most browsers have good error reporting facilities and are often used to help find errors in a document that aren't immediately obvious. They are usually very strict and will terminate processing on errors even if they are not defined as fatal. This is common with nearly all parsers and is in line with the specification that only states that they *may* recover. In practice it's easier to just stop when an error is encountered than try to repair it by divining the author's original intention. This would also lead to discrepancies in how parsers handled documents and lead to a similar unwanted situation to that previously mentioned in regards to web pages. The following Try It Out deliberately creates a badly-formed file to demonstrate how error reporting is handled in a browser.

TRY IT OUT Using a Browser to Find Errors

To see how errors are reported in a browser use the following code file:

Available for download on Wrox.com

```
<?xml version="1.0" encoding="utf-8"?>
<pangrams createdOn="2012-01-04T10:19:45'>
  <!-- This file is designed to show
  how errors are reported in a browser -->
  <pangram>The quick brown fox jumps over the lazy dog.</pangram>
  <pangram>Pack my box with five dozen liquor jugs.</pangram>
  <pangram>Glib jocks quiz nymph to vex dwarf.</pangram>
  <pangram>The five boxing wizards jump quickly.</Pangram>
  <pangram>What you write deserves better than a jiggling, shaky,
     inexact & questionably fuzzy approximation of blur</pangram>
</pangrams>
```

XmlFileWithErrors.xml

This file contains three errors, which may or may not be immediately apparent depending on your familiarity with XML and your general proofreading abilities. However, these errors are reported differently in the browser in Figure 2-2 than how you might describe them yourself. In each case the browser stops after reporting the error and simply shows content up to that point where possible. Google's Chrome browser is used for this demo.

1. Browse to the file locally and you see the first error report, shown in Figure 2-2.

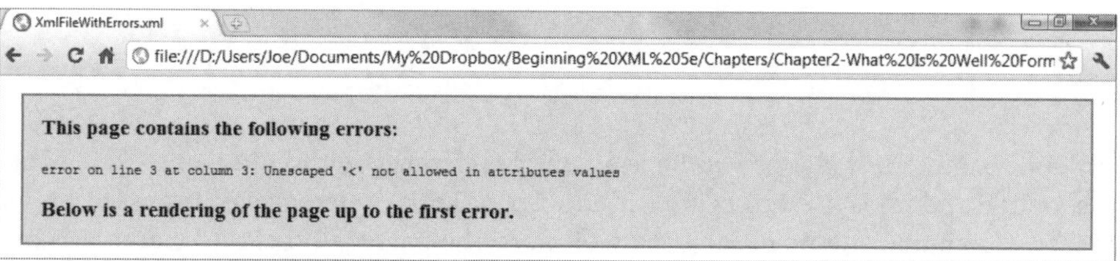

FIGURE 2-2

2. Look carefully at the file source you'll see that the `createdOn` attribute uses mismatched quotes — a double quote to start with and a single quote to finish. However, this isn't the error that's reported. Instead the parser complains that there is an unescaped < present. This is because it thinks the attribute hasn't been closed yet and suddenly it's found an illegal character. So far it hasn't read any textual content so there's nothing to display apart from the error message.

3. Correct the error by replacing the single quote with a double quote and reopen the file in Chrome. You get a new message as shown in Figure 2-3.

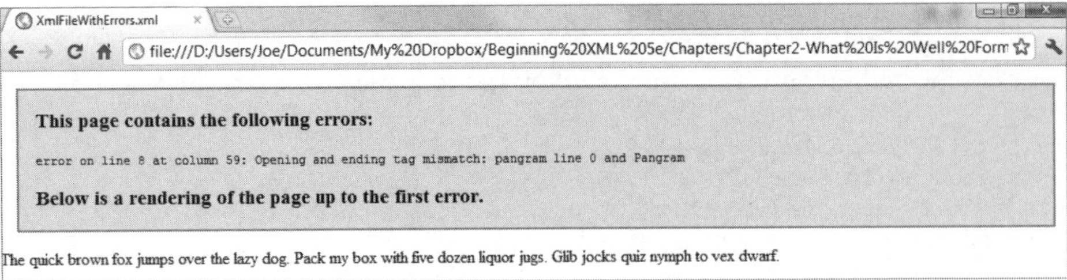

FIGURE 2-3

4. This time Chrome reports mismatching tag names. The fourth <pangram> element has <pangram> for a start tag but </Pangram> for the end tag and tags must match by case. This time, though, some content has been read and so the text of the first three <pangram> elements is shown. Correct the mismatch and reopen the file. The final error is reported, as shown in Figure 2-4.

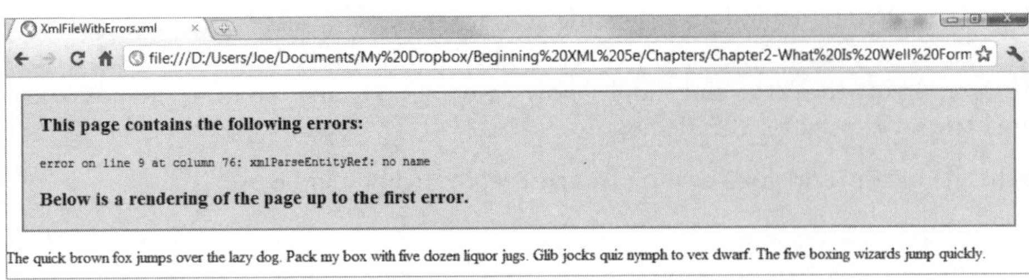

FIGURE 2-4

5. This slightly confusing report claims you have an entity reference without a name. This is because in XML the ampersand (&) is used to begin a character or entity reference as discussed previously. In the file there is no name and no closing semicolon, so the parser thinks the reference is malformed rather than the simpler explanation, which is that you've forgotten to escape the & altogether. Correct this final error and you see the entire file in Figure 2-5.

XmlFileWithErrors.xml

file:///D:/Users/Joe/Documents/My%20Dropbox/Beginning%20XML%205e/Chapters/Chapter2-What%20Is%20Well%20Form

This XML file does not appear to have any style information associated with it. The document tree is shown below.

```
▼<pangrams createdOn="2012-01-04T10:19:45">
  ▼<!--
     This file is designed to show how errors are reported in a browser
   -->
   <pangram>The quick brown fox jumps over the lazy dog.</pangram>
   <pangram>Pack my box with five dozen liquor jugs.</pangram>
   <pangram>Glib jocks quiz nymph to vex dwarf.</pangram>
   <pangram>The five boxing wizards jump quickly.</pangram>
  ▼<pangram>
     What you write deserves better than a jiggling, shaky, inexact & questionably fuzzy approximation of blur
   </pangram>
 </pangrams>
```

FIGURE 2-5

This time the file is displayed as a familiar tree and you can see the comment, plus you can expand and collapse various regions.

How It Works

XML parsers typically work in a sequential fashion when checking for errors. They start reading through the file and as soon as an error is encountered it is reported and any further parsing ceases. This explains how, on each occasion, only one error is displayed by Chrome and how, after fixing that error, the parser is able to get a little further in the parsing each time until, eventually, all three errors are removed and the browser can display the whole XML.

NOTE *If you're wondering about the file's contents, a* pangram *is a sentence in a language that uses each letter of the alphabet at least once.*

Read the XML specification carefully to learn more about determining which errors are defined as fatal and which are not. Fatal errors are clearly pointed out, and any other infringement is a recoverable error. As already noted, however, most parsers treat all errors as fatal and the best policy is to make sure any files you create are entirely free of them and that files received by you are perfect. If you do receive files that have errors your best choice, if you can't afford to simply reject them, is to correct them using non-XML means before moving them to your XML processing pipeline.

Now that you understand the building blocks of an XML file, the rules that need to be followed when creating them, and how errors are reported you can move on to the next stage. The next section deals with how a document is treated once it has been parsed.

THE XML INFOSET

Sometime after the W3C's XML recommendation was published a need arose for a common way to talk about the structure of an XML document after it had been parsed.

Up until this point there were many ways of describing a document depending on which technology it was being used with. The document object model (DOM) referred to elements and attributes as different types of nodes, as well as all the other building blocks such as comments and processing instructions. Other technologies (as you see in later chapters) had other terms, and part of the new model's job was to come up with a common vocabulary. This model was also meant to abstract away the individual differences in the way an original file had been written, such as whether it used single- or double–quotation marked attribute values. Additionally, the new model enables other XML-related applications, such as those used to transform XML, to work against an idealized picture of the document. The model was given the name the *XML Information Set* and is now commonly called the *XML Infoset.*

The XML Infoset consists of eleven components. This section takes a short look at each one to see how it relates to the underlying lexical representation. These components have the official title of *information items.*

The Document Information Item

Every XML document has one document information item. This item enables access to all the other items in the document as well as possessing a number of properties of its own. Some of these properties are those seen in the XML declaration such as character encoding and whether the document is standalone. Others are those such as the *Base URI*, which is essentially a pointer to the document's source, and the document element, which is the outermost element (what up until now has been referred to as the root element). In the older DOM terminology the document information item most closely resembles the root node of the entire XML.

To navigate from this item to other information items you can use the `Document Element` property, which points to the root element, and the `Children` property , which gives access to any comments or processing instructions that lie in the XML prolog (that is, before the root element).

Element Information Items

Element information items provide access to all element-related information, and each element has one associated item. The element information item has a number of properties, including:

- **Local Name:** The name of the element without any namespace prefixes (this is covered in the next chapter). For example, the local name of both `<pangram>` and `<ns:pangram>` would be `pangram`.
- **Children:** Any elements, comments, processing instructions, and references beneath this element.
- **Attributes:** An unordered list of all the attributes of this element. Note that attributes are not considered to be children of an element.
- **Parent:** The element, or in the case of the document element, the document, that has this element as its child.

Attribute Information Items

Attribute information items give access to each attribute found on an element. Properties include:

- **Local Name:** As for elements, this is the name without a namespace prefix.
- **Normalized Value:** The value of the attribute after the standard whitespace normalization, such as various line feeds, all being changed to a single newline character and all references being expanded.
- **Owner Element:** The element for which this attribute appears in its attributes property.

Processing Instruction Information Items

One processing instruction information item will be present for each processing instruction (PI) in the document. The properties include the target, which represents the target of the PI, and content, which is the rest of the text that appears. Quite often the content is split into what looks like attributes—set of name/value pairs—but that's not mandatory, so the information item does not parse the content any further.

Character Information Item

In theory each character that appears in the document, either literally as a character reference or within a CDATA section, will have an associated character information item. The properties of these include:

- **Character Code:** A value in the range of 0 to #x10FFFF indicating the character code. These codes are defined by the ISO 10646 standard which, for this interpretation, is the same as the Unicode one. Remember that some codes, such as 0, are not allowed in an XML document so you won't come across them if the XML is well-formed.
- **Element Content Whitespace:** This is a Boolean property indicating whether or not the character is whitespace within an element.
- **Parent:** The element that contains this item in its children property.

In practice, XML applications often group characters into strings of text because it's unlikely you'll want to process text one character at a time.

Comment Information Item

A comment information item refers to a comment in the source document. It has only two properties: `content`, which has the text of the comment, and `parent`.

Namespace Information Item

Each element in the document has one namespace information item for each namespace that is in scope. The wonderful world of namespaces is covered in the next chapter.

The Document Type Declaration Information Item

If a document has a document type declaration, this information item will have details about it. Properties include System Identifier and Public Identifier, which enable the XML to retrieve the DTD. This information item (as well as the following three: unexpected entity reference, unparsed entity, and notation) are only applicable when a document type definition is associated with the document.

Unexpanded Entity Reference Information Item

You're unlikely to come across these; they are placeholders for an external entity that has not been expanded. Most parsers will expand these references anyway, so they are quite rare.

Unparsed Entity Information Item

Again these are something declared in a DTD and you are unlikely to come across them.

Notation Information Item

One of these appears for each *notation* described in the DTD. Notations allow you to include references to non-XML content, such as images, in your XML document by declaring a reference to that content in the DTD.

In addition to the XML Infoset there is also a version known as the Post Schema Validation Infoset (PSVI), which brings additional information due to the fact that the XML has an associated schema and has been checked against that schema. You'll see some of this extra information in Chapter 5.

SUMMARY

- What exactly is meant by well-formed XML
- What characters are not allowed in an XML document
- What an encoding is and what is meant by Unicode
- The basic building blocks of XML, including elements and attributes
- How each of these blocks is formed and what rules need to be followed
- How some characters need to be escaped and how to represent characters that are not present in your chosen encoding
- How whitespace is handled
- How errors are handled
- What to think about when choosing between elements and attributes
- The XML Infoset and how it is an idealized model of an XML document

EXERCISES

Answers to exercises can be found in Appendix A.

1. What errors make the following file not well-formed?

```
<xmlLibrary>
  <play publicationYear=1898>
    <title>Arms & The Man</title>
    <author>George Bernard Shaw</author>
    <play description>Comedy dealing with the futility of war
 and the hypocrisy of human nature.</play description>
  <play>
  <play publicationYear=1950>
    <title>The Mousetrap</title>
    <author>Agatha Christie</author>
    <play description>A traditional whodunnit
 with an extraordinary twist.</play description>
  <play>
</xmlLibrary>
```

2. How would you declare an entity reference for your e-mail address so that you could easily change it in one place rather than many. Give a complete example.

▶ WHAT YOU LEARNED IN THIS CHAPTER

TOPIC	KEYPOINTS
Why it's essential that your XML is well-formed	If XML is not well-formed then it's not XML and an XML parser won't be able to read it.
Certain characters are not allowed in XML documents	The null character (0x0) is forbidden in XML 1.0 and is the only forbidden Unicode character in XML 1.1. XML 1.0 also forbids the characters in the range 0x1 to 0x19 with the exception the whitespace characters tab (0x9), newline (0xa), and carriage return (0xd).
Some characters have special meanings	& and < are used for references and tags respectively so they need to be escaped as & and < if they are needed as text.
XML files can use a variety of characters encodings	If your file isn't in the UTF-8 encoding then the encoding must be declared in the XML declaration.
Basic structure	XML files are mainly built from elements and attributes. An XML document must have one all-encompassing root or document element.
Whitespace receives special treatment	In general, line endings consisting of newline and carriage return characters are compressed into a single newline and multiple spaces into a single space unless the parser considers them to be significant.
Elements or Attributes	In general, choose elements for complex structures or data that is repeated. Choose attributes for single atomic values.
The XML Infoset	The infoset is an idealized version of an XML document created after a document has been successfully parsed. Applications that consume XML should base their behavior on this structure so that do not rely on insignificant differences in how the document was written.

3

XML Namespaces

WHAT YOU WILL LEARN IN THIS CHAPTER:

- What namespaces are
- Why you need namespaces
- How to choose a namespace
- How to declare a namespace
- How to show that items are in a namespace
- The relationship between namespaces and XML Schema
- When to use namespaces
- Common uses of namespaces

This chapter covers the thorny topic of XML Namespaces, something that should be quite simple and straightforward but often seems to lead to confusion, even among experienced developers. This chapter starts by explaining what is meant by the term namespace and how it's not limited to the world of XML. It then details when and why you would need them and shows the problems you can experience if they were not available. Then you delve into the implementation of namespaces, how they are declared in an XML document, and how you specify that an item resides in a particular namespace. You are then introduced to one of the main uses of namespaces, XML Schemas, which enable you to validate that a particular document conforms to a pre-determined structure. The final section lists some real-world examples of namespace usage that you are likely to encounter and gives a brief description of where and why they are used.

DEFINING NAMESPACES

At their simplest, *namespaces* are a way of grouping elements and attributes under a common heading in order to differentiate them from similarly-named items.

Take the following scenario: You overhear two people talking and one says to the other, "You need a new table." What does that mean? There could be quite a number of options depending on the context. For example it could be:

- Someone discussing a dinner party with their spouse and they need a bigger dining table.
- A database developer who's been asked to design a system to store user preferences on a website — a new database table.
- An HTML developer who has been told to display some extra information on the user's account page — an HTML table.

You can tell only if you know the context, or if the complete names are used — dining table, database table, or HTML table.

This is how namespaces work with elements and attributes. You can group these items under a namespace so that they keep their familiar name, such as `user`, but also have a namespace so that they can be differentiated, both by a human reader and a software application, from any other elements that may be called `user` by someone else.

WHY DO YOU NEED NAMESPACES?

For a more concrete example on the need for namespaces, take the following scenario: You have details about your company employees stored as XML and you want to be able to include a brief biography in the form of some HTML within the document. Your basic document looks something like Listing 3-1.

Available for download on Wrox.com

LISTING 3-1: employees-base.xml

```
<employees>
  <employee id="001">
    <firstName>Joe</firstName>
    <lastName>Fawcett</lastName>
    <title>Mr</title>
    <dateOfBirth>1962-11-19</dateOfBirth>
    <dateOfHire>2005-12-05</dateOfHire>
    <position>Head of Software Development</position>
    <biography><!-- biography here --></biography>
  </employee>
  <!-- more employee elements can be added here-->
</employees>
```

This document doesn't use namespaces, and it still works fine. Now say you want to add the biography and you're going to use XHTML. This is the perfect opportunity to use namespaces, but first, take a look at a document, shown in Listing 3-2, that doesn't declare any namespaces and which illustrates the problem:

Available for download on Wrox.com

LISTING 3-2: employees-with-bio.xml

```
<employees>
  <employee id="001">
    <firstName>Joe</firstName>
    <lastName>Fawcett</lastName>
    <title>Mr</title>
    <dateOfBirth>1962-11-19</dateOfBirth>
    <dateOfHire>2005-12-05</dateOfHire>
    <position>Head of Software Development</position>
    <biography>
      <html>
        <head>
          <title>Joe's Biography</title>
        </head>
        <body>
          <p>After graduating from the University of Life
 Joe moved into software development,
 originally working with COBOL on mainframes in the 1980s.</p>
        </body>
      </html>
    </biography>
  </employee>
  <!-- more employee elements -->
</employees>
```

Now without namespaces you have a clash — two <title> elements performing two distinct functions. One is for the employee's salutation and the other is for the title of the biography. For a human reader this isn't a problem; you can see from the type of data and the general context what each <title> element represents, but to a software program that isn't the case. If asked to find the employee's title, for example a report showing the title, first name, and last name, there could be a conflict because it can't choose the correct title without further help.

The way to get around this is to group the two sets of information — the employee data and the biographical information — into two different namespaces. You can see the final document later in the chapter, complete with namespaces, after you learn the methods by which you declare them.

If you didn't want to use namespaces, you could use a different element name for the employee's title — `salutation` perhaps. Given that you designed the format of the basic XML and decided the names of the elements, you're perfectly entitled to use this approach; however, the elements that you are using in the biography section are part of the XHTML standard and so you can't arbitrarily go and change the <title> element to be called something different.

However, the main reason why you would typically need namespaces is because you won't always be using your own XML formats entirely within your own systems. If you did that, you wouldn't have to worry about elements getting mixed up simply because they had the same name; you could ensure that all your element and attribute names were unique across all your systems. In the real world, though, it's not like that. One of XML's main purposes is to share data across systems and organizations. So, although you probably will invent some XML formats that are only for internal use, will never need to be shared, and will never come into contact with other formats, at some stage you are going to need namespaces.

HOW DO YOU CHOOSE A NAMESPACE?

Chapter 1, "What is XML?" mentioned how namespaces were already heavily used in many programming languages such as C# and Java. In C# they are actually called *namespaces* whereas Java prefers the term *packages*. So an example from C# could be the `Timer` class. The .NET library contains three different timers, each under its own namespace:

- `System.Windows.Forms.Timer`: Fires an event at regular intervals on the main user interface thread on a form.
- `System.Timers.Timer`: Fires an event on a worker thread.
- `System.Threading.Timer`: Designed for use in multi-threaded situations.

How these timers actually differ is unimportant. The point is that they all have a similar base name, `Timer`, but all live in a different namespace, respectively `System.Windows.Forms`, `System.Timers`, and `System.Threading`. When you declare one of these in code, the correct one is called because the full namespace name is used; if you don't declare the namespace correctly the compiler emits an error message saying that it can't find the `Timer` class that you need.

For XML you need a similar system, a way to make sure that your elements and attributes have a unique name. XML Namespaces provide a simple solution; you can choose virtually any string of characters to make sure your element's full name is unique. So you could choose your element to be `user`, as before, and decide that it is in the `BeginningXMLFifthEdition` namespace. However, that doesn't guarantee that the full name will be unique; several authors contributed to this book and one could also choose that string as the namespace. To avoid this problem in the real world you have two ways to create a unique namespace: using URIs or URNs. That's not to say people don't use other formats, but if you want to follow the W3C recommendation you'll stick with one of these.

URLs, URIs, and URNs

Before you begin to choose your namespace you need to understand the difference between URLs, URIs, and URNs.

A URL is a Uniform Resource Locator. It specifies the location of a resource, for example a web page, and how it can be retrieved. It has the following format:

```
[Scheme]://[Domain]:[Port]/[Path]?[QueryString]#[FragmentId]
```

The terms in square brackets are replaced by their actual values and the rest of the items other than `Scheme` and `Domain` are optional. So a typical web URL would be `http://www.wrox.com/remtitle.cgi?isbn=0470114878`.

The scheme is `http`, the domain is `www.wrox.com`, followed by the path and a querystring. This URL enables you to locate a resource, in this case a web page about the previous edition of this book, using the HTTP protocol. You can use many other schemes, such as FTP and HTTPS, but the main point about URLs is that they enable you to locate a resource, whether that is a web page, a file, or something else.

A URI, on the other hand, is a Uniform Resource Identifier; it can have the same format as a URL or it can be in the URN format, which you learn about next. It doesn't have to point to anything tangible — it's just a unique string that identifies something. All URLs are also URIs but the opposite is not necessarily true. You'll see that when designing your first namespace, you end up with a unique identifier, but one that does not have a physical representation on the Internet.

URNs are slightly different again; the letters stand for Uniform Resource Name. A URN is a name that uniquely defines something. In the non-computing world analogies would be Social Security numbers and ISBNs. They both uniquely identify something — U.S. citizens and editions of books, respectively.

URNs take the following format:

```
urn:[namespace identifier]:[namespace specific string]
```

As before, the items in square brackets need to be replaced by actual values and the three-character prefix, `urn`, is not case-sensitive.

The *namespace identifier* is a string of characters such as `isbn`, which identifies how the namespace specific string should be interpreted. Namespace identifiers can be registered with the Internet Assigned Numbers Authority (IANA) if they are expected to be utilized by many different organizations. The latter part of the URN, the *namespace specific string*, identifies the actual thing within the category set by the identifier. An example of a URN using a registered scheme would be:

```
urn:isbn:9780470114872
```

This URN uniquely identifies the fourth edition of this book, but because it's a URN, not a URL, it doesn't tell you anything about how to retrieve either the book itself or any information about it.

So, in brief, URLs and URNs are both URIs; a URL tells you the how and where of something, and the URN is simply a unique name. Both URLs and URNs are used to create XML Namespace URIs, as you'll see next.

Creating Your First Namespace

When creating your first namespace you should use the URI format. As stated earlier, the URI must be unique because you don't want it to clash with someone else's choice. Because most companies and independent software developers have their own registered domain, it's become fairly standard to use their domain name as a starting point. So your namespace starts with `http://wrox.com/`. Following the domain name you can use most any combination of characters you want, although you should avoid spaces and the question mark. The definitive list of what is and isn't allowed depends on whether you're using XML Namespace version 1.0 or version 1.1 (see the note in the later section on declaring namespaces for more details).

Now for your user element, which in the example scenario came from an application configuration file that may have been used by your HR system, you might choose the full namespace: `http://wrox.com/namespaces/applications/hr/config`.

This actual string of characters chosen is known as the *namespace URI*. Namespaces are case-sensitive so try to be consistent when inventing them; sticking to all lowercase can save having to remember which letters were capitalized.

***WARNING** As mentioned previously, don't be distracted by the fact that the preceding namespace looks like a URL — it definitely isn't one. If you type the namespace into a browser's address bar you won't see anything returned. This is one of the main problems experienced when first meeting namespaces; the domain part is there to make sure that the namespaces are unique across the globe and has no bearing on whether they can be browsed to.*

HOW TO DECLARE A NAMESPACE

You can declare a namespace in two ways, depending on whether you want all the elements in a document to be under the namespace or just a few specific elements to be under it. If you want all elements to be included, you can use the following style:

```
xmlns= "http://wrox.com/namespaces/applications/hr/config"
```

Therefore, if you take your `appUsers.xml` file from Chapter 1 you have what's shown in Listing 3-3.

LISTING 3-3: appUsers.xml

Available for download on Wrox.com

```
<applicationUsers>
  <user firstName="Joe" lastName="Fawcett" />
  <user firstName="Danny" lastName="Ayers" />
  <user firstName="Catherine" lastName="Middleton" />
</applicationUsers>
```

To add the namespace declaration, change it to the code shown in Listing 3-4.

LISTING 3-4: appUsersWithDefaultNamespace.xml

Available for download on Wrox.com

```
<applicationUsers
 xmlns="http://wrox.com/namespaces/applications/hr/config">
  <user firstName="Joe" lastName="Fawcett" />
  <user firstName="Danny" lastName="Ayers" />
  <user firstName="Catherine" lastName="Middleton" />
</applicationUsers>
```

This is known as declaring a default namespace, which is associated with the element on which it is declared, in this case `<applicationUsers>`, and any element contained within it. The namespace is said to be in scope for all these elements. Attributes, such as `firstName`, are not covered by a default namespace.

WARNING *One of the common complaints about the implementation of XML Namespaces is that the declarations themselves look very much like attributes. This can cause considerable confusion when trying to deal with the document programmatically. Although they do look like attributes, they are treated completely differently and won't appear in any attributes collection, for instance. There have been many proposals to change the way they are declared but this would mean breaking most existing parsers so it seems unlikely that a change will occur.*

Once an element has an associated namespace it no longer has a simple name such as `user`; the namespace has to be taken into account as well. There is no W3C standard for showing the element's full name but there is a convention, called Clark notation (after James Clark, one of the founding fathers of XML) that can be used. The Clark notation places the namespace URI in curly braces before what is known as the *local name*. Using Clark notation, the `user` element would have the full name:

```
{http://wrox.com/namespaces/applications/hr/config}user
```

WARNING *Not realizing that a default namespace is present is one of the most common causes of code failing to work in the XML world, particularly with XSLT, as you see in Chapter 8.*

As mentioned previously, a default namespace applies only to elements. Attributes need their namespaces to be specifically declared, and other components of an XML document, such as comments, don't have associated namespaces at all.

To declare a namespace explicitly you have to choose a prefix to represent it. This is partly because it would be very onerous having to use the full name every time you created a tag or an attribute. The prefix can be more or less whatever you like; it follows the same naming rules as an element or attribute, but cannot contain a colon (`:`).

WARNING *Some prefixes are reserved, such as* xml, xmlns, *and any other combinations beginning with the characters* xml. *This means that you are not allowed to use these prefixes to represent your chosen namespace URIs when designing your own XML.*

Say you decide to use hr as your prefix. You would then declare your namespace using the slightly modified form:

```
xmlns:hr="http://wrox.com/namespaces/applications/hr/config"
```

Note the hr prefix follows the xmlns in the declaration.

Listing 3-5 shows the full file, now including the namespace declaration that has a prefix of hr.

Available for download on Wrox.com

LISTING 3-5: appUsersWithNamespace.xml

```
<applicationUsers xmlns:hr="http://wrox.com/namespaces/applications/hr/config">
  <user firstName="Joe" lastName="Fawcett" />
  <user firstName="Danny" lastName="Ayers" />
  <user firstName="Catherine" lastName="Middleton" />
</applicationUsers>
```

However, this just means that you have a namespace URI that is identified by a prefix of hr; so far none of the elements or attributes are grouped in that namespace. To associate the elements with the namespace you have to add the prefix to the elements' tags. For example, start by showing that the <applicationUsers> element resides in the http://wrox.com/namespaces/applications/hr/config namespace (referred to from now on as the hr namespace). The document would then look like Listing 3-6.

Available for download on Wrox.com

LISTING 3-6: appUsersWithNamespaceUsedOnRoot.xml

```
<hr:applicationUsers xmlns:hr="http://wrox.com/namespaces/applications/hr/config">
  <user firstName="Joe" lastName="Fawcett" />
  <user firstName="Danny" lastName="Ayers" />
  <user firstName="Catherine" lastName="Middleton" />
</hr:applicationUsers>
```

Notice that the prefix, hr, has been added to both the start and the end tags and is followed by a colon and then the element's local name.

> **NOTE** *It's also possible to use a DTD to add namespace declarations to a document. In general I don't like this practice. It's often unclear what the namespace is because the DTD is usually referenced rather than embedded. Given that this practice is dying out it won't be covered in this chapter.*

If you want the attributes in the document to be also in the hr namespace you follow a similar procedure as shown in Listing 3-7:

LISTING 3-7: appUsersWithNamespaceUsedOnAttributes.xml

Available for download on Wrox.com

```
<hr:applicationUsers xmlns:hr="http://wrox.com/namespaces/applications/hr/config">
  <user hr:firstName="Joe" hr:lastName="Fawcett" />
  <user hr:firstName="Danny" hr:lastName="Ayers" />
  <user hr:firstName="Catherine" hr:lastName="Middleton" />
</hr:applicationUsers>
```

Again the namespace prefix is prepended to the attribute's name and followed by a colon. In most XML documents that use namespaces you'll see that it's very common that elements belong to a particular namespace, but less so for attributes. The reason for this is that attributes are always associated with an element; they can't stand alone. Therefore, if the element itself is in a namespace, the attribute is already uniquely identifiable and there's really no need for it to be a namespace.

> **NOTE** *An element or attribute name with a prefix is known as a* Qualified Name, *often abbreviated to* QName. *The part after the prefix is technically known as a* Local Name.

Remember that the namespace declaration must come either on the element that uses it or on one higher in the tree, an *ancestor* as it's often called. This means that the file in Listing 3-8 is not well-formed because the declaration is too far down the tree and therefore not in scope.

LISTING 3-8: appUsersWithIncorrectDeclaration.xml

Available for download on Wrox.com

```
<hr:applicationUsers>
  <user
         xmlns:hr="http://wrox.com/namespaces/applications/hr/config"
         firstName="Joe" lastName="Fawcett" />
  <user firstName="Danny" lastName="Ayers" />
  <user firstName="Catherine" lastName="Middleton" />
</hr:applicationUsers>
```

It isn't necessary to declare all your namespaces on the root element, but it is common practice to do so (unless you have a good reason not to) and usually makes the document that much easier to read.

If your document uses only one namespace and all the elements in the document belong to it, there's little to choose between using a default namespace and one with a defined prefix. As far as the XML parser is concerned there is no difference between the document in Listing 3-4, which used a default namespace declaration, and the one in Listing 3-9, which uses an explicit declaration with the prefix `hr`.

LISTING 3-9: appUsersWithExplicitNamespaceUsedThroughout.xml

Available for download on Wrox.com

```
<hr:applicationUsers xmlns:hr="http://wrox.com/namespaces/applications/hr/config">
  <hr:user firstName="Joe" lastName="Fawcett" />
  <hr:user firstName="Danny" lastName="Ayers" />
  <hr:user firstName="Catherine" lastName="Middleton" />
</hr:applicationUsers>
```

Notice how the declaration is made on the root element and all start and end tags have the hr prefix. This is a typical example of how a document with an explicitly-defined namespace looks and many of the documents you will encounter in real life follow this pattern.

How Exactly Does Scope Work?

The principle of being *in scope* applies to any namespaces declared in an XML document and it's important to clearly understand this concept. *In scope* means the same for XML Namespaces as it does in more traditional programming settings — the namespace is available to be used. Just because a namespace is in scope doesn't mean that an element belongs to it. Take Listing 3-10, which takes the current example and modifies it slightly, moving the declaration from the <applicationUsers> element.

LISTING 3-10: appUsersWithNarrowScopeDeclaration.xml

Available for download on Wrox.com

```
<applicationUsers>
  <hr:user xmlns:hr="http://wrox.com/namespaces/applications/hr/config"
        firstName="Joe" lastName="Fawcett" />
  <user firstName="Danny" lastName="Ayers" />
  <user firstName="Catherine" lastName="Middleton" />
</applicationUsers>
```

Now the namespace declaration is on the first <user> element. It is only in scope for that element, its attributes, and any elements it contains (in this case there aren't any). Because of this the namespace cannot be used on either the <applicationUsers> element or any of the other <user> elements — trying to assign a prefix to these elements would lead to an error when parsing the XML. It is usually considered good practice when designing an XML document to limit the scope of any namespace declarations by declaring them at as low a level as possible in the document, as long as you still only have to declare them once. This maintains standard programming practice in other languages, where it is frowned on to declare all variables as global and better to declare them only when they are needed and therefore limit their scope.

Declaring More Than One Namespace

Many documents use more than one namespace to group their elements. Typically, you have a number of choices when you need to design XML in this fashion. One option is to choose a default namespace for some elements and an explicit one for others. You can stick with the example document but you need to incorporate a few changes:

1. First, place the <applicationUsers> element in the hr namespace and the <user> elements themselves in a different one, which is used by <user> elements across all company documents. This namespace will be http://wrox.com/namespaces/general/entities.

2. Now create the hr namespace as the default and the entities namespace as explicit. You need a prefix for the newer one so choose ent. This means your document will look like Listing 3-11.

LISTING 3-11: appUsersWithTwoNamespaces.xml

```
<applicationUsers
      xmlns="http://wrox.com/namespaces/applications/hr/config"
      xmlns:ent="http://wrox.com/namespaces/general/entities">
  <ent:user firstName="Joe" lastName="Fawcett" />
  <ent:user firstName="Danny" lastName="Ayers" />
  <ent:user firstName="Catherine" lastName="Middleton" />
</applicationUsers>
```

Because both declarations are on the root element they are in scope for the whole of the document. Therefore any elements without a prefix fall into the hr namespace and any with an ent prefix fall into the entities namespace. None of the attributes in this document are in a namespace. If you wanted you could just as easily have declared the entities namespace as the default and used the hr prefix for the other one; in real life you would probably choose the default for the namespace that was most used.

Alternatively, if you want to avoid a default namespace because you think it makes which element is grouped under which namespace clearer, you could make both namespace declarations explicit as shown in Listing 3-12.

LISTING 3-12: appUsersWithTwoExplicitNamespaces.xml

```
<hr:applicationUsers
      xmlns:hr="http://wrox.com/namespaces/applications/hr/config"
      xmlns:ent="http://wrox.com/namespaces/general/entities">
  <ent:user firstName="Joe" lastName="Fawcett" />
  <ent:user firstName="Danny" lastName="Ayers" />
  <ent:user firstName="Catherine" lastName="Middleton" />
</hr:applicationUsers>
```

However, there is a third option to consider when dealing with multiple namespaces that occurs less commonly: declaring a namespace twice with different prefixes, as shown in Listing 3-13.

LISTING 3-13: appUsersWithNamespaceDeclaredTwice.xml

```
<hr1:applicationUsers
  xmlns:hr1="http://wrox.com/namespaces/applications/hr/config"
  xmlns:hr2="http://wrox.com/namespaces/applications/hr/config">
```

continues

LISTING 3-13 *(continued)*

```
    <hr2:user firstName="Joe" lastName="Fawcett" />
    <hr2:user firstName="Danny" lastName="Ayers" />
    <hr2:user firstName="Catherine" lastName="Middleton" />
  </hr1:applicationUsers>
```

Notice how both prefixes, `hr1` and `hr2`, point to the same namespace URI. The document element, `<applicationUsers>`, uses the `hr1` prefix whereas the other elements use `hr2`. It's not something you're likely to need but you do occasionally come across it when two different applications have had a part in creating an XML file and the prefixes were chosen independently.

What you can't have, though, is the same prefix pointing to different namespace URIs, as shown in Listing 3-14.

Available for download on Wrox.com

LISTING 3-14: appUsersWithPrefixedMappedTwiceIllegally.xml

```
<hr:applicationUsers
    xmlns:hr="http://wrox.com/namespaces/applications/hr/config"
    xmlns:hr="http://wrox.com/namespaces/general/entities">
  <hr:user firstName="Joe" lastName="Fawcett" />
  <hr:user firstName="Danny" lastName="Ayers" />
  <hr:user firstName="Catherine" lastName="Middleton" />
</hr:applicationUsers>
```

In this example, the parser can't tell which namespace URI to use when it encounters the `hr` prefix, so the XML is not well-formed or, to use the full technical terminology, it's not *namespace–well-formed*.

Changing a Namespace Declaration

Although it's not something that you would want to do regularly, there are a few instances in which you would want to change a namespace declaration; this is most likely when a document has been created from components coming from different sources. You can do this in one of three ways:

- Change the mapping between a prefix and a namespace URI
- Change the default namespace
- Remove a namespace from scope by undeclaring it

First, take an example of changing the mapping between a prefix and its namespace URI. In a realistic scenario, you need an XML document with at least two levels of nesting, shown in Listing 3-15.

Available for download on Wrox.com

LISTING 3-15: ChangingNamespaceBindings.xml

```
<hr:config xmlns:hr="http://wrox.com/namespaces/applications/hr/config">
  <hr:applicationUsers xmlns:hr="http://wrox.com/namespaces/general/entities">
      <hr:user firstName="Joe" lastName="Fawcett" />
      <hr:user firstName="Danny" lastName="Ayers" />
      <hr:user firstName="Catherine" lastName="Middleton" />
  </hr:applicationUsers>
</hr:config>
```

This is not a good practice, so this example is a little contrived, but it shows the namespace declaration on the `<config>` element being mapped to the `hr` prefix and then, on the `<applicationUsers>` element, a different namespace URI is mapped to the same prefix. Although this is confusing, it can happen when you receive different parts of an XML file from separate sources. There are certainly no benefits to using this technique unless it's absolutely necessary and, although a software application should have no trouble reading the document, it makes human consumption difficult.

You can also use this technique to change the document's default namespace as shown in Listing 3-16.

Available for download on Wrox.com

LISTING 3-16: ChangingDefaultNamespaceBindings.xml

```
<config xmlns="http://wrox.com/namespaces/applications/hr/config">
  <applicationUsers xmlns="http://wrox.com/namespaces/general/entities">
      <user firstName="Joe" lastName="Fawcett" />
      <user firstName="Danny" lastName="Ayers" />
      <user firstName="Catherine" lastName="Middleton" />
  </applicationUsers>
</config>
```

Now the `<config>` element is in the `http://wrox.com/namespaces/applications/hr/config` namespace but the other elements contained within it are in the `http://wrox.com/namespaces/general/entities` one. Again, this is not something you'd strive for yourself but it's a scenario that might occur in files you receive from others. For example you may have two documents that both use a default namespace but you need to embed one inside the other. As you know, an application can cope with reading this sort of hybrid document but if you also want humans to edit it, using more than one default namespace is definitely something to avoid.

A slightly different scenario occurs when you want to undeclare a namespace mapping completely. Whether you can do this depends on if it's a default mapping and which version of the XML Namespaces recommendation you are using. The default mapping can be undeclared in all versions (currently there are versions 1.0 and 1.1) and you just need to use an empty namespace URI as shown in Listing 3-17.

Available for download on Wrox.com

LISTING 3-17: UndeclaringTheDefaultNamespaceMapping.xml

```
<config xmlns="http://wrox.com/namespaces/applications/hr/config">
  <applicationUsers xmlns="">
      <user firstName="Joe" lastName="Fawcett" />
      <user firstName="Danny" lastName="Ayers" />
      <user firstName="Catherine" lastName="Middleton" />
  </applicationUsers>
</config>
```

In this variation the `<config>` element is in the `http://wrox.com/namespaces/applications/hr/config` namespace, but the other elements are not in any namespace (otherwise known as being in the empty or null namespace). This is because the `xmlns=""` on the `<applicationUsers>` element undeclares the namespace mapping.

If you want to do a similar operation when using an explicit namespace — one with a prefix defined — you need to specify that you're using version 1.1 in the XML declaration. This means that you need to check that the XML parser you're intending to use supports this newer version. Most of the big names do, although Microsoft's .NET parser doesn't and many other lesser-known ones don't either. Listing 3-18 shows an XML document that declares the correct version and then maps and unmaps a namespace to a prefix.

LISTING 3-18: UndeclaringAPrefixedNamespaceMapping.xml

Available for download on Wrox.com

```
<?xml version="1.1" ?>
<hr:config xmlns:hr="http://wrox.com/namespaces/applications/hr/config">
  <applicationUsers xmlns:hr=»»>
      <user firstName=»Joe» lastName=»Fawcett» />
      <user firstName=»Danny» lastName=»Ayers» />
      <user firstName=»Catherine» lastName=»Middleton» />
  </applicationUsers>
</hr:config>
```

Here the `hr` prefix is mapped to a namespace URI on the `<config>` element and then unmapped on the `<applicationUsers>` element. This means that it would be illegal to try to use the prefix from this point. Note that for this to be legal syntax you must declare that you're using version 1.1 as shown on the first line of the listing.

NOTE *Another change made in version 1.1 is that namespace URIs (Uniform Resource Identifiers) are now officially IRIs (Internationalized Resource Identifiers). This means that they can contain characters from sets other than the basic ASCII ones. You may have noticed that web addresses sometimes have characters that need to be escaped using the* `%xx` *format, where* `xx` *represents the Unicode code point for the character (refer to Chapter 2 for more on Unicode). With IRIs these characters can be used directly so, for example, a Russian website can use characters from the Cyrillic alphabet in its page names. You can find the full specification for URIs and IRIs on the W3C's website.*

Returning to the XML file showing the employee data example from earlier, you can see how you separate the two sets of information using namespaces. You use an explicit declaration for the basic employee data and a default declaration for the biographical data that uses elements from the XHTML namespace, as shown in Listing 3-19:

LISTING 3-19: employees.xml

Available for download on Wrox.com

```
<emp:employees xmlns:emp="http://wrox.com/namespaces/general/employee">
  <emp:employee id="001">
    <emp:firstName>Joe</emp:firstName>
```

```
        <emp:lastName>Fawcett</emp:lastName>
      <emp:title>Mr</emp:title>
      <emp:dateOfBirth>1962-11-19</emp:dateOfBirth>
      <emp:dateOfHire>2005-12-05</emp:dateOfHire>
      <emp:position>Head of Software Development</emp:position>
      <emp:biography>
        <html xmlns="http://www.w3.org/1999/xhtml">
          <head>
            <title>Joe's Biography</title>
          </head>
          <body>
            <p>After graduating from the University of Life
 Joe moved into software development, originally working with COBOL on mainframes in
the 1980s.</p>
          </body>
        </html>
      </emp:biography>
    </emp:employee>
    <!-- more employee elements can be added here -->
  </emp:employees>
```

The first declaration is on the `<emp:employees>` element, so it is in scope for the whole document. The second declaration is on the `<html>` element, so it applies only to this element and those contained within it. Now any software processing this document can easily differentiate between the two `<title>` elements because one has the full name of:

```
{ http://wrox.com/namespaces/general/employee}title
```

And the other has:

```
{ http://www.w3.org/1999/xhtml}title
```

Thus far you have learned the following important concepts about namespaces:

- Their main purpose is to group elements and to differentiate an element from others with a similar name.
- You can choose any string of characters for the namespace URI, although it's common practice to start it with your domain name.
- You can choose between a default namespace, where all elements are included automatically, or a prefixed namespace declaration, where you need to add the prefix to the start and end tags of any elements you wish to include.
- Your prefix can be more or less what you want, with the exception of being unable to use colons; it makes sense to use a short, simple character string.

The next section will introduce you to a number of real-world applications that make use of namespaces.

NAMESPACE USAGE IN THE REAL WORLD

You will most likely encounter namespaces whenever you use XML that has been designed for mass consumption rather than for just one application. Although the primary reason to use namespaces is still to group elements that are used together and to differentiate them from others with the same name, there are other common uses as well. These include the following:

- **XML Schemas:** Defining the structure of a document.
- **Combination documents:** Merging documents from more than one source.
- **Versioning:** Differentiating between different versions of an XML format.

This section shows some common uses of namespaces in some real-life situations, starting with XML Schema.

XML Schema

XML Schema gets a whole chapter to itself later in this book so this section just gives a quick overview of the basics and how namespaces are used within this branch of XML.

The basic idea behind XML Schemas is that they describe the legitimate format that an XML document can take. This goes beyond being well-formed, which is discussed in Chapter 2, and moves on to exactly which elements and attributes are allowed where, and what sort of content these items can contain. For example, an attribute of `creationDate` on an element of `<logEntry>` would normally be expected to contain a date or possibly a date and time. The schema associated with this document would detail that requirement. Besides the date and time data types there are a host of others such as decimal, string, and Boolean.

XML Schema works by assigning the format and content type based on namespaces; any rules target a single given namespace. If your XML format deals with elements from different namespaces, you need to create a schema for each one and then merge these together using techniques you learn in Chapter 5.

Given that the XML Schema recommendation has already declared a broad range of types dealing with numbers, text, dates, and times, it's handy to be able to use these types in other documents, not just when you're describing the content of elements and attributes. For example, XSLT, which is described in Chapter 8, was primarily designed to convert one XML format into another. It has the facility to create functions to help in this matter and these functions need a way to specify their return type, as is common in most programming languages. Rather than reinvent the wheel and come out with another long list of types that may be returned, XSLT can use the same types as XML Schema. You simply have to declare the XML Schema namespace, which is `http://www.w3.org/2001/XMLSchema`, and assign a prefix such as `xs` in your XSLT document. You can then declare that your function returns an `xs:string` or an `xs:boolean`, for example. You see some full examples of this in Chapter 8, which covers XSLT in depth.

Documents with Multiple Namespaces

Another common example of needing a document with more than one namespace is when you want to embed XML into a web page. For example, Scalable Vector Graphics (SVG) provides for a standardized XML representation of graphics. The advantages of being able to describe these as XML are that any manipulation of them, such as stretching or changing the colors or rotation, is now a relatively simple process of transforming the XML rather than processor-hungry manipulation of bitmaps. You can use SVG from within a web page but you need to be careful to make sure the browser knows which part is to be rendered as traditional HTML and which part needs to be processed by the SVG plug-in. You do this by creating different namespaces for the two distinct parts of the document. The following Try It Out takes you through the process of creating a simple web page and then adding extra content, in the form of SVG. It shows how the browser needs this extra content defined in the SVG namespace so that it can choose which plug-in parses the XML and renders it as an image.

TRY IT OUT SVG within a Web Page

Even with two different namespaces, the main browsers — such as Internet Explorer, Firefox, and Chrome — struggle. That's because, at heart, they are not strict XML processors but have to deal with plain HTML (possibly with incorrect syntax), XHTML, and a number of other formats. To get around this you should embed the SVG file within the XHTML using an iframe rather than have the two syntaxes intermingled on the one page. You will still need two namespaces, though, to make sure that elements are handled correctly.

1. Start with a bare-bones XHTML page as shown in the following snippet and save it as `EmbeddedSVG.htm`:

```
<!DOCTYPE html PUBLIC "-//W3C//DTD XHTML 1.0 Transitional//EN"
"http://www.w3.org/TR/xhtml1/DTD/xhtml1-transitional.dtd">
<html xmlns="http://www.w3.org/1999/xhtml" >
<head>
    <title>Embedded SVG</title>
</head>
<body>
<h1>Embedded SVG Example</h1>
<!-- SVG will go here -->
</body>
</html>
```

EmbeddedSVG.htm

Because this is XHTML rather than HTML it has a default namespace declared, `http://www.w3.org/1999/xhtml`, on the root element. It also has a doctype, which is not essential from an XML point of view but the browser needs this to know whether the document conforms to the agreed format for XHTML.

2. Now you need to create a simple SVG document. Using a simple text editor such as Notepad, create a file named `shapes.svg` and add the following code to form the basis of the document:

```
<?xml version="1.0" encoding="utf-8" standalone="no"?>
<!DOCTYPE svg PUBLIC "-//W3C//DTD SVG 1.0//EN"
"http://www.w3.org/TR/SVG/DTD/svg10.dtd">
<svg viewBox="0 0 270 400" width="100%" height="100%"
xmlns="http://www.w3.org/2000/svg">

  <!-- body of svg document -->
</svg>
```

3. Save it in the same folder as `EmbeddedSVG.htm`. Remember that SVG stands for Scalable Vector Graphics and the format is used to describe shapes, from very simple to highly complex ones. Your SVG file will display three basic shapes: a rectangle, a circle, and an ellipse. A caption will also be associated with each item. The SVG file also has a doctype and its own namespace, `http://www.w3.org/2000/svg`. You can see that after the XML prolog the root element is `<svg>` which is in the `http://www.w3.org/2000/svg` namespace.

4. Further down the hierarchy, after a `<g>` element (which represents a graphics item), come three elements named `<rect>`, `<circle>`, and `<ellipse>` as shown in the following snippet:

```
<g id="mainlayer">
  <rect fill="red" stroke="black" x="15" y="15" width="100" height="50"/>
  <circle fill="yellow" stroke="black" cx="62" cy="135" r="20"/>
  <ellipse fill="green" stroke="black" cx="200" cy="135" rx="50" ry="20"/>
  <!-- shape descriptions -->
</g>
```

5. After these comes another `<g>` element containing the three captions for the shapes:

```
<g font-size="20px">
  <text x="44" y="88">rectangle</text>
  <text x="36" y="180">circle</text>
  <text x="170" y="180">ellipse</text>
</g>
```

6. When you are finished, the full document should look like the following:

Available for download on Wrox.com

```
<?xml version="1.0" encoding="utf-8" standalone="no"?>
<!DOCTYPE svg PUBLIC "-//W3C//DTD SVG 1.0//EN"
"http://www.w3.org/TR/SVG/DTD/svg10.dtd">
<svg viewBox="0 0 270 400" width="100%" height="100%"
xmlns="http://www.w3.org/2000/svg">
  <g id="mainlayer">
    <rect fill="red" stroke="black" x="15" y="15" width="100" height="50"/>
    <circle fill="yellow" stroke="black" cx="62" cy="135" r="20"/>
    <ellipse fill="green" stroke="black" cx="200" cy="135" rx="50" ry="20"/>
    <g font-size="20px">
      <text x="44" y="88">rectangle</text>
      <text x="36" y="180">circle</text>
      <text x="170" y="180">ellipse</text>
    </g>
  </g>
</svg >
```

Shapes.svg

7. Now you need to embed the SVG in the web page. You have three possible ways of doing this:

   - Use an `<embed>` element. This works in most browsers but isn't part of strict XHTML.
   - Use an `<object>` element. This works in Firefox and Chrome but can be problematic in Internet Explorer.
   - Use an `<iframe>` element. Probably the simplest technique and one that you'll use here. It works in all browsers capable of displaying SVG.

Note that if you're using an older version of IE you may need to download the Adobe SVG plugin from `http://www.adobe.com/svg/viewer/install/`.

8. So your final file will look like this:

```
<!DOCTYPE html PUBLIC "-//W3C//DTD XHTML 1.0 Transitional//EN"
"http://www.w3.org/TR/xhtml1/DTD/xhtml1-transitional.dtd">
<html xmlns="http://www.w3.org/1999/xhtml">
<head>
  <title>Embedded SVG</title>
</head>
<body>
  <h1>
    Embedded SVG Example</h1>
  <iframe src="shapes.svg" width="400" height="400"></iframe>
</body>
</html>
```

The `shapes.svg` file needs to be in the same folder as `EmbeddedSVG.htm`. The final result looks something like Figure 3-1.

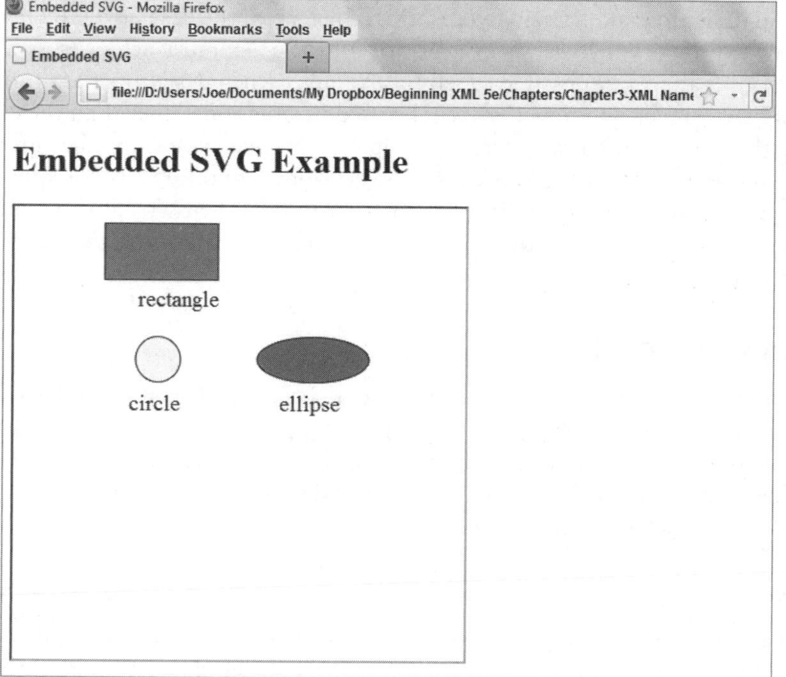

FIGURE 3-1

How it Works

All modern browsers can handle a variety of different data formats. The majority of web pages contain HTML formatted text and images, which can be JPGs, PNGs or GIFs to name but a few. Browsers can also handle a variety of other text-based formats provided that they have either native support or access to a suitable plug-in. Whichever of these two options apply, it is necessary for the browser to be able to differentiate which specific content is passed to each handler. The most common way that this occurs is by declaring XML-based content in a specific namespace. In this example the main content is XHTML, rendered by the standard browser display engine. XHTML elements are grouped under the `http://www.w3.org/1999/xhtml` namespace. The SVG content is contained in an iframe. When the browser encounters the SVG namespace, `http://www.w3.org/2000/svg`, it realizes that the standard XHTML parser won't suffice and it looks for a handler that can process the content. Some browsers come with a built-in SVG parser; others require you to have installed one separately. Whichever option is needed, any content in the SVG namespace is rendered using the rules defined in the SVG standards as a graphic.

WHEN TO USE AND NOT USE NAMESPACES

When designing an XML format for some data that doesn't already possess a standard representation, you should consider carefully whether or not the document should use a namespace. Although there are a number of good reasons to use one there are also scenarios where a namespace will only add to the work involved in designing and utilizing your XML. In general the case normally favors using a namespace, and the extra work involved is usually offset by the flexibility achieved as well as future-proofing your design; it's almost impossible to tell for example, when designing data formats, how long they will remain in existence and how they will be used in situations other than the ones which initially warranted their creation. For a concrete example of this, cast your mind back to the *Millennium Bug*. Masses of software rewriting was caused by developers in the 1970s not appreciating that the chosen date format using just two digits for the year limited their work to a twenty to thirty year life span. The next two sections cover common situations for when you should use namespaces and when you shouldn't.

When Namespaces are Needed

You've seen the main reason for using namespaces: to differentiate between elements that have the same name. This is one of the main reasons for using namespaces in your documents. The other reasons to do so are discussed in this section. Once you have got the hang of XML Namespaces you'll naturally assume that documents generally use them, and it's certainly unusual to find XML made for consumption by more than one client to not have any.

When There's No Choice

The first situation is the easiest; sometimes you have no choice in the matter. For example, if you choose to use a format designed by someone else to represent your data, the chances are that the format insists on the elements being in a namespace. If you decide to change this and just use the prescribed format but without namespaces, you'll find three things:

- You won't be able to validate whether the documents you create are in the correct format because, as was pointed out earlier, any XML Schema that describes the document's format will be targeting items in the relevant namespace.

- You won't be able to share these documents outside your own systems; others will expect the namespaced version.
- Your system won't accept documents from external sources because these will be namespaced.

If you decide that a previously-developed format suits your data, you should adopt it completely and not try to change it. This will leave you capable of using standard tools designed to work with that format and increase the chances of interoperability.

When You Need Interoperability

If you decide that an XML format is the best way to represent your data, your next question may well be, "Do I need to share this data with other systems, particularly those not developed externally?"

If the answer to this question is *yes*, you should probably group your elements under a namespace. Even if, in your local systems the document will always stand alone and there's no danger of a clash of element names, you can't tell how other systems will use this information. They may well need to embed your XML into a larger document and need the namespaces to differentiate your data from the complete structure.

When You Need Validation

Validation is covered in the next two chapters, but earlier you saw that XML Schemas provide a way to dictate the structure of an XML document and which content types the elements and attributes can contain. Although it's possible to have a schema that works without using namespaces it's quite rare and can cause problems when document collation is needed. So if you want to be able validate your document, it needs to use namespaces.

When Namespaces Are Not Needed

The main case for avoiding namespaces is when you have the need to store or exchange data for relatively small documents that will be seen only by a limited number of systems, ideally those developed internally by yourself or others in your organization.

A typical example of this situation might be when a web page needs to retrieve snippets of data from a web service using Ajax. If you have a page that accepts two numeric values and two currency descriptors that are used to convert from one denomination to another, you might be expecting a response that looks something like:

```
<conversion amount= "100" from= "USD" to= "GBP">60.86</conversion>
```

In this case the response is so small and the chance of the service being used externally is so low that it doesn't make sense to add the complexity of namespaces.

NOTE *Many might argue that with such small amounts of data and the fact that it's only going to be consumed directly by a browser, XML isn't a good choice for the data format in the first place, never mind whether you should worry about using a namespace. This sort of situation is where you might reject XML in favor of a more lightweight format such as JSON, which, along with AJAX, is covered in more depth Chapter 16.*

Versioning and Namespaces

One way in that people have used namespaces in the past is to differentiate between various versions of their formats. For example, if you go back to the `employees.xml` file from earlier, you used a namespace of `http://wrox.com/namespaces/general/employee`. Suppose you come out with a newer version of the format — you may decide to change it to `http://wrox.com/namespaces/general/employee/v2`. Superficially this seems like a good idea because the two formats will probably only differ slightly; there may be some extra elements and attributes in the later version but the general structure is likely to be similar. In practice, though, it rarely is.

The reason for this becomes clear when you ask the question, "How do I want the application to handle the two different versions?" There are four different scenarios:

- Version one of the application opens a version one file.
- Version one of the application opens a version two file.
- Version two of the application opens a version one file.
- Version two of the application opens a version two file.

The first and the last cases are easy, but the other two need some thought. If version one of the software opens a version two file, would you expect it to be able to read it or not? Will it just ignore any elements it does not recognize and process the rest as normal, or just reject the file out of hand? A similar issue applies in the third case. Should the version two system recognize an earlier XML version and just add some defaults for any missing values, or should it just announce that the file is not the correct format?

If you're happy for the applications to reject a mismatching file, you can safely use different namespaces for each version. It won't matter because, for all intents and purposes, to the version two application a version one file may as well be a random XML document such as an XHTML page; it's just not going to read it. If, however, you want the applications to be able to cope with both the earlier and the later formats it's important that the two namespaces are the same. If this isn't the case, the systems would need to know the namespaces of all possible future XML formats that could be accepted. This isn't very practical; in fact, the best way to cope with versioning is to have something like a separate attribute on the file, something like this:

```
<emp:employees
  xmlns:emp="http://wrox.com/namespaces/general/employee"
  version="1.0">
  <!-- rest of data -->
</emp:employee>
```

As stated earlier, more experienced XML developers tend to veer towards using namespaces in their documents as opposed to using their own formats, but ultimately the choice is up to you. And this choice isn't set in stone by any means. There are plenty of public data formats that began by not using namespaces in earlier versions but changed to using them in subsequent designs. There are also examples that show the opposite — documents that originally used a namespace but then decided that it wasn't needed and reverted to a simpler format. Now that you've seen the pros and cons regarding using namespaces in your own documents you should be in a better position to make your own decision. Next you look at some common namespaces used in XML documents.

COMMON NAMESPACES

Hundreds, possibly thousands, of namespaces are accepted as standard for different XML formats. However, you will likely find yourself using many of the same ones over and over. This section just discusses some of the most common namespaces you'll encounter if your systems accept documents from external sources.

The XML Namespace

The XML Namespace is a special case. The prefix *xml* is bound to the URI `http://www.w3.org/XML/1998/namespace` and this is hard-coded into all XML parsers so you don't need to declare it yourself. This means that you can use various special attributes in your XML document, such as *xml:lang*, which is used to denote which natural language an element's content is in. For example, you may want to store phrases in multiple languages, as shown in Listing 3-20.

Available for download on Wrox.com

LISTING 3-20: UsingXmlLangAttribute.xml

```
<phrases>
  <phrase id="1">
    <text xml:lang="en-gb">Please choose a colour</text>
    <text xml:lang="en-us">Please choose a color</text>
    <text xml:lang="es-es">Por favor, elija un color</text>
  </phrase>
  <phrase id="2">
    <text xml:lang="en-gb">How large is your organisation?</text>
    <text xml:lang="en-us">>How large is your organization?</text>
    <text xml:lang="es-es">¿Qué tan grande es su organización?</text>
  </phrase>
</phrases>
```

Here the translations can be found by using a combination of the `id` attribute and the contents of `xml:lang`, which uses the first two letters for the language and the second two for the region where it's spoken. So you have each phrase in British English, U.S. English, and Spanish as spoken in Spain. Of course, you could just use your own attribute, such as `lang`, but using the standard one means that you'll get alerted if you choose an invalid language-region combination such as `en-fr` because there's no official version of English particular to France.

The other attributes and identifiers you might encounter that are in the XML Namespace are:

- `xml:space`: You met this in Chapter 2. It is used so the author of the document can specify whether whitespace is significant or not. It takes the values `preserve` or `default`.
- `xml:base`: This is used in a similar way to the base attribute in HTML. It enables you to specify a base URL from which any relative URLs in the document will be resolved.
- `xml:id`: This specifies that the value of this attribute is a unique identifier within the document.
- `xml:Father`: Although rarely seen in practice, its existence proves that the W3C's XML committee is actually human. It refers to Jon Bosak, a leading light in the XML community who chaired the original XML working group. It could be used, for example, when specifying a document's author such as `<document author="xml:Father" />`.

There's no reason for you to declare the XML Namespace but you can if want to; what you must not do is either try to bind the `xml` prefix to another URI or undeclare it — that would lead to the parser throwing an error.

The XMLNS Namespace

As you've seen throughout this chapter the `xmlns` prefix is used to declare a prefixed namespace in an XML document. Again it is hard-coded into parsers and is bound to the URI `http://www.w3.org/2000/xmlns/`. Trying to declare it yourself, or trying to bind it to another URI, is an error. This makes sense because how would you do this anyway? You need the `xmlns` prefix itself to declare or undeclare so you're creating an infinite loop if you try to bind it yourself.

The XML Schema Namespace

This namespace, with a URI of `http://www.w3.org/2001/XMLSchema`, is used in schema documents describing the legitimate structure of a particular XML format. As mentioned earlier, the data types in this namespace, such as decimal, string, and Boolean, are often used by other schemas instead of having to re-invent the list themselves. They are usually bound to the prefix `xs` or `xsd` but that's purely a personal choice. With the exception of the `xml` and `xmlns` you can choose whatever prefix you like when binding a namespace. So it is perfectly acceptable if you want a document that looks like the following:

```
<myVeryLongPrefix:schema
  xmlns:myVeryLongPrefix="http://www.w3.org/2001/XMLSchema">
  <!-- rest of document here -->
</myVeryLongPrefix:schema>
```

The XSLT Namespace

XSLT, covered in Chapter 8, is primarily used to convert XML into a different format, either a differently-formatted XML or perhaps HTML or just plain text. Because XSLT is XML itself, it's essential that its elements are in a namespace; otherwise it would be impossible to tell which parts of the document are instructions for processing and which are new elements to be output. All but the most trivial XSLT documents, therefore, have elements in multiple namespaces. The XSLT Namespace URI is `http://www.w3.org/1999/XSL/Transform` and is most commonly bound to the `xsl` or `xslt` prefix.

The SOAP Namespaces

SOAP is covered in depth in Chapters 15 and 16. It's an XML format designed to enable method calls between a client and a web service. There are two namespaces depending on which version you use (presumably, as discussed in the section on versioning using namespaces, the authors of the specifications didn't want interoperability between the two formats). The original namespace URI for SOAP 1.1 is `http://schemas.xmlsoap.org/soap/envelope/` and is usually bound to the prefix `soap`. The later one, for version 1.2, is `http://www.w3.org/2003/05/soap-envelope`, which is commonly bound to the prefix `soap12`. The SOAP namespace contains such elements as `<soap:Envelope>`, which wraps the entire message; `<soap:Header>`, which contains details such as user credentials; and `<soap:Body>`, which contains the method being called and its arguments.

The WSDL Namespace

The Web Services Description Language (WSDL) is used to describe a web service in such a way that clients can programmatically connect to a server, know what methods are available, and format their method calls appropriately. It's closely associated with the SOAP specification from the preceding paragraph. The URI is `http://www.w3.org/ns/wsdl` for both versions 1.0 and 2.0 of this format and is usually bound to the prefix `wsdl` if it's not used as the default namespace.

The Atom Namespace

This namespace is used for publishing information (such as newsfeeds) and has also been adopted by Microsoft for use in ODATA, a format where results from database queries can be presented in an XML format. The URI is `http://www.w3.org/2005/Atom`.

Atom is a rival format to RSS, which has long been used for the XML formatting of informational lists, such as blog posts or news.

The MathML Namespace

MathML is used to describe mathematical notations such as equations and their content and structure. It uses the namespace URI `http://www.w3.org/1998/Math/MathML`. It is a rather verbose language compared to traditional ways of representation but is designed to be consumed only by suitable software applications. For example, the simple equation $ax^2 + bx + c$ could be represented by Listing 3-21.

LISTING 3-21: SimpleEquationInMathML.xml

```
<!DOCTYPE math
 PUBLIC "-//W3C//DTD MathML 2.0//EN"
        "http://www.w3.org/Math/DTD/mathml2/mathml2.dtd">
<math xmlns="http://www.w3.org/1998/Math/MathML"
xmlns:xlink="http://www.w3.org/1999/xlink" overflow="scroll">
<mrow xmlns="http://www.w3.org/1998/Math/MathML"
xmlns:xlink="http://www.w3.org/1999/xlink">
  <mi xmlns="http://www.w3.org/1998/Math/MathML"
```

continues

LISTING 3-21 *(continued)*

```
xmlns:xlink="http://www.w3.org/1999/xlink">a</mi>
- <mo xmlns="http://www.w3.org/1998/Math/MathML"
xmlns:xlink="http://www.w3.org/1999/xlink">
  ?
<!--  &InvisibleTimes;
  -->
  </mo>
<msup xmlns="http://www.w3.org/1998/Math/MathML"
xmlns:xlink="http://www.w3.org/1999/xlink">
  <mi xmlns="http://www.w3.org/1998/Math/MathML"
xmlns:xlink="http://www.w3.org/1999/xlink">x</mi>
  <mn xmlns="http://www.w3.org/1998/Math/MathML"
xmlns:xlink="http://www.w3.org/1999/xlink">2</mn>
  </msup>
  <mo xmlns="http://www.w3.org/1998/Math/MathML"
xmlns:xlink="http://www.w3.org/1999/xlink">+</mo>
  <mi xmlns="http://www.w3.org/1998/Math/MathML"
xmlns:xlink="http://www.w3.org/1999/xlink">b</mi>
- <mo xmlns="http://www.w3.org/1998/Math/MathML"
xmlns:xlink="http://www.w3.org/1999/xlink">
  ?
- <!--  &InvisibleTimes;
  -->
  </mo>
  <mi xmlns="http://www.w3.org/1998/Math/MathML"
xmlns:xlink="http://www.w3.org/1999/xlink">x</mi>
  <mo xmlns="http://www.w3.org/1998/Math/MathML"
xmlns:xlink="http://www.w3.org/1999/xlink">+</mo>
  <mi xmlns="http://www.w3.org/1998/Math/MathML"
xmlns:xlink="http://www.w3.org/1999/xlink">c</mi>
  </mrow>
  </math>
```

If you have Word 2007 or greater you can try this XML by pasting it into a new document. Word understands MathML and will simply show the equation rather than the markup.

The Docbook Namespace

Finally, the Docbook namespace is normally used to mark up such things as technical publications and software and hardware manuals, although there's no reason it can't be used for other topics. It has elements such as `<book>`, `<title>`, `<chapter>`, and `<para>` to represent the various stories of a document. The namespace URI is `http://docbook.org/ns/docbook`.

SUMMARY

This chapter introduced you to XML Namespaces. You should now understand:

- The primary purpose of namespaces is to group related elements and to differentiate them from elements with the same name that were designed to represent different types of data.

- The accepted way to choose a unique namespace is to use a domain name that you control combined with a unique string of characters indicating its usage.
- There are differences between URLs, URNs, and URIs; namespaces are not URLs.
- How to declare a namespace using `xmlns`.
- There are two ways of specifying namespaces: default and prefixed.
- Documents can have more than one namespace; this makes it possible for software applications to treat the two content types differently.
- The basics of XML Schemas and how they use namespaces.

The next few chapters cover how to describe the format and content types of an XML document and how to determine if it has the correct structure.

EXERCISES

Answers to Exercises can be found in Appendix A.

1. There are three things wrong with the following namespaced document. What are they?

```
<xmlData:document>
  <xmlData:item xmlns:xmlData="http://www.wrox.com/chapter3/exercise1/data">
    <ns:details>What's wrong with this document?</ns:details>
  </xmlData:item>
</xmldata:document>
```

Exercise1-question.xml

2. There are three reasons why the following namespace URI is a poor choice for an XML format you designed. What are they?

```
http://www.wrox.com/namespaces/HR application/%7eConfig
```

▸ WHAT YOU LEARNED IN THIS CHAPTER

TOPIC	KEY POINTS
The reason for namespaces	Namespaces exist to group-related elements and to differentiate them from other elements with the same name.
Choosing namespaces	Use a unique character string; for example, a domain that you control followed by a string giving an idea of what area it is used in.
Types of namespaces	There are two types: default namespaces and those using prefixes.
Declaring default namespaces	Add `xmlns="your namespace URI here"`. The element on which this declaration appears and any under it will be in this namespace; attributes will not be in a namespace.
Declaring prefixed namespaces	Add `xmlns:prefix="your namespace URI here"`. Elements must now be written as `<prefix:myElement/>` to be included in the namespace.
Reasons to use namespaces in your own documents	You are following a predefined schema. You need to incorporate your document into another XML format. You want to make validation easier. You expect your document to be consumed by many different applications.
Reasons not to use namespaces in your own documents	You are only using the documents internally on one system. You don't need to validate the documents.

PART II
Validation

Document Type Definitions

WHAT YOU WILL LEARN IN THIS CHAPTER:

- How to create DTDs
- How to validate an XML document against a DTD
- How to use DTDs to create XML documents from multiple files

As you have seen so far, you can write well-formed XML by following a few simple rules. In effect, these rules describe how to determine one of XML's key characteristics: its structure. Without the rules, the material is ambiguous. But well-formedness only goes so far. Several other technologies are available for validating XML documents, each with their own advantages and disadvantages. Document Type Definitions (DTDs) offer a way of specifying further rules that help in the interpretation of documents and their structure. By using namespaces (see Chapter 3) it's possible to create unambiguously distinct sets of elements and attributes according the purpose you have in mind. Whether or not they appear in a namespace, such special-purpose sets of terms are sometimes known as *vocabularies*. You can describe an XML language's structure and vocabulary in a software-friendly fashion, which can be used to check whether XML documents meet the requirements. This checking is known as *validation*.

WHAT ARE DOCUMENT TYPE DEFINITIONS?

When the vocabulary and structure of potential XML documents for a given purpose are considered together, you can talk about the *type* of the documents: the elements and attributes in these documents, and how they interrelate are designed to cover a particular subject of interest. Generally speaking, this isn't any more than using a specific XML language, for example XMLTV (used for television listings) or X3D (for 3D graphics). But for validation purposes, the nature of an XML language can be much more specific, and Document Type

Definitions (DTDs) are a way to describe fairly precisely the "shape" of the language. This idea has parallels in human language.

If you want to read or write in English or German, you must have some understanding of the grammar of the language in question. In a similar fashion, it's useful to make sure the structure and vocabulary of XML documents are valid against the grammatical rules of the appropriate XML language. Fortunately, XML languages are considerably simpler than human languages. As you would expect, the grammars of XML languages are expressed with computer processing in mind. The breaking down of a human-language sentence into its grammatical components is known as *parsing*. The same applies with XML, although being simpler, a machine parser can do the job.

As mentioned in Chapter 1, parsers are the software subsystems that read the information contained in XML documents into our programs. The XML specification separates parsers into two categories: validating and nonvalidating. Validating parsers must implement validity checking using DTDs. With a validating parser, a lot of content-checking code you might otherwise need in your application is unnecessary; you can depend on the parser to verify the content of the XML document against the DTD.

NOTE *Although you learn everything you need to know about DTDs in this chapter, you might like to see the XML Recommendation and its discussion of DTDs for yourself. If so, you can look it up at* `www.w3.org/TR/REC-xml#dt-doctype`.

Working with DTDs

There are two ways of associating a DTD with a document: internally and externally. The internal approach includes the DTD within the XML document. Although this isn't a very common way of using DTDs in the wild, it can be very useful during development because you can easily change the shape of the XML and associated DTD and you can quickly confirm they are consistent with each other. Once a DTD has been developed, typically XML documents will be associated with it by reference. It's very likely you will have seen such a reference already; a large proportion of HTML pages include a line like the following:

```
<!DOCTYPE html PUBLIC "-//W3C//DTD XHTML 1.0 Transitional//EN"
"http://www.w3.org/TR/xhtml1/DTD/xhtml1-transitional.dtd">
```

You will soon see what all of this means, but first you need to get equipped to write your own DTDs. To get started, the following section examines a text editor with DTD support that can be used to parse and validate XML documents.

Using jEdit

To author XML documents and DTDs all you need is a text editor, but if you want to experiment with validation you'll want something with dedicated support built in. Lots of free, open source, and commercial tools are available for XML, and many support validation. Most Integrated

Development Environments (IDEs), such as Eclipse and NetBeans, have some XML facilities, and if you're already using one of these you may want to read the appropriate parts of your IDE's documentation. For the practical examples in this chapter and the next, you'll be using the jEdit programmer's editor available from `www.jedit.org`. It's open source and a free download is available for all major operating systems. At its core jEdit is a simple, relatively lightweight text editor. But a vast number of plugins are available which enable you to customize it to the programming language(s) of your choice.

> **NOTE** *jEdit is built in Java so you will also need Java Virtual Machine (JVM) support. There's a good chance you'll already have JVM installed because lots of software depends on it. Check for this and if necessary download what's needed at* `www.java.com`.

Once you have downloaded and installed jEdit you will need to add XML support. This is very easy.

1. First run jEdit and click the Plugins menu.
2. On the submenus you will see Plugins Manager; click this. You will be presented with a table with three tabs at the top: Manage, Update, and Install.
3. Click Install. After a moment's delay (while jEdit downloads the latest plugin list) you will see a list of available plugins, each with a checkbox to the left.
4. Scroll down to the entry for XML and click the checkbox.
5. An Install button below will be enabled; click this.
6. Once the download has finished, close the Plugin Manager window and you're ready to go.

Now that you've set up your development environment, you'll use jEdit's DTD capabilities to validate an XML document. You'll also see what happens when the content doesn't match the structure specified in the DTD.

TRY IT OUT What's in a Name?

In this example, you embed a DTD that defines the `<name>` vocabulary directly within an XML document. The editor plugin is used to confirm that the XML is valid against the DTD. You can experiment to see what is and isn't considered valid. Later, you will see how the more common approach of separating the definition from the XML document can be useful in distributed environments.

1. Run jEdit and type in the following document, making sure you include the spaces as shown. This document simply holds details of a person's full name:

```
<?xml version="1.0"?>
<!DOCTYPE name [
  <!ELEMENT name (first, middle, last)>
  <!ELEMENT first (#PCDATA)>
  <!ELEMENT middle (#PCDATA)>
```

```
  <!ELEMENT last (#PCDATA)>
]>
<name>
  <first>Joseph</first>
  <middle>John</middle>
  <last>Fawcett</last>
</name>
```

2. Click File ➪ Save As and save the file as `name-dtd.xml`.
3. You are now ready to validate the document. Click the Plugins menu, and choose XML ➪ Parse XML. This will look like Figure 4-1. A Sidekick window will appear showing the structure of the XML. Just close this.

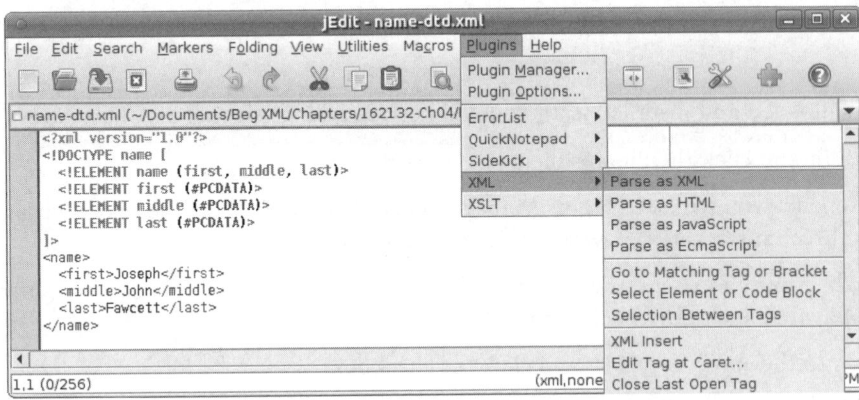

FIGURE 4-1

4. If any part of your document is now underlined in red, then the parser encountered an error. Moving the mouse over the red line will produce a pop-up describing the error. Correct the error and try again. When editing XML manually, it is common to make errors when you first begin. Very soon you will find yourself spotting and correcting errors as you go along.
5. Create a new document called `name-dtd-2.xml` by clicking File ➪ Save As again. Change the name of the `<first>` element to `<given>` within the document:

```
<?xml version="1.0"?>
<!DOCTYPE name [
  <!ELEMENT name (first, middle, last)>
  <!ELEMENT first (#PCDATA)>
  <!ELEMENT middle (#PCDATA)>
  <!ELEMENT last (#PCDATA)>
]>
<name>
   <given>Joseph</given>
   <middle>John</middle>
   <last>Fawcett</last>
</name>
```

6. Save the file and try validating again: Plugins ➪ XML ➪ Parse as XML. This time the program should indicate errors, as shown in Figure 4-2.

If you move your mouse over the red lines you will get the reports that (under the opening `<given>` tag), "Element type `given` must be declared" and (under the closing `</name>` tag), "The content of the element type `name` must match `(first, middle, last)`." The program is letting you know that the content of the XML document didn't match what was specified in the DTD.

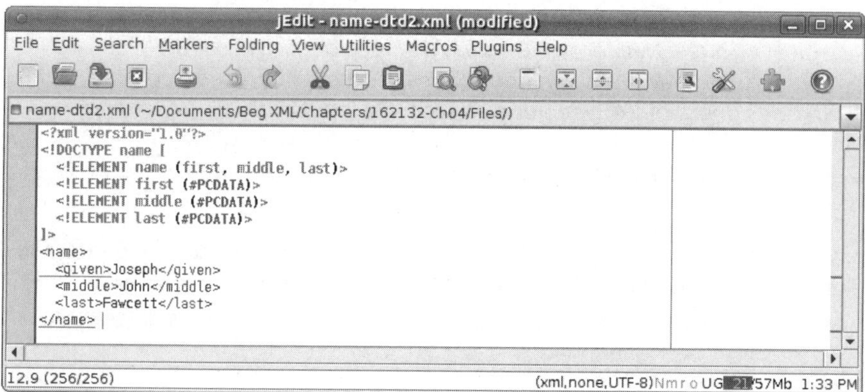

FIGURE 4-2

How It Works

This Try It Out used the DTD to check whether the content within the XML document matched the vocabulary. This was achieved using the DTD-aware parser built into the jEdit plugin. Internally, parsers handle these checks in different ways (usually it's best to think of them as black boxes). At the most basic level, the parser reads the DTD declarations and stores them in memory. Then, as it reads the document, it validates each element that it encounters against the matching declaration. If it finds an element or attribute that does not appear within the declarations or appears in the wrong position, or if it finds a declaration that has no matching XML content, it raises a validity error.

Let's break the DTD down into smaller pieces so that you can get a preview of what you will learn later. As you have learned so far, you begin with the XML declaration. This is optional, but it is recommended that you include it to avoid potential XML version conflicts in the future:

```
<?xml version="1.0"?>
```

Immediately following the XML header is the *document type declaration*, commonly referred to as the `DOCTYPE`:

```
<!DOCTYPE name [
```

The DOCTYPE informs the parser that a DTD is associated with this XML document. When using a DTD, the document type declaration must appear at the start of the document (preceded only by the XML header) — it is not permitted anywhere else within the document. The DOCTYPE declaration has an exclamation mark (!) at the start of the element name. The XML Recommendation indicates that *declaration elements* must begin with an exclamation mark. Declaration elements may appear only as part of the DTD. They may not appear within the main XML content.

WARNING *At this point, you may have noticed that the syntax for DTDs is very different from the rules for basic XML documents. DTDs were originally used with the Standard Generalized Markup Language (SGML). To maintain compatibility with SGML, the designers of XML decided to keep the declaration language similar.*

In the previous example, you created a relatively simple DOCTYPE declaration. Directly following the DOCTYPE declaration is the body of the DTD. This is where you declare elements, attributes, entities, and notations:

```
<!ELEMENT name (first, middle, last)>
<!ELEMENT first (#PCDATA)>
<!ELEMENT middle (#PCDATA)>
<!ELEMENT last (#PCDATA)>
```

In the preceding DTD, you have declared several elements that make up the vocabulary of the <name> document. Like the DOCTYPE declaration, the element declarations must start with an exclamation mark.

Finally, the declaration section of the DTD is closed using a closing bracket and a closing angle bracket (]>). This effectively ends the definition, and the XML document immediately follows.

Now that you have seen a DTD and a validating parser in action, you may feel ready to create DTDs for all of your XML documents. Bear in mind that validation uses more processing power than simply reading a document into an application, so it's a good idea to be systematic about your use of DTDs. But if you're hand-authoring with a tool like jEdit then it certainly makes sense to validate before saving.

The Document Type Declaration in Detail

The document type declaration, or DOCTYPE, informs the parser that your document should conform to a DTD. It also indicates where the parser can find the rest of the definition. In the first example, the DOCTYPE was simple:

```
<!DOCTYPE name [ ]>
```

The document type declaration always begins in the same way, with `<!DOCTYPE`, followed by some whitespace, just as there is after element names. Note that whitespace is not allowed to appear in between `DOCTYPE` and the opening `<!`.

After the whitespace, the name of the XML document's root element must appear *exactly* as it will in the document, including any namespace prefix. Because the document's root element is `<name>`, the word `name` follows the opening `<!DOCTYPE` in the previous declaration.

WARNING *Remember that XML is case sensitive. Therefore, anytime you see a name in XML, it is case sensitive. When the recommendation says the name must appear exactly as it will in the document, this includes character case. You will see this throughout the DTD; any reference to XML names implies case sensitivity.*

Following the name of the root element, you have several options for specifying the rest of the document type declaration. In the `<name>` example, the element declarations appeared between the `[` and `]` of the DTD. When declarations appear between the `[` and `]`, as in the example, they are called *internal subset declarations*. It is also possible to have some or all of your declarations in a separate document. DTD declarations that appear in external documents are *external subset declarations*. You can refer to an external DTD by either using system identifiers or public identifiers.

NOTE *Aside from experimentation and development, it's rarely necessary to use internal DTDs, and external DTDs have many advantages. For example, because the DTD appears in a single separate document, it is easier to make changes that apply to all documents that use the DTD. Later in the chapter, you look at XML documents and DTDs that consist of many files using entities.*

You must remember, however, that looking up the DTD file takes extra processing time. In addition, if the DTD file is located on the Internet, you have to wait for it to download. Usually it is better to keep a local copy of the DTD for validation purposes or ensure the tools you are using have a caching mechanism. If you are maintaining a local copy, you should check for changes to the DTD at the original location.

System Identifiers

A *system identifier* enables you to specify the location of an external file containing DTD declarations. It is comprised of two parts: the keyword `SYSTEM`, and a URI reference pointing to the document's location. A URI can be a file on your local hard drive, a file on your intranet or network, or even a file available on the Internet:

```
<!DOCTYPE name SYSTEM "name.dtd" [...]>
```

You must type the word `SYSTEM` after the name of the root element in your declaration. Following the `SYSTEM` keyword is the URI reference to the location of the file, in quotation marks. The following examples use system identifiers:

```
<!DOCTYPE name SYSTEM "file:///c:/name.dtd" [ ]>
<!DOCTYPE name SYSTEM "http://wiley.com/hr/name.dtd" [ ]>
<!DOCTYPE name SYSTEM "name.dtd">
```

Notice that the last example has no `[` and `]` characters. This is perfectly normal. Specifying an internal subset is optional. An XML document might conform to a DTD that uses only an internal subset, only an external subset, or both. If you do specify an internal subset, it appears between the `[` and `]`, immediately following the system identifier.

You'll see how to use an external DTD in the next Try It Out, but before you do, take a look at an alternative way to refer to external DTDs: public identifiers.

Public Identifiers

Public identifiers provide a second mechanism to locate DTD resources and look like this:

```
<!DOCTYPE name PUBLIC "-//Beginning XML//DTD Name Example//EN">
```

Much like the system identifier, the public identifier begins with a keyword, `PUBLIC`, followed by a specialized identifier. However, instead of a reference to a file, public identifiers are used to identify an entry in a catalog. According to the XML specification, public identifiers can follow any format; however, a commonly used format is called *Formal Public Identifiers*, or *FPIs*.

NOTE *The syntax for an FPI is defined in the document ISO 9070. ISO 9070 also defines the process for registration and recording of formal public identifiers. The International Organization for Standardization, or ISO, is a group that designs government-approved standards. You can learn more about the ISO by going to its website at* `www.iso.ch`.

The syntax for FPIs matches the following basic structure:

```
-//Owner//Class Description//Language//Version
```

At the most basic level, all public identifiers function similarly to namespace names, but public identifiers cannot be used to combine two different vocabularies in the same document. This makes namespaces much more powerful than public identifiers.

Following the public identifier string, you can include an optional system identifier as well. This enables the processor to find a copy of the document if it cannot resolve the public identifier (most processors cannot resolve public identifiers). When including the optional system identifier, the `SYSTEM` keyword shown earlier isn't required. A valid document type declaration that uses a public identifier might look like the following:

```
<!DOCTYPE name PUBLIC "-//Beginning XML//DTD Name Example//EN" "name.dtd">
```

The preceding declaration assumes you are defining a document type for a document whose root element is <name>. The definition has the following public identifier:

```
-//Beginning XML//DTD Name Example//EN
```

In case this cannot be resolved, there is a URI to a file called `name.dtd`. In the preceding example, no internal subset is included.

Now that you have learned how to use public and system identifiers, in the following Try It Out you create an external DTD file and associate it with the XML document. Remember that you can have an internal subset, an external subset, or both. When using an internal subset, the DTD declarations will appear within the XML document. When using an external subset, the DTD declarations will appear in a separate file.

TRY IT OUT The External DTD

By using an external DTD, you can easily share your vocabulary with others in your company, or even your own industry. Likewise, you can use vocabularies that others have already developed, by referring to external files they have created. This exercise reconfigures the <name> example so that the DTD is defined separately from the XML document:

1. Create a new document to form the external DTD. In jEdit, click File ➪ New and type in the following:

```
<!ELEMENT name (first, middle, last)>
<!ELEMENT first (#PCDATA)>
<!ELEMENT middle (#PCDATA)>
<!ELEMENT last (#PCDATA)>
```

2. Click File ➪ Save As and save the document as `name.dtd`.
3. Again click File ➪ New and type in the following:

```
<?xml version="1.0"?>
<!DOCTYPE name PUBLIC "-//Beginning XML//DTD Name Example//EN" "name.dtd">
<name>
   <first>Joseph</first>
   <middle>John</middle>
   <last>Fawcett</last>
</name>
```

4. Save this as `name-doc.xml`.
5. You are ready to validate the document again. Click Plugins ➪ XML ➪ Parse as XML (again, just close the Sidekick window that pops up).

If you received any errors, check whether you have typed everything correctly and try again.

How It Works

In this Try It Out, you used an external DTD to check the XML content. As you may have guessed, the syntax for the DTD changed very little. The main difference between the internal DTD and external DTD was the absence of a `DOCTYPE` declaration within the external DTD. The `DOCTYPE` declaration is always located within the main XML document. In addition, within the `name-doc.xml` document, there was no internal subset. Instead, you used a public identifier and system identifier to indicate which DTD the validation program should use.

In this case, the validation program had no way to resolve public identifiers. The processor instead used the optional URI reference that you included to find the correct DTD for validation. In this example, the XML parser had to find the file `name.dtd`. Because this is a relative reference (it does not contain a website address or drive letter), the parser began looking in the current directory — where the XML document it was parsing was located. The XML Recommendation does not specify how parsers should handle relative URL references, but most XML parsers will treat the path of the XML document as the base path, just as this example did. If, when working with another parser you find it doesn't locate the DTD, be sure to check your XML parser's documentation.

Sharing DTDs

In reality, most DTDs will be much more complex than the example here; for instance, the DocBook DTD (used for any kind of documentation) runs to over 4000 lines. Due to this complexity, it is better to use DTDs that are widely accepted, wherever possible. However, in the cases where you are covering new ground, you can actually share DTDs, which not only removes the burden for others to have to create the declarations, but it also enables you to more easily integrate with other companies and developers.

Many individuals and industries have developed DTDs that are de facto standards; your favorite search engine will probably find what you need. If you do want to publish your own, here are a few good practices to bear in mind:

- **It should be error-free:** This is rather obvious, but mistakes are easy to make. The best way to be sure is to use the DTD yourself for a while before making it public (or at least announcing it).
- **Choose a simple, informative URL:** Again this is something that applies more generally, but you should think particularly carefully about how you might publish any revisions — for instance, whether to include the date in the URL or reuse the same URL for subsequent versions.
- **Make sure your server is delivering the DTD using the correct media (MIME) type in the HTTP headers:** IETF RFC 3023: XML Media Types states that `application/xml-dtd` *should* be used for DTDs. This may happen automatically if the file is saved on the server with the extension `.dtd`. Online tools are available to check the HTTP MIME type, but every developer should have a copy of the cURL command-line tool. It's available from `http://curl.haxx.se`, free and open source. The command for showing the HTTP headers from a URL looks like this:

```
curl -I http://dannyayers.com/dtd/name.dtd
```

Somewhere in the results you also want to see the following:

```
Content-Type: application/xml-dtd
```

If that doesn't appear, you should check your server documentation.

- **Provide documentation:** Though you may prefer to provide explanatory documentation inside the DTD itself (comments use the same syntax as XML), keep in mind that your DTD may be repeatedly downloaded by tools that lack caching and therefore gobble up a lot of bandwidth. A good alternative is to just provide a single link to an HTML page describing the DTD, for example:

```
<!-- DTD for naming people, see http://example.org/name -->
```

ANATOMY OF A DTD

In addition to the different types of DTDs and their basic function, DTD declarations can be broken down into even more detail. Generally, DTDs consist of three basic parts:

- Element declarations
- Attribute declarations
- Entity declarations

The following sections examine these three parts. To achieve a full understanding of each DTD part, you will create an XML vocabulary for listing contacts — all of your friends and family. Note, however, that many existing vocabularies for contacts are available on the Internet and using a simplified format like that enables you to quickly create your own vocabulary.

Element Declarations

The beginning of this chapter demonstrated element declarations in use, but you have not yet looked at an element declaration in detail. When using a DTD to define the content of an XML document, you must declare each element that appears within the document. Additionally, DTDs can include declarations for *optional elements*: elements that may or may not appear in the XML document. Element declarations consist of three basic parts:

- The `ELEMENT` declaration
- The element name
- The element content model

```
<!ELEMENT name (first, middle, last)>
```

The `ELEMENT` declaration is used to indicate to the parser that you are about to define an element, and following the `ELEMENT` keyword is the name of the element that you are defining. Just as you saw in the `DOCTYPE`, the element name must appear exactly as it will within the XML document, including any namespace prefix.

NOTE *The fact that you must specify the namespace prefix within DTDs is a major limitation. Essentially this means that users are not able to choose their own namespace prefix but must use the prefix defined within the DTD. This limitation exists because the W3C completed the XML Recommendation before finalizing how namespaces would work. As you will see in the next two chapters, XML Schemas and RELAX NG documents are not limited in this way.*

After the element name, an element's *content model* defines the allowable content within the element. An element may contain element children, text, a combination of children and text, or the element may be empty. As far as the XML Recommendation is concerned, four kinds of content models exist:

- Element
- Mixed
- Empty
- Any

Let's look at each of these content models in more detail.

Element Content

When defining a content model with element content, simply include the allowable elements within parentheses. For example, if you have a `<contact>` element that is allowed to contain only a `<name>` element, the declaration should read as follows:

```
<!ELEMENT contact (name)>
```

In the contact list, however, the `<contact>` element needs to include more than just the name. This example includes as its children a `<name>`, `<location>`, `<phone>`, `<knows>`, and `<description>` element:

```
<!ELEMENT contact (name, location, phone, knows, description)>
```

Each element specified within this element's content model must also have its own definition within the DTD. Therefore, in the preceding example, `ELEMENT` declarations are included for the `<name>`, `<location>`, `<phone>`, `<knows>`, and `<description>` elements to complete the DTD. The processor needs this information so that it knows how to handle each element when it is encountered. You can put the `ELEMENT` declarations in any order you like.

NOTE *Even if an element is used in multiple content models, you should declare it only once. You cannot declare two elements with the same name inside a DTD.*

Of course, even in the small example at the start of the chapter the element had more than one child. There are two fundamental ways of specifying the element children:

- Sequences
- Choices

Sequences

Often the elements within these documents must appear in a distinct order. If this is the case, you define the content model using a *sequence*. When specifying a sequence of elements, you simply list the element names separated by commas, as in:

```
<!ELEMENT name (first, middle, last)>
```

The declaration indicates that the `<name>` element must have exactly three children — `<first>`, `<middle>`, and `<last>` — and that they must appear in this order. Likewise, here the `<contact>` element must have exactly five children in the order specified, like so:

```
<!ELEMENT contact (name, location, phone, knows, description)>
```

Take care when creating this line of code. The parser raises an error in three instances:

- If your XML document is missing one of the elements within the sequence
- If your document contains more elements
- If the elements appeared in another order

Choices

Suppose you needed to allow one element or another, but not both. Consider a `<location>` element, which specifies where each contact lives:

```
<!ELEMENT location (address)>
```

Instead of requiring one element, you could require a choice between two elements:

```
<!ELEMENT location (address | GPS)>
```

This declaration allows the `<location>` element to contain one `<address>` or one `<GPS>` element. If the `<location>` element were empty, or if it contained more than one of these elements, the parser would raise an error.

Constructing a choice content model is very similar to constructing a sequence content model. The main difference is that instead of separating the elements by commas, you must use the pipe (|) character. The pipe functions as an exclusive OR. An exclusive OR allows one and only one element of the possible options.

Combining Sequences and Choices

Many XML documents need to leverage much more complex rules. DTDs offer an intuitive way of achieving this: using both simple sequences and choices as building blocks.

Suppose you wanted to declare <latitude> and <longitude> elements within the <location> content model instead of the single <GPS> element. When creating the <location> declaration, you would need to specify that the content can include either an <address> element *or* the <latitude> and <longitude> sequence of elements, but not both. The model could be declared as follows:

```
<!ELEMENT location (address | (latitude, longitude))>
```

The entire content model is enclosed within parentheses as before, but here you have a second set of parentheses within the content model. Think of this as a content model within a content model. The inner content model is a sequence specifying the elements <latitude> and <longitude>. The XML Recommendation allows content models within content models within content models, and so on, indefinitely.

Mixed Content

The XML Recommendation doesn't really talk about mixed content or text content on its own. Instead, it specifies that any element with text in its content is a *mixed content model* element. Within mixed content models, text can appear by itself or it can be interspersed between elements.

NOTE *In everyday usage, people refer to elements that can contain only text as text-only elements or text-only content.*

The rules for mixed content models are similar to the element content model rules that you learned in the preceding section. You have already seen some examples of the simplest mixed content model — text-only:

```
<!ELEMENT first (#PCDATA)>
```

The preceding declaration specifies the keyword #PCDATA within the parentheses of the content model. PCDATA is a keyword derived from Parsed Character DATA. It simply indicates that the character data within the content model should be parsed by the parser. Here's an example element that conforms to this declaration:

```
<first>John</first>
```

Mixed content models can also contain elements interspersed within the text. Suppose you wanted to include a description of each contact in your XML document. You could create a new element <description>:

```
<description>Joe is a developer and author for <title>Beginning XML</title>, now in
 its <detail>5th Edition</detail></description>.
```

In this example, you have a <description> element. Within the <description> element, the text is interspersed with the elements <title> and <detail>.

There is only one way to declare a mixed content model within DTDs — by using the choice mechanism when adding elements. This means that each element within the content model must be separated by the pipe (|) character:

```
<!ELEMENT description (#PCDATA | title | detail)*>
```

The preceding example declares the new <description> element. Notice that you use the choice mechanism to describe the content model; a pipe separates each element. You cannot use commas to separate the choices.

When including elements in the mixed content model, the #PCDATA keyword must always appear first in the list of choices. Unlike element-only content models, you cannot have inner content models in a mixed declaration.

The * outside the parentheses of the content model indicates that the element may appear zero or more times. You can have an unlimited number of <title> elements, an unlimited number of <detail> elements, and any amount of text. All of this can appear in any order within the <description> element. This potential variation is a limitation of validation by DTD. Later you learn how XML Schema has improved validation of mixed content models.

In summary, every time you declare elements within a mixed content model, they must follow four rules:

- They must use the choice mechanism (the pipe (|) character) to separate elements.
- The #PCDATA keyword must appear first in the list of elements.
- There must be no inner content models.
- If there are child elements, the * cardinality indicator *must* appear at the end of the model.

Empty Content

Some elements within your XML documents may or may not have content, and some might *never* need to contain content. For example, if you were working on an HTML-like XML language you might have a <br> element indicating a line break. It wouldn't really make any sense for this to have any child elements or text content.

To define an element with an empty content model, simply include the word EMPTY following the element name in the declaration:

```
<!ELEMENT br EMPTY>
```

Remember that this requires the element to be empty within the XML document. Using the EMPTY keyword, you shouldn't declare elements that *may* contain content. For example, a <middle> element used to hold a middle name may or may not contain text, and therefore should not use the EMPTY keyword.

Any Content

Finally, you can declare an element using the ANY keyword. For example:

```
<!ELEMENT description ANY>
```

Here, the ANY keyword indicates that text (PCDATA) and/or any elements declared within the DTD can be used within the content of the <description> element and that they can be used in any order any number of times. However, the ANY keyword does not allow you to include elements that are not declared within the DTD.

The following Try It Out builds on the previous one. You'll see how to define more complicated structures that are more representative of real-life XML. These structures include mixed content, where you have text and XML interleaved, as well as situations where the author of a document has a choice of content type.

TRY IT OUT "Making Contact"

The first practical example you saw demonstrated how to define simple nested XML in DTDs. In this exercise, you will see how to extend the basic model to include coverage of mixed content and make use of combinations of sequences and choices.

1. Open jEdit and type in the following XML document:

```
<?xml version="1.0"?>
<!DOCTYPE contacts PUBLIC "-//Beginning XML//DTD Contact Example//EN"
"contacts1.dtd">
<contacts>
  <contact>
    <name>
      <first>Joseph</first>
      <middle>John</middle>
      <last>Fawcett</last>
    </name>
    <location>
      <latitude>50.7218</latitude>
      <longitude>-3.533617</longitude>
    </location>
    <phone>001-234-567-8910</phone>
    <knows>John Doe, Danny Ayers</knows>
    <description>Joseph is a developer and author for Beginning XML <em>5th
edition</em>.<br/>Joseph <strong>loves</strong> XML!</description>
  </contact>
</contacts>
```

2. Save it as contacts1.xml. Notice that you have added a document type declaration that refers to an external system file called contacts1.dtd. In addition, the root element in this document and the element name within the DOCTYPE declaration are the same.

3. Create a new document called contacts1.dtd. This file will be where you define your DTD.

   Because you have a sample XML document, you can base most of your declarations on the text that you have. When designing a DTD, it is much easier to create a sample and let the document evolve before the vocabulary is set in stone.

4. In the XML document, <contacts> is the root element. This is the easiest place to start, so begin by declaring it in the DTD:

```
<!ELEMENT contacts ()>
```

5. You haven't specified a content model. Looking at the sample document, you can see that the <contacts> element contains a <contact> element. There is only one child element, so this content model should be easy to define; enter the following line:

```
<!ELEMENT contacts (contact)>
```

Allowing for only one contact as you have done is a little clumsy, but you'll improve this content model a little later in the chapter.

6. Because you have specified a contact element in the content model, you now must declare it in the DTD:

```
<!ELEMENT contact (name, location, phone, knows, description)>
```

7. Remember to also declare each element that is used within the content model. Declare the <name> element and each of its children:

```
<!ELEMENT name (first, middle, last)>
<!ELEMENT first (#PCDATA)>
<!ELEMENT middle (#PCDATA)>
<!ELEMENT last (#PCDATA)>
```

The <first>, <middle>, and <last> elements represent each part of the contact's name. They are all text-only elements, so you have declared that they can contain only #PCDATA. Remember that this qualifies as a mixed content model even though there are no element children.

8. Use a complex content model for the <location> element, as shown earlier in the chapter in the "Combining Sequences and Choices" section:

```
<!ELEMENT location (address | (latitude, longitude))>
```

This declaration allows each location to include either an address or the latitude and longitude coordinates. Even though you didn't include the <latitude> or <longitude> elements in the <location> element in the sample, you should still include them in the content model declaration so that they can be used in other documents.

The <address>, <latitude>, and <longitude> elements are text-only elements:

```
<!ELEMENT address (#PCDATA)>
<!ELEMENT latitude (#PCDATA)>
<!ELEMENT longitude (#PCDATA)>
```

9. Declare the <phone> element in your DTD; this will also be text-only:

```
<!ELEMENT phone (#PCDATA)>
```

10. There is a <knows> element in the sample document. This contains structured information, so ideally that should be represented using XML's structure. But for the sake of simplicity in this example, declare it as text-only:

```
<!ELEMENT knows (#PCDATA)>
```

11. You can use a truly mixed content model for the description. This time you'll have some layout elements borrowed from HTML. Add the following line:

```
<!ELEMENT description (#PCDATA | em | strong | br)*>
```

12. Finally, you must include declarations for the <em>, <strong>, and <br> elements:

```
<!ELEMENT em (#PCDATA)>
<!ELEMENT strong (#PCDATA)>
<!ELEMENT br EMPTY>
```

At this point you have completed the DTD. All of the children that were listed in content models now have their own element declarations. The final DTD should look like the following:

```
<!ELEMENT contacts (contact)>
<!ELEMENT contact (name, location, phone, knows, description)>

<!ELEMENT name (first, middle, last)>
<!ELEMENT first (#PCDATA)>
<!ELEMENT middle (#PCDATA)>
<!ELEMENT last (#PCDATA)>

<!ELEMENT location (address | (latitude, longitude))>
<!ELEMENT address (#PCDATA)>
<!ELEMENT latitude (#PCDATA)>
<!ELEMENT longitude (#PCDATA)>

<!ELEMENT phone (#PCDATA)>
<!ELEMENT knows (#PCDATA)>

<!ELEMENT description (#PCDATA | em | strong | br)*>
<!ELEMENT em (#PCDATA)>
<!ELEMENT strong (#PCDATA)>
<!ELEMENT br EMPTY>
```

13. Now save the file and prepare to validate the document again. Open the `contacts1.xml` document (there's a drop-down list above the text area that gives quick access to recent files) and click Plugins ➪ XML ➪ Parse as XML. If you received any errors (red underlining), confirm that you input the documents correctly and click Validate again.

How It Works

Just as you saw with the original <name> example, the validator processed your XML document, checking that each element it encountered was declared in the DTD. The DTD for your contacts list used all choice and sequence content models, text-only content models, and mixed content models. You even declared an empty element.

The preceding example provides a great overview of using the four different types of element content, however, the contacts DTD is still limited. It allows only one contact. You now need a way to tell the processor that the `(contact)` sequence may appear many times or not at all.

Cardinality

An element's *cardinality* defines how many times it will appear within a content model. DTDs allow four indicators for cardinality, as shown here in Table 4-1:

TABLE 4-1: Cardinality Indicators

INDICATOR	DESCRIPTION
[none]	As you have seen in all of the content models thus far, when no cardinality indicator is used, it indicates that the element must appear once and only once. This is the default behavior for elements used in content models.
?	Indicates that the element may appear either once or not at all.
+	Indicates that the element may appear one or more times.
*	Indicates that the element may appear zero or more times.

These indicators are associated with elements in the DTD to correspond to the requirements of the document model. The following activity improves the example you have been working with by expressing the cardinality of the elements in the DTD, making it a more accurate description and hence allowing tighter validation of documents. As you will now see, the syntax for this is straightforward: the cardinality indicators are simply appended to the element names.

TRY IT OUT "Making Contact" — Part 2

Now that you have learned how to correct and improve the DTD, it is time to integrate cardinality requirements to certain of the elements.

1. Reopen the file `contacts1.dtd` and modify the highlighted sections:

```
<!ELEMENT contacts (contact*)>
<!ELEMENT contact (name, location, phone, knows, description)>

<!ELEMENT name (first+, middle?, last)>
<!ELEMENT first (#PCDATA)>
<!ELEMENT middle (#PCDATA)>
<!ELEMENT last (#PCDATA)>

<!ELEMENT location (address | (latitude, longitude))*>
<!ELEMENT address (#PCDATA)>
<!ELEMENT latitude (#PCDATA)>
<!ELEMENT longitude (#PCDATA)>
```

```
<!ELEMENT phone (#PCDATA)>
<!ELEMENT knows (#PCDATA)>

<!ELEMENT description (#PCDATA | em | strong | br)*>
<!ELEMENT em (#PCDATA)>
<!ELEMENT strong (#PCDATA)>
<!ELEMENT br EMPTY>
```

2. Save this modified version as `contacts2.dtd`.
3. Now that you have created a new DTD file, you need to update your XML document to refer to it. Reopen `contacts1.xml` and save it as `contacts2.xml`. In addition to modifying the `DOCTYPE` declaration so that it refers to the new DTD, make a few more changes as highlighted here:

```
<?xml version="1.0"?>
<!DOCTYPE contacts PUBLIC "-//Beginning XML//DTD Contact Example//EN"
"contacts2.dtd">
<contacts>
  <contact>
    <name>
      <first>Joseph</first>
      <first>John</first>
      <last>Fawcett</last>
    </name>
    <location>
      <address>Exeter, UK</address>
      <latitude>50.7218</latitude>
      <longitude>-3.533617</longitude>
    </location>
    <phone>001-234-567-8910</phone>
    <knows>John Doe, Danny Ayers</knows>
    <description>Joseph is a developer and author for Beginning XML <em>5th
    edition</em>.<br/>Joseph <strong>loves</strong> XML!</description>
  </contact>
  <contact>
    <name>
      <first>John</first>
      <last>Doe</last>
    </name>
    <location>
      <address>Address is not known</address>
    </location>
    <phone>321 321 3213</phone>
    <knows>Joseph Fawcett, Danny Ayers</knows>
    <description>Senior Technical Consultant for LMX.</description>
  </contact>
</contacts>
```

4. Save the modified file and prepare to validate the document again. Click Plugins ⇨ XML ⇨ Parse as XML.

Again, if anything is underlined in red, check whether you have typed everything correctly and try again.

How It Works

This Try It Out implements much of what you learned throughout this section. You set out to design a DTD that could be used to describe a complete list of contacts. You used an assortment of complex content models so that your DTD would reflect various XML documents. Of course, when you first began designing your DTD, you didn't include many options, but after you had the basic structure designed, you modified the DTD to correct some problems and add some features. This design strategy is very common among XML developers.

Attribute Declarations

Attribute declarations are similar to element declarations in many ways except one. Instead of declaring allowable content models for elements, you declare a list of allowable attributes for each element. These lists are called `ATTLIST` *declarations*, and look like this:

```
<!ELEMENT contacts (contact*)>
<!ATTLIST contacts source CDATA #IMPLIED>
```

The preceding example has the same element declaration for your `<contacts>` element from the contacts list example. This particular `ATTLIST` declares only one attribute, `source`, for the `<contacts>` element.

An `ATTLIST` declaration consists of three basic parts:

- The `ATTLIST` keyword
- The associated element's name
- The list of declared attributes

Following the `ATTLIST` keyword in the example is the name of the associated element, `contacts`. Each attribute is then listed in turn with three pieces of information:

- The attribute name
- The attribute type
- The attribute value declaration

In the example the name of the attribute is `source`. This `source` attribute can contain character data — the `CDATA` keyword is used to give the attribute's type. Lastly, the declaration indicates that the attribute has no default value, and that this attribute does not need to appear within the element using the `#IMPLIED` keyword. This third part of the attribute declaration is known as the *value declaration*; it controls how the XML parser handles the attribute's value.

Attribute Names

In addition to the basic XML naming rules, you must also ensure that you don't have duplicate names within the attribute list for a given element. To declare an attribute name, simply type the name exactly as it appears in the XML document, including any namespace prefix.

WARNING *As far as DTDs are concerned, namespace declarations, such as* `xmlns:contacts= "http://wiley.com/contacts"`*, are also treated as attributes. Although the Namespace Recommendation insists that* `xmlns` *statements are declarations and not attributes, DTDs must declare them in an* `ATTLIST` *declaration if they are used. This is because the W3C finalized the syntax for DTDs before the Namespace Recommendation was completed.*

Attribute Types

When declaring attributes, you can specify how the processor should handle the data that appears in the value. Within the element declarations, you could specify that an element contained text, but you couldn't specify how the processor should treat the text value. Several new features are available for attribute declaration.

Table 4-2 provides a summary of the different attribute types:

TABLE 4-2: Attribute Data Types

TYPE	DESCRIPTION
`CDATA`	Indicates that the attribute value is character data, the default type. Notice that this is slightly different from the `PCDATA` keyword in `ELEMENT` declarations. Unlike `PCDATA`, within `CDATA`, the parser can ignore certain reserved characters.
`ID`	Indicates that the attribute value uniquely identifies the containing element.
`IDREF`	Indicates that the attribute value is a reference, by `ID`, to a uniquely identifiable element.
`IDREFS`	Indicates that the attribute value is a whitespace-separated list of `IDREF` values.
`ENTITY`	Indicates that the attribute value is a reference to an external unparsed entity (you'll learn more about entities later).
`ENTITIES`	Indicates that the attribute value is a whitespace-separated list of `ENTITY` values.
`NMTOKEN`	Indicates that the attribute value is a name token. An `NMTOKEN` is a string of character data consisting of standard name characters.
`NMTOKENS`	Indicates that the attribute value is a whitespace-separated list of `NMTOKEN` values.
Enumerated List	Apart from using the default types, you can also declare an enumerated list of possible values for the attribute.

There isn't space here to go into these attribute types in depth, though a couple of the more common ones are used in the next example. As usual, the key reference for this material is the XML Recommendation (`http://www.w3.org/TR/xml`), and your favorite search engine will find you a lot more explanatory material on the Web.

Attribute Value Declarations

Within each attribute declaration you must specify how the value will appear in the document. The XML Recommendation allows you to specify that the attribute either:

- Has a default value
- Has a fixed value
- Is required
- Is implied (or *is optional*)

Default Values

By specifying a *default value* for the attribute, you can be sure that it is included in the final output. As the document is being processed, a validating parser automatically inserts the attribute with the default value if the attribute has been omitted. If the attribute has a default value but a value has also been included in the document, the parser uses the attribute included in the document, rather than the default.

So what does this look like in practice? Try starting with an enumerated list to say that the `kind` attribute of the `<phone>` element should have the value of one of several alternatives like so:

```
<!ATTLIST phone kind (Home | Work | Cell | Fax)>
```

Given this in the DTD, one possible valid form of the element with attribute would be:

```
<phone kind="Work">
```

You can then easily specify the default attribute by simply including the value in quotation marks after the attribute type:

```
<!ATTLIST phone kind (Home | Work | Cell | Fax) "Home">
```

Here, the default value is `Home`. When a validating parser is reading the `<phone>` element, if the `kind` attribute has been omitted, the parser will automatically insert the attribute `kind` with the value `Home`. If the parser encounters a `kind` attribute within the `<phone>` element, it will use the value that has been specified within the document.

Fixed Values

When an attribute's value can never change, you use the `#FIXED` keyword followed by the fixed value. *Fixed values* operate much like default values. As the parser is validating the file, if the fixed attribute is encountered, the parser checks whether the fixed value and attribute value match. If they do not match, the parser raises an error. If the parser does not encounter the attribute within the element, it inserts the attribute with the fixed value.

A common use of fixed attributes is specifying version numbers. Often, DTD authors fix the version number for a specific DTD, like this:

```
<!ATTLIST contacts version CDATA #FIXED "1.0">
```

So this would be valid:

```
<contacts version="1.0">
```

But this would not:

```
<contacts version="1.1">
```

Required Values

When you specify that an attribute is *required*, it must be included within the XML document. Suppose you require this `kind` attribute:

```
<!ATTLIST phone kind (Home | Work | Cell | Fax) #REQUIRED>
```

In the preceding example, the declaration indicates that the `kind` attribute must appear within every `<phone>` element in the document. If the parser encounters a `<phone>` element without a `kind` attribute as it is processing the document, it raises an error.

When declaring that an attribute is required, you are not permitted to specify a default value.

Implied Values

These are the most common form of values. When declaring an attribute, you must always specify a value declaration. If the attribute you are declaring has no default value, has no fixed value, and is not required, then you must declare that the attribute is *implied*. You can declare that an attribute is implied by simply adding the keyword `#IMPLIED` after the attribute's type declaration, like the following:

```
<!ATTLIST knows contacts IDREFS #IMPLIED>
```

Specifying Multiple Attributes

The `ATTLIST` declaration enables you to declare more than one attribute, like so:

```
<!ATTLIST contacts version CDATA #FIXED "1.0"
                   source CDATA #IMPLIED>
```

In the preceding `ATTLIST` declaration for the `<contacts>` element, there is both a `version` and a `source` attribute. These declarations don't have to be expressed together; an alternative is to use multiple `ATTLIST`s, each describing characteristics of the attributes one at a time:

```
<!ATTLIST contacts version CDATA #FIXED "1.0">
<!ATTLIST contacts source CDATA #IMPLIED>
```

Either style for declaring multiple attributes is legal; it's really a matter of taste.

Now that you have seen how to describe attributes in a DTD, you can try it in practice in the following activity.

TRY IT OUT "Making Contact" — Part 3

Once again you can revisit the contact list example and make further improvements. This time you'll add attributes to some of the elements to provide more information in the document.

1. Reopen `contacts2.xml` and save it as `contacts3.xml`. Now make the following modifications:

```
<?xml version="1.0"?>
<!DOCTYPE contacts PUBLIC "-//Beginning XML//DTD Contact Example//EN"
"contacts3.dtd">
<contacts source="Beginning XML 5E" version="1.0">
  <contact person="Joe_Fawcett" tags="author xml poetry">
    <name>
      <first>Joseph</first>
      <first>John</first>
      <last>Fawcett</last>
    </name>
    <location>
      <address>Exeter, UK</address>
      <latitude>50.7218</latitude>
      <longitude>-3.533617</longitude>
    </location>
    <phone kind="Home">001-234-567-8910</phone>
    <knows contacts="John_Doe Danny_Ayers"/>
        <description>Joseph is a developer and author for Beginning XML <em>5th
        edition</em>.<br/>Joseph <strong>loves</strong> XML!</description>
  </contact>
  <contact person="John Doe" tags="author consultant CGI">
    <name>
      <first>John</first>
      <last>Doe</last>
    </name>
    <location>
      <address>Address is not known</address>
    </location>
    <phone>321 321 3213</phone>
    <knows contacts="Joseph Fawcett Danny_Ayers"/>
    <description>Senior Technical Consultant for LMX.</description>
  </contact>
</contacts>
```

2. You now must declare these new attributes within the DTD. Create a new file named `contacts3.dtd`. Again, you can base this document on `contacts2.dtd`. Make the following modifications and save the file:

```
<!ELEMENT contacts (contact*)>
<!ATTLIST contacts version CDATA #FIXED "1.0">
<!ATTLIST contacts source CDATA #IMPLIED>

<!ELEMENT contact (name, location, phone, knows, description)>
```

```
<!ATTLIST contact person ID #REQUIRED>
<!ATTLIST contact tags NMTOKENS #IMPLIED>

<!ELEMENT name (first+, middle?, last)>
<!ELEMENT first (#PCDATA)>
<!ELEMENT middle (#PCDATA)>
<!ELEMENT last (#PCDATA)>

<!ELEMENT location (address | (latitude, longitude))*>
<!ELEMENT address (#PCDATA)>
<!ELEMENT latitude (#PCDATA)>
<!ELEMENT longitude (#PCDATA)>

<!ELEMENT phone (#PCDATA)>
<!ATTLIST phone kind (Home | Work | Cell | Fax) "Home">

<!ELEMENT knows EMPTY>
<!ATTLIST knows contacts IDREFS #IMPLIED>

<!ELEMENT description (#PCDATA | em | strong | br)*>
<!ELEMENT em (#PCDATA)>
<!ELEMENT strong (#PCDATA)>
<!ELEMENT br EMPTY>
```

3. You are ready to validate your document again. Open `contacts3.xml` and once again click Plugins ➪ XML ➪ Parse as XML.

How It Works

In this Try It Out example, you added several `ATTLIST` declarations to your DTD. You added the attributes `version` and `source` to your `<contacts>` element. The `version` attribute could be used to indicate to an application which version of the DTD this contact list matches. Using the `source` attribute, you can provide a friendly description of who provided the information. If you had omitted the `version` attribute the XML parser would have passed the value `1.0` to the application because you declared that it had a fixed value.

The unique identifiers were created by simply using the contact's name and replacing all the whitespace with underscores (so that it was a valid XML name). The `tags` attribute included names that weren't declared anywhere in the DTD but which still followed the rules for the `NMTOKEN` attribute type.

You also added a `kind` attribute that provided a list of possible phone number entries for the contact. Because there were only four choices for the value of the `kind` attribute, you used an enumerated list. You also set the default value to `Home` because many of the contacts you listed included home phone numbers and you didn't want to type it repeatedly. Note that there was no `kind` attribute on the phone number in the contact for David Hunter. Because the `kind` attribute was omitted, a processor, as it is parsing the document, will automatically insert the attribute with the default value.

Finally, the `<knows>` element was modified, specifying that it would be `EMPTY` and contain a single `IDREFS` attribute. This allowed you to connect contacts together through the `ID`/`IDREF` mechanism built into DTDs. This can be a very powerful feature. Unfortunately, though, the names you refer to must be present within your contacts list. Therefore, you couldn't say that Jeff knows `Andrew_Watt` because there is no `Andrew_Watt` `ID` within the contacts list.

Entity Declarations

In Chapter 2, you saw how you could escape characters or use entity references to include special characters within the XML document. You learned that five *entities* built into XML enable you to include characters that have special meaning in XML documents. In addition to these built-in entities, you also learned that you can use character references to include characters that are difficult to type, such as the (c) character in the following example:

```
<contacts source="Beginning XML 5E&apos;s Contact List" version="1.0">
 <description>Joseph is a developer and author for Beginning XML <em>5th
 edition</em> &#169; 2012 Wiley Publishing.
<br/>Joseph <strong>loves</strong> XML!</description>
```

The first entity reference here is an `'` within the attribute content. This allows you to include a (`'`) character without the XML parser treating it as the end of the attribute value. As part of the description there is an `©` character reference within the element content. This allows you to include the (c) character by specifying the character's Unicode value.

In fact, entities are not limited to simple character references within XML documents. Entities can be used throughout the XML document to refer to sections of replacement text, other XML markup, and even external files. You can separate entities into four primary types, each of which may be used within an XML document:

- Built-in entities
- Character entities
- General entities
- Parameter entities

You've already seen the roles the five built-in entities play in well-formed XML. Here they are again as a reminder:

- `&` — The `&` character
- `<` — The `<` character
- `>` — The `>` character
- `'` — The `'` character
- `"` — The `"` character

All XML parsers must support these. In general, you can use these *entity references* anywhere you can use normal text within the XML document, such as in element contents and attribute values. You can also use entity references in your DTD within default and fixed attribute value declarations, as well as entity declarations (as shown later). Although the built-in entities allow you to refer to markup characters, they cannot be used in place of XML markup. For example, the following is *legal*:

```
<description>Author &amp; programmer</description>
```

Here, the `&` built-in entity allows you to include an ampersand (`&`) in the content of the `<description>` element. This is allowed because it is within the element's text content. Conversely, the following would be *illegal*:

```
<contacts version=&quot;1.0&quot;>
```

The XML within the document is first checked for well-formedness errors; only then are entity references resolved.

There are actually three other general kinds of entities you can use within an XML document: character entities, general entities, and parameter entities. The latter two are of particular relevance to DTDs, but here's as good a place as any to mention character entities.

Character Entities

Character entities are typically used when unusual characters are needed in a document. Their form is similar to the built-in entities, beginning with an ampersand (`&`) and ending with a semicolon(`;`). In between there is a numeric reference to the required Unicode character code. For example, the Unicode value for the (c) character is 169, so to include a (c) in an XML document you can use the following:

```
&#169;
```

The extra `#` character before the number indicates that it's a decimal number. You can also refer to a character entity by using the hexadecimal Unicode value for the character:

```
&#x00A9;
```

Here, the hexadecimal value `00A9` is used in place of the decimal value `169`.

Charts listing the numeric values that correspond to different characters are available from `www.unicode.org/charts/`.

General Entities

General entities must be declared within the DTD before they can be used within an XML document. Most commonly, XML developers use general entities to create reusable sections of *replacement text*. Instead of representing only a single character, general entities can represent characters, paragraphs, and even entire documents.

You can declare general entities within the DTD in two ways. You can specify the value of the entity directly in the declaration or you can refer to an external file. Let's begin by looking at an *internal entity declaration*:

```
<!ENTITY source-text "Beginning XML">
```

Following the `ENTITY` keyword is the name of the entity, in this case `source-text`. You use this name when referring to the entity elsewhere in the XML document, like so:

```
&source-text;
```

After the entity name in the preceding declaration is a line of replacement text. Whenever an XML parser encounters a reference to this entity, it will supply the replacement text to the application at the point of the reference. This example is an internal entity declaration because the replacement text appears directly within the declaration in the DTD.

Within a general entity, the replacement text can consist of any well-formed XML content, although content without a root element is allowed. For example, the following are *legal* general entity values:

```
<!ENTITY address-unknown "The address for this location is &quot;Unknown&quot;">
<!ENTITY empty-gps "<latitude></latitude><longitude></longitude>">
```

Notice that entity references can be included within the replacement text. Although you can include entity references within replacement text, an entity is not permitted to contain a reference to itself. The following declaration is *not legal*:

```
<!ENTITY address-unknown "The address for this location is &address-unknown;">
```

Because no limits exist on the length of replacement text, your DTD can quickly become cluttered by sections of replacement text, making it more difficult to read. When declaring your entities, instead of declaring the replacement text internally you can refer to external files. In this case the entity is declared using an *external entity declaration*. For example, you could declare your entities as:

```
<!ENTITY joe-description SYSTEM "joe.txt">
```

or:

```
<!ENTITY joe-description PUBLIC
  "-//Beginning XML//Joe Description//EN" "joe.txt">
```

Just as you saw with the document type declaration, when referring to external files, you can use a system identifier or a public identifier. When you use a public identifier, you can also include an optional URI reference, as this example does. Each of these declarations refers to an external file named `jeff.txt`. As an XML parser is processing the DTD, if it encounters an external entity declaration, it *might* open the external file and parse it. If the XML parser is a validating parser, it *must* open the external file, parse it, and be able to use the content when it is referenced. If the XML parser is not a validating parser, it might or might not attempt to parse the external file; you need to check the parser documentation.

Parameter Entities

Parameter entities, much like general entities, enable you to create reusable sections of replacement text. However, parameter entities cannot be used in general content; you can refer to parameter entities only within the DTD. Unlike other kinds of entities, the replacement text within a parameter entity can be made up of DTD declarations or pieces of declarations.

Parameter entities can also be used to build *modular DTDs* from multiple files. This is very helpful in their reuse; you only need to use the parts relevant to your application.

Parameter entity declarations are very similar to general entity declarations. Here is an example:

```
<!ENTITY % DefaultPhoneKind "Home">
```

This example contains a declaration for an internal parameter entity named `DefaultPhoneKind`. The percent sign (`%`) before the name of the entity indicates this is a parameter entity.

Like general entities, parameter entities can also refer to external files using a system or public identifier. The references look like this:

```
<!ENTITY % NameDeclarations SYSTEM "name.dtd">
```

or:

```
<!ENTITY % NameDeclarations
  PUBLIC "-//Beginning XML//DTD External module//EN" "name.dtd">
```

Instead of redeclaring the `<name>`, `<first>`, `<middle>`, and `<last>` elements in the DTD for the contacts list, you could refer to the `name.dtd` from earlier in the chapter. Reusing existing declarations in your DTD through external parameter entities is a good way to modularize your vocabulary.

References to Parameter Entities

When referring to a parameter entity within a DTD, the syntax changes slightly. Instead of using an ampersand (`&`) you must use a percent sign (`%`), as shown in the following example:

```
%NameDeclarations;
```

The reference consists of a percent sign (`%`), followed by the entity name, followed by a semicolon (`;`). References to parameter entities are permitted only within the DTD. Suppose you wanted to make use of the `DefaultPhoneKind` parameter entity within the `ATTLIST` declaration for the `phone` element. You could change the declaration as follows:

```
<!ENTITY % DefaultPhoneKind "&#34;Home&#34;">
<!ATTLIST phone kind (Home | Work | Cell | Fax) %DefaultPhoneKind;>
```

In this example, the parameter entity called `DefaultPhoneKind` is used in place of the attribute value declaration. Parameter entity references can be used in place of DTD declarations or parts of DTD declarations. Unfortunately, you can't use the built-in entity `"` because general entities and built-in entities that appear in parameter entity values are not expanded as they are elsewhere. Therefore, you instead use character entities for the quotation marks. The following is perfectly legal:

```
<!ATTLIST phone kind (Home | Work | Cell | Fax) "%DefaultPhoneKind;">
```

Now that you have seen how to express the different kinds of entities, you're ready to try them in the following DTD activity.

TRY IT OUT "Making Contact" — Part 4

In this exercise you take what you just learned and use it to add a parameter entity reference to your contacts DTD. This will enable you to parameterize the phone attribute declaration within your DTD.

1. Begin by making the appropriate modifications to the DTD file. Create a new document called `contacts4.dtd`. You can copy the content from `contacts3.dtd`, adding the new `DefaultPhoneKind` parameter entity and modifying the `ATTLIST` declaration for the `<phone>` element. When you have made the changes, save the `contacts4.dtd` file:

```
<!ENTITY % DefaultPhoneKind '"Home"'>
<!ATTLIST phone kind (Home | Work | Cell | Fax) %DefaultPhoneKind;>
```

2. Change the XML file to refer to the new DTD. This is the only change you need to make within your XML document. Create a new document based on `contacts3.xml`, the document you created in the previous Try it Out. Change the Document Type Declaration to refer to your new DTD, and save the file as `contacts4.xml`:

```
<!DOCTYPE contacts PUBLIC "-//Beginning XML//DTD Contact Example//EN"
  "contacts4.dtd">
```

3. You are ready to validate the document again. Open `contacts4.xml` and click Plugins ➪ XML ➪ Parse as XML.

Your output should show a complete validation without errors. If you received any errors this time, confirm that you have typed everything correctly and try again.

How It Works

You were able to change `ATTLIST` declarations by using a parameter entity for the content model and a parameter entity for the attribute declarations. Just as you have seen throughout this section, parameter entities enable you to reuse DTD declarations or pieces of declarations. As the parser attempts to process the content model for the `<contact>` declaration, it encounters the parameter entity reference. It replaces the entity reference with the replacement text specified in the `ENTITY` declaration.

Note that the declaration of a parameter entity must occur in the DTD before any references to that entity.

NOTE *When a parser builds the replacement value for a parameter entity, it adds a single space character before and after the value you specify. This can create all kinds of confusion if you are not careful in defining your parameter entities. In fact, this is why you need to include the quotation marks as part of the parameter entity — so that there won't be extra spaces in the value.*

DTD LIMITATIONS

DTDs are a rather old technology and over time various limitations have become apparent. Most significantly, DTDs have:

- Poor support for XML namespaces
- Poor data typing
- Limited content model descriptions

However, it is important to remember that even with their limitations, DTDs are a fundamental part of the XML Recommendation. DTDs will continue to be used in many diverse situations, even as other methods of describing documents emerge.

SUMMARY

In this chapter, you learned the following:

- By using DTDs, you can easily validate your XML documents against a defined vocabulary of elements and attributes. This reduces the amount of code needed within your application.
- An XML parser can be used to check whether the contents of an XML document are valid according to the declarations within a DTD.
- DTDs enable you to exercise much more control over your document content than simple well-formedness checks do.
- Use a DTD to provide a description against which documents can be validated.
- Create element declarations using the `<!ELEMENT ... >` construct.
- Create attribute declarations using the `<!ATTLIST ... >` construct.
- Create entity declarations using the `<!ENTITY ... >` construct.
- Specify the DTD associated with an XML document using the `<!DOCTYPE ... >` construct.
- DTDs have several limitations. The next two chapters illustrate how these limitations have been addressed in newer standards, such as XML Schemas and RELAX NG.

EXERCISES

You can find suggested solutions to these questions in Appendix A.

1. Build a contact for yourself in the list based on the declarations in the contacts DTD. Once you have added the new contact, validate your document to ensure that it is correct.

2. Add a `gender` attribute declaration for the `<contact>` elements. The attribute should allow two possible values: `male` and `female`. Make sure the attribute is required.

3. Currently, each contact can have only one phone number. Modify the contact declaration so that each contact can have zero or more phone numbers. In addition, add declarations for `website` and `email` elements.

▶ WHAT YOU LEARNED IN THIS CHAPTER

<table>
<tr><th>TOPIC</th><th>KEY POINTS</th></tr>
<tr><td>Purpose of DTDs</td><td>To describe the structure of XML documents in a way that they may be validated.</td></tr>
<tr><td>Associating XML documents to DTDs</td><td>The DTD can be included within the XML document itself, or specified by reference in the document's DOCTYPE declaration.</td></tr>
<tr><td>Element declarations</td><td>Elements and their allowed children can be specified in DTDs, e.g. <!ELEMENT name (first, middle, last)>.</td></tr>
<tr><td>Content models</td><td>DTDs support four different kinds of content model: Element (child elements only); Mixed (elements and text); Empty (no content); and Any (unrestricted).</td></tr>
<tr><td>Child element structure</td><td>The structure of the children of an element may be specified using a combination of sequences (comma-separated lists) or choices (lists separated by the "|" character), e.g. <!ELEMENT location (address | (latitude, longitude))>.</td></tr>
<tr><td>Cardinality indicators</td><td>When no cardinality indicator is used on an element, by default it indicates that the element should appear once and once only. The indicators are: ? (zero or one occurrence of the element); + (one or more occurrences); and * (zero or more occurrences).</td></tr>
<tr><td>Attribute declarations</td><td>Attributes and the details of their nature can be specified in DTDs, e.g. <!ATTLIST phone kind (Home | Work | Cell | Fax)>.</td></tr>
<tr><td>Entity declarations</td><td>There are four kinds of entities to be found in XML: Built-in (for example & for the & character); Character (for example © for the copyright symbol); General (replacement text); and Parameter (replacement text for use in DTDs).</td></tr>
</table>

5

XML Schemas

WHAT YOU WILL LEARN IN THIS CHAPTER:

- The benefits of XML Schemas
- How to create and use XML Schemas
- How to document your XML Schemas

Like DTDs, XML Schemas are used for defining XML vocabularies. They describe the structure and content of XML documents in more detail than DTDs, and hence allow more precise validation.

Today, XML Schemas are a mature technology used in a variety of XML applications. Apart from their use in validation, aspects of XML Schemas are used in various other XML technologies such as XQuery and SOAP, which are covered in later chapters.

The XML Schema 1.0 specifications were first published by the W3C in 2001 and then revised to a Second Edition in 2004. The 2004 documents are currently the primary reference for XML Schema, although a 1.1 version is under development. At the time of this writing, these documents are at Candidate Recommendation status. The main ideas of the 1.1 specification are the same as the 1.0 version and this newer version is clearer and a little easier to read, so generally speaking it makes a better reference (a handful of changes and additions are covered at the end of this chapter). All the relevant specifications are available at `www.w3.org/XML/Schema`.

NOTE *In general, a schema is any type of model document that defines the structure of something, such as database layout or documents. For example, DTDs are a type of schema. The word* schema *is often interchangeable with the word* vocabulary. *But more specifically, the term XML Schema is used to refer to the W3C XML Schema technology. When referring to W3C XML Schemas, the "S" in "Schema" should be capitalized, and sometimes you will see "WXS" used to refer to this technology. A more common set of initials is "XSD" for XML Schema Document, referring to the actual definition files, which are typically saved with the filename extension* `.xsd`.

BENEFITS OF XML SCHEMAS

At this point you have already invested time in learning DTDs. You know the syntax and can create complex, even modular, definitions for your vocabulary. XML Schemas look a lot different from DTDs (and in many ways are!), but they use the same underlying principles in specifying a vocabulary and grammar for your XML documents. Before jumping in to the details, it's worth looking at the benefits of XML Schemas:

- XML Schemas are created using basic XML, whereas DTDs utilize a separate syntax.
- XML Schemas fully support the Namespace Recommendation.
- XML Schemas enable you to validate text element content based on built-in and user-defined data types.
- XML Schemas enable you to more easily create complex and reusable content models.
- XML Schemas enable the modeling of programming concepts such as object inheritance and type substitution.

The following sections look at some of these benefits in more detail.

XML Schemas Use XML Syntax

In the previous chapter, you spent most of your time learning the DTD syntax. When creating an XML Schema, the syntax is entirely in XML. But as with DTDs you are defining rules for XML documents, so there are similarities. For example, in the previous chapter you saw rules for elements that looked like this:

```
<!ELEMENT first (#PCDATA)>
```

The same rule (approximately) is expressed in XML Schema as:

```
<element name="first" type="string"/>
```

A big advantage of XML Schemas (written in XML) is that you can use generic XML tools for writing and processing them.

XML Schema Namespace Support

Because XML Schemas were finalized after the Namespace Recommendation, unlike DTDs, they support namespaces (which were covered in Chapter 3). With XML Schemas you can define vocabularies that use namespace declarations and mix namespaces in XML documents with more flexibility. For example, when designing an XML Schema, it is not necessary to specify namespace prefixes as you must in DTDs. Instead, the XML Schema (in line with the XML namespaces spec) leaves this decision to the user of the document.

XML Schema Data Types

When you develop DTDs, you can specify that an element has *mixed content*, *element content*, or *empty content*. Unfortunately, when your elements contain only text, you can't add any constraints on the format of the text. Attribute declarations give you some control, but even then the data types you can use in attribute declarations are very limited.

XML Schemas divide data types into two broad categories: complex and simple. Elements that may contain attributes or other elements are declared using complex types. Attribute values and text content within elements are declared using simple types.

For example, by utilizing these types you could specify that an element may contain only date values, only positive numbers, or only numbers within a certain range. Many commonly-used simple types are built into XML Schemas. This is, perhaps, the single most important feature within XML Schemas. By enabling you to specify the allowable type of data within an element or attribute, you can exercise more rigid control over documents. This enables you to easily create documents that are intended to represent databases, programming languages, and objects within programming languages. Simple types and complex types are exemplified later in this chapter.

XML Schema Content Models

To reuse a content model within a DTD, you have to utilize parameter entities. Using multiple parameter entities can lead to complex declarations within the DTD. XML Schemas provide several mechanisms for reusing content models. In addition to the simple models that you create in DTDs, XML Schema declarations can use object inheritance and content model inheritance. The advanced features of XML Schemas enable you to build content models upon content models, modifying the definition in each step.

XML Schema Specifications

The specification for XML Schemas (version 1.0) is provided in three documents available from `www.w3.org/XML/Schema`. These specification documents are as follows:

- **Part 0: Primer:** A (comparatively) easy-to-read overview of XML Schema.
- **Part 1: Structures:** This describes the concepts behind XML Schema and defines its component parts, how they are used to describe document structure, and how XML Schema is used for validation.
- **Part 2: Datatypes:** This defines the different kinds of data types XML Schema can support, including simple built-in types (such as decimal numbers). It additionally describes the system by which complex data types can be built up from simpler components (for example, a list of 10 negative integers).

***NOTE** Version 1.1 has revised versions of these three specification documents, together with a few auxiliary documents.*

Given the size and complexity of these specifications, XML Schemas cannot be covered completely in one chapter. But many tools don't support the advanced features properly; in fact, experts often recommend against many that don't. So this chapter covers the basic features — those that are most useful.

XML SCHEMAS IN PRACTICE

Most XML Schemas are stored within a separate document in a similar fashion to external DTDs; that is, an XML document contains a reference to the XML Schema that defines its vocabulary. An XML document that adheres to a particular XML Schema vocabulary is called an XML Schema *instance* document.

Like DTDs, XML Schemas can be used for a variety of purposes, including, for example, assisting in the authoring of documents. But their most common use is to validate XML documents.

As shown in the previous chapter, validating a document against its vocabulary requires the use of a special parser. The XML Schema Recommendation calls these parsers *schema validators*. Not only do schema validators render a verdict on the document's schema validity, but many also provide type information to the application. This set of type information is called the *Post Schema Validation Infoset* (*PSVI*). You may never need to use this notion in practice, but you are most likely to encounter the phrase in documentation. For example, PSVI output is used by XQuery and XPath2. The XML Infoset (defined at `http://www.w3.org/TR/xml-infoset/`) is an abstract view of the data contained in XML documents. It may not be made explicit anywhere, but if you are working with XML in an object-oriented programming language, this is the basic model you're dealing with. When using XML Schema, there's even more information to work with. The PSVI contains all of the information in the XML document plus a basic summary of everything declared in the schema.

RUNNING THE SAMPLES

Throughout this chapter, the examples assume you are using the jEdit editor (`www.jedit.org`). In addition to being able to work with DTDs, jEdit is capable of checking an XML Schema instance document against its XML Schema. It is possible to create a program that validates your XML against an XML Schema using a validating parser library. More information on using parsers in your own programs is available in the next chapter.

You have learned some of the benefits of XML Schemas, but it helps if you see an entire XML Schema before you look at each part in detail. To illustrate how the XML Schema works, in the following activity you will modify the name example from the previous chapter that used a DTD to define a vocabulary for documents providing contact information. Here you will use XML Schema to define a similar vocabulary, and use it to validate documents.

TRY IT OUT What's in a Name?

This example creates an XML Schema that defines the name vocabulary. It shows how to refer to the XML Schema from the instance document:

1. Begin by creating the XML Schema. Run jEdit and copy the following. Save the file as `name5.xsd`:

Available for download on Wrox.com

```
<?xml version="1.0"?>
<schema xmlns="http://www.w3.org/2001/XMLSchema"
xmlns:target="http://www.example.com/name"
targetNamespace="http://www.example.com/name" elementFormDefault="qualified">
  <element name="name">
    <complexType>
      <sequence>
        <element name="first" type="string"/>
        <element name="middle" type="string"/>
        <element name="last" type="string"/>
      </sequence>
      <attribute name="title" type="string"/>
    </complexType>
  </element>
</schema>
```

name5.xsd

2. Create the instance document. This document is very similar to the `name4.xml` example from the previous chapter. Instead of referring to a DTD, refer to the newly created XML Schema. Create a new document called `name5.xml` and copy the following; when you are finished, save the file:

Available for download on Wrox.com

```
<?xml version="1.0"?>
<name
  xmlns="http://www.example.com/name"
  xmlns:xsi="http://www.w3.org/2001/XMLSchema-instance"
  xsi:schemaLocation="http://www.example.com/name name5.xsd"
  title="Mr.">
   <first>John</first>
   <middle>Fitzgerald Johansen</middle>
   <last>Doe</last>
</name>
```

name5.xml

3. You are ready to validate your XML instance document against the XML Schema. Because you refer to your XML Schema within `name5.xml`, you don't need to select it within the validator. As in the previous chapter, in jEdit you validate by clicking the Plugins menu, selecting XML, and clicking the Parse as XML option. You should see something like Figure 5-1, with "XML parsing complete, 0 error(s)" in jEdit's status bar at the bottom. If the output suggests that the validation completed but there is an error in the document, correct the error and try again.

4. If you would like to see what happens when there is an error, simply modify your `name5.xml` document and try validating it again.

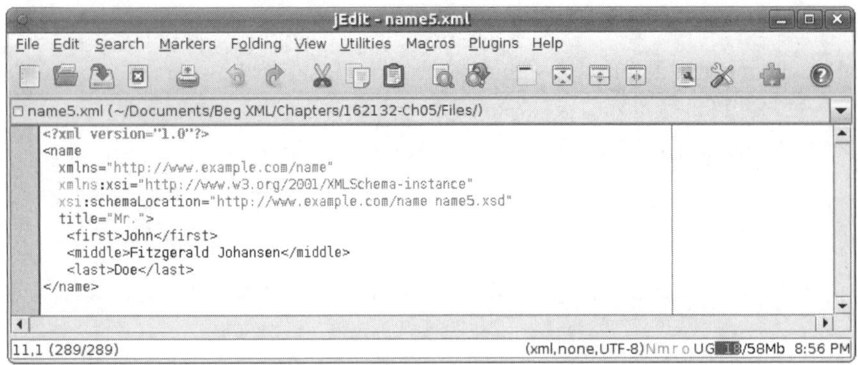

FIGURE 5-1

How It Works

In this Try It Out you created an XML Schema for the name vocabulary. You used the XML Schema to determine whether your instance document was schema-valid. To connect the two documents, you included a reference to the XML Schema within your instance document. The schema validator can then read the declarations within the XML Schema. As it is parsing the instance document, it validates each element that it encounters against the matching declaration. If it finds an element or attribute that does not appear within the declarations, or if it finds a declaration that has no matching XML content, it raises a schema validity error.

The XML begins like this:

```
<?xml version="1.0"?>
<schema xmlns="http://www.w3.org/2001/XMLSchema"
     xmlns:target="http://www.example.com/name"
     targetNamespace="http://www.example.com/name"
     elementFormDefault="qualified">
```

The root element within your XML Schema is the `<schema>` element. Within the `<schema>` element, you have its namespace declaration `http://www.w3.org/2001/XMLSchema`. You also include a `targetNamespace` attribute indicating that you are developing a vocabulary for the namespace `http://www.example.com/name`. You also declared a namespace that matches your `targetNamespace` with the prefix `target`. If you need to refer to any declarations within your XML Schema, you need this declaration, so you include it just in case. As with all namespace declarations, you are not required to use `target` as your prefix; you could choose any prefix you like.

You also included the attribute `elementFormDefault` with the value `qualified`. Essentially, this controls the way namespaces are used within your corresponding XML document. For now, it is best to get into the habit of adding this attribute with the value `qualified`, because it will simplify your instance documents. You will see what this means a little later in the chapter.

Next, in the XML you have:

```
<element name="name">
```

Within the <schema> element is an <element> declaration. Within this <element>, you specified that the name of the element is name. In this example, the content model is specified by including a <complexType> definition within the <element> declaration:

```
<complexType>
  <sequence>
    <element name="first" type="string"/>
    <element name="middle" type="string"/>
    <element name="last" type="string"/>
  </sequence>
  <attribute name="title" type="string"/>
</complexType>
```

Because the <name> element contains the elements <first>, <middle>, and <last>, it must be declared as a complex type. A <complexType> definition enables you to specify the allowable elements and their order as well as any attribute declarations.

In this example, you have indicated that you are using a sequence by including a <sequence> element. The <sequence> declaration contains three <element> declarations. Within these declarations, you have specified that their type is string. This indicates that the elements must adhere to the XML Schema simple type string, which allows any textual content.

In addition, within the <complexType> definition is an <attribute> declaration. This <attribute> declaration appears at the end of the <complexType> definition, after any content model information. By declaring a title attribute, you can easily specify how you should address the individual described by your XML document. Because the title attribute is declared in the <complexType> declaration for the <name> element, the attribute is allowed to appear in the <name> element in the instance document.

Before moving on, take a quick look at the instance document from the preceding activity:

```
<name
  xmlns="http://www.example.com/name"
  xmlns:xsi="http://www.w3.org/2001/XMLSchema-instance"
  xsi:schemaLocation="http://www.example.com/name name5.xsd"
  title="Mr.">
```

Within the root element of the instance document are two namespace declarations. The first indicates that the default namespace is http://www.example.com/name. This namespace matches the targetNamespace that you declared within your XML Schema. You also declare the namespace http://www.w3.org/2001/XMLSchema-instance. Several attributes from this namespace can be used within your instance document.

The instance document includes the attribute schemaLocation. This attribute tells the schema validator where to find the XML Schema document for validation. The schemaLocation attribute is declared within the namespace http://www.w3.org/2001/XMLSchema-instance, so the attribute has the prefix xsi. The value of the schemaLocation attribute is http://www.example.com/name name5.xsd. This is known as a *namespace-location pair*; it is the namespace of your XML document and the URL of the XML Schema that describes your namespace. This example used a very simple relative URL, `name5.xsd`. The XML Schema Recommendation allows you to declare several namespace-location pairs within a single `schemaLocation` attribute — simply separate the values with whitespace. This is useful when your XML document uses multiple namespaces.

The `schemaLocation` attribute is only a hint for the processor to use — the processor doesn't have to use the provided location. For example, the validator may have a local copy of the XML Schema instead of loading the file specified, to decrease processor usage. If your XML Schema has no `targetNamespace`, you cannot use a namespace-location pair. Instead, you must refer to the XML Schema using the `noNamespaceSchemaLocation` attribute within your instance document.

This has been an extremely brief overview of some difficult concepts in XML Schemas. Don't worry; the Try It Out from this section is intended to give you an overall context for what you will be learning throughout the chapter. Each of these concepts is covered in much greater detail.

DEFINING XML SCHEMAS

Now you have a general feel for what XML Schemas look like and how they are used, it's time to move onto the details of their construction. The following sections go over the structure and function of the various components and declarations in in an XML Schema.

<schema> Declarations

The `<schema>` element is the root element within an XML Schema and it enables you to declare namespace information as well as defaults for declarations throughout the document. You can also include a `version` attribute that helps to identify the XML Schema and the version of your vocabulary, like so:

```
<schema targetNamespace="URI"
  attributeFormDefault="qualified or unqualified"
  elementFormDefault="qualified or unqualified"
  version="version number">
```

The XML Schema Namespace

In the first example, the namespace `http://www.w3.org/2001/XMLSchema` was declared as the default within the `<schema>` element. This enables you to indicate that the `<schema>` element is part of the XML Schema vocabulary. Remember that because XML is case sensitive, namespaces are case sensitive.

Instead of making this the default, you could have used a prefix. For the following example, the XML Schema Recommendation itself uses the prefix `xs`:

```
<xs:schema xmlns:xs="http://www.w3.org/2001/XMLSchema">
```

As shown in Chapter 3, the namespace prefix is insignificant — it is only a shortcut to the namespace declaration. Which prefix you use is a matter of personal preference; just remember to be consistent throughout your document.

Target Namespaces

The primary purpose of XML Schemas is to declare vocabularies. These vocabularies can be identified by a namespace that is specified in the `targetNamespace` attribute. Not all XML Schemas will have a `targetNamespace`. Many XML Schemas define vocabularies that are reused in another XML Schema, or vocabularies that are used in documents where the namespace is not necessary.

When declaring a `targetNamespace`, it is important to include a matching namespace declaration. You can choose any prefix you like, or you can use a default namespace declaration. The namespace declaration is used when you are referring to declarations within the XML Schema. You will see what this means in more detail later in the section "Referring to an Existing Global Element."

Some possible `targetNamespace` declarations include the following:

```
<schema xmlns="http://www.w3.org/2001/XMLSchema"
  targetNamespace="http://www.example.com/name"
  xmlns:target="http://www.example.com/name">
```

or

```
<xs:schema xmlns:xs="http://www.w3.org/2001/XMLSchema"
  targetNamespace="http://www.example.com/name"
  xmlns="http://www.example.com/name">
```

Notice that in the first declaration the `<schema>` element uses the default namespace. Because of this, the target namespace `http://www.example.com/name` requires the use of a prefix. However, in the second declaration you see the exact opposite; the `<schema>` element requires the use of a prefix because the target namespace `http://www.example.com/name` is using a default namespace declaration. Again, user preference is the only difference.

Element and Attribute Qualification

Within the instance document, elements and attributes may be qualified or unqualified. An element or attribute is *qualified* if it has an associated namespace. For example, the following elements are qualified:

```
<name xmlns="http://www.example.com/name">
   <first>John</first>
   <middle>Fitzgerald</middle>
   <last>Doe</last>
</name>
```

Even though the elements in this example don't have namespace prefixes, they still have an associated namespace, `http://www.example.com/name`, making them qualified but *not prefixed*. Each of the child elements is also qualified because of the default namespace declaration in the `<name>` element. Again, these elements have no prefixes.

In the following example, all of the elements are qualified *and* prefixed:

```
<n:name xmlns:n="http://www.example.com/name">
   <n:first>John</n:first>
   <n:middle>Fitzgerald</n:middle>
   <n:last>Doe</n:last>
</n:name>
```

Unqualified elements have no associated namespace:

```
<n:name xmlns:n="http://www.example.com/name">
   <first>John</first>
   <middle>Fitzgerald</middle>
   <last>Doe</last>
</n:name>
```

The `<name>` element is qualified, but the `<first>`, `<middle>`, and `<last>` elements are not. The `<first>`, `<middle>`, and `<last>` elements have no associated namespace declaration (default or otherwise); therefore, they are unqualified. This mix of qualified and unqualified elements may seem strange; nevertheless, it is the default behavior in XML Schemas.

Within the `<schema>` element you can modify the defaults specifying how elements should be qualified by including the following attributes:

- `elementFormDefault`
- `attributeFormDefault`

The `elementFormDefault` and `attributeFormDefault` attributes enable you to control the default qualification form for elements and attributes in the instance documents. The default value for both `elementFormDefault` and `attributeFormDefault` is `unqualified`.

Even though the value of the `elementFormDefault` attribute is `unqualified`, some elements must be qualified regardless. For example, global element declarations must always be qualified in instance documents (global and local declarations are discussed in detail in the next section). In the preceding example, this is exactly what was done. The `<name>` element was qualified with a namespace, but not the `<first>`, `<middle>`, and `<last>` elements.

On some occasions you will want a mix of qualified and unqualified elements; for example, XSLT and SOAP documents may contain both. But as a rule of thumb it's best to qualify all of the elements in your documents. In other words, always include the `elementFormDefault` attribute with the value `qualified`. This makes reuse of the vocabulary a little easier.

NOTE *The default value for* `attributeFormDefault` *is* `unqualified`. *Usually you won't have to change this value, because most attributes in XML vocabularies are unqualified.*

Content Models

XML Schemas specify what may appear in a document by providing a structural model of the allowable content. Where elements and attributes could be seen as the "atoms" of XML, it's also possible to group these together into "molecules." These molecules are the content models.

In the first example you saw a <complexType> and a <sequence> declaration used to specify an element's allowable content. The <sequence> declaration is one of three distinct ways of interpreting a list of elements. All three are as follows:

- <sequence>: Elements must appear in the given order.
- <choice>: Only one of the elements in the list may appear.
- <all>: Elements can appear in any order, with each child element occurring zero or one time.

What's more, the contents of the <sequence> and <choice> elements aren't limited to individual elements. You can use these structures as components of other structures. For example:

```
<complexType name="NameOrEmail">
<choice>
  <element name="email" type="string"/>
  <sequence>
    <element name="first" type="string"/>
    <element name="middle" type="string"/>
    <element name="last" type="string"/>
  </sequence>
  </choice>
</complexType>
```

Here, the content model specifies that the NameOrEmail type is something that's *either* a string in an <email> element *or* an ordered list of <first>, <middle>, <last> elements containing strings.

There is also the <group> declaration, which, as you see later, can be used to wrap <sequence>, <choice>, or <all> blocks for reuse elsewhere in the schema.

The <sequence> and <choice> declarations are pretty straightforward in their interpretations, but there are some special rules that govern the use of <all>.

Restrictions on <all>

The <all> declaration says that the elements can appear in any order, with each child element occurring zero or one time.

To use this mechanism, you must adhere to several rules:

- The <all> declaration must be the only content model declaration that appears as a child of a <complexType> definition.
- The <all> declaration can contain only <element> declarations as its children. It is not permitted to contain <sequence>, <choice>, or <group> declarations.

- The <all> declaration's children may appear once each in the instance document. This means that within the <all> declaration, the values for minOccurs for maxOccurs are limited to 0 or 1.

Even with these additional restrictions, the <all> declaration can be very useful. It is commonly used when the expected content is known, but not the order.

Suppose you declared the <name> content model using the <all> mechanism:

```
<element name="name">
  <complexType>
    <all>
      <element name="first" type="string"/>
      <element name="middle" type="string"/>
      <element name="last" type="string"/>
    </all>
    <attribute name="title" type="string"/>
  </complexType>
</element>
```

Notice that the <all> element is the only content model declaration within the <complexType> (<attribute> declarations do not count as content model declarations). In addition, note that the <all> declaration contains only <element> declarations as its children. Because the default value for minOccurs and maxOccurs is 1, each element can appear in the instance document once and only once. By declaring the content model as shown in the preceding example, you can validate your element content but still allow your elements to appear in any order. The allowable content for a <name> element declared using an <all> declaration might include

```
<first>John</first>
<middle>Fitzgerald</middle>
<last>Doe</last>
```

or

```
<first>John</first>
<last>Doe</last>
<middle>Fitzgerald</middle>
```

As long as all of the elements you have specified appear, they can appear in any order. In the second example, the <middle> element was added last. Because the content model is declared using <all>, this is still allowable.

<element> Declarations

When declaring an element, you are actually performing two primary tasks — specifying the element name and defining the allowable content:

```
<element
  name="name of the element"
  type="global type"
  ref="global element declaration"
```

```
form="qualified or unqualified"
minOccurs="non-negative number"
maxOccurs="non-negative number or 'unbounded'"
default="default value"
fixed="fixed value">
```

When specifying the name, standard XML restrictions exist on what names you can give elements. Though XML names can *include* numerical digits, periods (.), hyphens (-), and underscores (_), they must *begin* with a letter or an underscore (_). Because of the way namespaces are dealt with in XML Schema, the colon (:) is also disallowed anywhere in the name.

An element's allowable content is determined by its *type*, which may be simple or complex. You can specify the type in three main ways: by creating a local type, using a global type, or by referring to a global element declaration.

Global versus Local

Before you can understand these different methods for declaring elements, you must understand the difference between global and local declarations:

- *Global declarations* are declarations that appear as direct children of the <schema> element. Global element declarations can be reused throughout the XML Schema.
- *Local declarations* do not have the <schema> element as their direct parent and can be used only in their specific context.

Look at the first example (name5.xsd) again:

```
<?xml version="1.0"?>
<schema xmlns="http://www.w3.org/2001/XMLSchema"
  xmlns:target="http://www.example.com/name"
  targetNamespace="http://www.example.com/name"
  elementFormDefault="qualified">
  <element name="name">
    <complexType>
      <sequence>
        <element name="first" type="string"/>
        <element name="middle" type="string"/>
        <element name="last" type="string"/>
      </sequence>
      <attribute name="title" type="string"/>
    </complexType>
  </element>
</schema>
```

This XML Schema has four element declarations. The first declaration, the <name> element, is a global declaration because it is a direct child of the <schema> element. The declarations for the <first>, <middle>, and <last> elements are considered local because the declarations are not direct children of the <schema> element. The declarations for the <first>, <middle>, and <last> elements are valid only within the <sequence> declaration — they cannot be reused elsewhere in the XML Schema.

Creating a Local Type

Of the two methods of element declaration, creating a local type should seem the most familiar. This model was used when declaring the <name> element in the example. To create a local type, you simply include the type declaration as a child of the element declaration, as in the following example:

```
<element name="name">
  <complexType>
    <sequence>
      <element name="first" type="string"/>
      <element name="middle" type="string"/>
      <element name="last" type="string"/>
    </sequence>
    <attribute name="title" type="string"/>
  </complexType>
</element>
```

or

```
<element name="name">
  <simpleType>
    <restriction base="string">
      <enumeration value="Home"/>
      <enumeration value="Work"/>
      <enumeration value="Cell"/>
      <enumeration value="Fax"/>
    </restriction>
  </simpleType>
</element>
```

These examples show that an element declaration can contain a <complexType> definition or a <simpleType> definition, but it cannot contain both at the same time.

Creating a Global Type

Often, many of your elements will have the same content. Instead of declaring duplicate local types throughout your schema, you can create a global type. Within your element declarations, you can refer to a global type by name. In fact, you have already seen this:

```
<element name="first" type="string"/>
```

Here, the `type` attribute refers to the built-in data type `string`. XML Schemas have many built-in data types, most of which will be described in the "Data Types" section later in the chapter. You can also create your own global declarations and refer to them. For example, suppose you had created a global type for the content of the <name> element like so:

```
<schema xmlns="http://www.w3.org/2001/XMLSchema"
  xmlns:target="http://www.example.com/name"
  targetNamespace="http://www.example.com/name"
  elementFormDefault="qualified">
  <complexType name="NameType">
```

```
    <sequence>
      <element name="first" type="string"/>
      <element name="middle" type="string"/>
      <element name="last" type="string"/>
    </sequence>
    <attribute name="title" type="string"/>
  </complexType>
  <element name="name" type="target:NameType"/>
</schema>
```

Even though the type is global, it is still part of the target namespace. Therefore, when referring to the type, you must include the target namespace prefix (if any). This example used the prefix `target` to refer to the target namespace, but it is equally correct to do the following:

```
<xs:schema xmlns:xs="http://www.w3.org/2001/XMLSchema"
  xmlns="http://www.example.com/name"
  targetNamespace="http://www.example.com/name"
  elementFormDefault="qualified">
  <xs:complexType name="NameType">
    <xs:sequence>
      <xs:element name="first" type="xs:string"/>
      <xs:element name="middle" type="xs:string"/>
      <xs:element name="last" type="xs:string"/>
    </xs:sequence>
    <xs:attribute name="title" type="xs:string"/>
  </xs:complexType>
  <xs:element name="name" type="NameType"/>
</xs:schema>
```

Here, the XML Schema namespace is declared using the prefix `xs`, and the target namespace has no prefix. Therefore, to refer to the global type `NameType`, you do not need to include any prefix.

Now that you know the theory behind global types, you can try them out in practice.

TRY IT OUT Creating Reusable Global Types

Creating global types within an XML Schema is straightforward. In this example you convert the `<name>` example to use a named global type, rather than a local type. Once a global type is defined you can use it anywhere in your schema, so you don't have to repeat yourself. Here's how it's done:

1. Begin by making the necessary changes to your XML Schema. Run jEdit and reopen `name5.xsd`. Then make the highlighted changes in the following code, and save the result as `name6.xsd`.

Available for download on Wrox.com

```
<?xml version="1.0"?>
<schema xmlns="http://www.w3.org/2001/XMLSchema"
  xmlns:target="http://www.example.com/name"
  targetNamespace="http://www.example.com/name"
  elementFormDefault="qualified">
  <complexType name="NameType">
    <sequence>
      <element name="first" type="string"/>
      <element name="middle" type="string"/>
```

```
      <element name="last" type="string"/>
    </sequence>
    <attribute name="title" type="string"/>
  </complexType>
  <element name="name" type="target:NameType"/>
</schema>
```

name6.xsd

2. Before you can validate your document, you must modify it so that it refers to your new XML Schema. Reopen name5.xml and change the xsi:schemaLocation attribute, as follows:

```
xsi:schemaLocation="http://www.example.com/name name6.xsd"
```

Save this modified version as name6.xml.

3. You are ready to validate your XML instance document against your XML Schema. In jEdit click Plugins ➪ XML ➪ Parse as XML. This should validate with no errors, as before.

How It Works

You had to make minor modifications to your schema in order to create a reusable complex type. First, you moved the <complexType> definition from within your <element> declaration to your <schema> element. Remember that a declaration is global if it is a direct child of the <schema> element. Once you made the <complexType> definition global, you needed to add a name attribute so that you could refer to it later. You named the <complexType> definition NameType so it would be easy to identify.

After you declared the NameType <complexType>, you modified your <name> element declaration to refer to it. You added a type attribute to your element declaration with the value target:NameType. Keep in mind that you have to include the namespace prefix target when referring to the type so the validator knows which namespace it should look in.

So within <complexType> definitions, you specify the allowable element content for the declaration:

```
<complexType
  mixed="true or false"
  name="Name of complexType">
```

Earlier, when you created a local declaration, you did not include a name attribute in your <complexType> definition. Local <complexType> definitions are *never* named; in fact, they are called *anonymous complex types*. As you have already seen, however, global <complexType> definitions are *always* named, so that they can be identified later.

Referring to an Existing Global Element

As shown in the preceding example, referring to global types enables you to reuse content model definitions within your XML Schema. Often, you may want to reuse entire element declarations instead of just the type. To refer to a global element declaration, simply include a `ref` attribute and specify the name of the global element as the value, like so:

```
<element ref="target:first"/>
```

Again, the name of the element must be qualified with the namespace. The preceding example is an element reference to a global element named `first` that was declared in the target namespace. Notice that when you refer to a global element declaration, you have no `type` attribute and no local type declaration. Your element declaration uses the type of the `<element>` declaration in the reference.

This is very straightforward; now you can add a reference to the global type.

TRY IT OUT Referring to Global Element Declarations

In the last Try It Out you created a global type. In this one you will modify the schema from the previous activity to refer to global element declarations. Here's how to do it:

1. Begin by making the necessary changes to the XML Schema. Reopen `name6.xsd` and save it as `name7.xsd`.
2. Make the following changes:

Available for download on Wrox.com

```
<?xml version="1.0"?>
<schema xmlns="http://www.w3.org/2001/XMLSchema"
  xmlns:target="http://www.example.com/name"
  targetNamespace="http://www.example.com/name"
  elementFormDefault="qualified">
  <element name="first" type="string"/>
  <element name="middle" type="string"/>
  <element name="last" type="string"/>
  <complexType name="NameType">
    <sequence>
      <element ref="target:first"/>
      <element ref="target:middle"/>
      <element ref="target:last"/>
    </sequence>
    <attribute name="title" type="string"/>
  </complexType>
  <element name="name" type="target:NameType"/>
</schema>
```

name7.xsd

3. Before you can schema-validate your XML document, you must modify it so that it refers to your new XML Schema. Reopen `name6.xml`, save it as `name7.xml`, and change the `xsi:schemaLocation` attribute to point to the new schema:

```
xsi:schemaLocation="http://www.example.com/name name7.xsd"
```

4. You are ready to validate your XML instance document against your XML Schema. In jEdit, click Plugins ➪ XML ➪ Parse as XML.

How It Works

This Try It Out utilized references to global element declarations within your content model. First you moved the declarations for the `<first>`, `<middle>`, and `<last>` elements from within your `<complexType>` definition to your `<schema>` element, making them global. After you created your global declarations, you inserted references to the elements within your `<complexType>`. In each reference, you prefixed the global element name with the prefix `target`.

What a Validator Does with Global Types

At this point, it might help to examine what the schema validator is doing in more detail. As the schema validator processes your instance document, it first encounters the root element, in this case `<name>`. When it encounters the `<name>` element, it looks it up in the XML Schema. When attempting to find the declaration for the root element, the schema validator looks through only the global element declarations.

Once the schema validator finds the matching declaration, it finds the associated type (in this case it is a global `<complexType>` definition `NameType`). It then validates the content of the `<name>` element within the instance against the content model defined in the associated type. When the schema validator encounters the `<element>` reference declarations, it imports the global `<element>` declarations into the `<complexType>` definition, as if they had been included directly.

Now that you have learned some of the basics of how elements are declared, the following sections look briefly at some of the features element declarations offer.

Cardinality

Cardinality specifies the number of times a particular element appears within a content model. In XML Schemas, you can modify an element's cardinality by specifying the `minOccurs` and `maxOccurs` attributes within the element declaration.

WARNING *The* `minOccurs` *and* `maxOccurs` *attributes are not permitted within global element declarations. Instead, use these attributes within the element references in your content models.*

Some possible uses of the `minOccurs` and `maxOccurs` attributes include the following:

```
<element name="first" type="string" minOccurs="2" maxOccurs="2"/>

<element ref="target:first" maxOccurs="10"/>

<element name="location" "minOccurs="0" maxOccurs="unbounded"/>
```

The first of the preceding examples declares that the element `<first>` must appear within the instance document a minimum of two times and a maximum of two times. The second example declares your element using a reference to the global `<first>` declaration. Even though it is declared using the `ref` attribute, you are permitted to use the `minOccurs` and `maxOccurs` attributes to specify the element's cardinality. In this case, a `maxOccurs` attribute was included with the value `10`. A `minOccurs` attribute was not included, so a schema validator would use the default value, `1`. The final example specifies that `<location>` may or may not appear within your instance document because the `minOccurs` attribute has the value `0`. It also indicates that it may appear an infinite number of times because the value of `maxOccurs` is `unbounded`.

The default value for the `minOccurs` attribute and the `maxOccurs` attribute is `1`. This means that, by default, an element must appear only once. You can use the two attributes separately or in conjunction. The `maxOccurs` attribute enables you to enter the value `unbounded`, which indicates there is no limit to the number of occurrences. The only additional rule you must adhere to when specifying `minOccurs` and `maxOccurs` is that the value of `maxOccurs` must be greater than or equal to the value for `minOccurs`.

Default and Fixed Values

When designing the DTD for your contacts list in the previous chapter, you made use of attribute default and fixed values. In XML Schemas, you can declare default and fixed values for elements as well as attributes. When declaring default values for elements, you can only specify a text value. You are not permitted to specify a default value for an element whose content model will contain other elements, unless the content model is mixed. By specifying a default value for your element, you ensure that the schema validator will treat the value as if it were included in the XML document — even if it is omitted.

To specify a default value, simply include the `default` attribute with the desired value. Suppose your `<name>` elements were being used to design the Doe family tree. You might want to make `"Doe"` the default for the last name element, like so:

```
<element name="last" type="string" default="Doe"/>
```

This example declares that the element `<last>` has the default value of `"Doe"`, so when a schema validator encounters the `<last>` element in the instance document, it inserts the default value if there is no content. For example, if the schema validator encounters:

```
<last></last>
```

or

```
<last/>
```

it would treat the element as follows:

```
<last>Doe</last>
```

Note that if the element does not appear within the document or if the element already has content, the default value is not used.

In some circumstances you may want to ensure that an element's value does not change, such as an element whose value is used to indicate a version number. As the schema validator processes an element declared to have a fixed value, it checks whether the element's content and fixed attribute values match. If they do not match, the validator raises a schema-validity error. If the element is empty, the parser inserts the fixed value.

To specify a fixed value, simply include the `fixed` attribute with the desired value, like so:

```
<element name="version" type="string" fixed="1.0"/>
```

The preceding example specifies that the `<version>` element, if it appears, must contain the value `1.0`. The fixed value is a valid `string` value (the type of the `<version>` element is `string`). Therefore, the following elements are *legal*:

```
<version>1.0</version>

<version></version>

<version/>
```

As the schema validator processes the file, it accepts elements with the value `1.0` or empty elements. When it encounters empty elements, it treats them as though the value `1.0` had been included. The following value is *not legal*:

```
<version>2.0</version>
```

When specifying fixed or default values in element declarations, you must ensure that the value you specify is allowable content for the type you have declared. For example, if you specify that an element has the type `positiveInteger`, you cannot use `Doe` as a default value because it is not a positive integer.

Element Wildcards: the <any> Declaration

You'll often want to include elements in your XML Schema without explicitly declaring which elements should be allowed. Suppose you want to specify that your element can contain any of the elements declared in your namespace, or any elements from another namespace. Declarations that allow you to include any element from a namespace are called *element wildcards*.

To declare an element wildcard, use the `<any>` declaration, like so:

```
<any
  minOccurs="non negative number"
  maxOccurs="non negative number or unbounded"
  namespace="allowable namespaces"
  processContents="lax or skip or strict">
```

The `<any>` declaration can appear only within a content model. You are not allowed to create global `<any>` declarations. When specifying an `<any>` declaration, you can specify the cardinality just as you would within an `<element>` declaration. By specifying the `minOccurs` or the `maxOccurs` attributes, you can control the number of wildcard occurrences allowed within your instance document.

The <any> declaration also enables you to control which namespace or namespaces the elements are allowed to come from. You do this by including the namespace attribute. The namespace attribute allows several values, shown in Table 5-1:

TABLE 5-1: Namespace Values

VALUE	DESCRIPTION
##any	Enables elements from all namespaces to be included as part of the wildcard.
##other	Enables elements from namespaces other than the targetNamespace to be included as part of the wildcard.
##targetNamespace	Enables elements from only the targetNamespace to be included as part of the wildcard.
##local	Enables any well-formed elements that are not qualified by a namespace to be included as part of the wildcard.
Whitespace-separated	Enables elements from any listed namespaces to be included as part of the list of allowable wildcards. Possible list values also include ##targetNamespace namespace URIs and ##local.

For example, suppose you wanted to allow any well-formed XML content from any namespace within the <name> element. To do this, you simply include an element wildcard within the content model for your NameType complex type, like so:

```
<complexType name="NameType">
  <sequence>
    <element ref="target:first"/>
    <element ref="target:middle"/>
    <element ref="target:last"/>
    <!-- allow any element from any namespace -->
    <any namespace="##any"
         processContents="lax"
         minOccurs="0"
         maxOccurs="unbounded"/>
  </sequence>
  <attribute name="title" type="string"/>
</complexType>
```

By setting the namespace attribute to ##any, you have specified that elements from all namespaces can be included as part of the wildcard. You have also included cardinality attributes to indicate the number of allowed wildcard elements. This case specifies any number of elements because the value of the `minOccurs` attribute is set to `0` and the value of `maxOccurs` is set to `unbounded`. Therefore, the content model must contain a `<first>`, `<middle>`, and `<last>` element in sequence, followed by any number of elements from any namespace.

When the schema validator is processing an element that contains a wildcard declaration, it validates the instance documents in one of three ways:

- If the value of the `processContents` attribute is set to `skip`, the processor skips any wildcard elements in the instance document.
- If the value of `processContents` attribute is set to `lax`, the processor attempts to validate the wildcard elements if it has access to a global XML Schema definition for them.
- If the value of the `processContents` attribute is set to `strict` (the default) or there is no `processContents` attribute, the processor attempts to validate the wildcard elements. However, in contrast to using the `lax` setting, the schema validator raises a validity error if a global XML Schema definition for the wildcard elements cannot be found.

Mixed Content

Mixed content models enable you to include both text and element content within a single content model. To create a mixed content model in XML Schemas, simply include the `mixed` attribute with the value `true` in your `<complexType>` definition, like so:

```
<element name="description">
  <complexType mixed="true">
    <choice minOccurs="0" maxOccurs="unbounded">
      <element name="em" type="string"/>
      <element name="strong" type="string"/>
      <element name="br" type="string"/>
    </choice>
  </complexType>
</element>
```

The preceding example declares a `<description>` element, which can contain an infinite number of `<em>`, `<strong>`, and `<br>` elements. Because the complex type is declared as mixed, text can be interspersed throughout these elements. An allowable `<description>` element might look like the following:

```
<description>Joe is a developer &amp; author for Beginning XML <em>5th
 edition</em></description>
```

In this `<description>` element, textual content is interspersed throughout the elements declared within the content model. As the schema validator is processing the preceding example, it skips over the textual content and entities while performing standard validation on the elements. Because the elements `<em>`, `<strong>`, and `<br>` may appear repeatedly (`maxOccurs="unbounded"`), the example is valid.

To declare an empty content model in a <complexType> definition, you simply create the <complexType> definition without any <element> or content model declarations. Consider the following declarations:

```
<element name="knows">
  <complexType>
  </complexType>
</element>

<element name="knows">
  <complexType/>
</element>
```

Each of these declares an element named knows. In both cases, the <complexType> definition is empty, indicating that knows will not contain text or element children. When used in your instance document, <knows> must be empty.

<group> Declarations

In addition to <complexType> definitions, XML Schemas also enable you to define reusable groups of elements. By creating a global <group> declaration like the following, you can easily reuse and combine entire content models:

```
<group name="name of global group">
```

Just as you have seen with global <complexType> definitions, all global <group> declarations must be named. Simply specify the name attribute with the desired name. Again, the name that you specify must follow the rules for XML names and should not include a prefix. The basic structure of a global <group> declaration follows:

```
<group name="NameGroup">
 <!-- content model goes here -->
</group>
```

In the following activity you will practice creating and naming a global <group> declaration.

TRY IT OUT Using a Global Group

This example redesigns the schema so that you can create a reusable global <group> declaration:

1. Begin by making the necessary changes to your XML Schema. Create a new document called name8.xsd. Copy the contents from name7.xsd and make the following changes:

Available for download on Wrox.com

```
<?xml version="1.0"?>
<schema xmlns="http://www.w3.org/2001/XMLSchema"
  xmlns:target="http://www.example.com/name"
  targetNamespace="http://www.example.com/name"
  elementFormDefault="qualified">
 <group name="NameGroup">
```

```
      <sequence>
        <element name="first" type="string" minOccurs="1" maxOccurs="unbounded"/>
        <element name="middle" type="string" minOccurs="0" maxOccurs="1"/>
        <element name="last" type="string"/>
      </sequence>
    </group>
    <complexType name="NameType">
      <group ref="target:NameGroup"/>
      <attribute name="title" type="string"/>
    </complexType>
    <element name="name" type="target:NameType"/>
  </schema>
```

name8.xsd

2. Before you can schema-validate your XML document, you must modify it so that it refers to your new XML Schema. Create a new document called name8.xml. Copy the contents from name7.xml and change the xsi:schemaLocation attribute as follows:

```
xsi:schemaLocation="http://www.example.com/name name8.xsd"
```

3. You are ready to validate your XML instance document against the XML Schema. Open the name8.xml document with jEdit and click Plugins ➪ XML ➪ Parse as XML. This should validate with no errors, as shown in the previous Try It Out.

How It Works

This Try It Out modified your XML Schema to use a global <group> declaration. Within the global <group> declaration named NameGroup, you declared the allowable elements for your content model. Instead of including element declarations in the <complexType> definition for your <name> element, you created a <group> reference declaration. When referring to the global <group> declaration, you included a ref attribute with the value target:NameGroup.

You also updated the <element> declarations to make use of the minOccurs and maxOccurs attributes. The values used in the minOccurs and maxOccurs attributes enabled you to mimic the various cardinality indicators used in the original DTD.

Notice that the <attribute> declaration still appeared within the <complexType> declaration and not within the <group> declaration. This should give you some indication of the difference between a <group> and a <complexType> definition. A <complexType> declaration defines the allowable content for a specific element or type of element. A <group> declaration simply allows you to create a reusable content model that can replace other content model declarations in your XML Schema.

As the schema validator is processing the instance document, it processes the <name> element, similarly to the earlier examples. When it encounters the <name> element, it looks it up in the XML Schema. Once it finds the declaration, it finds the associated type (in this case it is a local <complexType> definition). When the schema validator encounters the <group> reference declaration, it treats the items within the group as if they had been included directly within the <complexType> definition. Even though the <group> declaration is global, the <element> declarations within the <group> are not.

<attribute> Declarations

So far, you have spent most of this chapter learning how to create element declarations. Within XML Schemas, attribute declarations are very similar to element declarations. So rather than describe all the features of attribute declarations in detail, here is a quick overview, followed by an example of attributes used in practice through which you can work.

In the examples for the `<name>` element, you have already seen an attribute declaration for the `title` attribute. As with element declarations, you have two primary methods for declaring attributes: creating a local type and using a global type.

Unlike elements, which are divided into simple types and complex types, attribute declarations are restricted to simple types. Remember that complex types are used to define types that contain attributes or elements; simple types are used to restrict text-only content. A basic attribute declaration looks like this:

```
<attribute name="title">
  <simpleType>
    <!-- type information -->
  </simpleType>
</element>
```

Like elements, you can also reuse attributes by referring to global declarations.

At this point you have heard about most of the major features of XML Schema, and before you go on to learn the remaining ones, you should apply what you know so far in a longer example to see how everything thus far fits together.

***NOTE** There may be a few features of XML Schema in the following example that haven't been discussed in detail yet, but don't worry. You will get to them shortly after and you will still be able to perform the example in the meantime.*

An XML Schema for Contacts

In the previous chapter you saw a way of expressing contact lists in XML, backed by a DTD. Here, the same idea will be revisited using an XML Schema for validation.

Listing 5-1 provides a sample document to work from.

Available for download on Wrox.com

LISTING 5-1: contacts5.xml

```
<?xml version="1.0"?>
<contacts xmlns="http://www.example.com/contacts"
    xmlns:xsi="http://www.w3.org/2001/XMLSchema-instance"
    xsi:schemaLocation="http://www.example.com/contacts contacts5.xsd"
    source="Beginning XML 5E"
```

continues

LISTING 5-1 *(continued)*

```
    version="1.0">

  <contact>
    <name>
      <first>Joseph</first>
      <first>John</first>
      <last>Fawcett</last>
    </name>
    <location>
      <address>Exeter, UK</address>
      <latitude>50.7218</latitude>
      <longitude>-3.533617</longitude>
    </location>
    <phone kind="Home">001-234-567-8910</phone>
    <knows/>
    <description> Joseph is a developer and author for Beginning XML
<em>5th edition</em>.<br/>Joseph <strong>loves</strong> XML!</description>
  </contact>
  <contact>

    <name>

      <first>Liam</first>

      <last>Quin</last>

    </name>

    <location>

      <address>Ontario, Canada</address>

    </location>

    <phone>+1 613 476 8769</phone>

    <knows/>

    <description>XML Activity Lead at W3C</description>

  </contact>
</contacts>
```

This is very similar to the instance documents you saw in the previous chapter, but with one significant change: the declarations on the root element, highlighted here:

```
<contacts xmlns="http://www.example.com/contacts"
     xmlns:xsi="http://www.w3.org/2001/XMLSchema-instance"
     xsi:schemaLocation="http://www.example.com/contacts contacts5.xsd"
    source="Beginning XML 5E"
    version="1.0">
```

This document is associated with the identified XML Schema, which will live in the file `contacts5.xsd`.

To begin to build your XML, perform the following steps:

1. Start building your XML at root. Following is a suitable opening for the <schema> element:

```
<schema xmlns="http://www.w3.org/2001/XMLSchema"
  xmlns:contacts="http://www.example.com/contacts"
  targetNamespace="http://www.example.com/contacts"
  elementFormDefault="qualified">
```

   Here, the correct namespace is given for XML Schemas. This is followed by the namespace that will be used within instance documents, which is also specified as the targetNamespace for your vocabulary. Finally, there is the attribute elementFormDefault with the value qualified, which says the elements should be given a namespace (see the "Element and Attribute Qualification" section earlier).

2. Next, consider the contacts root element of the instance document. You created a global <element> declaration for your contacts element. Recall that this must be declared as a global <element> because you are using it as the root. When your schema validator eventually processes your instance document, it encounters the contacts element. The schema validator then opens your XML Schema document based on the xsi:schemaLocation attribute hint and finds the global declaration for the contacts element.

   Describe the contacts element by declaring a local <complexType> within your <element> declaration, and within that definition, use a <sequence> content model containing only one element. Even if you have only one element inside of a complex type, you still need to declare it as part of a suitable block container. Following the shape of the instance document, it makes sense to specify that the <contact> element could occur an unbounded number of times or not occur at all. These decisions lead to the following chunk in the XML Schema:

```
<element name="contacts">
    <complexType>
      <sequence>
        <element name="contact" minOccurs="0" maxOccurs="unbounded">
```

3. Next, use another local <complexType> to define the content model for this element. It is possible to use local <complexType> declarations inside of other <complexType> declarations. In fact, you could define an entire schema in this manner. In general, it is better to use global type definitions whenever possible, but for demonstration purposes there's a mix here. Use global <complexType> definitions for the name and location elements:

```
<complexType>
          <sequence>
            <element name="name" type="contacts:NameType"/>
            <element name="location" type="contacts:LocationType"/>
```

4. Now define the <phone> element in the schema like so:

```
<element name="phone">
       <complexType>
          <simpleContent>
             <extension base="string">
```

```
                <attribute name="kind" type="string" default="Home" />
              </extension>
            </simpleContent>
          </complexType>
        </element>
```

This is declared locally as another nested <complexType>. The <simpleContent> element indicates that the <complexType> cannot contain child elements, though it may contain attributes.

Within the <simpleContent> element, you have an <extension> declaration. This specifies what kind of data type should be used to validate your simple content. An <extension> declaration is necessary because you are extending an existing data type by adding attribute declarations.

In the <extension> declaration, the `base` attribute specifies the data type `string` to use as the basis for your element's content. Here, the built-in `string` type is the base type, but you are not limited to using built-in data types. You can also refer to any global <simpleType> in your XML Schema.

5. After specifying the base type, declare the attribute you want to use. The attribute declaration has a `name` and `type` just like element declarations. Here you also have a default value of `Home`. Any of the following examples are allowable <phone> elements based on the declaration:

```
<phone kind="Home">001-909-555-1212</phone>
<phone>001-909-555-1212</phone>
<phone />
```

In the first, the <phone> element contains a phone number string and a `kind` attribute. In the second example, the `kind` attribute is omitted. If a schema-aware parser encountered this element, it would use the default value `Home` specified in the attribute declaration.

6. The rest of the contact block is comprised of the <knows> element and the <description> element. Here, for the sake of experimentation, define their allowable content by the global `KnowsType` and `DescriptionType` declarations, and defer their definition until later in the schema:

```
        <element name="knows" type="contacts:KnowsType"/>
              <element name="description" type="contacts:DescriptionType"/>
            </sequence>
          </complexType>
        </element>
```

7. Zooming back out of the nesting, you can see that so far the contents of the <contacts> element have been described up to the <sequence> of elements it contains. But the <contacts> element itself has some attribute information; cover this like so:

```
<element name="contacts">
  <complexType>
    <sequence>
      <element name="contact" ...
```

```
...
      </sequence>
      <attributeGroup ref="contacts:ContactAttributes"/>
    </complexType>
  </element>
```

8. The <attributeGroup> here refers to a global grouping named ContactAttributes. Define this next in the schema like so:

```
<attributeGroup name="ContactAttributes">
  <attribute name="version" type="string" fixed="1.0" />
  <attribute name="source" type="string"/>
</attributeGroup>
```

When the schema validator encounters the <attributeGroup> reference declaration, it treats the source <attribute> declaration within the group as if it had been included directly within the <complexType> definition. It does this for each attribute declaration in the group.

The fixed declaration for the source attribute still applies even though you are using a group. Because the version of your contacts list is 1.0, it matches the fixed value. You could have omitted the version attribute altogether. As the document is being processed, the schema validator adds the fixed value from the XML Schema if no value is specified in the XML document.

9. Define the content model for the global NameType using a reference to a <group> as shown in the following code. To refer to the global <group> declaration, prefix the group name with the namespace prefix for your targetNamespace. In reality, you don't need to use a global group to specify the content of the <name> element, but the name elements are fairly common, and global groups can be more easily combined and reused. Global complex types are more useful when using type-aware tools such as XPath2 and XQuery. When designing your own schemas it is really a matter of personal preference and which tools you plan on using with your XML Schemas.

```
<group name="NameGroup">
  <sequence>
    <element name="first" type="string" minOccurs="1"
    maxOccurs="unbounded"/>
    <element name="middle" type="string" minOccurs="0" maxOccurs="1"/>
    <element name="last" type="string"/>
  </sequence>
</group>
```

The <group> declaration for the NameGroup is very straightforward. It lists the allowable elements for the content model within a <sequence> declaration. This should look very similar to the <name> examples you have already seen.

10. Next, in the LocationType <complexType> definition, use a choice declaration to allow either the element address or the sequence of elements, including latitude and longitude, like this:

```
 <complexType name="LocationType">
<choice minOccurs="0" maxOccurs="unbounded">
  <element name="address" type="string"/>
  <sequence>
    <element name="latitude" type="string"/>
```

```
          <element name="longitude" type="string"/>
        </sequence>
      </choice>
    </complexType>
```

Here you've specified that the choice may or may not appear and that it could appear an `unbounded` number of times.

11. The global declaration for `KnowsType` didn't contain a content model. Because of this, make the `<knows>` element in the instance document empty like so:

```
    <complexType name="KnowsType">
    </complexType>
    <complexType name="DescriptionType" mixed="true">
      <choice minOccurs="0" maxOccurs="unbounded">
        <element name="em" type="string"/>
        <element name="strong" type="string"/>
        <element name="br" type="string"/>
      </choice>
  </complexType>
```

The `DescriptionType` `<complexType>` definition here is a mixed declaration. To specify this, you have a `mixed` attribute with the value `true`. Within the mixed content model, to allow an `unbounded` number of `<em>`, `<strong>`, and `<br>` elements to be interspersed within the text, you used a `<choice>` declaration. Again, `minOccurs` is set to `0` and `maxOccurs` is set to `unbounded` so that the choice would be repeated.

12. Finally, close off your schema to finish up:

```
  </schema>
```

After reading and following along with all the preceding steps, you now know how to develop an XML Schema. The following activity builds on these steps to express a list of contacts using XML Schema.

TRY IT OUT Making Contact in XML Schema

This example recycles the idea of expressing contacts listings in XML that you saw in the previous chapter, only this time instead of using a DTD to specify the format you use an XML Schema. Before reading the How It Works section, take a few minutes to read through the listing and try to imagine what the XML documents it specifies might look like.

1. Begin by opening jEdit and enter the XML Schema you have just developed (refer to Listing 5-1). Save it as `contacts5.xsd`.

```
<?xml version="1.0"?>
<schema xmlns="http://www.w3.org/2001/XMLSchema"
xmlns:contacts="http://www.example.com/contacts"
targetNamespace="http://www.example.com/contacts" elementFormDefault="qualified">

  <element name="contacts">
    <complexType>
      <sequence>
        <element name="contact" minOccurs="0" maxOccurs="unbounded">
```

```
          <complexType>
            <sequence>
              <element name="name" type="contacts:NameType"/>
              <element name="location" type="contacts:LocationType"/>

              <element name="phone">
                 <complexType>
                    <simpleContent>
                       <extension base="string">
                          <attribute name="kind" type="string" default="Home" />
                       </extension>
                    </simpleContent>
                 </complexType>
              </element>
              <element name="knows" type="contacts:KnowsType"/>
              <element name="description" type="contacts:DescriptionType"/>
            </sequence>
          </complexType>
        </element>
      </sequence>
      <attributeGroup ref="contacts:ContactAttributes"/>
    </complexType>
  </element>

  <attributeGroup name="ContactAttributes">
    <attribute name="version" type="string" fixed="1.0" />
    <attribute name="source" type="string"/>
  </attributeGroup>

  <attribute name="title" type="string"/>

  <complexType name="NameType">
    <group ref="contacts:NameGroup"/>
  </complexType>

  <group name="NameGroup">
    <sequence>
      <element name="first" type="string" minOccurs="1" maxOccurs="unbounded"/>
      <element name="middle" type="string" minOccurs="0" maxOccurs="1"/>
      <element name="last" type="string"/>
    </sequence>
  </group>

  <complexType name="LocationType">
    <choice minOccurs="0" maxOccurs="unbounded">
      <element name="address" type="string"/>
      <sequence>
        <element name="latitude" type="string"/>
        <element name="longitude" type="string"/>
      </sequence>
    </choice>
  </complexType>

  <complexType name="KnowsType"></complexType>
```

```
    <complexType name="DescriptionType" mixed="true">
      <choice minOccurs="0" maxOccurs="unbounded">
        <element name="em" type="string"/>
        <element name="strong" type="string"/>
        <element name="br" type="string"/>
      </choice>
    </complexType>
  </schema>
```

2. Now enter the instance document from Listing 5-1.
3. You are ready to validate your XML instance document against your XML Schema. Click Plugins ➪ XML ➪ Parse as XML.

How It Works

The operation here is exactly the same as the one you've seen before, with jEdit's validator comparing the XML instance document against its schema.

Data Types

You have seen how to declare allowable elements and attributes using `<complexType>` definitions. In addition, you can define the allowable content for text-only elements and attribute values. The XML Schema Recommendation allows you to use two kinds of data types:

- Built-in data types
- User-defined data types

Built-in Data Types

The examples throughout this chapter have used the `string` type for our text-only content. The `string` type is a primitive data type that allows any textual content. XML Schemas provide a number of built-in simple types that allow you to exercise greater control over textual content in your XML document. Table 5-2 lists all of the simple types built into XML Schemas:

TABLE 5-2: XML Schema simple Types

TYPE	DESCRIPTION
`string`	Any character data
`normalizedString`	A whitespace-normalized string in which all spaces, tabs, carriage returns, and linefeed characters are converted to single spaces
`token`	A string that does not contain sequences of two or more spaces, tabs, carriage returns, or linefeed characters

TYPE	DESCRIPTION
`byte`	A numeric value from `-128` to `127`
`unsignedByte`	A numeric value from `0` to `255`
`base64Binary`	Base64-encoded binary information
`hexBinary`	Hexadecimal-encoded binary information
`integer`	A numeric value representing a whole number
`positiveInteger`	An integer whose value is greater than 0
`negativeInteger`	An integer whose value is less than 0
`nonNegativeInteger`	An integer whose value is 0 or greater
`nonPositiveInteger`	An integer whose value is less than or equal to 0
`int`	A numeric value from `-2147483648` to `2147483647`
`unsignedInt`	A numeric value from `0` to `4294967295`
`long`	A numeric value from `-9223372036854775808` to `9223372036854775807`
`unsignedLong`	A numeric value from `0` to `18446744073709551615`
`short`	A numeric value from `-32768` to `32767`
`unsignedShort`	A numeric value from `0` to `65535`
`decimal`	A numeric value that may or may not include a fractional part
`float`	A numeric value that corresponds to the IEEE single-precision 32-bit floating-point type defined in the standard IEEE 754-1985. `-0`, `INF`, `-INF`, and `NaN` are also valid values.
`double`	A numeric value that corresponds to the IEEE double-precision 64-bit floating-point type defined in the standard IEEE 754-1985. `-0`, `INF`, `-INF`, and `NaN` are also valid values.
`boolean`	A logical value, including `true`, `false`, `0`, and `1`
`time`	An instant of time that occurs daily as defined in Section 5.3 of ISO 8601. For example, `15:45:00.000` is a valid `time` value.
`dateTime`	An instant of time, including both a date and a time value, as defined in Section 5.4 of ISO 8601. For example, `1998-07-12T16:30:00.000` is a valid `dateTime` value.
`duration`	A span of time as defined in Section 5.5.3.2 of ISO 8601. For example, `P30D` is a valid `duration` value indicating a duration of 30 days.

continues

TABLE 5-2 *(continued)*

TYPE	DESCRIPTION
date	A date according to the Gregorian calendar as defined in Section 5.2.1 of ISO 8601. For example, 1995–05–25 is a valid date value.
gMonth	A month in the Gregorian calendar as defined in Section 3 of ISO 8601. For example, –07 is a valid gMonth value.
gYear	A year in the Gregorian calendar as defined in Section 5.2.1 of ISO 8601. For example, 1998 is a valid gYear value.
gYearMonth	A specific month and year in the Gregorian calendar as defined in Section 5.2.1 of ISO 8601. For example, 1998–07 is a valid gYearMonth value.
gDay	A recurring day of the month as defined in Section 3 of ISO 8601, such as the 12th day of the month. For example, --12 is a valid gDay value.
gMonthDay	A recurring day of a specific month as defined in Section 3 of ISO 8601, such as the 12th day of July. For example, –07–12 is a valid gMonthDay value.
name	An XML name according to the Namespace Recommendation. XML names must begin with a letter or an underscore. Though this type can allow for ":" characters, it is best to avoid them for compatibility.
QName	A qualified XML name as defined in the Namespaces Recommendation. QNames may or may not contain a namespace prefix and colon.
NCName	A noncolonized XML name that does not include a namespace prefix or colon as defined in the Namespaces Recommendation
anyURI	A valid Uniform Resource Identifier (URI)
language	A language constant as defined in RFC 1766, such as en-US (RFC 1766 can be found at www.ietf.org/rfc/rfc1766.txt)

In addition to the types listed, the XML Schema Recommendation also allows the types defined within the XML Recommendation. These types include ID, IDREF, IDREFS, ENTITY, ENTITIES, NOTATION, NMTOKEN, and NMTOKENS.

Although you have used the string type throughout most of the examples, any of the preceding types can be used to restrict the allowable content within your elements and attributes. Suppose you want to modify the declarations of the <latitude> and <longitude> elements within your contacts XML Schema. By specifying a more restrictive type, you could ensure that users of your XML Schema enter valid values. You could modify your declarations as follows:

```
<element name="latitude" type="float"/>
<element name="longitude" type="float"/>
```

Now, instead of allowing any textual content, you require that users specify a floating-point number. For a more in-depth look at these types, see the XML Schema Recommendation at `www.w3.org/TR/xmlschema-2`.

It will be straightforward to integrate built-in data types with the contacts example, as you will now see.

TRY IT OUT Making Contact — Built-in XML Schema Data Types

This Try It Out modifies the contacts example so that you can take advantage of the built-in XML Schema data types. You will also include some additional attributes that utilize the built-in types:

1. Begin by making the necessary changes to your XML Schema. Open the file `contacts5.xsd`, save it as `contacts6.xsd`, and make the following changes:

Available for download on Wrox.com

```
<?xml version="1.0"?>
<schema xmlns="http://www.w3.org/2001/XMLSchema"
  xmlns:contacts="http://www.example.com/contacts"
  targetNamespace="http://www.example.com/contacts"
  elementFormDefault="qualified">

  <attributeGroup name="ContactAttributes">
    <attribute name="version" type="decimal" fixed="1.0" />
    <attribute name="source" type="string"/>
  </attributeGroup>

  <element name="contacts">
    <complexType>
      <sequence>
        <element name="contact" minOccurs="0" maxOccurs="unbounded">
          <complexType>
            <sequence>
              <element name="name" type="contacts:NameType"/>
              <element name="location" type="contacts:LocationType"/>
              <element name="phone" type="contacts:PhoneType"/>
              <element name="knows" type="contacts:KnowsType"/>
              <element name="description" type="contacts:DescriptionType"/>
            </sequence>
            <attribute name="tags" type="token"/>
            <attribute name="person" type="ID"/>
          </complexType>
        </element>
      </sequence>
      <attributeGroup ref="contacts:ContactAttributes"/>
    </complexType>
  </element>

  <complexType name="NameType">
```

```
    <group ref="contacts:NameGroup"/>
    <attribute name="title" type="string"/>
  </complexType>

  <group name="NameGroup">
    <sequence>
      <element name="first" type="string" minOccurs="1" maxOccurs="unbounded"/>
      <element name="middle" type="string" minOccurs="0" maxOccurs="1"/>
      <element name="last" type="string"/>
    </sequence>
  </group>

  <complexType name="LocationType">
    <choice minOccurs="0" maxOccurs="unbounded">
      <element name="address" type="string"/>
      <sequence>
        <element name="latitude" type="float"/>
        <element name="longitude" type="float"/>
      </sequence>
    </choice>
  </complexType>

  <complexType name="PhoneType">
    <simpleContent>
      <extension base="string">
        <attribute name="kind" type="string" default="Home" />
      </extension>
    </simpleContent>
  </complexType>
  <complexType name="KnowsType">
    <attribute name="contacts" type="IDREFS"/>
  </complexType>

  <complexType name="DescriptionType" mixed="true">
    <choice minOccurs="0" maxOccurs="unbounded">
      <element name="em" type="string"/>
      <element name="strong" type="string"/>
      <element name="br" type="string"/>
    </choice>
  </complexType>

</schema>
```

contacts6.xsd

2. Before you can schema-validate your XML document, you must modify it so that it refers to your new XML Schema. You should also add some attributes. Open `contacts5.xml` and save it as `contacts6.xml`. Now change the `xsi:schemaLocation` attribute and add these highlighted attributes:

Available for download on Wrox.com

```
<?xml version="1.0"?>
<contacts source="Beginning XML 5E" version="1.0"
  xmlns="http://www.example.com/contacts"
  xmlns:xsi="http://www.w3.org/2001/XMLSchema-instance"
```

```
  xsi:schemaLocation="http://www.example.com/contacts contacts6.xsd">
  <contact person="Joe_Fawcett" tags="author xml poetry">

    <name>
      <first>Joseph</first>
      <first>John</first>
      <last>Fawcett</last>
    </name>

    <location>
      <address>Exeter, UK</address>
      <latitude>50.7218</latitude>
      <longitude>-3.533617</longitude>
    </location>

    <phone kind="Home">001-234-567-8910</phone>
    <knows contacts="Liam_Quin Danny_Ayers"/>
        <description>Joseph is a developer and author for Beginning XML <em>5th
edition</em>.<br/>Joseph <strong>loves</strong> XML!</description>
  </contact>

  <contact person="Liam_Quin" tags="author consultant w3c">

    <name>
      <first>Liam</first>
      <last>Quin</last>
    </name>

    <location>
      <address>Ontario, Canada</address>
    </location>

    <phone>+1 613 476 8769</phone>
    <knows contacts="Joe Fawcett Danny_Ayers"/>
    <description>XML Activity Lead at W3C</description>
  </contact>

</contacts>
```

contacts6.xml

3. You are ready to validate your XML instance document against your XML Schema. Open `contacts9.xml` and click Plugins ➪ XML ➪ Parse as XML in the jEdit editor. This should validate with no warnings and no errors, but if you do get a validation error, correct it and try validating it again.

How It Works

This Try It Out used some of the XML Schema built-in data types. These data types enable you to exercise more control over the textual content within your instance documents. Let's look at some of the types in a little more detail. You began by changing the type of your version attribute from string to decimal like so:

```
<attribute name="version" type="decimal" fixed="1.0" />
```

This is a perfect fit because your version number must always be a valid decimal number. (If you ever needed a complex version number such as 1.0.1, however, this data type would be insufficient.)

Next, you added a tags attribute to the <complexType> declaration for the contact element as shown here:

```
<attribute name="tags" type="token"/>
```

You specified that the type should be token, which allows you to use a whitespace-separated list as the value. You added a person attribute as well, specifying the type as ID as in the following:

```
<attribute name="person" type="ID"/>
```

To complement this attribute, you modified the KnowsType <complexType> declaration like so:

```
<complexType name="KnowsType">
  <attribute name="contacts" type="IDREFS"/>
</complexType>
```

Here you used the built-in types ID and IDREFS. Remember that these types were added to XML Schema for compatibility with DTDs and other XML tools. XML Schema actually allows you to build complex keys and key-references using its own built-in mechanism. Until recently these features were not widely supported, so it is usually better to use ID and IDREFS whenever possible.

Next, the phone <element> declaration was modified to refer to a new global type PhoneType shown here:

```
<element name="phone" type="contacts:PhoneType"/>
```

And the PhoneType was added to the XML Schema like so:

```
<complexType name="PhoneType">
    <simpleContent>
      <extension base="string">
        <attribute name="kind" type="string" default="Home" />
      </extension>
    </simpleContent>
</complexType>
```

The PhoneType <complexType> declaration allowed you to specify that the <phone> element could contain simple string content as well as a kind attribute.

Instead of using the built-in string type for the latitude and longitude <element> declarations, you modified these to use the built-in type float. The float type is similar to the decimal type, in that it allows you to have decimal numbers, but it offers even more control and compatibility. Because the `float` type is based on existing standards, it is useful across various computer languages. For example, some XML applications such as XQuery and XPath2 can natively understand floating-point arithmetic.

As the schema validator processes the document, not only is it checking whether the element content models you have specified are correct, it is also checking whether the textual data you included in your elements and attributes is valid based on the type you specified.

User-Defined Data Types

Although the XML Schema Recommendation includes a wealth of built-in data types, it doesn't include everything. As you are developing your XML Schemas, you will run into many elements and attribute values that require a type not defined in the XML Schema Recommendation. Consider the `kind` attribute for the `<phone>` element. Because you restricted its value to the `string` type, it still accepts unwanted values such as the following:

```
kind="Walkie-Talkie"
```

According to the declaration for the `kind` attribute, the value `Walkie-Talkie` is valid. What you need is to create a list of allowable values as you did in your DTD. No such built-in type exists within the XML Schema Recommendation, so you must create a new type using a `<simpleType>` definition.

<simpleType> Declarations

When designing your XML Schemas, you may need to design your own data types. You can create custom user-defined data types using the `<simpleType>` definition that follows:

```
<simpleType
  name="name of the simpleType"
  final="#all or list or union or restriction">
```

When you declare a `<simpleType>`, you must always base your declaration on an existing data type. The existing data type may be a built-in XML Schema data type, or it may be another custom data type. Because you must derive every `<simpleType>` definition from another data type, `<simpleType>` definitions are often called *derived types*. There are three primary derived types:

- Restriction types
- List types
- Union types

The following sections describe these three derived types in detail.

<restriction> Declarations

The most common `<simpleType>` derivation is the restriction type. Restriction types are declared using the `<restriction>` declaration as follows:

```
<restriction base="name of the simpleType you are deriving from">
```

A derived type declared using the `<restriction>` declaration is a subset of its base type. Facets control all simple types within XML Schemas. A *facet* is a single property or trait of a `<simpleType>`. For example, the built-in numeric type `nonNegativeInteger` was created by deriving from the built-in `Integer` type and setting the facet `minInclusive` to zero. This specifies that the minimum value allowed for the type is zero. By constraining the facets of existing types, you can create your own more restrictive types.

There are 12 constraining facets, described in Table 5-3:

TABLE 5-3: simpleType Constraining Facets

FACET	DESCRIPTION
`minExclusive`	Enables you to specify the minimum value for your type that excludes the value you specify
`minInclusive`	Enables you to specify the minimum value for your type that includes the value you specify
`maxExclusive`	Enables you to specify the maximum value for your type that excludes the value you specify
`maxInclusive`	Enables you to specify the maximum value for your type that includes the value you specify
`totalDigits`	Enables you to specify the total number of digits in a numeric type
`fractionDigits`	Enables you to specify the number of fractional digits in a numeric type (for example, the number of digits to the right of the decimal point)
`length`	Enables you to specify the number of items in a list type, or the number of characters in a string type
`minLength`	Enables you to specify the minimum number of items in a list type, or the minimum number of characters in a string type
`maxLength`	Enables you to specify the maximum number of items in a list type, or the maximum number of characters in a string type
`enumeration`	Enables you to specify an allowable value in an enumerated list
`whiteSpace`	Enables you to specify how whitespace should be treated within the type
`pattern`	Enables you to restrict string types using regular expressions

Not all types use every facet. In fact, most types can be constrained only by a couple of facets.

Within a <restriction> declaration, you must specify the type you are restricting using the base attribute. The value of the base attribute is a reference to a global <simpleType> definition or built-in XML Schema data type. As you have seen with all references in your XML Schema, the reference is a namespace-qualified value and, therefore, may need to be prefixed.

Suppose you want to create a restriction type that uses enumeration facets to restrict the allowable values for the kind attribute in your <phone> element. The declaration would look like this:

```
<attribute name="kind">
  <simpleType>
    <restriction base="string">
      <enumeration value="Home"/>
      <enumeration value="Work"/>
      <enumeration value="Cell"/>
      <enumeration value="Fax"/>
    </restriction>
  </simpleType>
</attribute>
```

This declaration contains a <restriction> declaration with the base type string. Within the restriction are multiple enumeration facets to create a list of all of the allowable values for your type.

Now that you have seen the theory, you can use the preceding Try It Out to practice.

TRY IT OUT Making Contact — Creating a Restriction Simple Type

As shown in the section "User-Defined Data Types" earlier in the chapter, the kind attribute should be more restrictive. Now that you know how to create your own <simpleType> definitions, this Try It Out enables you to create a <restriction> type for the kind attribute:

1. Begin by making the necessary changes to your XML Schema. Create a new document called contacts7.xsd. Copy the contents from the file contacts6.xsd and make the following changes. You only need to modify the <attribute> declaration for the kind attribute. The rest of the XML Schema remains the same:

```
<complexType name="PhoneType">
  <simpleContent>
    <extension base="string">
      <attribute name="kind" default="Home">
        <simpleType>
          <restriction base="string">
            <enumeration value="Home"/>
            <enumeration value="Work"/>
            <enumeration value="Cell"/>
            <enumeration value="Fax"/>
          </restriction>
        </simpleType>
      </attribute>
    </extension>
  </simpleContent>
</complexType>
```

2. Before you can schema-validate your XML document, you must modify it so that it refers to your new XML Schema. Create a new document called `contacts10.xml`. Copy the contents of the file `contacts9.xml` and change the `xsi:schemaLocation` attribute as follows:

```
xsi:schemaLocation="http://www.example.com/contacts contacts7.xsd
```

3. You are ready to validate your XML instance document against your XML Schema. Open `contacts10.xml` and click Plugins ➪ XML ➪ Parse as XML in the jEdit editor. This should validate without warnings or errors. If you do get a validation error, correct it and try validating it again.

How It Works

In this Try It Out, you modified the `kind` attribute declaration. You created a local `<simpleType>` definition that is a restriction derived from the built-in type `string`. This allowed you to limit which string values could be used within the `kind` attribute in your instance document. Each possible string was defined with a separate `<enumeration>` facet, as in the following:

```
<attribute name="kind" default="Home">
  <simpleType>
    <restriction base="string">
      <enumeration value="Home"/>
      <enumeration value="Work"/>
      <enumeration value="Cell"/>
      <enumeration value="Fax"/>
    </restriction>
  </simpleType>
</attribute>
```

Because you changed your attribute's type to a local `<simpleType>`, you had to remove the original type by removing the `type` attribute.

The changes you made here had the effect of tightening up the constraints allowed in the instance document. As always, there's a trade-off between the flexibility of allowing a wide range of values in the XML document and restricting those values to simplify processing.

<list> Declarations

You'll often need to create a list of items. Using a `<list>` declaration like the following, you can base your list items on a specific `<simpleType>`:

```
<list itemType="name of simpleType used for validating items in the list">
```

When creating your `<list>` declaration, you can specify the type of items in your list by including the `itemType` attribute. The value of the `itemType` attribute should be a reference to a global `<simpleType>` definition or built-in XML Schema data type. The reference is a namespace-qualified value, so it may need to be prefixed. The `<list>` declaration also allows you to specify your `itemType` by creating a local `<simpleType>` definition.

When choosing the `itemType`, remember that you are creating a whitespace-separated list, so your items cannot contain whitespace. Therefore, types that include whitespace cannot be used as `itemTypes`. A side effect of this limitation is that you cannot create a list whose `itemType` is itself a list.

Suppose you created a global `<simpleType>` called `ContactTagsType` whereby you enumerated all of the allowable tags for a contact, like so:

```
<simpleType name="ContactTagsType">
  <restriction base="string">
    <enumeration value="author"/>
    <enumeration value="xml"/>
    <enumeration value="poetry"/>
    <enumeration value="consultant"/>
    <enumeration value="CGI"/>
    <enumeration value="semantics"/>
    <enumeration value="animals"/>
  </restriction>
</simpleType>
```

This simple type only allows for one of the enumerated values to be used. If you want to allow for multiple items, you can make a type called `ContactTagsListType`, which allows for a list of tags using the `<list>` declaration, as in the following:

```
<simpleType name="ContactTagsListType">
    <list itemType="contacts:ContactTagsType"/>
  </simpleType>
```

If you use this within your contacts XML Schema, it would allow you to specify multiple tags within your instance document, but still require that they adhere to the enumerations you provide. In practice, you would probably want to expand your list of possible tags to include all kinds of values, but for now this ensures that each tag is validated.

<union> Declarations

Finally, when creating your derived types, you may need to combine two or more types. By declaring a `<union>` in the following example, you can validate the values in your instance document against multiple types at once:

```
<union memberTypes="whitespace separated list of types">
```

When creating a `<union>` declaration, you can specify the types you are combining by including the `memberTypes` attribute. The value of the `memberTypes` attribute should be a whitespace-separated list of references to global `<simpleType>` definitions or built-in XML Schema data types. Again, these references are namespace-qualified values, so they may need to be prefixed.

The <union> declaration also allows you to specify your memberTypes by creating local <simpleType> definitions.

Suppose that you wanted to allow the value Unknown in the <latitude> and <longitude> elements. To do this you could use a union of the built-in float type and a custom type that allows only the string Unknown, as shown in the following example:

```
<simpleType name="UnknownString">
  <restriction base="string">
    <enumeration value="Unknown"/>
  </restriction>
</simpleType>

<simpleType name="UnknownOrFloatType">
  <union memberTypes="float contacts:UnknownString"/>
</simpleType>
```

In this declaration, you have created the custom UnknownString type and a union of the two simple types, float and UnknownString. Note that when you refer to the names of the <simpleType> definitions, you must make sure they are qualified with a namespace. In this case, the reference to float has no prefix because the default namespace for this document is the XML Schema namespace. The prefix contacts is used when referring to the type UnknownString, however, because it was declared in the target namespace. By referring to your newly created type, you can specify that your <latitude> and <longitude> elements must contain either float values or the string Unknown, shown here:

```
<element name="latitude" type="contacts:UnknownStringOrFloatType"/>
<element name="longitude" type="contacts:UnknownStringOrFloatType"/>
```

Some *valid* elements include the following:

```
<latitude>43.847156</latitude>
<longitude>Unknown</longitude>
```

Some *invalid* elements include these:

```
<latitude>unknown</latitude>
<longitude>43.847156 Unknown</longitude>
```

The first two elements both contain valid values. The third element is invalid because the value unknown is not listed in either of the unioned types — the values are case sensitive. The fourth element is invalid because the schema validator treats this as a single value. Although Unknown and 43.847156 are allowable by themselves, the value 43.847156 Unknown is not listed in either of the union types.

In this section you have seen (and experimented with) many of the constructs that can be used inside XML Schema. In the next section you will zoom out a little to see a technique for simplifying the management of schemas.

CREATING A SCHEMA FROM MULTIPLE DOCUMENTS

So far, the XML Schemas in this chapter have used a single schema document to keep things simple. The XML Schema Recommendation introduces mechanisms for combining XML Schemas and reusing definitions. As mentioned in Chapter 4, “Document Type Definitions,” reusing existing definitions is good practice — it saves you time when creating the documents and increases your document’s interoperability.

The XML Schema Recommendation provides two primary declarations for use with multiple XML Schema documents:

- `<import>`
- `<include>`

<import> Declarations

The `<import>` declaration, as the name implies, allows you to import global declarations from other XML Schemas. The `<import>` declaration is used primarily for combining XML Schemas that have different `targetNamespaces`. By importing the declarations, the two XML Schemas can be used in conjunction within an instance document. Note that the `<import>` declaration allows you to *refer* to declarations only within other XML Schemas.

This is the typical shape of an import declaration:

```
<import
  namespace=""
  schemaLocation="">
```

The `<import>` declaration is always declared globally within an XML Schema (it must be a direct child of the `<schema>` element). This means that the `<import>` declaration applies to the entire XML Schema. When importing declarations from other namespaces, the schema validator attempts to look up the document based on the `schemaLocation` attribute specified within the corresponding `<import>` declaration. Of course, as shown earlier, the `schemaLocation` attribute serves only as a hint to the processor. The processor may elect to use another copy of the XML Schema. If the schema validator cannot locate the XML Schema for any reason, it may raise an error or proceed with lax validation.

To get a better idea of how this works, you need a sample XML Schema that uses the `<import>` declaration. Let’s combine the examples that you have been working with throughout this chapter.

Within the XML Schema for your contacts listing, import the declarations from your `<name>` vocabulary. Use the imported `<name>` declarations in place of the existing declarations. Though it means you need to remove some declarations in this case, it is better to reuse XML Schemas whenever possible.

Next, you will use `<import>` declarations to combine the example you have already worked on.

TRY IT OUT Making Contact — Importing XML Schema Declarations

This example modifies your contacts listing to introduce an <import> declaration using the name vocabulary that you developed earlier in the chapter. You need to remove some existing declarations and modify your instance document to reflect the changes in your XML Schemas:

1. Begin by modifying your contacts vocabulary. Import the name vocabulary and use the imported types. Create a new document called `contacts8.xsd`. Copy the contents of the file `contacts7.xsd` and make the following changes:

```
<schema xmlns="http://www.w3.org/2001/XMLSchema"
  xmlns:contacts="http://www.example.com/contacts"
  xmlns:name="http://www.example.com/name"
  targetNamespace="http://www.example.com/contacts"
  elementFormDefault="qualified">

  <import namespace="http://www.example.com/name" schemaLocation="name8.xsd"/>
```

2. You also need to modify the declaration of the <contact> element to refer to the global <name> element declared in `name8.xsd`:

```
<element name="contacts">
    <complexType>
      <sequence>
        <element name="contact" minOccurs="0" maxOccurs="unbounded">
          <complexType>
            <sequence>
              <element ref="name:name"/>
              <element name="location" type="contacts:LocationType"/>
              <element name="phone" type="contacts:PhoneType"/>
              <element name="knows" type="contacts:KnowsType"/>
              <element name="description" type="contacts:DescriptionType"/>
            </sequence>
            <attribute name="person" type="ID"/>
            <attribute name="tags" type="token"/>
          </complexType>
        </element>
      </sequence>
      <attributeGroup ref="contacts:ContactAttributes"/>
    </complexType>
</element>
```

3. Remove the NameType <complexType> declaration and the `NameGroup` <group> declaration from your schema.

4. Now that you have modified your XML Schema document, you can create an instance document that reflects the changes. This document is very similar to the `contacts10.xml` document. Only the <name> elements will change. Create a new document called `contacts11.xml`. Copy the contents of the file `contacts10.xml` and make the following changes:

```
<?xml version="1.0"?>
<contacts
  xmlns="http://www.example.com/contacts"
xmlns:name="http://www.example.com/name"
```

```
  xmlns:xsi="http://www.w3.org/2001/XMLSchema-instance"
  xsi:schemaLocation="http://www.example.com/contacts contacts8.xsd"

  source="Beginning XML 5E"
  version="1.0">
  <contact person="Joe_Fawcett" tags="author xml">
    <name:name title="Mr.">
      <name:first>Joseph</name:first>
      <name:middle>John</name:middle>
      <name:last>Fawcett</name:last>
    </name:name>

    <location>
      <address>Exeter, UK</address>
           <latitude>50.7218</latitude>
      <longitude>-3.533617</longitude>
    </location>
    <phone kind="Home">001-909-555-1212</phone>
    <knows contacts="Joe_Fawcett Danny_Ayers"/>
    <description>Joe is a developer and author for Beginning XML <em>5th edition</
em>.<br/>Joe <strong>loves</strong> XML!</description>
  </contact>
  <contact person="Liam_Quin" tags="author consultant w3c">
    <name:name>
      <name:first>Liam</name:first>
      <name:last>Quin</name:last>
    </name:name>

    <location>
      <address>Ontario, Canada</address>
    </location>
    <phone kind="Work">+1 613 476 8769</phone>
    <knows contacts="Joe_Fawcett Danny_Ayers"/>
    <description>XML Activity Lead at W3C</description>
  </contact>
  <contact person="Danny_Ayers" tags="author semantics animals">
    <name:name>
      <name:first>Daniel</name:first>
      <name:middle>John</name:middle>
      <name:last>Ayers</name:last>
    </name:name>

    <location>
      <latitude>43.847156</latitude>
      <longitude>10.50808</longitude>
      <address>Mozzanella, Italy</address>
    </location>
    <phone>+39-0555-11-22-33-</phone>
    <knows contacts="Joe_Fawcett Liam_Quin"/>
    <description>Web Research and Development.</description>
  </contact>
</contacts>
```

5. You are ready to validate your XML instance document against your XML Schema. Open `contacts11.xml` and click Plugin ➪ XML ➪ Parse as XML in the jEdit editor. As before, this should validate with no warnings and no errors. If not, then correct any errors and try validating it again.

How It Works

In this Try It Out, you imported one XML Schema into another. You used the `<import>` declaration because the two XML Schemas were designed for different `targetNamespaces`. Within your first XML Schema, you had already declared a single global element that could be used to describe names. In your second XML Schema, you were forced to do some more work:

```
<?xml version="1.0"?>
<schema xmlns="http://www.w3.org/2001/XMLSchema"
  xmlns:contacts="http://www.example.com/contacts"
  xmlns:name="http://www.example.com/name"
  targetNamespace="http://www.example.com/contacts"
  elementFormDefault="qualified">
```

The first addition you had to make was an XML namespace declaration in the root element. You added a namespace declaration for the namespace `http://www.example.com/name`. You needed to add this declaration so that you could refer to items declared within the namespace later in your XML Schema.

Next, you added an `<import>` declaration:

```
<import namespace="http://www.example.com/name"
  schemaLocation="name8.xsd"/>
```

This `<import>` declaration is straightforward. You are importing the declarations from the `http://www.example.com/name` namespace, which is located in the file `name8.xsd`. This declaration enables you to reuse the declarations from your `name8.xsd` XML Schema within your `contacts12.xsd` XML Schema. (If you are using another schema validator, you should check the documentation for special rules when referring to external files. For example, the Xerces parser handles relative URL references differently in older versions.)

Finally, you modified the `name` element declaration within your `<contact>` declaration:

```
<element ref="name:name" />
```

Notice that you use the namespace prefix declared within the root element when referring to the `name` element declaration from your `name8.xsd` file. Instead of using an element reference, you could have referred to the global type `NameType`.

Once you made these changes, you had to create a new, compliant instance document. The major difference (apart from the namespace declaration in the root element) was the modified content of your `<contact>` elements:

```
<contact person="Jeff_Rafter" tags="author xml poetry">
<name:name title="Mr.">
  <name:first>Jeff</name:first>
  <name:middle>Craig</name:middle>
  <name:last>Rafter</name:last>
```

```
    </name:name>
    <location>
      <address>Redlands, CA, USA</address>
      <latitude>34.031892</latitude>
      <longitude>-117.207642</longitude>
    </location>
    <phone kind="Home">001-909-555-1212</phone>
    <knows contacts="David_Hunter Danny_Ayers"/>
    <description>Jeff is a developer and author for Beginning XML <em>4th
edition</em>.<br/>Jeff <strong>loves</strong> XML!</description>
  </contact>
```

This might seem a little more confusing than you would expect. Because you declared that the `elementFormDefault` of both XML Schemas was `qualified`, you are required to qualify all your elements with namespace prefixes (or a default namespace declaration).

In your instance document you were already using the default namespace to refer to elements from the namespace `http://www.example.com/contacts`. Therefore, you had to use a namespace prefix, in this case `name`, when referring to the elements from the namespace `http://www.example.com/name`. The `<first>`, `<middle>`, and `<last>` elements are all declared within the `http://www.example.com/name` namespace; therefore, you must qualify them with the `name` prefix you declared in the root element of your instance document.

The `title` attribute doesn't need to be qualified, because you didn't modify the `attributeFormDefault` within your XML Schemas — so it uses the default value `unqualified`.

<include> Declarations

The `<include>` declaration is very similar to the `<import>` declaration, except that the `<include>` declaration allows you to combine XML Schemas that are designed for the same `targetNamespace` (or no `targetNamespace`) much more effectively. When a schema validator encounters an `<include>` declaration, it treats the global declarations from the included XML Schema as if they had been declared in the XML Schema that contains the `<include>` declaration. This subtle distinction makes quite a difference when you are using many modules to define a single vocabulary.

This is the shape of a typical `<include>` declaration:

```
<include
  schemaLocation="">
```

Notice that within the `<include>` declaration there is no `namespace` attribute. Again, unlike the `<import>` declaration, the `<include>` declaration can be used only on documents with the same `targetNamespace`, or no `targetNamespace`. Because of this, a `namespace` attribute would be redundant. Just as you saw before, the `schemaLocation` attribute allows you to specify the location of the XML Schema you are including. The `schemaLocation` value functions as a validator hint. If the schema validator cannot locate a copy of the XML Schema for any reason, it may raise an error or proceed with lax validation.

To demonstrate the `<include>` declaration, you will now create an example that utilizes two XML Schema documents with the same `targetNamespace`. To do this, you will break your contacts XML Schema into two parts — moving the type declarations for the `ContactTagsType` to a new XML Schema that can be included in your main document. The following Try It Out exemplifies this process.

TRY IT OUT Making Contact — Including XML Schema Declarations

In this Try It Out you divide your XML Schema into two parts and include one in the other. This is known as dividing an XML Schema into *modules* — separate files that make up the overall XML Schema:

1. Create a new XML Schema called `contact_tags.xsd` that declares all of the allowable tags in your contact listing. To create the declarations, you can simply copy the declarations from `contacts8.xsd`:

```
<?xml version="1.0"?>
<schema xmlns="http://www.w3.org/2001/XMLSchema"
  xmlns:contacts="http://www.example.com/contacts"
  targetNamespace="http://www.example.com/contacts"
  elementFormDefault="qualified">
  <simpleType name="ContactTagsType">
    <restriction base="string">
      <enumeration value="author"/>
      <enumeration value="xml"/>
      <enumeration value="poetry"/>
      <enumeration value="consultant"/>
      <enumeration value="CGI"/>
      <enumeration value="semantics"/>
      <enumeration value="animals"/>
    </restriction>
  </simpleType>
</schema>
```

Contact_tags.xsd

2. Now that you have created the `contact_tags.xsd` XML Schema, create a new document called `contacts9.xsd`. Copy the contents of the file `contacts8.xsd`. You need to insert an `<include>` declaration, and be sure to remove the `ContactTagsType` declaration. So the new `contacts9.xsd` document will begin like this:

```
<?xml version="1.0"?>
<schema xmlns="http://www.w3.org/2001/XMLSchema"
  xmlns:contacts="http://www.example.com/contacts"
  xmlns:name="http://www.example.com/name"
  targetNamespace="http://www.example.com/contacts"
  elementFormDefault="qualified">

  <include schemaLocation="contact_tags.xsd"/>

  <import namespace="http://www.example.com/name" schemaLocation="name8.xsd"/>
```

contacts9.xsd

3. Before you can schema-validate your instance document, you must modify it so that it refers to your new XML Schema. Create a new document called `contacts12.xml`. Copy the contents of the file `contacts11.xml` and change the `xsi:schemaLocation` attribute as follows:

```
xsi:schemaLocation="http://www.example.com/contacts contacts12.xsd"
```

4. You are ready to validate your XML instance document against your XML Schema. Open `contacts12.xml` and click Plugins ➪ XML ➪ Parse as XML in the jEdit editor. This should validate with no warnings or errors. If not, correct any errors and try validating it again.

How It Works

Dividing complex XML Schemas into modules can be an excellent design technique. In this Try It Out, you divided your contacts vocabulary into two modules. You declared these modules in separate XML Schema documents, each with `http://www.example.com/contacts` as the `targetNamespace`. Because the two documents utilized the same `targetNamespace`, you simply used an `<include>` declaration to combine them:

```
<include schemaLocation="contact_tags.xsd" />
```

As the schema validator processes `contacts13.xsd`, it includes the declarations from `contact_tags.xsd` with the declarations for `contacts13.xsd` as if they had been declared in one document. Therefore, you were able to use all of the types as if they were declared within `contacts13.xsd`. Because you didn't introduce any namespace complexities, there was no need to change the instance document to support the new modular design.

NOTE *Declarations within XML Schemas that have no* `targetNamespace` *are treated differently. These declarations are known as Chameleon components. Chameleon components take on the* `targetNamespace` *of the XML Schema that includes them. Therefore, even though they were declared with no* `targetNamespace`*, when they are included they take the* `targetNamespace` *of the XML Schema that is including them.*

DOCUMENTING XML SCHEMAS

For other people to be able to reuse your schemas, and for them to make sense to you at a later date, it's good practice to include documentation. The XML Schema Recommendation provides several mechanisms for documenting your code:

- XML comments
- Other-namespace components
- XML Schema annotations

You should already be reasonably familiar with the first two of these — they exploit the fact that XML Schemas are XML themselves. Standard XML techniques can be used to include information that won't be used by the primary processor, the validator, or any other tool. However, they will be available to any human reader and/or dedicated documentation tool.

But XML Schemas also have their own system for including documentation known as *annotations*. This is provided by three terms in the XSD namespace: `annotation`, `appinfo`, and `documentation`.

These are all very straightforward, so in a moment you will see an example that includes all three kinds of documentation. But first it's worth mentioning again the special XML attribute `xml:lang`. This is used to specify that a particular chunk of text is in a specific (human) language. Obviously this can be very important in documentation. The following example includes only English text (`xml:lang="en"`, the language codes being defined in `www.ietf.org/rfc/bcp/bcp47.txt`). But it's not uncommon to see pieces of text repeated in different languages within a document.

Listing 5-2 is a self-documenting XML Schema:

Available for download on Wrox.com

LISTING 5-2: name-documented.xsd

```
<?xml version="1.0"?>
<schema xmlns="http://www.w3.org/2001/XMLSchema"
  xmlns:target="http://www.example.com/name"
  xmlns:doc="http://www.example.com/documentation"
  targetNamespace="http://www.example.com/name"
  elementFormDefault="qualified">
    <annotation>
    <appinfo source="name-sample.xml"/>
    <documentation xml:lang="en">
        The name vocabulary was created for an example of a DTD. We have
        recycled it into an XML Schema.
    </documentation>
  </annotation>

  <!-- Specification of name elements -->
 <group name="NameGroup">
    <sequence>
      <element name="first" type="string" minOccurs="1" maxOccurs="unbounded"/>
      <element name="middle" type="string" minOccurs="0" maxOccurs="1"/>
      <element name="last" type="string"/>
    </sequence>
  </group>
  <!-- Specification of name datatype -->


<complexType name="NameType" doc:comments="This complexType allows you to
 describe a person's name broken down by first, middle and last parts of the
name. You can also specify a greeting by including the title attribute.">

    <group ref="target:NameGroup" />
    <attribute name="title" type="string"/>
  </complexType>
  <element name="name" type="target:NameType"/>
</schema>
```

The first thing to notice here is the added namespace declaration:

```
xmlns:doc="http://www.example.com/documentation"
```

This namespace has been invented for demonstration purposes. Its purpose here is effectively to hide an attribute from processors for which it has no meaning. That attribute is `doc:comments`, included here on the `<complexType>` element:

```
<complexType name="NameType" doc:comments="This complexType allows you to
describe a person's name broken down by first, middle and last parts of the name.
You can also specify a greeting by including the title attribute.">
```

When applied to an XML document, an XML Schema validator will read and apply the appropriate rules for the `<complexType>` element, but it will ignore this “foreign” attribute. However, you can write your own custom processing; for example, to convert the XML Schema to HTML for documentation purposes, which could pull out and display these comments as you see fit.

The `<annotation>` element is used as a block container with two distinct elements. The `<appinfo>` element is used to pass information to external tools (such as documentation formatters). The XML Schema specification includes the definition of one attribute for this element, `source`, which is used here to point to a sample document that conforms to this schema. You can also add any foreign-namespace attributes here as well. This is the shape of a typical `<annotation>` element:

```
<annotation>
<appinfo source="name-sample.xml"/>
```

The `<documentation>` element is used to wrap human-oriented text. It too may contain a `source` attribute, although one is not included here. What is included is an `xml:lang` attribute to say that the text is in English, as shown in the following code snippet:

```
    <documentation xml:lang="en">
        The name vocabulary was created for an example of a DTD. We have
        recycled it into an XML Schema.
    </documentation>
  </annotation>
```

The `<annotation>` element can contain as many `<appinfo>` and `<documentation>` sub-elements as you like (including zero), so providing documentation in multiple languages is straightforward.

Finally, the third kind of documentation in this document is the regular XML comment:

```
<!-- Specification of name elements -->
```

Primarily intended for readers of the document source, these will be ignored by most processors.

XML SCHEMA 1.1

As mentioned in the introduction, at the time of this writing the 1.1 revision of the specification is under development. Although not quite finished, it is at the W3C's Candidate Recommendation status, so only minor changes are likely to be made before it achieves full Recommendation status.

As the small increment suggests, this version isn't very much different from XML Schema 1.0. The important thing to note is that in general, schemas developed according to the 1.0 specification will still work with the 1.1 specification. Compatibility is maintained to the extent of reusing the same namespace URI (`http://www.w3.org/2001/XMLSchema`). So an XML document defined using a 1.0 schema can be validated using a 1.1 schema processor/validator.

The main changes in XML Schema 1.1 from 1.0 are:

- It relaxes certain rules
- Assertions can be defined over the document content
- The spec is clearer and a little easier to read

Relaxed Rules

One of the rules that has relaxed is when a particular block in the schema specifies both an explicit element and a wildcard that may include that element. When the validator encounters the element in a document, it can't tell whether to interpret it as specified by the explicit element (and check whatever other conditions apply there) or by the wildcard.

For example, say you have a schema containing the following:

```
<sequence>
   <element name="size" type="xsd:decimal" minOccurs="0"/>
   <any namespace="##any" minOccurs="0"/>
</sequence>
```

This could try to validate a document that contains:

```
<size>large</size>
```

Is that element valid, because the `<any>` declaration allows any element from any namespace, or invalid because the `<element>` declaration states it should be a decimal?

To avoid this situation XML Schema 1.0 disallowed any such ambiguity; such constructions are forbidden in the schema. However, in XML Schema 1.1 this kind of thing is allowed, with ambiguity being avoided by using the rule that named elements take precedence over wildcards. So in XML Schema 1.1 the `<size>` element is associated with the named element in the schema, and in this example is judged invalid because the content types don't match.

Other changes in XML Schema 1.1 relate to other restrictions but they are quite detailed, and beyond the scope of this book. Once the new specification has been finalized and published, status updates will be linked from `http://www.w3.org/XML/Schema`.

<assert>

XML Schema 1.1 adds an `<assert>` component to provide rule-based validation (along similar lines of Schematron, which you will see in the next chapter).

The rule is specified using a Boolean XPath expression. The assertion may pass (true) or fail (false) depending on the evaluation of the expression. Assertions are treated like other validation features; failure of the assertion means the document isn't valid.

Here's an example:

```
<element name="sizeRange">
  <complexType>
     <sequence>
         <element name="minSize" type="xsd:decimal"/>
         <element name="maxSize" type="xsd:decimal"/>
     </sequence>
    <assert test="minSize le maxSize"/>
</complexType>
</element>
```

Here, the schema specifies an element `<sizeRange>` with two nested elements, `<minSize>` and `<maxSize>`, each of which should contain a decimal value. The assertion tests whether the value in `<minSize>` is less than or equal to the value in `<maxSize>`. The XPath expression for this comparison is `le`.

As you will see later, XPath is a powerful language. In the context of XML Schema 1.1 this means much more sophisticated assertions are possible.

NOTE *Now that you understand the basics of XML Schemas, you are ready to create your own vocabularies. Even with the basics, however, you have many styles and options when designing your XML Schemas. Roger Costello, with the help of many volunteers, has created an XML Schemas Best Practices document that gives advice on what the best choice or style is for many different situations. See* `www.xfront.com/BestPracticesHomepage.html`.

SUMMARY

- XML Schemas can be used to schema-validate your XML documents.
- XML Schemas have many advantages over Document Type Definitions.
- You can associate XML Schema with an XML Document by declaring element and attribute groups.
- You can specify allowable XML content using simple types and complex types.
- You can create an XML Schema using multiple documents and namespaces.

EXERCISE

Answers to Exercises can be found in Appendix A.

1. Add a `gender` attribute declaration for the `<contact>` elements. The attribute should allow two possible values: `male` and `female`. Make sure the attribute is required.

2. Currently, each contact can have only one phone number. Modify the contact declaration so that each contact can have zero or more phone numbers.

3. Modify the `<description>` declaration to include an element wildcard. Within the wildcard, specify that the description element can accept any elements from the namespace `http://www.w3.org/1999/xhtml`. Set the `processContents` attribute to `lax`.

▶ WHAT YOU LEARNED IN THIS CHAPTER

TOPIC	KEY POINTS
Advantages of XML Schemas over DTDs	XML syntax
Associating an XML Schema with an XML document	Options include direct linking and association with a file and/or indirectly using `<import>` or `<include>` declarations
Declaring element and attribute types	These are based on the XML Schema depending on the `<element>` and `<attribute>` elements
Declaring groups and attribute groups	Use `<sequence>`, `<choice>`, and `<all>` blocks
Specifying allowable XML content	Constraints may build up from combinations of simple types and complex types
Creating an XML Schema using namespace and multiple documents	Various approaches are available, notably using `<import>` and `<include>`declarations

6

RELAX NG and Schematron

WHAT YOU WILL LEARN IN THIS CHAPTER:

- Why you need more ways of validating
- Definition of RELAX NG and its aims
- How to write and use RELAX NG
- How to convert between RELAX NG and other validation methods
- Definition of Schematron and its aims
- How to write and use Schematron

Validation of XML documents is an exceedingly common requirement, especially when your software is accepting XML from another source. Unfortunately, checking whether the XML you have received meets the expectations of the software that will process it can be difficult, as there are a myriad of rules that may need to be applied. You've already met two different ways of validating XML documents to make sure they conform to a specific format: *document type definitions* (*DTDs*) and *W3C XML Schema*. Both of these techniques have their uses but neither offers a full validation solution; in fact, most experts agree that there isn't a single technique that can cope with every validation rule that you may want to apply. In this chapter you meet two further solutions, *RELAX NG* and *Schematron*. Neither of these is expected to completely replace DTDs or Schemas; they are actually both designed to be used in conjunction with other validation methods. The expectation is that combining two or more techniques will enable users to completely specify the rules that a document must follow before it is said to be valid and therefore suitable for consumption by their business applications.

In this chapter you first see how RELAX NG and Schematron can be used in isolation to perform validation, and then you'll learn how they are used in conjunction with different aspects of XML Schemas to produce a complete solution.

NOTE *In keeping with the rest of the book, this chapter uses the capitalized form,* Schema *or* XML Schema*, when referring to the W3C standard;* schema*, in lowercase, is used as a more generic term.*

WHY DO YOU NEED MORE WAYS OF VALIDATING XML?

As you've seen in the preceding two chapters, it's important to be able to assert whether or not an XML document conforms to a predetermined structure. One of the main driving forces behind XML — interoperability — means that the XML output by one application will most likely be used as the input to another. If both of these applications are your own home-grown systems, you might be able to assume that everything will function correctly and validation is not a primary concern. If, however, you are receiving documents from external suppliers, especially if they are from people with whom you have had no previous contact, you need to be sure that the document is valid and will not, unintentionally or maliciously, cause an error in your systems.

People have not been satisfied with the two most popular validation methods, DTDs and XML Schema, for a few reasons. DTDs were designed long before XML was created to work with SGML. Although SGML is a superset of XML, DTDs are too limited in many respects to cope with the huge diversity of constraints that occur in many XML formats. They have very limited support for namespaces and only a very small range of data types. W3C XML Schemas are more versatile but extremely complicated; they have a wider variety of data types available as well as ways to extend and restrict these types. They also have built-in support for namespaces, and the advantage that they themselves are written in XML means that you can often use the same tools to create them as you would for the actual instance documents, something not possible with DTDs.

Both of the alternatives in this chapter seek to address these limitations. RELAX NG (usually pronounced as *relaxing*) tries to be a simple yet powerful and natural way to describe the format of an XML document, without some of the baggage carried by XML Schema, such as appending information to the document in the form of default attributes. Schematron's main selling point is that it provides a way of reporting errors in the document in a very friendly manner. The messages from Schematron, which are defined by the author, can be in a non-technical format such as *The book element must have an ID*, rather than the sometimes more cryptic output received from XML Schema–based parsers. Schematron can also cope with constraints in XML documents that are difficult or impossible to express using other validation methods.

The first stage in learning about these two validation techniques is to set up your environment.

SETTING UP YOUR ENVIRONMENT

The examples in this chapter use the <oXygen/> XML editor. This editor is widely acknowledged as one of the leading applications in its field. Unfortunately, but perhaps not surprisingly, it is not free, but it does have a 31-day trial period. One of the reasons it was chosen for the examples in this chapter is that it has good support for both RELAX NG and Schematron, which is a change from the command-line operations that you've been using a lot elsewhere in the book. It only takes a few steps to get started with the editor:

1. Download the editor at `http://www.oxygenxml.com/download_oxygenxml_editor.html`.
2. Choose the *XML Editor* version and either apply for a license from the site or wait until your first use, when you'll be prompted to register.
3. Once you've downloaded the install file, run it. Accepting the defaults when prompted is sufficient.
4. Start the application when asked and, if given a choice, ask for the enterprise license, which means you have access to all the functionality of the software.

Now that the environment is ready you can start to learn what RELAX NG is all about.

USING RELAX NG

RELAX NG came out shortly after XML Schema and one of its aims—simplicity—arose because many thought that W3C XML Schemas were too difficult to use. Users were also hopeful that having a more compact non-XML format would make it easier to hand-write RELAX NG, while the XML version would be more suitable for creation and use by software. The main precepts of RELAX NG include the following:

- Simple to learn
- Has two representations, both XML and textual
- Does not alter the target document in any way
- Can cope with namespaces
- Treats elements and attributes equally as far as possible
- Can use data types from other vocabularies such as W3C XML Schema
- Has a solid theoretical basis

There was also a feeling that DTDs suffered two main failings: they could be used to add default content to documents at run-time, making it difficult to determine what data the document held just by inspection, and could only deal with a very limited set of data types. Both these deficiencies are addressed in RELAX NG: no default content is added and data types from other technologies can be used if the built-in ones are insufficient. RELAX NG has therefore stood the test of time and is extensively used. In the rest of the chapter you cover all these points in detail and you should be able to judge if RELAX NG succeeds in its goals.

Understanding the Basics of RELAX NG

RELAX NG is built on the idea of pattern matching. The XML document you are trying to validate, commonly called the target document, can be visualized as a tree, starting with the root element and spreading out to cover all child elements and attributes. Other items, such as comments and processing instructions, cannot be validated using RELAX NG; this is similar to the situation with DTDs and XML Schema.

The following examples use an XML file that represents a collection of books. The document element is `<library>` and underneath are one or more `<book>` elements. Each book element has attributes and elements that contain information about the authors, the characters in the book, a description, and technical data such as publication date. The full file is shown in Listing 6-1.

NOTE *As stated previously, there are two representations for RELAX NG: an XML and a plain text version. When authoring strictly by hand it's usually considered easier to use the plain text version, known as the compact syntax. If you are using an editor such as <oXygen/> then it's more down to personal preference; you can easily convert between the two using the built-in schema converter (you'll be using this later). To start with you'll use the XML format. You'll see examples of both usages in the next few sections.*

Available for download on Wrox.com

LISTING 6-1: Library.xml

```
<library>
    <book id="ACMAS-20" publishedDate="1920" genre="Detective Fiction">
        <title>The Mysterious Affair at Styles</title>
        <authors count="1">
            <author id="AC">Agatha Christie</author>
        </authors>
        <characters>
            <character id="HP">
                <name>Hercule Poirot</name>
                <description>A former Belgian detective,
                now a private investigator.</description>
            </character>
            <character id="JJ">
                <name>James Japp</name>
                <description>A detective from London's
                Scotland Yard.</description>
            </character>
            <character id="AH">
                <name>Arthur Hastings</name>
                <description>The narrator of the tale
                and an old friend of Poirot.</description>
            </character>
            <character id="AI">
                <name>Alfred Inglethorpe</name>
                <description>The new husband of Emily Cavendish,
                who is disliked by her family.</description>
            </character>
        </characters>
        <description>Emily Cavendish, a wealthy widow,
        marries again to Alfred Inglethorp.
        One night she is found poisoned and
```

```
    Alfred immediately becomes the main suspect.</description>
  </book>
  <book id="EGOSC-77" publishedDate="1977" genre="Science Fiction">
      <title>Ender's Game</title>
      <authors count="1">
          <author id="OSC">Orson Scott Card</author>
      </authors>
      <characters>
          <character id="AW">
              <name>Andrew "Ender" Wiggin</name>
              <description>A young boy
              who is selected for Battle School following an incident
              with a local bully.</description>
          </character>
          <character id="MR">
              <name>Mazer Rackham</name>
              <description>A hero from the earlier Formic wars.</description>
          </character>
      </characters>
      <description>Earth is at war with an alien species known as Formics
      which nearly succeeded in destroying the human race.
      Ender is unwittingly thrust into combat against
          them.</description>
  </book>
</library>
```

If you were to describe this document in plain English, you would probably start by stating that:

- A <library> element is composed of:
  - one or more <book> elements that have
    - id, publishedDate, and genre attributes
    - a <title> element
    - an <authors> element
    - a <characters> element
    - a <description> element

RELAX NG tries to mimic this explanation, stating the patterns that different elements and attributes match. To show that an element matches a certain pattern you need to use an <element> element. So, because all XML documents start with an element, the basic RELAX NG schema starts with

```
<element xmlns="http://relaxng.org/ns/structure/1.0" name="library"></element>
```

where the name attribute of <element> is the document element of the target XML. Note that there is a default namespace associated with the document identifying it as a RELAX NG schema. So far you've provided a pattern for the <library> element but haven't described its children; you describe them by adding a pattern for the <book> element. There can be one or more <book> elements so you start with a <oneOrMore> element and within the <oneOrMore> element is another <element> to match <book>. The following snippet shows how the RELAX NG schema looks when the <book> element is included:

```
<element xmlns="http://relaxng.org/ns/structure/1.0" name="library">
    <oneOrMore>
     <element name="book"></element>
    </oneOrMore>
</element>
```

A <book> element has three attributes; these are described using an <attribute> matching element like so:

```
<element xmlns="http://relaxng.org/ns/structure/1.0" name="library">
    <oneOrMore>
        <element name="book">
            <attribute name="id"/>
             <attribute name="publishedDate"/>
             <attribute name="genre"/>
        </element>
    </oneOrMore>
</element>
```

You can now use your editor to see if your schema is accurate so far.

1. Create a new file, Library-1.xml, which contains just the <library> and <book> elements together with the latter's attributes. It will look like Listing 6-2. Save the file in a folder named *RELAXNG*.

Available for download on Wrox.com

LISTING 6-2: Library-1.xml

```
<library>
    <book id="ACMAS-20" publishedDate="1920" genre="Detective Fiction">

    </book>
    <book id="EGOSC-77" publishedDate="1977" genre="Science Fiction">

    </book>
</library>
```

2. Now save the schema you've created as Library-1.rng, again in the RELAXNG folder. The code is shown in Listing 6-3.

Available for download on Wrox.com

LISTING 6-3: Library-1.rng

```
<element xmlns="http://relaxng.org/ns/structure/1.0" name="library">
    <oneOrMore>
        <element name="book">
            <attribute name="id"/>
            <attribute name="publishedDate"/>
            <attribute name="genre"/>
```

```
        </element>
    </oneOrMore>
</element>
```

3. Now open both these files in the <oXygen/> editor. To validate, make sure that the `Library-1.xml` file is open in the front tab and choose Document ➪ Validate ➪ Validate with . . . from the menu. See the dialog box shown in Figure 6-1.

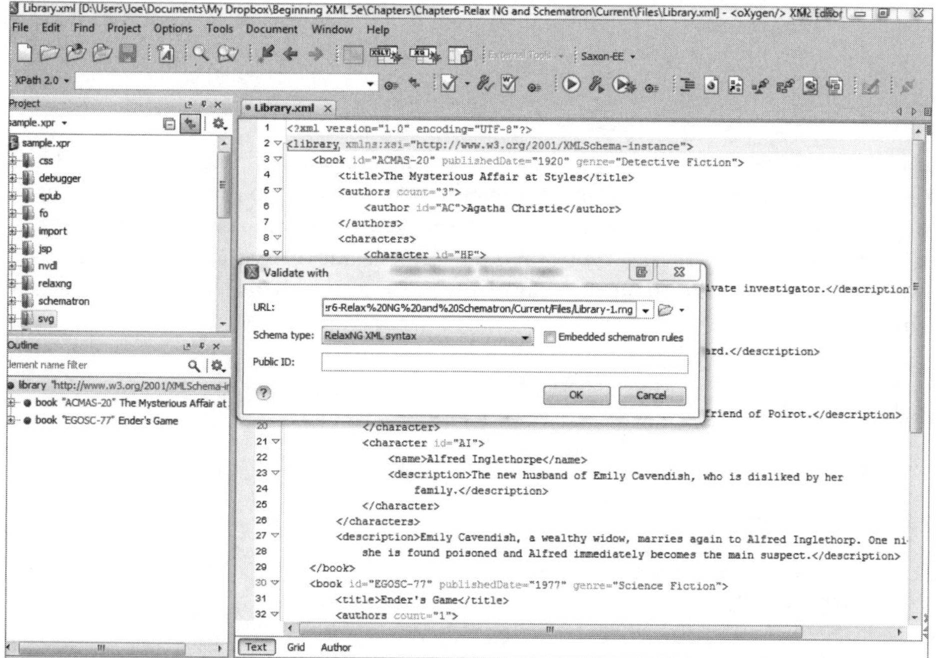

FIGURE 6-1

4. In the URL textbox, browse for the `Library-1.rng` file and in the Schema Type drop-down choose RelaxNG XML Syntax. Now click the OK button and you should see a green box in the application's status bar with the words "Validation successful." If you go and make a small change to `Library-1.xml`, perhaps by removing the `id` attribute from first book element and revalidating, you'll see a message stating that `element "book" missing required attribute "id"`.

5. The next stage to building up your schema is to add patterns that match the child elements of `<book>`. Modify the current schema, `Library-1.rng` to give the following:

```
<element xmlns="http://relaxng.org/ns/structure/1.0" name="library">
    <oneOrMore>
        <element name="book">
            <attribute name="id"/>
```

```
                <attribute name="publishedDate"/>
                <attribute name="genre"/>
                <element name="title">
                    <text/>
                </element>
                <element name="authors">
                    <attribute name="count"/>
                </element>
                <element name="characters"/>
                <element name="description">
                    <text/>
                </element>
            </element>
        </oneOrMore>
    </element>
```

6. Notice how the elements <title> and <description> contain a <text/> element. This pattern matcher states that these elements contain only text and no other markup. The final step is to fill in the patterns that match the <author> and <character> elements. Specify that there must be at least one <author> element but there don't have to be any <character> ones. Save the changes so far as `Library-2.rng`. This leads to the code shown in Listing 6-4.

LISTING 6-4: Library-2.rng

Available for download on Wrox.com

```
<element xmlns="http://relaxng.org/ns/structure/1.0" name="library">
    <oneOrMore>
        <element name="book">
            <attribute name="id"/>
            <attribute name="publishedDate"/>
            <attribute name="genre"/>
            <element name="title">
                <text/>
            </element>
            <element name="authors">
                <attribute name="count"/>
                <oneOrMore>
                    <element name="author">
                        <attribute name="id"/>
                        <text/>
                    </element>
                </oneOrMore>
            </element>
            <element name="characters">
                <zeroOrMore>
                    <element name="character">
                        <attribute name="id"/>
                        <element name="name">
                            <text/>
                        </element>
                        <element name="description">
                            <text/>
                        </element>
                    </element>
```

```
                </zeroOrMore>
            </element>
            <element name="description">
                <text/>
            </element>
        </element>
    </oneOrMore>
</element>
```

To specify that you want one or more <author> elements, you surround the block with a <oneOrMore> element. Conversely, you can omit <character> elements altogether, so there you use a <zeroOrMore> containing element.

7. You can now validate your complete `Library.xml` file against this schema; it should pass validation with no error messages. You can test if your <zeroOrMore> stipulation works by deleting or commenting out all the character elements from one of the <book> elements; the file will still validate. So far all the solitary elements and attributes have been mandatory; the only options you've had are how many <author> and <character> elements were allowed.

Now suppose you decide that the <description> element of the book is not mandatory — it can be omitted from the XML. To denote this in your RELAX NG schema you can make use of the <optional> element, which looks like the following:

```
<optional>
    <element name="description">
        <text/>
    </element>
</optional>
```

If you now comment out one of the <description> elements like this:

```
    </characters>
    <!-- <description>Emily Cavendish, a wealthy widow,
 marries again to Alfred Inglethorp. One night
        she is found poisoned and
  Alfred immediately becomes the main suspect.</description> -->
</book>
```

and then revalidate, you find the file still passes.

You've now covered the basics of RELAX NG, but only using the XML representation. You'll now see how to describe the same XML using the compact syntax.

Understanding RELAX NG's Compact Syntax

Instead of XML elements, the compact syntax makes use of curly braces (`{}`), parentheses (`()`), and commas (`,`) in its syntax. There are two ways to make a declaration:

- For your basic declaration — that the file starts with a <library> element — you use the following:

```
element library {}
```

- A similar structure can declare an attribute named `id` that has a data type of `text`, which is the only data type that is recognized by RELAX NG without recourse to external definition sets such as W3C XML Schema:

```
attribute id { text }
```

You can now use these two declarations to build your schema using the compact syntax:

1. Follow the common convention to put new declarations on separate lines as far as possible:

```
element library {
  element book {}+ }
```

   The preceding snippet says that the document element is `<library>` and underneath this are one or more `<book>` elements (as indicated by the + sign). You can use one of three signs for optionally occurring items:

   - ?: Indicates that the item is optional, zero or one occurrence at most
   - +: Indicates that the item occurs at least once with no maximum
   - *: Indicates that the item occurs zero or more times, again with no upper limit

   If none of these signs are used, the item must occur once and only once. Note that attributes can only use the ? sign because XML doesn't allow repetition of attribute names within a single element.

2. After defining the `<book>` element, fill in the attributes it needs. These need to be separated by commas:

```
element library {
  element book {
    attribute id { text },
    attribute publishedDate { text },
    attribute genre { text }
  }+
}
```

   The indentation is purely for readability. You have now described the basic structure of your library. You can use <oXygen/> to validate against the simplified version, `Library-1.xml`, as you did earlier.

3. Save the preceding code as `Library-1.rnc` (notice the different extension) and validate as before. The only thing you need to do differently is change your choice in the validation dialog box drop-down to be RelaxNG Compact Syntax.

4. Now add the remaining definitions to the `<book>` element to the compact version to give the following schema:

```
element library {
  element book {
    attribute id { text },
    attribute publishedDate { text },
    attribute genre { text },
```

```
        element title { text },
        element authors {
          attribute count { text }
        },
        element characters {},
        element description { text }?
      }+
    }
```

Notice how the <description> element is made optional by the addition of the question mark after the closing curly brace.

5. The final stage is to fill in the patterns covering the <author> and <character> elements. The full schema is shown in Listing 6-5.

LISTING 6-5: Library.rnc

Available for download on Wrox.com

```
element library {
  element book {
    attribute id { text},
    attribute publishedDate { text },
    attribute genre { text },
    element title { text },
    element authors {
      attribute count { text },
      element author {
        attribute id { text },
        text
      }+
    },
    element characters {
      element character {
        attribute id { text },
        element name { text },
        element description { text }
      }*
    },
    element description { text }?
  }+
}
```

In general, most people find it easier to write RELAX NG schema using the compact syntax. If you compare the two versions you'll see that the XML one is more than 65 percent longer for the same functionality. The best thing is that the two formats are completely interchangeable; you can test this out using the <oXygen/> editor.

Converting Between the Two RELAX NG Formats

Conversion using your chosen editor is very straightforward, as demonstrated by converting the XML version, `Library.rng`, to the compact version.

1. In the editor go to Tools ➪ Generate/Convert Schema. . . . In the dialog box that is displayed on the left-hand side, choose RELAX NG Schema - XML as the Input and browse to `Library.rng` in the file entry box. In the right-hand pane, choose RELAX NG Schema - Compact as the Output; browse to the same folder as your input but choose `Library-converted.rnc` as the file name.
2. Click the Convert button and open the newly created file; you'll find that it's exactly the same as the version created earlier, `Library.rnc`. If you try the reverse process, (converting from the compact syntax to the XML one), then you'll find that this works just as well with a copy of `Library.rng` being produced.

***NOTE** Although the conversion from compact to XML has produced the same version as the hand-crafted one, this won't always be the case because there is often more than one way to express an XML structure using the XML syntax. It worked nicely this time because the schema is a fairly simple one.*

So far, although you've described the format of the XML documents you want to validate, you haven't constrained the actual values that elements or attributes hold. For example, the `publishedDate` attribute should hold a valid year but your document just defines the content as `text`. In the next section you see how to further constrain content to suit your requirements.

Constraining Content

The first type of constraint you'll look at is limiting content to an enumeration — a list of specific values. For example, in your `Library.xml` file the `<book>` element has a `genre` attribute. It's likely that this is taken from a fixed list of values. You can specify this in your schema by using the following declaration in the XML format:

```
<attribute name="genre">
    <choice>
        <value>Detective Fiction</value>
        <value>Science Fiction</value>
        <value>General Fiction</value>
        <value>Non-fiction</value>
    </choice>
</attribute>
```

This limits the value of `genre` to one of four values. If you modify `Library.xml` so that the `genre` attribute of the first `<book>` is `Crime Fiction` the validator will mark it as an error. If you want to use the compact syntax, use this:

```
attribute genre {
  "Detective Fiction"
   | "Science Fiction"
   | "General Fiction"
   | "Non-fiction"
}
```

In compact syntax the pipe character (|) is used to indicate a choice.

RELAX NG has a deliberately limited set of data types; in fact, there are only two: *string* and *token*. You're no doubt familiar with the first of these, which represents a sequence of characters. Token is more difficult to describe. It's a way of normalizing string types such that insignificant whitespace is removed. In practice this means that leading and trailing whitespace is removed and any sequence of more than one whitespace character is combined to form a single space.

NOTE *As a reminder from earlier chapters,* whitespace, *in the XML world, is defined as one of the following Unicode characters: 0x9 (tab), 0xa (newline), 0xd (carriage return), and 0x20 (space). Any other characters, including the often-used non-breaking space in HTML, are not counted as whitespace.*

`Token` is the default data type used when no other is specified, as is the case with the `genre` attribute defined previously. If you want to explicitly state which type you want, use the `type` attribute, like so:

```
<attribute name="genre">
    <choice>
        <value type="token">Detective Fiction</value>
        <value type="token">Science Fiction</value>
        <value type="token">General Fiction</value>
        <value type="token">Non-fiction</value>
    </choice>
</attribute>
```

or, in the compact syntax:

```
attribute genre {
  token "Detective Fiction"
  | token "Science Fiction"
  | token "General Fiction"
  | token "Non-fiction"
}
```

Having only two data types is a bit limiting, so RELAX NG schemas are able to import data types from other libraries. The most common library used is the W3C XML Schema library; this then gives access to a host of useful types. To show that you want data types from the XML Schema library, use the `datatypeLibrary` attribute on the schema's document element, like so:

```
<element xmlns="http://relaxng.org/ns/structure/1.0"
    datatypeLibrary="http://www.w3.org/2001/XMLSchema-datatypes"
    name="library">
```

Now that you have access to the XML Schema data types, you can constrain content, such as the following `publishedDate` attribute:

```
<attribute name="publishedDate">
    <data type="gYear"></data>
</attribute>
```

Notice how the type is specified within a `<data>` element. The `<data>` element is more restrictive than the `<text>` pattern because, in theory, content specified with the `<text>` pattern can contain unlimited text nodes, whereas the `<data>` pattern can accept only one text node, which can be further constrained by the `type` attribute. If you want to use the XML Schema types within the compact syntax, it's slightly easier. The use is so common that these types are accessible without an initial declaration. All that is needed is to prefix the data type with `xsd:`:

```
attribute publishedDate { xsd:gYear }
```

The XML Schema data type `gYear` specifies a Gregorian year, which means a year without any associated month and day information. If the target document contains anything else, there will be a validation error.

An alternative library to the XML Schema library is the *DTD Compatibility Library*. You can specify that you're using this library by using the namespace `http://relaxng.org/ns/compatibility/datatypes/1.0` on the document element as before. Alternatively, you can declare it *in situ*, on the actual pattern that needs it. For example, using the following code you could use the `ID` type from this library for the `id` attribute on the `<book>` attribute while keeping the XML Schema library for the rest of the document:

```
<element name="book">
            <attribute name="id">
                <data
 datatypeLibrary="http://relaxng.org/ns/compatibility/datatypes/1.0"
type="ID"/>
            </attribute>
```

If you want to use the compact syntax, use this:

```
datatypes dtd = "http://relaxng.org/ns/compatibility/datatypes/1.0"

element library {
  element book {
    attribute id { dtd:ID }
```

NOTE *Be sure to put a declaration at the top of the file that nominates a prefix; this prefix is used to qualify the data type whenever it's used.*

As an alternative, or in combination with external data types, you can also use regular expressions to constrain data. For example, suppose you want to specify that the `id` attribute for characters must consist of two or three uppercase characters from the Latin alphabet. The regular expression for this is:

```
[A-Z]{2,3}
```

This means any character in the range A to Z. The curly braces indicate the minimum and maximum times the characters must appear. To use this expression in your schema you add the following code:

```
<element name="character">
        <attribute name="id">
                <data type="token">
                <param name="pattern">[A-Z]{2,3}</param>
                </data>
        </attribute>
```

In the RELAX NG compact version it looks like this:

```
element character {
  attribute id {
    xsd:token { pattern = "[A-Z]{2,3}" }
  }
```

The final aspect of RELAX NG is that of code re-use.

Reusing Code in RELAX NG Schema

In most programming languages there is the facility to define blocks of code that can be reused; RELAX NG is no exception in this regard. The idea behind this is similar to other languages — it

WARNING *If you change one of the characters' IDs to be something other than two characters, you'll get an error message on validating pointing out the correct pattern to use.*

saves having to write the same code more than once, and when modifications are needed the schema has to be changed only in one place. This facility enables patterns to be defined, which can then be used throughout the document. For example, suppose you want to reuse the constraint you developed for the `<character>` element's `id` attribute — that it must be two or three uppercase letters. You can define this constraint separately from the main schema and apply it when needed.

1. First you need a way to define the constraint, like so:

```
<define name="person-id">
    <attribute name="id">
        <data type="token">
            <param name="pattern">[A-Z]{2,3}</param>
        </data>
    </attribute>
</define>
```

The name attribute on the <define> element enables you to reference the definition later in the schema. The rest of the code is just the definition of the attribute as before. In the compact version you use a construct similar to defining a variable with the name before an equal sign and the definition itself on the right-hand side:

```
person-id =
  attribute id {
    xsd:token { pattern = "[A-Z]{2,3}" }
  }
```

2. Second, you need to be able to reference this definition, first for the <author> element:

```
<oneOrMore>
    <element name="author">
        <ref name="person-id"/>
        <text/>
    </element>
</oneOrMore>
```

In the <character> element it's similar:

```
<zeroOrMore>
   <element name="character">
       <ref name="person-id"/>
       <element name="name">
          <text/>
       </element>
       <element name="description">
          <text/>
       </element>
   </element>
</zeroOrMore>
```

The compact version looks like this in the <author> element:

```
element author { person-id, text }+
```

In the <character> element it's:

```
element character {
  person-id,
  element name { text },
  element description { text }
}*
```

3. There's one final tweak needed for the XML version. Because XML documents can have only one root element, you need to separate your definitions from the actual schema (which is contained within a <start> element) and then wrap all the content in a <grammar> element. The complete schema is shown in Listing 6-6.

Available for download on Wrox.com

LISTING 6-6: LibraryWithConstraints.rng

```
<?xml version="1.0" encoding="UTF-8"?>
<grammar xmlns="http://relaxng.org/ns/structure/1.0"
    datatypeLibrary="http://www.w3.org/2001/XMLSchema-datatypes">
    <define name="person-id">
        <attribute name="id">
            <data type="token">
                <param name="pattern">[A-Z]{2,3}</param>
            </data>
        </attribute>
    </define>
    <start>
        <element name="library">
            <oneOrMore>
                <element name="book">
                    <attribute name="id">
                        <data
 datatypeLibrary="http://relaxng.org/ns/compatibility/datatypes/1.0"
                            type="ID"/>
                    </attribute>
                    <attribute name="publishedDate">
                        <data type="gYear"/>
                    </attribute>
                    <attribute name="genre">
                        <choice>
                            <value type="token">Detective Fiction</value>
                            <value type="token">Science Fiction</value>
                            <value type="token">General Fiction</value>
                            <value type="token">Non-fiction</value>
                        </choice>
                    </attribute>
                    <element name="title">
                        <text/>
                    </element>
                    <element name="authors">
                        <attribute name="count"/>
                        <oneOrMore>
                            <element name="author">
                                <ref name="person-id"/>
                                <text/>
                            </element>
                        </oneOrMore>
                    </element>
                    <element name="characters">
                        <zeroOrMore>
                            <element name="character">
                                <ref name="person-id"/>
                                <element name="name">
                                    <text/>
                                </element>
                                <element name="description">
                                    <text/>
```

continues

LISTING 6-6 *(continued)*

```
                                            </element>
                                        </element>
                                    </zeroOrMore>
                                </element>
                                <element name="description">
                                    <text/>
                                </element>
                            </element>
                        </oneOrMore>
                    </element>
            </start>
        </grammar>
```

The complete version in the compact syntax is shown in Listing 6-7.

Available for download on Wrox.com

LISTING 6-7: LibraryWithConstraints.rnc

```
datatypes d = "http://relaxng.org/ns/compatibility/datatypes/1.0"

person-id =
  attribute id {
    xsd:token { pattern = "[A-Z]{2,3}" }
  }
start =
  element library {
    element book {
      attribute id { d:ID },
      attribute publishedDate { xsd:gYear },
      attribute genre {
        xsd:token "Detective Fiction"
        | xsd:token "Science Fiction"
        | xsd:token "General Fiction"
        | xsd:token "Non-fiction"
      },
      element title { text },
      element authors {
        attribute count { text },
        element author { person-id, text }+
      },
      element characters {
        element character {
          person-id,
          element name { text },
          element description { text }
        }*
      },
      element description { text }
    }+
  }
```

There's plenty more to RELAX NG — there are ways to describe most of the XML formats that you're likely to come across in real-world situations. Unless you're a dyed-in-the-wool XML

Schema aficionado, you'll almost certainly find them easier to write by hand, and converting them to other formats is easy enough with tools, such as the <oXygen/> editor you've used, and others, such as Trang, a free conversion tool, which you can find at `http://www.thaiopensource.com/relaxng/trang.html`.

That concludes your introduction to RELAX NG. Next, you meet Schematron and see what unique features it has that make it particularly attractive when designing schemas that will be used by more non-technical users.

***NOTE** There is an excellent guide to RELAX NG by Wrox author Eric van der Vlist at* `http://books.xmlschemata.org/relaxng/page2.html`.

USING SCHEMATRON

The second validation tool discussed is Schematron, which looks at the problem of describing and validating an XML document in a different way than the three methods you've encountered thus far. These other methods (DTDs, XML Schema, and RELAX NG) all set to create a model of the target document. If the document doesn't match that model, an error is raised. Schematron's approach uses hand-crafted rules to describe what should appear and where in a document. It's up to the author to decide how many rules are needed, how strict they are and, most importantly, what messages should appear if any of them are broken.

Understanding the Basics of Schematron

As stated, Schematron revolves around the concept of *rules*; you can create any number of rules, such as:

- The `<character>` element's `id` attribute must be two or three uppercase letters from the Roman alphabet.
- The `count` attribute on the `<authors>` element must equal the number of `<author>` elements.

You can add as many rules as you see fit and attach a message to each one alerting the user if it has been broken. Schematron uses XPath to express these rules; XPath is a fundamental part of many XML-related technologies and is covered in depth in Chapter 7. This section gives a very quick introduction and sticks to simple examples. This will give you enough to appreciate Schematron's power, which can be harnessed in full when your XPath skills are honed later on.

Understanding XPath

Similar to the way RELAX NG portrays an XML document, XPath also seeks to represent an XML document as a tree, starting at the root node and branching out through the document element and all its children. It uses a format similar to that used for paths in the filesystem. The root is represented by a forward slash (`/`) and then you can specify the direction or axis you want to travel and the name of any element you want to target. There are many directions that you can use but in this chapter you'll use only two: you can travel along the child axis or the attribute axis. So, if you want to single out the `<library>` element in your `Library.xml` file, you would use the following XPath expression:

```
/library
```

You have moved from the root (`/`) along the child axis (which is the default, so it doesn't need specifying) to all elements named `library`, which are directly under the root. In this case there is only one such element. You could then move to all the `<book>` elements by using:

```
/library/book
```

If you then change by switching onto the attribute axis, denoted by the `@` sign, you can pick out the `genre` attributes:

```
/library/book/@genre
```

Finally, you can filter these expressions using a *predicate*, which is denoted using square brackets (`[]`). For instance, if you want to target all `<book>` elements that have an `id` attribute of `ACMAS-20`, you can specify:

```
/library/book[@id = 'ACMAS-20']
```

Now that you have a basic understanding of XPath you can put this knowledge to good use by employing Schematron to validate XML. First though, you need to decide exactly which version of Schematron to use.

Choosing a Version of Schematron

Schematron comes in more than one flavor. The original version was developed by Rick Jelliffe in 1999 and is generally known as *Schematron 1.5*. Since Schematron's origin, there has been an effort for it to be recognized as an international standard, which led to the development of a new version known as *ISO Schematron*. The original, however, is typically more popular, probably because it seems easier to use. This is likely due to the fact that it was designed by one man rather than the newer version that was designed by a group of people, all with their own favorite parts that they wanted to include, forced to compromise over what exactly was left in and what was omitted. This group design led to a product that doesn't quite suit anybody. For these reasons you'll be using the original Schematron 1.5. Most of the examples will work in either version; where this is not the case it will be mentioned explicitly.

Understanding the Basic Process

Although Schematron relies on the creation of rules to describe an XML document, how those rules are tested deserves a mention. Once the rules are written, using an XML format, they are transformed using XSLT. The basic usage of XSLT is to transform XML from one format to another using templates (see Chapter 8, "XSLT" for more information). So Schematron takes the rules and uses XSLT to produce a second transformation. This is then applied to the XML to be validated, and the output produced lists whether the document passes all the tests or, if not, what rules have been broken. Although this may seem quite complicated, it's fairly straightforward once you've seen it in action. The <oXygen/> application you're using also hides a lot of the background processing, enabling you to concentrate on the core tasks in Schematron: rule creation and error messages.

Writing Basic Rules in Schematron

The first thing a rule needs is a *context* — when is this rule to be applied? Schematron rules start by defining this context using an attribute like so:

```
<rule context="...">
  <!-- rest of rule -->
```

The context is an XPath expression that defines when the rule should be tested. Say you want to define a rule relating to your `Library.xml` file you used in Listing 6-1. You know that `<book>` elements should possess three attributes: `id`, `publishedDate`, and `genre`. You can test that this is the case by choosing the `<book>` element as your context and adding three tests, one for each attribute.

In Schematron there are two types of tests: a positive one that says *this statement should be true; if it's not show an error message*; or a negative one that says *this statement should not be true; if it is show an error message*. The positive test is defined using an `<assert>` element and the negative test is defined using a `<report>` element.

You can therefore write your first test — that there is an `id` attribute — by using a positive `<assert>` element after setting the `context` attribute to `book`:

```
<rule context="book">
  <assert test="@id">The 'book' element must have an 'id' attribute.</assert>
</rule>
```

Here, the `test` is simple. The Schematron processor looks for an `id` attribute on all `<book>` elements. The XPath expression `@id` returns the `id` attribute if it exists, otherwise no value is returned. The `test` attribute on the `<assert>` element expects a Boolean. Using XPath's built-in rules, if there is no value returned then it is treated as `false`, if any value is returned then the test is `true`. So if an `id` attribute is returned, the `<assert>` succeeds; otherwise, if no `id` attribute is returned, the `test` is false and the `<assert>` fails. If the `<assert>` fails, the text within the element is shown to the user. In simple English this rule asserts that every `<book>` element has an `id` attribute.

You could equally well have written this `<rule>` using the `<report>` element, as follows:

```
<rule context="book">
  <report test="not(@id)">The 'book' element does not have
 an 'id' attribute.</report>
</rule>
```

This time the `test` has been changed; if any `<book>` element does *not* have an `id` attribute, the message is shown to the user. It's entirely up to you whether you use `<assert>` or `<report>` elements.

It's really a matter of style. Before you decide, think about the test you are going to write — which way will be easier, the positive assert or the negative report?

You can extend this rule to cover the other two attributes, `publishedDate` and `genre` like so:

```
<rule context="book">
  <assert
   test="@id">The 'book' element must have an 'id' attribute.</assert>
  <assert
   test="@publishedDate">
              The 'book' element must have a 'publishedDate' attribute.</assert>
  <assert
       test="@genre">The 'book' element must have a 'genre' attribute.</assert>
</rule>
```

Again, you could have used `<report>` elements for the tests or, if feeling very contrary, mixed the use of `<assert>` and `<report>`:

```
<rule context="book">
  <assert
   test="@id">The 'book' element must have an 'id' attribute.</assert>
  <report
   test="not(@publishedDate)">
      The 'book' element does not have a 'publishedDate' attribute.</report>
  <assert
       test="@genre">The 'book' element must have a 'genre' attribute.</assert>
</rule>
```

The practice of using both `<assert>` and `<report>` elements for the sake of it, rather than sticking to one or the other, isn't recommended, but it's perfectly legal in Schematron.

So far your rules have targeted a `<book>` element, but Schematron lets you target items other than elements; for example, comments, processing instructions, and text. This makes it stand out from other validation techniques. DTDs and W3C Schema can't handle comments and processing instructions. Schematron doesn't, however, let you target attributes directly; you need to target their parent element as you did in the previous examples.

NOTE *ISO Schematron differs from traditional Schematron in that it lets you set an attribute as a context. On the other hand, ISO Schematron can't target text items.*

So far you've seen how to write simple rules; it's now time to put these rules into the framework of a full Schematron document.

Creating a Schematron Document

A Schematron 1.5 document begins with a `<schema>` element that is in the `www.ascc.net/xml/Schematron` namespace. The `<rule>` elements themselves are grouped under `<pattern>` elements. The reason for this is that once a node has passed or failed a rule within a pattern, no more rules are processed against that node. Therefore, if you want two rules to be applied to a node, you need to put each <rule> into a separate <pattern> element. Your first Schematron document therefore looks like Listing 6-8.

LISTING 6-8: Library-1.sch

```
<schema xmlns="http://www.ascc.net/xml/schematron">
     <pattern name="book attributes">
          <rule context="book">
               <assert
   test="@id">The 'book' element must have an 'id' attribute.</assert>
               <assert
   test="@publishedDate">The 'book' element must have a 'publishedDate'
                    attribute.</assert>
               <assert
   test="@genre">The 'book' element must have a 'genre' attribute.</assert>
          </rule>
     </pattern>
</schema>
```

You've grouped the rule applying to <book> elements into a <pattern> element with the name book attributes (this name is just for your benefit; it is ignored by the validator).

You can use this schema to validate Library.xml. The process is similar to before — open Library.xml in <oXygen/> and choose Document ⇨ Validate ⇨ Validate with . . . from the menu. Then browse to Library-1.sch in the URL text box and click OK. You should see a Validation successful message next to a green square in the status bar. If you modify Library.xml by removing the id="EGOSC-77" from the second <book> element and revalidate, you'll see the message: The 'book' element must have an 'id' attribute. (@id) [assert]. The first part of this is the text from your <assert> element; the latter parts indicate the XPath of the test attribute and that an assert caused the message, rather than a report.

Although this message informs you of the problem, it doesn't specify which <book> caused the problem. This is an essential piece of information — after all, you could have thousands of <book> elements in your <library>. Next, you see how to add extra information to messages to help the user correct any errors.

Adding More Information to Messages

Two techniques are available that help you improve any error messages. The first is of limited use and only really makes your code less repetitious and more maintainable; this method is to make use of the <name> element.

Using the <name> Element

The <name> element enables you to output the name of any node that can be accessed from the current context. For example, instead of hard-coding the name book into your error message you could write:

```
<assert test="@id">
The '<name path="."/>' element must have an 'id' attribute.</assert>
```

Here the <name> element has an attribute, path, that points to the current context, which is the <book> element that is being processed.

NOTE *In XPath the period (.) is used to represent the context, much as the same symbol can be used in a file path to represent the current directory. This is covered fully in Chapter 7.*

For this example, using the <name> element is not very helpful. Your rule is set only to process <book> elements so it will always resolve to *book* in the output. However, your rule could have been specified differently such that knowing the name of the failing element would have been more helpful. In this example supplying the path attribute is actually unnecessary. It's so common to output the name of the element currently being processed that including just <name/> in the message is sufficient. It's only if you want the name of a different element that the path attribute is needed. So your full schema would now look like Listing 6-9:

Available for download on Wrox.com

LISTING 6-9: Library-2.sch

```
<schema xmlns="http://www.ascc.net/xml/schematron" >
     <pattern name="book attributes">
          <rule context="book">
               <assert test="@id">
 The '<name/>' element must have an 'id' attribute.</assert>
               <assert test="@publishedDate">
 The '<name/>' element must have a 'publishedDate' attribute.</assert>
               <assert test="@genre">
 The '<name/>' element must have a 'genre' attribute.</assert>
          </rule>
     </pattern>
</schema>
```

The second technique you can use to improve error messages is much more useful; this is the <diagnostic> element.

Using the <diagnostic> Element

The <diagnostic> element has three advantages:

- It allows you to easily reuse error messages that apply to more than one context.
- It allows you to display more than one error message for each rule violation.
- It enables more detailed inspection of the offending node.
- The <diagnostic> element has the following form:

```
<diagnostic id="id-attribute"><!-- error message --></diagnostic>
```

The id attribute needs to be unique and is used to associate the message with the <assert> or <report> that uses it. Within the error message you can use a <value-of> element that lets you obtain data from any part of the targeted XML document. This means you can show the user exactly where the error occurred.

To associate a <diagnostic> element with an <assert> or <report> that uses it, add a diagnostics attribute like so:

```
<assert
    diagnostics="id-attribute"
    test="@id">The 'book' element must have an 'id' attribute.</assert>
```

Now the <diagnostic> element with the relevant id will be called if this assertion fails.

You can add a <value-of> element to make the output even more useful. This has a select attribute, which takes an XPath expression. You can use this expression to retrieve the title of the invalid <book> element to make it easier for the user to identify where the target XML needs modifying.

To keep the <diagnostic> elements separate they are wrapped in a <diagnostics> element. The full schema is shown in Listing 6-10.

Available for download on Wrox.com

LISTING 6-10: Library-3.sch

```
<schema xmlns="http://www.ascc.net/xml/schematron" >
     <pattern name="book attributes">
          <rule context="book">
               <assert
                 diagnostics="id-attribute"
             test="@id">The 'book' element must have an
             'id' attribute.</assert>
               <assert test="@publishedDate">
             The 'book' element must have a 'publishedDate' attribute.</assert>
               <assert test="@genre">
             The 'book' element must have a 'genre' attribute.</assert>
          </rule>
     </pattern>

     <diagnostics>
          <diagnostic id="id-attribute">The 'id' was missing on book/title:
 <value-of select="title"/></diagnostic>
     </diagnostics>
</schema>
```

If you validate the example file with the id attribute missing from the second book, you'll get an error message this time like this one:

```
Diagnostics: [id-attribute] The 'id' was missing on book/title: Ender's Game
```

When it comes to choosing where to put what in error messages, again it's somewhat a matter of style. In general the <assert> and <report> elements should contain a simple explanation of the broken rule. The <diagnostic> elements should help narrow down exactly where the rule was broken. You can associate more than one <diagnostic> element to an <assert> or <report> element if you want; you just need to separate the id values by a single space. A common use of this facility is to display the more detailed message in more than one language, as shown in Listing 6-11.

Available for download on Wrox.com

LISTING 6-11: Library-4.sch

```
<schema xmlns="http://www.ascc.net/xml/schematron" >
     <pattern name="book attributes">
          <rule context="book">
               <assert
                 diagnostics="id-attribute-en id-attribute-fr"
             test="@id">The 'book' element must have an 'id' attribute.</assert>
               <assert test="@publishedDate">
               The 'book' element must have a 'publishedDate' attribute.</assert>
               <assert test="@genre">
               The 'book' element must have a 'genre' attribute.</assert>
          </rule>
     </pattern>

<diagnostics>
          <diagnostic id="id-attribute-en">
  The 'id' was missing on book/title: <value-of select="title"/></diagnostic>
          <diagnostic id="id-attribute-fr">
book/title: <value-of select="title"/> manque de l'attribut 'id'.
</diagnostic>
     </diagnostics>

</schema>
```

Now the user will see a full explanation in both English and French if the `id` attribute is missing.

So far your checks have been fairly perfunctory, just testing for the presence of an attribute. The next section details what to do if you want to test not only for the existence, but also that the value it contains is valid.

Constraining Values in Schematron

Testing for the existence of attributes is not really enough; you also need to make sure that the actual value is a valid one. For example, you tested that there was an `id` attribute on the `<book>` element; however, it could have been empty and the test would still have passed.

Using `publishedDate` as an example, you know that it represents the year the book was first published. You can express this in a test by seeing if the actual value can be cast to a `gYear`.

Because `gYear` is defined as one of the W3C XML Schema types, you'll need a way to reference these. You can declare a namespace mapping using the `<ns>` element, which takes two attributes to hold the namespace URI and the prefix you want to use to refer to it:

```
<schema xmlns="http://www.ascc.net/xml/schematron">
     <ns uri="http://www.w3.org/2001/XMLSchema" prefix="xs"/>
     <pattern name="book attributes">
     <!-- rest of schema -->
</schema>
```

You then need an assertion that the value is suitable. For this you'll use the `castable as` operator in XPath.

NOTE *For this example to work you need to make sure you're using XPath 2.0. Go to* Options ➪ Preferences ➪ XML ➪ XML Parser ➪ Schematron ➪ Schematron XPath Version *and make sure 2.0 is selected.*

You'll test whether the `publishedDate` is `castable as a gYear`:

```
<schema xmlns="http://www.ascc.net/xml/schematron">
     <ns uri="http://www.w3.org/2001/XMLSchema" prefix="xs"/>
     <pattern name="book attributes">
          <rule context="book">
               <assert
              diagnostics="id-attribute-en id-attribute-fr" test="@id">The 'book' element
                    must have an 'id' attribute.</assert>
               <assert test="@publishedDate">
               The 'book' element must have a 'publishedDate' attribute.</assert>
               <assert test="@publishedDate castable as xs:gYear">
               The publishedDate attribute must contain a valid year.</assert>
    <!-- rest of schema -->
</schema>
```

Now you can test your new schema. If you replace the date of the first book in your example file, `1920`, with an illegal entry, such as `xxxx`, you'll get an error message such as that shown in Figure 6-2.

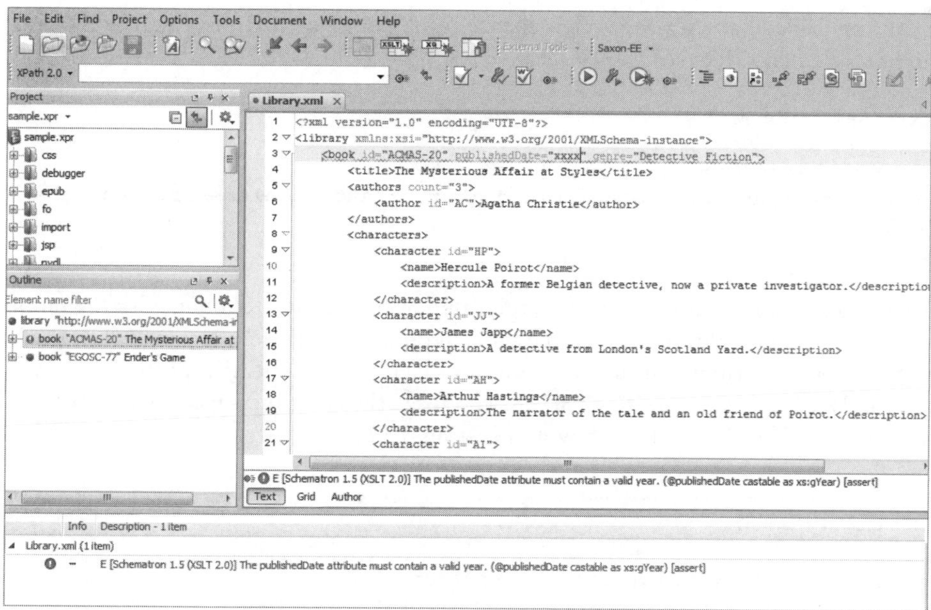

FIGURE 6-2

You've now covered the basics of Schematron and seen how it copes with some of the traditional validation requirements, such as mandatory content and checking whether data is of the correct type. However these things can be done equally well with XML Schemas. One of the reasons for Schematron being popular is that is can also cope with scenarios that can't be handled using constructs found in existing technologies. One of these situations is known as co-constraints, a common requirement that neither DTDs nor XML Schemas can handle but which is easy using Schematron.

Handling Co-Constraints in Schematron

A co-constraint refers to the situation where you want to say *if this then that.* This is impossible to with DTDs and is achievable in W3C XML Schema only if you are using version 1.1, which adds the `<assert>` element to provide this capability. Unfortunately, few products implement XML Schema 1.1 yet.

As an example, notice that the `<authors>` element in `Library-1.xml` document has a `count` attribute, the value of which is equal to the number of `<author>` elements contained within it. If you want to check that this is indeed the case you need to create a new rule to deal with it.

1. First you add a new `<pattern>` element and, within that, a `<rule>` that has `authors` as a context. Try the following:

```
<pattern name="authors">
  <rule context="authors">
    <!-- asserts to go here -->
  </rule>
</pattern>
```

2. Then you need to add an `<assert>` that checks if the `count` attribute is equal to the number of `<author>` elements, like so:

```
<pattern name="authors">
  <rule context="authors">
    <assert test="@count = count(author)">
The count attribute must equal the number of author elements.</assert>
  </rule>
</pattern>
```

3. The XPath expression compares `@count`, the value of the `count` attribute, with the number of `<author>` elements, obtained using the built-in `count()` function. If you change the value of the `count` attribute on the first `<author>` element to indicate that there are two authors for *The Mysterious Affair at Styles*, you'll see the error message reported when you try to validate. The full schema is shown in Listing 6-12.

Available for download on Wrox.com

LISTING 6-12: Library-6.sch

```
<schema xmlns="http://www.ascc.net/xml/schematron">
     <ns uri="http://www.w3.org/2001/XMLSchema" prefix="xs"/>
     <pattern name="book attributes">
          <rule context="book">
               <assert
    diagnostics="id-attribute-en id-attribute-fr" test="@id">
    The 'book' element must have an 'id' attribute.</assert>
```

```
                <assert
             test="@publishedDate">
 The 'book' element must have a 'publishedDate' attribute.</assert>
                <assert
      test="@publishedDate castable as xs:gYear">
      The publishedDate attribute must contain a valid year.</assert>
                <assert test="@genre">
        The 'book' element must have a 'genre' attribute.</assert>
           </rule>
      </pattern>

      <pattern name="authors">
           <rule context="authors">
                <assert test="@count = count(author)">
       The count attribute must equal the number of author elements.</assert>
           </rule>
      </pattern>

      <diagnostics>
           <diagnostic id="id-attribute-en">
     The 'id' was missing on book/title: <value-of select="title"/>
           </diagnostic>
           <diagnostic id="id-attribute-fr">
    book/title: <value-of select="title"/> manque de l'attribut 'id'.</diagnostic>
      </diagnostics>
 </schema>
```

You've looked at the basics of Schematron and it definitely has its advantages over XML Schema. However, it's inconvenient to have to write every rule by hand, and specifying the basic structure of the target document is tiresome. A better way to go about this is to have some basic validation performed using XML Schema and then use Schematron to add rules that are difficult or impossible to express otherwise. You can then also take advantage of Schematron's friendlier error messages. This is a supported scenario and achieved by embedding Schematron rules within a W3C XML Schema.

Using Schematron from Within XML Schema

The code download for this chapter contains a simple W3C XML Schema, `Library.xsd`, which can be used to validate your example file. You'll now go through the process of adding a Schematron rule to test the co-constraint that you used previously — that the `count` attribute on the `<authors>` element does in fact equal the number of `<author>` elements.

TRY IT OUT Embedding Schematron Rules in XML Schema

This Try It Out takes you through the process of combining a basic XML Schema validation with Schematron and shows how you can use XML Schema to do the grunt work while utilizing Schematron's flexible validation rules to supplement when necessary.

1. First, modify your XML Schema to accept Schematron rules. To do so just add the Schematron namespace to your XML Schema, `Library.xsd`:

```
<xs:schema xmlns:xs="http://www.w3.org/2001/XMLSchema"
xmlns:sch="http://www.ascc.net/xml/schematron" elementFormDefault="qualified">
```

2. Next, create the new rule. Simply take your old rule and reform it so that the elements use the `sch` prefix to show that they are in the Schematron namespace, like so:

```
<sch:pattern id="authors">
  <sch:rule context="authors">
    <sch:assert
     test="@count = count(author)">
     The count attribute must equal the number of author elements.
    </sch:assert>
  </sch:rule>
</sch:pattern>
```

   This is exactly the same as the original, but you use a prefixed namespace rather than the default one.

3. Add the rule to the XML Schema by taking advantage of the `<xs:annotation>` element. This enables you to embed user-friendly documentation or machine-readable data into the schema. Embed the latter, so underneath the `<xs:annotation>` you have an `<xs:appinfo>` element:

```
<xs:annotation>
  <xs:appinfo>
    <!-- Schematron patterns go here -->
  </xs:appinfo>
</xs:annotation>
```

4. The best place to put the Schematron rules is near the definitions of the elements they are testing, so put this block immediately after the definition of the `<authors>` element, like the following code snippet. Once these changes have been made, save the file as `LibraryWithSchematronRules.sch`:

```
<xs:element name="authors">
    <xs:annotation>
      <xs:appinfo>
        <sch:pattern id="authors">
          <sch:rule context="authors">
            <sch:assert
               test="@count = count(author)">
   The count attribute must equal the number of author elements.</sch:assert>
          </sch:rule>
        </sch:pattern>
      </xs:appinfo>
    </xs:annotation>
    <xs:complexType>
  <!-- rest of authors element definition -->
</xs:element>
```

5. The final step is to make two changes to `Library.xml`. Open the file in the <oXygen/> editor and add the `xsi:noNamespaceSchemaLocation` attribute to the `<library>` element, as well as a new namespace declaration for the Schema Instance library:

```
<library xmlns:xsi="http://www.w3.org/2001/XMLSchema-instance"
    xsi:noNamespaceSchemaLocation="LibraryWithSchematronRules.xsd">
```

The second change is purely for the benefit of the <oXygen/> editor. It needs to know that, as well as validating using the standard XML Schema, it must also extract the Schematron rules from the document and validate against those. This is accomplished by using an XML processing instruction, which is inserted at the top of the target XML:

```
<?oxygen SCHSchema="LibraryWithSchematronRules.xsd"?>
```

You then need to save the document as `LibraryForValidation.xml`.

6. To test the validation, open `LibraryForValidation.xml` in <oXygen/> and change the name of first `<book>` element to `<tome>`. Then validate by using the shortcut, Ctrl+Shift+V. You'll get an error about an unexpected element — `<tome>` where `<book>` was expected. This shows that the W3C XML Schema is being used to validate. Now change the element back to `<book>` and alter one of the `<authors>` element's `count` attributes to be incorrect. Re-validate and you'll see a message similar to the previous one, that the count is incorrect.

The full code for `LibraryWithSchematronRules.xsd` is shown in Listing 6-13.

LISTING 6-13: LibraryWithSchematronRules.xsd

Available for download on Wrox.com

```
<?xml version="1.0" encoding="UTF-8"?>
<xs:schema xmlns:xs="http://www.w3.org/2001/XMLSchema"
           xmlns:sch="http://www.ascc.net/xml/schematron"
           elementFormDefault="qualified">
  <xs:element name="library">
    <xs:complexType>
      <xs:sequence>
        <xs:element maxOccurs="unbounded" ref="book"/>
      </xs:sequence>
    </xs:complexType>
  </xs:element>
  <xs:element name="book">
    <xs:complexType>
      <xs:sequence>
        <xs:element ref="title"/>
        <xs:element ref="authors"/>
        <xs:element ref="characters"/>
        <xs:element ref="description"/>
      </xs:sequence>
      <xs:attribute name="genre" use="required"/>
      <xs:attribute name="id" use="required" type="xs:token"/>
      <xs:attribute name="publishedDate" use="required" type="xs:gYear"/>
    </xs:complexType>
  </xs:element>
  <xs:element name="title" type="xs:string"/>
  <xs:element name="authors">
    <xs:annotation>
      <xs:appinfo>
        <sch:pattern id="authors">
          <sch:rule context="authors">
            <sch:assert test="@count = count(author)">
```

continues

LISTING 6-13 *(continued)*

```
The count attribute must equal the number of author elements.</sch:assert>
          </sch:rule>
        </sch:pattern>
      </xs:appinfo>
    </xs:annotation>
    <xs:complexType>
      <xs:sequence>
        <xs:element ref="author"/>
      </xs:sequence>
      <xs:attribute name="count" use="required" type="xs:integer"/>
    </xs:complexType>
  </xs:element>
  <xs:element name="author">
    <xs:complexType mixed="true">
      <xs:attribute name="id" use="required" type="xs:token"/>
    </xs:complexType>
  </xs:element>
  <xs:element name="characters">
    <xs:complexType>
      <xs:sequence>
        <xs:element maxOccurs="unbounded" ref="character"/>
      </xs:sequence>
    </xs:complexType>
  </xs:element>
  <xs:element name="character">
    <xs:complexType>
      <xs:sequence>
        <xs:element ref="name"/>
        <xs:element ref="description"/>
      </xs:sequence>
      <xs:attribute name="id" use="required" type="xs:token"/>
    </xs:complexType>
  </xs:element>
  <xs:element name="name" type="xs:string"/>
  <xs:element name="description" type="xs:string"/>
</xs:schema>
```

How It Works

The <oXygen/> editor first validates using the XML Schema as indicated by the `xsi:noNamespaceSchemaLocation` attribute on the `<library>` element. Second, it extracts all the Schematron elements it can find that are within any `<xs:appinfo>` sections. It processes these just as it would a standalone Schematron schema.

Some of the features you haven't covered are *phases*, where you split the validation into separate sections and only validate specific phases at any one time. This is useful where the full validation takes a long time and you only want to check a specific part of the document. There are also *abstract* patterns and rules, where you can define commonly occurring functionality that can then be inherited by concrete ones later, similar to abstract classes in traditional computer languages. If you're interested you can find a list of online resources at `www.schematron.com`.

SUMMARY

- There is a need for other schema languages; no one language can express all possible rules.
- The reasons behind RELAX NG include simplicity and the ability to use data types from other languages.
- RELAX NG has two possible formats: an XML version where the files have a `.rng` extension and the compact syntax where the files have a `.rnc` suffix.
- Conversion between the two different schema formats or between other formats, such as XML Schema and RELAX NG, is possible and there are many tools that can do this.
- Schematron's idea of using XPath for validation rules enables complicated rules that are not possible in other languages.
- Schematron deals with co-constraints by comparing values from more than one item using XPath.
- XML Schema can combine with Schematron to get the best of both technologies.

In the next chapter, you see some of the different ways that you can extract data from XML documents.

EXERCISES

Answers to the exercises can be found in Appendix A.

1. Modify the RELAX NG schema for `Library.xml` to allow for an optional `url` attribute on `<book>` and make sure it's typed to allow only `xs:anyUri` as its value.

2. Add a Schematron rule to `LibraryWithSchematronRules.xsd` to make sure that a character's description is longer than the name of the character.

▸ WHAT YOU LEARNED IN THIS CHAPTER

TOPIC	KEY POINTS
The reasons for more validation languages	Each language has its own strong and weak points. None can manage to express every possible validation rule.
The main principles of RELAX NG	Simplicity. Two formats, XML and plain text. Can use data types from elsewhere. Does not add extra data.
The main principles of Schematron	Designed to be used in conjunction with other validation languages (mainly XML Schemas). Uses XPath to specify rules. Can define co-constraints (a constraint on data based on another item's data).
Combining Schematron with XML Schema	Standard practice is to use a basic XML Schema to describe the format of an XML document and then add Schematron rules where the ability to reference more than one information item is needed.

PART III
Processing

7

Extracting Data from XML

WHAT YOU WILL LEARN IN THIS CHAPTER:

- How XML is usually represented in memory
- What the DOW and the XDM are
- What XPath is
- How to read and write XPath expressions
- How to learn more about the XPath language when you need it

There's quite a lot packed into a small space here, but XPath is both important and useful. Most useful languages for querying and extracting data have fairly powerful expression languages and XPath is no exception. It's everywhere, too: XPath "engines" are available for pretty much every programming environment, from JavaScript to Java, from PHP and Perl to Python, from C to SQL. XPath is also central to XSLT and XQuery.

DOCUMENT MODELS: REPRESENTING XML IN MEMORY

XML is a text-based way to represent documents, but once an XML document has been read into memory, it's usually represented as a tree. To make developers' lives easier, several standard ways exist to represent and access that tree. All of these ways have differences in implementation, but once you have seen a couple, the others will generally seem very similar.

This chapter briefly introduces three of the most widely used models; you learn more about each of them later in the book. You also learn how to avoid using these data models altogether using XPath (in this chapter) and XQuery (in Chapter 9).

Meet the Models: DOM, XDM, and PSVI

The best-known data model for storing and processing XML trees is called the W3C document object model, or the DOM for short. The DOM was originally designed for handling HTML in web browsers; the XML DOM is actually a separate specification, but it's supported by all modern web browsers, and a host of other applications and libraries.

XPath 2 and 3, XQuery, and XSLT 2 all use the XQuery and XPath Data Model, or XDM, which is a slightly different data model than DOM. The XDM is more powerful than the DOM, includes support for objects with types described by W3C XML Schema, and also supports items such as floating-point numbers and sequences intermingled with the XML data.

Finally, W3C XML Schema defines an abstract model with the catchy name *Post-Validation Information Set*, or *PSVI*. The PSVI is the result of validating an XML document against a W3C XML Schema and "augmenting" the XML document with type annotations; for example, saying a `<hatsize>` element contains an integer. The term *information set* comes from a specification (the XML Information Set), which provides a standard set of terminology for other specifications (like XSD) to use. You will sometimes also hear people refer to the *infoset* as if it was a data model, but this is not strictly accurate.

This chapter focuses first on the DOM, and then on using XPath to get at XML elements and attributes, whether they are stored using the DOM or otherwise.

WARNING *The XPath 1.0 specification did not rely on the DOM, and, in fact, some slight incompatibilities exist between XPath 1 and the DOM. However, the DOM is so widely used with XPath 1.0 that this is not an issue in practice.*

A Sample DOM Tree

There are three main reasons why it is important to talk about the DOM in this book:

- Some of the most widely used XPath implementations return DOM node lists.
- jQuery and other similar libraries are built on top of the DOM and described in terms of the DOM.
- The XDM used by XPath 2 and later is based on the same principles as DOM.

To start off, take a look at Listing 7-1 that shows how the XML text is taken to represent a tree in memory:

LISTING 7-1: Armstrong.xml

Available for download on Wrox.com

```
<entry id="armstrong-john">
  <title>Armstrong, John</title>
  <body>
    <p>, an English physician and poet,
```

```
        was born in <born>1715</born> in the parish of Castleton in Roxburghshire,
        where his father and brother were clergymen; and having
        completed his education at the University of Edinburgh,
        took his degree in physics, Feb. 4, 1732, with much reputation.
        . . .
      </p>
    </body>
  </entry>
```

Figure 7-1 illustrates how an implementation might represent this short snippet of XML in memory. In the diagram, the element nodes are drawn as circles, text nodes as pentagons, and attribute properties as boxes. The dotted part of the diagram is there to remind you that the illustration is not complete. The snippet includes only one entry, although the actual full dictionary has a <book> element and more than 10,000 entries. You see a larger example later in this chapter.

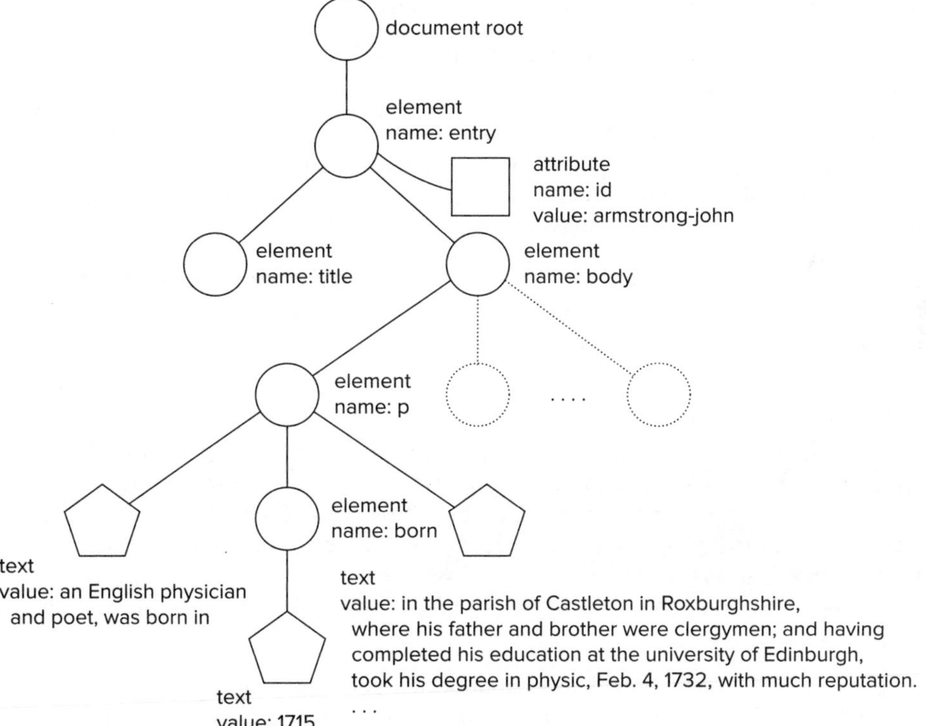

FIGURE 7-1

DOM Node Types

The in-memory representation of any XML item in a DOM tree such as an element, an attribute, a piece of text, and so on is called a *node*; XDM uses the word node in the same way. There are many different types of nodes; you take care not to get them confused. The following list helps spell the different node types out:

- **Document Node:** The node at the very top of the tree, *Document*, is special; it is not an element, it does not correspond to anything in the XML, but represents the entire document.
- **DocumentFragment Node:** A *DocumentFragment* is a node used for holding part of a document, such as a buffer for copy and paste. It does not need to meet all of the well-formedness constraints — for example, it could contain multiple top-level elements.
- **Element Node:** An *Element* node in a DOM tree represents a single XML element and its contents.
- **Attr (Attribute) Node:** *Attr* nodes each represent a single attribute with its name, value, and possibly, type information. They are normally only found hidden inside element nodes, and you have to use a method such as `getAttributeNode(name)` to retrieve them.
- **Text node:** A *text node* is the textual content of an element.
- **DocumentType, CDATASection, Notation, Entity, and Comment Nodes:** These are for more advanced use of the DOM.

DOM nodes also have *properties*; you just saw an example of this in Figure 7-1 — an element node has a property called `tagName`. Most DOM programs will contain code that tests the various properties of a node, especially its type (element, attribute, text and so on) and behaves accordingly, even though this is not usual in object-oriented design.

Look at the previous code example to put all of this information about nodes together in context: `<title>Armstrong, John</title>` has a start tag (`<title>`), text content (`Armstrong, John`), and an end tag (`</title>`), and as a whole, represents an element called `title`.

***NOTE** In this book the convention `<x>` is used in the text to refer to the element x. However, in the examples, and in actual XML files, `<title>` is a* tag *and not an element. The* element *is a logical idea, and the text representation of the element in an XML file includes the start tag, the end tag, and the content, which is everything between the tags.*

The resulting part of the DOM tree has an element node whose `tagName` property has the value `title`, and that element node contains a reference to a text node whose text value is `Armstrong, John`.

So a tag, an element, and a node are three different things. This may seem subtle, but it will really help you with XPath and XSLT.

DOM Node Lists

When you access parts of a DOM tree from a program, you generally get back a *node list*. As the name suggests, this is simply a list of nodes. You often then use an *iterator* to march through the list one item at a time. In particular, XPath queries return a node list.

An unusual thing about DOM node lists is that they are live: the items in the list are really references or pointers into the tree, so that if you generate a node list and then change one of the nodes in that list, those changes are reflected in the tree, and also in any other lists containing that node. Not all implementations support live node lists, however, so you should check the environment you plan to use before relying on the feature.

For example, code using the DOM, depending on the programming language, often looks something like this:

```
foreach (e in document.getelementsbytagname("p")) {
    if (e.attributes["role"] = "introduction") {
        document.delete(e);
    }
}
```

In this code, `document.getelementsbytagname("p")` is a DOM function that returns a node list, and the code then processes each element in turn, deleting the nodes whose role attribute is set to `introduction`. In some languages you would need to call string comparison functions to test against `"introduction"` and in others you might need to save the node list in a variable and *iterate* over it one item at a time using the `length` property of the node list. Although the details vary, the basic ideas are the same in all languages supporting the DOM.

The Limitations of DOM

The DOM provides a low-level application programming interface (API) for accessing a tree in memory. Although the DOM has some object-oriented features, it does not support the two most important features: *information hiding* (a concept alien to XML) and *implicit dispatch*, the idea that the compiler or interpreter chooses the right function or "method" to call based on the type or class of a target object. Therefore, since the DOM doesn't support implicit dispatch, you have to write code that says, "if the node is an element, do this; if it's a text node, do this," and so on, and it can be easy to forget a node type. In fact, it feels like playing snooker by giving a robot verbal commands — "left a bit, further, slower, right a bit, that's good." With XPath and XQuery, you just pick up the snooker cue and hit the ball.

The DOM nodes also have a lot of methods and properties, which use a lot of memory in many programming languages. It's not uncommon for DOM-based applications to get 10- to 100-times smaller when rewritten in XQuery, and for DOM expressions to find a node to get 10- to 100-times smaller and much easier to understand when they're rewritten in XPath. Additionally, because code using the DOM is verbose and tedious it is often expensive to maintain and error-prone.

Older languages and APIs restrict you to using the DOM, but these days in most cases you should be able to avoid it and use something higher-level. If you do end up using the DOM, see if there's a higher-level language or API that also returns a DOM node list. You should consider switching to XPath (described later in this chapter), XQuery (see Chapter 9), XSLT (see Chapter 8), or in JavaScript, jQuery. You will learn more about jQuery and JavaScript in Chapter 16, "AJAX". The rest of this chapter focuses on a higher-level language for accessing parts of a document, XPath.

THE XPATH LANGUAGE

The XML Path Language, XPath, is used to point into XML documents and select parts of them for later use. XPath was designed to be embedded and used by other languages — in particular by XSLT, XLink, and XPointer, and later by XQuery — and this means that XPath isn't a complete programming language. But when you use it from Python, PHP, Perl, C, C++, JavaScript, Schema, Java, Scala, XSLT, XQuery, and a host of other languages, you'll quickly come to like it!

XPath Basics

The most common way to use XPath is to pass an *XPath expression* and one or more XML documents to an *XPath engine*: the XPath engine evaluates the expression and gives you back the result. This can be via a programming language API, using a standalone command-line program, or indirectly, as when XPath is included in another language such as XQuery or XSLT.

NOTE *If your program is going to read the same XML document repeatedly, you can often get better performance using XQuery than with XPath alone. If, on the other hand, you want to process an entire document rather than just grab small parts, you should consider using XSLT. In any case, you'll need to know about XPath, because XQuery and XSLT are both based on it.*

With XPath version 1.0, the result of evaluating an XPath expression is a *node list*, and in practice this is often a DOM node list. With later versions of XPath you are more likely to get back an XDM sequence, but it depends on the exact API and environment of the language embedding the XPath engine. As of 2012, web browsers are still using XPath 1.

XPath is deceptively simple at first, and can be very easy to use. Following is an example from the start of the chapter showing how to get at John Armstrong's date of birth:

```
/entry/body/p/born
```

If there was a whole book with lots of entries, and you just wanted the one for John Armstrong, then you would use this instead:

```
/book/entry[@id = "armstrong-john"]/body/p/born
```

Each level of this XPath expression, from the root element down to `born` is a separate call to a DOM API, with a loop needed to handle the test for the attribute value. But what's equally as important is that an XPath engine has the freedom to evaluate this expression in any order, so, for example, it could start with the `<born>` element and work upward, which is sometimes a much faster strategy.

Understanding Context

In many environments using XPath you can "navigate" through the document and evaluate an XPath expression against any node in the tree. When an environment enables navigation and evaluation, the node becomes the *context item*.

The XPath context item can be set in three places: the first one you have seen before in the previous XPath examples that have all started with a slash (`/`), explicitly setting the initial context to the document node. The context can also be set before evaluation by the language or environment embedding XPath. You'll see examples of the "host language" setting the initial context outside XPath in Chapter 8, "XSLT" with `xsl:for-each` and `xsl:apply-templates`. Finally, when you use a predicate, the context is set by XPath inside the predicate. See the following example:

```
/book/entry[@id = "armstrong-john"]
```

Conceptually, the XPath engine finds the top-level `<book>` element, then makes a list of all `<entry>` elements underneath that `<book>` element. Then, for each of those `<entry>` elements, the XPath engine evaluates the predicate and keeps only the `<entry>` nodes for which the predicate is true — in this case, it keeps those `<entry>` elements having an `id` attribute whose value is equal to `"armstrong-john"`. The *context* for the predicate each time is a different `<entry>` element.

You'll see later that you can access the *initial* context node with the `current()` function, and that you can get at the *current* context node with a period (`.`). The names make more sense when XPath is used within XSLT, but for now all you need to remember is that there's always a context and you can access it explicitly if you need to.

XPath Node Types and Node Tests

So far you've seen XPath used only with XML elements, attributes, and text nodes, but XML documents can also contain node types such as processing instructions and comments. In addition, XPath 2 introduced *typed nodes*: all the types defined by W3C XML Schema are available.

Just as `entry` matches an element of that name, and `@id` matches an attribute called `id`, you can test for various node types including processing instructions, comments, and text. You can also match an element that was validated against a schema and assigned a particular type. Table 7-1 contains a list of all the different *node tests* you can use in XPath.

TABLE 7-1: XPath Node Types and Node Tests

NODE TEST	NODE TYPES MATCHED
`node()`	Matches any node at all.
`text()`	A text node.
`processing-instruction()`	A processing instruction.
`comment()`	A comment node (if the XML processor didn't remove them from the input!).
`prefix:name`	This is called a QName, and matches any element with the same namespace URI as that to which the prefix is bound and the same "local name" as *name* (see the section "XPath and Namespaces" later in this chapter for an English translation of this!). Examples: `svg:circle`, `html:div`.
`name`	An element with the given name (entry, body, and so on).

continues

TABLE 7-1 *(continued)*

NODE TEST	NODE TYPES MATCHED
`@attr`	An attribute of the given name (id, href, and so on); can be prefixed as a QName, for example, `@xlink:href`, but remember that attributes are not in any namespace by default.
`*`	Any element.
`element(name, type)`	An element of given name (use `*` for any), and of the given schema type, for example, `xs:decimal`. Examples: `entry/p/element(*, xs:gYear)` to find any element declared with XSD to have content of type `xs:gYear`; `entry/p/element(born, *)`, which is essentially the same as `entry/p/born`.
`attribute(name, type)`	Same as `element()` but for attributes.

You can use any of these node tests in a path. In Listing 7-1, for example, `/entry/body/title/text()` would match the text node inside the `<title>` element. The parentheses in `text()` are needed to show it's a test for a text node, and not looking for an element called `text` instead.

***NOTE** In practice it's pretty unusual to fetch processing instructions or comments from XML documents, but you do sometimes need to, especially if you're working on a general library for other people to use.*

XPath Predicates: The Full Story

Earlier in this chapter you saw a predicate used to select `<entry>` elements having an attribute called `id` with a particular value. The general pattern is that you can apply a predicate to any node list. The result is those nodes for which the predicate evaluated to a true, or non-zero, value. You can even combine predicates like so:

```
/book/chapter[position() = 2]/p[@class = 'footnote'][position() = 1]
```

This example finds all `<chapter>` elements in a book, then uses a predicate to pick out only those chapters that are the second child of the book (this is just the second chapter of the book). It then finds all the `<p>` children of that chapter, and uses a predicate to filter out all except those `<p>` elements that have a `class` attribute with the value `footnote`, Finally, it uses yet another predicate to choose only the first node in the list — that is, the first such `<p>` element.

The expression inside the predicate can actually be *any* XPath expression! Wow! So you could write something like this:

```
/entries/entry[body/p/born = /entries/entry/@born]
```

This expression finds all the entry elements that contain a born element whose value is equal to the born attribute on some (possibly different) entry element. You'll see more examples like this in Chapter 9, "XQuery"). For now, just notice that you can have fairly complex expressions inside predicates.

Positional Predicates

Let's slow down a bit and look at a simpler example for a moment. The simplest predicate is just a number, like `[17]`, which selects only the seventeenth node. You could write `/book/chapter[2]` to select the second chapter: that's because it's exactly the same as writing `/book/chapter[position() = 2]`. This is often called a *positional predicate*. It's really still a boolean (true or false) expression because of the way it expands to `position() = 17`.

NOTE *The predicate is not like an array dereference in many programming languages, but rather a filter with a boolean expression inside. An expression like* `p[0]` *is actually like* `p[false()]` *and does not select anything at all. The first node is therefore numbered node one, and* `p[1]` *gets you the first* `p` *node.*

So the full story on XPath predicates is that they can have any XPath expression in them, and that it will be evaluated to true or false for each node in the current list, winnowing down the list to leave only the nodes for which the predicate was true. And a plain number will be true if it matches the position in the list.

WARNING *A common source of confusion is the difference between* `//table/tbody/tr[1]` *and* `(//table/tbody/tr)[1]`*. The first expression selects all* `tr` *elements that are the first child of* `tbody` *elements. The second expression finds all* `tr` *elements that are any direct child of a* `tbody` *element, makes a list of them all in document order, and takes the first one. In most cases it's the second form that you actually want!*

The Context in Predicates

At the start of this chapter you learned how every XPath expression is evaluated in a *context*. The step (/) and the predicate change the context. For example, if the initial context is the top-level document node in Figure 7-1, then given the expression `/entry[@id]`, the context for the predicate after /entry will be the <entry> element, and so the expression looks for an id element on each *entry* node in turn; in this example there's only one such node, so it won't take long!

The shorthand ". " (a dot, or period) refers to the context node (the <entry> element), and the function current() refers to the initial context (the document node in this example).

For example, if you're processing an SVG document you might want to know if a definition is used, so, in the context of a <def> element, you might look for

```
//*[@use = current()/@id]
```

to find every element with an attribute called use whose value is equal to the id attribute on the current <def> element. You couldn't just write

```
//*[@use = @id]
```

because that would look for every element having use and id attributes with the same value, which is not at all what you want.

Effective Boolean Value

You've learned, informally, that a predicate is evaluated for each node, and that if it's true the node is kept. Formally this is called the *effective boolean value* of the expression in the predicate. Here are the rules XPath uses for working out whether a predicate is true (add the node to the list of results) or false (don't add the node to the list):

- An empty sequence is false.
- Any sequence whose first item is a *node* is true.
- A boolean value, true() or false(), returns its value.
- A string or string-like value is false if it is zero length, and true otherwise. String-like values are xs:string, xs:anyURI, xs:untypedAtomic, and types derived from them using XML Schema.
- Numeric values are false if they are zero or NaN, and true otherwise.

XPath Steps and Axes

An XPath axis is really just a direction, like up or down. (Note that the plural, axes, is pronounced *akseez* and is not related to chopping wood.) And a *step* moves you along the axis you have chosen.

The most common XPath axis is called *child*, and is the direction the XPath engine goes when you use a slash. Formally,

```
/book/chapter
```

is just a shorthand for

```
/child::book/child::chapter
```

You won't need the long form of the child axis very often, but it's there for completeness. The slash (`/`) is the actual step. Similarly, there's an attribute axis, and you can probably guess that the shorthand for it is the at sign (`@`).

Table 7-2 shows all of the different XPath axes, together with the short forms where they exist.

TABLE 7-2: XPath Axes

SHORTHAND	FULL NAME	MEANING
`name`	`child::`	The default axis; `/a/child::b` matches `<a>` elements that contain one or more `<b>` elements.
`//`	`descendant::`	`descendant::born` is true if there's at least one born element anywhere in the tree beneath the context node. `a//b` matches all `b` elements anywhere under `a` in the tree; a leading `//` searches the whole document.
`@`	`attribute::`	Matches an attribute of the context node, with the given name; for example, `@href`.
	`self::`	Matches the context node. For example, `self::p` is true if the context node is an element named "p."
	`descendant-or-self::`	Matches the current node or any child or child's child, all the way to the bottom. `p/descendant-or-self::p` matches the first `p` as well as the descendants called `p`.
	`following-sibling::`	Elements that come after the context node in the document are at the same level and have the same immediate parent.
	`following::`	Elements anywhere in the document *after* the current node.
`..`	`parent::`	The parent of the current node.
	`ancestor::`	Parent, grandparent, and so on up to the top. For example, `ancestor::div` returns all the div elements that enclose (are above) the context node.
	`preceding-sibling::`	The reverse of `following-sibling`.
	`preceding::`	The reverse of `following`.
	`ancestor-or-self::`	The reverse of `descendant-or-self`.
	`namespace::`	See Chapter 8 on XSLT.

***NOTE** Strictly speaking,* `a//b` *is equivalent to* `a/descendant-or-self::node()/child::b` *rather than being shorthand for the descendant axis. The difference is only really visible in obscure cases, but reference books often say* `//` *is short for* `descendant-or-self`*; don't be misled by this!*

Now take a look at an example XPath expression that uses some of these axes:

```
//a[preceding-sibling::a/@href = ./@href]
```

This expression matches <a> elements anywhere in the document (because `//a` at the start is the same as `/descendant::a`), and then uses a predicate to choose only those <a> elements that have a preceding sibling — that is, another <a> element earlier in the document, but only going back as far as the start of the parent element — where that other <a> element has the same value for its `href` attribute as this one (the dot meaning the node you're testing with the predicate). You might use this expression to match the second and subsequent links in a paragraph to the same footnote, for example.

XPath Expressions

Like most computer languages, XPath has expressions. In XPath 1 the outermost expression had to match nodes in the XPath 1 data model; more recent versions of XPath remove this restriction. This means that the following are all valid XPath expressions:

- `count(//p)`: The number of <p> elements in the document.
- `2 + 2`: Five. Wait, three. No, four, that's it, four!
- `1 + count(//p) + string-length(@id)`: One more than the number of <p> elements in the whole document, plus the number of characters in the `id` attribute of the current element (the context node).
- `10 idiv 4`: Two (*idiv* is integer division). XPath can't use "/" for division because that's already used for paths.
- `(1, 2, 3)`: In XPath 2 and later, this makes a *sequence*, in this case a sequence of integers (whole numbers).
- `(1 to 100)[. mod 5 eq 0]` (XPath 2 and later): Those numbers between 1 and 100 (inclusive) that are divisible by five.

Table 7-3 lists the operators you can use in an XPath expression.

***NOTE** Check* `www.w3.org/TR/` *for the latest version of the XPath and XQuery Functions and Operators document; at the time this book was written the latest stable version of XPath was 2.0, and 3.0 was still being developed.*

TABLE 7-3: XPath Operators

XPATH OPERATOR	MEANING
`+ - * idiv div mod`	Addition, subtraction, multiplication, integer division (`3 idiv 2` gives `1`), division (`3 div 2` gives `1.5`), modulus, or remainder (`12 mod 7` gives `5`).
`eq, ne, gt, lt, ge, le`	Equals, not equals, greater than, less than, greater than or equal, less than or equal. See the section "Equality in XPath," later in the chapter.
`<<, >>`	`A << B` is true if `A` and `B` are nodes in a document (for example, elements) and `A` occurs before `B`; `A >> B` is true if `A` comes after `B`. Note that these operators generally need to be escaped in XML documents.
`union, intersect, |, except`	`A union B` gives all nodes matched by either `A` or `B`, and is the same as `A|B`; `A intersect B` gives nodes in both `A` and `B`. See the section "XPath Set Operations."
`to`	`3 to 20` gives a sequence of integers `3, 4, 5,...18, 19, 20.`
`,`	The comma separates items in sequences, as well as arguments to functions.
`+, -`	The so-called *unary* operators, for negative and positive numbers, like `-2` and `+42`.
`e(list)`	Calls `e` as a function with the given arguments; `e` can be the literal name of a function, like `concat("hello", " ", "world")`, or can be an expression returning a "function item." See the section "Defining Your Own Functions" later in this chapter.
`(e1, e2, e3...)`	A sequence of values.

Equality in XPath

Two values are said to be *equal* if they are the same, and checking to see if things are equal is called testing for equality. The reason a precise term is needed for this action is because equality is a very important and precise concept in computing, and in XPath in particular. The following sections describe the main ways XPath has to compare items and their values to see if they are equal. There are also some sneaky unofficial ways you'll see mentioned as well.

The = Operator Works on Lists

The `=` operator in XPath actually operates on sequences (or, in XPath 1, on node lists). If A and B are two sequences, you could read `A = B` as "there's at least one value that appears in both A *and* B." Here are some examples:

- `(1, 2, 3) = (2, 4, 6, 8)`: True, because 2 appears on both sides.
- `("a", "hello", "b") = ("c", "Hello", "A")`: False (XPath, like XML, is case-sensitive).
- `3 = (1, 2, 3)`: True, the single value on the left is just treated like a short sequence.

NOTE *If you're ever feeling lonely at a party, you can quickly become the center of attention by explaining that the equals sign in XPath stands for "implicit existential quantification," a term from predicate calculus (the mathematical study of logic).*

This behavior may seem odd at first, but it's very useful with XML documents. Consider the following example:

```
/book/entry[p/place = "Oxford"]
```

This finds all the `<entry>` elements that contain a `<p>` element, which, in turn, contains a `<place>` element whose string value is equal to Oxford. There might be lots of `<place>` elements, and that's perfectly normal: if any of them has the value Oxford, the predicate will be true, and the containing `<entry>` will be returned.

The = operator works on simple (*atomic*) values; see the `deep-equal()` function for comparing structure.

The eq Operator Works on Single Values

If you know you intend to compare exactly one pair of values, you can use the singleton operator `eq` instead: `@chapterNumber eq 7`, for example. Two reasons to use this are: first, that if your assumption is incorrect and there's more than one value, you'll get an error; second, that `eq` is often slightly faster than =. But it is much better for code to be correct and slow than wrong and fast, so use `eq` only when you are sure there will only be one value on the left and one on the right.

The is Operator Works on Identity

In larger programs you'll often have variables that refer to nodes, and you may want to know if two variables refer to the same node. If you used the `eq` operator you'd be asking if you have two nodes whose contents have the same value, but with `is` you can ask if the two nodes are actually the same node, in the same place on the tree. In XQuery, you might write the following to treat a particular node differently:

```
if ($input is $target) then $target
else process ($input)
```

NOTE *If you are using XPath 1, and don't have the "`is`" operator available, you can use `count()` like this:*

```
count($input) = count($input|.)
```

This will be true if the current node (.) is in the list of nodes referred to by `$input`.

The deep-equal() Function Works on Subtrees

Finally, you can compare two entire subtrees to see if they are the same:

```
deep-equal(e1, e2)
```

This will be true if the structures *and* content are equal. Consider Listing 7-2:

LISTING 7-2: try.xml

Available for download on Wrox.com

```
<?xml version="1.0"?>
<store>
    <item id="shoes"><quantity>12</quantity></item>
    <street-address>12</street-address>
    <name>Shoe Store</name>
</store>
```

The XPath expression `/store/item = /store/street-address` is true. But `deep-equal(/store/item, /store/street-address)` is false.

> ***NOTE*** *The* `deep-equal` *function was added in XPath 2, so you can't see this with the widely-used* xmllint *program, which implements only XPath 1. The oXygen XML editor does include XPath 2 support, so you could experiment with* `deep-equal` *in oXygen; in Chapter 9 on XQuery you'll be using BaseX, which also has XPath 2 and 3 support.*

XPath Literal Values, Types, and Constructors

You've already seen quite a few examples of literal values in XPath. Table 7-4 puts them all together in one place, and you can also look back to Chapter 5, "XML Schemas" for more examples of XSD simple types. The table also shows the constructors, which are functions that take a string and return a value of the given type. In most cases you don't need to use the constructors, however in a few cases they can make your code clearer, and they *are* needed when you want to distinguish between values of different types, such as a number that's a shoe size and another that's a price. For example, the following two snippets of XSLT have the same effect, but it's easy to miss the single quotes in the first line:

```
<xsl:value-of select="'/'"/>
<xsl:value-of select="string('/')"/>
```

> ***NOTE*** *In XPath 2 and later, the functions are in a namespace that by default is bound to the prefix* `fn:`*, so instead of* `string()` *you can write* `fn:string()` *if you prefer. If you define your own functions (for example in PHP, Python, XSLT, or XQuery), you should put them in your own namespace.*

TABLE 7-4: XPath Literal Values and Types

VALUE TYPE	DESCRIPTION
Integer	0, 1, 2, and so on. Note that -1 is (strictly speaking) a unary minus operator applied to a number. Constructor: xs:integer("12")
Float, double	Same as for XSD, for example, 2.5, NaN. Constructors: xs:double("2.5e-17"), xs:float("42")
String	Use either double or single quotes, like XML attribute values. See also the following section "XPath String Quoting." Constructors: string("hello world") and xs:string("hello world")
Boolean	Use true() or false() to make them, and combine them with and, or, and the pseudo-function not(expr).
xs:dateTime, xs:anyURI, other Schema types	You can make any XSD simple type using the name of the type and a string, just as with float. See Chapter 5 "XML Schemas" for examples of values.
Function Items and Inline Functions	See the section "Defining Your Own Functions" later in this chapter.
Sequences	The comma constructs a sequence in XPath 2 and later: (1, 2, 42, 3)

XPath alone can never construct or remove document nodes. An XPath expression that returns a node will therefore also return all of the descendants of that node. If you want to do more extensive changes to the input, use XSLT or XQuery. Once you've learned XPath, XSLT and XQuery are plain sailing.

XPath String Quoting

Sometimes you need to include an apostrophe in a string, and this can get tricky. In XPath 2 or later you can double the apostrophe, 'can''t', but in XPath 1 you may have to resort to tricks using the concat() function to join its arguments together and make a single string. In XSLT 1 you could also sometimes use numeric character references — " for the double quote and ' for the single quote (apostrophe). In all versions of XPath, a string with single quotes around it can contain double quotes, and a string with double quotes around it can contain single quotes without a problem.

Variables in XPath Expressions

XPath is a *declarative language*. This means that you describe the results you want, and it's up to the computer to figure out how to get there. There's no looping, and no way to change the value of variables. In fact, you can't even set variables in the first place in XPath 1, so all XPath variables come from the host language outside of XPath.

Variables are marked by a dollar sign ($); they can contain node lists or sequences as well as the "atomic" types like numbers and strings. Here is an example in which $year is given the value 1732 and $e is the top-level <book> element in a large biographical dictionary:

```
$e/entry[@born le $year and @died ge $year]
```

This expression gets all the entry elements for people alive during the given year.

In XPath 2 and 3 you can define variables using `for` and `let`, although you still can't change their values.

New Expressions in XPath 2

XPath 2 introduces `for`, `let`, `if`, `some`, and `every` expressions, as well as casts. All of these expressions are really useful, but only work in XPath 2 and later. You won't be able to try them in the popular open-source *xmllint* program, nor in other programs based on libxml2, because that supports only XPath 1. However, if you have a version of the oXygen XML editor that uses the Saxon XPath engine, you can type them into the XPath 2.0 box in the upper right of the XML editor program. They also work in XQuery, so you could try the BaseX open source XQuery program used for some of the examples in Chapter 9, "XQuery."

XPath "for" Expressions

The format of a `for` expression is simple. Take a look at the following one that is a complete XPath expression that returns the numbers 5, 10, 15, 20, and so on up to 100:

```
for $i in (1 to 20)
return $i * 5
```

Figure 7-2 shows a screenshot of oXygen after entering this expression.

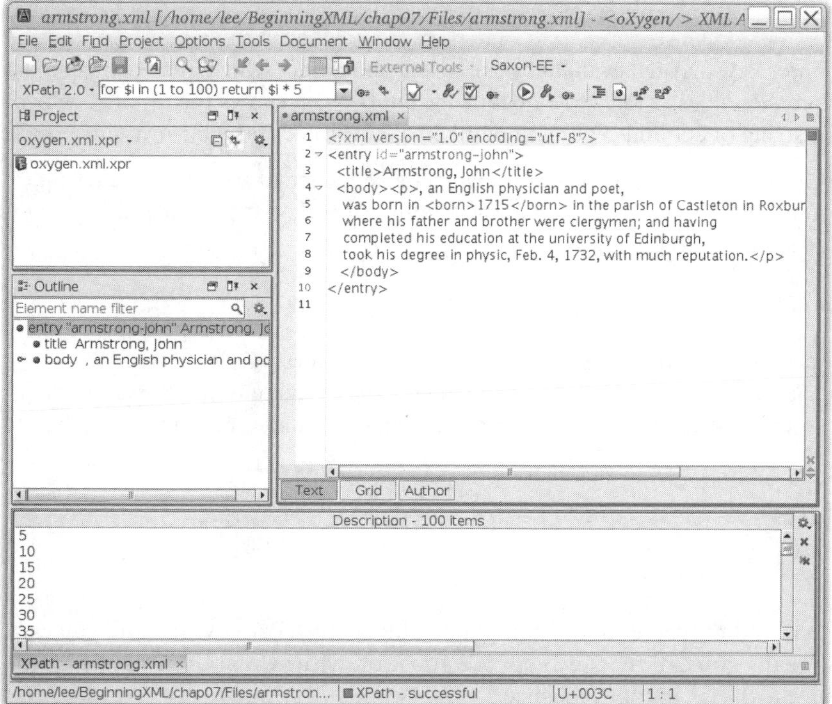

FIGURE 7-2

The `return` clause is evaluated once for each distinct value of `$i` and the result is a sequence.

You can also include multiple variables with a comma between them, like this:

```
for $lastname in (//person/name/last),
    $i in (1 to string-length($lastname))
return substring($lastname, 1, $i)
```

If you have a single `<last>` element containing `Smith`, this XPath expression generates `SSmSmiSmitSmith`.

Now you've seen some examples it's time to try something yourself. In the activity that follows, you'll learn how XPath expressions can return any sequence of values, and you'll experience XPath in action.

TRY IT OUT XPath for Expressions

In this Try It Out you generate a sequence of numbers separated by commas and spaces. You also learn about another way to explore XPath expressions and XML documents, using the oXygen XML editor, and also start to see how to join together, or "compose," XPath expressions.

1. Open the oXygen XML editor; you can use an XML document from one of the earlier chapters or the biography example `armstrong.xml` from Listing 7-1.
2. Because oXygen supports XPath 2, try a `for` expression. Type this into the XPath 2 box and press Enter:

    ```
    for $i in (1 to 20) return $i * 5
    ```

3. When you press the Enter key, oXygen evaluates the expression against whichever document you have loaded; your expression doesn't refer to a document, but oXygen shows the results one per line. It's not the single string of comma-separated numbers you wanted though, so you need to fix it.
4. The XPath function `string-join` takes two arguments—a sequence of strings and a string, respectively—and produces a single string as output. It sounds ideal, except that you're generating a sequence of numbers. You could try it anyway:

    ```
    string-join(for $i in (1 to 20) return $i * 5, ", ")
    ```

5. When you press the Enter key this time, oXygen gives you an error message, because `string-join` works on strings, not numbers. So now you need to convert the individual numbers in your sequence into strings, which will give you a sequence of strings! Change the entry in the box to be like this:

    ```
    string-join(for $i in (1 to 20) return string($i * 5), ", ")
    ```

How It Works

The key insight you need here is that wherever you can put a value in an XPath expression, you can put a whole expression. So really you call the `string-join` function with two arguments: a sequence, and a string to put between the things in that sequence.

The sequence will start out `("5", "10", "15", ...)`.

If you need more convincing, try just the following:

```
string-join(("apple", "orange", "banana"), "===")
```

This results in:

```
apple===orange===banana
```

You can explore more XPath expressions this way. If your expression selects part of the document, such as `//*[3]` to get all elements anywhere in the document (recall that the leading `//` searches the whole document) that are the third child of their parent element), you can click in the results list in oXygen to see the corresponding parts of the document.

XPath "let" Expressions

The syntax of a `let` expression is very simple; see the following:

```
let $v := 6 return $v + 1
```

As with the `for` expression, you can have more than one variable like so:

```
let $entry := //entry[@id = "galileo"],
    $born := $entry/@born, $died := $entry/@died
 return $died - $born
```

XPath "if" Expressions

Like many programming and query languages, XPath 2 introduced `if/then/else`. Unlike many other languages, though, the `else` is always required. See the following:

```
if (name() eq "entry") then "yes" else "no"
```

Note that you can't use `if-then-else` to guard against errors:

```
if (true()) then population/$i else population/0
```

This will likely raise a divide-by-zero error even though the "else" part is never used. The XPath 2 and XQuery languages were designed this way to give implementations as much power as possible to rewrite your expressions to make them go faster.

XPath "some" and "every" Expressions

XPath calls `some` and `every` *quantified expressions*; they are like the "implicit existential quantifier" that you learned about: the "=" operator. For example the following code could be read as "some node `$n2` whose value appears in `$list1` is equal to some other node `$n2` whose value appears in `$list2`."

```
$list1 = $list2
```

You could also write this as:

```
some $v in $list1 satisfies length(index-of($list2, $v)) ge 1
```

The "some . . . satisfies" expression returns true if the expression after "satisfies" is true, using the variable (or variables) you bind after the keyword, for at least one value in `$list1`.

Similarly, if you replace `some` by `every`, the expression returns true if the expression is true for every separate value in the list. Here is a longer example:

```
let $list := (1, 2, 3, 4, 5),
    $squares := (1, 4, 9, 25)
return
    every $i in $list satisfies ($i * $i) intersect $squares
```

The example makes use of *effective boolean value* — the expression intersecting a list with one item, the square of `$i`, with the list of squares will be true if it's not an empty set. The result of the whole XPath expression is false though because the value sixteen is missing from the list of squares.

These four expressions — `if-then-else`, `let-return`, `some-satisfies`, and `every-satisfies` — are all very useful in their place, and you should be aware of them in case you have to work with someone else's XPath expressions! The last two in particular, `some` and `every`, are often used simply because they were used as examples in the W3C XQuery 1.0 Use Cases document that you can find on `http://www.w3.org/TR/`.

XPath Cast and Type Expressions

XPath 2 added expressions that work on the XML Schema type of expressions and values: `instance of`, `cast`, `castable`, and `treat as`. In practice these may be useful when XPath is embedded in SQL expressions or when XPath is used inside XSLT and XQuery, but tend not to be useful when XPath is used alone because it's rare to have Schema-type information available outside of type-aware environments.

instance of

You can use instance of to determine if a value is in fact of a particular type. The following example will copy a `<sock>` element to its output, but will ignore anything else:

```
if ($input instance of element(sock))
then $input
else ()
```

cast

Sometimes you need to convert a value from one type to another. The way you do this is usually with a `cast`, although in some more complex cases, especially for complex user-defined types, you may end up writing a function to do it instead. You can only cast to *atomic* types, not elements, and, unlike in languages like C++, casting can affect the value. For example, you could cast an attribute to an integer in order to pass its value to a function expecting numbers. In the following snippet, if you tried to compare `@born` to 1700 directly, you'd get a type error unless the XPath engine knew that `@born` attribute held an integer, perhaps because of some XML Schema *validation episode* that had already happened:

```
//entry[(@born cast as xs:integer) gt 1700]
```

castable

In XPath 2 there's no way to catch errors, so if a cast fails you end up with no results. The `castable` expression lets you do the cast only if it is going to work:

```
if ($entry/@born castable as xs:integer)
then $entry/@born cast as xs:integer
else 42
```

> **NOTE** *Optimization rules enable the XPath processor to evaluate the* `then` *and* `else` *parts of* `if-then-else` *expressions in either order, even before the test, but any dynamic errors in the branch not used are silently ignored.*

treat as

The `treat as` expression is used as a sort of assertion: `A treat as T` says that the XPath compiler is to behave as if A really does have type T, and allows you to write anything that you could write in that case. If, at runtime, A does *not* have type T, the XPath processor will raise an error. Normally XPath is actually interpreted rather than compiled, and the compiler part is called *static analysis;* this is done before evaluating expressions to make sure there are no type errors. The difference between `cast` and `treat as` is that cast affects the dynamic type of the value that is actually supplied, and maybe even changes it, whereas `treat as` does not change the value and will raise a runtime error if the value does not have the right type, but will allow you to write expressions like `math:sqrt($x treat as xs:double)`.

XPath Functions

A *function* in mathematics is way of giving a name to a calculation; in XPath, functions work in much the same way. A function is said to take *arguments*, also called *parameters*, meaning that they have input; the output is called the *result* of the function.

For example, `string-length("Jerusalem")` is a call to the function `string-length` with argument `"Jerusalem"`, and the result is, of course, 9. Like most computer languages XPath includes quite a few predefined functions. XPath 2 added considerably to their number, and XPath 3 will add even more. Most of the new functions since XPath 1 come from one of two sources: first, from handling XML Schema types, since that ability was added for XPath 2; second, because users wanted them and showed a compelling reason to add them, often on the W3C public "bugzilla" tracking system, and sometimes by asking their vendor or implementer to add a feature.

WARNING *Not everything that looks like a name followed by parentheses is a function in XPath! You have already seen some node tests like* `text()` *and* `comment()`*, and those are not functions; you also have sequences like (*`a, b,` *c).*

There's a complete list of the XPath functions in Appendix B at the back of this book, along with a list of the W3C XML Schema types. This section looks at a few of the functions to give you a feel for some of the things you can do.

Document Handling

The `doc()` and `document()` functions read an external XML document and return the document node, through which you can access the rest of the document. The document must, of course, parse as well-formed XML.

NOTE *The* `document()` *function belongs to XSLT 1.0 rather than XPath, and is slightly more complex than the* `doc()` *function. You should use* `doc()` *with XPath 2 or later, but you may still see* `document()` *in older XSLT style sheets.*

Take Listing 7-3, which contains extra information about people in the biography, such as this:

Available for download on Wrox.com

LISTING 7-3: extra.xml

```
<?xml version="1.0" encoding="utf-8"?>
<people>
  <person id="armstrong-john">
    <p>W. J. Maloney's 1954 book
    "George and John Armstrong of Castleton,
     2 Eighteenth-Century Medical Pioneers"
     was reviewed by Dr. Jerome M Schneck.</p>
  </person>
  <person id="newton-sir-isaac">
    <p>Invented the apple pie.</p>
  </person>
</people>
```

Now you could use XPath to extract the names of people who are in both the biography and the extra file like so:

```
/entry[@id = doc("extra.xml")//person/@id]/title
```

If you try this in oXygen with the `armstrong.xml` (Listing 7-1) file open, and with `extra.xml` (Listing 7-3) in the same folder as `armstrong.xml`, you will find the result shown is Armstrong, John.

You won't be able to try this example with *xmllint* or other XPath 1 programs, because XPath 1 didn't have a function to load a file; it came from XSLT.

String-Handling Functions

People do a lot of string-handling in XPath, especially from XSLT or XQuery. String functions include `substring()`, `substring-before()`, `substring-after()`, `translate()`, `matches()`, `replace()`, `concat()`, `string-length()`, and more. See Appendix B, "Xpath Functions" for a full list.

It's worth learning about `substring-before()` and `substring-after()` because they're a little unusual. The call `substring-before("abcdefcdef", "cd")` returns `ab`, and `substring-after("abcdefcdef", "cd")` returns `efcdef`. In other words, the functions search the string you give, and look for the *first* occurrence of the second argument (`"cd"` in this example). Then they return either everything *before* that first occurrence or everything after it.

The `matches()` and `replace()` functions use regular expressions. They were introduced in XPath 2, although you can find implementations for XSLT 1 at `www.exslt.org`. Regular expressions, also called patterns, are extremely useful for anyone working extensively with text, and if that's your situation, it's worth using an XSLT 2 or XPath 2 processor such as Saxon just for that single feature.

Numeric Functions

XPath 1 includes only a very few numeric functions: `sum()`, `floor()`, `ceiling()`, `round()`, and, to construct a number from a string, `number()`. There were also some named operators such as `div`, `idiv`, and `mod`.

XPath 2 adds `abs()`, `round-half-to-even()`, and trigonometric and logarithmic functions such as `sin()`, `sqrt()`, and so forth.

The XPath 3 draft adds `format-number()`.

One reason to add the trigonometric functions to XPath was that people are now using XSLT and XQuery to generate graphics using SVG. You will learn more about SVG in Chapter 18, "Scalable Vector Graphics (SVG)".

Defining Your Own Functions

You can define your own functions for use in XPath expression in two ways. The first, starting in XPath 3, is by using *inline functions* like so:

```
let $addTax := function($a as xs:double) {
    $a * 1.13
} return $addTax(/invoice/amounts/total)
```

Inline functions are mainly useful with XQuery and XSLT; if you're using XPath from a traditional programming language, you're more likely to want to do that processing in the parent language. However, inline functions in XPath 3 can help to simplify large and complex XPath expressions.

The second way to define your own function is to write (or call) an *external function*. For example, if you are using the Saxon XSLT engine, which is written in Java, you can call out to functions that are implemented in XSLT (the host language) as well as to external functions written in Java. They're called *external* because they're outside not only XPath, but also the language (in this case XSLT) that is using XPath. Chapter 8 returns to this topic and gives you examples of defining functions.

In XPath 3 you can also refer to functions using *function items*. A function item is the name of a function (complete with namespace prefix if needed) followed by a hash (#) and the number of arguments. For example you could use `fn:round#1` because `round()` has only one argument. If you define a variable to contain a function item you can use the variable like the function. For example, the following expression returns the value 4:

```
let $r := round#1 return $r(3.5)
```

XPath Set Operations

XPath node lists are not really sets: every time you do a step, they are sorted into document order and duplicate nodes are eliminated. But it's still useful to do set-like operations on them.

Suppose `$a` and `$b` are two unimaginatively named node lists. Table 7-5 shows some set-like operations you can do using XPath 1, XPath 2, or later.

TABLE 7-5: XPath Set-like Operations

OPERATION	XPATH EXPRESSION
. occurs within `$a`	`count($a|.) = count($a)`

All nodes in `$a` or `$b`	`$a|$b`
	or, in Xpath 2 or later,
	`$a union $b`

Only nodes in both `$a` and `$b`	`$a[count(.|$b) = count($b)]`
	or, in XPath 2 or later,
	`$a intersect $b`

Nodes in `$a` but not in `$b`	`$a[not(count(.|$b) = count($b)]`
	or, in XPath 2 or later,
	`$a except $b`

XPath and Namespaces

One of the most common questions people ask when they start to use XPath is "why doesn't my XPath expression match anything?"

By far the most common reason is that the elements in the document have an associated XML namespace, and the XPath expression don't account for this.

XPath does not give a complete way to handle namespaces itself: you need the cooperation of the host language. You have to *bind* (connect) a prefix string that you choose to the *exact* same URI, byte for byte, that's in the document.

Take a look at Listing 7-4 for an example:

Available for download on Wrox.com

LISTING 7-4: tiny.html

```
<?xml version="1.0" encoding="UTF-8"?>

<!DOCTYPE html PUBLIC "-//W3C//DTD XHTML 1.0 Transitional//EN"
"http://www.w3.org/TR/xhtml1/DTD/xhtml1-transitional.dtd">

<html xmlns="http://www.w3.org/1999/xhtml">

  <head>
    <title>This is not a title</title>
  </head>
  <body>
    <h1>No h1 here</h1>
    <p>No p here</p>
  </body>
</html>
```

You might think (as most people do at first) that you could extract the title of this document like this:

```
/html/head/title
```

But if you try this you'll discover it doesn't work. Recall that a namespace URI is actually a part of the element's name in XML. So there's no element called `"title"` in this document. Instead, there's one whose namespace URI is that of XHTML and whose *local name* is `"title"`.

The following will work but is cumbersome:

```
/*[local-name() = "html"]/*[local-name() = "head"]/*[local-name() = "title"]
```

Strictly speaking, you should also test `namespace-uri()` in each of those predicates too, in case there are elements from some other namespace in the document with the same local names, but it's already too complicated to work with. Use this approach only as a last resort.

The preferred way to use XPath in documents with namespaces is to bind a prefix to the document's namespace and use that. For example, in PHP you might do something like this:

```
$sxe = new SimpleXMLElement($html);


$sxe->registerXPathNamespace('h', 'http://www.w3.org/1999/xhtml');
$result = $sxe->xpath('/h:html/h:body/h:title');

foreach ($result as $title) {

  echo $title . "\n";

}
```

The loop at the end is because XPath returns a node list, although in this case of course you'll only get one item back.

WARNING *You can use any prefix you like, because it's the namespace URI that matters, but the URI you use must be character-for-character, byte-for-byte identical to the one in the document. If the URI in the document has an escape, like* `%7e` *for a tilde, then yours must use the same escape in the same place, and* `%7e` *and* `%7E` *would not be the same!*

The same sort of technique works in most other languages, including Java, JavaScript, Perl, Python, Ruby, C, C++, Scala, and so forth. XSLT and XQuery also provide ways to work with XML namespaces, as you'll learn in Chapters 8 and 9.

SUMMARY

- XML is often stored in memory in a tree structure like DOM.
- XPath is a terse, powerful way to refer to parts of an XML document.
- XPath works on trees, including both DOM and XDM; not on tags.
- XPath uses node tests, predicates, and steps.
- XPath works with W3C XML Schema types as well as with plain untyped XML.
- XPath provides the foundation for XSLT and XQuery, and is also available in most programming languages.
- XPath cannot change the document, and cannot return elements that are not part of the document; to do those things you need a language such as XSLT, the subject of the next chapter.

EXERCISES

You can find answers to these exercises in Appendix A.

1. Write an XPath expression to find all `<entry>` elements (anywhere in the input document) having a `born` element anywhere inside them.
2. What does the XPath expression `/html/body//div[1]` return?
3. Write an XPath expression to find all `<div>` elements (anywhere in the input document) that do not have an `id` attribute.

▶ WHAT YOU LEARNED IN THIS CHAPTER

TOPIC	KEY POINTS
How XML is stored in memory	XML is usually stored in trees, using DOM, XDM, or some other data model.
What is XPath?	XPath is an expression language used primarily for finding items in XML trees.
Is XPath a programming language?	Although XPath is a complete language, it is designed to be "hosted" in another environment, such as XSLT, a Web browser, Query, or Java.
XPath and Namespaces	You generally have to bind a prefix to a namespace URI outside of XPath and use expressions like `/h:html/h:body/h:div` to match elements with an associated namespace.
Can XPath change the document, or return elements without their children, or make new elements?	No. Use XQuery or XSLT for that.
When should I program with the DOM?	The DOM API is low-level; use XPath, XQuery, or XSLT in preference to direct access of the DOM.

8

XSLT

WHAT YOU WILL LEARN IN THIS CHAPTER:

- What XSLT is used for
- How writing XSLT code is different than writing code in traditional languages
- The basic XSLT constructs
- How XSLT uses XPath
- The more advanced XSLT constructs
- XSLT 2.0 improvements
- The future of XSLT

XSLT stands for Extensible Stylesheet Language Transformations and is one of the big success stories among the various XML technologies. In this chapter you'll find out why there is constant need for transformations from one XML format to another, or from an XML format to a plain text document. You will see how XSLT, as a declarative language (you tell it what you want done in a specific circumstance and you let the XSLT processor decide how it should be done), differs from the majority of common coding languages such as Java and C# because they are procedural (essentially a series of low-level instructions on how to manipulate data). You'll then be introduced to the mainstay of XSLT, the *template*, and see how judicious use of this makes processing XML simpler than having to provide detailed instructions. You will also see how XSLT is a functional language where results are defined as the result of function calls, rather than data being directly manipulated. Programming with declarative, functional languages can take some getting used to; it needs a different mindset from that used in procedural code, and this puts off many people when they start with XSLT. You shouldn't fall into that group because the examples shown in this chapter will make you appreciate the simplicity and power that XSLT possesses. You'll also see how XPath integrates closely with XSLT; it pops up in a number of places so what you learned in Chapter 7 will be invaluable. After demonstrating a number of basic techniques you'll take a look at version 2.0 of XSLT and see how its new features have been designed to cope with many day-to-day problems that people have struggled with in version 1.0. The chapter concludes with a brief look at what's scheduled to appear in version 3.0, which promises to make XSLT an extremely powerful functional language, along the lines of Haskell, Lisp, or F#.

WHAT XSLT IS USED FOR

At its heart, XSLT has a simple use case: to take an existing XML document and transform it to a different format. The new format might be XML, HTML, or just plain text, such as a comma-separated values (CSV) file. This is an extremely common scenario. One of the main reasons for XML is to have a facility to store data in a presentation- and application-neutral format so that it can easily be reused. XSLT is used in two common situations:

- To convert from XML into a presentation-specific format, such as HTML.
- To convert from the format understood by one application into the structure required by another. This is particularly common when exchanging data between different organizations.

Since XSLT was originally conceived it has grown and now has the ability to process non-XML files too, so you can take a plain text file and transform it into XML or any other format.

NOTE *Two technologies come under the umbrella of XSL: XSLT, dealt with in this chapter, and XSL-FO (the FO stands for Formatting Objects). XSL-FO is a technique that enables you to define the layout, structure, and general format of content designed to be published; for example, an article or book that will be issued in electronic format, perhaps as a PDF, or printed in a traditional way. You can find out more about XSL-FO at* `www.w3.org/standards/xml/publishing`.

XSLT differs from many mainstream programming languages such as C# or Java in two main ways. First, XSLT is a *declarative* language, and second, it is a *functional* language.

XSLT as a Declarative Language

Most mainstream programming languages are considered procedural. Data is fed to the software, which then manipulates it step-by-step. Each code statement or block generally has a clearly defined task which is responsible for minor changes to the data; these individual changes are combined to produce the overall data transformation required. Take a typical example: you have a collection of `Author` objects, each of which has a `FirstName` and a `LastName` property. You are asked to display the full name of each `Author` in the collection. The `Author` collection is zero-based so the first `Author` has an index of zero and the last has an index of one less than the total number of

Author objects. Your code will probably look something like this (this code is not written in any particular language but uses the C#/Java style):

```
int index;
for (index = 0; index < allAuthors.Count; index++)
{
  Author thisAuthor = allAuthors[index];
  Console.WriteLine(thisAuthor.FirstName + " " + thisAuthor.LastName);
}
```

This is a standard piece of coding. You loop through all the authors by using an index that is gradually incremented from zero to the number of Author objects minus one. At each pass through the loop, you assign the current Author to a variable, thisAuthor, and then access the two properties you are interested in, FirstName and LastName. Now, this is fairly low-level coding; you have to determine the total number of Author objects using the Count property and keep track of which Author you are processing using an index. Many languages let you write this code at a more declarative level, where it's not necessary to keep track of these things. In C#, for example, you can use the foreach construct:

```
foreach (Author thisAuthor in allAuthors)
{
  Console.WriteLine(thisAuthor.FirstName + " " + thisAuthor.LastName);
}
```

This is more declarative code. You're not worried about keeping track of the individual Author objects—you just ask for each Author, one by one, and display its details. Another example of declarative programming is SQL, used to query relational databases. In SQL, if you wanted to see the names of all the authors in a table you'd use something like this:

```
SELECT FirstName, LastName FROM Authors;
```

Again, in this code, you don't need to keep track of the individual rows in the Authors table. You let the database query engine worry about the low-level operations.

XSLT takes this idea of letting the processor look after the low-level details one stage further. It is designed from the ground up as a declarative language, so you needn't concern yourself with how something is done. Rather, you concentrate on describing what you want done. For example, if you want to perform a similar operation to output all author names from an XML document containing many <author> elements, such as this one:

```
<authors>
  <author>
    <firstName>Danny</firstName>
    <lastName>Ayers</lastName>
  </author>
  <author>
    <firstName>Joe</firstName>
    <lastName>Fawcett</lastName>
  </author>
  <author>
    <firstName>William</firstName>
```

```
    <lastName>Shakespeare</lastName>
  </author>
</authors>
```

you'd use an XSLT template such as:

```
<xsl:template match="author" />
  <xsl:value-of select="firstName" /> <xsl:value-of select="lastName" />
</xsl:template>
```

As you can see, you haven't had to declare a variable to keep track of the `<author>` elements or write any code that loops through them. You just tell the XSLT processor to output the value of the `<firstName>` and the `<lastName>` element whenever you come across an `<author>` element. You'll learn more about how this all works when you've dealt with another aspect of XSLT programming—the fact that it's a *functional* language.

How Is XSLT a Functional Language?

If you've grown up with languages such as Java, C++, C#, PHP, or others, you've used what are known as *imperative* programming languages; imperative literally means that you order the computer exactly what you want it to do. Imperative languages tend to manipulate the state of an object to represent changes of circumstance. To stick with the current example, if an author changed his last name, the standard paradigm to reflect this in code would be to get a reference to an `Author` object representing the particular person and modify the `LastName` property. The pseudo-code for this would look like:

```
Author authorToEdit = getAuthor(12345); //Get the required author using their ID
authorToEdit.LastName = "Marlowe"; //Change last name
```

A functional language takes a different approach. The output is considered the result of one or more functions applied to the input. In a strict functional language you cannot change the value of a variable, nor have any functions that have side effects, such as incrementing a counter while reading a value. XSLT follows this pattern, the main advantage of which is that often the order of execution of a complete transformation is irrelevant, leaving the processor free to optimize the proceedings. The main downside to functional programming is that it takes some getting used to at first. You are likely far too accustomed to be able to re-assign values to variables, rely on the order of your code to determine the order of operations, and have functions that have global side effects. However, once you get the hang of the functional way of doing things you'll find that tasks such as testing become much easier and also that making changes to any particular piece of code is much less likely to break something elsewhere.

SETTING UP YOUR XSLT DEVELOPMENT ENVIRONMENT

Before you start to run any XSLT code, you need to set up an environment to write and process your transformations. The Saxon processor runs the examples in this chapter for three reasons:

- It's the acknowledged leader in its field with the most up-to-date implementation of XSLT.
- It's free to use (although commercial versions have more features).
- It has both a Java and a .NET version, making it suitable to run on nearly all environments.

The version used for this chapter is 9.3HE (home edition), which you can download from `http://saxon.sourceforge.net/`. As stated before, you can choose to use the .NET or the Java version. If you're running a machine with .NET installed, this version is slightly easier to use but it's really a personal preference.

To begin set-up, create a folder called `saxon` on your C Drive and download the .NET or Java version of the zip file to:

```
C:\saxon
```

Once the zip file has downloaded you will need to take a few further steps, which differ slightly depending on whether you are going to run the .NET version or the Java one. The following sections cover each scenario.

Setting Up Saxon for .NET

Running the Saxon for .NET installation should add the path to the Saxon executables to your machine's PATH environment variable. It's worth checking, however, because sometimes security settings prevent this from happening. The advantage of having the Saxon in your PATH is that you won't have to type the full path to the executable each time you want to run a transformation from the command line.

How to change the PATH environment variable depends slightly on which version of Windows you are running. For Windows 7:

1. Right-click My Computer and choose Properties.
2. Then choose Advanced System Settings from the left-hand menu and click the Environment Variables button toward the bottom of the tab that is shown.
3. Click Path in the upper panel and then click the Edit button.
4. If necessary, add the path to the Saxon bin folder, preceded by a semicolon if there's not one there already. For example, on my machine I needed to add `;c:\Program Files\Saxonica\SaxonHE9.3N\bin`. Then click OK on each of the three dialog boxes.

You can now test whether everything is working as expected by opening a command window (Start ➪ Run, type in **cmd**, and press Enter). When the command window appears type **`Transform -?`** and press Enter. You should see some information regarding Saxon and a miniature help screen. If you don't get this screen, check that you are on the correct drive where Saxon is installed—if it's on the C: drive, type **C:** and press Enter. If you are on the correct drive and still don't get the help screen, double-check that the PATH environment variable is set correctly. That's all you need to do to enable command-line transformations. If you need more help with the installation there is a full online guide at `www.saxonica.com/documentation/about/installationdotnet.xml`.

NOTE *Another option to actually run the transformations is Kernow, available from* `http://kernowforsaxon.sourceforge.net/`. *This provides a graphical user interface on top of Saxon.*

Setting Up Saxon for Java

If you want to run the Java version of Saxon you need a Java Virtual Machine (JVM) installed. You can find out if this is the case by opening a command window, as described previously, and typing:

```
java -version
```

If Java is installed, you'll see something like this:

```
java version "1.6.0_23"
Java(TM) SE Runtime Environment (build 1.6.0_23-b05)
Java HotSpot(TM) 64-Bit Server VM (build 19.0-b09, mixed mode)
```

Otherwise you'll see this:

```
'java' is not recognized as an internal or external command,
operable program or batch file.
```

If the latter happens, you can download the required files from `www.oracle.com/technetwork/java/javase/downloads/index.html`. If you just want to perform command-line transformations, download and install the JVM (or JRE as it is referred to on the download site); otherwise, if you want to use Saxon programmatically, i.e. calling it from within code rather than from the command line, download the full Java SDK. To run the examples in this chapter you'll only need the JVM, not the full JDK. You'll also need to add the Saxon jar file to your machine's CLASSPATH variable.

Adding Saxon to your CLASSPATH environment variable for Windows is much the same process as editing the PATH environment variable. Follow the initial steps but look for a variable named CLASSPATH. This might be in the upper panel, as was PATH, or in the lower panel with the system environment variables. If it's not there, click the New button in the upper panel and add the variable name, CLASSPATH, and the path to the Saxon jar, such as `<installation path>/saxon9he.jar`.

You should now be able to test whether everything is set up by opening a command window (Start ➪ Run ➪ CMD [Enter]) and typing:

```
java net.sf.saxon.Transform -?
```

You should see a mini help screen detailing various Saxon options. If this doesn't happen, double-check that the CLASSPATH environment variable is set correctly. If you need more help with the installation, there is a full online guide at `www.saxonica.com/documentation/about/installationjava.xml`. That completes the set up needed for both the .NET and the Java versions.

WHICH XSLT EDITOR TO USE?

XSL transformations are themselves XML documents, so to create them you can use anything from a simple text editor such as Notepad or Vim to a fully-fledged XML designer such as Altova's XML Spy, jEdit or the <oXygen/> editor. At the time of writing, both of these products have trial versions available that are suitable for trying out the examples in this chapter. They also have the facility to run transformations from within the development environment, although you'll have to configure them to use Saxon as their XSLT processor.

Next, you look at the basic elements used in XSLT and how they are combined to produce both simple and sophisticated transformations.

FOUNDATIONAL XSLT ELEMENTS

XSLT is based on the idea of templates. The basic concept is that you specify a number of templates that each match XML in the source document. When the matching XML is found, the template is activated and its contents are added to the output document. For example, you may have a template that matches a `<Person>` element. For each `<Person>` element encountered in the source document the corresponding template will be activated. Any code inside the template will be executed and added to the output. The code within the templates can be complex and has full access to the item that was matched and caused the template to run as well as other information about the input document.

Using templates to process various parts of the source document in this manner is one of the most powerful features of XSLT and one that you'll be exploring in this section. Initially you'll be introduced to the following basic XSLT constructs that enable you to write basic transformations:

- `<xsl:stylesheet>`: This is the all-encompassing document element used to hold all your templates. You also use it for some configuration, such as setting which version of XSLT you want to use.
- `<xsl:template>`: This is the bedrock of XSLT and has two main features. It details what items from the source document it should handle and uses its content to specify what should be added to the output when it is executed.
- `<xsl:apply-templates>`: This element is responsible for deciding which items in the source document should be processed; they are then handled by the appropriate template.
- `<xsl:value-of>`: This element is used to evaluate an expression and add the result to the output. For example, you may be processing a `<Person>` element and use `<xsl:value-of>` to add the contents of its `<Name>` element to the output.
- `<xsl:for-each>`: Occasionally you need to process a number of items in a similar fashion but using an `<xsl:template>` isn't a good option. In that case you can use this element to group the items and produce output based on each one.

Before you start learning about these templates, you are going to need an XML input document for your transformations. Listing 8-1 is a fairly simple document that details some famous politicians.

LISTING 8-1: People.xml

```
<People>
  <Person bornDate="1874-11-30" diedDate="1965-01-24">
    <Name>Winston Churchill</Name>
    <Description>
      Winston Churchill was a mid-20th century British politician who
      became famous as Prime Minister during the Second World War.
    </Description>
  </Person>
  <Person bornDate="1917-11-19" diedDate="1984-10-31">
    <Name>Indira Gandhi</Name>
    <Description>
      Indira Gandhi was India's first female prime minister and was
      assassinated in 1984.
    </Description>
  </Person>
  <Person bornDate="1917-05-29" diedDate="1963-11-22">
    <Name>John F. Kennedy</Name>
    <Description>
      JFK, as he was affectionately known, was a United States president
      who was assassinated in Dallas, Texas.
    </Description>
  </Person>
</People>
```

The style of this XML, mixing attributes and elements in the way it does, is probably not the best, but it's typical of files that you'll have to deal with and demonstrates the different techniques needed to deal with these items. Your first XSLT concentrates on a common use case: transforming the XML into an HTML page.

NOTE *The current version of XSLT is 2.0, but few processors other than Saxon completely support this version. Therefore the first examples you'll see stick to version 1.0. Later in the chapter you'll move on to the new features in version 2.0. Unfortunately, Microsoft has abandoned attempts to produce a version 2.0 for .NET so if you need the extra facilities in a .NET environment you have little choice but Saxon.*

The <xsl:stylesheet> Element

Listing 8-2 shows the basic shell used by all XSL transformations.

LISTING 8-2: Shell.xslt

Available for download on Wrox.com

```
<xsl:stylesheet version="1.0" xmlns:xsl="http://www.w3.org/1999/XSL/Transform">
  <!-- rest of XSLT here -->
</xsl:stylesheet>
```

NOTE *XSLT has something quite unusual in regards to its schema; you have a choice of document elements—either* `<xsl:transform>` *or* `<xsl:stylesheet>`*. The reason for this is that in its early days the W3C committee was torn between the two aspects of the technology: transforming from one format to another or creating a presentation-specific format, such as HTML. This latter process was considered something akin to using cascading style sheets (CSS) to alter a web page's appearance. Although it's legal to use either element at the start of your XSLT,* `<xsl:stylesheet>` *is favored most in the XML community.*

An analysis of this file shows that the XSLT elements are in the `http://www.w3.org/1999/XSL/Transform` namespace. The second point is that the version number is declared as 1.0. Although Saxon is a version 2.0 processor it will run files marked as version 1.0 in backward-compatibility mode. This namespace URI doesn't change between the two versions, so to change the version you'd just need change this attribute.

NOTE *The* `<xsl:stylesheet>` *element doesn't have many attributes but one useful one that can appear is* `exclude-result-prefixes`*. You use this attribute to prevent unnecessary namespace URIs appearing in your output. You will see this attribute being used a few times in some of the examples in this chapter.*

Although Listing 8-2 is a legal style sheet, it doesn't actually do anything very useful. (It will produce some output if run against your example XML, but you'll see why this is after you've covered the other basic elements.)

To actually create a new output you need to do two things: you have to select some elements or attributes to process; and you need to describe the output required based on these items. The element used to describe what output to create is the `<xsl:template>` instruction.

The <xsl:template> Element

The `<xsl:template>` element is a cornerstone of the entire technology, so understanding how it works is key to the entire process. If you add an `<xsl:template>` element to your example transformation you get Listing 8-3.

LISTING 8-3: PeopleToHtml-Basic.xslt

Available for download on Wrox.com

```
<xsl:stylesheet version="1.0" xmlns:xsl="http://www.w3.org/1999/XSL/Transform">

  <xsl:template match="/">
    <!-- basic output here -->
  </xsl:template>
</xsl:stylesheet>
```

This instruction, as it's known in XSLT terminology, essentially says to the processor: *Execute the code in this template whenever you meet an item that matches those specified in my match attribute.* Because the `match` attribute specifies `/` as its value, the template is called when the root node is encountered by the XSLT processor.

XSL PATTERN

The `match` attribute in Listing 8-3 (as well as a small number of other attributes in XSLT) uses a similar syntax to XPath, which was described in Chapter 7. This syntax is actually called *XSL Pattern* and is a subset of XPath. The main difference is that XSL Pattern has access to a much more limited number of axes, namely the forward-looking, `child` and `attribute`, rather than ones such as `preceding-sibling`. For the full specification see `www.w3.org/TR/xslt#patterns`.

The contents of the template are then evaluated using the root element as the *context*. In XSLT the term context has a very specific meaning as most XPath expressions are evaluated relative to the context.

NOTE *In Listing 8-3 there is no direct inner textual content, other than a comment, so nothing will be added to the output.*

What Exactly Is Meant by Context?

Context has a specific meaning when it comes to XSLT. Nearly all processing is executed in the context of a particular item, or node as they are termed in XSLT, of the document. In Listing 8-3 the root is the context node. This means that any requests for data that use XPath are made relative to the root node. Take the following XPath in relation to the Listing 8-1 document shown previously:

```
People/Person
```

This XPath, executed in the context of the root node, will bring back three elements named `<Person>`. This is because you are starting at the root, then moving one level down, along the child axis, to the <People> element, and then, following the child axis once more, to reach the <Person> elements. If you change the XPath to read

```
Person
```

and then execute this in the context of the root node, you'll find that no elements are returned. This is because if you start at the root node and move one step along the child axis there are no <Person> elements. For this XPath to succeed you'd need to execute it in the context of the <People> element. You'll be meeting the concept of context many times in this chapter; so remember that within an XSL transformation the context will determine the starting point of any relative XPath statements that occur.

You now need to see how you can add some output to the <xsl:template> element.

Adding Output to a Template

Adding output to an <xsl:template> element is easy. Anything appearing between the start tag and the end tag will be sent to the *result tree*, the technical term for the output from a transformation. You'll start by using your template to create an HTML shell as shown in Listing 8-4

Available for download on Wrox.com

LISTING 8-4: PeopleToHtml-BasicStructure.xslt

```
<xsl:stylesheet version="1.0"
 xmlns:xsl="http://www.w3.org/1999/XSL/Transform">
  <xsl:template match="/">
    <html>
      <head>
        <title>Famous People</title>
      </head>
      <body>
        <h1>Famous People</h1>
        <hr />
      </body>
    </html>
  </xsl:template>
</xsl:stylesheet>
```

You've now added some basic HTML elements to the template; note that because an XSLT document is XML, the contents must be well-formed. This means that you have to use constructs such as <hr /> rather than just <hr>. XSLT processors have the special rules about HTML embedded in them, so they'll automatically output these elements correctly if they can recognize that you're creating an HTML file.

You can now try to run this transformation, just to see if everything's working as expected. Open a command window and navigate to the folder where the People.xml and PeopleToHtml-BasicStructure.xslt files (from Listings 8-3 and 8-4) are located. If you're using the Java version, type the following line before pressing Enter (this command needs to be all on one line):

```
java net.sf.saxon.Transform -s:People.xml
               -xsl:PeopleToHtml-BasicStructure.xslt -o:People-BasicStructure.html
```

If you are using the .NET version use the following command:

```
Transform -s:People.xml -xsl:PeopleToHtml-BasicStructure.xslt
 -o:People- BasicStructure.html
```

The command options used in these transformation examples are:

- `-s`: The source document, that is, the XML you want to transform.
- `-xsl`: The path to the XSL transform.
- `-o`: The name of the output file you want to create. It can be left blank if you want the results to be displayed in the console.

Once you run this transformation, you should see that a new file, `People-BasicStructure.html`, has been created in the same directory as the XML and XSLT. This is shown in Listing 8-5.

Available for download on Wrox.com

LISTING 8-5: People-BasicStructure.html

```
<html>
  <head>
    <META http-equiv="Content-Type" content="text/html; charset=utf-8">
    <title>Famous People</title>
  </head>
  <body>
    <h1>Famous People</h1>
    <hr>
  </body>
</html>
```

You can see that the basics of an HTML page have been created, along with a `<META>` element to declare the content type. You now need to include some of the information from Listing 8-1. As a first step you'll just output their names using a bulleted list. To do this, first you need to create a new template to process the individual `<Person>` elements and add this to the transformation as shown in Listing 8-6.

Available for download on Wrox.com

LISTING 8-6: PeopleToHtml-PersonTemplate.xslt

```
<xsl:stylesheet version="1.0"
      xmlns:xsl="http://www.w3.org/1999/XSL/Transform">
  <xsl:template match="/">
    <html>
      <head>
        <title>Famous People</title>
      </head>
      <body>
        <h1>Famous People</h1>
        <hr />
      </body>
    </html>
  </xsl:template>
```

```
  <xsl:template match="Person">
    <li><!-- Person details here --></li>
  </xsl:template>
</xsl:stylesheet>
```

Next, you need to instruct the transform to actually process these elements, and for this you'll need a new instruction.

The <xsl:apply-templates> Element

The `<xsl:apply-templates>` element uses a `select` attribute to choose which nodes to process. The processor then searches the XSLT for an `<xsl:template>` element that has a `match` attribute that matches those nodes. To instruct the XSLT engine to process the `<Person>` elements add the `<xsl:apply-templates>` instruction to your transformation code and put it inside HTML unordered list tags (`<ul>`), as shown in Listing 8-7.

Available for download on Wrox.com

LISTING 8-7: PeopleToHtml-ProcessPerson.xslt

```
<xsl:stylesheet version="1.0"
            xmlns:xsl="http://www.w3.org/1999/XSL/Transform">
  <xsl:template match="/">
    <html>
      <head>
        <title>Famous People</title>
      </head>
      <body>
        <h1>Famous People</h1>
        <hr />
        <ul>
          <xsl:apply-templates select="People/Person" />
        </ul>
      </body>
    </html>
  </xsl:template>

  <xsl:template match="Person">
    <li><!-- Person details here --></li>
  </xsl:template>
</xsl:stylesheet>
```

You can see that you used the XPath mentioned earlier, `People/Person`, to choose the nodes you want to display. This will select the three `<Person>` elements and pass them to the template that matches them.

Finally, you'll need to extract some data—in this case, the first and last names—from the `<Person>` elements. You have a number of ways to extract information from nodes in an XML document; when it's simply textual content the normal choice is to use `<xsl:value-of>`.

The <xsl:value-of> Element

The `<xsl:value-of>` element is very simple to use. It has an attribute, named `select`, which takes an XPath to the node you need. If you specify an element as the target you get all the text within that element; if you specify an attribute you get the value of the attribute as a string. Because you are inside the template that matches the `<Person>` element, this is the current context; therefore, the XPath you need is just `Name`. You wrap this inside a list item as shown in Listing 8-8.

Available for download on Wrox.com

LISTING 8-8: PeopleToHtml-PersonName.xslt

```
<?xml version="1.0" encoding="utf-8"?>
<xsl:stylesheet version="1.0" xmlns:xsl="http://www.w3.org/1999/XSL/Transform">

  <xsl:template match="/">
    <html>
      <head>
        <title>Famous People</title>
      </head>
      <body>
        <h1>Famous People</h1>
        <hr />
        <ul>
          <xsl:apply-templates select="People/Person" />
        </ul>
      </body>
    </html>
  </xsl:template>

  <xsl:template match="Person">
    <li>
      <xsl:value-of select="Name" />
    </li>
  </xsl:template>
</xsl:stylesheet>
```

Now run one of the following command lines (the first is for Java, the second for .NET):

```
java net.sf.saxon.Transform -s:People.xml
 -xsl:PeopleToHtml-PersonName.xslt -o:People-PersonName.html
```

or:

```
Transform -s:People.xml -xsl:PeopleToHtml-PersonName.xslt -o:People-PersonName.html
```

The output created will now look like Listing 8-9.

Available for download on Wrox.com

LISTING 8-9: People-PersonName.html

```
<html>
  <head>
    <META http-equiv="Content-Type" content="text/html; charset=utf-8">
    <title>Famous People</title>
  </head>
  <body>
```

```
      <h1>Famous People</h1>
      <hr>
      <ul>
        <li>Winston Churchill</li>
        <li>Indira Gandhi</li>
        <li>John F. Kennedy</li>
      </ul>
    </body>
  </html>
```

You now have a complete working transformation using a combination of <xsl:apply-templates> to specify the nodes to be processed and <xsl:template> elements to handle them. This method is often known as *push processing* because the processor marches through the source XML and pushes the nodes selected by <xsl:apply-templates> to the relevant <xsl:template>. Sometimes, however, it's more convenient to use *pull processing* by grabbing nodes directly and using their contents. For this type of processing you need the <xsl:for-each> element.

The <xsl:for-each> Element

The <xsl:for-each> element enables you to select a group of nodes and to apply an operation to each of them. It does not work like the similarly named construct in other languages, which is used to loop through an array or collection. As stated earlier, XSLT is a functional language, and within the processing there is no guarantee to the order of processing within the group of nodes selected. Similarly, you can exit the loop using a `break` statement. Listing 8-10 shows how the example XSLT you have so far looks if you replace the call to <xsl:apply-templates> with an <xsl:for-each> instruction.

Available for download on Wrox.com

LISTING 8-10: PeopleToHtml-ForEach.xslt

```
<?xml version="1.0" encoding="utf-8"?>
<xsl:stylesheet version="1.0" xmlns:xsl="http://www.w3.org/1999/XSL/Transform">

  <xsl:template match="/">
    <html>
      <head>
        <title>Famous People</title>
      </head>
      <body>
        <h1>Famous People</h1>
        <hr />
        <ul>
          <xsl:for-each select="People/Person">
            <li>
              <xsl:value-of select="Name" />
            </li>
          </xsl:for-each>
        </ul>
      </body>
    </html>
  </xsl:template>
</xsl:stylesheet>
```

The <xsl:for-each> element has a select attribute that points to the nodes you want to process. For each node in the group the contents of the <xsl:for-each> instruction is executed. Therefore, the select attribute uses the People/Person XPath as before and for each <Person> a list item is created. For this XSLT, the output is identical to that of the previous version.

Push-Processing versus Pull-Processing

So now you have two ways of processing nodes: pushing them to an <xsl:template> or pulling them using <xsl:for-each>. Which one is best? Although there's no firm rule, it's typically best to start by trying to use an <xsl:template>. They are more flexible and, as later examples show, they are usually easier to maintain. They also give you the chance to build up XSL transformations from smaller modules, something not really possible using <xsl:for-each>. In general I use <xsl:for-each> only for quick and dirty code or small snippets that I don't think will need to change over time.

Before you move on to using some of the other XSLT instructions, you need to understand the role of XPath.

The Role of XPath in XSLT

You've already seen a number of cases of XPath being used in XSLT as the select attribute. These have included:

- <xsl:apply-templates>
- <xsl:for-each>
- <xsl:value-of>

Typically, a select attribute takes an XPath expression to the set of nodes you want to process. There is, however, no golden rule about which attributes can take an XPath expression—you just have to refer to the specification if you're in doubt. The XSLT 2.0 version is located at www.w3.org/TR/xslt20.

WARNING *Remember that the* match *attribute on an* <xsl:template> *element does not take an XPath expression, but an XSL Pattern. This is also generally the case for other elements that have a* match *attribute.*

In addition to the select attribute, there are many more XSLT instructions that use XPath, and this section takes a look at these alternative instructions. You can start by extending the example in Listing 8-8 in two ways: first you'll make the output page more interesting by using an HTML table and displaying the born and died dates as well as the description. You are going to stick with the <xsl:apply-templates> version, using push-processing. This means that you only need to modify the main template so that the basic HTML table is created and then alter the template that matches the Person elements. The new XSLT looks like Listing 8-11.

Available for download on Wrox.com

LISTING 8-11: PeopleToHtml-WithTable.xslt

```
<xsl:stylesheet version="1.0"
     xmlns:xsl="http://www.w3.org/1999/XSL/Transform">

  <xsl:template match="/">
    <html>
      <head>
        <title>Famous People</title>
      </head>
      <body>
        <h1>Famous People</h1>
        <hr />
        <table>
          <caption>Famous People</caption>
          <thead>
            <tr>
              <th>Name</th>
              <th>Born</th>
              <th>Died</th>
              <th>Description</th>
            </tr>
          </thead>
          <tbody>
            <xsl:apply-templates select="People/Person" />
          </tbody>
        </table>
      </body>
    </html>
  </xsl:template>

  <xsl:template match="Person">
    <tr>
      <td>
        <xsl:value-of select="Name" />
      </td>
      <td>
        <xsl:value-of select="@bornDate" />
      </td>
      <td>
        <xsl:value-of select="@diedDate" />
      </td>
      <td>
        <xsl:value-of select="Description" />
      </td>
    </tr>
  </xsl:template>
</xsl:stylesheet>
```

Notice how you selected the two date attributes using the XPath `@bornDate` and `@diedDate`. You can see the results of running the transformation in Figure 8-1.

Famous People

Famous People

Famous People

Name	Born	Died	Description
Winston Churchill	1874-11-30	1965-01-24	Winston Churchill was a mid 20th century British politician who became famous as Prime Minister during the Second World War.
Indira Gandhi	1917-11-19	1984-10-31	Indira Gandhi was India's first female prime minister and was assassinated in 1984.
John F. Kennedy	1917-05-29	1963-11-22	JFK, as he was affectionately known, was a United States president who was assassinated in Dallas, Texas.

FIGURE 8-1

You can see that the dates aren't in a very user-friendly format; they are still using the official XML format of year-month-date. If you want to change that you need to process that value before displaying it. In version 2.0 you have a number of choices but in version 1.0 you are going to have to use named templates. These act in a similar way to the templates you've already seen; they process nodes. The difference is that they are called by name, rather than by using a `match` attribute, which makes them similar to functions in standard programming languages.

NOTE *The XML date format is actually an ISO format known as ISO 8601. There's a good explanatory article at* `http://en.wikipedia.org/wiki/ISO_8601`.

Using Named Templates

Your final addition to the HTML page is to display the full date in an unambiguous fashion. Named templates can act in a similar way to functions and do some basic processing on the date so that the year falls at the end. You can also remove the ambiguity about which value represents the month by using the month's name instead of a two-digit code. This will give you a chance to use a named template and also show how to use XPath functions to manipulate a string value. Start by creating a named template that accepts a parameter of a date in the standard XML format as shown in the following snippet:

```
<xsl:template name="iso8601DateToDisplayDate">
    <xsl:param name="iso8601Date" />
    <xsl:variable name="yearPart"
                  select="substring($iso8601Date, 1, 4)" />
    <xsl:variable name="monthPart"
                  select="substring($iso8601Date, 7, 2)" />
    <xsl:variable name="datePart"
                  select="substring($iso8601Date, 9, 2)" />
    <xsl:value-of
                  select="concat($datePart, '/', $monthPart, '/', $yearPart)" />
</xsl:template>
```

A named template obviously needs a name and, not surprisingly, there is a name attribute that reflects this. You normally have an <xsl:template> that has either a match or a name attribute. In some instances, however, it's useful for them to have both. You can't have an <xsl:template> with neither a match nor a name attribute though.

A named template can also have any number of <xsl:param> elements as its children. These are used in the same way that parameters are used in functions within standard programming languages—they let you pass values into the template. The preceding example has one parameter that is passed in, the date from which you will extract the individual components of year, month and day. You extract the different parts of the full date—the date, month, and year—and place them into three variables named $datePart, $monthPart, and $yearPart, respectively. To do this you use the XPath substring function. This takes three parameters, of which the third is optional:

- The string on which to operate
- The character on which to start the operation
- The length of the result string

If the third parameter is omitted, the whole of the string, starting at the character in the second parameter, is returned. So to access the month part, start with the full date and take two characters starting at the sixth character. You then repeat this operation for the day by taking two characters starting at the ninth character. Once you have the three separate parts you use another XPath function, concat(), to chain them back together separated by a suitable delimiter.

The <xsl:variable> element is a little strange compared to its counterpart in standard non-functional languages. It can be initialized only once within its lifetime. You can do this in two ways: use a select attribute, as was exhibited earlier, or use the contents of the element itself. This second method looks like this:

```
<xsl:variable name="myVariable">
  <myElement>Some content</myElement>
</xsl:variable>
```

In general, if you can use the select attribute to specify what you want in the variable, you should. The second way can lead to complications because a new tree has to be constructed and an outer node added. This can lead to problems when using the variable. Once you have set the contents of a variable, you can access it by using the name of the variable preceded by a $ sign. It is important to note that the scope of variables is enforced strictly by the processor. If you declare a variable as a top-level element, a direct child of <xsl:stylesheet>, then it can be used anywhere in the document. If you create it within an <xsl:template>, it can only be used there, and it can only be used within the parent in which it was created. As an example, the following code snippet contains two attempts to use the variable named $demo. The first time is fine because $demo is declared with the <xsl:for-each> element as its parent and is used within that element. The second attempt will produce an error because an attempt is made to access $demo outside of the parent in which it was created.

```
<xsl:template name="usingVariables">
  <xsl:for-each select="someElements/someElement">
    <xsl:variable name="demo" select="'Some text'" />
    <!-- this next line is okay as $demo is in scope -->
```

```
      <xsl:value-of select="concat(someElement, $demo)" />
    </xsl:for-each>
    <!-- this next line is an error as $demo is out of scope -->
    <xsl:value-of select="$demo" />
  </xsl:template>
```

To utilize this template you need to modify the code that creates the table and take advantage of the `<xsl:call-template>` element; the new version of the style sheet that does just that is shown in Listing 8-12.

NOTE *Note how two sets of quotes are needed to set the value of* `$demo` *to a string—one to enclose the attribute value itself and a second pair for the string. If the inner quotes were missing the processor would treat* `Some text` *as an XPath expression, which, in this case, would lead to an error.*

Available for download on Wrox.com

LISTING 8-12: PeopleToHtml-FriendlyDate.xslt

```
<xsl:stylesheet version="1.0"
    xmlns:xsl="http://www.w3.org/1999/XSL/Transform">
  <xsl:template match="/">
    <html>
      <head>
        <title>Famous People</title>
      </head>
      <body>
        <h1>Famous People</h1>
        <hr />
        <table>
          <caption>Famous People</caption>
          <thead>
            <tr>
              <th>Name</th>
              <th>Born</th>
              <th>Died</th>
              <th>Description</th>
            </tr>
          </thead>
          <tbody>
            <xsl:apply-templates select="People/Person" />
          </tbody>
        </table>
      </body>
    </html>
  </xsl:template>

  <xsl:template match="Person">
    <tr>
      <td>
```

```
        <xsl:value-of select="Name" />
      </td>
      <td>
        <xsl:call-template name="iso8601DateToDisplayDate">
          <xsl:with-param
                name="iso8601Date" select="@bornDate" />
        </xsl:call-template>
      </td>
      <td>
        <xsl:call-template name="iso8601DateToDisplayDate">
          <xsl:with-param
                name="iso8601Date" select="@diedDate" />
        </xsl:call-template>
      </td>
      <td>
        <xsl:value-of select="Description" />
      </td>
    </tr>
  </xsl:template>

  <xsl:template name="iso8601DateToDisplayDate">
    <xsl:param name="iso8601Date" />
    <xsl:variable name="yearPart"
           select="substring($iso8601Date, 1, 4)" />
     <xsl:variable name="monthPart"
           select="substring($iso8601Date, 6, 2)" />
     <xsl:variable name="datePart"
           select="substring($iso8601Date, 9, 2)" />
    <xsl:value-of
          select="concat($datePart, '/', $monthPart, '/', $yearPart)" />
  </xsl:template></xsl:stylesheet>
```

The <xsl:call-template> Element

The `<xsl:call-template>` element has an attribute, `name`, that identifies which template to call. Contained within the element can be any number of `<xsl:with-param>` elements that pass values to the `<xsl:template>`. These values are received by the `<xsl:param>` elements within the called template. The `<xsl:with-param>` elements have a `select` attribute to retrieve whatever values are required. The results of this new transformation are shown in Figure 8-2.

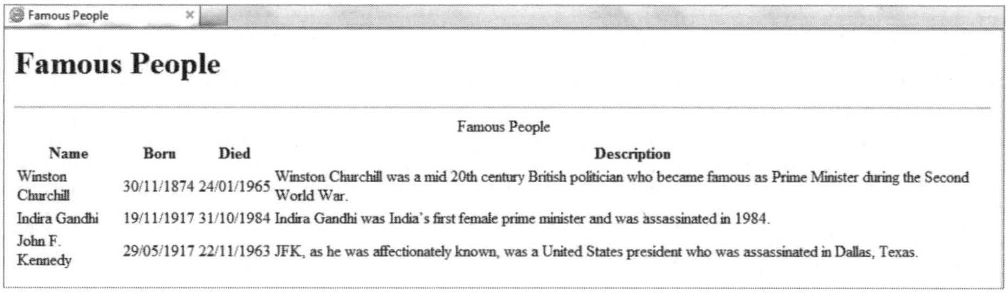

Famous People

Famous People

Famous People

Name	Born	Died	Description
Winston Churchill	30/11/1874	24/01/1965	Winston Churchill was a mid 20th century British politician who became famous as Prime Minister during the Second World War.
Indira Gandhi	19/11/1917	31/10/1984	Indira Gandhi was India's first female prime minister and was assassinated in 1984.
John F. Kennedy	29/05/1917	22/11/1963	JFK, as he was affectionately known, was a United States president who was assassinated in Dallas, Texas.

FIGURE 8-2

As you can see, though, the date format, although clear enough in this instance, is not really suitable for a page that may be viewed in many different countries. It follows the European standard of date-month-year rather than the U.S. standard of month-date-year. To remove this ambiguity you can modify the named template to show the month using its name. This will give you a chance to see a new aspect of XSLT—how to embed and retrieve lookup information both from an external source and within the transformation using the `document()` function.

The document() Function in XSLT

The `document()` function is one of the most useful functions in the XSLT library. At its simplest it takes one argument, which is a string pointing to an external document, usually in the form of a URL. XSLT processors can support schemes other than HTTP and HTTPS but those tend to be the only ones that most can cope with. So if you have an XSL transformation that processes an XML file but you also want to incorporate information from a document held at `http:// www.wrox.com/books.xml`, you'd use code similar to the following:

```
<xsl:variable name="books" select="document('http://www.wrox.com/books.xml')" />
```

Assuming the URL `http://www.wrox.com/books.xml` points to a well-formed document and is accessible, the variable `$books` will now hold a reference to the root node of the document and other nodes can be accessed in the usual way using XPath. For example, each book might be found using the expression:

```
$books/Books/Book
```

NOTE *You can call the document function in some other ways. For example, a node-set passed as an argument will retrieve a document composed of each individual document found after each node in the set is turned into a URL. For the full details see* `http://www.w3.org/TR/xslt#document`.

You'll now see how the `document()` function can help you complete your current task, turning the month represented as a number into the full month name.

1. Start by constructing a lookup "table," some XML that lets you map the number of a month to its name as shown in Listing 8-13.

LISTING 8-13: Months.xml

```
<?xml version="1.0" encoding="utf-8"?>
<Months>
  <Month index="1">January</Month>
  <Month index="2">February</Month>
  <Month index="3">March</Month>
  <Month index="4">April</Month>
```

```
  <Month index="5">May</Month>
  <Month index="6">June</Month>
  <Month index="7">July</Month>
  <Month index="8">August</Month>
  <Month index="9">September</Month>
  <Month index="10">October</Month>
  <Month index="11">November</Month>
  <Month index="12">December</Month>
</Months>
```

2. Nothing dramatic here—just what is effectively a serialized array of the months. Now use the `document()` function to access this file from within your transformation. Use a variable to hold the results:

```
<xsl:variable name="allMonths" select="document('months.xml')" />
```

3. This will be a top-level element; that is, a direct child of `<xsl:stylesheet>`. Alter the template that manipulates the date so that it finds the text of the month where the index attribute matches the value held in `$monthPart`:

```
<xsl:template
 name="iso8601DateToDisplayDate">
<xsl:param name="iso8601Date" />
<xsl:variable
   name="yearPart" select="substring($iso8601Date, 1, 4)" />
<xsl:variable
  name="monthPart" select="substring($iso8601Date, 6, 2)" />
<xsl:variable
   name="monthName"
   select="$allMonths/Months/Month[@index = number($monthPart)]" />
<xsl:variable
  name="datePart" select="substring($iso8601Date, 9, 2)" />
<xsl:value-of select="concat($datePart, ' ', $monthName, ' ', $yearPart)" />
</xsl:template>
```

4. Next, remove the forward slashes from the final `<xsl:value-of>` and replace them with a single space. The new XSLT is shown in Listing 8-14.

Available for download on Wrox.com

LISTING 8-14: PeopleToHtml-MonthNames.xslt

```
<?xml version="1.0" encoding="utf-8"?>
<xsl:stylesheet version="1.0" xmlns:xsl="http://www.w3.org/1999/XSL/Transform">

  <xsl:variable name="allMonths" select="document('months.xml')" />

  <xsl:template match="/">
    <html>
      <head>
        <title>Famous People</title>
      </head>
      <body>
```

continues

LISTING 8-14 *(continued)*

```
        <h1>Famous People</h1>
        <hr />
        <table>
          <caption>Famous People</caption>
          <thead>
            <tr>
              <th>Name</th>
              <th>Born</th>
              <th>Died</th>
              <th>Description</th>
            </tr>
          </thead>
          <tbody>
            <xsl:apply-templates select="People/Person" />
          </tbody>
        </table>
      </body>
    </html>
  </xsl:template>

  <xsl:template match="Person">
    <tr>
      <td>
        <xsl:value-of select="Name" />
      </td>
      <td>
        <xsl:call-template name="iso8601DateToDisplayDate">
          <xsl:with-param name="iso8601Date" select="@bornDate" />
        </xsl:call-template>
      </td>
      <td>
        <xsl:call-template name="iso8601DateToDisplayDate">
          <xsl:with-param name="iso8601Date" select="@diedDate" />
        </xsl:call-template>
      </td>
      <td>
        <xsl:value-of select="Description" />
      </td>
    </tr>
  </xsl:template>

  <xsl:template
       name="iso8601DateToDisplayDate">
    <xsl:param name="iso8601Date" />
    <xsl:variable
       name="yearPart" select="substring($iso8601Date, 1, 4)" />
    <xsl:variable
       name="monthPart" select="substring($iso8601Date, 6, 2)" />
    <xsl:variable
  name="monthName" select="$allMonths/Months/Month[@index = number($monthPart)]" />
    <xsl:variable
       name="datePart" select="substring($iso8601Date, 9, 2)" />
```

```
    <xsl:value-of select="concat($datePart, ' ', $monthName, ' ', $yearPart)" />
  </xsl:template>

</xsl:stylesheet>
```

The results of running this transformation are shown in Figure 8-3.

Famous People

Famous People

Famous People

Name	Born	Died	Description
Winston Churchill	30 November 1874	24 January 1965	Winston Churchill was a mid 20th century British politician who became famous as Prime Minister during the Second World War.
Indira Gandhi	19 November 1917	31 October 1984	Indira Gandhi was India's first female prime minister and was assassinated in 1984.
John F. Kennedy	29 May 1917	22 November 1963	JFK, as he was affectionately known, was a United States president who was assassinated in Dallas, Texas.

FIGURE 8-3

The `document()` function opens some exciting possibilities. There's no reason, for instance, that the file you try to access has to be a static file—it could be the results of a web service call. As long as the content returned is well-formed, the `document()` function will treat what is returned as a valid XML document. However, there's no way of posting data—the web service has to be able to accept parameters in the querystring or be a RESTful type. For example, you might have coded a web service that accepts the number of the month and returns the full name. It might be called like this, using querystring parameters:

```
<xsl:variable name="monthName"
   select="document('http://www.wrox.com/services/getMonthName.asmx?index=3')" />
```

or this, using a RESTful-style service:

```
<xsl:variable name="monthName"
   select="document('http://www.wrox.com/services/months/3')" />
```

To be fair, the example with an external lookup file for the months was somewhat overkill—in many cases you might just want to embed the lookup data within the actual XSLT. To embed something within the XSLT, you use the same format for the data; the only small change is to ensure the processor understands that this is your data and that it is clearly separate from both the XSLT itself and any elements you want to appear in the output. To ensure this separation, you need to group the elements under a namespace.

1. First, add an extra namespace declaration to the `<xsl:stylesheet>` element and then add the lookup information to the beginning of the XSLT:

```
<xsl:stylesheet version="1.0" xmlns:xsl="http://www.w3.org/1999/XSL/Transform"
xmlns:myData="http://wrox.com/namespaces/embeddedData" >

  <xsl:variable name="allMonths" select="document('months.xml')" />
```

```
  <myData:Months>
    <Month index="1">January</Month>
    <Month index="2">February</Month>
    <Month index="3">March</Month>
    <Month index="4">April</Month>
    <Month index="5">May</Month>
    <Month index="6">June</Month>
    <Month index="7">July</Month>
    <Month index="8">August</Month>
    <Month index="9">September</Month>
    <Month index="10">October</Month>
    <Month index="11">November</Month>
    <Month index="12">December</Month>
  </myData:Months>

  <!-- rest of stylesheet -->
</xsl:stylesheet>
```

PeopleToHtml-LocalDocument.xslt

2. To access this XML from within the transformation use the `document()` function, but this time you will need to access the style sheet itself rather than an external file. Use an empty string as the argument to the function. This gives you a reference to the currently executing XSLT.

3. Change the variable declared at the beginning of the transformation as in the following—it no longer refers to the months so you'll call it `thisDocument`:

```
<xsl:variable name="thisDocument" select="document('')" />
```

4. Now drill down further to the `<myData:Months>` element. Because this element is in a namespace, you need to include the namespace prefix in the path `$thisDocument/xsl:stylesheet/myData:Months/Month[@index = number($monthPart)]`. Remember that only the `<myData:Months>` element was put into the `http://wrox.com/namespaces/embeddedData` namespace so only that one needs the `myData` prefix. The final style sheet looks like Listing 8-15. The result of this transformation will be exactly the same as the previous one.

Available for download on Wrox.com

LISTING 8-15: PeopleToHtml-LocalDocument.xslt

```
<?xml version="1.0" encoding="utf-8"?>
<xsl:stylesheet version="1.0"
              xmlns:xsl="http://www.w3.org/1999/XSL/Transform"
              xmlns:myData="http://wrox.com/namespaces/embeddedData">

  <xsl:variable name="thisDocument" select="document('')" />

  <myData:Months>
    <Month index="1">January</Month>
    <Month index="2">February</Month>
```

```
  <Month index="3">March</Month>
  <Month index="4">April</Month>
  <Month index="5">May</Month>
  <Month index="6">June</Month>
  <Month index="7">July</Month>
  <Month index="8">August</Month>
  <Month index="9">September</Month>
  <Month index="10">October</Month>
  <Month index="11">November</Month>
  <Month index="12">December</Month>
</myData:Months>

<xsl:template match="/">
  <html>
    <head>
      <title>Famous People</title>
    </head>
    <body>
      <h1>Famous People</h1>
      <hr />
      <table>
        <caption>Famous People</caption>
        <thead>
          <tr>
            <th>Name</th>
            <th>Born</th>
            <th>Died</th>
            <th>Description</th>
          </tr>
        </thead>
        <tbody>
          <xsl:apply-templates select="People/Person" />
        </tbody>
      </table>
    </body>
  </html>
</xsl:template>

<xsl:template match="Person">
  <tr>
    <td>
      <xsl:value-of select="Name" />
    </td>
    <td>
      <xsl:call-template name="iso8601DateToDisplayDate">
        <xsl:with-param name="iso8601Date" select="@bornDate" />
      </xsl:call-template>
    </td>
    <td>
      <xsl:call-template name="iso8601DateToDisplay">
        <xsl:with-param name="iso8601Date" select="@diedDate" />
      </xsl:call-template>
    </td>
    <td>
```

continues

LISTING 8-15 *(continued)*

```
        <xsl:value-of select="Description" />
      </td>
    </tr>
  </xsl:template>

  <xsl:template name="iso8601DateToDisplayDate">
    <xsl:param name="iso8601Date" />
    <xsl:variable name="yearPart"
             select="substring($iso8601, 1, 4)" />
    <xsl:variable name="monthPart"
             select="substring($iso8601Date, 6, 2)" />
    <xsl:variable name="monthName" select=
"$thisDocument/xsl:stylesheet/myData:Months/Month[@index = number($monthPart)]"
    />
    <xsl:variable name="datePart"
                  select="substring($iso8601Date, 9, 2)" />
    <xsl:value-of select="concat($datePart, ' ', $monthName, ' ', $yearPart)" />
  </xsl:template>

</xsl:stylesheet>
```

Now there's one main area of processing that you haven't covered yet and that is conditional logic—how can you change what processing occurs depending on a condition?

Conditional Logic

There are two main ways to use conditional logic in XSLT version 1.0, with a third appearing in version 2.0 courtesy of the enhanced powers of XPath available in the later version. The first way is to use an `<xsl:if>` element. This enables you to make simple tests but doesn't give you the option of an `else` statement. The basic structure of the element is:

```
<xsl:if test="test condition goes here">
  <!-- instructions if the condition is true -->
</xsl:if>
```

The `<xsl:if>` element has an attribute named `test`. The value of this attribute is an XPath expression that produces a Boolean value of true or false. If the condition evaluates to true, the instructions within the element are carried out. Example tests might be:

- `Person`: Evaluates to true if there is at least one `Person` element.
- `Name = 'Indira Gandhi'`: Evaluates to true if the `Name` element has the text `'Indira Gandhi'`.
- `number(substring(Person/@bornDate, 1, 2)) = 19`: Takes the first two characters of the `bornDate` attribute and returns true if they are equal to 19.

You can use this last test in your current transformation to mark the names of people born in the twentieth century in a different color. To do so, add the test to the template that matches the `<Person>` element and then perform the following steps:

1. Declare an `<xsl:variable>` element named `nameCSS` to hold the relevant style information.
2. Then test the `bornDate` attribute as described previously. If this evaluates true, set the value of the variable to `color:red;`, otherwise it will remain blank.
3. Next add a `style` attribute to the `<td>` element holding the name. To retrieve the value of `$nameCSS` you can use a common shortcut: enclose the name of the variable in curly braces to tell the XSLT processor that the value needs to be evaluated as an XPath expression.

The final result looks like the following code snippet:

```
<xsl:template match="Person">
  <xsl:variable name="nameCSS">
    <xsl:if
        test="number(substring(@bornDate, 1, 2)) = 19">color:red</xsl:if>
  </xsl:variable>
  <tr>
    <td style="{$nameCSS}">
      <xsl:value-of select="Name" />
    </td>

    <!-- remainder of template -->

</xsl:template>
```

PeopleToHtml-ColoredNames.xslt

When you run the transformation you get the result shown in Figure 8-4 where the first politician, Winston Churchill, is in black and the others are colored red.

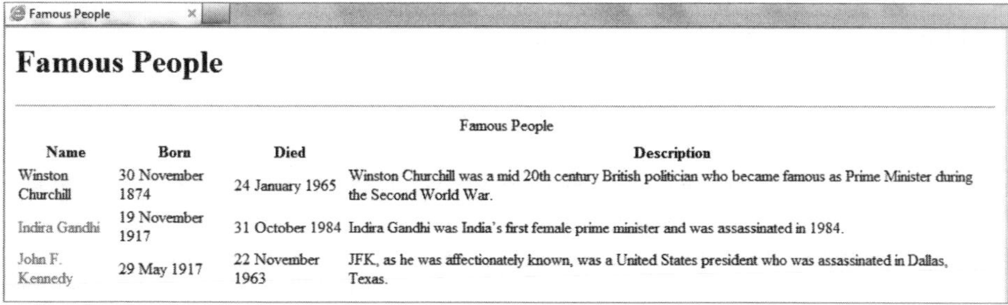
Famous People

Famous People

Famous People

Name	Born	Died	Description
Winston Churchill	30 November 1874	24 January 1965	Winston Churchill was a mid 20th century British politician who became famous as Prime Minister during the Second World War.
Indira Gandhi	19 November 1917	31 October 1984	Indira Gandhi was India's first female prime minister and was assassinated in 1984.
John F. Kennedy	29 May 1917	22 November 1963	JFK, as he was affectionately known, was a United States president who was assassinated in Dallas, Texas.

FIGURE 8-4

`<xsl:if>` is quite limited. When you need something more powerful to handle more than one condition, use `<xsl:choose>`. This instruction takes the following form:

```
<xsl:choose>
  <xsl:when test="test condition goes here">
    <!-- instructions if the condition is true -->
  </xsl:when>
  <!-- more when elements can go here -->
```

```
    <!-- the otherwise is optional -->
    <xsl:otherwise>
      <!-- instructions if all when conditions fail -->
    </xsl:otherwise>
  </xsl:choose>
```

Basically, you can have any number of <xsl:when> elements inside <xsl:choose>. You can also have an optional <xsl:otherwise> that is executed if all the previous tests have failed. As an example of using choose suppose you want to improve the look of your output document by giving every odd numbered row in the table a different background color than the even numbered ones. You can accomplish this by testing against the results of the position() function, which gives the index of the node being processed starting at one. So in your Person template you can add the following:

Available for download on Wrox.com

```
<xsl:template match="Person">
  <xsl:variable name="rowCSS">
    <xsl:choose>
      <xsl:when test="position() mod 2 = 0">color:#0000aa;</xsl:when>
      <xsl:otherwise>color:#006666;</xsl:otherwise>
    </xsl:choose>
  </xsl:variable>

  <!-- rest of template -->
</xsl:template>
```

PeopleToHtml-ColoredRows.xslt

The test here uses the position() function, which tells you which <Person> element you are processing, and the mod operator, which returns the remainder after dividing the position by two. If the remainder is zero, it's an even numbered row and you assign a color of #0000aa, otherwise you assign a color of #006666.

You can then add this variable to the style attribute of the <tr> element:

```
<tr style="{$rowCSS}">
    <td style="{$nameCSS}">
      <xsl:value-of select="Name" />
    </td>
```

The complete template now looks like:

Available for download on Wrox.com

```
<xsl:template match="Person">
  <xsl:variable name="rowCSS">
    <xsl:choose>
      <xsl:when test="position() mod 2 = 0">color:#0000aa;</xsl:when>
      <xsl:otherwise>color:#006666;</xsl:otherwise>
    </xsl:choose>
  </xsl:variable>
  <xsl:variable name="nameCSS">
    <xsl:if test="number(substring(@bornDate, 1, 2)) = 19">color:red;</xsl:if>
  </xsl:variable>
  <tr style="{$rowCSS}">
    <td style="{$nameCSS}">
      <xsl:value-of select="Name" />
```

```
        </td>
        <td>
          <xsl:call-template name="iso8601DateToDisplayDate">
            <xsl:with-param name="iso8601Date" select="@bornDate" />
          </xsl:call-template>
        </td>
        <td>
          <xsl:call-template name="iso8601DateToDisplayDate">
            <xsl:with-param name="iso8601Date" select="@diedDate" />
          </xsl:call-template>
        </td>
        <td>
          <xsl:value-of select="Description" />
        </td>
      </tr>
    </xsl:template>
```

PeopleToHtml-ColoredRows.xslt

When you run this transformation using one of the following command lines you get the result shown in Figure 8-5 where the first name, Winston Churchill, is in black but the names after that are in red:

```
java net.sf.saxon.Transform -s:People.xml
 -xsl:PeopleToHtml-ColoredRows.xslt -o:People-ColoredRows.html
```

or:

```
Transform -s:People.xml -xsl:PeopleToHtml-ColoredRows.xslt
 -o:People-ColoredRows.html
```

Famous People

Famous People

Famous People

Name	Born	Died	Description
Winston Churchill	30 November 1874	24 January 1965	Winston Churchill was a mid 20th century British politician who became famous as Prime Minister during the Second World War.
Indira Gandhi	19 November 1917	31 October 1984	Indira Gandhi was India's first female prime minister and was assassinated in 1984.
John F. Kennedy	29 May 1917	22 November 1963	JFK, as he was affectionately known, was a United States president who was assassinated in Dallas, Texas.

FIGURE 8-5

NOTE *Occasionally you will need to test explicitly against the values true or false. XPath does not have any keywords to represent those values; if you do use true or false, the processor will just assume they are element names. To remedy this situation, there are two built-in functions,* `true()` *and* `false()`*, which return the values true and false, respectively.*

The technique of using a variable or any XPath expression within an attribute's value, as used in the preceding snippet, is a powerful one. In the snippet the variable, `$rowCSS` was embedded inside the `style` attribute's value as shown here:

```
<tr style="{$rowCSS}" >
```

The variable is surrounded by braces, `{}`, to inform the XSLT processor that the contents need to be treated as XPath and replaced with whatever value the XPath expression evaluates to. These braces are only needed when the element whose attribute they appear in is not a built-in XSLT instruction. For example in the following snippet the braces are not required as the `<xsl:value-of>` element is intrinsic to XSLT and its `select` attribute expects the following XPath expression:

```
<xsl:value-of select="$rowCSS" />
```

So the rule to decide whether or not an XPath expression needs to be surrounded by braces is simple: *Does the attribute expect XPath or not?* If it does, just write the XPath expression; if it doesn't, use the XPath surrounded by braces. The technique of embedding XPath within attributes that usually take literal values is known as *attribute value templates* (AVT) and if you look at the XSLT specification you will see that attributes definitions are accompanied with whether or not attribute value templates can be used with them.

So far you've seen how to process both a main input document and how to take advantage of external documents using the `document()` function. Next you see how to pass in simple pieces of information to a transformation using the `<xsl:param>` element.

The <xsl:param> element

To make your transformations reusable it's often necessary to pass arguments to them that affect the processing. To do that you can declare any number of `<xsl:param>` elements as children of the `<xsl:stylesheet>` element. These can be set before the transformation takes place. The way these parameters are initialized is not defined by the XSLT specification but is left to the designer of the processor. The processor you are using, Saxon, enables parameters to be set on the command line or via Java or .NET code. In reference to the ongoing example, suppose you want to modify the part of the transform that highlights the name in the resulting HTML. Currently you highlight anyone born in the twentieth century or later by checking the first two digits of the year. To change that, pass in a parameter specifying a year and highlighting anyone born after that by performing the following steps.

1. First, add an `<xsl:param>` element to the XSLT, like so:

```
<xsl:stylesheet version="1.0"
      xmlns:xsl="http://www.w3.org/1999/XSL/Transform"
      xmlns:myData="http://wrox.com/namespaces/embeddedData">

  <xsl:param name="targetYear" select="3000" />
```

PeopleToHtml-BornAfter

2. The parameter is named `targetYear` and is given a default value of 1000, which makes sure the XSLT works as expected if no year is passed in. Now change the logic that tests the `bornDate` attribute, like so:

```
<xsl:variable name="nameCSS">
<xsl:if test="number(substring(@bornDate, 1, 4)) > $targetYear">color:red;</xsl:if>
</xsl:variable>
```

PeopleToHtml-BornAfter

3. This time you take the first four characters of the date, the complete year, and only highlight if the value is greater than the `$targetYear` parameter. To test this XSLT, set the parameter on the command line by using the following syntax (all on one line):

```
java net.sf.saxon.Transform -s:people.xml -xsl:peopleToHtml-BornAfter.xslt
                        -o:People-BornAfter.html targetYear=1916
```

or:

```
Transform -s:people.xml -xsl:peopleToHtml-BornAfter.xslt
                     -o:People-BornAfter.html targetYear=1916
```

4. The result should look the same as Figure 8-5. If you change the `targetYear` parameter to be 1816, all names will be highlighted; if you leave the declaration off entirely, the default value of 3000 is used so no names are colored red.

When processing nodes from the source document it's sometimes important to be able to sort them based on various criteria rather than just have them appear in the output in the same order as the input. For this task you can use the `<xsl:sort>` element.

The <xsl:sort> Element

The `<xsl:sort>` element is fairly simple. It can be used as a child of `<xsl:apply-templates>` or `<xsl:for-each>`. It has the following attributes to control the sorting process:

- `select`: An XPath expression pointing to the node(s) to sort on.
- `data-type`: How to treat the node values, usually either text or number.
- `order`: Either ascending or descending. Ascending is the default.

Say you want to sort the people in your HTML table based on their year of birth. This is going to need two stages: first you need to convert the full date, which is currently in the format yyyy-mm-dd, into a number that can be sorted; and second, you need to use the `<xsl:sort>` element.

For the first stage you need to make use of the `translate()` function. This function takes three arguments. The first is an expression pointing to the data to work on, the second parameter is what to search for, and the third is what to replace any found characters with. For example:

```
translate('The first of the few ', 'fiw', 'wot')
```

This would look for the characters *f*, *i*, and *w* and change them to *w*, *o*, and *t*, respectively. This would result in:

```
The worst of the wet.
```

WARNING *The* `translate()` *function can only cope with one-to-one mappings. In XSLT version 2.0 you can use the* `replace()` *function if you need more flexibility.*

Now back in the example, use the `translate()` function to remove the hyphens from the dates:

```
translate(@bornDate, '- ', '')
```

This leaves you with an eight-digit string that can be compared with directly with another similarly treated date meaning that a number of different dates can be sorted solely on their numeric value. The `<xsl:sort>` element is a child of the call to `<xsl:apply-templates>`, as shown in the following:

```
<xsl:apply-templates select="People/Person">
  <xsl:sort select="translate(@bornDate, '-', '')" data-type="number"/>
</xsl:apply-templates>
```

The `select` attribute in this snippet uses the `@bornDate` but with the hyphens removed and the `data-type` attribute set to `number`.

Now that you have enabled sorting the dates by translating them into numeric values and then added the `<xsl:sort>` instruction within the call to `<xsl:apply-templates>`, you can try the transformation again. When this new code is run the HTML table produced looks like Listing 8-16.

Available for download on Wrox.com

LISTING 8-16: People-SortedRows.html

```
<html xmlns:myData="http://wrox.com/namespaces/embeddedData">
  <head>
    <META http-equiv="Content-Type" content="text/html; charset=utf-8">
    <title>Famous People</title>
  </head>
  <body>
    <h1>Famous People</h1>
    <hr>
    <table>
      <caption>Famous People</caption>
      <thead>
        <tr>
          <th>Name</th>
          <th>Born</th>
```

```
          <th>Died</th>
          <th>Description</th>
        </tr>
      </thead>
      <tbody>
        <tr style="color:#006666;">
          <td style="">Winston Churchill</td>
          <td>30 November 1874</td>
          <td>24 January 1965</td>
          <td>
      Winston Churchill was a mid-20th century British politician who
      became famous as Prime Minister during the Second World War.
    </td>
        </tr>
        <tr style="color:#0000aa;">
          <td style="">John F. Kennedy</td>
          <td>29 May 1917</td>
          <td>22 November 1963</td>
          <td>
      JFK, as he was affectionately known, was a United States president
      who was assassinated in Dallas, Texas.
    </td>
        </tr>
        <tr style="color:#006666;">
          <td style="">Indira Gandhi</td>
          <td>19 November 1917</td>
          <td>31 October 1984</td>
          <td>
      Indira Gandhi was India's first female prime minister and was
      assassinated in 1984.
    </td>
        </tr>
      </tbody>
    </table>
  </body>
</html>
```

Note that the order of the people has now changed with Indira Gandhi appearing last because she was born latest.

When extracting information from the source document you have so far only used the `<xsl:value-of>` instruction. This is handy when you want snippets of data but less useful when you need to copy entire elements. `<xsl:value-of>` always returns the text from an element or the value of an attribute. If it is passed a set of nodes, it returns the text of the first element or the value of the first attribute (in version 1.0 at least). In XSLT terminology it returns an atomic value as opposed to a node or a node set. If you want to copy elements in their entirety you have two options: `<xsl:copy>` and `<xsl:copy-of>`.

<xsl:copy> and <xsl:copy-of> Elements

Both these elements can be used to copy content from the source to the output tree. `<xsl:copy>` performs a shallow copy—it just copies the current node without any children, or attributes if it's an element. If you want any other nodes to appear you need to add them manually. <xsl:copy-of> performs a deep copy—it copies the specified node with all its children and attributes. Creating a simple transformation can better examine the difference between <xsl:value-of>, <xsl:copy>, and <xsl:copy-of. Listing 8-17 shows a basic XSLT that processes each of the <Person> elements.

Available for download on Wrox.com

LISTING 8-17: CopyingNodes.xslt

```
<xsl:stylesheet version="1.0" xmlns:xsl="http://www.w3.org/1999/XSL/Transform">
  <xsl:output method="xml" indent="yes"/>

 <xsl:template match="/">
   <People>
     <xsl:apply-templates select="People/Person" />
   </People>
  </xsl:template>

  <xsl:template match="Person">
    <valueOf>
      <xsl:value-of select="." />
    </valueOf>

    <copy>
      <xsl:copy />
    </copy>

    <copyOf>
      <xsl:copy-of select="."/>
    </copyOf>
  </xsl:template>
</xsl:stylesheet>
```

WARNING *If you are generating HTML for use on the Web, you should use* `xsl:output method="html"`*; XSLT 2 also introduces* `method="xhtml"`*. See Chapter 17, "XHTML and HTML 5", for more information on why you need to do this.*

After the initial <xsl:stylesheet> element you have added an <xsl:output> element. This has a number of uses. Its primary purpose is to specify what format the output will take using the method attribute. The options are *xml* (the default), *html*, and *text*, with the fourth option of *xhtml* available if you are using XSLT version 2.0. So far you haven't had to use this element because any output document starting with an <html> tag is assumed to be HTML. Similarly, any document beginning with any other element is treated as XML. The reason you use the element in this transformation is that you want to specify that the output is indented to make it easier to read—this is achieved when the indent attribute is set to yes. Another attribute often seen on <xsl:output> is encoding. This allows you to state whether the output should be in something other than *utf-8*, for example *iso-8859-1*.

In Listing 8-17, the first `<xsl:template>` matches the root node (`/`), and this simply adds a `<People>` element at the document element of output. Then `<xsl:apply-templates>` is called as before and the `<Person>` elements are selected for processing. They are caught by the second `<xsl:template>`, which outputs three different views of each `<Person>`. The first, contained within a `<valueOf>` element, uses `<xsl:value-of>`. This just extracts all the text and ignores all attributes and child elements. The second outputs a `<copy>` element and then uses `<xsl:copy>`. This just outputs the `<Person>` element itself without any attributes or children. The third view of the `<Person>` element uses the `<xsl:copy-of>` instruction. This makes a deep copy and includes the `<Person>` element along with its attributes and all children, including the text nodes. The results of the transformation are shown in Listing 8-18.

Available for download on Wrox.com

LISTING 8-18: CopyingNodes.xml

```
<?xml version="1.0" encoding="utf-8"?>
<People>
  <valueOf>
    Winston Churchill

      Winston Churchill was a mid-20th century British politician who
      became famous as Prime Minister during the Second World War.

  </valueOf>
  <copy>
    <Person />
  </copy>
  <copyOf>
    <Person bornDate="1874-11-30" diedDate="1965-01-24">
    <Name>Winston Churchill</Name>
    <Description>
      Winston Churchill was a mid-20th century British politician who
      became famous as Prime Minister during the Second World War.
    </Description>
  </Person>
  </copyOf>
  <valueOf>
    Indira Gandhi

      Indira Gandhi was India's first female prime minister and was
      assassinated in 1984.

  </valueOf>
  <copy>
    <Person />
  </copy>
  <copyOf>
    <Person bornDate="1917-11-19" diedDate="1984-10-31">
    <Name>Indira Gandhi</Name>
    <Description>
      Indira Gandhi was India's first female prime minister and was
      assassinated in 1984.
    </Description>
```

continues

LISTING 8-18 *(continued)*

```
    </Person>
    </copyOf>
    <valueOf>
      John F. Kennedy

        JFK, as he was affectionately known, was a United States president
        who was assassinated in Dallas, Texas.

    </valueOf>
    <copy>
      <Person />
    </copy>
    <copyOf>
      <Person bornDate="1917-05-29" diedDate="1963-11-22">
      <Name>John F. Kennedy</Name>
      <Description>
        JFK, as he was affectionately known, was a United States president
        who was assassinated in Dallas, Texas.
      </Description>
    </Person>
    </copyOf>
  </People>
```

REUSING CODE IN XSLT

Another important facet of development, in any language, is code reuse. XSLT has two ways to let you write style sheets that can be used in more than one place: `<xsl:include>` and `<xsl:import>`.

The <xsl:include> Element

`<xsl:include>` allows you to include one style sheet within another. This has the same effect as simply copying and pasting the code from the included style sheet into the main one, but enables you to build up modules of useful code. For example, the template you used earlier to convert a date into a more user-friendly format could be extracted from the main transformation. It could then be included in a number of other transformations without having to write the code again.

The following Try It Out takes you through a scenario that is often found in software development, refactoring code into separate and reusable modules. These modules can then be incorporated into multiple transformations. Reusing code in this fashion has two main advantages. First, it means not having to write the same functionality time and again; and second, if you find a mistake within the reusable code module, you can simply correct it in one place and any other transformation using that module will benefit.

TRY IT OUT Using <xsl:include>

The following steps extract the code used to replace an XML formatted date with a user friendly version and place it in its own transformation. You will then incorporate this stylesheet into another one using the `<xsl:include>` element.

1. Extract the template named `iso8601DateToDisplayDateToDisplayDate` to its own style sheet and then include it in the main XSLT.

2. Create a new XSLT, `DateTemplates.xslt`, and include the code in Listing 8-19.

Available for download on Wrox.com

LISTING 8-19: DateTemplates.xslt

```
<?xml version="1.0" encoding="utf-8"?>
<xsl:stylesheet version="1.0"
          xmlns:xsl="http://www.w3.org/1999/XSL/Transform"
          xmlns:myData="http://wrox.com/namespaces/embeddedData"
          exclude-result-prefixes="myData">

  <xsl:variable name="thisDocument" select="document('')" />

  <myData:Months>
    <Month index="1">January</Month>
    <Month index="2">February</Month>
    <Month index="3">March</Month>
    <Month index="4">April</Month>
    <Month index="5">May</Month>
    <Month index="6">June</Month>
    <Month index="7">July</Month>
    <Month index="8">August</Month>
    <Month index="9">September</Month>
    <Month index="10">October</Month>
    <Month index="11">November</Month>
    <Month index="12">December</Month>
  </myData:Months>

  <xsl:template name="iso8601DateToDisplayDate">
    <xsl:param name="iso8601Date" />
    <xsl:variable name="yearPart"
         select="substring($iso8601Date, 1, 4)" />
    <xsl:variable name="monthPart"
         select="substring($iso8601Date, 6, 2)" />
    <xsl:variable name="monthName"select=
"$thisDocument/xsl:stylesheet/myData:Months/Month[@index = number($monthPart)]" />
    <xsl:variable name="datePart"
         select="substring($iso8601Date, 9, 2)" />
    <xsl:value-of select="concat($datePart, ' ', $monthName, ' ', $yearPart)" />
  </xsl:template>

</xsl:stylesheet>
```

This contains all the code from the actual template plus the lookup data for the months and the variable that holds the reference to the document itself.

3. Now create a second XSLT, `PeopleToHtml-UsingIncludes.xslt`, with the code in Listing 8-20.

Available for download on Wrox.com

LISTING 8-20: PeopleToHtml-UsingIncludes.xslt

```
<?xml version="1.0" encoding="utf-8"?>
<xsl:stylesheet version="1.0" xmlns:xsl="http://www.w3.org/1999/XSL/Transform"
                xmlns:myData="http://wrox.com/namespaces/embeddedData">

  <xsl:include href="DateTemplates.xslt" />

  <xsl:param name="targetYear" select="3000" />

  <xsl:template match="/">
    <html>
      <head>
        <title>Famous People</title>
      </head>
      <body>
        <h1>Famous People</h1>
        <hr />
        <table>
          <caption>Famous People</caption>
          <thead>
            <tr>
              <th>Name</th>
              <th>Born</th>
              <th>Died</th>
              <th>Description</th>
            </tr>
          </thead>
          <tbody>
            <xsl:apply-templates select="People/Person">
              <xsl:sort
                 select="translate(@bornDate, '-', '')"
                 data-type="number"/>
            </xsl:apply-templates>
          </tbody>
        </table>
      </body>
    </html>
  </xsl:template>

  <xsl:template match="Person">
    <xsl:variable name="rowCSS">
      <xsl:choose>
        <xsl:when test="position() mod 2 = 0">color:#0000aa;</xsl:when>
        <xsl:otherwise>color:#006666;</xsl:otherwise>
      </xsl:choose>
    </xsl:variable>
    <xsl:variable name="nameCSS">
      <xsl:if
     test="number(substring(@bornDate, 1, 4)) > $targetYear">color:red;</xsl:if>
    </xsl:variable>
    <tr style="{$rowCSS}">
      <td style="{$nameCSS}">
        <xsl:value-of select="Name" />
```

```
        </td>
        <td>
          <xsl:call-template name="iso8601DateToDisplay">
            <xsl:with-param name="iso8601Date" select="@bornDate" />
          </xsl:call-template>
        </td>
        <td>
          <xsl:call-template name="iso8601DateToDisplayDate">
            <xsl:with-param name="iso8601Date" select="@diedDate" />
          </xsl:call-template>
        </td>
        <td>
          <xsl:value-of select="Description" />
        </td>
      </tr>
    </xsl:template>

  </xsl:stylesheet>
```

Note how the `<xsl:include>` element points to `DateTemplates.xslt`.

4. Use one of the following command lines to run the transformation:

```
java net.sf.saxon.Transform -s:people.xml -xsl: PeopleToHtml-UsingIncludes.xslt
                              -o:People-UsingIncludes.html
```

or:

```
Transform -s:people.xml -xsl: PeopleToHtml-UsingIncludes.xslt
                              -o:People-UsingIncludes.html
```

The results are the same as Listing 8-16.

How It Works

The `<xsl:include>` element uses the `href` attribute to point to another XSLT file. The processor takes the code from the referenced file, removes the outer `<xsl:stylesheet>` element, and builds an in-memory representation consisting of both the main style sheet and any included ones. Then the transformation is carried out in the usual fashion.

The <xsl:import> Element

This element acts in a very similar way to `<xsl:include>` with one difference—if the templates imported clash with any already in the main XSLT, they take a lower precedence. This means that if you have two templates that match `<Person>`, for example, the one in the main style sheet is executed rather than the template in the imported one. For many transformations this is irrelevant, and as long as you don't have any templates that match the same nodes then `<xsl:import>` and `<xsl:include>` behave in the same way.

Another common use case that arises is when you want to process the same node more than once. This can occur when you want to show a summary or a table of contents. To process nodes more than once you need to use two `<xsl:template>` elements and specify a *mode* attribute.

The <xsl:template> Mode Attribute

Say you want to add a menu to your `People.html` page. This will take the form of three anchors at the start of the HTML that link to the relevant section in the table below. To create this new menu, perform the following:

1. First you need to create a new `<xsl:template>` to create your menu. Notice in the following code snippet that this template has a `mode` attribute, which has the value `menu`. The template simply creates three `<a>` elements with an `href` of `#Person` followed by the position of the person in the node set. This means the links will point to `Person1`, `Person2`, and so on.

```
<xsl:template match="Person" mode="menu">
  <a href="#Person{position()}">
    <xsl:value-of select="Name" />
  </a>
  <br />
</xsl:template>
```

2. To call this template, add an `<xsl:apply-templates>` instruction with a mode also set to `menu` toward the start of the XSLT:

```
<body>
        <h1>Famous People</h1>
        <hr />
        <xsl:apply-templates select="People/Person" mode="menu">
          <xsl:sort select="translate(@bornDate, '-', '')" data-type="number"/>
        </xsl:apply-templates>
        <hr />
        <table>
```

3. Next, add an anchor when you create the cell holding the name:

```
<td style="{$nameCSS}">
        <a name="Person{position()}">
          <xsl:value-of select="Name" />
        </a>
      </td>
```

4. Again create an `<a>` element but with a name attribute consisting of `#Person` followed by a digit indicating the position in the set.

5. Finally, add a mode to the original `<xsl:template>` that matches `<Person>` and include this when you use `<xsl:apply-templates>` to process the `<Person>` nodes for a second time:

```
<tbody>
  <xsl:apply-templates select="People/Person" mode="details">
    <xsl:sort
```

```
select="translate(@bornDate, '-', '')" data-type="number"/>
    </xsl:apply-templates>
  </tbody>
```

The complete style sheet is shown in Listing 8-21.

Available for download on Wrox.com

LISTING 8-21: PeopleToHtml-WithMenu.xslt

```
<?xml version="1.0" encoding="utf-8"?>
<xsl:stylesheet version="1.0"
      xmlns:xsl="http://www.w3.org/1999/XSL/Transform"
      xmlns:myData="http://wrox.com/namespaces/embeddedData"
      exclude-result-prefixes="myData">

  <xsl:include href="DateTemplates.xslt" />
  <xsl:param name="targetYear" select="3000" />

  <xsl:template match="/">
    <html>
      <head>
        <title>Famous People</title>
      </head>
      <body>
        <h1>Famous People</h1>
        <hr />
        <xsl:apply-templates select="People/Person" mode="menu">
          <xsl:sort select="translate(@bornDate, '-', '')" data-type="number"/>
        </xsl:apply-templates>
        <hr />
        <table>
          <caption>Famous People</caption>
          <thead>
            <tr>
              <th>Name</th>
              <th>Born</th>
              <th>Died</th>
              <th>Description</th>
            </tr>
          </thead>
          <tbody>
            <xsl:apply-templates select="People/Person" mode="details">
              <xsl:sort
        select="translate(@bornDate, '-', '')" data-type="number"/>
            </xsl:apply-templates>
          </tbody>
        </table>
      </body>
    </html>
  </xsl:template>

  <xsl:template match="Person" mode="menu">
    <a href="#Person{position()}">
      <xsl:value-of select="Name" />
```

continues

LISTING 8-21 *(continued)*

```
      </a>
      <br />
    </xsl:template>

    <xsl:template match="Person" mode="details">
      <xsl:variable name="rowCSS">
        <xsl:choose>
          <xsl:when test="position() mod 2 = 0">color:#0000aa;</xsl:when>
          <xsl:otherwise>color:#006666;</xsl:otherwise>
        </xsl:choose>
      </xsl:variable>
      <xsl:variable name="nameCSS">
        <xsl:if
     test="number(substring(@bornDate, 1, 4)) > $targetYear">color:red;</xsl:if>
      </xsl:variable>
      <tr style="{$rowCSS}">
        <td style="{$nameCSS}">
          <a name="Person{position()}">
            <xsl:value-of select="Name" />
          </a>
        </td>
        <td>
          <xsl:call-template name="iso8601DateToDisplayDate">
            <xsl:with-param name="iso8601Date" select="@bornDate" />
          </xsl:call-template>
        </td>
        <td>
          <xsl:call-template name="iso8601DateToDisplayDate">
            <xsl:with-param name="iso8601Date" select="@diedDate" />
          </xsl:call-template>
        </td>
        <td>
          <xsl:value-of select="Description" />
        </td>
      </tr>
    </xsl:template>

  </xsl:stylesheet>
```

If you've been experimenting with your own style sheets, or when you do so in future, you may experience a strange phenomenon—some of the text from the source document will appear in the output even when you didn't ask for it. This is a problem often encountered and occurs because of two features of XSLT: *built-in templates* and *built-in rules*.

UNDERSTANDING BUILT-IN TEMPLATES AND BUILT-IN RULES

Before the built-in templates and rules are explained in depth it will be best to start with an example of how they operate. Create a basic shell transformation consisting entirely of an `<xsl:stylesheet>` element, as shown in the following snippet:

```
<xsl:stylesheet version="1.0" xmlns:xsl="http://www.w3.org/1999/XSL/Transform">
</xsl:stylesheet>
```

Now if you run it against the People.xml file you'll find that, although there are no <xsl:templates> in the transformation, the output consists of all the actual text within the XML. However, no elements are output. This happens because there is a built-in rule for each of the different item types in a document—elements, attributes, comments, and so on—that is applied if you haven't specified an explicit one yourself. The basic rule for the root node or an element is simply: apply templates to the children of the root node or element. This means that the empty style sheet in the preceding code is the equivalent of the following:

```
<xsl:stylesheet version="1.0" xmlns:xsl="http://www.w3.org/1999/XSL/Transform">

  <xsl:template match="/">
    <xsl:apply-templates select="*" />
  </xsl:template>
</xsl:stylesheet></xsl:stylesheet>
```

Now there isn't a template matching the child of the root node, which is <People>, so the built-in template kicks in. This simply outputs all text content of the element. In effect there is a template added for <People>, which just selects the element's value, like so:

```
<xsl:stylesheet version="1.0" xmlns:xsl="http://www.w3.org/1999/XSL/Transform">

  <xsl:template match="/">
    <xsl:apply-templates select="*" />
  </xsl:template>

  <xsl:template match="People">
    <xsl:value-of select="."/>
  </xsl:template>
</xsl:stylesheet>
```

As long as you provide templates for any elements you select you won't have this problem; if you do select elements using <xsl:apply-templates> and there are no matching <xsl:template> elements to process them, you'll most likely encounter unwanted text in your output. You can always get around this by overriding the built-in template with one of your own that outputs nothing; in the following simple example a template matches all text nodes and effectively discards them getting rid of all the output created by the built-in rules:

```
<xsl:stylesheet version="1.0" xmlns:xsl="http://www.w3.org/1999/XSL/Transform">
  <xsl:template match="text()" />
</xsl:stylesheet>
```

If you run this transformation against People.xml, or any other file, you shouldn't see any output because there is now an <xsl:template> element that matches any text found and ignores it.

You've now covered the majority of elements and their attributes found in version 1.0 of XSLT. You've seen how the whole idea of the language is based on the premise of <xsl:template> elements that deal with specific parts of the input document. You've also seen how these templates are executed, either being called by name using an `<xsl:call-template>` instruction or by matching the nodes selected by `<xsl:apply-templates>`. You also saw that inside `<xsl:template>` it was possible to extract values relative to the node being processed, known as the context node. You saw how you have a number of different choices of what format this information takes, using `<xsl:value-of>` to extract a simple string value or using `<xsl:copy>` and `<xsl:copy-of>` to output full nodes as XML. The other main elements covered were `<xsl:include>` and `<xsl:import>` which are designed to enable reusable XSLT modules to be designed that can then be incorporated in other transformations.

You are now going to look at version 2.0 of XSLT and see what new features were introduced and what problems they are designed to help solve.

USING XSLT 2.0

After XSLT 1.0 had been in use for some time, it became apparent that there were a number of areas that could be improved and a number of use cases that it couldn't cope with, at least in a relatively simple manner.

NOTE *Use cases are scenarios that occur in real-life situations. They are often used to help document software requirements before development begins.*

Some of the new features in version 2.0 that you'll be looking at in this section include:

- **Stronger data typing:** Version 1.0 only really dealt with numbers, text, Booleans, and, to a limited extent, dates. In version 2.0 there is much more granular control.
- **User-defined functions:** Although you can use `<xsl:call-template>` as a limited function substitute in version 1.0, version 2.0 enables you to create your own functions that can be called from within an XPath expression.
- **Multiple result documents:** In version 2.0 you can produce more than one file from a single transformation; this is a common use case when you need to split a large XML document into smaller ones.
- **Multiple input documents:** Version 1.0 allowed extra input by way of the `document()` function. Version 2.0 adds a `collection()` function that allows processing of multiple documents; for example, you could process a whole folder.
- **Support for grouping:** Grouping in version 1.0 was very difficult; in version 2.0 it's much simpler.
- **The ability to process non-XML input:** You can now take a CSV file, for example, and turn it into XML.

- **Better text handling:** A number of new elements can assist in the parsing of textual content; for example, using a regular expression to break long pieces of text into smaller chunks.
- **Support for XPath 2.0:** XPath 2.0 contains a wealth of new functions that can all be used in the newer version of XSLT.

You'll take a look at these features in the next few sections and see how they help solve problems that were difficult or impossible in version 1.0.

Understanding Data Types in XSLT 2.0

XSLT 1.0 had very limited type support—basically text, numbers, and Booleans. There was no support for other common types found in many other languages and even dates were often manipulated as numbers. In version 2.0 you can specify a much wider range of types based on those found in XML Schema; this includes integers, doubles, and decimals as well as support for time durations such as day, month, and year. You can also import types from other XML Schemas if you are using a schema-aware processor.

NOTE *XSLT 2.0 allows for two types of processors: basic and schema-aware. The latter allows you to use data types from third-party schema as well as the built-in ones from XML Schema; they also allow validation of both the input and the output document based on a schema. Saxon has a schema-aware version but it requires a paid-for license so this aspect of version 2.0 in is not covered in the examples.*

Support for these extra types means that you can now label variables, templates and functions as holding, outputting and returning, respectively, a particular type. This means that if you try to use text where an integer had been expected, the processor will flag an error rather than try to perform a silent conversion. This makes debugging much easier. The full list of built-in types is available at `http://www.w3.org/TR/xpath-functions/#datatypes`. You'll see how to use some of the newer date time types when you've covered the next new feature, functions.

Creating User-Defined Functions

The ability to create functions was sorely missing in version 1.0. In version 2.0 this is remedied by adding the `<xsl:function>` element. The resulting function can be used anywhere the built-in XPath functions, such as `concat()` and `substring()`, can be used.

The following Try It Out shows how to write a function in XSLT using the `<xsl:function>` element. You'll see the process involved in converting a named template to a function, how the code differs, and what advantages a function has over a template.

TRY IT OUT Creating a User-Defined Function

You're going to take another look at the example shown in Listing 8-19 where you converted a date in the standard XML format, *yyyy-mm-dd*, to a more user-friendly *date month-name year*. This time you'll replace the named template with a function.

1. Create the file in Listing 8-22, `DateFunctions.xslt`, which will replace `DateTemplates.xslt`.

Available for download on Wrox.com

LISTING 8-22: DateFunctions.xslt

```
<xsl:stylesheet version="2.0"
     xmlns:xsl="http://www.w3.org/1999/XSL/Transform"
     xmlns:myData="http://wrox.com/namespaces/embeddedData"
     xmlns:myFunc="http://wrox.com/namespaces/functions/datetime"
     xmlns:xs="http://www.w3.org/2001/XMLSchema"
     exclude-result-prefixes="myFunc">

  <xsl:variable name="thisDocument" select="document('')" />

  <myData:Months>
    <Month index="1">January</Month>
    <Month index="2">February</Month>
    <Month index="3">March</Month>
    <Month index="4">April</Month>
    <Month index="5">May</Month>
    <Month index="6">June</Month>
    <Month index="7">July</Month>
    <Month index="8">August</Month>
    <Month index="9">September</Month>
    <Month index="10">October</Month>
    <Month index="11">November</Month>
    <Month index="12">December</Month>
  </myData:Months>

  <xsl:function name="myFunc:iso8601DateToDisplayDate" as="xs:string">
    <xsl:param name="iso8601Date" as="xs:date" />
    <xsl:variable name="yearPart"
         select="year-from-date($iso8601Date)" as="xs:integer" />
    <xsl:variable name="monthPart"
        select="month-from-date($iso8601Date)" as="xs:integer" />
    <xsl:variable name="monthName" select=
"$thisDocument/xsl:stylesheet/myData:Months/Month[@index = number($monthPart)]"
/>
    <xsl:variable name="datePart"
           select="day-from-date($iso8601Date)" as="xs:integer" />
    <xsl:value-of select="concat($datePart, ' ', $monthName, ' ', $yearPart)" />
  </xsl:function>
</xsl:stylesheet>
```

Notice how you need to add two new namespaces to the top of the file: one for the function you are going to declare, and one to use the data types from the XML Schema namespace. You also need to make sure that the version attribute is now set to 2.0; this will be the case for all transforms from now on.

2. Modify Listing 8-21 so that instead of calling the named templates, it uses the newly created function as shown in Listing 8-23. Notice how you need to add the `myFunc` namespace to the top of this file too.

LISTING 8-23: PeopleToHtml-UsingFunctions.xslt

Available for download on Wrox.com

```
<xsl:stylesheet version="2.0" xmlns:xsl="http://www.w3.org/1999/XSL/Transform"
                 xmlns:myFunc="http://wrox.com/namespaces/functions/datetime">

  <xsl:include href="DateFunctions.xslt" />
  <xsl:param name="targetYear" select="3000" />

  <xsl:template match="/">
    <html>
      <head>
        <title>Famous People</title>
      </head>
      <body>
        <h1>Famous People</h1>
        <hr />
        <xsl:apply-templates select="People/Person" mode="menu">
          <xsl:sort select="translate(@bornDate, '-', '')" data-type="number"/>
        </xsl:apply-templates>
        <hr />
        <table>
          <caption>Famous People</caption>
          <thead>
            <tr>
              <th>Name</th>
              <th>Born</th>
              <th>Died</th>
              <th>Description</th>
            </tr>
          </thead>
          <tbody>
            <xsl:apply-templates select="People/Person" mode="details">
              <xsl:sort select="translate(@bornDate, '-', '')"
                   data-type="number"/>
            </xsl:apply-templates>
          </tbody>
        </table>
      </body>
    </html>
  </xsl:template>

  <xsl:template match="Person" mode="menu">
    <a href="#Person{position()}">
      <xsl:value-of select="Name" />
    </a>
    <br />
  </xsl:template>
```

continues

LISTING 8-23 *(continued)*

```
    <xsl:template match="Person" mode="details">
      <xsl:variable name="rowCSS">
        <xsl:choose>
          <xsl:when test="position() mod 2 = 0">color:#0000aa;</xsl:when>
          <xsl:otherwise>color:#006666;</xsl:otherwise>
        </xsl:choose>
      </xsl:variable>
      <xsl:variable name="nameCSS">
        <xsl:if
        test="number(substring(@bornDate, 1, 4)) > $targetYear">color:red;</xsl:if>
      </xsl:variable>
      <tr style="{$rowCSS}">
        <td style="{$nameCSS}">
          <a name="Person{position()}">
            <xsl:value-of select="Name" />
          </a>
        </td>
        <td>
          <xsl:value-of select="myFunc:iso8601DateToDisplayDate(@bornDate)" />
        </td>
        <td>
          <xsl:value-of select="myFunc:iso8601DateToDisplayDate(@diedDate)" />
        </td>
        <td>
          <xsl:value-of select="Description" />
        </td>
      </tr>
    </xsl:template>

  </xsl:stylesheet>
```

3. Run the transformation using one of the following command lines:

```
java net.sf.saxon.Transform -s:people.xml
 -xsl:peopleToHtml-UsingFunctions.xslt -o:people-usingFunctions.html
```

or:

```
transform -s:people.xml -xsl:peopleToHtml-UsingFunctions.xslt -o:people-usingFunctions
.html
```

The results will be the same as the named template version.

How It Works

The following code snippet shows the basic structure of the function:

```
<xsl:function name="myFunc:iso8601DateToDisplayDate" as="xs:string">
    <xsl:param name="iso8601Date" as="xs:date" />
    <!-- rest of function -->
</xsl:function>
```

The function is declared using the new `<xsl:function>` element. This has a name parameter, which must take a qualified name, that is, one with a prefix referring to a previously declared namespace. It's also good practice to specify the return type of the function; in this case it will be an `xs:string` as defined in the XML Schema specification so this too will be a qualified name. Inside the function you have an `<xsl:param>` as before—the only difference is that this too has its type declared; in this case it will be an `xs:date` as shown in the following code:

```
<xsl:function name="myFunc:iso8601DateToDisplayDate" as="xs:string">
  <xsl:param name="iso8601Date" as="xs:date" />
  <xsl:variable name="yearPart"
       select="year-from-date($iso8601Date)" as="xs:integer" />
  <xsl:variable name="monthPart"
       select="month-from-date($iso8601Date)" as="xs:integer" />
  <xsl:variable
   name="monthName" select=
 "$thisDocument/xsl:stylesheet/myData:Months/Month[@index = number($monthPart)]" />
  <xsl:variable name="datePart"
     select="day-from-date($iso8601Date)" as="xs:integer" />
  <xsl:value-of select="concat($datePart, ' ', $monthName, ' ', $yearPart)" />
</xsl:function>
```

The body of the function is similar to the named template from Listing 8-19. You separate the parts of the date into different variables; this time, though, you don't use string manipulation but take advantage of some of XPath's newer date handling functions, such as `year-from-date()`. Again the variables have an `as` attribute to specify the type they will hold.

To be fair, this hasn't added a lot of value; the function is still much the same size and complexity. The bigger win comes in using it. The ungainly call to the named template is now a simple one-line `<xsl:value>` instruction:

```
<td>
  <xsl:value-of select="myFunc:iso8601DateToDisplayDate(@bornDate)" />
</td>
```

In fact, although this example used converting a date to a more user-friendly format as an example of how to write a function, this was such a common request from version 1.0 users that XSLT now has a built-in `format-date()` function. This can take a standard date and an output pattern. This allows you to dispense with your included `DateFunctions.xslt` and just use the following:

Available for download on Wrox.com

```
<td>
  <xsl:value-of select="format-date(@bornDate, '[D1] [MNn] [Y]')" />
</td>
```

PeopleToHtml-FormatDate.xslt

The full file is included in the code download as `PeopleToHtml-FormatDate.xslt`.

You can find plenty of examples of how to use the `format-date()` function and the different options available for the pattern, as well as how to request different languages for the month names, at `www.w3.org/TR/xslt20/#format-date`.

The next new features you'll cover are how to create multiple documents from one transformation and how to use multiple documents as input.

Creating Multiple Output Documents

Many people using version 1.0 requested the ability to produce more than one output document from a single transformation. A common use case was where the input document had many child elements underneath the root, perhaps a list of employees, and each one was to be formatted and output separately. Many processor vendors added extensions to their products to allow this but in XSLT 2.0 there is a new instruction, `<xsl:result-document>`, that allows this task to be performed quite simply. For this example you'll take `People.xml` and create a transformation that splits it into three documents, one for each `<Person>` element. The code is shown in Listing 8-24.

Available for download on Wrox.com

LISTING 8-24: PeopleToSeparateFiles.xslt

```
<xsl:stylesheet version="2.0"
                xmlns:xsl="http://www.w3.org/1999/XSL/Transform">

  <xsl:template match="/">
    <personCount>
      <xsl:value-of select="count(People/Person)"/>
    </personCount>
    <xsl:apply-templates select="People/Person" />
  </xsl:template>

  <xsl:template match="Person">
    <xsl:result-document href="Person{position()}.xml">
      <xsl:copy-of select="." />
    </xsl:result-document>
  </xsl:template>

</xsl:stylesheet>
```

The first template matches the root node and outputs an element containing the number of `<Person>` elements in the source file. This acts as a report for the transformation. The `Person` elements are then selected using `<xsl:apply-templates>` and matched by the second template. To output a second document you use the `<xsl:result-document>` element along with its `href` attribute to specify the name of the output file. Here you've said that the name should be `PersonN.xml` with the *N* replaced by the position of the `Person` element in the set. Within the `<xsl:result-document>` you've simply done a deep copy of the current node, so all of the `<Person>` elements will appear. If you run one of the following command lines:

```
java net.sf.saxon.Transform -s:people.xml
 -xsl:peopleToSeparateFiles.xslt -o:peopleReport.xml
```

or:

```
transform -s:people.xml -xsl:peopleToSeparateFiles.xslt -o:peopleReport.xml
```

you'll get four new files. There will be a standard output, which will contain the following code:

Available for download on Wrox.com

```
<personCount>3</personCount>
```

peopleReport.xml

Then there will be three files named `Person1.xml`, `Person2.xml`, and `Person3.xml` produced in the same folder as the XSLT. They will each contain one `<Person>` element. For example, `Person2.xml` looks like:

Available for download on Wrox.com

```
<Person bornDate="1917-11-19" diedDate="1984-10-31">
  <Name>Indira Gandhi</Name>
  <Description>
    Indira Gandhi was India's first female prime minister and was
    assassinated in 1984.
  </Description>
</Person>
```

Person2.xml

This technique of splitting a larger XML document into smaller ones is often used in situations where orders are received via XML. The actual orders, from various clients, are typically aggregated by a third party into one large document and need to be treated separately. They are first split into individual orders and then processed. The advantages of splitting before processing are to make it easier to identify which order is a problem if an error should arise as well as being able to process each order differently if, for example, there were varying business rules for each customer.

Using the collection() Function

The opposite task of splitting one file into many is processing many files at once, and this is achieved using the `collection()` function. The `collection()` function can be used in a number of ways, but commonly it is used to process a complete folder or tree of folders. As a simple example you'll create a style sheet that takes the three `PersonN.xml` files created in Listing 8-24 and recombines them. The way that processors fully implement the `collection()` function is vendor dependent and Saxon has a number of extra features that allow the documents in the folder to be filtered based on their name. You will pass a filter along with the name of the folder to be treated so that only the target files are combined. The XSLT is shown in Listing 8-25.

Available for download on Wrox.com

LISTING 8-25: CombinePersonElements.xslt

```
<xsl:stylesheet version="2.0"
                xmlns:xsl="http://www.w3.org/1999/XSL/Transform">

  <xsl:template name="main">
    <People>
      <xsl:for-each
       select="collection('file:///C:/Xml/Examples/Files?select=Person*.xml')">
        <xsl:copy-of select="."/>
```

continues

LISTING 8-25 *(continued)*

```
      </xsl:for-each>
    </People>
  </xsl:template>

</xsl:stylesheet>
```

The first thing to note is the `name` attribute on the `<xsl:template>` element. Because you won't be processing a single source document you need to be able to specify where processing starts. The template contains a literal element, `<People>`, which will hold all the combined `<Person>` elements. It then uses `<xsl:for-each>` to process all files returned from the `collection()` function. This takes a single string parameter, which takes the URI to a folder and then adds a querystring parameter named `select`. This accepts a pattern that any found files must match if they are to be returned. The pattern says the name must start with `Person`, be followed by some extra characters, and end with `.xml`. The path to the folder needs to be a URI so even in Windows it uses the forward slash as a folder delimiter and must start with the `file://` scheme. You'll obviously have to modify the path to your files if you want to test this example. To run this transformation you need a slightly different command line, like so:

```
java saxon.net.sf.Transform -it:main
  -xsl:combinePersonElements.xslt -o:CombinedPerson.xml
```

or:

```
transform -it:main -xsl:combinePersonElements.xslt -o:CombinedPerson.xml
```

Instead of supplying a source document with the `-s` switch you specify an initial template with the `-it` switch. The output file will be the same as your initial `People.xml`.

Grouping in XSLT 2.0

A common use case in XSLT is to group elements in various ways and then process them together. For example, an input file may contain a list of all employees and the requirement is to group them alphabetically before displaying their information. This was a challenge in version 1.0 but has become much simpler in version 2.0 with the addition of the new elements and functions.

The file used for the examples so far, `People.xml` from Listing 8-1, doesn't have enough `<Person>` elements for grouping to be demonstrated so another file, `Employees.xml`, is used for this example. The file is shown in Listing 8-26.

Available for download on Wrox.com

LISTING 8-26: Employees.xml

```
<employees>
  <employee firstName="Joe" lastName="Fawcett"
            jobTitle="Developer" department="IT"/>
  <employee firstName="Max" lastName="Bialystock"
            jobTitle="CEO" department="Management"/>
```

```
  <employee firstName="Phineas" lastName="Barnum"
            jobTitle="Head of Sales" department="Sales and Marketing"/>
  <employee firstName="Leo" lastName="Bloom"
            jobTitle="Auditor" department="Accounts"/>
  <employee firstName="Danny" lastName="Ayers"
            jobTitle="Developer" department="IT"/>
  <employee firstName="Carmen" lastName="Ghia"
            jobTitle="PA to the VP of Products" department="Management"/>
  <employee firstName="Ulla" lastName="Anderson"
            jobTitle="Head of Promotions" department="Sales and Marketing"/>
  <employee firstName="Grace" lastName="Hopper"
            jobTitle="Developer" department="IT"/>
  <employee firstName="Bob" lastName="Cratchit"
            jobTitle="Bookkeeper" department="Accounts"/>
  <employee firstName="Charles" lastName="Babbage"
            jobTitle="Head of Infrastructure" department="IT"/>
  <employee firstName="Roger" lastName="De Bris"
            jobTitle="VP of Products" department="Management"/>
  <employee firstName="Willy" lastName="Loman"
            jobTitle="Salesman" department="Sales and Marketing"/>
  <employee firstName="Franz" lastName="Liebkind"
            jobTitle="Developer" department="IT"/>
  <employee firstName="Luca" lastName="Pacioli"
            jobTitle="Accountant" department="Accounts"/>
  <employee firstName="Lorenzo" lastName="St. DuBois"
            jobTitle="Project Manager" department="IT" />
</employees>
```

Your requirement is to output each department in a separate element and, within each department, output the employees in alphabetical order. You'll be using the new `<xsl:for-each-group>` instruction as well as the `current-group()` and `current-grouping-key()` functions.

The style sheet is shown in Listing 8-27.

Available for download on Wrox.com

LISTING 8-27: EmployeesByDepartment.xslt

```
<xsl:stylesheet version="2.0" xmlns:xsl="http://www.w3.org/1999/XSL/Transform">

  <xsl:template match="/">
    <employeesByDepartment>
      <xsl:for-each-group select="employees/employee" group-by="@department">
        <xsl:sort select="@department" data-type="text" />
        <department name="{current-grouping-key()}">
          <xsl:apply-templates select="current-group()">
            <xsl:sort select="@lastName" data-type="text" />
            <xsl:sort select="@firstName" data-type="text" />
          </xsl:apply-templates>
        </department>
      </xsl:for-each-group>
    </employeesByDepartment>
  </xsl:template>
```

continues

LISTING 8-27 *(continued)*

```
  <xsl:template match="employee">
    <employee jobTitle="{@jobTitle}">
      <xsl:value-of select="concat(@lastName, ', ', @firstName)"/>
    </employee>
  </xsl:template>
</xsl:stylesheet>
```

The following steps explain how the transformation is accomplished and what role the newly introduced elements, such as `<xsl:for-each-group>`, play in the proceedings:

1. After matching the root node and creating an `<employeesByDepartment>` element to hold your results, use the new `<xsl:for-each-group>` element to select all the `<employee>` elements.
2. Then specify, via the `group-by` attribute, that you want to group on the department attribute.
3. Follow this with a standard `<xsl:sort>` to make sure that the department names are output in alphabetical order.
4. After sorting, output a `<department>` element with its `name` attribute set to the value of the `current-grouping-key()` function. This is a handy way to find out the actual value of each department.
5. Once the `<department>` element is output, use `<xsl:apply-templates>` to process the individual `<employee>` elements. Select these by using the `current-group()` function, which holds all of the nodes currently being processed as part of the `<xsl:for-each-group>` element. Again these elements are sorted, first on the `lastName` attribute and then by `firstName`.

The second template, matching the `<employee>` elements, just uses standard methods to output a new `<employee>` element along with their department and their full name. If you run one of the following commands (on one line):

```
java net.sf.saxon.Transform  -s:employees.xml
          -xsl:EmployeesByDepartment.xslt -o:EmployeesByDepartment.xml
```

or:

```
transform -s:employees.xml
          -xsl:EmployeesByDepartment.xslt -o:EmployeesByDepartment.xml
```

you'll see the resulting file as shown in Figure 8-6.

D:\Users\Joe\Documents\...

```
<?xml version="1.0" encoding="UTF-8"?>
- <employeesByDepartment>
  - <department name="Accounts">
       <employee jobTitle="Auditor">Bloom, Leo</employee>
       <employee jobTitle="Bookkeeper">Cratchit, Bob</employee>
       <employee jobTitle="Accountant">Pacioli, Luca</employee>
    </department>
  - <department name="IT">
       <employee jobTitle="Developer">Ayers, Danny</employee>
       <employee jobTitle="Head of Infrastructure">Babbage, Charles</employee>
       <employee jobTitle="Developer">Fawcett, Joe</employee>
       <employee jobTitle="Developer">Hopper, Grace</employee>
       <employee jobTitle="Developer">Liebkind, Franz</employee>
       <employee jobTitle="Project Manager">St. DuBois, Lorenzo</employee>
    </department>
  - <department name="Management">
       <employee jobTitle="CEO">Bialystock, Max</employee>
       <employee jobTitle="VP of Products">De Bris, Roger</employee>
       <employee jobTitle="PA to the VP of Products">Ghia, Carmen</employee>
    </department>
  - <department name="Sales and Marketing">
       <employee jobTitle="Head of Promotions">Anderson, Ulla</employee>
       <employee jobTitle="Head of Sales">Barnum, Phineas</employee>
       <employee jobTitle="Salesman">Loman, Willy</employee>
    </department>
  </employeesByDepartment>
```

FIGURE 8-6

NOTE *If you only have access to version 1.0 and need to fulfill this requirement, the best approach is known as Muenchian grouping. It's not easy but it is doable; there are some good examples at* `www.jenitennison.com/xslt/grouping/muenchian.html`.

The next new feature you'll cover is how to process non-XML input using XSLT.

Handling Non-XML Input with XSLT 2.0

As with most of the new features in version 2.0, many 1.0 users requested that 2.0 be equipped to handle input documents that were not XML. A typical use case is to convert a traditional CSV file, maybe exported from Excel or a legacy database system, into an XML format that could then be consumed by a separate application. There are two new features in version 2.0 that make this possible. First is the `unparsed-text()` function, which, as the name implies, enables the retrieval of a text file the URI of which is specified as an argument, similar to the `document()` function. The second feature is the XPath `tokenize()` function, which is used to split the text into separate tokens based on a regular expression. The example that follows takes a simple three-column CSV file and uses these two new features to create an XML representation of the data.

The first file is shown in Listing 8-28. This is the CSV that you should import to perform the following steps. It has three columns for last name, first name, and job title.

Available for download on Wrox.com

LISTING 8-28: Employees.csv

```
Fawcett, Joe, Developer
Ayers, Danny, Developer
Lovelace, Ada, Project Manager
```

1. Start the XSLT by declaring a variable to hold the path to the CSV file; this is passed to the transformation on the command line:

```
<xsl:stylesheet version="2.0"
                xmlns:xsl="http://www.w3.org/1999/XSL/Transform"
                xmlns:xs="http://www.w3.org/2001/XMLSchema">

  <xsl:param name="dataPath" select="''" as="xs:string"/>
</xsl:stylesheet>
```

2. Next add a variable that uses `dataPath` as the argument to `unparsed-text()` and stores it for use later:

```
<xsl:stylesheet version="2.0"
                xmlns:xsl="http://www.w3.org/1999/XSL/Transform"
                xmlns:xs="http://www.w3.org/2001/XMLSchema">

  <xsl:param name="dataPath" select="''" as="xs:string"/>
  <xsl:variable name="employeesText" select="unparsed-text($dataPath)"
                as="xs:string" />
</xsl:stylesheet>
```

3. Now comes the main template. First take the CSV data and split it into separate lines by using the `tokenize()` function with a second argument of `\r?\n`; this means split the data whenever you encounter either a carriage return followed by a newline character or just a newline character.

```
<xsl:stylesheet version="2.0"
                xmlns:xsl="http://www.w3.org/1999/XSL/Transform"
                xmlns:xs="http://www.w3.org/2001/XMLSchema">

  <xsl:param name="dataPath" select="''" as="xs:string"/>
  <xsl:variable name="employeesText" select="unparsed-text($dataPath)"
                as="xs:string" />

  <xsl:template name="main">
    <xsl:variable name="lines" select="tokenize($employeesText, '\r?\n')"
                  as="xs:string*" />

  </xsl:template>
</xsl:stylesheet>
```

4. Then use `<xsl:for-each>` to process each line and use `tokenize()` once more, this time splitting on a comma followed by optional whitespace as indicated by the regular expression, `\s*`:

```
<xsl:stylesheet version="2.0"
                xmlns:xsl="http://www.w3.org/1999/XSL/Transform"
                xmlns:xs="http://www.w3.org/2001/XMLSchema">

 <xsl:param name="dataPath" select="''" as="xs:string"/>
 <xsl:variable name="employeesText" select="unparsed-text($dataPath)"
                as="xs:string" />

 <xsl:template name="main">
   <xsl:variable name="lines" select="tokenize($employeesText, '\r?\n')"
                  as="xs:string*" />
   <employees>
     <xsl:for-each select="$lines">
       <employee>
       <xsl:variable name="employeeData" select="tokenize(., ',\s*')"
                     as="xs:string+" />

       </employee>
     </xsl:for-each>
   </employees>
 </xsl:template>
</xsl:stylesheet>
```

5. Finally, add the XML elements you need and use the information held in `employeeData`. Because there were three columns in your CSV there will be three tokens that can be accessed by position. The full XSLT is shown in Listing 8-29.

Available for download on Wrox.com

LISTING 8-29: EmployeesFromCSV.xslt

```
<xsl:stylesheet version="2.0"
                xmlns:xsl="http://www.w3.org/1999/XSL/Transform"
                xmlns:xs="http://www.w3.org/2001/XMLSchema">

  <xsl:param name="dataPath" select="''" as="xs:string"/>
  <xsl:variable name="employeesText" select="unparsed-text($dataPath)"
                as="xs:string" />

  <xsl:template name="main">
    <xsl:variable name="lines" select="tokenize($employeesText, '\r?\n')"
                  as="xs:string*" />
    <employees>
      <xsl:for-each select="$lines">
        <employee>
        <xsl:variable name="employeeData" select="tokenize(., ',\s*')"
                      as="xs:string+" />
          <lastName>
            <xsl:value-of select="$employeeData[1]"/>
          </lastName>
          <firstName>
            <xsl:value-of select="$employeeData[2]"/>
          </firstName>
          <jobTitle>
            <xsl:value-of select="$employeeData[3]"/>
```

continues

LISTING 8-29 *(continued)*

```
            </jobTitle>
          </employee>
        </xsl:for-each>
      </employees>
    </xsl:template>
  </xsl:stylesheet>
```

If you run this by using the following command line (on one line):

```
java saxon.net.sf.Transform -it:main -xsl:EmployeesFromCSV.xslt
 dataPath=Employees.csv -o:EmployeesFromCSV.xml
```

or:

```
transform -it:main -xsl:EmployeesFromCSV.xslt
      dataPath=Employees.csv -o:EmployeesFromCSV.xml
```

then, assuming `Employees.csv` is in the same directory as the style sheet, you'll see the results as in Listing 8-30.

Available for download on Wrox.com

LISTING 8-30: EmployeesFromCSV.xml

```
<employees xmlns:xs="http://www.w3.org/2001/XMLSchema">
  <employee>
    <lastName>Fawcett</lastName>
    <firstName>Joe</firstName>
    <jobTitle>Developer</jobTitle>
  </employee>
  <employee>
    <lastName>Ayers</lastName>
    <firstName>Danny</firstName>
    <jobTitle>Developer</jobTitle>
  </employee>
  <employee>
    <lastName>Lovelace</lastName>
    <firstName>Ada</firstName>
    <jobTitle>Project Manager</jobTitle>
  </employee>
</employees>
```

NOTE *You'll notice there's an unused namespace declaration in the output file. This is because you declared it in the XSLT and it was copied to the output, just in case it was needed. If you want to tidy the output and remove it you can modify the* `<xsl:stylesheet>` *element by adding an* `exclude-result-prefixes` *attribute and giving it the value of xs, hence:* `<xsl:stylesheet exclude-result-prefixes="xs" ...... />`*. This tells the processor that you don't need the declaration appearing in the output XML.*

As well as incorporating plain text from external sources and being able to use the `tokenize()` function to break it into smaller parts there is also a powerful new element in XSLT 2.0 that can be used to separate textual content into two groups, those that match a regular expression and those that don't. This element is `<xs:analyze-string>`.

For an example of its use take a look at the source document in Listing 8-31:

LISTING 8-31: Addresses.xml

```
<addresses>
  <address name="The White House">
    1600 Pennsylvania Ave NW,  Washington, DC 20500-0001
  </address>
  <address name="The Statue of Liberty">
    Liberty Island, New York, NY 10004
  </address>
  <address name="The Empire State Building">
    350 5th Avenue,  New York, NY 10118
  </address>
  <address name="Utopia">
    Who knows?
  </address>
</addresses>
```

Listing 8-31 shows the addresses of three famous landmarks and a fictitious address, designed to show that it can cope with data that is in an unexpected format. The aim is to transform this file so that each valid address is split into four constituent parts representing the first line of the address, city, state and zip code. The transformation will use the `<xsl:analyze-string>` element as shown in Listing 8-32:

LISTING 8-32: Analyze-String.Xslt

```
xsl:stylesheet version="2.0"
               xmlns:xsl="http://www.w3.org/1999/XSL/Transform">

  <xsl:output indent="yes" />

  <xsl:template match="addresses">
    <addresses>
      <xsl:apply-templates select="address" />
    </addresses>
  </xsl:template>

  <xsl:template match="address">
   <address name="{@name}">
     <xsl:analyze-string select="."
      regex=
  "^\s*([^,]+)\s*,\s*([^,]+)\s*,\s*([A-Z]{{2}})\s*(\d{{5}}(\-\d{{4}})?)\s*$">
       <xsl:matching-substring>
         <addressLine1><xsl:value-of select="regex-group(1)"/></addressLine1>
```

continues

LISTING 8-32 *(continued)*

```
          <city><xsl:value-of select="regex-group(2)"/></city>
          <state><xsl:value-of select="regex-group(3)"/></state>
          <zip><xsl:value-of select="regex-group(4)"/></zip>
        </xsl:matching-substring>
        <xsl:non-matching-substring>
          <xsl:value-of select="." />
        </xsl:non-matching-substring>
      </xsl:analyze-string>
    </address>
  </xsl:template>
</xsl:stylesheet>
```

The code starts in the usual way, matching the `<addresses>` element and, within that template, calling `<xsl:apply-templates>` to process each individual `<address>`.

The second template, the one that matches `<address>`, contains the new `<xsl:analyze-string>` element. This has two attributes: `select`, that chooses what text to process, and `regex` which defines the regular expression used to break down the text into smaller units.

The regular expression is little complex, but it can be broken down into four main parts:

- `^\s*([^,]+)\s*,`

  The first section starts with the caret (`^`), which means match from the beginning of the string, and `\s*` means any number of spaces, including none should come first. These are followed by a group, in parentheses, which is defined as `[^,]+` representing any character that is not a comma occurring one or more times. This is followed by any number of spaces (`\s*`) and then another comma (`,`). This will be your first regular expression group and is used as the value for `<addressLine1>`.

- `\s*([^,]+)\s*,`

  The next part of the expression is almost identical; again it looks for any number of spaces (`\s*`) followed by a number of non-comma characters, some more spaces, and a comma. This group is used for the `<city>` element.

- `\s*([A-Z]{{2}})`

  The third part of the regular expression is used to populate the `<state>` element. It looks for a number of spaces followed by two uppercase characters in the range A to Z (`[A-Z]`). Notice how the quantity specifier, `2`, must appear between doubled braces, `{{2}}`, as opposed to the standard single braces, `{}`, normally used in regular expressions. This is because single braces are used to define embedded XPath in XSLT.

- `\s*(\d{{5}}(-\d{{4}})?)\s*$`

  The last part of the expression is used to extract the contents for the `<zip>` element. It searches for some spaces followed by digits (`\d`) that occur precisely five times (`{{5}}`). It then looks for a hyphen followed by four digits (`\d{{4}}`). This secondary group is followed by a question mark (`?`) meaning that the latter part of the zip code is optional. The final `$` sign is used to show that the regular expression extends to cover all the way to the end of the string being analyzed.

The `<xsl:matching-substring>` element is called whenever the regex succeeds (as shown in the following code). Within this element you use the regex-group(n) function to output any matching sections of the regular expression that appear within parentheses. You specify which section by passing in an index to regex-group(). There are five sets of parentheses in the expression, but only four are needed as the last one is for the second part of the zip code and this group is also contained within the fourth one.

```
        <xsl:matching-substring>
          <addressLine1><xsl:value-of select="regex-group(1)"/></addressLine1>
          <city><xsl:value-of select="regex-group(2)"/></city>
          <state><xsl:value-of select="regex-group(3)"/></state>
          <zip><xsl:value-of select="regex-group(4)"/></zip><!--    -->
        </xsl:matching-substring>
        <xsl:non-matching-substring>
          <xsl:value-of select="." />
        </xsl:non-matching-substring>
      </xsl:analyze-string>
```

The final part of the code is called if the regular expression doesn't match all or part of the string being analyzed. In this case you use it when an address does not appear in the expected format. In this case the original address is simply output verbatim.

You can try the code for yourself by using one of the following command lines:

```
java net.sf.saxon.Transform -s:addresses.xml -xsl:analyze-string.xslt
  -o:ParsedAddresses.xml
```

or:

```
Transform -s:addresses.xml -xsl:analyze-string.xslt -o:ParsedAddresses.xml
```

You should get a result similar to Listing 8-33:

Available for download on Wrox.com

LISTING 8-33: ParsedAddresses.xml

```
<addresses>
   <address name="The White House">
      <addressLine1>1600 Pennsylvania Ave NW</addressLine1>
      <city>Washington</city>
      <state>DC</state>
      <zip>20500-0001</zip>
   </address>
   <address name="The Statue of Liberty">
      <addressLine1>Liberty Island</addressLine1>
      <city>New York</city>
      <state>NY</state>
      <zip>10004</zip>
   </address>
   <address name="The Empire State Building">
      <addressLine1>350 5th Avenue</addressLine1>
      <city>New York</city>
```

continues

LISTING 8-33 *(continued)*

```
      <state>NY</state>
      <zip>10118</zip>
   </address>
   <address name="Utopia">
    Who knows?
  </address>
</addresses>
```

NOTE *There is a much better all-purpose CSV-to-XML converter available from* `http://andrewjwelch.com/code/xslt/csv/csv-to-xml_v2.html` *that allows for quoted values and column headings. A study of it will provide further insight into the string handling features of XSLT 2.0 such as the* `<xsl:analyze-string>` *element shown in Listing 8-32.*

That concludes your tour of XSLT 2.0; you'll now take a brief look at what's possibly coming in version 3.0.

XSLT AND XPATH 3.0: WHAT'S COMING NEXT?

XSLT 3.0 is currently at draft status. By looking at the W3C's specifications it seems like the main drive is to make it a much more powerful functional language. Most functional languages share certain features, the main one being the ability to treat functions as arguments to other functions; for example, the `map()` function, which takes two arguments, a sequence of nodes, and a function to apply to each node in turn. This and similar functions are present in the current XPath draft and it seems certain that they'll be included in the final spec.

There are also a number of new instructions for XSLT. These include `<xsl:try>` and `<xsl:catch>` for better error handling; and `<xsl:iterate>` which can select a sequence of nodes and then process them one by one but which also has the ability to cease processing and break out of the loop if required—something not currently possible with `<xsl:for-each>` because there is no guaranteed order of processing. There is also `<xsl:evaluate>`, which enables dynamic evaluation of XPath. You can construct a string and have it treated as an XPath expression; this is something that has been requested since XSLT launched.

If you're desperate to try out these new features some of them are implemented already in the Saxon processor. Go to `www.saxonica.com/documentation/using-xsl/xslt30.xml` for more information on how to turn on version 3.0 processing, but note that currently it's still in an experimental state and is only available for the paid for versions of Saxon.

SUMMARY

In this chapter you've learned:

- The basic premise behind XSLT is transforming an XML document to a different XML format, HTML or plain text.
- The basic `<xsl:template>` element matches specified XML and outputs new content
- `<xsl:apply-templates>` groups nodes that are then processed by their matching `<xsl:template>`.
- XPath is used throughout XSLT to specify nodes to process and to extract specific data items.
- The more advanced elements `<xsl:include>` and `<xsl:import>` enable you to write reusable code modules.
- Improvements in XSLT 2.0 include better handling of non-XML content using the `unparsed-text()` function as well as better processing of text through regular expressions by using functions such as `tokenize()` and elements such as `<analyze-string>`.
- Better error handling using `<try>`/`<catch>` and dynamic evaluation of strings as XPath using `<xsl:evaluate>` are coming up in the next version of XSLT.

EXERCISES

Answers to Exercises can be found in Appendix A.

1. Give three examples of functions that are available in XSLT but not in pure XPath.
2. Write a style sheet that accepts two currency codes and an amount as parameters and outputs the appropriate converted values using a simulated web service that is actually a hard-coded XML document (or write a web service if you're feeling adventurous).

▸ WHAT YOU LEARNED IN THIS CHAPTER

TOPIC	KEY POINTS
XSLT 1.0 Uses	To transform XML to another XML format, HTML, or plain text.
XSLT 2.0 Uses	Same as for 1.0 but can also transform plain text.
Language Style	**Declarative**: Specify what you want not how you want **Functional**: Output is a function of input
Main Elements:	<xsl:template> elements are executed when the processor encounters items that correspond to their match attribute. <xsl:apply-templates> elements are used to select groups of nodes that will then be tested against each <xsl:template> elements are used to see if they match.
Code Reusability	Achieved using <xsl:import> and <xsl:include>.
XSLT 2.0 Improvements	Plain text input to transformations. Ability to declare functions. Better text analysis using regular expressions. Ability to group nodes and process them as a group.

PART IV
Databases

9

XQuery

WHAT YOU WILL LEARN IN THIS CHAPTER:

- Why you should learn XQuery
- How XQuery uses and extends XPath
- Introduction to the XQuery language
- How to make and search an XML database
- When to use XQuery and when to use XSLT
- The future of XQuery, and how to learn more

XQuery is a language for searching and manipulating anything that can be represented as a tree using the XQuery and XPath Data Model (the "XDM" that you heard about in Chapter 7, "Extracting Data from XML"). XQuery programs (or *expressions* as they are called) can access multiple documents, or even multiple databases, and extract results very efficiently.

XQuery builds on and extends XPath. This means that XQuery's syntax is like XPath and not XML element–based like XSLT.

In this chapter you will learn all about this XQuery language: what it is and how to use it. You will also learn some rough guidelines for when to use XQuery, when to use XSLT, and when to use both, in Chapter 19, "Case Study: XML in Publishing." The short story is that XSLT is often best if you expect to process entire XML documents from start to finish and XQuery is often best if you are processing only part of a document, if you work with the same document repeatedly, or if you are processing a large number of documents.

XQUERY, XPATH, AND XSLT

XQuery, XPath, and XSLT share a lot of components. The best way to break down the various relationships though is this: where XSLT *uses* XPath — for example, in match expressions and in `<xslt:value-of>` — XQuery *extends* XPath. Any XPath 2 expression that you can write is also an XQuery expression. Let's look at each relationship separately.

NOTE *Because XSLT 1 and XPath 1 were released a long time before XQuery, XQuery 1 extends XPath version 2. W3C published a draft of XQuery 1.1 that extended an XPath 2.1, but it was all starting to get confusing, especially since W3C was working on XSLT 2.1 at the same time. W3C decided to rename XPath 2.1, XSLT 2.1, and XQuery 1.1 to XPath 3, XSLT 3 and XQuery 3 before they were released as standards.*

The latest versions (at the time of this writing) were still drafts, but were 3.0, so that XQuery 3.0 and XSLT 3.0 both used XPath 3.0, built on the Data Model (XDM) 3.0, used the Serialization 3.0 specification, and so on.

In this chapter "XQuery" means XQuery 1.0 or later, and "XPath" means XPath 2 or later, unless specified otherwise (for example, XPath 1).

XQuery and XSLT

Like XSLT (see Chapter 8), XQuery implementations often support a `collection()` function to work on databases or on the filesystem (for example, with `collection("*.xml")`); however, whereas XSLT's greatest strength lies in *apply-templates* and processing entire documents, XQuery is often best for extracting and processing small parts of documents, perhaps doing "joins" across multiple documents. The two languages are largely equivalent, but implementations tend to be optimized for these two different usages.

XQuery and XPath

Both XPath (starting with version 2) and XQuery are built on the same abstract data model, the XDM. Because of this, XQuery is not defined to operate over XML documents. Instead, like XPath 2, it is defined to work on abstract trees called *data model instances*; these could be constructed from XML documents, but they could also come from relational databases, RDF triple stores, geographical information systems, remote databases, and more.

NOTE *If you have already worked through Chapter 7, you have seen two widely-used tree structures for storing XML in memory: the document object model (DOM) and the XPath and XQuery Data Model (XDM). If you haven't read that chapter, go take a quick look now, because XQuery is built on top of XPath, the main topic of Chapter 7.*

Some differences do exist between XQuery and XPath, of course. The biggest one you'll see in practice is that there is no default *context item* in XQuery. For example, if you try a query like the following you'll get an error about no default context item.

```
/dictionary/entry[6]
```

This is because XQuery is commonly used to get information out of databases, or out of whole collections of documents. So, instead you write

```
doc("dictionary.xml")/dictionary/entry[6]
```

and all is well.

The biggest difference between XQuery and XPath, though, and by far the most important, is that there's *more* of XQuery: it's a full language in its own right. You look at some more examples in a moment, but first you should learn a little about where and how XQuery is used.

XQUERY IN PRACTICE

XQuery is widely used today, and lots of different implementations exist. The examples in this chapter focus on two implementations, Saxon and BaseX. In addition, this section covers some of the other areas in which XQuery has been quietly transforming whole industries.

Standalone XQuery Applications

In the previous chapter you used Saxon, a Java-based XSLT engine that you ran from the command line. Saxon also implements XQuery, so you could use Saxon to run the examples later in this chapter. Saxon reads your XML document, reads your query, runs the query against the document, and then prints the result.

Another open source standalone application for running XQuery is BaseX, which can be used either standalone or as a server, and which also has a graphical user interface. Dozens of other similar XQuery programs are available.

Part of SQL

Recent editions of the SQL standard from the International Organization for Standards (ISO, not an acronym) include a way to embed XQuery expressions in the middle of SQL statements. The major relational databases such as Oracle, IBM DB2, and Microsoft SQL Server all implement XQuery.

Callable from Java or Other Languages

Saxon, BaseX, Qizx, and a host of other programs come with Java libraries so that Java programmers can use XQuery instead of, or alongside, the document object model (DOM). Java programmers have reported that their programs became 100 times smaller when they moved to using XQuery instead of the DOM, and therefore much easier to understand and maintain.

XQuery libraries are also available for other languages, such as PHP, C++, and Perl: BaseX, Zorba, Berkeley DB XML, and others.

A Native-XML Server

BaseX, MarkLogic (commercial), eXist, Qizx, and several other programs exist that make an index of any number of XML documents, and can run queries against those documents using a server, so that there's no large startup time.

Some of these programs can also be called from a web server, using the servlet API or even as an Apache HTTP Web Server module; some of them include web servers so that you can write entire web-based applications in XQuery.

These programs tend to be mature, solid, robust, and very fast.

XQuery Anywhere

You can use XQuery on the cloud, in web browsers, on mobile devices, embedded inside devices — there are too many variations to list them all! Sometimes XQuery is hidden, or forms an inconspicuous part of a system. Apple's Sherlock program was extensible using XQuery; a number of commercial decision management and business support systems use XQuery, but don't generally make a big deal out of it.

In this chapter you'll use two different XQuery programs. One, Saxon, is a command-line program that reads an XQuery expression and one or more XML documents and produces a result. The second, BaseX, is a database server that's fast and easy to install and configure. BaseX runs XQuery expressions too, but instead of loading XML documents from your hard drive it can also use a database for better performance. You have already used Saxon in its XSLT mode. In the following exercise you'll install BaseX and see how easy it is to use.

TRY IT OUT Install BaseX and Run a Query

In this Try It Out you start by installing an XQuery engine to run the examples. The examples will work in Saxon, BaseX, Qizx, Zorba, or any of a number of other XQuery programs, and you can even run them directly from the oXygen XML editor. But, for these examples you'll use BaseX so as to have something specific to talk about.

1. Go to `www.basex.org` and find the Download link. It's usually at the end of the text introducing the product, right there on the front page.
2. Choose the Official Release. BaseX has frequent releases — at the time of writing, the current one is `BaseX 7.0.2.exe`. There are a few files to choose from: a Windows installer as well as a `.dmg` archive for Mac OS X users, and a Zip archive for others such as Linux. Download whichever file is appropriate for your operating system.
3. When you extract the archive you'll end up with a folder that contains, amongst other things, `BaseX.jar`, and possibly a batch or shell script called `bin/basexgui`. Either run `basexgui`, find

and double-click the `BaseX.jar` file, or run the following at a command prompt, taking care to keep the spaces and remembering that uppercase and lowercase are different:

```
java -cp BaseX.jar org.basex.BaseXGUI
```

4. Make the following simple XML document (for example, in jEdit or oXygen), and call it `armstrong.xml` — you could also use the file from Chapter 7 if you have it, or download it from this book's website.

Available for download on Wrox.com

```
<?xml version="1.0"?><?xml version="1.0" encoding="utf-8"?>
<entry id="armstrong-john">
  <title>Armstrong, John</title>
  <body><p>, an English physician and poet,
    was born in <born>1715</born> in the parish of Castleton in Roxburghshire,
    where his father and brother were clergymen; and having
    completed his education at the university of Edinburgh,
    took his degree in physic, Feb. 4, 1732, with much reputation.</p>
   </body>
</entry>
```

armstrong.xml

5. You might want to check your file by running the following command; if the file is well-formed (no mistakes), there will be no errors:

```
xmllint --noout armstrong.xml
```

6. If `xmllint` worked, your file is OK. If you don't have `xmllint` installed you can install it from `www.libxml.org`, or just move on, because BaseX will also tell you if there are problems.

7. Now go back to the BaseX window and, from the Database menu, choose Open And Manage. Create a new database called "armstrong" using the `armstrong.xml` file. You should see something like Figure 9-1, although the actual layout may vary if you have a version of BaseX newer than 7.0.2. In the Editor region, in the tab marked File, type the following short query:

```
collection("armstrong")//title
```

8. Run the query by clicking the green triangular icon at the bottom-right of the File area, near the middle of the entire BaseX window. You'll see the result appear in the area underneath the arrow, and as well as some statistics about how long the query took to run — 1.72 milliseconds in Figure 9-1. That was running on a laptop computer; XQuery can run very fast indeed!

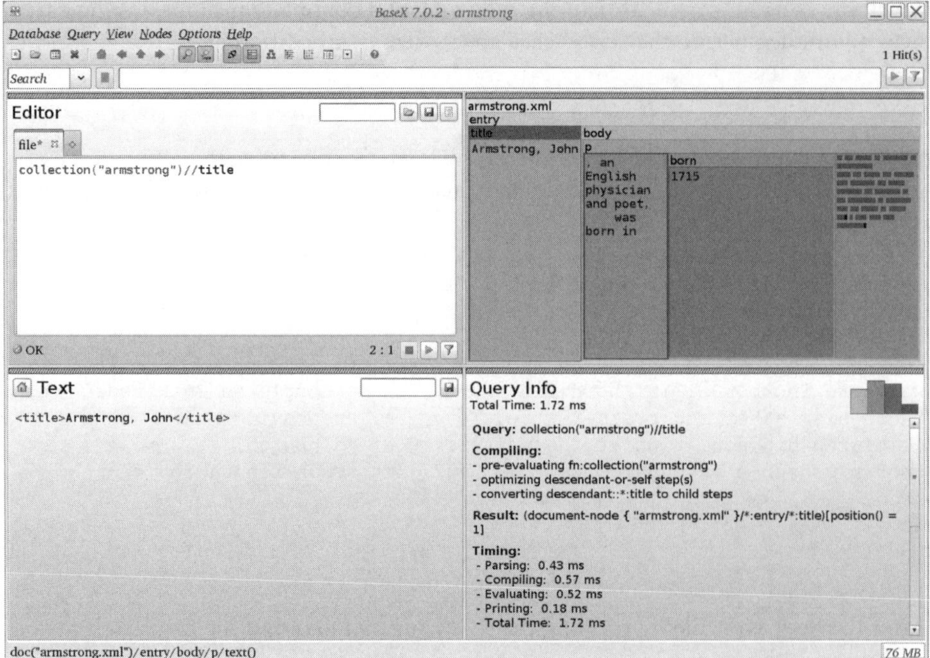

FIGURE 9-1

How It Works

In this Try It Out you have done three things. First, you downloaded and installed a database program. Second, you loaded an XML document into a database. Third, you ran a query against the database and saw the results. That's quite a lot to do all at once! But it's worth it, because now you can try the other examples in this chapter in BaseX when you get to them.

The little query you just ran first tells BaseX which database to use, with `collection("armstrong")`, and then uses the descendant-or-self/child shorthand `//` to find all child elements named `title` anywhere in the database. The database is rather small, with only one document, and only a single `<title>` element in it, so that's what was found.

Notice that BaseX has loaded your XML document into a database, so that it doesn't need to parse the XML each time. Not all XQuery implementations do that, but the ones that do can be very fast.

If you prefer, you can put your XQuery expression into a file, call it `thetitle.xq` (for example), and run it with Saxon; you'll also need to change `collection("armstrong")` into `doc("armstrong.xml")` because Saxon doesn't use a database. You can run Saxon in a command prompt window like this:

```
java -cp saxon9he.jar net.sf.saxon.Query thetitle.xq
```

You should see the same result, after the Java virtual machine has loaded.

BUILDING BLOCKS OF XQUERY

In the previous section you saw a very simple XQuery expression, just to get something working. Your sample query was just one line long, and a lot of useful XQuery expressions are like that in practice. But just as often you'll see longer and more complicated constructions, some scaling up to entire applications.

Before you learn about XQuery in detail, there are some things you should know that will help you. This section takes a more in-depth look at some building blocks of XQuery.

FLWOR Expressions, Modules, and Functions

You learn about each of these things in detail later, but for now, you should know that whereas templates are the heart of XSLT, the heart of XQuery is in "FLWOR" expressions, in functions, and in modules.

FLWOR (pronounced "flower") stands for `For`, `Let`, `Where`, `Order by`, `Return`; you can think of it as XQuery's equivalent to the SQL `SELECT` statement. Here is a simple example:

```
for $boy in doc("students.xml")/students/boy
where $boy/eye-color = "yellow"
return $boy/name
```

students.xml

The keywords are bold just so you can see how they fit in with the FLWOR idea; you don't have to type them in bold, of course. If you downloaded BaseX or Saxon, you can fetch `students.xml` from the website for this book and run the example just as it is.

Although this short example doesn't use all the components — it has no `let` or `order by` clauses — it is still a FLWOR expression.

Following is a slightly bigger example, using a much larger XML document The sample XML document is 4,000 lines long, and too large to print in this book; it is from the two-hundred-year-old dictionary of biography edited by Chalmers. The full 32-volume dictionary is online at `http://words.fromoldbooks.org/`, but this is just a tiny fraction of it, with simplified markup:

```
for $dude in doc("chalmers-biography-extract.xml")//entry
where xs:integer($dude/@died) lt 1600
order by $dude/@died
return $dude/title
```

dudes-simple.xq

On the first line you can see there's a `for` expression starting. If you're familiar with procedural languages like PHP or C, note that this `for` is very different! In XQuery, `for` generates a sequence of values. It does this by making a sequence of *tuples*, evaluating the body of the `for` expression for each tuple, and constructing a sequence out of the result.

Here is a simple example to help you understand tuples:

```
for $a in 1 to 5, $b in ("a", "b", "c")
return <e id="{$b}{$a}"/>
```

If you type this into the BaseX query window and run it, or put it in a text file and run Saxon on it in XQuery mode (not XSLT mode), you will see this result:

```
<e id="a1"/>
<e id="b1"/>
<e id="c1"/>
<e id="a2"/>
<e id="b2"/>
<e id="c2"/>
<e id="a3"/>
<e id="b3"/>
<e id="c3"/>
<e id="a4"/>
<e id="b4"/>
<e id="c4"/>
<e id="a5"/>
<e id="b5"/>
<e id="c5"/>
```

This shows fifteen lines of output, one for each possible combination of the numbers 1 through 5 and the letters a, b, and c. The XQuery processor has generated all fifteen combinations and, for each combination, has evaluated the query body on the second line. The results are then put into the sequence you see as the result. Each combination, such as `(3, a)`, represents a single *tuple*.

A multi-threaded XQuery processor might evaluate the query body in parallel; on a large database it might be faster to generate the tuples in some particular order, making best use of an in-memory cache. All that matters is that the results end up in the right order. This is generally true in XQuery: optimizers can rearrange your query, sometimes in quite surprising ways, as long as the result is the same. Most times you won't have to think about this, but if you call external functions that interact with the outside world, you might be able to see this happening.

Now that you know a bit about tuples and `for`, let's return to the code example:

Available for download on Wrox.com

```
for $dude in doc("chalmers-biography-extract.xml")//entry
where xs:integer($dude/@died) lt 1600
order by $dude/@died
return $dude/title
```

dudes-simple.xq

The first line starts the FLWOR expression: the tuples consist of a single item each, bound to `$dude`, and the items are each `<entry>` elements.

The next line weeds out the results, keeping only tuples in which the dude (or dudette) died after the year 1600. The `xs:integer()` function converts the attribute to a number so that you can do the comparison.

The third line tells the XQuery processor to sort the resulting sequence by the (string) value of the `$dude/@died` attribute. Hmm, that's going to go wrong if someone died before the year 1000, so you should change it like so:

```
order by xs:integer($dude/@died) ascending
```

`ascending` is the default, but now you can guess how to sort with most recent first, using `descending` instead. The default, if there is no `order by` clause, is to use document order if that applies, but otherwise it's in the order in which the tuples are generated.

Finally, the fourth line of the listing says what to generate in the result for each tuple that was accepted: return the title element. If you run this, you'll get output that starts like this:

```
<title>
  <csc>Abu</csc>-<csc>Nowas</csc>
</title>
<title>
  <csc>Ado</csc>
</title>
<title>
  <csc>Alfes</csc>,<csc>Isaac</csc>
</title>
<title>
  <csc>Algazeli</csc>,<csc>Abou</csc>-<csc>Hamed</csc>-<csc>Mohammed</csc>
</title>
```

There are two difficulties with the output generated by this example. The first is that it's hard to read, and the second is that there's no outermost element to make it legal XML output. It turns out to be rather easy to generate XQuery output that is not well-formed XML, a problem that may be partly addressed in XQuery 3.0 with an option to validate the output automatically. In the following exercise you'll make a version of the query that generates nicer output.

TRY IT OUT Formatting Query Results

In this exercise you'll start with the `dudes-simple.xq` example file but change it very slightly so that the output is formatted more readably.

1. Type the following code into a file called `dudes.xq`; it's similar to the previous example, so the differences are highlighted.

Available for download on Wrox.com

```
<results>{
  for $dude in doc("chalmers-biography-extract.xml")//entry
  let $name := normalize-space(string-join($dude/title//text(), "")),
      $died := xs:integer($dude/@died)
  where $died lt 1600
  order by $died ascending
  return <dude>{$name} (d. {$died})</dude>
}</results>
```

dudes.xq

2. Run the BaseX GUI program. In the Editor area (usually on the upper left of the BaseX window, depending on the View options you have chosen) use the Open File icon to load `dudes.xq` into the editor, or copy and paste the text into the tab, or type it in directly.

3. You will need the `chalmers-biography-extract.xml` file for this activity; you can get it from the website for this book or from `http://words.fromoldbooks.org/xml/` instead.

4. Press the green triangle in BaseX to run the query. Alternatively, you can also run the same query with Saxon:

```
java -jar saxon9he.jar -query dudes.xq > results.xml
```

5. Here are the first few results:

```
<?xml version="1.0" encoding="UTF-8"?>
<results>
   <dude>Abu-Nowas (810)</dude>
   <dude>Ado (875)</dude>
   <dude>Alfes, Isaac (1103)</dude>
   <dude>Algazeli, Abou-Hamed-Mohammed (1111)</dude>
   <dude>Aben-Ezra (1165)</dude>
   <dude>Ailred (1166)</dude>
   <dude>Accorso, Francis (1229)</dude>
   . . .
</results>
```

How It Works

The revised version of the query is a little more complex.

In this version of the query you can see that a variable, `$name`, was used; this is the purpose of the `let` part of the FLWOR expression. You can have any number of `let` expressions, separated by commas.

The definition of `$name` is a little more complex. Because the definition is inside a FLWOR expression, `$name` is defined once for each tuple — in this case, once for each `<entry>` element in the document.

First, you make a list of all the text nodes in the entry, with this XPath expression:

```
$dude/title//text()
```

Recall from what you learned about XPath in Chapter 7 that `//text()` is short for `descendant-or-self::text()`. You can use either form, but the important thing is to get all the text nodes. For example, in the following snippet, the `<title>` element contains five text nodes:

```
<title>
  <csc>Abel</csc>, <csc>Gaspar</csc>
</title>
```

They are (1) the space between `<title>` and `<csc>`, (2) `Abel`, (3) “`, `”, (4) `Gaspar`, and (5) the space between `</csc>` and `</title>`. It’s the newlines at the start and end that were messing up the output before, along with the clutter of the `<csc>` elements. But you don't want to lose the spaces between words. So you make `$name` be the result of taking all those text nodes and joining them together with `string-join()`, but then strip leading and trailing spaces and turning multiple consecutive blanks, including newlines, into a single space, with the `normalize-space()`, as follows:

```
normalize-space(string-join($dude/title/descendant-or-self::text(), ""))
```

After defining `$name`, the query defines `$died` to be the result of casting the `<entry>` element's `died` attribute to an integer. This step would not be needed in a schema-aware XQuery processor, if a suitable schema had been applied. The `$died` variable is just used to avoid repeating that type conversion to integer, since the value is used twice. In general, it's good style to avoid duplicating code.

The `where` clause is the same as before, except that it uses `$died` instead of `xs:integer ($entry/@died)`.

The `order by` clause is new, and sorts the results so the people who died earlier in history are listed sooner in the results.

The `return` clause previously returned a `<title>` element for each entry in the dictionary, and now constructs a new `<dude>` element containing the person's name and the year in which he died. But this time the person's name is formatted nicely, because of the work you did in defining the `$name` variable.

Finally, note that the entire query is inside a `<results>` element, and uses `{…}` to put the query expression inside the constructor for `<results>`. Having a single top-level element means the results are now well-formed XML.

WARNING *When you create a database or import a file with BaseX, there is an option to drop spaces between elements, which will make the first and last name run together in the result. Dropping spaces is appropriate for data-oriented XML, but not for document-oriented XML such as this example.*

XQuery Expressions Do Not Have a Default Context

In XSLT or XPath, there's usually a current node and a context item. You can write things like `//boy[eye-color = "yellow"]` or `<xsl:apply-templates/>`, and because there's a default context, the right thing happens.

In XQuery you have to be explicit, and write things like:

```
doc("students.xml")//boy[eye-color = "yellow"]/name
```

or, more commonly:

```
for $boy in doc("students.xml")/students/boy
where $boy/eye-color = "yellow"
return $boy/name
```

THE ANATOMY OF A QUERY EXPRESSION

Now that you've learned a bit more about XQuery, this section gets more formal and goes over the basic parts of a query.

Every complete query has two parts: the *prolog* and the *query body*. There is also an optional third part, the *version declaration*. Often the optional version declaration is left out and the prolog is empty, making the entire query just a query body. This is how the examples in the chapter thus far have been constructed, but not for long. Look at the following example for a complete query.

NOTE *If you like, you can follow along in the XQuery Specification (informally known as the "Language Book" to its friends): the Language Book is much easier to read than most formal computer language, and of course it's always the first place to go if you need to answer a question about the language.*

In section 4 of `http://www.w3.org/TR/xquery-30/` you will see the following:

```
[1]Module     ::= VersionDecl? (LibraryModule | MainModule)
[3]MainModule ::= Prolog QueryBody
```

Rule [1] says that, in XQuery, a module starts with a version declaration, which (because of that question mark after it) is optional; then there is either a `LibraryModule` or a `MainModule`. If you look at the definition of `MainModule` on the next line, it consists of a prolog followed by a query body.

NOTE *These names —* `VersionDecl`, `LibraryModule`, `MainModule` *— do not appear in the actual query. They are just names the specification uses, so as to be able to talk about the various parts of a query.*

You'll come back to modules later in this chapter. For now, the important part to know is that every complete XQuery consists of a version declaration, a prolog, and a body. (Remember that in the examples so far the optional version declaration was left out and the prolog was empty.)

The following sections introduce the version declaration and the various things you can put into the query prolog; you'll see some examples along the way, and after the prolog you'll come back to the query body, which is where your FLWOR expressions go.

The Version Declaration

Every XQuery query body can begin with a version declaration like so:

```
xquery version "1.0" encoding "utf-8";
```

The values `1.0` (for the version of XQuery in use) and `utf-8` (for the encoding of the file containing the query) are defaults. If you use features from versions of XQuery newer than 1.0, you should indicate the minimum required version in the version declaration. If you don't use a version declaration, the default is 1.0. You can leave out the encoding or the version if you like, as shown here:

```
xquery version "1.0";
xquery encoding "utf-8";
```

WARNING *All XQuery implementations are defined to use Unicode internally, or at least to behave as if they do. If you use some encoding other than UTF-8 or UTF-16 for your query file, it just means that query processors will have to transcode the file into the Unicode character set before interpreting it. It is generally best to stick to UTF-8 on Linux or Macintosh systems, and either UTF-8 or UTF-16 on Windows or in Java.*

The Query Prolog

The XQuery prolog is a place for definitions and settings to go, before the actual query body itself. The prolog is everything after the (optional) version declaration but before the start of the query.

You can define functions, bind prefixes to namespaces, import schemas, define variables, and more. The items can appear in any order, although, for example, a namespace declaration has to appear *before* you try to use the namespace it declares.

Namespace Declarations

Use a namespace declaration to connect a short name, called a *prefix*, to a namespace URI like so:

```
declare namespace fobo = "http://www.fromoldbooks.org/ns/";
```

The prefix `fobo` here is said to be *bound* to the namespace URI `http://www.fromoldbooks.org/ns/`.

XQuery comes with a number of namespace bindings already built in:

```
xml = http://www.w3.org/XML/1998/namespace
xs = http://www.w3.org/2001/XMLSchema
xsi = http://www.w3.org/2001/XMLSchema-instance
fn = http://www.w3.org/2005/xpath-functions
local = http://www.w3.org/2005/xquery-local-functions
```

You can bind them yourself too if you prefer, using `declare namespace` in the same way. The `local` namespace is for use in your own functions, as you'll learn shortly.

Importing Schemas

You can "import" a W3C XML Schema into your query so that you can then refer to the types it defines, and so that an XQuery engine can use it for validation. The schema must be an XSD-format XML document, or at least, that's the only format that the XQuery specification demands. The following example shows you how to import an XML Schema:

```
import schema fobo="http://www.fromoldbooks.org/Search/";
import schema "http://www.exmple.org/" at "http://www.example.org/xsdfiles/";
import schema fobo="http://www.fromoldbooks.org/Search/"
    at "http://www.fromoldbooks.org/Search/xml/search.xsd",
       "http://www.fromoldbooks.org/Search/xml/additional.xsd";
```

The first example instructs the XQuery processor to import a schema associated with the namespace URI `http://www.fromoldbooks.org/Search` and also to bind that URI to prefix `fobo`, but does not tell the XQuery processor where to find the schema.

The second example imports a schema for a given namespace URI, and gives the URI for its location. You can use a relative URI for the location hint if you like, but it's up to the implementation as to how to fetch the schema, unfortunately.

The third example gives all three elements: a prefix, a namespace URI, and then not one, but two, location hints. Again, it's up to the individual implementation as to whether both locations are used or only the first one found.

If you want to import an XML Schema document that does not use namespaces, use the empty string (`""`) as the target namespace.

When you import a schema into a query, two things happen: first, the things defined in the schema (types, elements, attributes) become available in the "in-scope schema definitions" in the query. You can use the types defined in the schema just as if they were built-in types, and you can validate XML fragments against the schema definitions. Second, validated XML document nodes have schema type information associated with them (this attribute's value is an integer, that element contains a *BirthplaceCity*, and so on).

You can use the imported schema types in XPath element tests — for example, `element(*, my:typename)` to match any element whose type is declared in an imported schema to be `typename` in the namespace associated in the query with the prefix `my`. You can use `element(my:entry, my:entrytype)` to match only an element called *entry* and of schema type `entrytype`, again in an appropriately declared namespace. You can leave out the type name and use `element(student:boy)` to match any element whose name is `boy`; you can also write `element()` or `element(*)` to match any element.

You see more examples of how you can use the schema types when you write your own functions in just a moment; see Chapter 5 for examples of defining your own types, although not all XQuery implementations support user-defined types. Because not all XQuery implementations support user-defined schema types, a detailed description is out of the scope of this book, but most implementations do at least support types for variables and function arguments, and queries can run much faster if you use them.

Importing Modules and Writing Your Own Modules

You can also import *modules*. A module is a collection of XQuery definitions. Following is how you'd tell your XQuery processor that you wanted to use a module:

```
import module namespace fobo="http://www.example.org/ns/" at "fobo-search.xqm";
import module "global-defs.xqm";
```

As with schemas, you can assign a prefix; unlike importing schemas, however, modules always associate their names with a namespace URI, so you can't just use an empty string. The location URI is a hint, and different implementations may do different things with it.

Once you import a module you can use the public functions and variables that it defines.

Modules are most often written in XQuery, and are just the same as the main XQuery file, except that they start with a module *declaration* instead of a module *import statement*, like so:

```
import module namespace fobo = "http://www.example.org/ns/";
```

Modules are very useful. They let you:

- Organize larger applications into more manageable parts
- Manage having multiple people working on the same application
- Have multiple implementations of an API, to separate out the non-portable (implementation-dependent) parts clearly
- Share libraries of code with other people

You can find some community-contributed library modules at `www.exquery.org` that you can try.

Variable Declarations

XQuery is a *declarative* language, like XSLT, so the "variables" are really more like the symbols used in algebra than variables in a regular programming language: you can't change their values! There's no assignment.

Here are some example variable declarations:

```
declare variable $socks := "black";
declare variable $sockprice as xs:decimal := 3.6;
declare variable $argyle as element(*) := <sock>argyle</sock>;
```

The full syntax is:

```
declare variable $name [ as type] := [external] value;
```

The brackets (`[]`) mean you can leave off the things inside of them (don't include the brackets either, of course!). Notice how XQuery is a language in which values can include XML elements: anything that can go in an XDM instance can be used as a value.

You can refer to variables outside the query — for example, variables exported in a host language such as PHP or Java — by calling them external.

One common use for a variable is to put configuration at the top of a program or module like so:

```
declare variable $places as xs:string := doc("places.xml");
```

Putting the call to `doc()` in a variable in the query prolog is no different from putting it everywhere you want to use it: the document will still be loaded only once. But this way you only have to change it in once place.

The value used to initialize a variable can be any expression. You can also give an explicit type to a variable like so:

```
declare variable $items-per-page as xs:integer := 16;
declare variable $config as element(config, mytype:config) :=
    <config>36</config>;
```

WARNING *Support for XML Schema and for the optional "static typing" feature in XQuery varies considerably between implementations; you may well be restricted to type names from the XSD specification itself, rather than being able to define your own types. It's still worth marking the types of variables, because the query optimizer can make use of it, and also because it can help the system to find errors in your query.*

Functions and Function Items

Just as XQuery variables are a useful way to give a name to some meaningful value, a *function* is a way to give a name to a meaningful expression.

Although XQuery expressions can use all of the functions defined by XPath (see Appendix B for a full list), it's often useful to define your own. If you find yourself repeating some fragment of XQuery over and over again, or if naming a calculation will make the query clearer, you should use a function. Here is a complete example of a query with a variable, a function, and a one-line query body:

Available for download on Wrox.com

```
declare variable $james := <person><name>James</name><socks>argyle</socks></person>;
declare function local:get-sock-color(
    $person as element(person)) as xs:string
{
    xs:string($person/socks)
};
local:get-sock-color($james)
```

function.xq

The first line declares a variable called `$james` as a fragment of XML.

The next line declares a function called `local:get-sock-color()`. The local namespace is reserved in XQuery for user-defined functions like this.

The function takes as input a `<person>` element and uses a simple XPath expression to return the value of the `<socks>` subelement, converted to a string.

Finally, you have a *query body*, the actual part that does the work, and all it does here is pass the variable as an argument, or *parameter*, to the function and return the result, which shows that James wears argyle socks.

User-defined functions are the second-most important aspect of XQuery, after the FLWOR expression.

Recursive Functions

Although this topic is often considered advanced in programming language courses, recursion, once grasped, is a fundamental part of XML processing. The idea is very simple: you write a function that handles the first part of its input, and then, to handle the rest, the function calls another copy of itself! Here is a very simple example you can try:

Available for download on Wrox.com

```
declare variable $numbers as xs:integer* := (1, 2, 3, 4, 5, 6);
declare function local:sum-of-squares($input as xs:integer*) as xs:integer
{
  if (empty($input)) then 0
  else
    let $first := $input[1]
    return $first * $first + local:sum-of-squares($input[position() gt 1])
};

local:sum-of-squares($numbers)
```

recursive-function.xq

In this example the function is declared to be in the predefined *local* namespace. The function `sum-of-squares` takes a list of numbers as input and returns a single number as a result.

On the fourth line the function checks to see if the input is empty, and, if it is, returns zero (nothing to do). *Every recursive function must do something like this* or it will never stop, and your query will never finish!

If the input is not empty, there must be at least one number, so you take the first such number and multiply it by itself. If the input list had only one number inside it, that would be all the function ever had to do. But the input might have more than one number, so you need to produce the square of the *first* number in the list *added to the sum of the squares of the rest of the numbers.* You already have (most of) a function to calculate the sum of squares, so you call it to do the work. Notice that you give it not `$input` but `$input` with the first element removed, `$input[position() gt 1]`, so that the list is shorter. That way you know that eventually the entire list will be processed and the function will finish.

Recursion turns out to be a very natural fit for working with XML, because XML trees are themselves recursive: elements can contain elements, which in turn can contain more elements, all the way down! If you work with XQuery (or XSLT) a lot, you should take the time to become comfortable with recursion.

External Functions

When XQuery is called from another "host" programming language, such as Java, C++, or Perl, you might want to call functions in that host language from within your XQuery expressions. Not all implementation support this, and restrictions usually exist on the sorts of functions you can call, so you'll have to read the documentation that came with the XQuery engine or host environment.

External functions usually consist of two steps: the first is to expose the function from the host language, and the second is to declare it inside your query. It is really only feasible to give you an example for the second part. Here's the part you'd put in your query:

```
declare function java:imagesize($imgfile as xs:anyURI) as xs:integer* external;
```

Now you can use that function in XQuery just like any other. The host language or the XQuery implementation's documentation will tell you which namespace to use and how to declare it (or it should, at least!).

Module Imports

XQuery lets you write collections of functions and variables and save them; later, you can reuse such a named collection as a *library module*. This can be an excellent way to structure larger applications, and even with smaller queries, it can help if more than one person or department is involved. You could provide a set of functions that hide the representation of information behind a set of functions, so that you can later change the representation; you could also provide a set of functions that work the same way across multiple XQuery implementations just by importing the appropriate version of a module.

The following example shows how to import a module called `wikidates` that might provide functions for finding birth and death dates for people based on the XML version of Wikipedia:

```
import module namespace
    wiki = "http://www.example.org/wikidates" at "wikidates.xqm";
```

This is a fictional example, and uses `example.org`, a domain intended only for use in books and examples.

You can leave out the `namespace wiki =` part if you like, but that would be a fairly advanced usage.

The only difference between the main query itself (also called the *main module* in the specification) and a module file is this: a module file must have, immediately after the optional version and encoding declaration, a module declaration, like so:

```
module namespace w = "http://www.example.org/wikidates";
```

As usual with XML namespaces, when you import the module you must use the exact same namespace URI, although the prefix (`w` in this example) doesn't have to be the same. Within the module a function might be named `w:getDateOfBirth`, and if you imported the module using the prefix `wiki`, you'd call the function as `wiki:getDateOfBirth()`. The XQuery engine knows you mean the same function because the prefixes are bound to the same namespace URI, once in the library module and once in the main module.

In addition, where the main module has a prolog followed by a query body, the library module has only a prolog, and no query body.

Some XQuery modules are available at `www.exquery.org` and are worth exploring, and some XQuery engines also come with module libraries of their own.

Optional Prolog Features

You can specify various options in the prolog; these are defined by specific XQuery engines, so you should look at the documentation for the product you're using.

The most common options have to do with serialization: the way that the results are written out. If you are using an in-memory query that just returns a tree or stores results directly back to a database, serialization is probably not an issue. If you are creating HTML (or, more likely, XHTML), you need to use the right options: XHTML is not the same as writing HTML elements in XML syntax. For example, the `<br>` HTML element must be written `<br />` in HTML, with a space between the `r` and `/` — it cannot be written as `<br></br>`. In XQuery 3.0, serialization is likely to be a standard part of the language, but for now just be aware that you'll probably need to read the documentation for the XQuery engines you use.

The Query Body

You have now seen all of the main parts of the query prolog, and you have also seen some sample queries. The query body is a single XQuery expression after the prolog; it's the actual query, and although it's only a single expression, it can be very long! You can also give a sequence of expressions, separated by commas. Because the items in the prolog are all optional, an entire query could be a single simple expression. When XQuery is used from within Java or SQL, this is not uncommon; when XQuery is used to handle complex business transactions, much longer queries are more likely.

Because XQuery extends XPath, you can use pretty much any XPath expression in XQuery. The biggest extensions after FLWOR are described in the following sections.

Typeswitch Expressions

The idea of a typeswitch expression is that you can write code to behave differently based on the type of an expression, such as the argument to a function.

Suppose in the dictionary of biography you have what are called *blind entries*; these are entries that just have a headword or title, such as "Isaac Newton," and then just say, "See Newton, Isaac."

You might define two separate types in your schema for the dictionary, *entry* and *blindentry* perhaps, even though both use the same element name. Then you could process them differently like so:

```
typeswitch ($entry)
    case $e as element(entry, blindEntry) return ()
    case $e as element(entry, entry) return process-entry($e)
    default return fn:error(xs:QName("my:err042"), "bad entry type")
```

Element Constructors

XPath expressions can only ever return pointers into the document tree (or, more correctly, references into XDM instances). People frequently want to do things like "return all of the *school* elements without any of their children" or to make entirely new elements not in the input. For this you need to use XQuery.

Anywhere you can have an expression or literal value, you can have an element constructor. Two types of element constructors exist: *direct* and *computed*.

Direct Element Constructors

You have already seen some examples of direct element constructors:

```
let $isaac := <entry id="newton-isaac" born="1642" died="1737">
  <title>Sir Isaac Newton</title>
</entry>
return $isaac/title
```

A direct element constructor can also have namespace declarations, and can contain expressions; you'll come back to this next example in Chapter 18, "Scalable Vector Graphics (SVG)," but for now all that matters is you could generate a `<rect>` element with some expressions in the attribute values or content, like so:

```
let $box:= <rect xmlns="http://www.w3.org/2000/svg"
    width="{$width}" height="{$width * 2}"
    x="{$isaac/@born}" y="{math:sin(xs:integer($isaac/@died))}" />,
    $text := <text>His name was {$isaac/title/text()}.</text>
```

Your XQuery implementation may provide an option to say whether space at the start and end of elements is included or ignored; this space is called *boundary space.*

You can also make comments and processing instructions like so:

```
let $c := <--* this is an example of a direct XML comment constructor *-->,
    $p := <?php echo date() ?>
```

WARNING *If you are working with XML and PHP, you will have to configure your server to use the* `<?php ...?>` *syntax rather than just* `<? ...?>` *so that your files can be legal XML documents. To do this on most systems, edit* `/etc/php.ini` *and set* `short_open_tag = Off`*, noting that it may occur in more than one place in the file.*

Computed Element Constructors

If you don't know the name of an element in advance, sometimes you have to use a computed element constructor. You can mix the two styles, and you can always use the computed element constructors, so some people choose to use these all the time, but they can be harder to read. The following example shows computed element constructors:

```
declare namespace svg = "http://www.w3.org/2000/svg";
let $width := 30,
    $height := 20,
    $isaac := <entry id="newton-isaac" born="1622" died="1736">
               <title>Sir Isaac Newton</title>
    </entry>,
$box := element svg:box {
    attribute width { $width },
    attribute height { $height },
    attribute x { $isaac/@born },
    attribute y { math:sin(xs:integer($isaac/@died)) }
},
    $p := element text {
      fn:concat(
        "His name was ",
        data($isaac/title),
        ".")
    } return ($box, $p)
```

This example generates the following output:

```
<svg:box xmlns:svg="http://www.w3.org/2000/svg" width="30" height="20" x="1622"
 y="0.96375518644307"/>
<text>His name was Sir Isaac Newton.</text>
```

The computed syntax is harder to work with when you are mixing text and values (*mixed content*). In that case, it's usually best to use the direct constructors, or to mix the two syntaxes like so:

```
    $p := elememt wrapper {
    <text>His name was {data($isaac/title)) }</text>
};
```

You can also construct text nodes and documents, using `text` and `document` instead of `element` or `attribute`.

FLWOR Expressions Revisited

It's time to give the full syntax for FLWOR expressions. You have already seen most of the parts in the "Building Blocks of XQuery" section. Note that XQuery 1, the stable version of XQuery, has a very basic FLWOR expression, and XQuery 3 extends it (there was no XQuery 2). In what follows, the parts that were introduced in 3.0 are marked like this: $^{3.0}$.

A FLWOR expression starts with one of the keywords `for`, `let`, or `window`$^{3.0}$, and its associated clause like so:

```
for | let | window3.0
```

After the initial `for`, `let`, or `window`$^{3.0}$, there can be any number of optional clauses as shown here:

```
(for | let | window3.0 | where | group by3.0 | order by | count3.0)*
```

The end of the FLWOR expression is signaled by a return clause:

```
return ExprSingle
```

Here, `ExprSingle` in the XQuery grammar means any single XQuery expression. Figure 9-2 shows a railroad diagram in which you start on the left and follow arrows until you get to the right. You can go round the middle loop as many times as you like, or not at all.

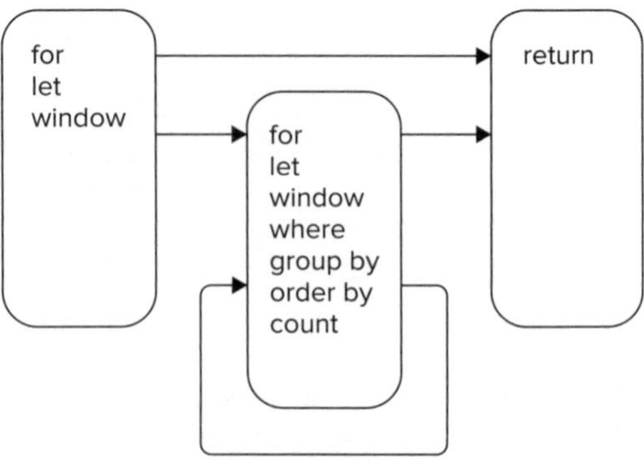

FIGURE 9-2

The individual parts of the FLWOR expression expand as shown in the following sections. In the explanations square brackets are used to mean something can be left out: `[at $pos]` means either put `at $pos` there, or don't. The square brackets are just to show you it's optional, and are not part of the query. The following explanations also use *italics* to show where you where you can put a value of your own, so `as` *`type`* means you'd type the literal word `as` followed by a space, and then the name of any type you wanted, such as `xs:integer*` to mean a sequence of whole numbers.

A type can be `empty-sequence()` to mean (of course) the empty sequence, or it can be a type name, such as `xs:integer`, optionally followed by an occurrence indicator: `*` to mean zero or more, `?` to mean zero or one, `+` to mean one or more, or with no indicator to mean exactly one. Thus, `xs:integer?` will accept either the empty sequence (no integers) or exactly one number. You can't put an occurrence indicator after `empty-sequence()` because XQuery does not support sequences of sequences.

The for Clause

Every FLWOR expression starts with a `for` clause, a `let` clause, or a `window` clause. The `for` clause has the following syntax:

```
for $var [as xs:integer] [allowing empty] [at $pos] in expr
```

Here are some examples; you can try them in the BaseX query window:

- Using the `at position` feature:

```
for $entry as element(entry) at $n in //entry
return <li>{$n}. {$entry/@id}</li>
```

- Using two variables:

```
for $a in (1, 2, 3),
```

```
        $b in (4, 5)
    return $a + $b
```

- Generating a tuple even for the empty sequence:

```
    for $a allowing empty in ()
    return 42
```

The let Clause

Use `let` to bind a variable to a value; you can have more than one `let` clause by separating them with commas. The syntax is:

```
let $var [as type] := expression
```

Here are two examples:

- Specifying a type:

```
let $x as xs:decimal := math:sin(0.5)
return $x
```

- With both `for` and `let`, and a direct element constructor:

```
for $a in (1, 2, 3)
let $b := $a * $a
return <r>{$b}</r>
```

The window Clause

The `window` clause lets you process several adjacent tuples at a time; it's described in the section "Coming In XQuery 3.0" later in this chapter.

The where Clause

The `where` part of a FLWOR is used to weed out tuples, leaving just the ones you want. If you have only a single bound variable in your `for` part, it's the same as using a predicate. For example:

```
for $person in /dictionary/entry[@born lt 1750]
```

has the same effect as

```
for $person in /dictionary/entry
where #born lt 1750
```

However, because the `where` clause operates on tuples rather than nodes, if you have more than one item in each tuple, you have to use a `where` clause like so:

```
for $a in (1 to 50), $b in (2, 3, 5, 7)
where $a mod $b eq 0
return $a * $b
```

Some implementations also do different optimizations on predicates and `where`, so one may be faster than the other, but in most cases you should concentrate on making your query as easy to read as possible.

The group by Clause

Grouping is introduced in XQuery 3.0, and is described later in this chapter.

The order by Clause

Use the `order by` clause to sort the tuples based on the value of an expression. The following complete example sorts all the people in the dictionary by their date of birth, lowest (earliest) first:

```
for $person in //entry[@born]
order by xs:integer(@born) ascending
return $person/title
```

The syntax is:

```
[stable] order by expression [direction] [collation "URI"]
```

You can have any number of the clauses after `order by`, separated by commas. The *direction* looks like this:

```
ascending|descending [ empty (greatest|least) ]
```

`empty greatest` and `empty least` say how the empty sequence is to be compared: whether it goes after all other values or before them.

The `stable` keyword tells the query processor to keep items in the same order if they have equal keys; sometimes it's much faster if the implementation can return items with equal sort keys in any order, but that's not always what you want.

`ascending` and `descending` say whether to put the results least first or greatest first.

The `collation` names a set of sorting rules, usually for comparing strings. For example, your implementation might provide a collation that's case insensitive, or one in which letters with accents or diacriticals (é, ô, Æ, ñ, ü) sort the same as if they did not have the marks (e, o, AE, n, u, or ue). The actual URIs you can use are *implementation defined*, meaning you have to look them up in the manual for the XQuery engine you're using.

Here are some more examples, showing just the `order by` clause:

```
order by $b ascending empty least
order by $b descending empty greatest
order by $b stable ascending
order by $e
```

The count Clause

Earlier, you saw how the `for` clause has an optional `at $n` to associate a variable with the position in the sequence selected by the `for` clause.

The `count` clause is similar, but numbers the overall tuples. The following example shows the difference:

Available for download on Wrox.com

```
for $boy at $boypos in ("Simon", "Nigel", "David"),
    $game at $gamepos in ("pushups", "situps")
    count $count
return
    <tuple n="{$count"}>
      boy {$boypos} is {$boy}, item {$gamepos}: {$game}
    </tuple>
```

Count-boys-games.xq

The output is as follows:

```
<tuple n="1">boy 1 is Simon, item 1: pushups</tuple>
<tuple n="2">boy 1 is Simon, item 2: situps</tuple>
<tuple n="3">boy 2 is Nigel, item 1: pushups</tuple>
<tuple n="4">boy 2 is Nigel, item 2: situps</tuple>
<tuple n="5">boy 3 is David, item 1: pushups</tuple>
<tuple n="6">boy 3 is David, item 2: situps</tuple>
```

The `count` clause was introduced for XQuery 3.0, and at the time of writing was not yet widely implemented. You can simulate it, if needed:

```
for $activity at $n in (
    for $boy at $boypos in ("Simon", "Nigel", "David"),
        $game at $gamepos in ("pushups", "situps")
    return
        concat("boy ", $boypos, " is ", $boy,
            " item ", $gamepos, ": ", $game)
        )
return <tuple n="{$n}">{$activity}</tuple>
```

The trick here is to use a *nested* FLWOR expression. The inner expression generates a sequence of strings, each one corresponding to the content of one of those `<tuple>` elements from the previous example. Then the outer FLWOR maps each of those strings to a `<tuple>` element, and because there's only one input sequence, the list of strings, the `at $pos` clause numbers the strings.

This is a fairly advanced example, and shows how you can use a FLWOR expression wherever you can use as a sequence.

NOTE *There's actually an extra open and close parenthesis in the example, around the inner FLWOR expression. They are not needed, and if you take them away you can see you get the same output, for example with Saxon or BaseX. They are there for readability, to try to make clear how the* `for` *and* `return` *clauses go together and nest. Tricks like this can also make your queries more robust in the face of careless editing!*

SOME OPTIONAL XQUERY FEATURES

At the same time that the XQuery language itself was being developed, three fairly large add-on facilities were being developed. They are Full Text Search, XQuery Update, and XQuery Scripting. The first two are widely supported; scripting is less widely used, but still useful to know about.

Describing these facilities in much depth is beyond the scope of a "Beginning" book; they could easily each have a chapter on their own. But you will learn in this section what these three facilities are for, see some examples, and learn how to find out more.

XQuery and XPath Full Text

This optional facility adds the idea of an external index to words or tokens occurring in the database, so that you can find all elements containing a given phrase very quickly. The Full Text language extends XPath, but in practice only really makes sense in XQuery, even though it could also be used with XSLT. Because the Full Text facility was finalized after XQuery 1.0, implementations vary a lot in how they support it. However, where it's available it can be very powerful.

One advantage of using full text searching is that it's usually pretty fast, even when you have terabytes or petabytes of data in your database. The speed is also predictable, which makes it useful for implementing interactions with human users.

Here is an example, using the biographical dictionary:

```
for $e in //entry where $e//p contains text "Oxford"
return (normalize-space($e/title), "&#xa;")
```

This returns results like this:

```
Adams, Fitzherbert
Airay, Henry
Aldrich, Robert
```

The entries returned are those for which the `where` clause is true: the entries that have a `<p>` element (a paragraph) that contains the word "Oxford." The query actually returns a sequence of two items for each matching entry. The first item is the title, converted to a string and with leading and trailing spaces removed, and the second item in the sequence is a newline, represented in hexadecimal as an XML character reference, `"
"` — the newline is just to make each title be on a separate line.

WARNING *The most often requested feature for the Full Text facility in XQuery is the ability to highlight matches, showing the actual words that were found. This is not, in general, possible today, but a new version of the Full Text specification is in preparation that will probably offer this functionality. Some implementations do have ways to identify matches as a vendor extension.*

The Full Text specification has a lot of features: you can enable *stemming*, so that *hop* might also match *hopped*, *hopping*, and *hops*; you also can enable a thesaurus, so that *walk* might also match *amble*, *shuffle*, *stroll*, *path*, and so on.

The XQuery Update Facility

So far all of the XQuery expressions you have seen return some fraction of the original document, and leave the document unchanged. If you're using a database, the chances are high that you'll need to change documents from time to time. A content management system might let users edit articles, or might represent users and their profiles as XML documents.

You might insert a new entry at the end of the biography like so:

```
insert nodes
    <entry id="bush-george"><title>George Bush</title></entry>
as last into doc("dictionary.xml")/dictionary
```

The XQuery Update Facility Use Cases, which you can find at `http://www.w3.org/TR/`(choose the "all items sorted by date" option), has many more examples. However, you will need to check the documentation for your system to see if it supports the Update Facility and, if so, exactly how.

XQuery Scripting Extension

This specification is still a draft at the time of writing. The XQuery Working Group at W3C does not have agreement on the language. However, some aspects are very useful and are widely implemented. In particular, whereas the Update Facility does not let what it calls an *updating expression* return a value, the scripting extension makes it possible to mix updates and value returns. You could, for example, report on whether a database insert was successful, something not possible with just the Update Facility.

The scripting extension also adds procedural-programming constructs such as loops, variable assignment, and blocks.

COMING IN XQUERY 3.0

When this book was written, XQuery 1.0 was well-established, and the W3C XML Query Working Group (in conjunction with the W3C XSLT Working Group) had skipped over 2.0 and was working on XQuery 3.0. The details were not final (XQuery was a "working draft" and not a "Recommendation") and you should consult `http://www.w3.org/TR/` for the latest published version of XQuery; the specification is readable and has examples. If you've followed along this far you should have little difficulty in reading the specification, especially after reviewing this section with its introductory descriptions of some of the new features. You can also find Use Cases documents parallel to the specifications, containing further examples, and these do generally get updated as the language specification evolves.

The following sections will give you an idea of what's coming in XQuery 3.0.

Grouping and Windowing

Suppose you want to make a table showing all the entries in your XML extract from the dictionary of biography, but you want to sort the entries by where the people were born. The following query generates such a list, putting a `<group>` element around all the people born in the same place:

```
for $e in /dictionary/entry[@birthplace]
let $d := $e/@birthplace
group by $d
order by $d
return
  if (count($e) eq 1) then () else
  <group birthplace="{$e[1]/@birthplace}">
    {
        for $person in $e
        return
            <person id="{$person/id}"
                    born="{$person/@born}"
                    died="{$person/@died}"
             >{
                data($person/title)
              }
            </person>
    }
  </group>
```

Here is a snippet of the output, showing the first two groups:

```
<group birthplace="Amsterdam">
  <person id="" born="1519" died="1585">
      Aersens, Peter
    </person>
  <person id="" born="1622" died="1669">
      Anslo, Reiner
    </person>
</group>
<group birthplace="Bologna">
  <person id="" born="1466" died="1558">
      Achillini, John
      Philotheus
    </person>
  <person id="" born="1574" died="1640">
      Achillini, Claude
    </person>
  <person id="" born="1570" died="1632">
      Agucchio, John
      Baptista
    </person>
  <person id="" born="1479" died="1552">
      Alberti, Leander
    </person>
  <person id="" born="1578" died="1638">
      Alloisi, Balthazar
    </person>
</group>
```

More formally, the syntax of a windowing expression (in the XQuery 3.0 draft document, at least) is that you can have either:

```
for tumbling window $var [as type] in expression windowStart [windowEnd]
```

or

```
for sliding window $var [as type] in expression windowStart windowEnd
```

The first form, the `tumbling window`, is for processing the tuples one clump at a time. Each time the `windowStart` expression is true, a new clump is started. If you give an end condition, the clumps will contain all the tuples from the start to when the end is true, inclusive; if you don't give an end condition, a new clump of tuples starts each time the start condition is true.

In the second form, the `sliding window`, a tuple can appear in more than one window.
For example, you could use a tumbling window to add a running average of the most recent five items to a table of numbers. Each row of the table would be processed five times, and you might add a table column showing the average of the number on that row and the numbers on the four rows before it.

The count Clause

The `count` clause in the FLWOR expression has already been described in this chapter, but since this is a list of XQuery 3.0 additions you should know that `count` was added for XQuery 3.

Try and Catch

`Try` and `catch` are familiar to programmers using Java or C++; it's a way to evaluate some code and then, if the code raised an error, instead of ending the query right then and there, you use the emergency fallback code you supply in the `catch` clause.

The syntax of a `try/catch` expression is very simple:

```
try { expression } catch errorlist { expression }
```

You can also have multiple `catch` clauses, one after the other with no comma between them.

Here is a complete `try/catch` example:

```
for $i in (2, 0.2, 0.0, 4)
return
    try {
        12 div $i
    } catch * {
        42
}
```

If you try this with BaseX, you will see the following result:

```
6 60 42 3
```

When the XQuery engine (BaseX) came to find the resulting value for the input tuple `(0.0)`, it had to evaluate 12 divided by zero, and that's an error. Because the error happened inside a `try` clause, BaseX checked to see if there was a `catch` clause that matched the error. There was indeed: the `*` means to catch any error. So BaseX used the expression in the `catch` block for the value, and returned 42.

If you try without the `try/catch`,

```
for $i in (0.5, 0.2, 0.0, 4)
return 12 div $i
```

you'll see the following error in the BaseX Query Info window:

```
Error: [FOAR0001] '12' was divided by zero.
```

You can catch specific errors, and even more than one error at a time like so:

```
for $i in (2, 0.2, 0.0, 4)
return
    try {
        12 div $i
    } catch FOAR0001|FOAR0002 { 42 }
```

The error codes in XQuery are designed so that the first two letters tell you which specification defines them: for example, Functions and Operators for `FO`. You can look in the corresponding specification to see what the code means.

WARNING *Because of optimization, XQuery processors might raise errors other than the one you expect. It's wise to use a catch-all clause if error recovery is important, perhaps using multiple* `catch` *blocks:*

```
try { 12 div $i }
catch FOAR0001 { 42 } catch * { 43 }
```

switch Expressions

The `switch` expression was introduced because long chains of if-then-else conditions can be hard to read, and, more importantly, because sometimes `switch` expresses the writer's intent more clearly. Take the following example:

```
for $word in ("the", "an", "a", "apple", "boy", "girl")
return (" ",
```

```
switch (substring($word, 1, 1))
case "a" return upper-case($word)
case "t" return $word
case "b" case "B" return <b>{$word}</b>
default return $word)
```

This example produces the following output:

```
the AN A APPLE <b>boy</b> girl
```

The `switch` statement looks at the first letter of the item it was given, and behaves differently depending on the value, converting words starting with an "a" to uppercase, and surrounding words starting with a "b" with a `<b>` element, and so on. Notice the two *case expression* clauses for `"b"` and `"B"`, which share an action.

The rather sparse syntax of `switch`, with no punctuation between cases and no marking at the end, means that if you get syntax errors you may want to put the entire construct in parentheses, to help you find the mistake. In this example there's a FLWOR `for` clause with its *`return`*, constructing a sequence of a single space followed by whatever the `switch` expression returns, for each item (actually each tuple) in the `for`.

Function Items and Higher Order Functions

With XQuery 3.0, the language designers finally admitted that XQuery is a functional language, and added a number of functional programming tools. Some of these are very advanced, and some are very straightforward. This section sticks to the straightforward parts.

Function Items

A "function item" is really just the name of a function together with the number of arguments it takes. For example, you can make a function item to refer to the `math:sqrt()` function, which takes a single numeric argument and returns its square root, just by writing `sqrt#1` in your query.

Why on earth would you want to do this? Read on!

Higher Order Functions

A *higher order function* is just a fancy name for a function that works with other functions. Consider the following simple function:

```
declare function local:double-root($x as xs:double)
as xs:double
{
    2 * math:sqrt($x)
};

local:double-root(9.0)
```

If you try this, you'll discover that, because the square root of nine is three, you get two times three, which is six, as a result.

But what if you wanted to write `local:double-sin($x)` as well? Or `local:double-cos($x)`? After a while you start to wonder if you could pass in the name of the function to call instead of `sqrt()`. And you can, as shown in the following code.

Available for download on Wrox.com

```
declare function local:double-f(
    $x as xs:double,
    $f as function($x as xs:double) as xs:double
) as xs:double {
    2 * $f($x)
};

local:double-it(9.0, math:sqrt#1)
```

higher-order.xq

Now you could call `double-it()` with any function, not only `math:sqrt()`.

This ability to use functions as arguments also lets you write XQuery modules that can accept functions for defining their configuration options, or to change the way they behave.

You can also declare functions inside expressions (actually an XPath 3 feature), and LISP programmers will be pleased to see `map` and `apply` as well as `fold`.

JSON Features

At the time of writing, support for JSON was under discussion in the W3C XQuery Working Group, but no definite resolution had been reached. One proposal is called JSONIQ. In any case, it seems likely that interoperability between JSON and XML will be a part of XQuery in the future. See Chapter 16, "AJAX" for more about JSON.

XQuery, Linked Data, and the Semantic Web

If you are working with RDF, whether as RSS feeds or as Semantic Web Linked Data, XQuery has something to offer you.

You can fairly easily generate RSS and RDF/XML with XQuery, of course. The query language for RDF is called SPARQL, and there's even a SPARQL query processor written in XQuery that turns out to be faster than many native SPARQL engines. SPARQL engines can produce results in XML, and that too can be processed with XQuery.

XML and RDF both have their separate uses, as do SPARQL and XQuery, and you can use them together when it makes sense.

SUMMARY

- XQuery is a W3C-standardized language for querying documents and data.
- XQuery operates on instances of the XPath and XQuery Data Model, so you can use XQuery to work with anything that can build a suitable model. This often includes relational databases and RDF triple stores.

- Objects in the data model and objects and values created by XQuery expressions have types as defined by W3C XML Schema.
- XQuery and XSLT both build on XPath; XSLT is an XML-syntax language which includes XPath expressions inside attributes and XQuery uses XPath syntax extended with more keywords.
- There are XQuery processors (sometimes called XQuery engines) that work inside relational databases, accessing the underlying store directly rather than going through SQL. There are also XML-native databases, and some XQuery engines just read files from the hard drive, from memory, or over the network.
- XQuery Update is a separate specification for making changes to data model instances.
- XPath and XQuery Full Text is a separate specification for full-text searching of XML documents or other data model instances.
- XQuery Scripting is a separate specification that adds procedural programming to XQuery, but it is currently not a final specification.
- The two most important building-blocks of XQuery are the FLWOR expression and functions.
- XQuery FLWOR stands for `for-let-where-order by-return`.
- User-defined functions can be recursive, and can be collected together along with user-defined read-only "variables" into separate library files called modules.

EXERCISES

You can find suggested solutions to these exercises in Appendix A.

1. Write a query expression to take the sequence of numbers from 1 to 100 and produce a list of their squares.
2. Find all of the people in the dictionary of biography who lived longer than 88 years; sort the list with the person who lived the longest at the start.
3. Build an interstellar space ship and travel to a place where all XML documents are well formed.
4. Find all entries in the dictionary of biography that have five or more paragraphs (`<p>` elements) in them.

▸ WHAT YOU LEARNED IN THIS CHAPTER

TOPIC	KEY POINTS
What is XQuery?	XQuery is a database query language, and also a general-purpose language in which XML elements are a native data type. XQuery is widely implemented, fairly popular, and easy to learn. There are standalone XQuery implementations, embedded implementations, and implementations that work with XML databases.
XQuery and XPath	XQuery extends the XPath syntax, unlike XSLT, which embeds XPath inside XML attributes in the XSLT language.
FLWOR expressions	The most important part of XQuery; use them to do joins, to construct and manipulate sequences, to sort, and to filter.
Functions and modules	You can define function libraries, called modules, with XQuery.

10

XML and Databases

WHAT YOU WILL LEARN IN THIS CHAPTER:

- Why databases need to handle XML
- The differences between relational and native XML databases
- What basic XML features are needed from a database
- How to use the XML features in MySQL
- How to use the XML features in SQL Server
- How to use features in eXist

Not very along ago, you had two main options when deciding where to store your data. You could go for the traditional solution, a relational database such as Oracle, Microsoft's SQL Server, or the ever-popular open source MySQL. Alternatively, you could choose to use XML. A relational database has the advantage of efficiently storing data that can be expressed in a tabular form, although performance can be a problem if you need to join many tables together. XML has the advantage of coping with nested data or documents that can't be easily broken down further. After a while, it became apparent that a hybrid of the two was needed: a system that could store tabular data alongside XML documents, giving the user the ability to query and modify the XML as well as perform standard operations against the relational data. This would create an all-purpose storage center giving the best of both worlds.

UNDERSTANDING WHY DATABASES NEED TO HANDLE XML

Relational databases grew from the work of Edgar Codd in the 1970s. He was the first to provide a solid mathematical foundation for the main concepts found in these systems, such as tables (which he called relations), primary keys, normalization (where efforts are made to reduce any duplication of data), and relationships, such as one-to-many and many-to-many. Nowadays, hundreds of relational database management systems are available. They range from top-end databases such as Oracle, SQL Server, and DB2, to ones designed for desktop use, such as Microsoft's Access.

These systems have widely different feature sets, but they generally have two things in common. First, they use a special language called Structured Query Language (SQL) to query the data that resides in them. Second, they cope well with data that can be broken down and stored in a tabular form, where items are typically represented as rows in a table. The different properties of these items are represented by the different fields, or columns, of these rows.

If you are trying to represent data for your customers and their orders, a relational system is fine. You probably have one table for basic customer details, one for the order summary, and another table for the order items. You can combine these tables to extract and report on the state of your business; the orders table has a reference to the customer who made the order and the order details table has a reference to the order number.

However, in many situations you need to store data that doesn't fit easily into this pattern. If you expand the customer and order scenario further, how would you store information regarding an actual order once it has been dispatched? It is not enough to keep a record of the actual items and their quantity because the price will almost certainly change in the future. If you wanted to go with this model, you'd need to keep track of historic prices, tax rates, and discounts. One solution is to store a copy of the order document as a binary file; this is a little inflexible because it can't be queried if necessary. A better alternative is to store the order details as an XML document detailing the actual items and their prices, customer, and shipping information and any discounts that were applied. This XML document can then be transformed to provide a confirmation e-mail, a delivery note, or the order itself. Because it is XML, it can also be queried easily using the techniques shown in this book and precludes the need to keep historical data. This makes the database schema and any associated queries much simpler.

An alternative to storing these documents within a database is to just keep them as documents in a filesystem. This is quite easy to do, but leads to a number of problems:

- You need to set up a folder structure manually and decide on a naming convention to aid easy retrieval.
- You need to have two systems: the database (to manage the tabular style data) and a separate XML processor (to query the XML documents).
- Retrieving whole documents is straightforward, but retrieving a fragment is more difficult.
- It's extremely difficult to index the data to allow queries that perform well. Maintaining the indexing system is yet one more system to manage.
- You need two separate backups, one for the database and one for the XML files.

Having a database that can both store XML documents and query them solves these problems and is much easier to use.

You can take two approaches if you want to store your documents in a database. You can use a traditional relational database such as SQL Server, which comes with the capability to store, query, and modify XML documents. Alternatively, you can choose a native XML database, one designed from the ground up to store XML documents efficiently; these usually have limited relational capabilities. Your decision should therefore be based on what data it is you want to store. If your data consists of a large number of XML documents that need to be accessed or queried then a native XML database is probably your best option. This might be the case if your software is a content management system where different snippets of data can be merged to form complete texts. If, however, you have a situation where you store details of customers but need to attach some XML documents, a traditional relational database with XML capabilities is a better choice.

Now that you understand why XML documents and databases are a good mix, you will next learn which XML features you usually need in a database to accomplish common tasks.

ANALYZING WHICH XML FEATURES ARE NEEDED IN A DATABASE

Whether you've chosen a relational or native XML database, you'll need a number of features to address the common tasks associated with XML documents. Not every application will necessarily need all features, and some will definitely be used less frequently than others. This section deals with each task separately, and gives an indication of how important each one is likely to be. This will help you choose between the many systems available.

Retrieving Documents

This is a must-have requirement; there's little use in storing documents that can't be accessed later. However, you have a couple of points to consider:

- **How will you specify which document you want?** If it's just a question of retrieving an order associated with a customer in a relational database, as detailed previously, there's no problem. All systems allow that. On the other hand, if you need to specify a document by some data held within it (such as an invoice number or a specific date) you'll need some sort of XML querying facility. The standard way to specify documents is by using XPath to target a particular value and return any documents that match what you need. (See Chapter 7 for a review of XPath) For example, you may want to view all invoices over $1000, so you'd specify an XPath expression similar to `/order[total > 1000]`.
- **How efficient does the search need to be?** This will probably depend on how many documents you have stored, but once you get past a few hundred your system will have to do some background indexing to prevent searches being slow.

Retrieving Data from Documents

It's quite likely that you'll want to retrieve sections of a document rather than the entire thing. For example, you may want to see the shipping address or all the line items with their respective discounts. You may also need the information in a slightly different format. This is where XQuery, covered in Chapter 9, becomes invaluable. Nearly all XML-enabled databases that expose this sort of functionality have settled on XQuery as the standard way of querying and transforming XML data (if necessary) before returning it to the user.

However, there is a huge variation in how much of the standard is supported. The winners here are the native XML databases. These databases often implement the full capabilities of XQuery, whereas some of the relational databases that have had XML features added on support only a limited subset. If this sort of operation is likely to be used heavily in your application, you'll want to check carefully just how much of XQuery is implemented before you decide which application to use.

Updating XML Documents

Although it seems like updating XML documents should be standard, this feature is more likely to be needed in a native XML database rather than a relational one. This is because in a relational database, XML documents are often used more as snapshots of the data at a point in time and therefore it doesn't make sense to change them. In a native application all your data is in the form of XML, so you'll probably need to modify it at some time. Again, the facilities for such modifications vary widely between databases; one reason for this is that the standard syntax for updating an XML document was agreed on much later than the one for retrieval.

Displaying Relational Data as XML

Displaying relational data as XML applies only to relational databases. Many relational databases have the capability to present the results of a standard SQL query as XML instead of the usual tabular format. Some have just a basic capability that wraps each row and each column in an element. With others, you can specify the format more precisely, perhaps by introducing nesting (where appropriate). Some systems also allow you to insert an XSL transformation into the pipeline. Although this is something that can be achieved easily enough once the data has been returned, it's often easier and more efficient to incorporate the transformation as part of the whole data retrieval process and let the client concentrate on the presentational aspect.

Presenting XML as Relational Data

Again, presenting XML as relational data really applies only to relational databases. Sometimes you need to combine a data from a relational source and an XML source—perhaps your XML refers to a customer's ID and you want to include some data from the customer table in your query. One way to do this is to present the XML document as a regular table and join it to the customer table. This works if the XML data is fairly regular and doesn't use a hierarchical structure.

A companion problem is called *shredding*, which means taking all or parts of an XML document and storing them in a regular database table. This is common when you receive the data from a third party and decide that the benefits of XML storage are outweighed by the need to integrate with an existing database structure. It's quite common in this situation to place the data you require into a table and retain the XML document as an extra column on that table. This way you can still use the XML if needed, but have the advantage of being able to join on other tables easily with the data you've extracted.

Now that you've seen some of the features that are available, the following section looks at three applications that implement some or all of these features, beginning with the XML functionality in MySQL.

USING MYSQL WITH XML

The driving factors to add XML support within open source *Relational Database Management Systems* (RDBMS) are the same as those of their commercial competitors, except that open-source RDBMSs appear to lag well behind in this area of functionality. The reasons are diverse. Open-source projects are often less prone than commercial companies to "get big fast" and absorb all their surroundings. They are also more used to collaborating with other projects. In addition, it is possible that they are less influenced to incorporate what many regard as just another trendy feature, XML in this case. In addition, open-source projects usually have fewer financial resources for their development.

MySQL is one of the leading open source databases, although the management of its development was taken over by Oracle a short time ago. It is used heavily in conjunction with both PHP- and Java-based websites. It has a few XML features, although in comparison to the other two commercial products examined in this chapter, it's sadly lacking. In fact, MySQL is the only database discussed in this chapter that hasn't added anything to its XML features since the last edition of this book in 2007.

Installing MySQL

You can download MySQL from `www.my.mysql.com/downloads/`. Follow the links to Community Server and choose version 5.5 (or later if available). Stable versions of MySQL are available for both Windows and Unix/Linux platforms.

The download page includes a sources download and a number of binary downloads for the most common platforms, including Windows, many Linux distributions, and Mac OS X. Choose the option that is the best match for your platform and follow the instructions.

For this chapter, you need to install the server and the client programs. If you are a Debian or Ubuntu user, select "Linux x86 generic RPM (dynamically linked) downloads," convert the `.rpm` packages into `.deb` packages using the Debian alien package and `alien` command, and install it like any other package using the Debian `dpkg -i` command.

You can also install the front-end tools, which give you a graphical user interface. However, for these examples you can just use the command shell, which is reminiscent of a Windows command prompt.

If you are installing a MySQL database for anything other than test purposes, it is recommended that you set up proper users and passwords to protect your database. For the tests covered in this chapter, you can just choose a password for the root/admin account. You'll be prompted to do that during the install, and you will access the system using that account.

Adding Information in MySQL

You can use a GUI tool to interact with MySQL, but if you really want to understand what's going on behind the scenes, the `mysql` command-line utility is your best friend. Open a Unix or Windows command window and navigate to the bin folder of the installation, for example: `C:\Program Files\MySQL\MySQl Server 5.5\bin`. Then type **`mysql -u root -p`**. If everything is working correctly, you should see the `mysql` prompt asking for the password you chose during installation:

```
C:\Program Files\MySQL\MySQl Server 5.5\bin>mysql -u root -p
Enter password: **********
Welcome to the MySQL monitor.  Commands end with ; or \g.
Your MySQL connection id is 4
Server version: 5.5.15 MySQL Community Server (GPL)

Copyright (c) 2000, 2010, Oracle and/or its affiliates. All rights reserved.

Oracle is a registered trademark of Oracle Corporation and/or its
affiliates. Other names may be trademarks of their respective
owners.

Type 'help;' or '\h' for help. Type '\c' to clear the current input statement.

mysql>
```

In the following Try It Out, you will create a new database and add information.

TRY IT OUT Creating and Populating a MySQL Database

Before you can add information in MySQL, you must create a database. A database acts as a container in which you group information related to a project.

1. To create a database named `Blog` with UTF-8 as a character set, type the following:

```
mysql> create database Blog DEFAULT CHARACTER SET 'utf8';
Query OK, 1 row affected (0.00 sec)

mysql>
```

2. Move into the newly created database by typing the following:

```
mysql> use Blog;
Database changed
mysql>
```

A big difference between a native XML database, such as eXist (which you look at later), and a relational database is that a relational database is highly structured. An XML database can learn the structure of your documents when you load them, without needing any prior definition. This isn't possible with a relational database. In a relational database, information is stored in tables with rows and columns. These tables are similar to spreadsheet tables, except that the name and type of the columns need to be defined before you can use them.

3. Create one of these tables to hold the information needed for the exercises in this chapter. Name it `BlogPost` and, for the sake of simplicity, give it only two columns:

   - A column named `PostId` that will be used as a primary key when you want to retrieve a specific blog entry
   - A column named `Post` to hold the blog entry in XML

Of course, this is a very minimal schema. You might want to add more columns to this table to simplify and optimize specific queries.

To create this table, type the following:

```
mysql> create table BlogPost (
    -> PostId INT PRIMARY KEY,
    -> Post LONGTEXT
    -> );

Query OK, 0 rows affected (0.27 sec)

mysql>
```

Note that you don't have to type the -> at the beginning of the second and subsequent lines of the `create table` SQL instruction; these are just prompts sent by the `mysql` command-line utility.

4. The database is now ready to accept your blog entries. In a real-world application, these entries would be added by a nice web application, but this chapter continues to use the `mysql` command-line utility to add them. In SQL, you add information through an `insert` statement. Enter a couple of your own blog entries following this pattern:

Available for download on Wrox.com

```
mysql> INSERT BlogPost (PostId, Post) SELECT 1,
'<post xmlns:x="http://www.w3.org/1999/xhtml"
 id="1" author="Joe Fawcett" dateCreated="2011-09-18">
  <title>A New Book</title>
  <body>
    <x:p>
      <x:b>I\'ve been asked to co-author a new edition of <x:a
 href="http://www.wrox.com/WileyCDA/WroxTitle/productCd-470114878.html">
Beginning XML</x:a> by Wrox</x:b>
    </x:p>
    <x:p>It\'s incredible how much has changed since the book was
 published nearly five years ago. XML
 is now a bedrock of many systems, contrarily you see less of it
 than previously as it\'s buried under more layers.</x:p>
 <x:p>There are also many places where it has stopped being an automatic
 choice for data transfer,
 JSON has become a popular replacement where the data is to
 be consumed directly by a
      JavaScript engine such as in a browser.</x:p>
    <x:p>The new edition should be finished towards the end of the year
 and be published early in 2012.</x:p>
  </body>
</post>';
Query OK, 1 row affected (0.34 sec)

mysql>
```

CreateAndLoadDatabse.sql

NOTE *The XML document that you're including is embedded in a SQL string delimited by single quotes. Any single quotes within your XML document must be escaped to fit in that string, and the SQL way to escape is by preceding it with a backslash as follows:* `\'`.

If you don't want to bother typing in the individual statements to create the database, the table, and to insert the data, you can run the following command from the `mysql` shell, which processes the file found in the code download. You will need to make sure the path to the file that the previous code snippet was from is correct for your machine:

```
source C:\mySQL\CreateAndLoadDatabase.sql
```

How It Works

In this Try It Out, you created a database that serves as the container where information is stored, and a table that defines the structure of your data. Then you entered data in this structure. So far none of this has been XML-specific; you've just used standard SQL statements as supported by all relational database systems.

Querying MySQL

Now that you have your first two blog entries, what can you do with them? Because MySQL is a SQL database, so you can use all the power of SQL to query the content of your database. To show all the entries, just type the following:

```
SELECT * FROM BlogPost;
```

The result is too verbose to print in a book, but if you want something more concise, you can select only the first characters of each entry:

```
mysql> SELECT PostId, substring(Post, 1, 60) FROM BlogPost;
+--------+-----------------------------------------------------------------------+
| PostId | substring(Post, 1, 70)                                                |
+--------+-----------------------------------------------------------------------+
|      1 | <post xmlns:x="http://www.w3.org/1999/xhtml" id="1" author="Joe Fawc |
|      2 | <post xmlns:x="http://www.w3.org/1999/xhtml" id="2" author="Joe Fawc |
|      3 | <post xmlns:x="http://www.w3.org/1999/xhtml" id="3" author="Joe Fawc |
+--------+-----------------------------------------------------------------------+
3 rows in set (0.02 sec)

mysql>
```

Or, if you just want the number of entries:

```
mysql> SELECT COUNT(*) FROM BlogPost;
+----------+
| COUNT(*) |
+----------+
|        3 |
+----------+
1 row in set (0.13 sec)

mysql>
```

This is pure SQL, however, and could be done with any SQL database without XML support. But what if you wanted, for instance, to display the content of the title element?

The XML support in MySQL 5.5 comes from two XML functions documented at `http://dev.mysql.com/doc/refman/5.5/en/xml-functions.html`. These are `ExtractValue` and `UpdateXML`. The following Try It Out shows you how to use `ExtractValue` to query data.

TRY IT OUT Using ExtractValue to Extract Title Data

In this Try It Out you'll use one of MySQL's XML functions, `ExtractValue`, to burrow into the XML representing a blog post and extracting its title. You'll be using the MySQL command shell to carry out the tasks, as in previous examples.

1. The `ExtractValue` function evaluates the result of an XPath expression over an XML fragment passed as a string. Only a fairly restricted subset of XPath is currently implemented, which severely limits your ability to query XML fragments, but this is still enough to extract the title from content columns:

```
mysql> SELECT PostId, ExtractValue(Post, '/post/title') Title FROM BlogPost;
+--------+-------------------------+
| PostId | Title                   |
+--------+-------------------------+
|      1 | A New Book              |
|      2 | Go, Neutrino, Go!       |
|      3 | Size of the Solar System |
+--------+-------------------------+
3 rows in set (0.01 sec)

mysql>
```

2. You are not limited to using the `ExtractValue` function in the `SELECT` statement; you can also use it in the `WHERE` clause. To retrieve the ID of the blog entry with a specific title, use the following:

```
mysql> SELECT PostId FROM BlogPost
    -> WHERE ExtractValue(Post, '/post/title') =
    -> 'A New Book';
```

```
+--------+
| PostId |
+--------+
|      1 |
+--------+
1 row in set (0.00 sec)

mysql>
```

How It Works

ExtractValue works by taking an XPath expression and evaluating it against the target document. It doesn't, however, return an exact copy of any XML it finds. Instead, it returns any text that is a child of the element selected, or, in the case that an attribute is selected, its value. This means that you extract the title of a post easily because the actual title is directly contained in a <title> element. You can also filter results by using ExtractValue in a WHERE clause; providing the value you want to test is simple text and not a full element.

If you are familiar with XPath, the behavior of ExtractValue is often somewhat counterintuitive. For instance, if you try to apply the same technique to fetch the <body> of your blog entries, you'll get the following:

```
mysql> SELECT PostId, ExtractValue(Post, 'post/body') Body
    -> FROM BlogPost;
+--------+--------------------------------------------------------+
| PostId | Body                                                   |
+--------+--------------------------------------------------------+
|      1 |




                                       |
|      2 |




                     |
|      3 |






        |
+--------+--------------------------------------------------------+
3 rows in set (0.04 sec)

mysql>
```

If you are used to the XPath behavior that translates elements into strings by concatenating the text nodes from all their descendants, you might assume that `ExtractValue` would do the same, but that's not the case: `ExtractValue` only concatenates the text nodes directly embedded in elements. In this case, the only text nodes that are direct children from description elements are whitespaces, which explains the preceding output.

To get the default XPath behavior, you need to explicitly state that you want the text nodes at any level like so:

```
mysql> SELECT PostId, ExtractValue(Post, 'post/body//text()') Body
    -> FROM BlogPost;
+| PostId | Body
+--------+----------------------------------------------------------------
|      1 |

       I've been asked to co-author a new edition of  Beginning XML
        by Wrox

     It's incredible how much has changed since the book was published
 nearly five years ago. XML
      is now a bedrock of many systems, contrarily you see less of it
than previously as it's buried....

3 rows in set (0.00 sec)

mysql>mysql>
```

Note that this listing has been edited for conciseness.

How would you select entries that contain images? In XPath, you use `//img` directly in a test, and this would be considered `true` if and only if there were at least one `<img>` element somewhere in the document. If you're familiar with XPath, you might be tempted to write something like this:

```
mysql> SELECT PostId, ExtractValue(Post, '/post/title') Title
    -> FROM BlogPost
    -> WHERE ExtractValue(Post, '//x:img') != '';
Empty set (0.00 sec)

mysql>
```

NOTE *MySQL's XML functions don't really understand namespaces. You don't have a way of binding a namespace URI to a prefix, so you just have to use the same prefix that exists in the source document.*

This doesn't work, however, because `<img>` elements are empty: they don't have any child text nodes, and `ExtractValue` converts them into empty strings. To make that query work, you need to select a node that will have a value (such as `//x:img/@src`) or count the number of `<img>` elements and test that the result is greater than zero. This method is shown in the following code snippet:

```
mysql> SELECT PostId, ExtractValue(Post, '/post/title') Title
    -> FROM BlogPost
    -> WHERE ExtractValue(Post, '//x:img/@src') != '';
+--------+-------------------------+
| PostId | Title                   |
+--------+-------------------------+
|      3 | Size of the Solar System |
+--------+-------------------------+
1 row in set (0.02 sec)

mysql> SELECT PostId, ExtractValue(Post, '/post/title') Title
    -> FROM BlogPost
    -> WHERE ExtractValue(Post, 'count(//x:img)') > 0;
+--------+-------------------------+
| PostId | Title                   |
+--------+-------------------------+
|      3 | Size of the Solar System |
+--------+-------------------------+
1 row in set (0.04 sec)

mysql>
```

You'll hit another limitation pretty soon if you use this function. Most of the string functions of XPath are not implemented. For instance, if you want to find entries with links to URIs from `www.wrox.com`, you might be tempted to write something such as the following:

```
mysql> SELECT PostId, ExtractValue(Post, '/post/title') Title
    -> FROM BlogPost
    -> WHERE ExtractValue
    -> (Post, 'count(//x:a[starts-with(@href, "http://www.wrox.com")])') > 0;
```

Unfortunately, the `starts-with` function is not implemented, so you'll get an error message—and not an informative one at that. It will just state that there's a syntax error; you need to use SQL to do what you can't do with XPath:

```
mysql> SELECT PostId, ExtractValue(Post, '/post/title') Title
    -> FROM BlogPost
    -> WHERE ExtractValue(Post, '//x:a/@href')
    -> LIKE 'http://www.wrox.com/%';
+--------+------------+
| PostId | Title      |
+--------+------------+
|      1 | A New Book |
+--------+------------+
1 row in set (0.06 sec)

mysql>
```

This ensures that any `href` attribute begins with the Wrox domain.

Now that you've seen how to make the most of MySQL's somewhat limited select functionality, it's time to try updating an XML document.

Updating XML in MySQL

The second XML function introduced by MySQL 5.5 is called `UpdateXML`. Like any SQL function, `UpdateXML` doesn't perform database updates, but it is handy when you use it in update statements.

`UpdateXML` takes three parameters:

- A string containing an XML document
- An XPath expression that points to an element
- An XML fragment

`UpdateXML` takes the XML document, looks for the content pointed to by the XPath expression passed as the second parameter and replaces it with the XML fragment passed as the third parameter. It then returns the new XML formed by the function as a string.

To change the title of the second blog entry, for example, use the following:

```
mysql> UPDATE BlogPost
    -> SET Post = UpdateXml(Post, '/post/title',
    -> '<title>Faster Than Light?</title>')
    -> WHERE PostId = 2;
Query OK, 1 row affected (0.13 sec)
Rows matched: 1  Changed: 1  Warnings: 0

mysql> SELECT PostId, ExtractValue(Post, '/post/title') Title
    -> FROM BlogPost;
+--------+-------------------------+
| PostId | Title                   |
+--------+-------------------------+
|      1 | A New Book              |
|      2 | Faster Than Light?      |
|      3 | Size of the Solar System |
+--------+-------------------------+
3 rows in set (0.00 sec)

mysql>
```

This function is obviously handy in this situation, but note that the XPath expression must point to an element. This means that the granularity of updates is at element level, so if you want to update an attribute value, you are out of luck.

Usability of XML in MySQL

After this introduction to the XML features of MySQL 5.5, you may be wondering, how usable these features are in real-world applications? To answer this question, first note that support of XML in MySQL 5.5 is limited to the two string functions already shown. In other words, there's no such thing as an XML column type. Your documents are stored as text and need to be parsed each time you use one of these functions.

Consider one of the queries that you have seen:

```
SELECT PostId FROM BlogPost WHERE
ExtractValue(Post, '/post/title') = 'A New Book';
```

To process this query, the database engine needs to read the full content of all the blog entries, parse this content, and apply the XPath expression that extracts the title. That's fine with your couple of blog entries, but likely not something you want to do if you are designing a WordPress clone able to store millions of blog entries.

To optimize the design of the sample database that you created, you would extract the information that is most commonly used in user queries and move it into table columns. In the `Blog` example created earlier, obvious candidates would be the title, the author, and the publication date. Having this data available as columns enables direct access for the engine. If you need further optimization, you can use these columns to create indexes.

The other consideration to keep in mind is the mismatch between the current implementation and the XPath usages. You saw an example of that when you had to explicitly specify that you wanted to concatenate text nodes from all the descendants. If you use these functions, you will see more examples where behavior differs from the generally accepted XML standards. This mismatch may be reduced in future releases, and is something to watch carefully because it could lead to incompatible changes.

With these restrictions in mind, if you are both a MySQL and an XML user, you will find these first XML features most welcome, and there is no reason to ignore them. They don't turn MySQL into a native XML database yet, but they are a step in the right direction!

Client-Side XML Support

The features that you have seen so far are all server-side features implemented by the database engine. You don't need anything to support XML on the client side, and it is very easy to use any programming language to convert SQL query results into XML. However, you might find it disappointing to leave this chapter without at least a peek at an XML feature that can be handy when you use the `mysql` command-line utility. To see this feature in action, start a new session but add the `--xml` option:

```
C:\Program Files\MySQL\MySQL Server 5.5\bin>mysql -u root -p --xml
Enter password: **********
Welcome to the MySQL monitor.  Commands end with ; or \g.
Your MySQL connection id is 15
Server version: 5.5.15 MySQL Community Server (GPL)

Copyright (c) 2000, 2010, Oracle and/or its affiliates. All rights reserved.

Oracle is a registered trademark of Oracle Corporation and/or its
affiliates. Other names may be trademarks of their respective
owners.

Type 'help;' or '\h' for help. Type '\c' to clear the current input statement.

mysql>
```

The `--xml` option has switched on the XML mode, and the query results will now be output as XML:

```
mysql> USE Blog
Database changed
mysql> SELECT PostId, ExtractValue(Post, '/post/title') Title
    -> FROM BlogPost;
<?xml version="1.0"?>

<resultset statement="SELECT PostId, ExtractValue(Post, '/post/title') Title
FROM BlogPost" xmlns:xsi="http://www.w3.org/2001/XMLSchema-instance">
  <row>
        <field name="PostId">1</field>
        <field name="Title">A New Book</field>
  </row>

  <row>
        <field name="PostId">2</field>
        <field name="Title">Faster Than Light?</field>
  </row>

  <row>
        <field name="PostId">3</field>
        <field name="Title">Size of the Solar System</field>
  </row>
</resultset>
3 rows in set (0.00 sec)

mysql>
```

Although that's not very readable as is, it's a useful feature when you use `mysql` in shell or DOS scripts. When you get your results as XML documents, you can run XML tools such as XSLT transformations. If you need a truly simple way to turn out a query result in XHTML, this is definitely something that you'll find useful.

Now that you've seen an open source implementation, it's time to move on to a commercial product, SQL Server.

USING SQL SERVER WITH XML

Microsoft's SQL Server has had XML functionality since version 2000. Version 2005 added a lot more, but since then there haven't been many changes. The version you use in this section is 2008 R2, but the examples work with any version from 2005 upwards unless otherwise specified.

Installing SQL Server

For these examples you'll use the free Express edition of SQL Server. You can download it from `www.microsoft.com/sqlserver/en/us/editions/express.aspx`. You'll need to choose the appropriate option depending on whether you need the 32 or 64 bit version. Make sure you select the install that comes with the developer tools so that you can use SQL Server Management

Studio to run the examples. You will also need to download a sample database to work with. The `AdventureWorks` OLTP database is available at `http://msftdbprodsamples.codeplex.com/releases/view/55926` and represents a fictitious bicycle manufacturing company. When downloaded into SQL Server Management Studio, the database is referred to as `AdventureWorks`.

DOWNLOADING DATABASES FOR SQL SERVER

If you are having trouble downloading and installing the sample databases you can use the files in the code download for this chapter and perform the following steps:

1. Copy `AdventureWorks_Data.mdf` and `AdventureWorks_Data_log.ldf` to a suitable folder and then open SQL Server Management Studio (SSMS).
2. Connect to the local instance and right-click the Databases node in the object explorer and choose Attach....
3. Use the Add button to browse for the `AdventureWorks_Data.mdf` file and Click OK and then OK again.
4. You can then refresh the Databases node by pressing F5 and the new database should appear. You can then right-click on it and choose Rename and call it `AdventureWorks2008R2` and hit F5 to complete the task.

The first piece of functionality discussed is how to present standard relational data as XML.

Presenting Relational Data as XML

Transforming tabular data to an XML format is a rather common requirement. SQL Server offers a number of options to achieve this, and they all involve appending the phrase `FOR XML <mode>` to the end of a regular `SELECT` query. You can use four different modes; each one enables you to tailor the results to a lesser or greater degree. The most basic mode of `FOR XML` is `RAW`.

Using FOR XML RAW

The simplest mode you can use is `RAW`. Suppose you have the following query, which selects the basic details of orders that have a value greater than $300,000:

Available for download on Wrox.com

```
SELECT [PurchaseOrderID]
      ,[RevisionNumber]
      ,[Status]
      ,[EmployeeID]
      ,[VendorID]
      ,[ShipMethodID]
```

```
      ,[OrderDate]
      ,[ShipDate]
      ,[SubTotal]
      ,[TaxAmt]
      ,[Freight]
      ,[TotalDue]
      ,[ModifiedDate]
  FROM [Purchasing].[PurchaseOrderHeader]
  WHERE [TotalDue] > 300000;
```

ForXmlQueries.sql

The example queries in this section are available in the code download for the chapter in a file named `ForXmlQueries.sql`. The results, three rows, are shown in Figure 10-1.

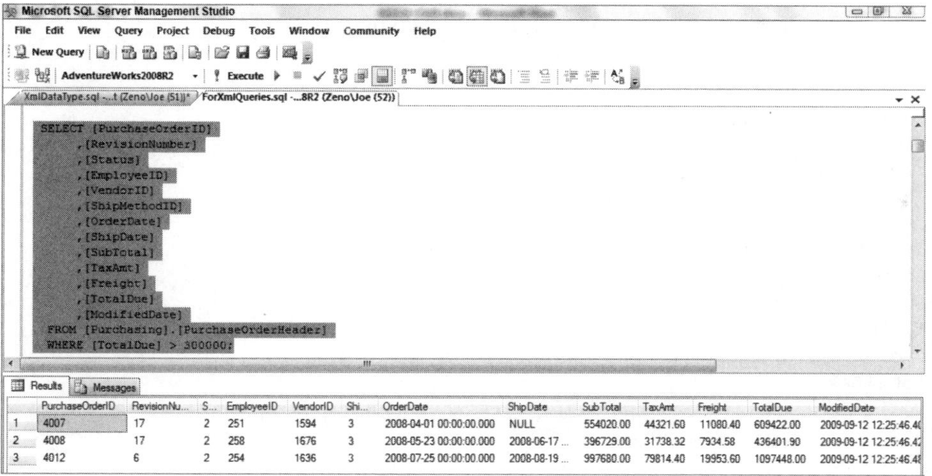

FIGURE 10-1

To return XML, add `FOR XML RAW` to the query:

Available for download on Wrox.com

```
SELECT [PurchaseOrderID]
      ,[RevisionNumber]
      ,[Status]
      ,[EmployeeID]
      ,[VendorID]
      ,[ShipMethodID]
      ,[OrderDate]
      ,[ShipDate]
      ,[SubTotal]
      ,[TaxAmt]
      ,[Freight]
```

```
      ,[TotalDue]
      ,[ModifiedDate]
  FROM [Purchasing].[PurchaseOrderHeader]
  WHERE [TotalDue] > 300000
  FOR XML RAW;
```

ForXmlQueries.sql

You'll now get an attribute-centric XML view of the data, with each row wrapped in a <row> element. However, there's no document element added so it's actually an XML fragment. One of the rows is shown in the following code:

```
<row PurchaseOrderID="4007" RevisionNumber="13" Status="2"
     EmployeeID="251" VendorID="1594" ShipMethodID="3"
     OrderDate="2008-04-01T00:00:00" ShipDate="2008-04-26T00:00:00"
     SubTotal="554020.0000" TaxAmt="44321.6000" Freight="11080.4000"
     TotalDue="609422.0000" ModifiedDate="2009-09-12T12:25:46.407" />
```

If you want an element-centric view, add the ELEMENTS directive to the query:

Available for download on Wrox.com

```
SELECT [PurchaseOrderID]
      ,[RevisionNumber]
      ,[Status]
      ,[EmployeeID]
      ,[VendorID]
      ,[ShipMethodID]
      ,[OrderDate]
      ,[ShipDate]
      ,[SubTotal]
      ,[TaxAmt]
      ,[Freight]
      ,[TotalDue]
      ,[ModifiedDate]
  FROM [Purchasing].[PurchaseOrderHeader]
  WHERE [TotalDue] > 300000
  FOR XML RAW, ELEMENTS;
```

ForXmlQueries.sql

You'll then get rows like the following:

```
<row>
  <PurchaseOrderID>4007</PurchaseOrderID>
  <RevisionNumber>13</RevisionNumber>
  <Status>2</Status>
  <EmployeeID>251</EmployeeID>
  <VendorID>1594</VendorID>
  <ShipMethodID>3</ShipMethodID>
  <OrderDate>2008-04-01T00:00:00</OrderDate>
  <ShipDate>2008-04-26T00:00:00</ShipDate>
  <SubTotal>554020.0000</SubTotal>
  <TaxAmt>44321.6000</TaxAmt>
```

```
    <Freight>11080.4000</Freight>
    <TotalDue>609422.0000</TotalDue>
    <ModifiedDate>2009-09-12T12:25:46.407</ModifiedDate>
  </row>
```

As mentioned before, the query returns an XML fragment rather than a full document. To add a surrounding root element, use the ROOT directive combined with the name of the root element you want:

```
SELECT [PurchaseOrderID]
      ,[RevisionNumber]
      ,[Status]
      ,[EmployeeID]
      ,[VendorID]
      ,[ShipMethodID]
      ,[OrderDate]
      ,[ShipDate]
      ,[SubTotal]
      ,[TaxAmt]
      ,[Freight]
      ,[TotalDue]
      ,[ModifiedDate]
  FROM [Purchasing].[PurchaseOrderHeader]
  WHERE [TotalDue] > 300000
  FOR XML RAW, ELEMENTS, ROOT('orders');
```

ForXmlQueries.sql

You'll now get an <orders> element around all the <row> elements.

You may also want to change the name of the default row container, which is <row>. Simply add the name in parentheses after the RAW keyword:

```
SELECT [PurchaseOrderID]
      ,[RevisionNumber]
      ,[Status]
      ,[EmployeeID]
      ,[VendorID]
      ,[ShipMethodID]
      ,[OrderDate]
      ,[ShipDate]
      ,[SubTotal]
      ,[TaxAmt]
      ,[Freight]
      ,[TotalDue]
      ,[ModifiedDate]
  FROM [Purchasing].[PurchaseOrderHeader]
  WHERE [TotalDue] > 300000
  FOR XML RAW('order'), ELEMENTS, ROOT('orders');
```

This will give you results similar to the following:

```
<orders>
  <order>
    <PurchaseOrderID>4007</PurchaseOrderID>
    <RevisionNumber>13</RevisionNumber>
    <Status>2</Status>
    <EmployeeID>251</EmployeeID>
    <VendorID>1594</VendorID>
    <ShipMethodID>3</ShipMethodID>
    <OrderDate>2008-04-01T00:00:00</OrderDate>
    <ShipDate>2008-04-26T00:00:00</ShipDate>
    <SubTotal>554020.0000</SubTotal>
    <TaxAmt>44321.6000</TaxAmt>
    <Freight>11080.4000</Freight>
    <TotalDue>609422.0000</TotalDue>
    <ModifiedDate>2009-09-12T12:25:46.407</ModifiedDate>
  </order>
 <!-- more order elements -->
</orders>
```

Another issue that commonly arises is how to treat nulls in the results. The default is to not output the element or attribute at all if its value is null. Sometimes it's easier to process the results if the element is there, but empty; to differentiate between an element that contains a null value and one which has an empty string there needs to be a marker on the element to signify that its value is null rather than an empty string. The marker used is `xsi:nil="true "`. This is a standard attribute from the schema instance namespace, so SQL Server also needs to add the correct namespace binding. If you want this treatment, use the `XSINIL` directive after the `ELEMENTS` keyword. The following code shows how to ensure that elements that have a null value are output rather than being omitted:

```
SSELECT [PurchaseOrderID]
      ,[RevisionNumber]
      ,[Status]
      ,[EmployeeID]
      ,[VendorID]
      ,[ShipMethodID]
      ,[OrderDate]
      ,[ShipDate]
      ,[SubTotal]
      ,[TaxAmt]
      ,[Freight]
      ,[TotalDue]
      ,[ModifiedDate]
  FROM [Purchasing].[PurchaseOrderHeader]
  WHERE [TotalDue] > 300000
  FOR XML RAW('order'), ELEMENTS XSINIL, ROOT('orders');
```

ForXmlQueries.sql

The result is as follows:

```
<orders xmlns:xsi="http://www.w3.org/2001/XMLSchema-instance">
  <order>
    <PurchaseOrderID>4007</PurchaseOrderID>
```

```
    <RevisionNumber>14</RevisionNumber>
    <Status>2</Status>
    <EmployeeID>251</EmployeeID>
    <VendorID>1594</VendorID>
    <ShipMethodID>3</ShipMethodID>
    <OrderDate>2008-04-01T00:00:00</OrderDate>
    <ShipDate xsi:nil="true" />
    <SubTotal>554020.0000</SubTotal>
    <TaxAmt>44321.6000</TaxAmt>
    <Freight>11080.4000</Freight>
    <TotalDue>609422.0000</TotalDue>
    <ModifiedDate>2009-09-12T12:25:46.407</ModifiedDate>
  </order>
  <!-- more order elements -->
</orders>
```

If your copy of the database doesn't have a null shipping date, you can always change one—the code in `ForXmlQueries.sql` makes the requisite change and then restores it at the end.

One final feature that might be useful, especially if your data is being passed to a third party, is the ability to add an XML schema. This is done by appending the previous code with the `XMLSCHEMA` directive like so:

Available for download on Wrox.com

```
SELECT [PurchaseOrderID]
      ,[RevisionNumber]
      ,[Status]
      ,[EmployeeID]
      ,[VendorID]
      ,[ShipMethodID]
      ,[OrderDate]
      ,[ShipDate]
      ,[SubTotal]
      ,[TaxAmt]
      ,[Freight]
      ,[TotalDue]
      ,[ModifiedDate]
  FROM [Purchasing].[PurchaseOrderHeader]
  WHERE [TotalDue] > 300000
  FOR XML RAW('order'), ELEMENTS XSINIL, ROOT('orders'), XMLSCHEMA;
```

ForXmlQueries.sql

The schema (highlighted here) is included just after the document element and before the actual results:

```
<orders xmlns:xsi="http://www.w3.org/2001/XMLSchema-instance">
  <xsd:schema targetNamespace="urn:schemas-microsoft-com:sql:SqlRowSet1"
        xmlns:xsd="http://www.w3.org/2001/XMLSchema"
        xmlns:sqltypes="http://schemas.microsoft.com/sqlserver/2004/sqltypes"
        elementFormDefault="qualified">
  <xsd:import namespace="http://schemas.microsoft.com/sqlserver/2004/sqltypes"
       schemaLocation=
```

```
"http://schemas.microsoft.com/sqlserver/2004/sqltypes/sqltypes.xsd" />
 <xsd:element name="order">
  <xsd:complexType>
   <xsd:sequence>
    <xsd:element name="PurchaseOrderID" type="sqltypes:int" nillable="1" />
    <xsd:element name="RevisionNumber" type="sqltypes:tinyint" nillable="1"/>
    <xsd:element name="Status" type="sqltypes:tinyint" nillable="1" />
    <xsd:element name="EmployeeID" type="sqltypes:int" nillable="1" />
    <xsd:element name="VendorID" type="sqltypes:int" nillable="1" />
    <xsd:element name="ShipMethodID" type="sqltypes:int" nillable="1" />
    <xsd:element name="OrderDate" type="sqltypes:datetime" nillable="1" />
    <xsd:element name="ShipDate" type="sqltypes:datetime" nillable="1" />
    <xsd:element name="SubTotal" type="sqltypes:money" nillable="1" />
    <xsd:element name="TaxAmt" type="sqltypes:money" nillable="1" />
    <xsd:element name="Freight" type="sqltypes:money" nillable="1" />
    <xsd:element name="TotalDue" type="sqltypes:money" nillable="1" />
    <xsd:element name="ModifiedDate" type="sqltypes:datetime" nillable="1" />
   </xsd:sequence>
   </xsd:complexType>
 </xsd:element>
</xsd:schema>
<order xmlns="urn:schemas-microsoft-com:sql:SqlRowSet1">
  <PurchaseOrderID>4007</PurchaseOrderID>
  <RevisionNumber>14</RevisionNumber>
  <Status>2</Status>
  <EmployeeID>251</EmployeeID>
  <VendorID>1594</VendorID>
  <ShipMethodID>3</ShipMethodID>
  <OrderDate>2008-04-01T00:00:00</OrderDate>
  <ShipDate xsi:nil="true" />
  <SubTotal>554020.0000</SubTotal>
  <TaxAmt>44321.6000</TaxAmt>
  <Freight>11080.4000</Freight>
  <TotalDue>609422.0000</TotalDue>
  <ModifiedDate>2009-09-12T12:25:46.407</ModifiedDate>
</order>
<!-- rest of order elements -->
</orders>
```

Although the RAW mode has a few options, it fails miserably when dealing with hierarchical data. To have more control and to be able to handle hierarchical data more effectively you can use FOR XML AUTO.

Using FOR XML AUTO

If you try to use the RAW mode with nested data, such as orders along with the line items, you'll get a repetitive block of XML in which the order is repeated for every line item. One of the strengths of XML is the ability to show hierarchical data cleanly, so this sort of repetition is something to be avoided. You examine how the AUTO mode copes with this in the following activity.

TRY IT OUT Using FOR XML AUTO

In this Try It Out you'll be using the more sophisticated `FOR XML AUTO` directive. You'll see how this gives greater control than the `FOR XML RAW` queries that you met earlier. Primarily `FOR XML AUTO` is much better at handling the XML returned when two or more tables are joined in a query, for example when joining `PurchaseOrderHeader` with `PurchaseOrderDetail` to give a full view of an order.

1. To try `FOR XML AUTO`, simply replace the `RAW` keyword with `AUTO` in the basic query introduced in the preceding section:

```
SELECT [PurchaseOrderID]
      ,[RevisionNumber]
      ,[Status]
      ,[EmployeeID]
      ,[VendorID]
      ,[ShipMethodID]
      ,[OrderDate]
      ,[ShipDate]
      ,[SubTotal]
      ,[TaxAmt]
      ,[Freight]
      ,[TotalDue]
      ,[ModifiedDate]
FROM [Purchasing].[PurchaseOrderHeader]
WHERE [TotalDue] > 300000
FOR XML AUTO;
```

ForXmlQueries.sql

You won't see much difference in the results of this query compared to the `RAW` version, other than the fact that the name of the element holding the data is derived from the table name rather than being a generic `row` element:

```
<Purchasing.PurchaseOrderHeader PurchaseOrderID="4007" RevisionNumber="14"
 Status="2" EmployeeID="251" VendorID="1594" ShipMethodID="3"
 OrderDate="2008-04-01T00:00:00" SubTotal="554020.0000" TaxAmt="44321.6000"
 Freight="11080.4000" TotalDue="609422.0000"
 ModifiedDate="2009-09-12T12:25:46.407" />
```

Again, the result is a fragment with no all-enclosing document element.

2. The real difference becomes apparent when a query extracting data from two linked tables is executed. The following SQL shows all the previous orders along with their individual line items:

```
SELECT POH.[PurchaseOrderID]
      ,POH.[RevisionNumber]
      ,POH.[Status]
      ,POH.[EmployeeID]
      ,POH.[VendorID]
      ,POH.[ShipMethodID]
      ,POH.[OrderDate]
      ,POH.[ShipDate]
```

```
      ,POH.[SubTotal]
      ,POH.[TaxAmt]
      ,POH.[Freight]
      ,POH.[TotalDue]
      ,POH.[ModifiedDate]
      ,POD.[OrderQty]
      ,POD.[ProductID]
      ,POD.[UnitPrice]
  FROM [Purchasing].[PurchaseOrderHeader] POH
  INNER JOIN Purchasing.PurchaseOrderDetail POD
  ON POH.PurchaseOrderID = POD.PurchaseOrderID
  WHERE [TotalDue] > 300000;
```

ForXmlQueries.sql

Here, the tables have been joined on the `PurchaseOrderId` field and the tables have been aliased to use the shorter names, `POH` and `POD`. The results of this query are shown in Figure 10-2.

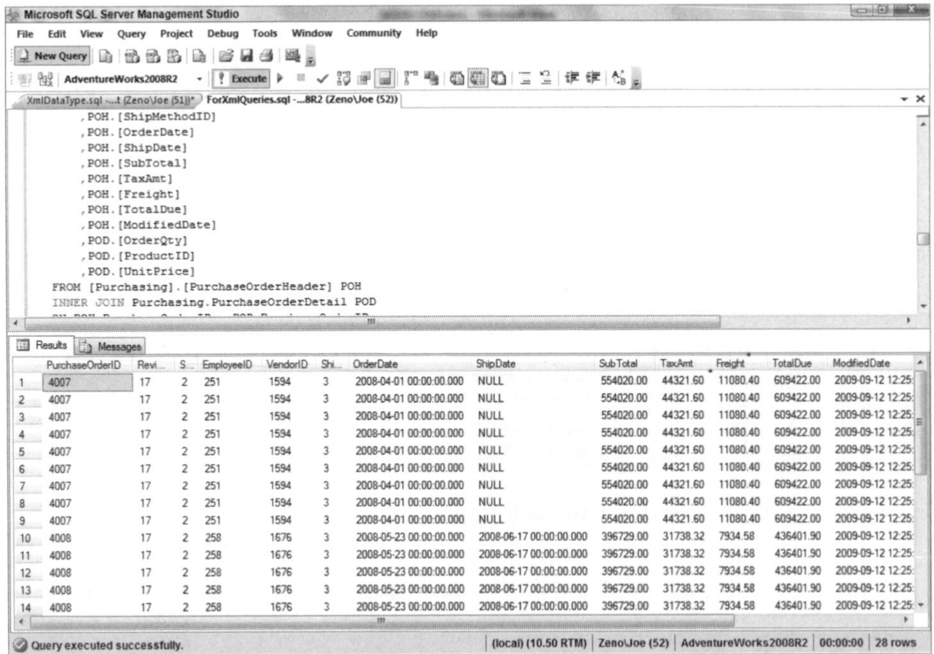

FIGURE 10-2

3. Now modify the query by adding `FOR XML AUTO`:

```
SELECT POH.[PurchaseOrderID]
      ,POH.[RevisionNumber]
```

```
      ,POH.[Status]
      ,POH.[EmployeeID]
      ,POH.[VendorID]
      ,POH.[ShipMethodID]
      ,POH.[OrderDate]
      ,POH.[ShipDate]
      ,POH.[SubTotal]
      ,POH.[TaxAmt]
      ,POH.[Freight]
      ,POH.[TotalDue]
      ,POH.[ModifiedDate]
      ,POD.[OrderQty]
      ,POD.[ProductID]
      ,POD.[UnitPrice]
  FROM [Purchasing].[PurchaseOrderHeader] POH
  INNER JOIN Purchasing.PurchaseOrderDetail POD
  ON POH.PurchaseOrderID = POD.PurchaseOrderID
  WHERE [TotalDue] > 300000
  FOR XML AUTO, ROOT('orders');
```

ForXmlQueries.sql

Notice that a root element has been specified, as with the RAW option. The results appear as follows with the hierarchical nature much more apparent:

```
<orders>
  <POH PurchaseOrderID="4007" RevisionNumber="16" Status="2" EmployeeID="251"
   VendorID="1594" ShipMethodID="3" OrderDate="2008-04-01T00:00:00"
   SubTotal="554020.0000" TaxAmt="44321.6000" Freight="11080.4000"
   TotalDue="609422.0000" ModifiedDate="2009-09-12T12:25:46.407">
    <POD OrderQty="5000" ProductID="849" UnitPrice="24.7500" />
    <POD OrderQty="5000" ProductID="850" UnitPrice="24.7500" />
    <POD OrderQty="5000" ProductID="851" UnitPrice="24.7500" />
    <POD OrderQty="750" ProductID="852" UnitPrice="30.9400" />
    <POD OrderQty="750" ProductID="853" UnitPrice="30.9400" />
    <POD OrderQty="750" ProductID="854" UnitPrice="30.9400" />
    <POD OrderQty="1050" ProductID="855" UnitPrice="37.1000" />
    <POD OrderQty="1000" ProductID="856" UnitPrice="37.1000" />
    <POD OrderQty="1000" ProductID="857" UnitPrice="37.1000" />
  </POH>
  <!-- more POH elements -->
</orders>
```

Note that the elements have taken on the names of the table aliases used in the query, which gives you a way to name them anything you like.

How It Works

The original query, without the FOR XML AUTO directive, leads to a very repetitive result set with each order line also containing the full details from the header. Adding FOR XML AUTO, ROOT('orders') to the query produces a nested set of records, something XML excels at, making each order header an element with its details such as order date and ID displayed as attributes. Underneath each `<POH>` element is one `<POD>` element representing a line from the order. Again each of these elements uses attributes to show values such as order quantity and product ID.

The other options available to `FOR XML RAW`, such as `ELEMENTS`, `XSINIL`, and `XMLSCHEMA`, are also available to `FOR XML AUTO`.

NOTE *Also available are several less commonly used features, such as those to return binary data and to use* `GROUP BY` *in XML queries. These are covered at length in the SQL Server Books Online (BOL), available from within the SQL Server Management Studio or online at* `msdn.microsoft.com/en-us/library/ms130214.aspx`.

Despite the different options available to both the `RAW` and the `AUTO` versions of `FOR XML`, you will likely encounter cases where neither alternative produces the output needed. The most common scenario is when you need a combination of elements and attributes, rather than one or the other. Two options are available for this purpose: `FOR XML EXPLICIT` and `FOR XML PATH`; the latter is available only in post-2000 versions.

Using FOR XML EXPLICIT

The `EXPLICIT` option enables almost unlimited control over the resulting XML format, but this comes at a price. The syntax is difficult to grasp, and because the mechanism used to construct the resulting XML is based on a forward-only XML writer, the results must be grouped and ordered in a very specific way. Unless you are stuck with SQL Server 2000, the advice from Microsoft and other experts is to use the `PATH` option instead. If you do need to use `EXPLICIT`, the full details are available in the SQL Server BOL.

Using FOR XML PATH

The `PATH` option, based on using XPath to specify the format of the output, makes building nested XML with combinations of elements and attributes relatively simple. Take one of the earlier query result examples, in which orders over $300,000 were retrieved and returned as attribute-centric XML using the `AUTO` option:

```
<orders>
  <Purchasing.PurchaseOrderHeader PurchaseOrderID="4007" RevisionNumber="16"
   Status="2" EmployeeID="251" VendorID="1594" ShipMethodID="3"
   OrderDate="2008-04-01T00:00:00" SubTotal="554020.0000" TaxAmt="44321.6000"
   Freight="11080.4000" TotalDue="609422.0000"
   ModifiedDate="2009-09-12T12:25:46.407" />
</orders>
```

What if a different layout was needed, one where the `PurchaseOrderID`, `EmployeedID`, and `status` were attributes but the other data appeared as elements? The `PATH` option uses aliases of the columns to specify how the XML is structured. The syntax is similar to XPath (covered in Chapter 7), hence the `PATH` keyword.

The `PATH` query for the order data as a mix of attributes and elements would be as follows:

```
SELECT [PurchaseOrderID] [@PurchaseOrderID]
    ,[Status] [@Status]
    ,[EmployeeID] [@EmployeeID]
    ,[VendorID]
    ,[ShipMethodID]
    ,[OrderDate]
    ,[ShipDate]
    ,[SubTotal]
    ,[TaxAmt]
    ,[Freight]
    ,[TotalDue]
FROM [Purchasing].[PurchaseOrderHeader] POH
WHERE [TotalDue] > 300000
FOR XML PATH('order'), ROOT('orders');
```

ForXmlQueries.sql

Notice how data that needs to be returned as attributes is aliased to a column name beginning with `@`. Unaliased columns are returned as elements. The results of this query would resemble the following XML:

```
<orders>
  <order PurchaseOrderID="4007" Status="2" EmployeeID="251">
    <VendorID>1594</VendorID>
    <ShipMethodID>3</ShipMethodID>
    <OrderDate>2008-04-01T00:00:00</OrderDate>
    <SubTotal>554020.0000</SubTotal>
    <TaxAmt>44321.6000</TaxAmt>
    <Freight>11080.4000</Freight>
    <TotalDue>609422.0000</TotalDue>
  </order>
  <!-- more order elements -->
</orders>
```

The `PATH` option also provides control over nesting. The usual way to do this, rather than use a SQL `JOIN` as shown previously, is to use a subquery. The following snippet shows the order header as attributes, with the order details as nested elements:

```
SELECT [POH].[PurchaseOrderID] [@PurchaseOrderID]
  ,[POH].[Status] [@Status]
  ,[POH].[EmployeeID] [@EmployeeID]
  ,[POH].[VendorID] [@VendorID]
```

```
    ,[POH].[ShipMethodID] [@ShipMethodID]
    ,[POH].[OrderDate] [@OrderDate]
    ,[POH].[ShipDate] [@ShipDate]
    ,[POH].[SubTotal] [@SubTotal]
    ,[POH].[TaxAmt] [@TaxAmt]
    ,[POH].[Freight] [@Freight]
    ,[POH].[TotalDue] [@TotalDue]
    ,(
       SELECT [POD].[OrderQty]
             ,[POD].[ProductID]
             ,[POD].[UnitPrice]
       FROM [Purchasing].[PurchaseOrderDetail] POD
       WHERE POH.[PurchaseOrderID] =
                                 POD.[PurchaseOrderID]
       ORDER BY POD.[PurchaseOrderID]
       FOR XML PATH('orderDetail'), TYPE
    )
 FROM [Purchasing].[PurchaseOrderHeader] POH
 WHERE [POH].[TotalDue] > 300000
 FOR XML PATH('order'), ROOT('orders');
```

ForXmlQueries.sql

The main part of the query, without the inner `SELECT`, is much the same as before except all the output columns are specified as attributes, as shown by the alias name beginning with the `@` symbol:

```
SELECT [POH].[PurchaseOrderID] [@PurchaseOrderID]
  ,[POH].[Status] [@Status]
  ,[POH].[EmployeeID] [@EmployeeID]
  ,[POH].[VendorID] [@VendorID]
  ,[POH].[ShipMethodID] [@ShipMethodID]
  ,[POH].[OrderDate] [@OrderDate]
  ,[POH].[ShipDate] [@ShipDate]
  ,[POH].[SubTotal] [@SubTotal]
  ,[POH].[TaxAmt] [@TaxAmt]
  ,[POH].[Freight] [@Freight]
  ,[POH].[TotalDue] [@TotalDue]
  (
          -- Inner query here
      )
FROM [Purchasing].[PurchaseOrderHeader] POH
WHERE [POH].[TotalDue] > 300000
FOR XML PATH('order'), ROOT('orders');
```

ForXmlQueries.sql

The inner query returns the order detail relating to the customer specified in the outer query. This is accomplished by equating the `PurchaseOrderDetail.PurchaseOrderId` field in the outer query to the `PurchaseOrderDetail.PurchaseOrderID` in the nested query as shown in the following code snippet. (In SQL terms, this is known as a *correlated subquery*.)

Available for download on Wrox.com

```
SELECT [POD].[OrderQty]
      ,[POD].[ProductID]
      ,[POD].[UnitPrice]
FROM [Purchasing].[PurchaseOrderDetail] POD
WHERE POH.[PurchaseOrderID] =
                          POD.[PurchaseOrderID]
ORDER BY POD.[PurchaseOrderID]
FOR XML PATH('orderDetail'), TYPE
```

ForXmlQueries.sql

Note the `TYPE` option at the end of the subquery. This specifies that the resulting data should be converted to the XML data type (this is covered in more detail later in the chapter). This option ensures that the data is inserted as XML, rather than a string. The actual output from the query appears as follows:

```
<orders>
  <order PurchaseOrderID="4007" Status="2" EmployeeID="251" VendorID="1594"
  ShipMethodID="3" OrderDate="2008-04-01T00:00:00" SubTotal="554020.0000"
  TaxAmt="44321.6000" Freight="11080.4000" TotalDue="609422.0000">
    <orderDetail>
      <OrderQty>5000</OrderQty>
      <ProductID>849</ProductID>
      <UnitPrice>24.7500</UnitPrice>
    </orderDetail>
    <orderDetail>
      <OrderQty>5000</OrderQty>
      <ProductID>850</ProductID>
      <UnitPrice>24.7500</UnitPrice>
    </orderDetail>
    <orderDetail>
      <OrderQty>5000</OrderQty>
      <ProductID>851</ProductID>
      <UnitPrice>24.7500</UnitPrice>
    </orderDetail>
    <orderDetail>
      <OrderQty>750</OrderQty>
      <ProductID>852</ProductID>
      <UnitPrice>30.9400</UnitPrice>
    </orderDetail>
    <!-- more orderDetail elements -->
  </order>
  <!-- more order elements -->
</orders>
```

Because no aliasing was applied to the inner query, the columns are represented by XML elements.

WARNING *If you remove the* `, TYPE` *from the inner query, the order details are inserted as escaped XML because they are treated as text data, not markup.*

Plenty of other options are available to customize the results returned from a FOR XML PATH query. The final example shows how to group data within elements. The two dates associated with the order are grouped under a <Dates> element, and an <orderDetail> element is used to hold the individual line items:

```
SELECT [POH].[PurchaseOrderID] [@PurchaseOrderID]
  ,[POH].[Status] [@Status]
  ,[POH].[EmployeeID] [@EmployeeID]
  ,[POH].[VendorID] [@VendorID]
  ,[POH].[ShipMethodID] [@ShipMethodID]
  ,[POH].[SubTotal] [@SubTotal]
  ,[POH].[TaxAmt] [@TaxAmt]
  ,[POH].[Freight] [@Freight]
  ,[POH].[TotalDue] [@TotalDue]
  ,[POH].[OrderDate] [Dates/Order]
  ,[POH].[ShipDate] [Dates/Ship]

  ,(
     SELECT [POD].[OrderQty]
           ,[POD].[ProductID]
           ,[POD].[UnitPrice]
     FROM [Purchasing].[PurchaseOrderDetail] POD
     WHERE POH.[PurchaseOrderID] =
                                POD.[PurchaseOrderID]
     ORDER BY POD.[PurchaseOrderID]
     FOR XML PATH('orderDetail'), TYPE
  )
FROM [Purchasing].[PurchaseOrderHeader] POH
WHERE [POH].[TotalDue] > 300000
FOR XML PATH('order'), ROOT('orders');
```

ForXmlQueries.sql

In the preceding code, the key change is to the OrderDate and ShipDate in the outer SELECT. The columns are aliased to Date/Order and Dates/Ship, so SQL Server creates a new element, Dates, to hold these two values. There is also an alias on the entire subquery, OrderDetails, that causes all of its results to be grouped under one element. The resulting XML looks like this:

```
<orders>
  <order PurchaseOrderID="4008" Status="2" EmployeeID="258" VendorID="1676"
 ShipMethodID="3" SubTotal="396729.0000" TaxAmt="31738.3200" Freight="7934.5800"
 TotalDue="436401.9000">
    <Dates>
      <Order>2008-05-23T00:00:00</Order>
      <Ship>2008-06-17T00:00:00</Ship>
    </Dates>
    <orderDetail>
      <OrderQty>700</OrderQty>
      <ProductID>858</ProductID>
      <UnitPrice>9.1500</UnitPrice>
    </orderDetail>
    <orderDetail>
```

```
      <OrderQty>700</OrderQty>
      <ProductID>859</ProductID>
      <UnitPrice>9.1500</UnitPrice>
    </orderDetail>
    <!-- more orderDetail elements -->
  </order>
  <order PurchaseOrderID="4012" Status="2" EmployeeID="254" VendorID="1636"
ShipMethodID="3" SubTotal="997680.0000" TaxAmt="79814.4000" Freight="19953.6000"
TotalDue="1097448.0000">
    <Dates>
      <Order>2008-07-25T00:00:00</Order>
      <Ship>2008-08-19T00:00:00</Ship>
    </Dates>
    <orderDetail>
      <OrderQty>6000</OrderQty>
      <ProductID>881</ProductID>
      <UnitPrice>41.5700</UnitPrice>
    </orderDetail>
    <!-- more orderDetail elements -->
  </order>
</orders>
```

NOTE *Dozens of additional options for* `PATH` *queries are available, including how to produce comments, how to create text content, and how to add namespace declarations. For a full discussion, refer to Books Online,* `http://msdn.microsoft.com/en-us/library/ms130214.aspx`.

That covers the basics of the `FOR XML` instruction. Next you take a look at storing XML within a table, starting with the `xml` data type.

Understanding the xml Data Type

SQL Server 2005 added an `xml` data type to those available, which means that XML documents can be stored in a SQL Server 2005 (or later) database. This is a vast improvement on earlier versions where there were two options for storing XML, neither of which was satisfactory. The first alternative was to shred the data into its constituent parts, which were then stored in multiple relational tables—defeating the purpose of using XML. The second choice was to convert the XML to a simple string of characters, which loses the logical content of the XML document. The additional ability to store XML data as an `xml` data type means that such data can be treated as if it were still an XML document. In reality, the `xml` data type is stored in a proprietary binary format, but, as far as the developer is concerned, it is accessible as XML, with its logical structure intact.

NOTE *One or two differences exist between the data stored by SQL Server and the original document, and it is not possible to round-trip between the two and get an identical copy, although the XML Infoset is preserved (see Chapter 2 for details).*

The existence of the `xml` data type means that XML documents stored as this type can be treated as if they were collections of XML documents sitting on your hard drive. Of course, the details of the interface to that XML is specific to SQL Server. Other advantages to having a specific data type devoted to XML are that you can store intermediate results in queries that return XML and you can use the methods of the `xml` data type to search and modify the XML stored in it.

There are several general advantages to storing your data in SQL Server. For one, XML storage benefits from the security, scalability, and other aspects of an enterprise-level database management system. You can also associate XML schemas with the column and, when querying the document, the appropriate type will be returned. This is a vast improvement over the previous version, where `CAST`ing or `CONVERT`ing was needed.

XML documents stored in SQL Server can be treated as XML in any other setting. One practical effect of that is that you can use XQuery (introduced in Chapter 9) to query these XML columns. Surprisingly, two XML document instances cannot be compared in this release, in part because of the flexibility of XML syntax. Consider, for example, the subtleties of trying to compare two lengthy XML documents that can have paired apostrophes or paired quotes to contain attribute values, differently-ordered attributes, different namespace prefixes although the namespace URI may be the same, and empty elements written with start tags and end tags or with the empty element tag.

Documents stored as the `xml` data type can be validated against a specified W3C XML Schema document. XML data that is not associated with a schema document is termed *untyped*, and XML associated with a schema document is termed *typed*.

In the following activity you create a simple table to contain XML documents in SQL Server. SQL Server Management Studio is the main graphical tool for manipulating database objects and writing SQL code, although Visual Studio and a number of third-party applications are also available. Refer to the "Installing SQL Server" section for instructions on how to download SQL Server Management Studio.

TRY IT OUT Creating XML Documents in SQL Server

The following Try It Out shows how to create a table designed specifically to hold XML documents in their native state, rather than as text. Once the table has been created you'll see how to insert a few sample XML documents and then retrieve them using SQL.

1. Open the SQL Server Management Studio (SSMS) and connect to the local instance of SQL Server (or whichever server you want to create the test database on).

2. In the Object Explorer, expand the nodes so that User Databases is shown. Right-click and select the New Database option. When dialog box opens, insert the name of the database—for this example, `XMLDocTest`. Before clicking OK, make sure that the Full Text Indexing option is checked.

3. Create a table called `Docs` using the following SQL:

```
CREATE TABLE dbo.Docs (
 DocID INTEGER IDENTITY PRIMARY KEY,
 XMLDoc XML
 )
```

XmlDataType.sql

The column `XMLDoc` is of type `xml`. Because this is a SQL statement, the data type is not case sensitive. Now you have an empty table.

4. For the purposes of this example, add simple XML documents with the following structure:

```
<Person>
 <FirstName></FirstName>
 <LastName></LastName>
</Person>
```

5. Insert XML documents using the SQL `INSERT` statement, as follows, which shows insertion of a single XML document:

```
INSERT Docs
VALUES ('<Person><FirstName>Joe</FirstName>
<LastName>Fawcett</LastName></Person>'
)
```

XmlDataType.sql

6. After modifying the values of the `FirstName` and `LastName` elements and adding a few documents to the `XMLDoc` column, confirm that retrieval works correctly using the following SQL statement:

```
SELECT * FROM Docs
```

The result of this SQL Query is shown in Figure 10-3.

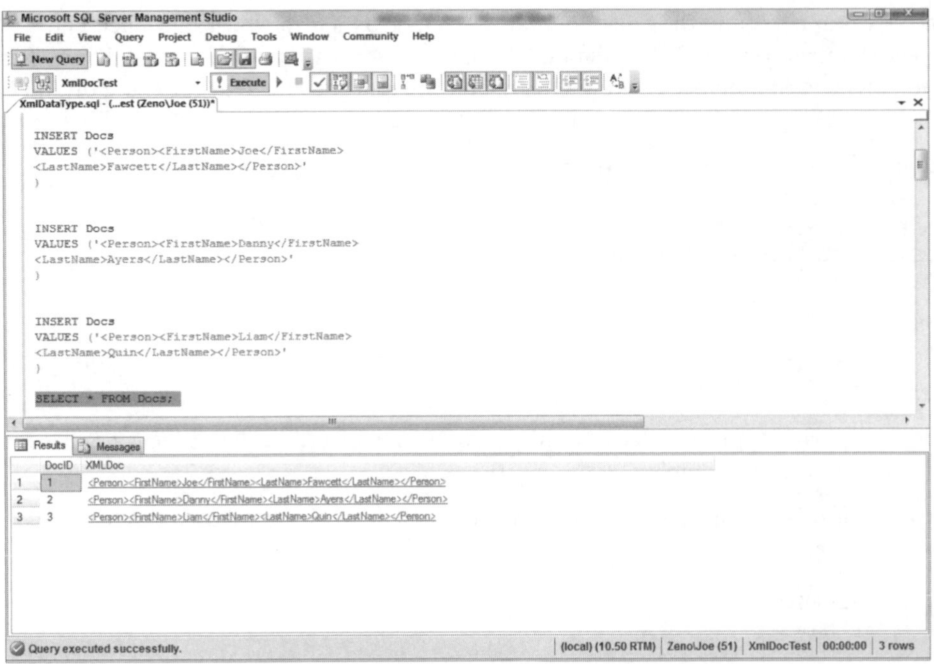

FIGURE 10-3

The values contained in the `XMLDoc` column are displayed in the lower pane of the figure. A little later, you will create some simple XQuery queries.

How It Works

The first step created a table, `Docs`, which had one of the columns, `XmlDoc`, defined as the new XML type. The next stage used a traditional `INSERT` query to add some text to this column. Because the column was defined as XML, the data was converted from text to an XML document. The document can be retrieved by using a traditional `SELECT` query.

As an alternative to retrieving the whole XML document, you can also select only parts of it (see the upcoming sections starting with "Using the query() Method").

Creating Indexes with the xml Data Type

XML documents in SQL Server can also be indexed for more efficient retrieval, and a full-text index can be created. To create a full-text index on a document, use a command like the following:

```
--If no catalog exists so far
CREATE FULLTEXT CATALOG ft ON DEFAULT
CREATE FULLTEXT INDEX ON dbo.Docs(XmlDoc) KEY INDEX <primary key name>
```

The `xml` data type enables you to use the following methods to manipulate the data and to extract it in various forms: `modify()`, `query()`, `value()`, `exist()`, and `nodes()`. The following sections look at each method in turn and describe how they are used.

Using the modify() Method

The `xml` data type can be queried using the XQuery language, which was introduced in Chapter 9. In SQL Server, XQuery expressions are embedded inside Transact-SQL. Transact-SQL is the flavor of the SQL language used in SQL Server.

Microsoft introduced the `modify()` method before XQuery had finalized a syntax. At the time there was talk of updating to the official standard when it appeared, but so far that hasn't happened.

The W3C XQuery 1.0 specification is limited in that it can query only an XML (or XML-enabled) data source. There is no facility in XQuery 1.0 to carry out deletions, to insert new data, or (combining those actions) to modify data. In SQL Server, the XML Data Modification Language (DML) adds three keywords to the functionality available in XQuery 1.0. You can see these keywords in action in the following exercise:

- `delete`
- `insert`
- `replace value of`

WARNING *Note that although SQL itself is not case sensitive, the commands used to manipulate XML within the* `modify()` *method are. For example, if you use* `DELETE` *instead of* `delete`*, you will receive a cryptic error message.*

TRY IT OUT Deleting with XML DML

This Try It Out looks at how to delete part of an XML document using the `modify()` method in conjunction with the `delete` keyword. You'll use a simple XML document stored in a local variable rather than a table and then target a specific part for deletion. The following code shows an example of how it can be used:

Available for download on Wrox.com

```
DECLARE @myDoc xml;
SET @myDoc = '<Person><FirstName>Joe</FirstName>
 <LastName>Fawcett</LastName></Person>';

SELECT @myDoc;
SET @myDoc.modify(' delete /Person/*[2]');
SELECT @myDoc;
```

XmlDataType.sql

To try this out in SSMS, follow these steps:

1. Open the SQL Server Management Studio.
2. Connect to the default instance.
3. From the toolbar, select New SQL Server Query, which appears on the far left.
4. Enter the preceding code.
5. Press F5 to run the SQL code. If you have typed in the code correctly, the original document should be displayed, with the modified document displayed below it. In the modified document, the `LastName` element has been removed.
6. Adjust the width of the columns to display the full XML.

How It Works

The first line of the code declares a variable, `myDoc`, and specifies the data type as `xml`. The `SET` statement specifies a value for the `myDoc` variable, shown in the following snippet. It's a familiar `Person` element with `FirstName` and `LastName` child elements and corresponding text content.

```
SET @myDoc = '<Person><FirstName>Joe</FirstName>
 <LastName>Fawcett</LastName></Person>';
```

The `SELECT` statement following the `SET` statement causes the value of `myDoc` to be displayed. Next, the `modify` function is used to modify the value of the `xml` data type:

```
SET @myDoc.modify(' delete /Person/*[2]');
```

The Data Modification Language statement inside the `modify()` function is, like XQuery, case sensitive. The `delete` keyword is used to specify which part of the XML document is to be deleted. In this case, the XPath expression `/Person/*[2]` specifies that the second child element of the `Person` element is to be deleted, which is the `LastName` element.

The final `SELECT` statement shows the value of `myDoc` after the deletion has taken place. Figure 10-4 shows the results of both `SELECT` statements.

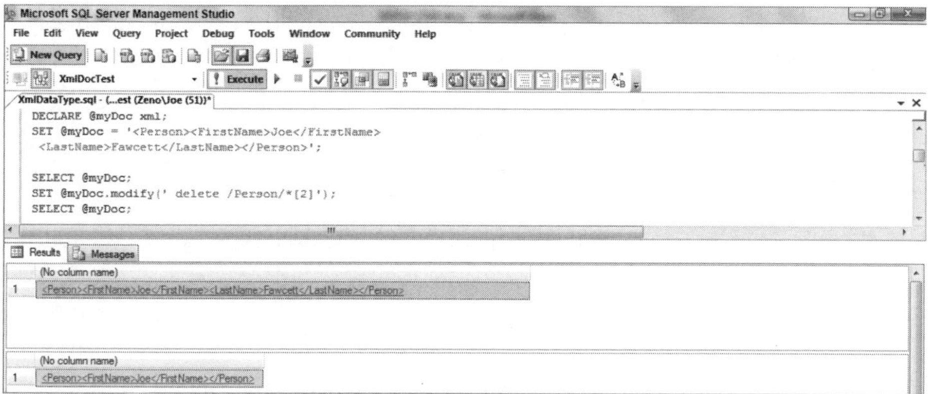

FIGURE 10-4

The following Try It Out again uses the `modify()` method but this time, instead of deleting unwanted XML, you insert a new element into the document.

TRY IT OUT Inserting with XML DML

This Try It Out shows how to add data to existing XML. It uses the `modify()` method together with the `insert` keyword. Again you'll see the operation performed on an `xml` data type represented by a local variable rather than that found in a table. The Transact-SQL code is shown here:

```
DECLARE @myDoc XML;

SET @myDoc = '<Person><LastName>Fawcett</LastName></Person>';
SELECT @myDoc;
SET @myDoc.modify(' insert <FirstName>Joe</FirstName> as first into /Person[1]');
SELECT @myDoc;
```

XmlDataType.sql

To run this code, follow these steps:

1. Open the SQL Server Management Studio.
2. Connect to the default instance.
3. From the toolbar, select New SQL Server Query which appears on the far left.
4. Enter the preceding code.

5. Press F5 to run the SQL code. If you have typed in the code correctly, the original document should be displayed, with the modified document displayed below it. The modified document has a new `FirstName` element.

6. Adjust the width of the columns to display the full XML.

How It Works

In the first line you declare a variable, `myDoc`, and specify that it has the data type `xml`. In the following code:

```
SET @myDoc = '<Person><LastName>Fawcett</LastName></Person>';
```

you set the value of the `myDoc` variable. You then specify a `Person` element that contains only a `LastName` element, which contains the text `Fawcett`.

The `modify()` function is used to contain the XQuery extension that you want to use. The `insert` keyword specifies that the modification is an `insert` operation, that is, you are going to introduce new content into an existing document rather than create a complete document or replace some pre-existing XML. The XML to be inserted follows the `insert` keyword. Notice that it is not enclosed by apostrophes or quotes. The clause `as first` specifies that the inserted XML is to be inserted first. The `into` clause uses an XPath expression, `/Person`, to specify that the `FirstName` element and its content is to be added as a child element to the `Person` element. Given the `as first` clause, you know that the `FirstName` element is to be the first child of the `Person` element.

As alternatives to `into`, you could also use `after` or `before`. Whereas `into` adds children to a parent node, `after` and `before` add siblings. The preceding query could be rewritten as follows:

Available for download on Wrox.com

```
DDECLARE @myDoc XML;
SET @myDoc = '<Person><LastName>Fawcett</LastName></Person>';
SELECT @myDoc;
SET @myDoc.modify(' insert <FirstName>Joe</FirstName> before
  (/Person/LastName)[1]');
SELECT @myDoc;
```

XmlDataType.sql

When you run the Transact-SQL, the first `SELECT` statement causes the original XML to be displayed, and the second `SELECT` statement causes the XML to be displayed after the `insert` operation has completed.

The final example of the `modify()` function shows how you can update, or replace, a section of XML.

TRY IT OUT Updating with XML DML

The final example using the Data Modification Language updates the content of an XML variable so that the value of the FirstName element is changed from Joe to Gillian. The code is shown here:

```
DECLARE @myDoc XML;
SET @myDoc =
'<Person><FirstName>Joe</FirstName><LastName>Fawcett</LastName></Person>'
SELECT @myDoc;
SET @myDoc.modify(' replace value of (/Person/FirstName/text())[1] with
 "Gillian" ');
SELECT @myDoc;
```

XmlDataType.sql

To run this code, follow these steps:

1. Open the SQL Server Management Studio.
2. Connect to the local instance or the server you want to run the query on.
3. From the toolbar, select New SQL Server Query which appears on the far left .
4. Enter the preceding code.
5. Press F5 to run the SQL code. If you have typed in the code correctly, the original document should be displayed, with the modified document displayed below it. The document now has Gillian instead of Joe for the FirstName element's contents.
6. Adjust the width of the columns to display the full XML.

How It Works

Notice the modify function:

```
SET @myDoc.modify(' replace value of (/Person/FirstName/text())[1] with
 "Gillian" ');
```

The replace value of keyword indicates an update, and an XPath expression indicates which part of the XML the update is to be applied to. In this case it is the text node that is the child of the FirstName element—in other words, the value of the FirstName element—specified by the XPath expression /Person/FirstName/text().

The results of the two SELECT statements are shown in Figure 10-5.

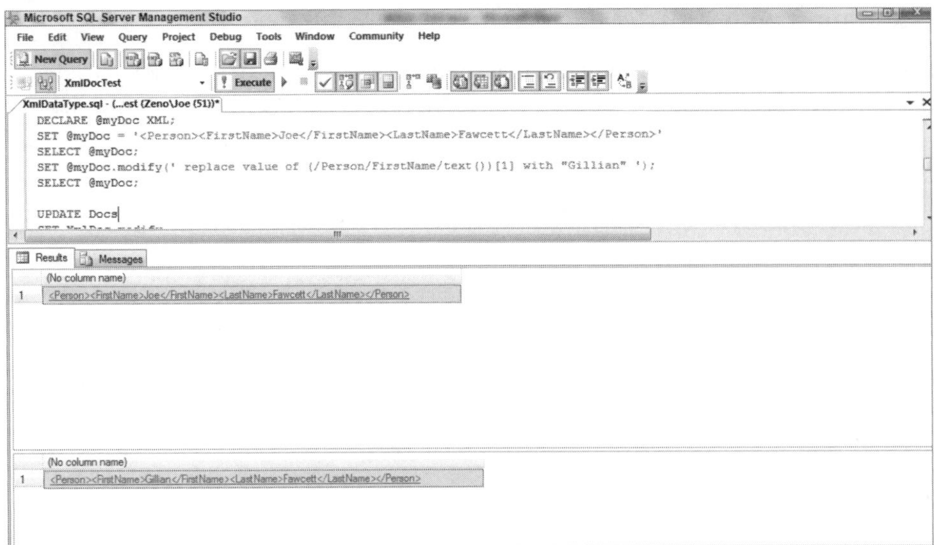

FIGURE 10-5

One of the main problems with using the `modify()` method is that it expects a hard-coded string as its argument. It is therefore difficult to make dynamic queries that are needed in the real world—for example, queries in which the new XML is brought in from another table. You have two ways around this. First, you can construct the query as a string and execute it dynamically using `EXEC`. Alternatively, you can use the built-in functions `sql:column` and `sql:function`. An example of each of these techniques follows.

For these examples you can use the `Docs` table created earlier. First, here's a reminder of what a static update looks like:

Available for download on Wrox.com

```
UPDATE Docs
SET XmlDoc.modify
(' replace value of (/Person/FirstName/text())[1] with "Joseph"')
WHERE DocId = 1;
```

XmlDataType.sql

Now suppose you want to replace the hard-coded value `Joseph` with a variable. You might first try this:

Available for download on Wrox.com

```
DECLARE @NewName NVARCHAR(100);
SET @NewName = N'Joseph';
UPDATE Docs
SET XmlDoc.modify(' replace value of (/Person/FirstName/text())[1] with "'
 + @NewName + '"')
WHERE DocId = 1;
```

XmlDataType.sql

Unfortunately, that won't work. The `modify()` method complains that it needs a string literal. One way around this is to build the whole SQL statement dynamically:

Available for download on Wrox.com

```
DECLARE @NewName NVARCHAR(100);
SET @NewName = N'Joseph';
DECLARE @SQL NVARCHAR(MAX);
SET @SQL = 'UPDATE Docs SET XmlDoc.modify('' replace value of (/Person/FirstName/text())
[1] with "' + @NewName + '"'')
 WHERE DocId = 1';
PRINT(@SQL);
EXEC(@SQL);
```

XmlDataType.sql

You can see the SQL before it is executed by running only as far as the `PRINT` statement, that is, not executing the last line, `EXEC (@SQL);` (the following is displayed on a single line):

```
UPDATE Docs SET XmlDoc.modify(' replace value of (/Person/FirstName/text())[1] with
"Joseph"')
 WHERE DocId = 1
```

This is exactly the same as the code you started with.

The recommended way to update based on data that will only be known at run-time, however, is to use the built-in functions `sql:column` or `sql:variable`. The `sql:column` function is used when the new data is being retrieved from a table, so here `sql:variable` is needed:

Available for download on Wrox.com

```
DECLARE @NewName NVARCHAR(100);
SET @NewName = N'Joseph';
UPDATE Docs
SET XmlDoc.modify
(' replace value of (/Person/FirstName/text())[1] with sql:variable("@NewName")')
WHERE DocId = 1;
```

XmlDataType.sql

The basic syntax is the name of the variable enclosed in double quotes as an argument to `sql:variable()`. Next you will see how to use standard XQuery against the `xml` data type.

Using the query() Method

The `query()` method enables you to construct XQuery statements in SQL Server. The syntax follows the XQuery syntax discussed in Chapter 9, and all the queries in that chapter can be run against a suitable XML data column.

The following query uses the `query()` method to output the names of each person in a newly constructed `Name` element, with the value of the `LastName` element followed by a comma and then the value of the `FirstName` element. The code is shown here:

```
SELECT XMLDoc.query
('for $p in /Person return
 <Name>{$p/LastName/text()}, {$p/FirstName/text()}</Name>')
FROM Docs;
```

XmlDataType.sql

The first line indicates that a selection is being made using the `query()` method applied to the `XMLDoc` column (which, of course, is of data type `xml`).

The `for` clause specifies that the variable `$p` is bound to the `Person` element node.

The `return` clause specifies that a `Name` element is to be constructed using an element constructor. The first part of the content of each `Name` element is created by evaluating the XQuery expression `$p/LastName/text()`, which, of course, is the text content of the `LastName` element. A literal comma is output, and then the XQuery expression `$p/FirstName/text()` is evaluated.

Figure 10-6 shows the output when the `SELECT` statement containing the XQuery query is run.

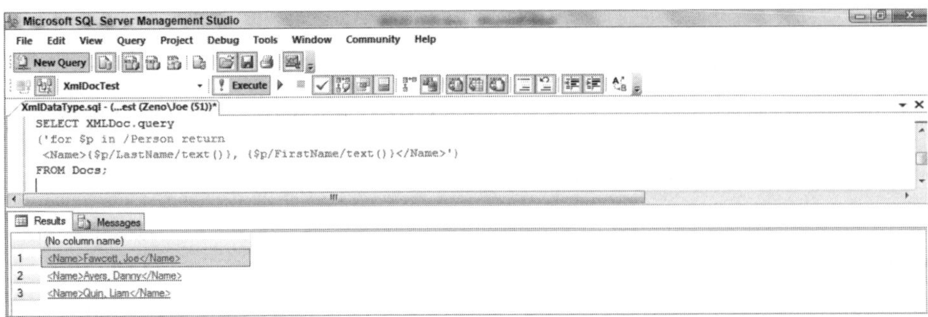

FIGURE 10-6

Using the value() Method

The `value()` method uses XPath to pinpoint specific data in an XML document and then converts it into a standard SQL Server data type. It's often used in the `WHERE` part of a SQL query. Suppose you want to return all the people in your `Docs` table who have the first name of Joe. This is one way of doing it:

```
SELECT * FROM Docs
WHERE XmlDoc.value('(/*/FirstName)[1]', 'nvarchar(100)') = 'Joe';
```

XmlDataType.sql

This returns just one row for the first document you added. Notice how the data type that you are converting to needs to be quoted; it's quite a common mistake to forget this. Obviously, you can also use the `value()` method in the `SELECT` list as well. If you just wanted the last name of everyone, you'd use the following:

```
SELECT DocId, XmlDoc.value('(/*/LastName)[1]', 'nvarchar(100)') LastName
FROM Docs;
```

XmlDataType.sql

This returns a standard two-column result set.

Using the exist() Method

The `exist()` method does what its name suggests—it checks if a value exists. It returns a `0` if it doesn't, a `1` if it does, and `null` if the XML column contains null.

So, you could rewrite the query to return people with a first name of Joe this way:

```
SELECT * FROM Docs
WHERE XmlDoc.exist('/*/FirstName[. = "Joe"]') = 1;
```

XmlDataType.sql

This returns the same results as the query using the `value()` method to do the filter did previously.

Using the nodes() Method

The `nodes()` method is used to present an XML document as a regular SQL table. You often need this when your query needs one row of data from a table combined with a child element of your XML. For a simple example, look at the following code:

```
DECLARE @People xml;
SET @People =
'<people><person>Joe</person>
         <person>Danny</person>
         <person>Liam</person></people>'
SELECT FirstName.value('text()[1]', 'nvarchar(100)') FirstName FROM
@People.nodes('/*/person') Person(FirstName);
```

XmlDataType.sql

The `nodes()` method takes an XPath that points to some repetitive child elements of the main document. You then provide a table name and a column name to use later in the form *`TableName(ColumnName)`*. Here, the table is `Person` and the column is `FirstName`. The `FirstName` column is then queried using `value()` to get the text. The results are shown in Figure 10-7.

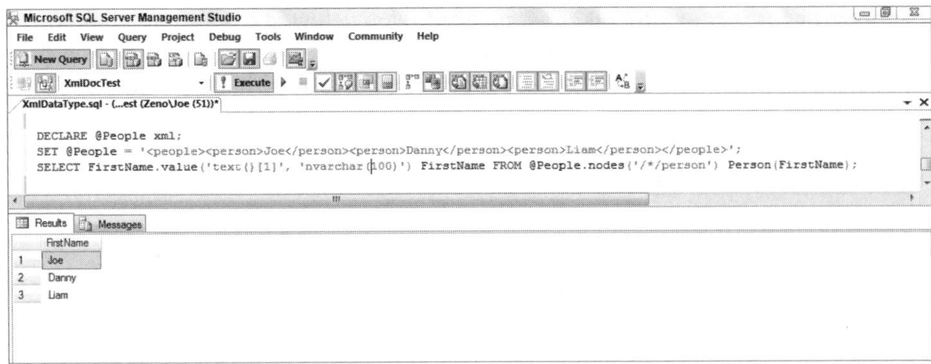

FIGURE 10-7

One thing that can affect how queries are written and processed is whether SQL Server knows the structure of the XML document held in a column. There needs to be some way to specify a schema alongside an XML data type. The following section explains how you tell SQL Server exactly what format the XML stored as an `xml` data type should take.

W3C XML Schema in SQL Server

It was mentioned earlier that the new `xml` data type is now a first-class data type in SQL Server. This data type can be used to store untyped and typed XML data, so it shouldn't be surprising that, just as relational data is specified by a schema, the new `xml` data type can be associated with a W3C XML Schema document to specify its structure.

Take a look at how you can specify a schema for data of type `xml`. The first task is to create a schema collection together with its first XML Schema. You need to give the collection a name—in this example, `EmployeesSchemaCollection`—and the W3C XML Schema document itself needs to be delimited with single quote marks. For example, if you wanted to create a very simple schema for a document that could contain a `Person` element and child elements named `FirstName` and `LastName`, you could do so using the following syntax:

Available for download on Wrox.com

```
CREATE XML SCHEMA COLLECTION EmployeesSchemaCollection AS
'<xsd:schema xmlns:xsd="http://www.w3.org/2001/XMLSchema" targetNamespace=
"http://wiley.com/namespaces/Person" xmlns="http://wiley.com/namespaces/Person">
 <xsd:element name="Person">
  <xsd:complexType>
   <xsd:sequence>
    <xsd:element name="FirstName" />
    <xsd:element name="LastName" />
   </xsd:sequence>
  </xsd:complexType>
 </xsd:element>
</xsd:schema>'
```

XmlDataType.sql

If you want to drop the XML Schema collection, you need to issue a `DROP XMLSCHEMA` statement:

```
DROP XML SCHEMA COLLECTION EmployeesSchemaCollection
```

Once you have a collection, you can add new schemas using the following syntax:

```
ALTER XML SCHEMA COLLECTION EmployeesSchemaCollection ADD
'<xsd:schema>
  <!--new schema inserted here -->
</xsd:schema>'
```

Untyped and typed XML data can be used in a SQL Server column, variable, or parameter. If you want to create a `Docs` table and associate it with a W3C XML Schema document, you can do so using code like the following:

```
CREATE TABLE [dbo].[Docs](
 [DocID] [int] IDENTITY(1,1) PRIMARY KEY,
 [XMLDoc] [xml] (EmployeesSchemaCollection))
```

The advantage of applying a schema collection is twofold. First, it acts as a validation check; XML not conforming to one of the schemas in the collection will be rejected in the same way that a column declared as an `INT` will not accept random textual data. Second, queries against the XML will return typed data as specified by the schema, rather than generic text.

For optimization, XML Schemas are shredded and stored internally in a proprietary format. Most of the schema can be reconstructed as an XML document from this proprietary format using the `xml_schema_namespace` intrinsic function. Therefore, if you had imported the schema into the `EmployeesSchemaCollection` shown in the `XmlDataType.sql` snippet, you could retrieve it using the following code:

```
SELECT xml_schema_namespace(N'dbo', N'EmployeesSchemaCollection')
```

Remember, too, that there can be multiple ways of writing a functionally equivalent W3C XML Schema document—for example, using references, named types, or anonymous types. SQL Server will not respect such differences when reconstituting a schema document.

In addition, the parts of the schema that are primarily documentation—for example, annotations and comments—are not stored in SQL Server's proprietary format. Therefore, to ensure precise recovery of an original W3C XML Schema document, it is necessary to store the serialized XML Schema document separately. One option is to store it in a column of type `xml` or `varchar(max)` in a separate table.

Your final look at SQL Server concerns how to specify namespaces.

Dealing with Namespaced Documents

Often the documents you are working with will have namespaced elements or attributes, and you'll need to specify a prefix to namespace URI binding in order to query them. You accomplish this by using the `WITH XMLNAMESPACES` statement.

The following example creates a document with a namespace and then queries it:

Available for download on Wrox.com

```
DECLARE @NamespacedData xml;
SET @NamespacedData = '<x:data xmlns:x="http://wrox.com/namespaces/examples">
                       <x:item id="1">One</x:item>
                       <x:item id="2">Two</x:item>
                       <x:item id="1">Three</x:item>
                       </x:data>';
WITH XMLNAMESPACES ('http://wrox.com/namespaces/examples' as x)
SELECT @NamespacedData.value('(/x:data/x:item[@id = 2])[1]', 'nvarchar(10)') Item;
```

XmlDataType.sql

This returns the value of the element that has an `id` equal to 2; in this case the result is `Two`.

The key point here is that you specify the namespace URI and a suitable prefix. The prefix chosen doesn't have to match the one in the document. One thing to note is that `WITH XMLNAMESPACES` must be preceded by a semicolon. If the previous statement doesn't end in a semicolon, place it before the `WITH`:

```
;WITH XMLNAMESPACES ('http://wrox.com/namespaces/examples' as x)
```

You can also specify a default namespace if you need to:

Available for download on Wrox.com

```
DECLARE @NamespacedData xml;
SET @NamespacedData = '<data xmlns="http://wrox.com/namespaces/examples">
                       <item id="1">One</item>
                       <item id="2">Two</item>
                       <item id="1">Three</item>
                       </data>';
WITH XMLNAMESPACES (DEFAULT 'http://wrox.com/namespaces/examples')
SELECT @NamespacedData.value('(/data/item[@id = 2])[1]', 'nvarchar(10)') Item;
```

XmlDataType.sql

This produces the same result as when you used an explicit prefix, `x`, bound to the namespace as shown in the `XmlDataType.sql` snippet.

So far you've seen two examples of how XML features and functionality have been added on to an existing relational database. In the next section you take the next step and examine an application designed from the ground up for the express purpose of storing and managing large numbers of XML documents.

USING EXIST WITH XML

The eXist XML database has been around since 2000, and has a solid reputation in its field. It is used as the basis for many systems, particularly those concerned with document and content management. Your first step is to download and install it.

Downloading and Installing eXist

Before doing anything with eXist, visit its website at `http://exist-db.org/`. From there, you'll find links to download the latest version. The download is available for different platforms: a `.jar` file suitable for Unix/Linux and an `.exe` for Windows. The examples in this chapter use the Windows installation, version 1.4.1. You may need to make sure that the version of Java installed is recent enough for the version of eXist. For version 1.4.x, you'll need Java 1.4 or higher.

NOTE *If you are not sure which version of Java is installed on your computer, type* **java -version** *in a DOS or Unix terminal.*

Once you have your download ready and have the right version of Java installed, you should be able to install eXist by clicking the `.jar` or `.exe` file on any properly configured workstation. If that's not the case, open a command window and type the following:

```
java -jar eXist-<version>.jar
```

A fancy graphical installer will pop up and guide you through the installation, which is very straightforward.

WARNING *When installing on Windows, you should install to somewhere other than the traditional Program Files. A good alternative is* `C:\Exist` *if you are on Windows Vista or later because the install package was designed before the User Account Control (UAC) security measures were introduced. Alternatively, you can temporarily disable UAC before running the install.*

WARNING *At some stage during the install you'll be prompted for a master password. Do not make the mistake of choosing one with an ampersand (&) in it. There's a bug in the installer that causes the ampersand and anything after it to be truncated.*

When that's done, you have a ready-to-run native XML database that can be used in three different modes:

- You can use eXist as a Java library to embed a database server in your own Java application.
- You can run it as a standalone database server as you would run a SQL database server.
- You can run it embedded in a web server and get the features of both a standalone database and a web interface to access the database.

After the installation, eXist can be used in the last two modes using a different set of scripts that you can find in its `bin` subdirectory:

- `server` (`.sh` or `.bat` depending on your platform) is used to run eXist as a standalone database server.
- `startup` (`.sh` or `.bat`) is used to start eXist embedded in a web server, and `shutdown` (`.sh` or `.bat`) is used to stop this web server. This is the mode that you will use for the exercises in this chapter because it is the one that includes most features.

To check that the installation is correct, launch `startup.sh` or `startup.bat` in a terminal. If you chose to install to the default directory on Windows (`Program Files\Exist`), you'll need to run the command prompt as administrator because standard users can't write to this folder. You should see a series of warnings and information, concluding with (if everything is okay) the following lines with the date and time reflecting that of installation:

```
29 Sep 2011 14:03:57,021 [main] INFO  (JettyStart.java [run]:175)
 - eXist-db has started on port 8080. Configured contexts:
29 Sep 2011 14:03:57,022 [main] INFO  (JettyStart.java [run]:177)
 - http://localhost:8080/exist
29 Sep 2011 14:03:57,023 [main] INFO  (JettyStart.java [run]:179)
 - -----------------------------------------------------
```

These lines mean that jetty (the Java web server that comes with this eXist download) is ready to accept connections on port 8080.

NOTE *By default, the web server listens to port 8080. This means that it will fail to start if another service is already bound to this port on your computer. If that's the case, either stop this service before you start eXist or change eXist's configuration to listen to another port. You can find instructions how to do so on eXist's website at* `http://exist-db.org/exist/quickstart.xml#installation`.

The last step to check that everything runs smoothly is to open your favorite web browser to `http://localhost:8080/exist/` and confirm that eXist's home page, shown in Figure 10-8, opens.

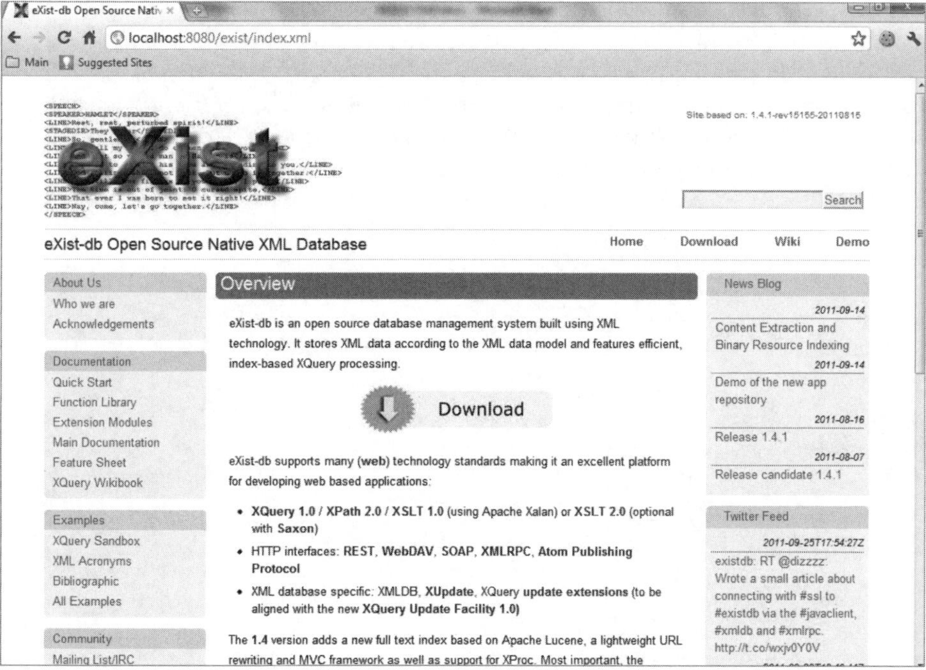

FIGURE 10-8

Interacting with eXist

Congratulations—you have your first native XML database up and running! Now it's time to find out how you can interact with it. You will soon see that eXist is so open that you have many options.

Using the Web Interface

The first option is to use the web interface at `http://localhost:8080/exist/`. Scroll down this web page to the Administration section (on the left side). Click Admin to go to `http://localhost:8080/exist/admin/admin.xql`, where you need to log in as user *admin* with the password you chose during the installation process.

Once you're logged in, you have access to the commands from the left-side menu. Feel free to explore by yourself how you can manage users and set up the example that eXist suggests you install.

When you are ready to continue this quick tour of eXist, click Browse Collection (see Figure 10-9).

NOTE *XML documents are organized in* collections; *a collection is equivalent to a directory on a file system. They are really the same concept. You can think of an eXist database as a black box that packages the features you lack when you store XML documents on disk, while retaining the same paradigm of a hierarchical structure of collections, or directories.*

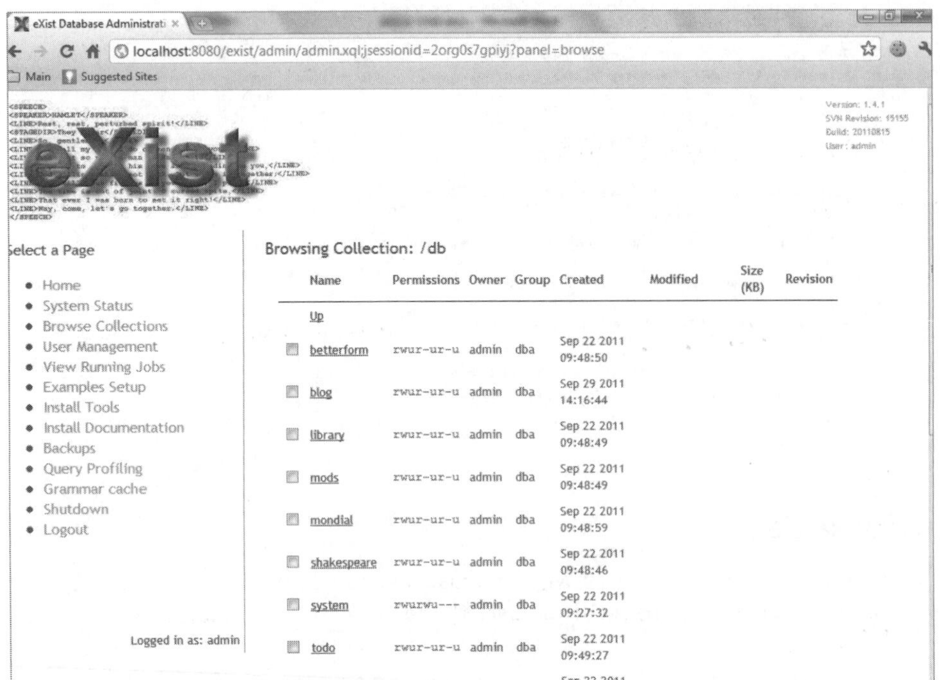

FIGURE 10-9

A brand-new eXist installation has a number of existing collections, but you will create a new one named `blog` using the Create Collection button in Listing 10-1. Once this collection is created, follow the link to browse it. This new collection is empty. Using the Upload button, upload the documents `blog-1.xml`, `blog-2.xml`, and `blog-3.xml`, which you can download from the code samples for this chapter on the Wrox site. These documents are sample blog entries such as the one shown in Listing 10-1.

Available for download on Wrox.com

LISTING 10-1: Blog-1.xml

```
<?xml version="1.0" encoding="UTF-8"?>
<post xmlns:x="http://www.w3.org/1999/xhtml" id="1"
 author="Joe Fawcett" dateCreated="2011-09-18">
  <title>A New Book</title>
```

```
   <body>
     <x:p>
       <x:b>I've been asked to co-author a new edition of <x:a
 href="http://www.wrox.com/WileyCDA/WroxTitle/productCd-0470114878.html">
Beginning XML</x:a>
         by Wrox</x:b>
     </x:p>
     <x:p>It's incredible how much has changed since the
 book was published nearly five years ago. XML
       is now a bedrock of many systems, contrarily you see less of it than
 previously as it's buried
       under more layers.</x:p>
     <x:p>There are also many places where it has stopped being an automatic
 choice for data transfer,
       JSON has become a popular replacement where the data
 is to be consumed directly by a
       JavaScript engine such as in a browser.</x:p>
     <x:p>The new edition should be finished towards the end of the year
 and be published early in
       2012.</x:p>
   </body>
</post>
```

After you have uploaded these documents, you can display them by clicking their links. Now that you have documents in the `/db/blog` collection, you can query these documents, still using the web interface. To do so, click the Home link to go back to the home page and follow the link to the XQuery sandbox, which you can reach at `http://localhost:8080/exist/sandbox/sandbox.xql`.

Recall what you learned of XPath in Chapter 7 and XQuery in Chapter 9: the large text area surrounded by a yellow border expects a query written in XPath or XQuery. If you start with something simple, such as `/item[@id='1']`, and click Send, you'll get all the documents from all the collections that have an `item` root element with an `id` attribute equal to `1`. If you've followed the instructions that led to this point, you should get only the content of the first blog entry.

Of course, you can write more complex queries. For example, if you want to determine the titles, IDs, and links of blog entries with a link on the Wrox site, you can write the following (Listing 10-2).

LISTING 10-2: PostsWithWroxLinks.xquery

Available for download on Wrox.com

```
xquery version "1.0";
declare namespace x="http://www.w3.org/1999/xhtml";

for $item in /post
  where .//x:a[contains(@href, 'wrox.com')]
  return <match>
     <id>{string($item/@id)}</id>
     {$item/title}
     {$item//x:a[contains(@href, 'wrox.com')]}
  </match>
```

Note that you need to bind the namespace URI to a prefix as XQuery, and eXist has full support for namespaces.

Feel free to try as many queries as you like, and then move on to discover the eXist client.

Using the eXist Client

The eXist client is a standalone graphical tool that can perform the same kind of operations as the web interface. To start the client, perform the following steps:

1. Click the `client.sh` or `client.bat` script, depending on your environment. You should see a login screen. Enter the password that you set up for the admin user. Before you click the OK button, note the URL entry field. By default, this field has the value `xmldb: exist://localhost:8080/exist/xmlrpc`. Details about the different components of this URL won't be covered here, but note the `localhost:8080` piece: it means that this client tool uses HTTP to connect to the eXist database and that you can administer eXist databases on other machines.
2. The next screen enables you to browse the collections or your database. Click the `blog` link in the `Name` column to find your three blog entries; and, if you click one of them, you get a window where you can edit the entry.
3. Back at the main window, click the button with binoculars to open the Query dialog. Here you can try your XPath and XQuery skills again. Paste the same query from Listing 10-2 into the upper panel and click the button that has a pair of binoculars and the word Submit. Note the Trace tab in the Results window at the bottom. There you find the execution path of your queries, which may contain useful information to debug or optimize them. Figure 10-10 shows the query in Listing 10-2 run in the eXist client.

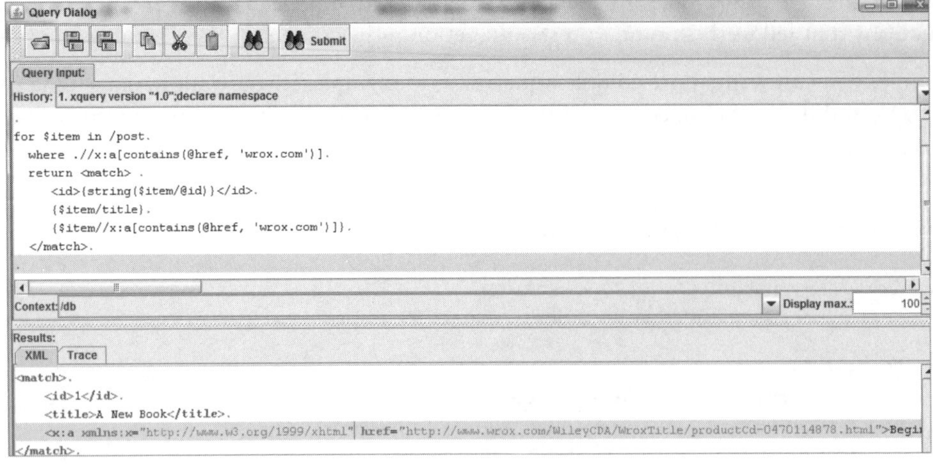

FIGURE 10-10

There is much more to explore with this client. For example, you can also save and restore collections or full databases. Once you're done exploring, read on to see how eXist can be used as a WebDAV server.

Using WebDAV

WebDAV stands for Web-based Distributed Authoring and Versioning. It designates a set of IETF RFCs that define how HTTP can be used to not only read resources, but also to write them. WebDAV is widely and natively implemented in most common operating systems and tools, and eXist's capability to expose its collections as WebDAV repositories can greatly facilitate the way you import and export documents.

NOTE *The IETF (Internet Engineering Task Force) is the standardization organization that publishes most of the protocol-oriented Internet specifications, including HTTP. Its specifications are called RFCs (Requests For Comments); and despite this name, they are de facto standards.*

As a first contact with WebDAV, point your web browser to `http://localhost:8080/exist/webdav/db/`. You need to enter the login and password of your database admin again. Then you will see a page where you can browse the collections and content of your database. Without browser extensions, you have read-only access; you need to set up your WebDAV client to gain write access and see the eXist database as a repository.

The eXist documentation available on your local database at `http://localhost:8080/exist/webdav.xml` includes detailed instructions for setting up Microsoft Windows, KDE Konqueror, oXygen, and XML Spy to use WebDAV. WebDAV support is also built into the finder on Mac OS X. In Windows XP and later, this feature is known as *web folders* and is fairly easy to configure; just note that if you are using IE8 or later, you'll need to open the File Explorer, choose Map Network Drive from the Tools menu, and use the Connect to a Website that You can Use to Store Your Documents and Pictures link. Because these setups are well described in the eXist documentation, they aren't covered here.

The only feature that you lack using the WebDAV interface is the capability to execute queries, but you'll see next that you can regain this feature if you use an XML IDE.

Using an XML IDE

Your favorite XML IDE can probably access your eXist database through WebDAV. If it is interfaced with eXist, you can also execute queries from the IDE itself. This is the case with oXygen 8.0 which is available as a 30-day evaluation license from its site at `www.oxygenxml.com/`.

To configure the connection to your eXist database, perform the following steps:

1. Select the database perspective using either its icon on the toolbar or Windows ➪ Open Perspective ➪ Database from the main menu. Then click the Configure Database Sources button situated at the upper-right corner of the Database Explorer window. This opens the database preferences window.
2. Create a new data source with type eXist and add the following files:
    - `exist.jar`
    - `lib/core/xmlrpc-client-3.1.1.jar`
    - `lib/core/xmlrpc-common-3.1.1.jar`
    - `lib/core/xmlrpc-common-3.1.1.jar`
    - `lib/core/ws-commons-util-1.0.2.jar`

    (The version numbers may be slightly different, but there will be only one version of each.)
3. Save this data source and create a connection using it with the eXist connection parameters. Save this connection and the database preferences, and you're all set.

The Database Explorer shows the newly created connection, and you can now browse and update the eXist database as you would browse and open documents on your local filesystem.

So far, all this could be done through WebDAV, but not the following, which interrogates the data. To execute a query, perform the following steps:

1. Create a new document through the File New icon or menu item.
2. Choose type XQuery for this document and type your query. When you're done, click the Apply Transformation Scenario button on the toolbar or select this action though the Document ➪ XML Document ➪ Apply Transformation Scenario menu item. Because no scenario is attached to this document yet, eXist opens the Configure Transformation Scenario dialog. The default scenario uses the Saxon XQuery engine.
3. To use the eXist XQuery engine, create a new scenario and select your eXist database connection as the Transformer.
4. Save this scenario and click Transform Now to run the query. You should get the same results as previously.
5. Now that this scenario is attached to your query document, you can update the query and click the Apply Transformation Scenario button to run it without needing to go through this configuration again.

Thus far you've seen a number of different ways to interact with the XML data using a variety of graphical tools, but you still need to see how web applications can access your database. This is discussed in the next section.

Using the REST Interface

What better way to interface your database with a web application could there be than using HTTP as it was meant to be used? This is the purpose of the REST interface.

***NOTE** REST stands for Representational State Transfer and is seen, in many cases, as a simpler and more efficient alternative to using SOAP based web services. It uses the intrinsic HTTP commands to create, update and retrieve data from a remote web service. REST and SOAP are covered in depth in Chapters 14 and 15.*

As a first step, you can point your browser to `http://localhost:8080/exist/rest/`. Doing so shows you the content of your database root exposed as an XML document. This XML format is less user-friendly than browsing the content of your collections through the admin web interface or even through browsing the WebDAV repository, but far more easy to process in an application!

The full content of the database is available through this interface. For instance, `http://localhost:8080/exist/rest/db/blog/` shows the content of the blog collection, and `http://localhost:080/exist/rest/db/blog/blogItem1.xml` gets you the first blog item. This becomes more interesting when you start playing with query strings. The REST interface accepts a number of parameters, including a `_query` parameter that you can use to send XPath or XQuery simple queries straight away!

For instance, if you want to get all the titles from all the documents in the collection `/db/blog`, you can query `http://localhost:8080/exist/rest/db/blog/?_query=//title`. The results are shown in Figure 10-11.

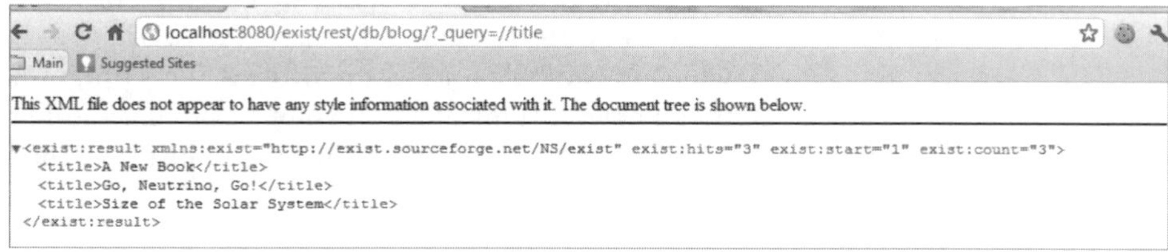

FIGURE 10-11

This XML deserves an XSLT transformation to be presented as HTML; and if you remember what you learned in Chapter 8, a simple transformation such as the one shown in Listing 10-3 would display the results better than the raw XML shown in Figure 10-11.

LISTING 10-3: Links.xslt

Available for download on Wrox.com

```
<xsl:stylesheet xmlns:xsl="http://www.w3.org/1999/XSL/Transform"
    xmlns:exist="http://exist.sourceforge.net/NS/exist" version="1.0">
    <xsl:template match=»/exist:result»>
        <html>
            <head>
                <title>Query results</title>
```

continues

LISTING 10-3 *(continued)*

```
            </head>
            <body>
                <h1>eXist query results</h1>
                <p>Showing results
<xsl:value-of select="@exist:start"/> to
<xsl:value-of
 select="@exist:end"/> out of <xsl:value-of select="@exist:hits"/>:</p>
                <xsl:apply-templates/>
            </body>
        </html>
    </xsl:template>
    <xsl:template match="*">
        <p>
            <xsl:copy-of select="."/>
        </p>
    </xsl:template>
</xsl:stylesheet>
```

The good news is that the eXist REST interface can execute this transformation for you if you like. But before you can do that, you need to store the transformation in the database. To do so, you can use any of the methods you have seen so far to upload documents in the database (the web interface, the eXist client, WebDAV, or your favorite XML IDE). Because this section is about the REST interface, you can use REST to upload the document.

Storing documents with the REST interface uses an `HTTP PUT` request; unfortunately, you can't do that with your web browser. To send an `HTTP PUT` request, you need to either do a bit of programming (all the programming languages have libraries available to support this) or use a utility such as curl (`http://curl.haxx.se/`), which is available for most platforms. This program has a lot of different command-line options. If you have curl installed on your machine, to store the document `Links.xslt` at location `http://localhost:8080/exist/rest/db/xslt/`, just type the following command in a Unix or Windows command window:

```
curl -T links.xslt http://localhost:8080/exist/rest/db/xslt/
```

This command simply sends this document through an `HTTP PUT`. The eXist REST interface also supports `HTTP DELETE` requests, and you can also delete this document. To do so, use the `-X` option, which enables you to define the HTTP method that you want to use and write:

```
curl -X DELETE localhost:8080/exist/rest/db/xslt/links.xslt
```

Of course, if you have run the previous command, you need to upload the transformation again before you can use it! Now that your style sheet is stored in the database, to use it just add an `_xsl` parameter, specifying its location. Then paste or type this URL in your browser: `http://localhost:8080/exist/rest/db/blog/?_query=//title&_xsl=/db/xslt/links.xslt`. The result is shown in Figure 10-12.

XQuery Sandbox | localhost:8080/exist/rest/db
localhost:8080/exist/rest/db/blog/?_query=//title&_xsl=/db/xslt/links.xslt
Main | Suggested Sites

This XML file does not appear to have any style information associated with it. The document tree is shown below.

```
▼<html xmlns:exist="http://exist.sourceforge.net/NS/exist">
  ▼<head>
     <title>Query results</title>
   </head>
  ▼<body>
     <h1>eXist query results</h1>
     <p>Showing results 1 to out of 3:</p>
    ▼<p>
       <title>A New Book</title>
     </p>
    ▼<p>
       <title>Go, Neutrino, Go!</title>
     </p>
    ▼<p>
       <title>Size of the Solar System</title>
     </p>
   </body>
 </html>
```

FIGURE 10-12

You have now seen how to use `HTTP GET`, `PUT`, and `DELETE` methods. If you are familiar with HTTP, you may be wondering whether the REST interface supports the `HTTP POST` method. The answer is yes; this method is used to send requests that are too big to be easily pasted in the query string of an `HTTP GET` request. These queries have to be wrapped into an XML document, the structure of which is defined in the eXist documentation. For instance, the query encountered in Listing 10-3 would need to be in the format shown in Listing 10-4.

Available for download on Wrox.com

LISTING 10-4: PostsWithWroxLinks.xml

```
<?xml version="1.0" encoding="UTF-8"?>
<query xmlns="http://exist.sourceforge.net/NS/exist">
  <text>
    <![CDATA[
  declare namespace x="http://www.w3.org/1999/xhtml";

for $item in /post
  where .//x:a[contains(@href, 'wrox.com')]
  return <match>
      <id>{string($item/@id)}</id>
      {$item/title}
      {$item//x:a[contains(@href, 'wrox.com')]}
  </match>
  ]]>
  </text>
</query>
```

Note how the query itself has been cautiously embedded within a `CDATA` section so that it qualifies as well-formed XML. To send this query using the REST interface, you can use curl and a `-d` option. The command looks like the following:

```
curl -d @linksToWrox.xml http://localhost:8080/exist/rest/db/
```

Other Interfaces

You've already seen four ways to interact with eXist, but there are many more out there. The following list briefly covers a few.

- **XML:DB API:** The XML:DB API is a common API defined by a number of XML database editors. Its original purpose was to define a vendor-neutral API to play the same role with XML databases that JDBC plays with SQL databases. Unfortunately, the project failed to attract commercial vendors and seems to have lost all its momentum. The XML:DB is still the API of choice to access your eXist database if you are developing in Java.
- **XML-RPC:** XML-RPC interface has the same functionality as the REST interface together with some added features—for example, you can update an XML fragment without uploading whole documents and administer your database entirely within this interface.
- **SOAP:** A SOAP interface is also available with the same features of the XML-RPC interface for those of you who prefer SOAP over XML-RPC.
- **Atom Publishing Protocol (APP):** An APP interface has been recently developed so that you can see your collections as Atom feeds.

Choosing an Interface

With so many options, how do you decide which one you should be using? Ask yourself whether it really matters. You can think of your eXist database as a black box that encapsulates your XML documents. These documents are located in collections that are similar to file directories. The black box acts like a filesystem with XQuery capabilities and provides a number of different interfaces to access the same set of documents in different ways. Whichever interface is used, the effect is the same. You can choose, case by case, the interface that is most convenient for the task you have to do. The following is a list of tips to help you decide:

- If you need a filesystem-like type of access to your documents, WebDAV is a sure choice.
- If all you have is a browser, the web interface is what you need.
- If your XML IDE supports eXist, that makes your life easier. If you're using a tool that is a good web citizen and can use the different HTTP, you can plug the REST interface directly.
- If you're developing in Java, have a look at the XML:DB API.
- If you want to integrate your database with Atom tools, the APP interface is designed for you.
- If you're a web services fan, you will choose either the XML-RPC or the SOAP interface.

The richness of this set of interfaces means that your documents will never be locked in the database and can remain accessible in any environment.

SUMMARY

In this chapter you've learned about the following:

- Much of today's data comes in the form of tabular data and XML combined.
- You need a dedicated storage type for XML rather than just use a text field. You also need methods to extract specific values and fragments of XML as well as methods to create new XML formats combining the relational and XML data. You will probably want the facility to update XML documents although this is not always a necessity.
- A relational database handles both tabular data and XML documents, whereas a native XML database is designed to cope solely with XML documents.
- High-end systems such as Oracle and SQL Server XML have their own data type and there are suitable methods available on these types for retrieval and manipulation of the XML.
- The features available in a native XML database include the ability to store large document collections as well as the ability to efficiently query across these documents.

EXERCISES

You can find suggested answers to these questions in Appendix A.

1. List the main reasons to choose a relational database with XML features over a native XML database.
2. What five methods are available against an XML data type? (No peeking!)
3. MySQL has only two XML-related functions. If you could ask for one more feature or function, what would it be?

▶ WHAT YOU LEARNED IN THIS CHAPTER

TOPIC	KEY POINTS
Storage needs	There is a big difference between relational data, data in a tabular format, and XML data. Therefore, special mechanisms are needed to store XML within relational systems.
Essential features in databases.	XML needs to be stored in a native format, rather than as text. There must also be ways to query it for specific values and a way to return fragments of XML. Ideally there should also be a way to treat XML as tabular data if possible.
Choosing an application	Most commercial relational databases have fairly advanced XML features, particularly Oracle and SQL Server. Native XML databases are designed to cope with the situation in which all data is held as XML.

PART V
Programming

11

Event-Driven Programming

WHAT YOU WILL LEARN IN THIS CHAPTER:

- Necessity of XML data access methods: SAX and .NET's XMLReader
- Why SAX and XMLReader are considered event-driven methods
- How to use SAX and XMLReader
- The right time to choose one of these methods to process your XML

There are many ways to extract information from an XML document. You've already seen how to use the document object model and XPath; both of these methods can be used to find any relevant item of data. Additionally, in Chapter 12 you'll meet LINQ to XML, Microsoft's latest attempt to incorporate XML data retrieval in its universal data access strategy.

Given the wide variety of methods already available, you may be wondering why you need more, and why in particular do you need event-driven methods? The main answer is because of memory limitations. Other XML processing methods require that the whole XML document be loaded into memory (that is, RAM) before any processing can take place. Because XML documents typically use up to four times more RAM than the size of the file containing the document, some documents can take up more RAM than is available on a computer; it is therefore necessary to find an alternative method to extract data. This is where event-driven paradigms come into play. Instead of loading the complete file into memory, the file is processed in sequence. There are two ways to do this: SAX and .NET's `XMLReader`. Both are covered in this chapter.

UNDERSTANDING SEQUENTIAL PROCESSING

There are two main ways of processing a file sequentially. The first relies on events being fired whenever specific items are found; whether you respond to these events is up to you. For example, say an event is fired when the opening tag of the root element is encountered, and the name of this element is passed to the event handler. Any time any textual content is found after this, another event is fired. In this scenario there would also be events that capture the closing of any elements with the final event being fired when the closing tag of the root element is encountered.

The second method is slightly different in that you tell the processor what sort of content you are interested in. For example, you may want to read an attribute on the first child under the root element. To do so, you instruct the XML reader to move to the root element and then to its first child. You would then begin to read the attributes until you get to the one you need. Both of these methods are similar conceptually, and both cope admirably with the problem of larger memory usage posed by using the DOM that requires the whole XML document to be loaded into memory before being processed.

Processing files in a sequential fashion includes one or two downsides, however. The first is that you can't revisit content. If you read an element and then move on to one of its siblings or children, you can't then go back and examine one of its attributes without starting from the beginning again. You need to plan carefully what information you'll need. The second problem is validation. Imagine you receive the document shown here:

```
<document>
  <data>Here is some data.</data>
  <data>Here is some more data.</data>
</document>
```

This document is well-formed, but what if its schema states that after all `<data>` elements there should be a `<summary>` element? The processor will report the elements and text content that it encounters, but won't complain that the document is not valid until it reaches the relevant point. You may not care about the extra element, in which case you can just extract whatever you need, but if you want to validate before processing begins, this usually involves reading the document twice. This is the price you pay for not needing to load the full document into memory.

In the following sections you'll examine the two methods in more detail. The pure event-driven method is called *SAX* and is commonly used with Java, although it can be used from any language that supports events. The second is specific to .NET and uses the `System.Xml.XmlReader` class.

USING SAX IN SEQUENTIAL PROCESSING

SAX stands for the Simple API for XML, and arose out of discussions on the XML-DEV list in the late 1990s.

NOTE *The archives for the XML-DEV list are available at* `http://lists.xml.org/archives/xml-dev/`*. The list is still very active and any XML-related problems are usually responded to within hours, if not minutes.*

Back then people were having problems because different parsers were incompatible. David Megginson took on the job of coordinating the process of specifying a new API with the group. On May 11, 1998, the SAX 1.0 specification was completed. A whole series of SAX 1.0–compliant parsers then began to emerge, both from large corporations, such as IBM and Sun, and from enterprising individuals, such as James Clark. All of these parsers were freely available for public download.

Eventually, a number of shortcomings in the specification became apparent, and David Megginson and his colleagues got back to work, finally producing the SAX 2.0 specification on May 5, 2000. The improvements centered on added support for namespaces and tighter adherence to the XML specification. Several other enhancements were made to expose additional information in the XML document, but the core of SAX was very stable. On April 27, 2004, these changes were finalized and released as version 2.0.2.

SAX is specified as a set of Java interfaces, which initially meant that if you were going to do any serious work with it, you were looking at doing some Java programming using Java Development Kit (JDK) 1.1 or later. Now, however, a wide variety of languages have their own version of SAX, some of which you learn about later in the chapter. In deference to the SAX tradition, however, the examples in this chapter are written in Java.

All the latest information about SAX is at `www.saxproject.org`. It remains a public domain, open source project hosted by SourceForge. To download SAX, go to the homepage and browse for the latest version, or go directly to the SourceForge project page at `http://sourceforge.net/projects/sax`.

This is one of the extraordinary things about SAX — it isn't owned by anyone. It doesn't belong to any consortium, standards body, company, or individual. In other words, it doesn't survive because some organization or government says that you must use it to comply with their standards, or because a specific company supporting it is dominant in the marketplace. It survives because it's simple and it works.

Preparing to Run the Examples

The SAX specification does not limit which XML parser you use with your document. It simply sits on top of it and reports what content it finds. A number of different parsers are available out in the wild, but these examples use the one that comes with the JDK.

If you don't have the JDK already installed, perform the following steps to do so:

1. Go to `http://www.oracle.com/technetwork/java/javase/downloads/index.html`. Download the latest version under the SE section. These examples use 1.6 but 1.7 is the latest available version and will work just as well.

2. Once you have completed the download and installed the files, make sure that the `<install location>\bin` folder is in your `PATH` environment variable. This will mean that you can access the Java compiler and other necessary files from any folder on your machine.
3. Next, create a folder where you will keep your Java code, for example `C:\Java\`.
4. Open a command prompt and navigate to this folder (alternatively, in modern Windows systems you can right-click with the Shift key down within the folder pane of Windows Explorer). Then run the following command:

    ```
    java -version
    ```

    You should see output similar to the following:

    ```
    java version "1.6.0_25"
    Java(TM) SE Runtime Environment (build 1.6.0_25-b06)
    Java HotSpot(TM) 64-Bit Server VM (build 20.0-b11, mixed mode)
    ```

    where the version number matches the JDK you downloaded earlier. If you get a message saying that `java` is not recognized as an internal or external command, you haven't set up the `PATH` environment variable correctly. See this link (which also advises on how to set it on other operating systems) for help on this: `http://www.java.com/en/download/help/path.xml`.

Once you have the correct output showing, you are all set to try the examples in this chapter.

Receiving SAX Events

SAX works by firing an event each time it comes across any content. An abbreviated list of events is shown in Table 11-1.

TABLE 11-1: SAX Events

EVENT NAME	DESCRIPTION	EXAMPLE CONTENT
`startDocument`	Processing has started and the first event fired.	
`endDocument`	The document is fully read, the last event fired.	
`startElement`	The opening tag of an element is encountered.	`<document>`
`endElement`	The closing tag of an element is encountered.	`</document>`
`characters`	A string of pure text is encountered, and can be fired multiple times for the same text node.	`This is some example text`

EVENT NAME	DESCRIPTION	EXAMPLE CONTENT
`processingInstruction`	A processing instruction was encountered.	`xml-stylesheet href="web.xsl" type="text/xml"`
`ignorableWhitespace`	Called when whitespace that is not an inherent part of the document is encountered.	
`skippedEntity`	Called when an external entity has been skipped.	
`setDocumentLocator`	Enables the parser to pass a `Locator` object to the application.	

When SAX was originally developed, it was quite a chore to create a class that handled all these events. Even if you didn't care about any comments or processing instructions, you still had to write a method to cope with them being fired from the SAX processor. The situation has improved since then and you can base your class on what is known as the `DefaultHandler`. This handles all the events for you, and you have to write methods only for those in which you are interested. For example, the `startDocument`, `startElement`, and `characters` events are the most commonly handled ones.

The following Try It Out puts the previous theory into practice. You'll use SAX to read a simple XML file and report back on some of the events that are received.

TRY IT OUT Using SAX to Read an XML File

This Try It Out guides you through the steps needed to create a SAX handler that can read a simple XML file and show the data that is contained within it.

1. Create or download the file in Listing 11-1 and save it as `People.xml`.

Available for download on Wrox.com

LISTING 11-1: People.xml

```
<People>
  <Person bornDate="1874-11-30" diedDate="1965-01-24">
    <Name>Winston Churchill</Name>
    <Description>
      Winston Churchill was a mid-20th century British politician who
      became famous as Prime Minister during the Second World War.
    </Description>
  </Person>
  <Person bornDate="1917-11-19" diedDate="1984-10-31">
```

continues

LISTING 11-1 *(continued)*

```
      <Name>Indira Gandhi</Name>
      <Description>
        Indira Gandhi was India's first female prime minister and was
        assassinated in 1984.
      </Description>
    </Person>
    <Person bornDate="1917-05-29" diedDate="1963-11-22">
      <Name>John F. Kennedy</Name>
      <Description>
        JFK, as he was affectionately known, was a United States president
        who was assassinated in Dallas, Texas.
      </Description>
    </Person>
  </People>
```

2. Create or download the file in Listing 11-2 and save it as `SaxParser1.java` (you can just use a simple text editor, or, if you have a Java development environment such as Eclipse, use a full Java editor).

Available for download on Wrox.com

LISTING 11-2: SaxParser1.java

```
import org.xml.sax.*;
import org.xml.sax.helpers.*;
import java.io.*;

public class SaxParser1 extends DefaultHandler {

  public void startDocument( ) throws SAXException {
    System.out.println( "SAX Event: START DOCUMENT" );
   }

  public void endDocument( ) throws SAXException {
    System.out.println( "SAX Event: END DOCUMENT" );
   }

  public void startElement(String namespaceURI,
                           String localName,
                           String qName,
                           Attributes attr ) throws SAXException {
    System.out.println( "SAX Event: START ELEMENT[ " + localName + " ]");
   }

  public void endElement(String namespaceURI,
                         String localName,
                         String qName ) throws SAXException {
    System.out.println( "SAX Event: END ELEMENT[ " + localName + " ]" );
   }

  public void characters(char[] ch,
                         int start,
```

```
                         int length ) throws SAXException {
    System.out.print( "SAX Event: CHARACTERS[ " );

    try {
      OutputStreamWriter output = new OutputStreamWriter(System.out);
      output.write( ch, start,length );
      output.flush();
    } catch ( Exception e ) {
     e.printStackTrace();
    }

    System.out.println( " ]" );
   }

  public static void main( String[] argv ){
    String inputFile = argv[0];
    System.out.println( "Processing '" + inputFile + "'." );
    System.out.println( "SAX Events:" );
    try {
      XMLReader reader = XMLReaderFactory.createXMLReader();
      reader.setContentHandler( new SaxParser1() );
      reader.parse( new InputSource(
                 new FileReader( inputFile )));
    } catch ( Exception e ) {
       e.printStackTrace();
    }
  }
}
```

3. Open a command window and navigate to the folder where you stored the two files just created. Enter the following command, which compiles the code in `SaxParser1.java` and produces the file `SaxParser1.class` (note that the executable file is called `javac`, the Java compiler):

```
javac SaxParser1.java
```

4. Execute the code you have just created by using the following command. Note that you do not have any extension on `SaxParser1` and that you are passing in the name of the XML file to process:

```
java SaxParser1 People.xml
```

5. You should see the following output displayed:

```
SAX Events:
SAX Event: START DOCUMENT
SAX Event: START ELEMENT[ People ]
SAX Event: CHARACTERS[
     ]
SAX Event: START ELEMENT[ Person ]
SAX Event: CHARACTERS[
     ]
SAX Event: START ELEMENT[ Name ]
SAX Event: CHARACTERS[ Winston Churchill ]
SAX Event: END ELEMENT[ Name ]
```

```
SAX Event: CHARACTERS[
     ]
SAX Event: START ELEMENT[ Description ]
SAX Event: CHARACTERS[
      Winston Churchill was a mid-20th century British politician who
      became famous as Prime Minister during the Second World War. ]
SAX Event: CHARACTERS[
     ]
SAX Event: END ELEMENT[ Description ]
SAX Event: CHARACTERS[
     ]
SAX Event: END ELEMENT[ Person ]
SAX Event: CHARACTERS[
     ]
SAX Event: START ELEMENT[ Person ]
SAX Event: CHARACTERS[
     ]
SAX Event: START ELEMENT[ Name ]
SAX Event: CHARACTERS[ Indira Gandhi ]
SAX Event: END ELEMENT[ Name ]
SAX Event: CHARACTERS[
     ]
SAX Event: START ELEMENT[ Description ]
SAX Event: CHARACTERS[
      Indira Gandhi was India's first female prime minister and was
      assassinated in 1984. ]
SAX Event: CHARACTERS[
     ]
SAX Event: END ELEMENT[ Description ]
SAX Event: CHARACTERS[
     ]
SAX Event: END ELEMENT[ Person ]
SAX Event: CHARACTERS[
     ]
SAX Event: START ELEMENT[ Person ]
SAX Event: CHARACTERS[
     ]
SAX Event: START ELEMENT[ Name ]
SAX Event: CHARACTERS[ John F. Kennedy ]
SAX Event: END ELEMENT[ Name ]
SAX Event: CHARACTERS[
     ]
SAX Event: START ELEMENT[ Description ]
SAX Event: CHARACTERS[
      JFK, as he was affectionately known, was a United States president
      who was assassinated in Dallas, Texas. ]
SAX Event: CHARACTERS[
     ]
SAX Event: END ELEMENT[ Description ]
SAX Event: CHARACTERS[
     ]
SAX Event: END ELEMENT[ Person ]
SAX Event: CHARACTERS[
     ]
```

```
SAX Event: END ELEMENT[ People ]
SAX Event: END DOCUMENT
```

How It Works

For each item of the XML document you are interested in, you override the event receiver in the `DefaultHandler` class with one of your own. The `DefaultHandler` class simply receives the events; it doesn't actually do anything with them.

The `startDocument` override is executed at the very start of the processing as shown here; there's no extra information made available, and you simply output that the event has occurred:

```
public void startDocument( ) throws SAXException {
  System.out.println( "SAX Event: START DOCUMENT" );
}
```

The following handler is the last to fire, and again, there's no information available so you just note that it has happened:

```
public void endDocument( ) throws SAXException {
  System.out.println( "SAX Event: END DOCUMENT" );
}
```

The `startHandler` handler fires whenever a new opening tag is encountered and gives you four potentially useful pieces of information as shown in the following code: the namespace URI that the element is in, the local name, the prefix (if there is one) that is mapped to the namespace URI, and a collection of attributes appearing on the element. You'll see how to use this collection shortly:

```
public void startElement(String namespaceURI,
                         String localName,
                         String qName,
                         Attributes attr ) throws SAXException {
  System.out.println( "SAX Event: START ELEMENT[ " + localName + " ]" );
}
```

The `endElement` is the complementary handler to the `startElement` one. It executes when an end tag is encountered and gives you the same information as before, with the exception of the attributes collection:

```
public void endElement(String namespaceURI,
                       String localName,
                       String qName ) throws SAXException {
  System.out.println( "SAX Event: END ELEMENT[ " + localName + " ]" );
}
```

The final handler is used to notify you about text content. The content is presented as an array of characters with two integers, which point to the first character in the array and the number of characters available:

```
public void characters(char[] ch,
                       int start,
                       int length ) throws SAXException {
  System.out.print( "SAX Event: CHARACTERS[ " );

  try {
    OutputStreamWriter output = new OutputStreamWriter(System.out);
```

```
    output.write( ch, start,length );
    output.flush();
  } catch (Exception e) {
   e.printStackTrace();
  }

  System.out.println( " ]" );
}
```

It's possible that pieces of text will be broken up into multiple calls to the characters handler, so don't assume that you will get all the text appearing in a block in one go; you'll see how to cope with this in a later example.

The rest of the class is simply the entry point. It first reads the single argument from the command line to see which file to process. It then creates an `XMLReader` that reads the XML and passes to it the class that will be used as a `ContentHandler`; in this case, itself. Invoking the `parse()` method on the `XMLReader` causes the file to be read and the SAX events to be fired:

```
public static void main( String[] argv ){
  String inputFile = argv[0];
  System.out.println( "Processing '" + inputFile + "'." );
  System.out.println( "SAX Events:" );
  try {
    XMLReader reader = XMLReaderFactory.createXMLReader();
    reader.setContentHandler( new SaxParser1() );
    reader.parse( new InputSource(
               new FileReader( inputFile )));
  }catch ( Exception e ) {
     e.printStackTrace();
  }
}
```

Now that you've seen the basics in action, in the following activity you see how you can deal with attributes within an XML document.

TRY IT OUT Using SAX to Read Attributes

This Try It Out builds on the code form Listing 11-2 and adds the ability to display any attributes, along with their values, when they are encountered.

1. Modify `SaxParser1.java` so that the `startElement` method now contains code to handle attributes:

```
                          public void startElement
                         (String namespaceURI,
                          String localName,
                          String qName,
                          Attributes attr ) throws SAXException {
  System.out.println( "SAX Event: START ELEMENT[ " + localName + " ]" );
  for ( int i = 0; i < attr.getLength(); i++ ){
  System.out.println( " ATTRIBUTE: " + attr.getLocalName(i) +  " VALUE: "
  + attr.getValue(i) );
  }
}
```

2. Save this file as `SaxParser2.java`.

3. Repeat the command to compile the code, this time with `SaxParser2.java`:

```
javac SaxParser2.java
```

4. Run the code as before:

```
java SaxParser2 People.xml
```

5. You should see similar results, but the attributes showing the dates of birth and death will also appear, as shown in the following snippet:

```
SAX Event: START ELEMENT[ Person ]
 ATTRIBUTE: bornDate VALUE: 1917-05-29
 ATTRIBUTE: diedDate VALUE: 1963-11-22
SAX Event: CHARACTERS[
     ]
SAX Event: START ELEMENT[ Name ]
SAX Event: CHARACTERS[ John F. Kennedy ]
SAX Event: END ELEMENT[ Name ]
SAX Event: CHARACTERS[
     ]
SAX Event: START ELEMENT[ Description ]
SAX Event: CHARACTERS[
      JFK, as he was affectionately known, was a United States president
      who was assassinated in Dallas, Texas. ]
SAX Event: CHARACTERS[
     ]
SAX Event: END ELEMENT[ Description ]
SAX Event: CHARACTERS[
     ]
SAX Event: END ELEMENT[ Person ]
SAX Event: CHARACTERS[
     ]
SAX Event: END ELEMENT[ People ]
```

How It Works

The following code simply uses the `attr` parameter, which is passed by the SAX parser to the `startElement` event handler. `attr` is a special collection of type `Attributes`. It provides various methods such as `getLocalName()` and `getValue()`, which take an integer specifying which attribute in the collection you need:

```
for ( int i = 0; i < attr.getLength(); i++ ){
System.out.println( " ATTRIBUTE: " + attr.getLocalName(i) +  " VALUE: "
 + attr.getValue(i) );
}
```

Although there is no inherent order to the attributes, if you want to just read the value of a specific one you can use the `getValue()` method, which takes either a string representing the attribute's qualified name, or two strings representing the namespace URI and the local name.

The two previous Try It Outs have both used the `characters` event to directly display any text nodes in the XML document reported by the SAX parser. There are two problems with this approach. First is the fact that you simply wrote any content directly to the output stream, in this case the console window. Usually you will want to store the text in a variable for processing. The second problem with the `characters` event is that it is not guaranteed to return all of an element's content in one call. Many times you'll find that a long block of text is broken down into one or more `characters` events. The next section shows a more sophisticated way to handle one or more `characters` events.

Handling the characters Event

A better way to handle the `characters` event is to build up the entire text content from the multiple firings of the event using the `startElement` and `endElement` events to indicate which characters belong to each element. To do so, follow these steps:

1. Start by declaring a `StringBuffer` in the class to hold the character data:

```
public class SaxParser3 extends DefaultHandler {

  private StringBuffer buffer = new StringBuffer();
```

2. Then, in the `startElement` event handler, make sure the buffer is cleared:

```
public void startElement(String namespaceURI,
                         String localName,
                         String qName,
                         Attributes attr ) throws SAXException {
    System.out.println( "SAX Event: START ELEMENT[ " + localName + " ]" );
    for ( int i = 0; i < attr.getLength(); i++ ){
    System.out.println( " ATTRIBUTE: "
    + attr.getLocalName(i) +  " VALUE: " + attr.getValue(i) );
    }

    buffer.setLength(0);
  }
```

3. In the `characters` event, append any text to the buffer:

```
  public void characters(char[] ch,
                         int start,
                         int length ) throws SAXException {
    try {
      buffer.append(ch, start, length);
    } catch (Exception e) {
     e.printStackTrace();
    }
  }
```

4. Then, in the `endElement` event, convert the buffer to a string and, in this instance, output it to the screen:

```
  public void endElement(String namespaceURI,
                         String localName,
                         String qName ) throws SAXException {
```

```
        System.out.print( "SAX Event: CHARACTERS[ " );
        System.out.println(buffer.toString());
        System.out.println( " ]" );
        System.out.println( "SAX Event: END ELEMENT[ " + localName + " ]" );
      }
```

The entire code is shown in Listing 11-3.

Available for download on Wrox.com

LISTING 11-3: SaxParser3.java

```
import org.xml.sax.*;
import org.xml.sax.helpers.*;
import java.io.*;

public class SaxParser3 extends DefaultHandler {

  private StringBuffer buffer = new StringBuffer();

  public void startDocument( ) throws SAXException {
    System.out.println( "SAX Event: START DOCUMENT" );
  }

  public void endDocument( ) throws SAXException {
    System.out.println( "SAX Event: END DOCUMENT" );
  }

  public void startElement(String namespaceURI,
                           String localName,
                           String qName,
                           Attributes attr ) throws SAXException {
    System.out.println( "SAX Event: START ELEMENT[ " + localName + " ]");
    for ( int i = 0; i < attr.getLength(); i++ ){
    System.out.println( " ATTRIBUTE: "
    + attr.getLocalName(i) +  " VALUE: " + attr.getValue(i) );
    }

    buffer.setLength(0);
  }

  public void endElement(String namespaceURI,
                         String localName,
                         String qName ) throws SAXException {
    System.out.print( "SAX Event: CHARACTERS[ " );
    System.out.println(buffer.toString());
    System.out.println( " ]" );
    System.out.println( "SAX Event: END ELEMENT[ " + localName + " ]" );
  }

  public void characters(char[] ch,
                         int start,
                         int length ) throws SAXException {
    try {
      buffer.append(ch, start, length);
    } catch (Exception e) {
```

continues

LISTING 11-3 *(continued)*

```
        e.printStackTrace();
      }
    }

    public static void main( String[] argv ){
      String inputFile = argv[0];
      System.out.println( "Processing '" + inputFile + "'." );
      System.out.println( "SAX Events:" );
      try {
        XMLReader reader = XMLReaderFactory.createXMLReader();
        reader.setContentHandler( new SaxParser3() );
        reader.parse( new InputSource(
                   new FileReader( inputFile )));
      }catch ( Exception e ) {
         e.printStackTrace();
      }
    }
  }
```

The results from running this are the same as the earlier version, but now you have a much more flexible way of coping with textual data. This technique does not work, however, if you have mixed content. In that case you would need to have separate buffers for each element's content and keep track of which one was needed via flags set in `startElement` and `endElement`.

So far you've treated all character data as significant, even the whitespace that comes between elements such as `<Name>` and `<Description>`, which is only there to make the XML more human-readable. The next section shows how you can use the `ignorableWhitespace` event to treat significant and insignificant whitespace differently.

Using the ignorableWhitespace Event

The `ignorableWhitespace` event is very similar to the `characters` event. It has the same signature:

```
public void ignorableWhitespace(char[ ] ch, int start, int len)
   throws SAXException
```

As with the `characters` event, it can be called multiple times for a block of contiguous whitespace. The reason that the event was not called at all when parsing the `People.xml` file is that the parser can tell if whitespace is significant or not only by referring to a document type definition (DTD). If there were a DTD associated with your document that said that each `<Person>` element contained only parsed character data (PCDATA), the linefeeds between elements would be taken as insignificant whitespace and reported accordingly.

Another event that is thrown by the SAX parser is when an external entity is encountered, but for some reason not retrieved or expanded.

Understanding the skippedEntity Event

The `skippedEntity` event, much like the `ignorableWhitespace` event, alerts the application that the SAX parser has encountered information it believes the application can or must skip. In the case of the skippedEntity event, the SAX parser has not expanded an entity reference it encountered in the XML document. An entity might be skipped for several reasons:

- The entity is a reference to an external resource that cannot be parsed or cannot be found
- The entity is an external general entity and the http://xml.org/sax/features/external-general-entities feature is set to false
- The entity is an external parameter entity and the http://xml.org/sax/features/external-parameter-entities feature is set to false

You learn more about the external-general-entities and external-parameter-entities features later in this chapter. The skippedEntity event is declared as follows:

```
public void skippedEntity(String name)
  throws SAXException
```

The name parameter is the name of the entity that was skipped. It begins with % in the case of a parameter entity. SAX considers the external DTD subset an entity, so if the name parameter is [dtd], it means the external DTD subset was not processed. For more information on DTDs, refer to Chapter 4.

Applications can make use of processing instructions within an XML document, although they are not that common. The most common one is xml-stylesheet, which is recognized by browsers as an instruction to transform the current XML using the specified XSLT.

Handling the processingInstruction Event

The signature of the processingInstruction event is as follows:

```
public void processingInstruction(String target, String data)
   throws SAXException
```

If you were writing an application that needed to process the common xml-stylesheet instruction and it encountered the following:

```
<?xml-stylesheet type="text/xsl" href="myTransform.xsl"?>
```

The target parameter would be set to xml-stylesheet and the data parameter would contain type="text/xsl" href="myTransform.xsl". Notice how the data is not broken into separate attributes; this is because processing instructions don't have them. The fact that two pieces of data are referred to as type and href is really just coincidental — these two items are usually called pseudo-attributes.

You probably don't need to be reminded at this point that the XML declaration at the start of an XML document is *not* really a processing instruction, and as such it shouldn't result in a processingInstruction event. If it does, you should switch to another parser quickly.

Handling Invalid Content

What happens if, while you are parsing a document, you come across some data that is invalid? Hopefully this would have already been caught by an earlier validation process, either via a DTD, XML Schema, or one of the other methods discussed in previous chapters. However, sometimes business rules exist that cannot be expressed easily in the chosen validation language. For example, in DTDs and version 1.0 of XML Schema, it's not possible to say: if attribute *x* equals *y* then the next element should be *<a>*, otherwise it should be *<b>*. If you come across this sort of situation or a similar one where you want to report a fatal error, the standard way to do so is to throw a *SAXException*. You may have noticed that all the standard parser events throw this. The `SAXException` has three constructors. The simplest takes a string as its parameter; this can be used to specify the reason for the error and any other information such as the location. The second constructor takes an `Exception` as its sole argument. This is for when you have already trapped an `Exception` and want to wrap it. The third constructor takes both a string and an `Exception`. This means you can trap an `Exception` and then add your own message to add details about where the error occurred, and so on. One way to do this is to use another event handler, `setDocumentLocator`.

Using the setDocumentLocator Event

The `setDocumentLocator` event has only one argument, an instance of the `Locator` class. The methods for this class are shown in Table 11-2:

TABLE 11-2: Locator Methods

METHOD	DESCRIPTION
`getLineNumber()`	Retrieves the line number for the current event.
`getColumnNumber()`	Retrieves the column number for the current event (the SAX specification assumes that the column number is based on right-to-left reading modes).
`getSystemId()`	Retrieves the system identifier of the document for the current event. Because XML documents may be composed of multiple external entities, this may change throughout the parsing process.
`getPublicId()`	Retrieves the public identifier of the document for the current event. Because XML documents may be composed of multiple external entities, this may change throughout the parsing process.

Although it is often used for increasing the helpfulness of error messages, it can be used elsewhere, as the following activity shows.

TRY IT OUT Using the setDocumentLocator Event

This Try It Out shows how you can use the `setDocumentLocator` event to retrieve information about the XML document you are parsing and use this information to add line number information to the output.

1. Modify `SaxParser3.java` so that you have a variable to hold the current instance of the `Locator` and change the name of the class to `SaxParser4`:

```
public class SaxParser4 extends DefaultHandler {

  private Locator docLocator = null;
  private StringBuffer buffer = new StringBuffer();
```

2. Add a new method to handle the `setDocumentLocator` event:

```
public void setDocumentLocator(Locator locator)
{
  docLocator = locator;
}
```

3. In the `startElement` method add the following code to check if `docLocator` is not null and retrieve the current line number:

```
public void startElement(String namespaceURI,
                         String localName,
                         String qName,
                         Attributes attr ) throws SAXException {
  int lineNumber = 0;
  if (docLocator != null)
  {
    lineNumber = docLocator.getLineNumber();
  }
  System.out.println( "SAX Event: START ELEMENT[ " + localName + " ]");
  if (lineNumber != 0)
  {
    System.out.println(\t"(Found at line number: " + lineNumber + ".)");
  }
  for ( int i = 0; i < attr.getLength(); i++ ){
  System.out.println( " ATTRIBUTE: " + attr.getLocalName(i) +
  " VALUE: " + attr.getValue(i) );
  }
```

4. Change the code in the `main()` method to use `SaxParser4`:

```
try {
   XMLReader reader = XMLReaderFactory.createXMLReader();
   reader.setContentHandler(new SaxParser4());
   reader.parse( new InputSource(
              new FileReader( inputFile )));
}
```

5. Save the file as `SaxParser4.java` and compile it in the usual manner.

6. Run using:

```
java SaxParser4 People.xml
```

You should see similar results as the previous Try It Out but this time with a line number shown after each element's start tag, as shown in the following snippet:

```
Processing 'people.xml'.
SAX Events:
SAX Event: START DOCUMENT
SAX Event: START ELEMENT[ People ]
```

```
(Found at line number: 1.)
SAX Event: START ELEMENT[ Person ]
(Found at line number: 2.)
 ATTRIBUTE: bornDate VALUE: 1874-11-30
 ATTRIBUTE: diedDate VALUE: 1965-01-24
SAX Event: START ELEMENT[ Name ]
(Found at line number: 3.)
SAX Event: CHARACTERS[ Winston Churchill
 ]
SAX Event: END ELEMENT[ Name ]
SAX Event: START ELEMENT[ Description ]
(Found at line number: 4.)
SAX Event: CHARACTERS[
      Winston Churchill was a mid 20th century British politician who
      became famous as Prime Minister during the Second World War.
 ]
SAX Event: END ELEMENT[ Description ]
SAX Event: CHARACTERS[
      Winston Churchill was a mid 20th century British politician who
      became famous as Prime Minister during the Second World War.

 ]
SAX Event: END ELEMENT[ Person ]
```

How It Works

There is not much to the code. The `setDocumentLocator` event handler stores the instance of the `Locator` class in a local variable, `docLocator` like so:

```
public void setDocumentLocator(Locator locator)
{
  docLocator = locator;
}
```

The `startElement` handler checks to make sure the `docLocator` isn't null (this is a standard safety measure) and then calls its `getLineNumber()` method. After the element's name is reported, you check if the `lineNumber` variable has been updated, from zero to a real line number, and, if so, output it to the screen.

```
int lineNumber = 0;
if (docLocator != null)
{
  lineNumber = docLocator.getLineNumber();
}
System.out.println( "SAX Event: START ELEMENT[ " + localName + " ]" );
if (lineNumber != 0)
{
  System.out.println("\t(Found at line number: " + lineNumber + ".)");
}
```

The full code is shown in Listing 11-4.

Available for download on Wrox.com

LISTING 11-4: SaxParser4.java

```
import org.xml.sax.*;
import org.xml.sax.helpers.*;
import java.io.*;

public class SaxParser4 extends DefaultHandler {

  private Locator docLocator = null;
  private StringBuffer buffer = new StringBuffer();

  public void setDocumentLocator(Locator locator)
  {
    docLocator = locator;
  }

  public void startDocument( ) throws SAXException {
    System.out.println( "SAX Event: START DOCUMENT" );
  }

  public void endDocument( ) throws SAXException {
    System.out.println( "SAX Event: END DOCUMENT" );
  }

  public void startElement(String namespaceURI,
                           String localName,
                           String qName,
                           Attributes attr ) throws SAXException {
    int lineNumber = 0;
    if (docLocator != null)
    {
      lineNumber = docLocator.getLineNumber();
    }
    System.out.println( "SAX Event: START ELEMENT[ " + localName + " ]");
    if (lineNumber != 0)
    {
      System.out.println("\t(Found at line number: " + lineNumber + ".)");
    }
    for ( int i = 0; i < attr.getLength(); i++ ){
    System.out.println( " ATTRIBUTE: " + attr.getLocalName(i) +  " VALUE: "
                       + attr.getValue(i) );
    }

    buffer.setLength(0);
  }

  public void endElement(String namespaceURI,
                         String localName,
                         String qName ) throws SAXException {
    System.out.print( "SAX Event: CHARACTERS[ " );
    System.out.println(buffer.toString());
    System.out.println( " ]" );
    System.out.println( "SAX Event: END ELEMENT[ " + localName + " ]" );
  }
```

continues

LISTING 11-4 *(continued)*

```
  public void characters(char[] ch,
                         int start,
                         int length ) throws SAXException {
    try {
      buffer.append(ch, start, length);
    } catch (Exception e) {
     e.printStackTrace();
    }
  }

  public static void main( String[] argv ){
    String inputFile = argv[0];
    System.out.println ("Processing '" + inputFile + "'." );
    System.out.println( "SAX Events:" );
    try {
      XMLReader reader = XMLReaderFactory.createXMLReader();
      reader.setContentHandler(new SaxParser4());
      reader.parse( new InputSource(
                  new FileReader( inputFile )));
    }catch ( Exception e ) {
       e.printStackTrace();
    }
  }
}
```

It's easy to see how using `setDocumentLocator` and storing the reference to the input document could be used to improve the information produced by an error handler. Instead of just the reason for the error, the location of the offending item could also be given.

Using the ErrorHandler Interface

So far all the information about the XML has been passed via the `ContentHandler` interface. Error information, however, comes from `ErrorHandler`. Fortunately, the `DefaultHandler` class also provides stubs for the three events this interface fires. The three events are shown in the Table 11-3.

TABLE 11-3: Events Fired By ErrorHandler

EVENT	DESCRIPTION
`warning`	Allows the parser to notify the application of a warning it has encountered in the parsing process. Though the XML Recommendation provides many possible warning conditions, very few SAX parsers actually produce warnings.
`error`	Allows the parser to notify the application of an error it has encountered. Even though the parser has encountered an error, parsing can continue. Validation errors should be reported through this event.
`fatalError`	Allows the parser to notify the application of a fatal error it has encountered and that it cannot continue parsing. Well-formedness errors should be reported through this event.

The default implementation within DefaultHandler simply throws a SAXException when these events are fired. If you want to do anything other than that, such as include the line number of the offending code, you need to do two things:

1. Use the SetErrorHandler method on the reader to make sure errors are passed through the interface:

```
XMLReader reader = XMLReaderFactory.createXMLReader();
SaxParser5 parser = new SaxParser5();
reader.setContentHandler(parser);
reader.setErrorHandler(parser);
```

2. Write a method that handles one or more of the three events shown in Table 11-3; for example, warning.

If you want to trap specific errors, such as those generated when document validation fails, you will also need to use feature activation to enable this. Feature activation is covered later in the chapter.

The following Try It Out shows how to make use of the events of ErrorHandler. It demonstrates the preliminary steps you need to take to turn on full error handling and then deliberately gives the parser a flawed document to see the events in action.

TRY IT OUT Using the ErrorHandler Interface

This Try It Out demonstrates the full process needed to configure ErrorHandler. You'll need to specify which class will be used to receive the ErrorHandler events and also turn on the SAX validation feature. Once those two tasks are complete you'll also need to specify what format the document should take, otherwise it wouldn't be possible to say that it's invalid; this is done using a DTD.

1. Modify SaxParser4.java so that the class is now SaxParser5 and change the main() method to set the ErrorHandler as shown previously:

```
public static void main( String[] argv ){
  String inputFile = argv[0];
  System.out.println("Processing '" + inputFile + "'.");
  System.out.println( "SAX Events:" );
  try {
    XMLReader reader = XMLReaderFactory.createXMLReader();
    SaxParser5 parser = new SaxParser5();
    reader.setContentHandler(parser);
    reader.setErrorHandler(parser);
    reader.parse( new InputSource(
               new FileReader( inputFile )));
  }catch ( Exception e ) {
     e.printStackTrace();
  }
}
```

2. Add in the following lines to activate the validation feature:

```
        reader.setErrorHandler(parser);
try
{
  reader.setFeature("http://xml.org/sax/features/validation", true);
} catch (SAXException e) {
```

```
    System.err.println("Cannot activate validation");
    }

    reader.parse( new InputSource(
              new FileReader( inputFile )));
```

3. Create a DTD for `People.xml` and add it to the top of a new file, `PeopleWithDTD.xml`, with the older content underneath:

```
<!DOCTYPE People [
  <!ELEMENT People (Person*)>
  <!ELEMENT Person (Name, Description)>
  <!ATTLIST Person bornDate CDATA #REQUIRED>
  <!ATTLIST Person diedDate CDATA #REQUIRED>
  <!ELEMENT Name (#PCDATA)>
  <!ELEMENT Description (#PCDATA)>
]>
<People>
<!-- rest of people.xml -->
</People>
```

4. Add three methods to override the `ErrorHandler` interface:

```
public void warning (SAXParseException exception)
  throws SAXException {
  System.err.println("[Warning] " +
    exception.getMessage() + " at line " +
    exception.getLineNumber() + ", column " +
    exception.getColumnNumber() );
}

public void error (SAXParseException exception)
  throws SAXException {
  System.err.println("[Error] " +
    exception.getMessage() + " at line " +
    exception.getLineNumber() + ", column " +
    exception.getColumnNumber() );
}

public void fatalError (SAXParseException exception)
  throws SAXException {
  System.err.println("[Fatal Error] " +
    exception.getMessage() + " at line " +
    exception.getLineNumber() + ", column " +
    exception.getColumnNumber() );
  throw exception;
}
```

5. Compile and run the class against `PeopleWithDTD.xml`. You shouldn't see any change in the output.

6. Now remove the `diedDate` attribute from the second `<Person>` element, Indira Gandhi. This time you'll get an error message displayed as the element is parsed:

```
[Error] Attribute "diedDate" is required and must be specified for element type
"Person" at line 17, column 33
```

```
SAX Event: START ELEMENT[ Person ]
        (Found at line number: 17.)
 ATTRIBUTE: bornDate VALUE: 1917-11-19
```

How It Works

The `ErrorHandler` interface is brought into play by using the `setErrorHandler` code in `main()`. The next stage is to activate the validation feature, which is covered in more detail shortly. Finally, methods are declared that override the `DefaultHandler's` implementation of `warning`, `error`, and `fatalError`.

The full code for `SaxParser5` is shown in Listing 11-5.

Available for download on Wrox.com

LISTING 11-5: SaxParser5.java

```
import org.xml.sax.*;
import org.xml.sax.helpers.*;
import java.io.*;

public class SaxParser5 extends DefaultHandler {

  private Locator docLocator = null;
  private StringBuffer buffer = new StringBuffer();

  public void setDocumentLocator(Locator locator)
  {
    docLocator = locator;
  }

  public void startDocument( ) throws SAXException {
    System.out.println( "SAX Event: START DOCUMENT" );
  }

  public void endDocument( ) throws SAXException {
    System.out.println( "SAX Event: END DOCUMENT" );
  }

  public void startElement(String namespaceURI,
                           String localName,
                           String qName,
                           Attributes attr ) throws SAXException {
    int lineNumber = 0;
    if (docLocator != null)
    {
      lineNumber = docLocator.getLineNumber();
    }
    System.out.println( "SAX Event: START ELEMENT[ " + localName + " ]" );
    if (lineNumber != 0)
    {
      System.out.println("\t(Found at line number: " + lineNumber + ".)");
    }
    for ( int i = 0; i < attr.getLength(); i++ ){
    System.out.println( " ATTRIBUTE: " + attr.getLocalName(i) +
```

continues

LISTING 11-5 *(continued)*

```
" VALUE: " + attr.getValue(i) );
    }

    buffer.setLength(0);
  }

  public void endElement(String namespaceURI,
                         String localName,
                         String qName ) throws SAXException {
    System.out.print( "SAX Event: CHARACTERS[ " );
    System.out.println(buffer.toString());
    System.out.println( " ]" );
    System.out.println( "SAX Event: END ELEMENT[ " + localName + " ]" );
  }

  public void characters(char[] ch,
                         int start,
                         int length ) throws SAXException {
    try {
      buffer.append(ch, start, length);
    } catch (Exception e) {
     e.printStackTrace();
    }
  }

  public void warning (SAXParseException exception)
    throws SAXException {
    System.err.println("[Warning] " +
      exception.getMessage() + " at line " +
      exception.getLineNumber() + ", column " +
      exception.getColumnNumber() );
  }

  public void error (SAXParseException exception)
    throws SAXException {
    System.err.println("[Error] " +
      exception.getMessage() + " at line " +
      exception.getLineNumber() + ", column " +
      exception.getColumnNumber() );
  }

  public void fatalError (SAXParseException exception)
    throws SAXException {
    System.err.println("[Fatal Error] " +
      exception.getMessage() + " at line " +
      exception.getLineNumber() + ", column " +
      exception.getColumnNumber() );
    throw exception;
  }


  public static void main( String[] argv ){
    String inputFile = argv[0];
```

```
        System.out.println( "Processing '" + inputFile + "'." );
        System.out.println( "SAX Events:" );
        try {
          XMLReader reader = XMLReaderFactory.createXMLReader();
          SaxParser5 parser = new SaxParser5();
          reader.setContentHandler(parser);
          reader.setErrorHandler(parser);
          try
          {
            reader.setFeature("http://xml.org/sax/features/validation", true);
          } catch (SAXException e) {
          System.err.println("Cannot activate validation");
          }

          reader.parse( new InputSource(
                      new FileReader( inputFile )));
        }catch ( Exception e ) {
           e.printStackTrace();
        }
      }
    }
```

You may want to use two other interfaces to receive notifications when the document is parsed. These are covered in the next two sections.

Using the DTDHandler Interface

Now that you have added a DTD to your document, you may want to receive some events about the declarations. The logical place to turn is the `DTDHandler` interface. Unfortunately, the `DTDHandler` interface provides you with very little information about the DTD itself. In fact, it allows you to see the declarations only for notations and unparsed entities. Table 11-4 shows the two events produced by the `DTDHandler` interface and their use.

TABLE 11-4: DTDHandler Events

EVENT	DESCRIPTION
`notationDecl`	Allows the parser to notify the application that it has read a notation declaration.
`unparsedEntityDecl`	Allows the parser to notify the application that it has read an unparsed entity declaration.

When parsing documents that make use of notations and unparsed entities to refer to external files — such as image references in XHTML or embedded references to non-XML documents — the application must have access to the declarations of these items in the DTD. This is why the creators of SAX made them available through the `DTDHandler`, one of the default interfaces associated with an `XMLReader`.

The declarations of elements, attributes, and internal entities, however, are not required for general XML processing. These declarations are more useful for XML editors and validators. Therefore, the events for these declarations were made available in one of the extension interfaces, `DeclHandler`. You look at the extension interfaces in more detail later in the chapter.

Using the `DTDHandler` interface is very similar to using the `ContentHandler` and `ErrorHandler` interfaces. The `DefaultHandler` class you used as the base class of the `TrainReader` also implements the `DTDHandler` interface, so working with the events is simply a matter of overriding the default behavior, just as you did with the `ErrorHandler` and `ContentHandler` events. To tell the `XMLReader` to send the `DTDHandler` events to your application, you can simply call the `setDTDHandler` function, as shown in the following code:

```
reader.setDTDHandler(SaxParser5);
```

> **WARNING** *You may be wondering if there is an interface for receiving XML Schema events. Surprisingly, there isn't. In fact, no events are fired for XML Schema declarations either. The creators of SAX wanted to ensure that all the information outlined in the XML Recommendation was available through the interfaces. Remember that DTDs are part of the XML Recommendation, but XML Schemas are defined in their own, separate recommendation.*

The second interface is `EntityResolver`, used for providing information and control when an external entity reference is encountered.

EntityResolver Interface

The `EntityResolver` interface enables you to control how a SAX parser behaves when it attempts to resolve external entity references within the DTD, so much like the `DTDHandler`, it is frequently not used. However, when an XML document utilizes external entity references, it is highly recommended that you provide an `EntityResolver`.

The `EntityResolver` interface defines only one function, `resolveEntity`, which enables the application to handle the resolution of entity lookups for the parser.

As shown with the other default interfaces, the `EntityResolver` interface is implemented by the `DefaultHandler` class. Therefore, to handle the event callback, you simply override the `resolveEntity` function in the `TrainReader` class and make a call to the `setEntityResolver` function like so:

```
reader.setEntityResolver(SaxParser5);
```

Consider the following entity declaration:

```
<!ENTITY People PUBLIC "-//People//people xml 1.0//EN"
    "http://wrox.com/people.xml">
```

In this case, the `resolveEntity` function would be passed — `//People//people xml 1.0//EN` as the public identifier, and `http://wrox.com/people.xml` as the system identifier. The `DefaultHandler` class's implementation of the `resolveEntity` function returns a null `InputSource` by default. When handling the `resolveEntity` event, however, your application can take any number of actions. It could create an `InputSource` based on the system identifier, or it could create an `InputSource` based on a stream returned from a database, hash table, or catalog lookup that used the public identifier as the key. It could also simply return `null`. These options and many more enable an application to control how the processor opens and connects to external resources.

Earlier you saw how validation was turned on by setting a feature; in the next section you'll look at this in more detail.

Understanding Features and Properties

As shown earlier in this chapter, some of the behavior of SAX parsers is controlled through setting features and properties. For example, to activate validation, you needed to set the `http://xml.org/sax/features/validation` feature to `true`. In fact, all features in SAX are controlled this way, by setting a flag to `true` or `false`. The feature and property names in SAX are full URIs so that they can have unique names — much like namespace names.

Working with Features

To change a feature's value in SAX, you simply call the `setFeature` function of the `XMLReader` like so:

```
public void setFeature(String name, boolean value)
  throws SAXNotRecognizedException, SAXNotSupportedException
```

When doing this, however, it is important to remember that parsers may not support, or even recognize, every feature. If a SAX parser does not recognize the name of the feature, the `setFeature` function raises a `SAXNotRecognizedException`. If it recognizes the feature name but does not support a feature (or does not support changing the value of a feature at a certain time), the `setFeature` function raises a `SAXNotSupportedException`. For example, if a SAX parser does not support validation, it raises a `SAXNotSupportedException` when you attempt to change the value to `true`.

The `getFeature` function enables you to check the value of any feature like so:

```
public boolean getFeature(String name)
  throws SAXNotRecognizedException, SAXNotSupportedException
```

Like the `setFeature` function, the `getFeature` function may raise exceptions if it does not recognize the name of the feature or does not support checking the value at certain times (such as before, during, or after the `parse` function has been called). Therefore, place all of your calls to the `setFeature` and `getFeature` functions within a `try/catch` block to handle any exceptions.

All SAX parsers should recognize, but may not support, the following features in Table 11-5:

TABLE 11-5: Configurable SAX Features

FEATURE	DEFAULT	DESCRIPTION
`http://xml.org/sax/features/validation`	*Unspecified*	Controls whether the parser will validate the document as it parses. In addition to controlling validation, it also affects certain parser behaviors. For example, if the feature is set to `true`, all external entities must be read.
`http://xml.org/sax/features/namespaces`	`true`	In the latest version of SAX, this feature should always be `true`, meaning that namespace URI and prefix values will be sent to the element and attribute functions when available.
`http://xml.org/sax/features/namespace-prefixes`	`false`	In the latest version of SAX, this feature should always be `false`. It means that names with colons will be treated as prefixes and local names. When this flag is set to `true`, raw XML names are sent to the application.
`http://xml.org/sax/features/xmlns-uris`	`false`	Enables you to control whether `xmlns` declarations are reported as having the namespace URI `http://www.w3.org/2000/xmlns/`. By default, SAX conforms to the original namespaces in the XML Recommendation and will not report this URI. The 1.1 Recommendation and an erratum to the 1.0 edition modified this behavior. This setting is used only when `xmlns` declarations are reported as attributes.
`http://xml.org/sax/features/resolve-dtd-uris`	`true`	Controls whether the SAX parser will "absolutize" system IDs relative to the base URI before reporting them. Parsers will use the `Locator`'s `systemID` as the base URI. This feature does not apply to `EntityResolver.resolveEntity`, nor does it apply to `LexicalHandler.startDTD`.
`http://xml.org/sax/features/external-general-entities`	*Unspecified*	Controls whether external general entities should be processed. When the validation feature is set to `true`, this feature is always `true`.
`http://xml.org/sax/features/external-parameter-entities`	*Unspecified*	Controls whether external parameter entities should be processed. When the validation feature is set to `true`, this feature is always `true`.
`http://xml.org/sax/features/lexical-handler/parameter-entities`	*Unspecified*	Controls the reporting of the start and end of parameter entity inclusions in the `LexicalHandler`.

FEATURE	DEFAULT	DESCRIPTION
`http://xml.org/sax/features/is-standalone`	*None*	Enables you to determine whether the standalone flag was set in the XML declaration. This feature can be accessed only after the `startDocument` event has completed. This feature is read-only and returns `true` only if the standalone flag in the XML declaration has a value of `yes`.
`http://xml.org/sax/features/use-attributes2`	*Unspecified*	Check this read-only feature to determine whether the `Attributes` interface passed to the `startElement` event supports the `Attributes2` extensions. The `Attributes2` extensions enable you to examine additional information about the declaration of the attribute in the DTD. Because this feature was introduced in a later version of SAX, some SAX parsers will not recognize it.
`http://xml.org/sax/features/use-locator2`	*Unspecified*	Check this read-only feature to determine whether the `Locator` interface passed to the `setDocumentLocator` event supports the `Locator2` extensions. The `Locator2` extensions enable to you determine the XML version and encoding declared in an entity's XML declaration. Because this feature was introduced in a later version of SAX, some SAX parsers will not recognize it.
`http://xml.org/sax/features/use-entity-resolver2`	`true` (if recognized)	Set this feature to `true` (the default) if the `EntityResolver` interface passed to the `setEntityResolver` function supports the `EntityResolver2` extensions. If it does not support the extensions, set this feature to `false`. The `EntityResolver2` extensions allow you to receive callbacks for the resolution of entities and the external subset of the DTD. Because this feature was introduced in a later version of SAX, some SAX parsers will not recognize it.
`http://xml.org/sax/features/string-interning`	*Unspecified*	Enables you to determine whether the strings reported in event callbacks were interned using the Java function `String.intern`. This allows for fast comparison of strings.
`http://xml.org/sax/features/unicode-normalization-checking`	`false`	Controls whether the parser reports Unicode normalization errors as described in Section 2.13 and Appendix B of the XML 1.1 Recommendation. Because these errors are not fatal, if encountered they are reported using the `ErrorHandler.error` callback.
`http://xml.org/sax/features/xml-1.1`	*Unspecified*	Read-only feature that returns `true` if the parser supports XML 1.1 and XML 1.0. If the parser does not support XML 1.1, this feature will be `false`.

Working with Properties

Working with properties is very similar to working with features. Instead of `boolean` flags, however, properties may be any kind of object. The property mechanism is most often used to connect helper objects to an `XMLReader`. For example, SAX comes with an extension set of interfaces called `DeclHandler` and `LexicalHandler` that enable you to receive additional events about the XML document. Because these interfaces are considered extensions, the only way to register these event handlers with the `XMLReader` is through the `setProperty` function:

```
public void setProperty(String name, Object value)
  throws SAXNotRecognizedException, SAXNotSupportedException

public Object getProperty(String name)
  throws SAXNotRecognizedException, SAXNotSupportedException
```

As you saw with the `setFeature` and `getFeature` functions, all calls to `setProperty` and `getProperty` should be safely placed in `try`/`catch` blocks, because they may raise exceptions. Some of the default property names are listed in Table 11-6:

TABLE 11-6: Configurable SAX Properties

PROPERTY NAME	DESCRIPTION
`http://xml.org/sax/properties/declaration-handler`	Specifies the `DeclHandler` object registered to receive events for declarations within the DTD.
`http://xml.org/sax/properties/lexical-handler`	Specifies the `LexicalHandler` object registered to receive lexical events, such as comments, `CDATA` sections, and entity references.
`http://xml.org/sax/properties/document-xml-version`	Read-only property that describes the actual version of the XML document, such as `1.0` or `1.1`. This property can only be accessed during the parse and after the `startDocument` callback has been completed.

Using the Extension Interfaces

The two primary extension interfaces are `DeclHandler` and `LexicalHandler`. Using these interfaces, you can receive events for each DTD declaration and specific items such as comments, `CDATA` sections, and entity references as they are expanded. It is not required by the XML specification that these items be passed to the application by an XML processor. All the same, the information can be very useful at times, so the creators of SAX wanted to ensure that they could be accessed.

The `DeclHandler` interface declares the following events in Table 11-7:

TABLE 11-7: DeclHandler Interface Definition

EVENT	DESCRIPTION
`attributeDecl`	Allows the parser to notify the application that it has read an attribute declaration.
`elementDecl`	Allows the parser to notify the application that it has read an element declaration.
`externalEntityDecl`	Allows the parser to notify the application that it has read an external entity declaration.
`internalEntityDecl`	Allows the parser to notify the application that it has read an internal entity declaration.

The `LexicalHandler` interface declares the following events in Table 11-8:

TABLE 11-8: LexicalHandler Interface Definition

EVENT	DESCRIPTION
`comment`	Allows the parser to notify the document that it has read a comment. The entire comment is passed back to the application in one event call; it is not buffered, as it may be in the `characters` and `ignorableWhitespace` events.
`startCDATA`	Allows the parser to notify the document that it has encountered a `CDATA` section start marker. The character data within the `CDATA` section is always passed to the application through the `characters` event.
`endCDATA`	Allows the parser to notify the document that it has encountered a `CDATA` section end marker.
`startDTD`	Allows the parser to notify the document that it has begun reading a DTD.
`endDTD`	Allows the parser to notify the document that it has finished reading a DTD.
`startEntity`	Allows the parser to notify the document that it has started reading or expanding an entity.
`endEntity`	Allows the parser to notify the document that it has finished reading or expanding an entity.

Because these are extension interfaces, they must be registered with the `XMLReader` using the property mechanism, as you just learned. For example, to register a class as a handler or `LexicalHandler` events, you might do the following:

```
reader.setProperty("http://xml.org/sax/properties/lexical-handler", lexHandler);
```

NOTE *The `DefaultHandler` class, which you used as the basis of the `SaxParser` classes, does not implement any of the extension interfaces. In the newer versions of SAX, however, an extension class was added called `DefaultHandler2`. This class not only implements the core interfaces, but the extension interfaces as well. Therefore, if you want to receive the `LexicalHandler` and `DeclHandler` events, it is probably a good idea to descend from `DefaultHandler2` instead of the `DefaultHandler` class.*

The great thing about SAX is that it's not just limited to Java. Implementations exist for C++, PHP, and Microsoft's COM as well as many other languages. People have accepted the fact that a good way to handle large documents is to use an event-based method.

Now that you've seen how SAX copes with documents using events, in the next section you look at .NET's answer to the problems posed by large documents, `System.Xml.XmlReader`.

USING XMLREADER

Whereas with SAX you handle events thrown by the parser, `XmlReader` takes a different approach, albeit one that needs a similar mindset to work with. Again you are working through the document in a serial fashion, but whereas with SAX the process is somewhat akin to watching a conveyor belt loaded with goods go by, with you plucking items from it as it passes, with `XmlReader` the process is more like the XML being laid out like a long buffet, where you need to move along picking up whatever items you want.

`XmlReader` has similar advantages and disadvantages to SAX, too. It is very efficient from a memory point of view because the whole document is not loaded into RAM. This also means that once you've passed a particular spot, you can't go back; you have to begin the process anew. You also can't validate a complete document. You can only know that the XML is valid or invalid up to the furthest point you've reached. If you want full validation before you start processing, you'll need two passes.

In the following activity you see how to get started with `XmlReader`. You'll start out with the basics: how to load an XML document and how to use basic navigation to read its content.

TRY IT OUT Loading a Document with XmlReader

This Try It Out walks you through creating an `XmlReader`, loading a document, and reading the name of the document's root element. If you just want to follow along, the code is available in the download for this chapter. The solution is named `XmlReaderDemo`.

1. If you are using the full version of Visual Studio then open it and create a blank solution named `XmlReaderDemo` as shown in Figure 11-1. If you are using Visual Studio Express open the C# version and move on to step 2.

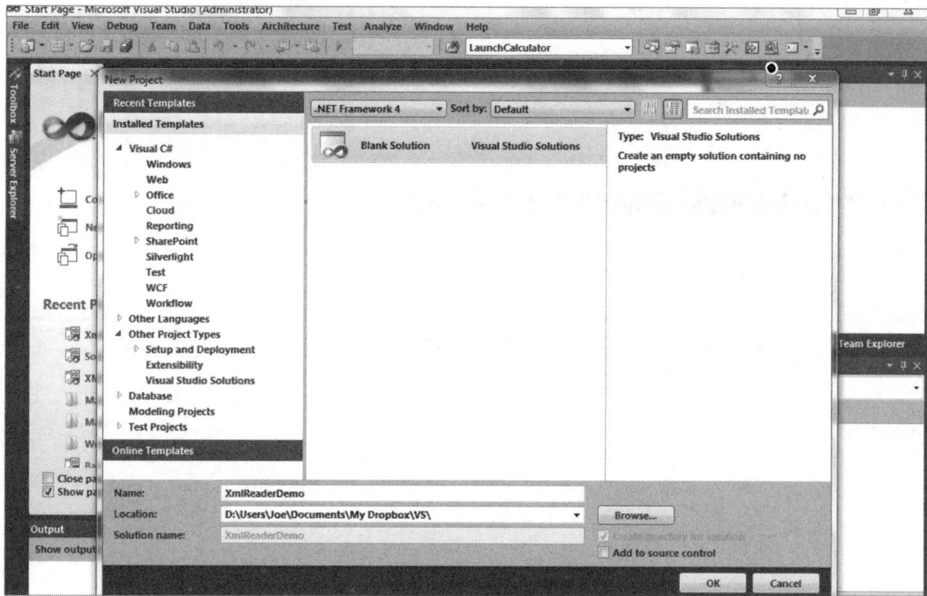

FIGURE 11-1

2. Add a new Windows Console project named `XmlReaderBasics`.
3. Right-click the project and choose Add ➪ Existing Item. Choose the `People.xml` file shown earlier in the chapter in Listing 11-1.
4. Go to the properties of `People.xml` and make sure that Copy to Output Directory is set to Copy If Newer as shown in the bottom right corner of Figure 11-2. This makes it easier to locate because it will be in the same folder as the application.
5. Replace the code in `Program.cs` with the code in Listing 11-6.

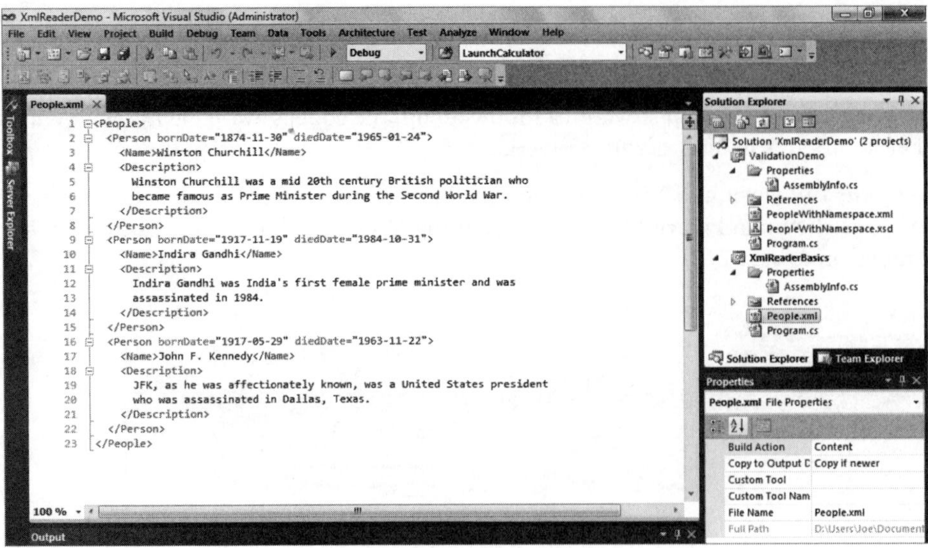

FIGURE 11-2

Available for download on Wrox.com

LISTING 11-6: Program.cs (in project XmlReaderBasics)

```
using System;
using System.Xml;

namespace XmlReaderBasics
{
  internal class Program
  {
    private static void Main(string[] args)
    {
      var xmlUri = "People.xml";
      var reader = DisplayRootElement(xmlUri);
      Console.ReadLine();
    }

    private static XmlReader DisplayRootElement(string uri)
    {
      var reader = XmlReader.Create(uri);
      reader.MoveToContent();
      var rootElementName = reader.Name;
      Console.WriteLine("Root element name is: {0}", rootElementName);
      return reader;
    }
  }
}
```

6. Save all files (Ctrl+Shift+S) and then build (Ctrl+Shift+B).
7. Assuming there are no build errors, run the program using F5.

8. You should see the following output in the console window. Press Enter to close the window.

```
Root element name is: People
```

How It Works

The `DisplayRootElement()` method first creates an `XmlReader` using a static factory method on the `XmlReader` class as shown in the following code. `XmlReader` is actually an abstract class and it therefore can't have an instance:

```
var reader = XmlReader.Create(uri);
```

What is actually returned in this example is an `XmlTextReader`, the simplest implementation of the abstract class. It's also possible to create other versions such as an `XmlValidatingReader` if you want document validation; you learn how to do this later in the chapter in the "Using XMLReaderSettings" section.

The `Create()` method takes the path to the file. In this case, this is a relative path because the file is in the same folder as the executable, but you can also pass in a full path or a URL. The `Create()` method can take other parameters, some of which you see later.

If there is a problem loading the XML — for example, the file cannot be found or there is a permissions problem — a suitable exception will be thrown such as `FileNotFoundException` or `SecurityException`.

Once the `XmlReader` has loaded the XML, the most common action is to use the `MoveToContent()` method to position the reader's cursor on the root element:

```
reader.MoveToContent();
```

The `MoveToContent()` method checks to see if the cursor is currently located at content; if not, it moves to the first content it can find. Content is defined as non-whitespace text, an element, or entity reference. Comments, processing instructions, document types, and whitespace are skipped over. This means that everything between the start of the document and the actual root element will be ignored and the cursor will be pointing to the first element in the document. Microsoft terms this the *current node* in the `XmlReader` documentation.

Once the reader has a current node, properties of this node are available. In this case you used the `Name` property as shown here but you could use dozens of others such as `Attributes`, `Value`, and `NamespaceURI`:

```
var rootElementName = reader.Name;
```

Finally, the name of the element is displayed and the reader is returned so that it can be used to extract more information:

```
Console.WriteLine("Root element name is: {0}", rootElementName);
return reader;
```

So far you've seen the basics in action — loading a document and moving to the document element. The next step is to read some useful information from the document, which you do in the following activity.

TRY IT OUT Getting Element and Attribute Data

This Try It Out shows you how to do basic navigation through a document and read element and attribute values.

1. Using the `XmlReaderBasics` project, add a new method named `DisplayPeopleWithDates` to `Program.cs` as shown here:

```
private static XmlReader DisplayPeopleWithDates(XmlReader reader)
{
  while (reader.Read())
  {
    if (reader.NodeType == XmlNodeType.Element
        && reader.Name == "Person")
    {
      DateTime bornDate = new DateTime();
      DateTime diedDate = new DateTime();
      var personName = string.Empty;
      while (reader.MoveToNextAttribute())
      {
        switch (reader.Name)
        {
          case "bornDate":
            bornDate = reader.ReadContentAsDateTime();
            break;
          case "diedDate":
            diedDate = reader.ReadContentAsDateTime();
            break;
        }
      }

      while (reader.Read())
      {
        if (reader.NodeType == XmlNodeType.Element
            && reader.Name == "Name")
        {
          personName = reader.ReadElementContentAsString();
          break;
        }
      }
      Console.WriteLine("{0} was born in {1} and died in {2}",
                        personName,
                        bornDate.ToShortDateString(),
                        diedDate.ToShortDateString());
    }
  }

  return reader;
}
```

2. Now add the following line to the `Main()` method:

```
private static void Main(string[] args)
{
  var xmlUri = "People.xml";
  var reader = DisplayRootElement(xmlUri);
  reader = DisplayPeopleWithDates(reader);
  Console.ReadLine();
}
```

3. Rebuild the project and press F5 to run. This time you'll see the names of the three politicians along with the dates on which they were born and died, as shown in the following code. The actual format of the date may differ, depending on the regional settings on your machine:

```
Root element name is: People
Winston Churchill was born in 30/11/1874 and died in 24/01/1965
Indira Gandhi was born in 19/11/1917 and died in 31/10/1984
John F. Kennedy was born in 29/05/1917 and died in 22/11/1963
```

How It Works

The `DisplayPeopleWithDates()` method accepts an `XmlReader` as a parameter. The current node for the reader is `People` so any operations will begin from there:

```
private static XmlReader DisplayPeopleWithDates(XmlReader reader)
{
  while (reader.Read())
```

One of `XmlReader`'s most commonly called methods, `Read()`, is used to move through the nodes within the XML. This method reads the next node from the input stream; the node can be any one of the types defined by the `XmlNodeType` enumeration.

If a node is successfully read, the `Read()` method returns `true`, otherwise it returns `false`. This means that the standard way to traverse a document is to use the `Read()` method in a `while` loop, which will automatically exit when the method returns `false`. In the body of the loop you can see which node type the reader is pointing at and then use other information, such as its name if it's an element, to garner whatever data you need.

In your method you test to see if you have an element and whether its name is `Person`:

```
if (reader.NodeType == XmlNodeType.Element
    && reader.Name == "Person")
{
  DateTime bornDate = new DateTime();
  DateTime diedDate = new DateTime();
  var personName = string.Empty;
```

If that is the case, you initialize three variables that will hold the three pieces of data that you're going to display: two dates and a string for the person's name.

You then use the `MoveToNextAttribute()` method, which cycles through an element's attributes.

```
while (reader.MoveToNextAttribute())
{
  switch (reader.Name)
  {
    case "bornDate":
      bornDate = reader.ReadContentAsDateTime();
      break;
    case "diedDate":
      diedDate = reader.ReadContentAsDateTime();
      break;
  }
}
```

Again, this method returns a Boolean, so a `while` loop is the easiest way to make sure you've read all the attributes you need. To read the attribute's value you use one of several `ReadContentAs...()` methods, in this case `ReadContentAsDateTime()`.

You next move to the `<Name>` element and you use a similar tactic as before, wrapping the `Read()` method in a `while` loop and testing that you have an element that has the appropriate name.

```
while (reader.Read())
{
  if (reader.NodeType == XmlNodeType.Element
      && reader.Name == "Name")
  {
    personName = reader.ReadElementContentAsString();
    break;
  }
}
```

You can read the text content of an element in many ways; here you use `ReadElementContentAsStrin g()`. Again, many variations of this return different types.

Once you have the three data items you need, you output them to the console. The outer `while` loop now continues until the `Read()` method returns `false`:

```
Console.WriteLine("{0} was born in {1} and died in {2}",
                  personName,
                  bornDate.ToShortDateString(),
                  diedDate.ToShortDateString());
```

The preceding Try It Out example made use of the `XmlNodeType` enumeration. The most common test is for elements but there are times when you are targeting other content types. The full list of values returned by `XmlReader` is shown in Table 11-9.

TABLE 11-9: XmlNodeType Enumeration

NAME	DESCRIPTION
`None`	The `Read()` method has not yet been called.
`Element`	An element has been read.
`Attribute`	An attribute has been read.
`Text`	The text content of a node, such as an element or an attribute, has been read.
`CDATA`	A `CDATA` section was read.
`EntityReference`	An entity reference, such as `é`, has been read.
`ProcessingInstruction`	A processing instruction has been read.
`Comment`	A comment has been read.
`DocumentType`	A document type declaration has been read.
`Whitespace`	Whitespace between markups has been read.
`SignificantWhitespace`	Whitespace that is known to be significant (because a schema or DTD has been used, for instance) has been read.
`EndElement`	The closing tag of an element has been read.
`XmlDeclaration`	The document's XML declaration has been read.

There are other members of the enumeration, such as Document, but these are never returned by the XmlReader.

So far you've used the basic `XmlReader.Create()` method to get a standard `XmlTextReader`. In the next section you see how you can use the `XmlReaderSettings` class to more tightly control how the reader will work.

Using XmlReaderSettings

Many questions can arise when parsing and reading XML, for example:

- How do you want to treat whitespace?
- Do you want validation?

- If you do want validation, where are the relevant schemas?
- Do you want attention paid to any document type definition?
- Are you interested in comments, or can they be ignored?
- What should be done with the stream after reading? Should it be closed or left open?
- How do you provide credentials to access secured online resources?

All these questions, along with others, can be answered by using the `XmlReaderSettings` class — to create a new instance of the class, set the appropriate properties, and then pass it as a second argument to the `XmlReader.Create()` method.

For example, suppose you want to ignore any comments in the document; you are not going to do anything with them so they'll only get in the way. The following code shows how to do this:

```
var settings = new XmlReaderSettings();
settings.IgnoreComments = true;
var reader = XmlReader.Create(xmlUri, settings);
```

The next example shows a more complicated scenario: how to provide credentials for a secured online resource. Any time an `XmlReader` needs to access a resource, it uses an `XmlResolver`. The built-in resolver uses the credentials of the account running the code, which may not be sufficient. You can access the resolver and change the credentials via the `XmlReaderSettings` in the following manner:

```
var settings = new XmlReaderSettings();
var resolver = new XmlUrlResolver();
var credentials = new Syystem.Net.NetworkCredential(username,
                                                    password,
                                                    domainName);
resolver.Credentials = credentials;
settings.XmlResolver = resolver;
var reader = XmlReader.Create(xmlUri, settings);
```

***NOTE** You can use a standard string to specify the password, but you should really use the `SecureString` class, which makes sure that the data is wiped from memory as soon as is practical.*

The next activity illustrates another common scenario: how to use an `XmlReader` to validate a document. You'll see how you need to specify in advance that you want a validating reader and how any validation errors are handled.

TRY IT OUT Validating a Document with XmlReader

This Try It Out will show you how to validate a document using `XmlReader`. You'll see how to use the `XmlReaderSettings` class to specify that you want validation and what validation method is required. You'll then see how validation messages are reported when reading an invalid document.

1. If you are using the full version of Visual Studio in the `XmlReaderDemo` solution, right-click the solution icon and choose Add ➪ New Project. If using the Express version then close any existing projects and choose File ➪ New Project.
2. Choose a Windows Console Application and call it `ValidationDemo`.
3. Within the project add a new item, an XML file named `PeopleWithNamespace.xml`.
4. Copy the XML from the `People.xml` in Listing 11-1 file and add the following namespace declaration to the document element to put all the elements into a default namespace:

```
<People xmlns="http://wrox.com/namespaces/BeginningXml/People">
```

5. Add another new file to the project, this time an XSD schema, and call it `PeopleWithNamespace.xsd`.
6. Add the code in Listing 11-7 to the XSD.

Available for download on Wrox.com

LISTING 11-7: PeopleWithNamespace.xsd

```
<?xml version="1.0" encoding="utf-8"?>
<xs:schema attributeFormDefault="unqualified"
           elementFormDefault="qualified"
           targetNamespace="http://wrox.com/namespaces/BeginningXml/People"
           xmlns:xs="http://www.w3.org/2001/XMLSchema">
  <xs:element name="People">
    <xs:complexType>
      <xs:sequence>
        <xs:element maxOccurs="unbounded" name="Person">
          <xs:complexType>
            <xs:sequence>
              <xs:element name="Name" type="xs:string" />
              <xs:element name="Description" type="xs:string" />
            </xs:sequence>
            <xs:attribute name="bornDate" type="xs:date" use="required" />
            <xs:attribute name="diedDate" type="xs:date" use="required" />
          </xs:complexType>
        </xs:element>
      </xs:sequence>
    </xs:complexType>
  </xs:element>
</xs:schema>
```

7. Make sure that Copy to Output Directory property for both these files is set to Copy If Newer.
8. Open `Program.cs` and replace the code with the code in Listing 11-8.

LISTING 11-8: Program.cs (in project ValidationDemo)

```
using System;
using System.Xml;
using System.Xml.Schema;

namespace ValidationDemo
{
  internal class Program
  {
    private static void Main(string[] args)
    {
      var xmlUri = "PeopleWithNamespace.xml";
      var targetNamespace =
         "http://wrox.com/namespaces/BeginningXml/People";
      var schemaUri = "PeopleWithNamespace.xsd";
      ValidateDocument(xmlUri, targetNamespace, schemaUri);
      Console.ReadLine();
    }

    private static void ValidateDocument(string uri,
                                         string targetNamespace,
                                         string schemaUri)
    {
      var schemaSet = new XmlSchemaSet();
      schemaSet.Add(targetNamespace, schemaUri);
      var settings = new XmlReaderSettings();
      settings.ValidationType = ValidationType.Schema;
      settings.Schemas = schemaSet;
      settings.ValidationEventHandler += ValidationCallback;
      var reader = XmlReader.Create(uri, settings);
      while (reader.Read()) ;
      Console.WriteLine("Validation complete.");
    }

    private static void ValidationCallback(object sender,
                                           ValidationEventArgs e)
    {
      Console.WriteLine(
            "Validation Error: {0}\n\tLine number {1}, position {2}.",
                        e.Message,
                        e.Exception.LineNumber,
                        e.Exception.LinePosition);
    }
  }
}
```

9. Right-click the project and set it as the startup project for the solution as shown in Figure 11-3.

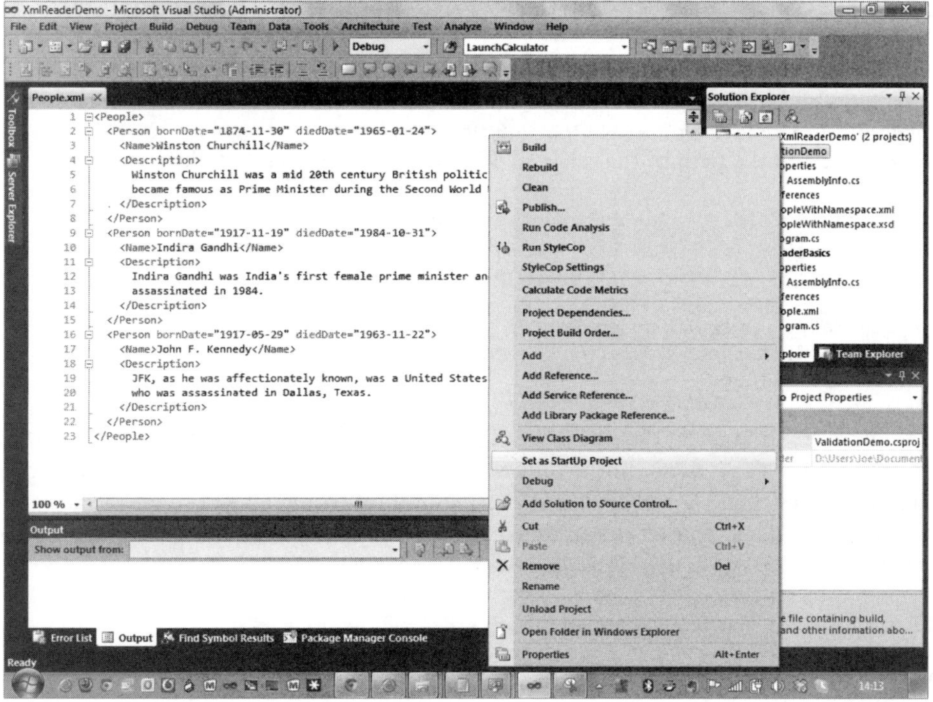

FIGURE 11-3

10. Save (Ctrl+Shift+S) and build (Ctrl+Shift+B) the project and run with F5.
11. You should see the following message in the console:

```
Validation complete.
```

12. Modify `PeopleWithNamespace.xml` by removing the `diedDate` attribute from the second `<Person>` element, as shown here:

```
<Person bornDate="1917-11-19">
  <Name>Indira Gandhi</Name>
```

13. Rerun the solution. This time you should see a message reporting a validation error as follows:

```
Validation Error: The required attribute 'diedDate' is missing.
        Line number 9, position 4.
Validation complete.
```

How It Works

`ValidateDocument` begins by setting up an `XmlSchemaSet` that will hold the necessary schema for validating your document. In this case there is only one, `PeopleWithNamespace.xsd`. You add this using the `Add()` method, which specifies the target namespace, `http://wrox.com/namespaces/BeginningXml/People`, and the path to the schema. The corresponding code follows:

```
private static void ValidateDocument(string uri,
                                     string targetNamespace,
                                     string schemaUri)
{
  var schemaSet = new XmlSchemaSet();
  schemaSet.Add(targetNamespace, schemaUri);
  // method continues
```

The next stage involves creating an `XmlReaderSettings` object and specifying the `ValidationType`. This defaults to `ValidationType.None`. In the following code you set it to `ValidationType.Schema`, which means that instead of the `XmlReader.Create()` method returning an `XmlTextReader`, you'll get an `XsdValidatingReader`. Then you set the settings' Schemas property to be the `XmlSchemaSet` previously created:

```
  var settings = new XmlReaderSettings();
  settings.ValidationType = ValidationType.Schema;
  settings.Schemas = schemaSet;
```

The next step is to provide a method that is called whenever a validation error occurs; here the method is named `ValidationCallback`:

```
  settings.ValidationEventHandler += ValidationCallback;
```

The last lines of the method create the `XmlReader`, passing in the all-important settings, and then call the `Read()` method in the familiar `while` loop. Notice how you are not doing anything extra within the loop; this is just to make sure the whole XML document is read and validated:

```
  var reader = XmlReader.Create(uri, settings);
  while (reader.Read()) ;
  Console.WriteLine("Validation complete.");
```

The callback that handles any errors is fairly straightforward, shown here:

```
private static void ValidationCallback(object sender,
                                       ValidationEventArgs e)
{
  Console.WriteLine("Validation Error: {0}\n\tLine number {1}, position {2}",
                    e.Message,
                    e.Exception.LineNumber,
                    e.Exception.LinePosition);
}
}
```

Whenever an error occurs, the method is called with the familiar .NET signature of the `sender` as an `object` and an `EventArgs`. In this case, the `EventArgs` is of type `ValidationEventArgs` and provides both a Message property, which is the reason the validation failed, and an Exception property, which can be used to garner more details. In this case the line number and position of the error is extracted. If you wanted more detail, you could cast the sender object to an XmlReader and use properties such as Name to find out which node was being read when the error occurred.

Now that you've covered most of the standard scenarios in reading data, using Read() to move through the XML and returning content from elements and attributes, next you'll look at the role of the XmlResolver more deeply and see how you can limit where external resources are loaded from.

Controlling External Resources

You saw earlier how an XmlReaderSettings class has a property, XmlResolver, which, by default, returns an instance of an XmlUrlResolver. By default, the XmlUrlResolver handles requests for files using the file:// and http:// protocols, but it's possible to write your own class that inherits from XmlResolver, which knows how to handle other ones. The XmlResolver class is also used when transforming XML using the System.Xml.Xsl.CompiledTransform, again to govern how external resources are dealt with. A common requirement when loading or especially transforming a file is to have access to data that resides in a traditional SQL database. Many people have therefore written XmlResolvers that can do this. Most of them allow you to specify a resource such as the following:

```
sql://executeProcedure?name=GetAllCustomers&City=Seattle
```

This would cause the data returned by the procedure — all customers who reside in Seattle — to be embedded in the XML.

Another common request is to be able to call a web service. This can be achieved in a limited way if the service is a RESTful one that only uses the querystring to provide data, but is impossible to do so where a post is required, as is the case for most SOAP-based services.

Both of the preceding scenarios involve writing your own implementation of XmlResolver, but there is another case that is so common that Microsoft has done the work for you. This is when you want to restrict access to external files, normally based on where they reside. Why would you want to do this? The common reason is that you are accepting XML files from a third party. Maybe your web orders are sent from other businesses using a business-to-business (B2B) system and you need to process these. Although it's legitimate for these files to contain references to external resources (maybe a schema, a DTD, or an entity), these resources should only reside on servers that have been approved beforehand. To prevent the chance of infected files getting on to your servers, or to prevent a denial of service (DoS) attack, it's essential to have a way of limiting the locations from where files are retrieved.

NOTE *A DoS attack is one which tries to use all the resources on a machine by either issuing an extremely large number of requests or by injecting very large files into the processing pipeline.*

For these and related reasons, Microsoft offers the *XmlSecureResolver* class, whereby you can easily restrict which domains can be accessed.

For this scenario, assume that any external resources can only come from two specific URLs, `http://myWebServer.com` and `http://myDataServer.com`. Now perform the following steps:

1. To limit access, first define a new System.Net.WebPermission:

```
var permission = new WebPermission(PermissionState.None);
```

   This creates a `WebPermission` that, by default, blocks all external access.

2. Next, add your two exceptions:

```
permission.AddPermission(NetworkAccess.Connect, "http://myWebServer.com");
permission.AddPermission(NetworkAccess.Connect, "http://myDataServer.com");
```

3. Then add the `WebPermission` to a `PermissionSet`, which enables you to create different permissions with different criteria if necessary:

```
var permissionSet = new PermissionSet(PermissionSet.None);
permissionSet.AddPermission(permission);
```

   Again, the `PermissionSet` blocks everything by default. Then your `WebPermission` is added that allows access to your two safe URLs.

4. Finally, create the `XmlSecureResolver` and give it your `PermissionSet`:

```
var resolver = new XmlSecureResolver(new XmlUrlResolver(), permissionSet);
```

5. Once that is complete, you use the resolver as shown earlier:

```
var settings = new XmlReaderSettings();
settings.XmlResolver = resolver;
var reader = XmlReader.Create(xmlUri, settings);
```

SUMMARY

- There are two new methods for processing XML: SAX and .NET's `XmlReader`.
- SAX is an event-driven paradigm whereby the SAX parser fires events when different types of content are found. Registered listeners can react to these events.
- In `XmlReader` the programmer instigates moving through the document and stops when the target content is reached.

EXERCISES

Answers to the exercises can be found in Appendix A.

1. Add a `LexicalHandler` to the `SaxParser5` class so that you can read any comments in the `PeopleWithDTD.xml` file. Add some comments to test it out.

2. Write a working example that shows how to use `XmlSecureResolver` to limit file access to the local machine.

▶ WHAT YOU LEARNED IN THIS CHAPTER

TOPIC	KEY POINTS
The need for event-driven methods	Building an XML tree in memory consumes a lot of RAM. Large documents need a more efficient way of being processed.
SAX	Developed with Java in mind but available in many other languages, SAX is an interface that relies on events being fired as content is encountered when a document is read sequentially.
Features	Extra features, such as validation, can be configured by specifying them using the `setFeature(name, value)` method.
Properties	Properties, such as which handlers are registered, can be configured using the `setProperty(name, value)` method.
`XmlReader`	.NET's `XmlReader` also reads a document sequentially. However, it does not fire events but relies on the developer to pinpoint a target by specifying its features. For example: *Is it an element or an attribute? What is its name?*
`XmlReaderSettings`	Advanced options, such as wanting validation for an XML document, can be configured by using the `XmlReaderSettings` class which is then passed to the `XmlReader.Create()` method.
`XmlResolver`	Access to supplementary documents that are needed to complete processing of the XML, such as DTDs and external entities, is controlled via the `XmlResolver` used by `XmlReader`. For example, you can limit file access to specific locations using `XmlSecureResolver` combined with a `PermissionSet`.

12

LINQ to XML

WHAT YOU WILL LEARN IN THIS CHAPTER:

- What LINQ is and how it is used
- Why you need LINQ to XML
- The basic LINQ to XML process
- More advanced features of LINQ to XML
- XML Literals in .NET

So far you've seen a number of ways that you can read, process, and create XML. You can use the document object model (DOM), which loads the whole document into memory, or one of the streaming methods covered in the previous chapter, such as Microsoft's `XmlReader` or the SAX interface. This chapter presents yet another option, which unifies the task of interacting with XML with one of Microsoft's core programming technologies, LINQ.

WHAT IS LINQ?

One aim of most programming languages is to be consistent. One area in which most languages fail in this respect is querying. The codes to query a database, a collection of objects, and an XML file are radically different. Microsoft has tried to abstract the querying process so that these, and other data sources, can be treated in a similar fashion. To this end, Microsoft invented *Language Integrated Query*, or *LINQ*.

LINQ is loosely based on SQL (the standard way to query a relational database), but gives you two ways to specify your query. The first, and some would say easier of the two because it tries to imitate natural language, takes the following form:

```
from <range variable> in <collection>
where <predicate>
select <something using the range variable>
```

Here, `range variable` is a standard identifier that is used to refer to the items selected, `collection` is a collection of objects to be queried, and `predicate` is an expression that yields `true` or `false` to determine whether to include the objects in the final results. It's not essential to have a predicate, and you can also incorporate ordering, grouping, and all the standard operations you may need. For a concrete example, take the simple task of extracting the even numbers from an array (these examples are in C#, although there's little difference from VB.NET or other .NET languages):

```
// Define an array of integers
int[] numbers = new int[10] { 0, 1, 2, 3, 4, 5, 6, 7, 8, 9};

var evenNumbers =
                      from num in numbers
                      where (num % 2) == 0
                      select num;
```

Here the range variable is `num`, the collection is an array of numbers named `numbers`, and the predicate is `(num % 2) == 0`. (The remainder after dividing by two is zero; in other words, the number is even.)

With LINQ, the query isn't executed immediately. For now, `evenNumbers` holds the details of the query, not the actual results. The query will actually run when the results are used as shown in the following snippet:

```
// Define an array of integers
int[] numbers = new int[10] { 0, 1, 2, 3, 4, 5, 6, 7, 8, 9};

var evenNumbers =
                      from num in numbers
                      where (num % 2) == 0
                      select num;
// Output the even numbers to the console
// This will actually execute the LINQ operation
foreach(int number in evenNumbers)
{
  Console.WriteLine(number);
}
```

If you execute this code in the debugger and step through it line by line, you'll see that the LINQ operation doesn't execute until the `foreach` loop outputs the results.

Using keywords to define the query is a very similar process across all the .NET languages. It has the advantage of being easy to read, but unfortunately many LINQ operations don't have keywords associated with them. That's why there's another way of specifying a query: using standard method syntax. In standard method syntax, the preceding example would now look like this:

```
// Define an array of integers
int[] numbers = new int[10] { 0, 1, 2, 3, 4, 5, 6, 7, 8, 9};

var evenNumbers = numbers.Where(num => num % 2 == 0);
// Output the even numbers to the console
// This will actually execute the LINQ operation
```

```
foreach(int number in evenNumbers)
{
  Console.WriteLine(number);
}
```

This time you just use an extension method, `Where()`, which takes a lambda expression as its argument. This lambda expression is equivalent to the predicate used in the first example.

NOTE *Because this chapter delves into LINQ only for the purpose of processing XML, it doesn't cover the background topics of expression trees, lambdas, extension methods, and implicitly typed local variables, which are all part of how LINQ works. If you want to learn more about these topics, go to* `http://www.4guysfromrolla.com/articles/021809-1.aspx.`

So far you've seen how you can query a locally-defined array. If this were all you could do with LINQ, it wouldn't be worth the trouble. However, LINQ can also deal with queries against database objects using, among other things, either *LINQ to SQL* or *LINQ to Entities*. Following is a sample query that (after you have set up the required database connection) queries for all customers who live in the USA:

```
// Get database context by opening the SQL Server mdf file
var northwind = new Northwind("Northwnd.mdf");
var customersInUSA = from customer in northwind.Customers
                     where customer.Country == "USA"
                     select customer;
// Do something with customersInUSA
```

This book doesn't cover the intricacies of how the `northwind` object is created from the database file, but you can see how the actual query has the same format as the one that processed the integer array.

You've seen in this section how LINQ can cope with many different types of collections; strictly speaking though, LINQ doesn't work against collections, it operates against the `IEnumerable<T>` interface. This interface represents any collection of objects that can be enumerated and contain objects of type `T`. Any collection that implements this interface then acquires all the methods, such as `Where()`, `OrderBy()`, and so on, that are defined using *extension methods* (methods that are added to the class using external assemblies). The reason LINQ to XML works is that the classes it exposes implement `IEnumerable<T>`, enabling you to use the same syntax for querying as you use against other data sources.

This is the beauty of LINQ. It means that when you work with collections you always use a similar syntax to query them, and this applies to XML as well. At this stage, though, you may be asking yourself, "Why do I need yet another way of working with XML? I already have a number of other options." The following section explains the importance of this new method.

Why You Need LINQ to XML

LINQ to XML is a useful addition to your XML armory for several reasons, spelled out in the following list:

- LINQ to XML enables you to use a similar technique to query a wide variety of data sources.
- LINQ to XML offers a way to extract data from an XML document that is much easier than both the DOM and the streaming/event-driven styles of .NET's XmlReader and SAX (which were covered in the previous chapter).

LINQ to XML offers a new way of creating XML documents that is easier than using the DOM or an *XmlWriter*, including a simple way to deal with namespaces that mimics how they are declared in XML. It is recommended that if you are developing in .NET and have to extract information from an XML document, your default choice should be LINQ to XML. You should choose some other way only if there is a good reason to—for example, the document is too large to load into memory and needs one of the streaming handlers. These advantages are discussed in greater detail later in this chapter, but first you need to learn how to use LINQ to XML.

Using LINQ to XML

Now that you know a little about LINQ and why it might be a good choice for reading or creating XML, this section shows you how LINQ works in practice.

NOTE *The examples in this chapter are in both C# and VB.NET. If you want to run them and don't have the full version of Visual Studio installed you can download the free edition, Visual Studio Express, at* `http://www.microsoft.com/visualstudio/en-us/products/2010-editions/express`. *You need to separately install both the C# and the VB version. These examples were tested against the 2010 versions but the newer 2011 version should work, although the user interface may be slightly different. If you do stick with the 2010 version you will also need to install Service Pack 1, available at:* `http://www.microsoft.com/download/en/details.aspx?displaylang=en&id=23691`. *Refer to the introduction of this book for more details on installing Visual Studio.*

Often, with LINQ to XML tutorials, you're presented with a sample XML document and shown how to query it. You're going to do the opposite here: you'll see how to create an XML document using what is known as *functional construction*. The standard way of creating XML using the document object model is to create the root element and then append whatever child elements and attributes are needed. A small sample in C# that creates an XML file describing a music collection is shown here:

Available for download on Wrox.com

```
XmlDocument doc = new XmlDocument();
XmlElement root = doc.CreateElement("musicLibrary");
doc.DocumentElement = root;
XmlElement cd = doc.CreateElement("cd");
cd.SetAttribute("id", "1");
XmlElement title = doc.CreateElement("title");
title.InnerText = "Parallel Lines";
cd.AppendChild(title);
XmlElement year = doc.CreateElement("year");
year.InnerText = "2001";
cd.AppendChild(year);
XmlElement artist = doc.CreateElement("artist");
artist.InnerText = "Blondie";
cd.AppendChild(artist);
XmlElement genre = doc.CreateElement("genre");
genre.InnerText = "New Wave";
cd.AppendChild(genre);
doc.DocumentElement.AppendChild(cd);
// Add more <cd> elements
```

Program.cs in XmlDocumentDemo project

The preceding code adds one <cd> element with its attributes and children to the collection. By repeating the code, other <cd> elements can be added to form the complete music collection. You will end up with the file shown in Listing 12-1:

Available for download on Wrox.com

LISTING 12-1: MusicLibrary.xml

```
<musicLibrary>
  <cd id="1">
    <title>Parallel Lines</title>
    <year>2001</year>
    <artist>Blondie</artist>
    <genre>New Wave</genre>
  </cd>
  <cd id="2">
    <title>Bat Out of Hell</title>
    <year>2001</year>
    <artist>Meatloaf</artist>
    <genre>Rock</genre>
  </cd>
  <cd id="3">
    <title>Abbey Road</title>
    <year>1987</year>
    <artist>The Beatles</artist>
    <genre>Rock</genre>
  </cd>
  <cd id="4">
    <title>The Dark Side of the Moon</title>
    <year>1994</year>
    <artist>Pink Floyd</artist>
    <genre>Rock</genre>
```

continues

LISTING 12-1 *(continued)*

```
  </cd>
  <cd id="5">
    <title>Thriller</title>
    <year>2001</year>
    <artist>Michael Jackson</artist>
    <genre>Pop</genre>
  </cd>
</musicLibrary>
```

Although this code gets the job done, it's not particularly easy to read and it's quite long-winded, having to create, set, and append values for every element. LINQ to XML's functional approach is shorter and more legible, as shown here:

Available for download on Wrox.com

```
XElement musicLibrary =
        new XElement("musicLibrary",
          new XElement("cd",
            new XAttribute("id", 1),
            new XElement("title", "Parallel Lines"),
            new XElement("year", 2001),
            new XElement("artist", "Blondie"),
            new XElement("genre", "New Wave")));
```

Program.cs in BasicDocumentCreation project

This code uses classes form the `System.Linq.Xml` namespace. The basic building blocks in this library are `XElement` and `XAttribute`. The first one, `XElement`, has an overloaded constructor; two of the most commonly used constructors take the name of the element, or more technically an `XName`, followed by its content or an array of content objects. The full definitions of these two overloads are:

```
public XElement(XName name, object content);
public XElement(XName name, params object[] content);
```

For the `XName` you can just use a string, which is automatically cast to an `XName`. The content is defined as an object, so you can either have a simple value such as a string, or include other `XElements` and `XAttributes`. The only thing you have to worry about is making sure your parentheses match, and this is fairly easy if you indent the code to follow the actual structure of the XML you are aiming to create.

You don't have to create a document from scratch, of course. You can also load it from a file, a URL, an XmlReader, or a string value. To load from a file or URL, use the static `Load()` method:

```
XElement musicLibrary.Load(@"C:\XML\musicLibrary.xml") ;
```

or

```
XElement musicLibrary.Load(@"http://www.wrox.com/samples/XML/musicLibrary.xml") ;
```

If you want to turn a string into an XML document, use the static `Parse()` method (shown in the following code snippet), which takes the string to convert to XML as its argument:

```
XElement musicLibrary = XElement.Parse(
@"<musicLibrary>
    <cd id="1">
      <title>Parallel Lines</title>
      <year>2001</year>
      <artist>Blondie</artist>
      <genre>New Wave</genre>
    </cd>
    <!-- more <cd> elements here -->
  </musicLibrary") ;
```

The next section takes you a bit further into using LINQ to XML with an introduction to creating documents using XDocument class.

CREATING DOCUMENTS

So far you've seen the XElement and the XAttribute classes. You may be wondering why you haven't used an XDocument class; after all, if you create an XML document using the DOM you need to make heavy use of the DomDocument. This is where LINQ to XML and the DOM differ most. LINQ to XML does have an XDocument class, but you don't have to use it; most of the time you just use the XElement class to load XML or build elements. However, in some instances the XDocument class is invaluable.

The XDocument class is useful when you need to add some metadata to the XML document—an XML declaration, for example—or when you want a comment or processing instruction to appear before the document element. Say you want the standard XML declaration declaring that the version is 1.0, the encoding is UTF-8, and that the document is standalone. Following is the output you're looking for:

```
<?xml version="1.0" encoding="utf-8" standalone="yes"?>
```

You achieve this by first using the XDocument class at the top level, and then by using the XDeclaration class, which takes three parameters to represent the version, the encoding, and the value for the standalone attribute. See the following example:

Available for download on Wrox.com

```
XDocument musicLibrary =
  new XDocument(
    new XDeclaration("1.0", "utf-8", "yes"),
      new XElement("musicLibrary",
        new XElement("cd",
        new XAttribute("id", 1),
        new XElement("title", "Parallel Lines"),
        new XElement("year", 2001),
        new XElement("artist", "Blondie"),
        new XElement("genre", "New Wave"))));
```

Program.cs in project BasicXDocumentUse

WARNING *There is a slight problem with the previous code snippet: the* `ToString()` *method used to display the XML ignores the declaration. To see it you'll have to insert a breakpoint and examine the object in the Locals window.*

If you want to add a comment, use the `XComment` class like so:

```
XDocument musicLibrary =
  new XDocument(
    new XDeclaration("1.0", "utf-8", "yes"),
      new XComment("This document holds details of my music collection"),
      new XElement("musicLibrary",
        new XElement("cd",
        new XAttribute("id", 1),
        new XElement("title", "Parallel Lines"),
        new XElement("year", 2001),
        new XElement("artist", "Blondie"),
        new XElement("genre", "New Wave"))));
```

This leads to the following document:

```
<?xml version="1.0" encoding="utf-8" standalone="yes"?>
<!-- This document holds details of my music collection -->
<musicLibrary>
  <cd id="1">
    <title>Parallel Lines</title>
    <year>2001</year>
    <artist>Blondie</artist>
    <genre>New Wave</genre>
  </cd>
</musicLibrary>
```

Finally, you can also use the `XProcessingInstruction` in a similar way. For example, if you want to associate an XSL transformation with the document you'd use the following code:

```
XDocument musicLibrary =
  new XDocument(
    new XDeclaration("1.0", "utf-8", "yes"),
      new XProcessingInstruction("xml-stylesheet", "href='music.xslt'"),
      new XComment("This document holds details of my music collection"),
      new XElement("musicLibrary",
        new XElement("cd",
        new XAttribute("id", 1),
        new XElement("title", "Parallel Lines"),
        new XElement("year", 2001),
        new XElement("artist", "Blondie"),
        new XElement("genre", "New Wave"))));
```

This code produces the following result:

```
<?xml version="1.0" encoding="utf-8" standalone="yes"?>
<?xml-stylesheet href='music.xslt'?>
<!-- This document holds details of my music collection -->
<musicLibrary>
  <cd id="1">
    <title>Parallel Lines</title>
    <year>2001</year>
    <artist>Blondie</artist>
    <genre>New Wave</genre>
  </cd>
</musicLibrary>
```

So far the documents you have created have all been free of namespaces. What happens when you need to create elements or attributes that belong to a particular namespace? The next section addresses this situation.

Creating Documents with Namespaces

Creating elements in namespaces is always a little trickier than those without one, whatever programmatic method you are using. LINQ to XML tries to make it as easy as possible by having a separate class, `XNamespace`, that can be used to declare and apply a namespace to an element or an attribute.

To create a document with a namespace, perform the following steps:

1. Create a new version of the music library, one where the elements are all under the namespace `http://www.wrox.com/namespaces/apps/musicLibrary`.
2. Make this the default namespace (don't use a prefix; all elements in the document will automatically belong under this namespace). The document you're aiming to create looks like this:

```
<musicLibrary xmlns="http://www.wrox.com/namespaces/apps/musicLibrary">
  <cd id="1">
    <title>Parallel Lines</title>
    <year>2001</year>
    <artist>Blondie</artist>
    <genre>New Wave</genre>
  </cd>
  < !-- more cd elements -->
</musicLibrary>
```

3. To accomplish this, use the `XNamespace` class to declare and apply the namespace as in the following snippet:

```
XNamespace ns = "http://www.wrox.com/namespaces/apps/musicLibrary" ;
XElement musicLibrary =
    new XElement(ns + "musicLibrary",
      new XElement(ns + "cd",
        new XAttribute("id", 1),
```

```
            new XElement(ns + "title", "Parallel Lines"),
            new XElement(ns + "year", 2001),
            new XElement(ns + "artist", "Blondie"),
            new XElement(ns + "genre", "New Wave")));
```

Program.cs in DocumentWithDefaultNamespace project

Notice how the `XNamespace` class doesn't use a constructor; you simply set the namespace URI as a string. When you create elements that belong in a namespace (in this example they all do), you concatenate the namespace with the actual name. `XNamespace`'s class overrides the plus (+) operator so that this action doesn't merge the two strings, but creates a true namespaced element.

Creating Documents with Prefixed Namespaces

The code for using a prefixed namespace is quite similar to the code for a default namespace; the main difference is that you need to use the `XAttribute` class to define your namespace URI to prefix mapping like so:

Available for download on Wrox.com

```
XNamespace ns = "http://www.wrox.com/namespaces/apps/musicLibrary";
XElement musicLibrary =
  new XElement(ns + "musicLibrary",
    new XAttribute(XNamespace.Xmlns + "ns", ns.NamespaceName),
      new XElement(ns + "cd",
      new XAttribute("id", 1),
      new XElement(ns + "title", "Parallel Lines"),
      new XElement(ns + "year", 2001),
      new XElement(ns + "artist", "Blondie"),
      new XElement(ns + "genre", "New Wave")));
```

The highlighted line uses the `XAttribute` class and a static member of the `XNamespace` class, `Xmlns`, to create the familiar `xmlns:ns="http://www.wrox.com/namespaces/apps/musicLibrary"` code on the root element. Now that LINQ to XML knows the namespace URI is bound to the prefix `ns`, all the elements in this namespace will automatically be given this prefix. The subsequent document looks like this:

```
<ns:musicLibrary xmlns:ns="http://www.wrox.com/namespaces/apps/musicLibrary">
  <ns:cd id="1">
    <ns:title>Parallel Lines</ns:title>
    <ns:year>2001</ns:year>
    <ns:artist>Blondie</ns:artist>
    <ns:genre>New Wave</ns:genre>
  </ns:cd>
  <!-- more cd elements -->
</ns:musicLibrary>
```

So far you've seen how to create documents from scratch and how to load them from an existing source. The next section covers how to extract data from an XML document.

EXTRACTING DATA FROM AN XML DOCUMENT

This section looks at some common scenarios that involve loading an existing XML file and retrieving specific parts of it. For the following activity, you load `MusicLibrary.xml` and display a list of all the CD titles. For this you'll be making use of the `Elements()` method.

TRY IT OUT Extracting Data Using the Elements() Method

This Try It Out introduces the `Elements()` method which is used to retrieve elements and their contents. You start by loading an existing file and then see how to navigate to the specific content you need, in this case the `<title>` elements of your CDs.

1. To start, create a new C# Console Application project in Visual Studio and name it `BasicDataExtraction`. This step is shown in Figure 12-1:

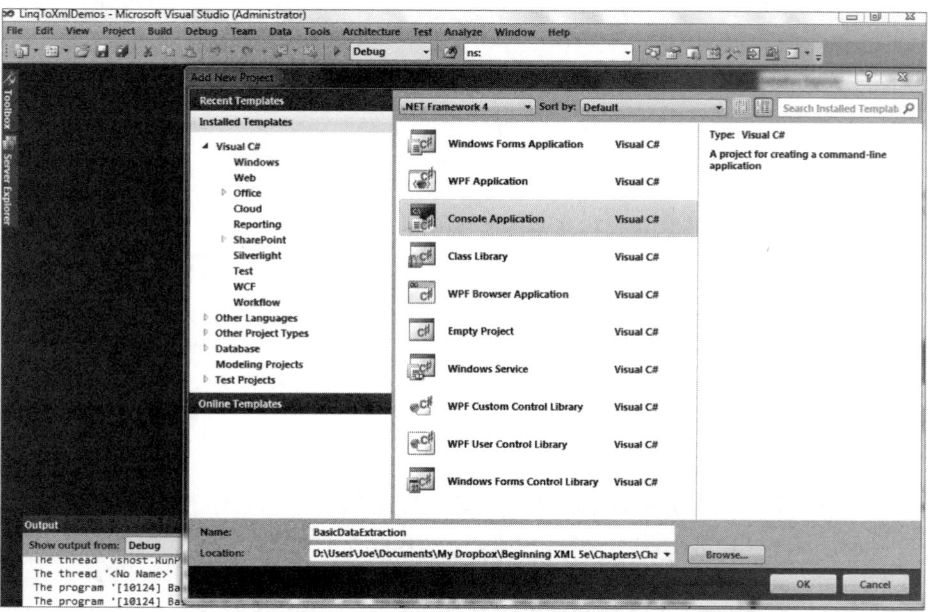

FIGURE 12-1

2. Next, add the `MusicLibrary.xml` file to the project as an existing item. Do this by right-clicking the project in the Solution Explorer and choosing Add ➪ Existing Item . . . and browsing to the file. You can find this file in the code download for the chapter (the project is also included there if you just want to test the code).

3. After you add this file, right-click it in the Solution Explorer and choose Properties. In the Properties window, find the Copy to Output Directory setting and change this to Copy if Newer. This ensures that the file ends up in the same directory as the executable, and means you can refer to it in code by just its name, rather than the full path.

4. Now open `program.cs`. Delete all the code that it currently contains, and replace it with the following:

Available for download on Wrox.com

```
using System;
using System.Xml.Linq;

namespace BasicDataExtraction
{
  class Program
  {
    static void Main(string[] args)
    {
      XElement musicLibrary = XElement.Load(@"MusicLibrary.xml");
      ShowTitles(musicLibrary);
      Console.ReadLine();
    }

    static void ShowTitles(XElement musicLibrary)
    {
      foreach (XElement t in musicLibrary.Elements("cd").Elements("title"))
      {
        Console.WriteLine(t.Value);
      }
    }
  }
}
```

Program.cs in BasicDataExtraction project

5. Save the file and press F5 to run the application. You should see a console window pop up, as shown in Figure 12-2:

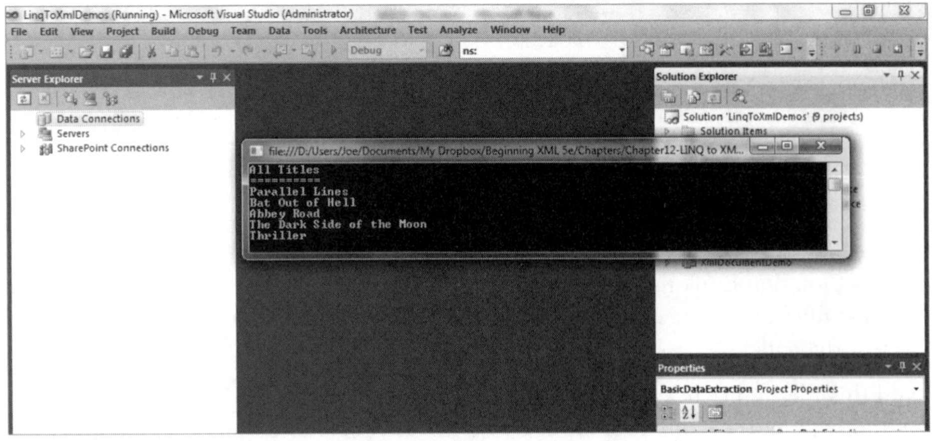

FIGURE 12-2

How It Works

To use LINQ to XML features, you need a reference to the `System.Xml.Linq.dll` assembly. This is added automatically to the project when it is created, but you still need to add the second `using` statement shown in the following snippet to be able to use the short form of the class names (that is, `XElement` instead of `System.Xml.Linq.XElement`) and, more importantly, to be able to access the LINQ extension methods:

```
using System;
using System.Xml.Linq;
```

The `Main()` method is the initial entry point for the application. You use the static `Load()` method of `XElement` to load the music library:

```
static void Main(string[] args)
{
  XElement musicLibrary = XElement.Load(@"MusicLibrary.xml");
```

After that, the `XElement`, `musicLibrary`, is passed to the `ShowTitles()` method:

```
{
  static void Main(string[] args)
  {
    XElement musicLibrary = XElement.Load(@"MusicLibrary.xml");
    ShowTitles(musicLibrary);
```

The `ShowTitles()` method uses the `Elements()` method twice. This method has two variations, one with no parameters and the other with the name of an element. If you don't pass it a parameter, it returns all the children of the element; if you pass the name of an element, it returns all elements with that name. In the following code you have specified the children named `cd`, then used `Elements()` again to extract the `<title>` elements:

```
  static void ShowTitles(XElement musicLibrary)
  {
    foreach (XElement t in musicLibrary.Elements("cd").Elements("title"))
    {
      Console.WriteLine(t.Value);
    }
  }
}
```

Once the `<title>` elements are found, you loop through all of them using a standard `foreach` and output the value of each. This equates to the text within the element.

Because there is a `Console.ReadLine()` call at the end of the `Main()` method, you'll need to press a key, such as the space bar or Enter, to dismiss the console window.

***NOTE** Technically, the two uses of `Elements()` in the previous activity use different methods. The first use involves a built-in method of `XElement`. The second is an extension method on the collection of elements returned. This method is found in the `System.Xml.Linq` namespace. This extension method works because the collection implements `IEnumerable<T>`, as discussed in the "What Is LINQ?" section earlier in the chapter.*

The `Elements()` method solely navigates down the child axis. Chapter 7, which covered XPath, also described the other axes that can be traversed, and many of these have corresponding methods in LINQ to XML. For example, instead of using the `Elements()` method, you could use `Descendants()`, which retrieves all descendants rather than just the immediate ones. The code from the previous activity would look like the following if you used `Descendants()` instead of `Elements()`:

```
    static void ShowTitles(XElement musicLibrary)
    {
      foreach (XElement t in musicLibrary.Descendants("title"))
      {
        Console.WriteLine(t.Value);
      }
    }
  }
```

It's preferable from a performance point of view to use the `Elements()` method rather than `Descendants()` if you can, because you typically want to only search specifically in the child axis. Sometimes though, you can make the search more generic by using the `Descendants()` method, and for small documents the gains in performance are going to be tiny anyway. Alongside the `Descendants()` method you can also find `DescendantNodes()`. `DescendantNodes()` differs from `Descendants()` in that it finds any nodes, comments, processing instructions, and so on, whereas the `Descendant()` returns only elements. Note that none of the methods discussed so far include attributes in the collections they return. If you want to examine these you'll need either the `Attributes()` method to fetch all attributes or the `Attribute(`*`attributeName`*`)` method, whereby you can specify the name of the attribute you're interested in.

A selection of the more commonly used methods is shown in Table 12-1.

TABLE 12-1: Common Axis Traversal Methods in LINQ to XML

METHOD NAME	DESCRIPTION
`Ancestors*`	Returns all the ancestor elements.
`AncestorsAndSelf*`	Returns all Ancestors but includes the current element.
`Attributes*`	Returns the attributes of the current element.

METHOD NAME	DESCRIPTION
`Descendants*`	Returns elements that are descendants of the current element.
`DescendantsAndSelf*`	Returns all Descendants but includes the current element.
`DescendantNodes*`	Returns all Descendants but includes other node types such as comments (but not attributes).
`Elements*`	Returns child elements of the current element.
`ElementsAfterSelf*`	Returns a collection of sibling elements that come after this element in document order.
`ElementsBeforeSelf*`	Returns a collection of sibling elements that come before this element in document order.
`Nodes`	Returns any child nodes of this element.
`NodesAfterSelf`	Returns any sibling nodes that come after this element in document order.
`NodesBeforeSelf`	Returns any sibling nodes that come before this element in document order.

* Those marked with an asterisk can also take a parameter specifying a name. Only nodes that match the name will be included in the return value.

The methods that include `Before` or `After` are used when you need to get elements based on their document order. For example, suppose you have a reference to the `<cd>` element that has an `id` of 3 and you want to display the titles of all the `<cd>` elements before that in document order. The following code retrieves the third `<cd>` element to do just that:

```
static void ShowTitlesBefore(XElement musicLibrary)
{
  XElement cd3 = (from cd in musicLibrary.Elements("cd")
                  where cd.Attribute("id").Value == "3"
                  select cd).FirstOrDefault();
  // code continued
}
```

This example uses the built-in LINQ keywords rather than the functional style. First, you select all the `<cd>` elements, then you test the `id` attribute to see if it equals 3.

Once you have a reference to the `<cd>` element you want, use the `ElementsBeforeSelf()` method to retrieve the preceding `<cd>` elements and their `<title>` elements as shown in the following snippet:

Available for download on Wrox.com

```
static void ShowTitlesBefore(XElement musicLibrary)
{
  XElement cd3 = (from cd in musicLibrary.Elements("cd")
                  where cd.Attribute("id").Value == "3"
```

```
                    select cd).FirstOrDefault();
    foreach (XElement t in cd3.ElementsBeforeSelf("cd").Elements("title"))
    {
      Console.WriteLine(t.Value);
    }
  }
```

Program.cs in BasicDataExtraction project

You then loop through the collection and display the `Value` of each `<title>` as before. The code displays the titles for the `<cd>` element that have an `id` of 1 and 2.

The next example uses the functional style to show all the titles after the third `<cd>`. It also uses `ElementsAfterSelf()` to find the siblings after the third CD in the document:

```
static void ShowTitlesAfter(XElement musicLibrary)
{
  XElement cd3 = musicLibrary.Elements("cd")
              .Where(cd => cd.Attribute("id").Value == "3")
              .FirstOrDefault();
    foreach (XElement t in cd3.ElementsAfterSelf("cd").Elements("title"))
    {
      Console.WriteLine(t.Value);
    }
  }
```

Program.cs in BasicDataExtraction project

Selecting elements based on an attribute can be a bit mundane, but there are more advanced features of LINQ, especially as they apply to XML. One of these features is *grouping*. A common requirement when processing any data is to group items based on a specific property. For example, you might want to group your CDs based on their genre. You can use the standard LINQ operators to accomplish this task, which can be broken down into two parts. First, you group the `<cd>` elements based on the `<genre>` element as shown in the following code:

```
static void GroupOnGenre(XElement musicLibrary)
{
  var groupQuery = from cd in musicLibrary.Elements("cd")
                   group cd by cd.Element("genre").Value into genreGroup
                   orderby genreGroup.Key
                   select new
                   {
                     Genre = genreGroup.Key,
                     Titles = from title in genreGroup.Elements("title")
                             select title.Value
                   };
  // code continues
}
```

Here you select the <cd> elements as before, but add a group operator that uses the <genre> element's `Value` as the property to group on. The results are held in `genreGroup`. They are then ordered using the built-in `Key` property of any grouping variable created using LINQ; in this case the `Key` holds the genre value. Using `genreGroup` you create an anonymous type that has two members. The first, `Genre`, is filled using the same `Key` property that was used for sorting. The second member, `Titles`, uses a second LINQ query to extract all the <title> elements.

The second part of the function is used to output the results as shown in the following code snippet:

Available for download on Wrox.com

```
static void GroupOnGenre(XElement musicLibrary)
{
  var groupQuery = from cd in musicLibrary.Elements("cd")
                   group cd by cd.Element("genre").Value into genreGroup
                   orderby genreGroup.Key
                   select new
                   {
                     Genre = genreGroup.Key,
                     Titles = from title in genreGroup.Elements("title")
                              select title.Value
                   };
  foreach (var entry in groupQuery)
  {
    Console.WriteLine(«Genre: {0}», entry.Genre);
    Console.WriteLine(«----------------»);
    foreach (var title in entry.Titles)
    {
      Console.WriteLine(«\t{0}», title);
    }
    Console.WriteLine();
  }
}
```

Program.cs in BasicDataExtraction project

The outer-level `foreach` loops through all items in the `groupQuery`, which contains a collection of your anonymous types. The code then outputs the `Genre` property and uses a second `foreach` to loop through the `Titles` collection to show each `Title` in the group.

If you add the `ShowTitlesBefore()`, `ShowTitlesAfter()` and `GroupOnGenre()` methods to the original `Program.cs` file, underneath the `ShowTitles()` method and press F5 to run the code, you will see the results shown in Figure 12-3.

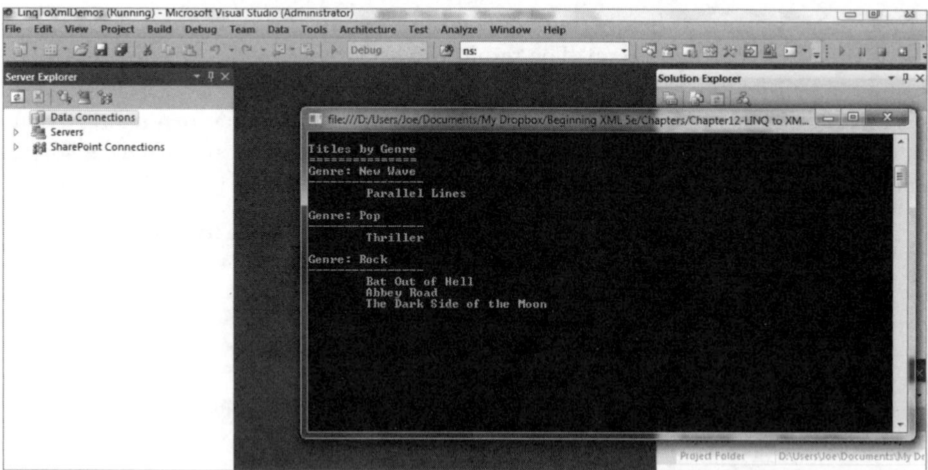

FIGURE 12-3

You have seen how to extract nodes and their values from a document. The next feature of LINQ to XML to investigate is how to modify an XML document.

MODIFYING DOCUMENTS

LINQ to XML has a plethora of methods that enable you to modify an existing XML document. This means that you can add new nodes, delete existing ones, and update values such as attributes and text content.

Adding Content to a Document

One of the most common operations is to add a new node. You can try this by adding a new `<cd>` element to your music library. To do so, perform the following steps:

1. First, use the following code to create a reusable method that returns a new `<cd> XElement` once it has passed the relevant values such as `id`, `title`, and `year`:

Available for download on Wrox.com

```
static XElement CreateCDElement(string id,
                                string title,
                                int year,
                                string artist,
                                string genre)
{
  return new XElement("cd",
          new XAttribute("id", id),
          new XElement("title", title),
          new XElement("year", year),
          new XElement("artist", artist),
          new XElement("genre", genre));
```

This method just mimics the code you saw earlier that had the values hard-coded.

2. Next use the `XElement`'s `Add()` method to append the new element to the existing `<cd>` elements like so:

```
static void AddNewCD(XElement musicLibrary)
{
  XElement cd = CreateCDElement("6", "Back in Black", 2003, "AC/DC", "Rock");
  musicLibrary.Add(cd);
}
```

Program.cs in ModifyingDocuments project

The result of this code is to make the example music file now look like the following:

```
<musicLibrary>
  <cd id="1">
    <title>Parallel Lines</title>
    <year>2001</year>
    <artist>Blondie</artist>
    <genre>New Wave</genre>
  </cd>
  <!-- cd elements 2, 3 and 4 -->
  <cd id="5">
    <title>Thriller</title>
    <year>2001</year>
    <artist>Michael Jackson</artist>
    <genre>Pop</genre>
  </cd>
  <cd id="6">
    <title>Back in Black</title>
    <year>2003</year>
    <artist>AC/DC</artist>
    <genre>Rock</genre>
  </cd>
</musicLibrary>
```

The `Add()` method is quite flexible. As well as specifying the node you want to add (as was done in the previous code example), you can also pass in a functionally constructed tree. You might want to do this if you are adding different elements and don't want to bother constructing a function that creates each one. The following code produces the same result as before, but doesn't use the helper function `CreateNewCD()`:

```
static void AddNewCDDirectly(XElement musicLibrary)
{
  musicLibrary.Add(
      new XElement("cd",
        new XAttribute("id", 6),
        new XElement("title", "Back in Black"),
        new XElement("year", 2003),
        new XElement("artist", "AC/DC"),
        new XElement("genre", "Rock")));
}
```

When you add an XElement to a document there is a lot going on behind the scenes. An XElement has a Parent property. When you first create the XElement, this property is set to null. When you use the Add() method, the Parent is set to the node that the Add() method was called from. So in all the previous examples the Parent property is set to the <musicLibrary> element.

Removing Content from a Document

Now that you've seen how to add content, try the opposite: removing content. The easiest way to accomplish this is to navigate to the node you want to delete and call its Remove() method. See the following example:

```
static void RemoveCD(XElement musicLibrary)
{
  XElement cd = (from entry in musicLibrary.Elements("cd")
                 where entry.Attribute("id").Value == "6"
                 select entry).FirstOrDefault();
  if (null != cd)
  {
    cd.Remove();
  }
}
```

This code first targets the <cd> that has an id of 6, which is the <cd> you just added with the AddNewCD() method. The code then calls the Remove() method, which leaves you with just five <cd> elements in your library.

The Remove() method also works on sets of elements. The following snippet removes all of the <cd> elements from the document:

```
musicLibrary.Elements("cd").Remove();
```

Updating and Replacing Existing Content in a Document

The last technique is how to update an existing document. Two operations need to be carried out on a regular basis: one is updating data within the document (either the value of an attribute or the text content of an element); and the second is replacing an entire element or tree of elements.

You have quite a few ways to update the text content of an element. One way is to use the ReplaceNodes() method, which replaces the nodes of the XElement it is called from. Suppose you want to update the <year> element of the *Abbey Road* CD, which has an id of 3. The following code finds this element and changes the year to 1986:

```
static void UpdateYearWithReplaceNodes(XElement musicLibrary)
{
  XElement cd = (from entry in musicLibrary.Elements("cd")
                 where entry.Attribute("id").Value == "3"
                 select entry).FirstOrDefault();
  cd.Element("year").ReplaceNodes("1986");
}
```

ReplaceNodes() also works with trees of nodes and just simple text content.

A second way to update the text is to use the `SetElementValue()` method like so:

```
static void UpdateYearWithSetElementValue(XElement musicLibrary)
{
  XElement cd = (from entry in musicLibrary.Elements("cd")
                 where entry.Attribute("id").Value == "3"
                 select entry).FirstOrDefault();
  cd.SetElementValue("year", "1987");
}
```

Again, you single out the target element using a standard LINQ query and then use `SetElementValue()` on the parent of the element you want to change. This method also has other uses. You can remove an element completely by setting the second argument to `null`. You can also create new elements. If the `<year>` element hadn't existed already for the `<cd>` you chose, it would have been created automatically by the code.

There is a similar technique to update, create, or remove an attribute's value name: `SetAttributeValue()`. If you want to update the `id` of the *Abbey Road* `<cd>` element, the following code will accomplish that:

```
static void UpdateAttributeValue(XElement musicLibrary)
{
  XElement cd = (from entry in musicLibrary.Elements("cd")
                 where entry.Attribute("id").Value == "3"
                 select entry).FirstOrDefault();
  cd.SetAttributeValue("id", "7");
}
```

The last method to look at is `ReplaceContent()`. This replaces the currently chosen node with the specified XML. For example, if you want to replace the first `<cd>` in the collection with a different one altogether, you'd use `ReplaceContent()` as follows:

```
static void ReplaceCD(XElement musicLibrary)
{
  XElement cd = (from entry in musicLibrary.Elements("cd")
                 where entry.Attribute("id").Value == "1"
                 select entry).FirstOrDefault();

  cd.ReplaceWith( new XElement("cd",
                    new XAttribute("id", 1),
                    new XElement("title", "Back in Black"),
                    new XElement("year", 2003),
                    new XElement("artist", "AC/DC"),
                    new XElement("genre", "Rock")));
}
```

This targets the first `<cd>` element, then calls `ReplaceContent()` and passes in a new tree.

In Chapter 8 you saw how you can use XSLT to change the format of an XML document. The output of a transformation might be a differently formatted XML or a text document.

TRANSFORMING DOCUMENTS

Using a combination of the techniques you've seen so far, it's possible to transform an XML document to a different format using LINQ to XML. In general, it's not as powerful as using XSLT, but has the advantage of being simpler for a lot of transformations and precludes the need to learn a completely different programming paradigm.

The following Try It Out takes you through the steps of transforming your current music library to a different format.

TRY IT OUT Transformations Using LINQ to XML

Currently musicLibrary.xml is element-centric, meaning, other than the id attribute on the <cd> element, the data is in the form of elements. This Try It Out shows you how to use LINQ to XML to turn the file into an attribute-centric one whereby each of the <cd> elements will look like this:

```
<newMusicLibrary>
  <cd id="1" year="2001" artist="Blondie" genre="New Wave">Parallel Lines</cd>
  <!-- nore cd elements -->
</newMusicLibrary>
```

Basically, all the properties of the <cd> element, except the title, are now defined by attributes. The title itself is just text content.

1. The first step is to create a new console application in Visual Studio as you did earlier. Name the project TransformingXml.

2. Once this project has been created, add the current musicLibrary.xml as before, and again find the Copy to Output Directory setting and change this to Copy if Newer.

3. Open program.cs from the Solution Explorer and replace the current using statements with the following three:

```
using System;
using System.Linq;
using System.Xml.Linq;
```

   These steps are all you need to make sure you can use both the standard LINQ keywords and the classes from LINQ to XML, such as XElement.

4. Next, replace the Main() method with the one shown here:

```
static void Main(string[] args)
{
  XElement musicLibrary = XElement.Load(@"MusicLibrary.xml");
  XElement newMusicLibrary = TransformToAttributes(musicLibrary);
  Console.WriteLine(newMusicLibrary);
  newMusicLibrary.Save(@"newMusicLibrary.xml");
  Console.ReadLine();
}
```

This code loads the music library XML and passes it to the `TransformToAttributes()` method. This method returns a new `XElement` containing the new format that was desired. The new XML will be written to the console and also saved to a new file named `newMusicLibrary.xml` when the code is run.

The method that does all the actual work is as follows:

```
static XElement TransformToAttributes(XElement musicLibrary)
{
  XElement newMusicLibrary =
    new XElement("newMusicLibrary",
                 from cd in musicLibrary.Elements("cd")
                 select new XElement("cd",
                   new XAttribute("id", cd.Attribute("id").Value),
                   new XAttribute("year", cd.Element("year").Value),
                   new XAttribute("artist", cd.Element("artist").Value),
                   new XAttribute("genre", cd.Element("genre").Value),
                   cd.Element("title").Value));
  return newMusicLibrary;
}
```

5. You can now run the project by pressing F5. The console window should show the new style XML and, if you look in the `bin\debug` folder underneath where `program.cs` is held, you should find a file named `newMusicLibrary.xml`, which is in the new format.

How It Works

`TransformToAttributes()` works by initially creating an `XElement`. The content of the new element is created by first finding all the current `<cd>` elements like so:

```
from cd in musicLibrary.Elements("cd")
```

It then selects each one and forms a new style `<cd>` element that uses the values from the old element—its `id` attribute and elements—to create a set of attributes and some plain text content like so:

```
select new XElement("cd",
  new XAttribute("id", cd.Attribute("id").Value),
  new XAttribute("year", cd.Element("year").Value),
  new XAttribute("artist", cd.Element("artist").Value),
  new XAttribute("genre", cd.Element("genre").Value),
  cd.Element("title").Value));
```

The new `XElement` is then returned to the calling function where the content is both displayed and saved to a file named `newMusicLibrary.xml`.

The full project, `TransformingXml`, is available in the code download for this chapter.

One of the downsides of transforming documents using LINQ to XML is that, although it is good for changes similar to the example of modifying the music library, where the new document follows a similar ordering to the original, it can't cope so well where a lot of re-ordering is needed or where the output is not an XML format. For those sorts of problems you are probably better off using XSLT.

The final section of this chapter deals with two XML features that are particular to VB.NET: *XML Literals* and *Axis Properties* syntax.

USING VB.NET XML FEATURES

VB.NET has two features that are not supported so far in either C# or any other .NET language. These are XML Literals and Axis Properties. XML Literals includes new ways of creating XML documents and easier ways of managing namespaces. Axis Properties mean you can navigate through a document and retrieve elements, attributes, and their values with a succinct syntax.

Using VB.NET XML Literals

It is often the case that you need to build a new XML document based on an existing template rather than create the whole thing from scratch. In the past you had two choices: embed the template as a string of XML, either in the code itself or within a resource file; or load it as a file. Neither of these two solutions is entirely satisfactory. The string representation can be tricky to handle—often there are problems with quote marks and there is no checking of the XML for well-formedness. Loading from a file means that there is an extra item, the file itself, to include in any installation package, and the application needs to be able to read from the relevant area of the disk.

Luckily, VB.NET has a third alternative: XML Literals, which enable you to embed XML directly into your code. XML Literals also facilitate including namespace declarations, should you need them, and putting placeholders within the XML that can be filled in later by code.

Start with a simple example. The music library you've seen so far could be declared as follows:

```
Dim musicLibrary As XElement =
<musicLibrary>
  <cd id="1">
    <title>Parallel Lines</title>
    <year>2001</year>
    <artist>Blondie</artist>
    <genre>New Wave</genre>
  </cd>
  <cd id="2">
    <title>Bat Out of Hell</title>
    <year>2001</year>
    <artist>Meatloaf</artist>
    <genre>Rock</genre>
  </cd>
  <cd id="3">
    <title>Abbey Road</title>
    <year>1987</year>
    <artist>The Beatles</artist>
    <genre>Rock</genre>
  </cd>
  <cd id="4">
    <title>The Dark Side of the Moon</title>
```

```
      <year>1994</year>
      <artist>Pink Floyd</artist>
      <genre>Rock</genre>
    </cd>
    <cd id="5">
      <title>Thriller</title>
      <year>2001</year>
      <artist>Michael Jackson</artist>
      <genre>Pop</genre>
    </cd>
  </musicLibrary>
```

In the previous code the variable `musicLibrary` is exactly the same as if `musicLibrary.xml` had been loaded using the `Load()` method shown earlier. In the preceding sections, the variable was specifically typed as `System.Xml.Linq.XElement`, but you could have used an implicit declaration instead, like so:

```
Dim musicLibrary =
<musicLibrary>
  <cd id="1">
    <title>Parallel Lines</title>
    <year>2001</year>
    <artist>Blondie</artist>
    <genre>New Wave</genre>
  </cd>
  <!-- rest of cd elements -->
</musicLibrary
```

If you try this code and then hover over the `musicLibrary` variable, you'll see that it is still an `XElement`. If you had included an XML declaration, or any form of prolog, such as in the following code, `musicLibrary` would have been typed as `System.Xml.Linq.XDocument`:

```
Dim musicLibrary =
<?xml version="1.0" encoding="utf-8"?>
<musicLibrary>
  <cd id="1">
    <title>Parallel Lines</title>
    <year>2001</year>
    <artist>Blondie</artist>
    <genre>New Wave</genre>
  </cd>
  <!-- rest of cd elements -->
</musicLibrary
```

However, embedding a complete file like this is unusual. It's more likely that you will have a basic structure that needs to be populated with data from an external source. XML Literals gives you an easy way to do this that is reminiscent of how classic ASP pages were coded. The following activity walks you through using XML Literals combined with placeholders to demonstrate the ease with which VB.NET allows you to define XML documents.

TRY IT OUT XML Literals with Placeholders

In this Try It Out you create the music library using an external data source and combine it with an XML Literal. This scenario would typically be seen when you need to present data residing in a relational database in an XML format and the database's native XML features were unsuitable.

1. If you are using the full version of Visual Studio then create a new project using the Visual Basic section. Otherwise create a new project using Visual Basic Express. The project will be a console application which you should name `VbXmlFeatures`.

2. You need a class to represent your CD data, so open `Module1.vb` and add the following code within the `Module Module1/End Module` keywords:

```
Private Class CD
  Public Property ID As String
  Public Property Title As String
  Public Property Year As Integer
  Public Property Artist As String
  Public Property Genre As String
End Class
```

   The `CD` class, which is marked private because it's used only within the module, simply defines the five properties needed for the XML of each `<cd>` element.

3. You now need a function that simulates retrieving the data from an external source such as a database. For this example, you'll simply hard-code the data as shown here:

Available for download on Wrox.com

```
Private Function GetCDs() As List(Of CD)
  Dim cdList As New List(Of CD) From
    {
      New CD() With {.ID = "1", .Title = "Parallel Lines",
                     .Year = 2001, .Artist = "Blondie", .Genre = "New Wave"},
      New CD() With {.ID = "2", .Title = "Bat Out of Hell",
                     .Year = 2001, .Artist = "Meatloaf", .Genre = "Rock"},
      New CD() With {.ID = "3", .Title = "Abbey Road",
                     .Year = 1987, .Artist = "The Beatles", .Genre = "Rock"},
      New CD() With {.ID = "4", .Title = "The Dark Side of the Moon",
                     .Year = 1994, .Artist = "Pink Floyd", .Genre = "Rock"},
      New CD() With {.ID = "5", .Title = "Thriller",
                     .Year = 2001, .Artist = "Michael Jackson", .Genre = "Pop"}
  }
  Return cdList
End Function
```

Module1.vb

4. Now for the principal function that combines the data with an XML Literal add the following code to `Module1`:

```
Private Function CreateMusicLibrary() As XElement
  Dim cdData = GetCDs()
  Dim musicLibrary =
```

```
      <musicLibrary>
        <%= From item In cdData
          Select <cd id=<%= item.ID %>>
                   <title><%= item.Title %></title>
                   <year><%= item.Year %></year>
                   <artist><%= item.Artist %></artist>
                   <genre><%= item.Genre %></genre>
                 </cd> %>
      </musicLibrary>
    Return musicLibrary
  End Function
```

5. Finally the code is initiated from the entry point to the module, `Sub Main()`:

```
Sub Main()
  Dim musicLibrary As XElement = CreateMusicLibrary()
  Console.WriteLine(musicLibrary)
  Console.ReadLine()
End Sub
```

6. To run the code press F5 and see the results in the console window that appears.

How It Works

The `CD` class is standard; it uses the newer automatic property syntax introduced in VB.NET 10 to define the five properties of a `CD`, `ID`, `Title`, `Year`, `Artist` and `Genre`. The backing variable that was previously needed to hold each of these values is now automatically taken care of rather than having to be defined explicitly.

The code that returns the CD data is also fairly straightforward. It uses VB.NET's syntax of object and collection initializers to create five `CD` objects within a generic list.

The salient code is in the `CreateMusicLibrary()` function. This combines the technique of using an XML Literal with using dynamic code, enclosed between the `<%= %>` brackets, to produce a complete document.

You should notice two things about using these brackets. First, they can be nested. There is one pair that begins the internal LINQ query that starts with `From item In cdData`, and then others pair around each use of `item`. Second, you need to avoid adding quotes around attribute values (in this example, when filling in the `ID` attribute—something I always forget) because these are appended automatically when the code is executed.

Although here you have used a LINQ query within the XML Literal, you're not limited to that technique. A traditional `For Each` loop or virtually any other code is allowable within the `<%= %>` brackets.

The result of running this code will be the familiar music library showing the five `<cd>` elements and their content.

The complete project, `VbXmlFeatures`, is available in the code download.

WARNING *One caveat is that using XML Literals is not allowed within an ASP.NET page; the parser just isn't able to cope with distinguishing the literal brackets from the standard ASP.NET ones. This applies only to the actual* `.aspx` *file, though; if your page has a code-behind file, you can use XML Literals there.*

At the moment these literals are available only in VB.NET, but there's nothing stopping you from having a VB.NET project in an otherwise C# solution. You can also include both C# and VB.NET code files in the same web project if you put them in different folders and make a small change to your config file as described here: `http://msdn.microsoft.com/en-us/library/t990ks23.aspx`.

Next take a look at the second unique feature in VB.NET, *Axis Properties*.

Understanding Axis Properties in VB.NET

Axis Properties are another XML feature that are only found in VB.NET. They are intended to make navigation through an XML document easier as well as to facilitate the retrieval of values from the XML.

Four Axis properties in VB.NET's XML features considerably simplify the code needed when extracting data from an XML source. Three of these take the form of shortcuts that can be used in place of the various `Elements()`, `Attributes()`, and `Descendants()` methods and the fourth is a convenient way to retrieve an element or attribute's value. The four properties are known as:

- The Child Axis Shortcut
- The Attribute Axis Shortcut
- The Descendants Axis Shortcut
- The Value Property Shortcut

The following sections will explain each shortcut in more detail and provide an example of how to use each one.

Using the Child Axis Shortcut

The first Axis Property shortcut is used when you want to access elements that lie on the child axis.

If you have loaded your music library into memory and want to access all the `<cd>` elements, you have so far used the following code:

```
musicLibrary.Elements("cd")
```

Using the child axis shortcut however, you can write:

```
musicLibrary.<cd>
```

This is shorter and easier to read, but performs the same function.

Using the Attribute Axis Shortcut

The next shortcut is used to retrieve attributes. Previously, to find attributes you used the `Attributes()` or `Attribute()` methods. To show the `id` attribute of a `<cd>` element, you used the following :

```
cd3.Attribute("id")
```

Using the attribute axis shortcut you can write the following instead of the preceding:

```
cd3.@id
```

This uses the familiar `@` symbol used in XPath to signify you are searching the attributes collection.

Using the Descendants Axis Shortcut

Not surprisingly, Descendants Axis Shortcut is used to find descendants.

Although children are limited to the level just below an element, descendants can be anywhere underneath. In earlier code you had to write the following to find all the `<title>` elements anywhere beneath `<musicLibrary>`:

```
musicLibrary.Descendants("title")
```

Now with the `descendants` axis shortcut, you can use three dots (. . .) as a shortcut:

```
musicLibrary...<title>
```

Using the Value Property Shortcut

The final shortcut, called an Axes Shortcut by Microsoft but really just operating on values, enables a quicker way to find an item's value.

If you retrieve a collection of elements, you normally need to either use `FirstOrDefault()` or an indexer to find the first item and then use the `Value` property to get its content. For example, to get the first `<title>` element's value you use:

```
musicLibrary...<title>(0).Value
```

The `Value` shortcut removes the need for the indexer and retrieves the value of the first element or attribute in the collection. The following code gives the same result as the preceding snippet:

```
musicLibrary...<title>.Value
```

The subroutine `ShortcutsDemo()` in the `VbXmlFeatures` project shows all these features in action.

The final VB.NET XML feature discussed in this chapter is how to manage namespaces.

Managing Namespaces in VB.NET

Assigning prefixes to namespace URIs is always a bit haphazard, and every XML technology seems to handle it differently. VB.NET has decided to use the same strategy as XML itself, which uses the following form:

```
<ns:musicLibrary xmlns:ns="http://www.wrox.com/namespaces/apps/musicLibrary">
  <!-- rest of document -->
</ns:musicLibrary>
```

The code in VB.NET to declare this namespace would be as follows:

```
Imports <xmlns:ns="http://www.wrox.com/namespaces/apps/musicLibrary">
```

This line needs to be at the top of the code file, outside the module declaration. The prefix `ns` can now be used to represent the namespace URI when searching. The following code shows how to load a namespaced version of the music library and find the second `<title>` element's value:

```
'At the top of the module
Imports <xmlns:ns="http://www.wrox.com/namespaces/apps/musicLibrary">

'Within the module
  Private Sub NamespaceDemo()
    Dim musicLibrary = XElement.Load(«musicLibraryWithNamespaces.xml»)
    Dim secondTitle = musicLibrary...<ns:title>(1).Value
    Console.WriteLine(«Second Title: {0}», secondTitle)
  End Sub
```

The working code is contained in the VB.NET project for this chapter.

SUMMARY

In this chapter you learned:

- LINQ is intended to unify access and manipulation of data collections from different sources.
- LINQ to XML is needed to make creation of XML documents simpler and to make navigation and data retrieval from XML a similar process to any fetching data from any other collection.
- Functional creation of XML documents means that the `XElement` class can take another `XElement` as part of its constructor, leading to a simpler way of defining an XML document.
- Using LINQ to XML to extract data is accomplished mainly through the `Elements()` and `Attributes()` methods.
- Using LINQ to XML to modify data is accomplished using methods such as `ReplaceNodes()` and `SetElementValue()`.

- Transforming documents with LINQ to XML is possible but it doesn't quite have the power of XSLT. It is a good choice if the basic ordering of the source and target XML are similar.
- VB.NET's extra XML features are XML literals, to declaratively define XML documents and Axis properties to simplify navigation to a target item and retrieve its value.

EXERCISES

1. You can find suggested answers to these questions in Appendix A. Use XML Literals and placeholders to create an attribute-centric version of the music library, as shown in the section on transformations.

▶ WHAT YOU LEARNED IN THIS CHAPTER

TOPIC	KEY POINTS
The Purpose of LINQ	To provide a consistent way to treat any collection, whether it be objects, relational data, or arrays.
Why LINQ to XML	To make manipulating XML similar to handling any other data.
The Main Classes	`XElement`, representing an XML element and `XAttribute` representing an XML attribute.
Other Classes	`XName` to represent an item's name and `XNamespace` to represent an XML namespace.
Main Methods	`Elements()`, to retrieve specified elements and `Attributes()` to retrieve attributes.
XML Literals	Available only in VB.NET and enable you to specify XML documents in declarative syntax with optional place holders for data that changes.
Axis Properties	Available only in VB.Net and enable shortcuts to be used to navigate to targeted content.

PART VI
Communication

13

RSS, Atom, and Content Syndication

WHAT YOU WILL LEARN IN THIS CHAPTER:

- Concepts and technologies of content syndication and meta data
- A brief look at the history of RSS, Atom, and related languages
- What the feed languages have in common and how they differ
- How to implement a simple newsreader/aggregator using Python
- Examples of XSLT used to generate and display news feeds

One of the interesting characteristics of the web is the way that certain ideas seem to arise spontaneously, without any centralized direction. Content syndication technologies definitely fall into this category, and they have emerged as a direct consequence of the linked structure of the web and general standardization regarding the use of XML.

This chapter focuses on a number of aspects of content syndication, including the RSS and Atom formats and their role in such areas as blogs, news services, and the like. It's useful to understand them not just from an XML-format standpoint, but also in terms of how they are helping to shape the evolving Internet.

There is a lot more to RSS, Atom, and content syndication than can be covered in a single chapter, so the aim here is to give you a good grounding in the basic ideas, and then provide a taste of how XML tools such as SAX and XSLT can be used in this field.

SYNDICATION

Over the course of the twentieth century, newspapers evolved into different kinds of news organizations with the advent of each new medium. Initially, most newspapers operated independently, and coverage of anything beyond local information was usually handled by dedicated reporters in major cities. However, for most newspapers, such reporters are typically very costly to maintain. Consequently, these news organizations pool their resources together to create syndicates, feeding certain articles (and columns) to the syndicates, who would then license them out to other publishers. These news syndicates, or services, specialize in certain areas. Associated Press (AP) and United Press International (UPI) handle syndication within the United States, while Reuters evolved as a source for European news. Similarly, comic strips are usually handled by separate syndicates (such as King Features Syndicate).

The news services aggregate news from a wide variety of different sources and, hopefully alongside original material, publish the result as a unified whole, the newspaper. One advantage of this approach is that it is possible to bundle related content together, regardless of the initial source. For instance, a sports-dedicated publication may pull together all articles on baseball, football, and basketball, but the feed wouldn't include finance articles unless they were sports-related.

A *syndication feed* is an online parallel to the syndicated publication of a cartoon strip or sports paper. If a website (or any other source) has information that appears in little, topically-categorized chunks over time, it's probably a good idea to create a syndication feed for it. For the web publisher it offers another kind of exposure, and for the web consumer it offers alternative ways of getting up-to-date information. For the developer, it's an established platform on which useful and interesting tools can be built.

In practice, syndication feeds are published as single XML files comprised of meta data elements and, in most cases, content as well. Several distinct standard formats exist. Each format shares a common basic model of a syndication feed. There is the *feed* itself, which has characteristics such as a title and publication date. The overall structure of a feed can be seen in Figure 13-1. The feed carries a series of discrete blocks of data, known as *items* or *entries*, each of which also has a set of individual characteristics, again such as title and date. These items are little chunks of information, which either describe a resource on the web (a link is provided) or are a self-contained unit, typically carrying content along with them.

Typically, a feed contains 10–20 entries. Note that in addition to the elements described in the specifications, each of the format types support extensions through various mechanisms.

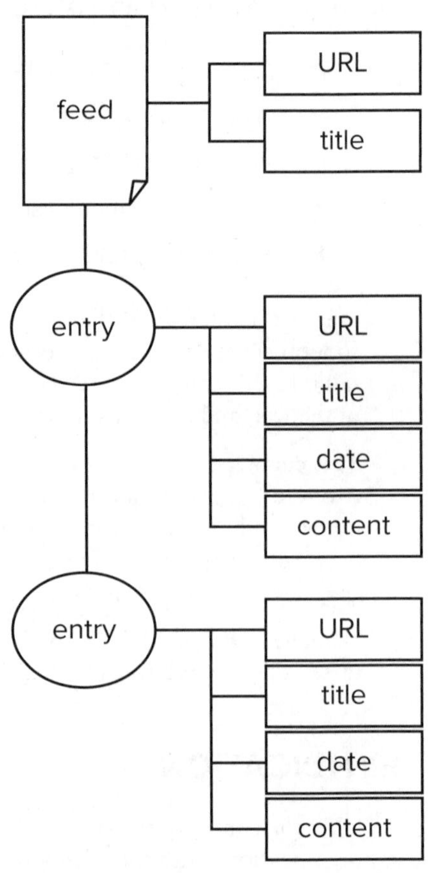

FIGURE 13-1

XML Syndication

The three primary XML formats for syndication are RSS 1.0, RSS 2.0, and Atom. Despite having a very similar data model (refer to Figure 13-1), they are largely incompatible with each other in terms of syntax. In practice they can generally be used interchangeably, and that's how they're mostly found in the wild. For the consumer of syndicated feeds, this is bad news: essentially you have to support all three species (and variants). For the producer it could be seen as good news; each format has advantages and may be best suited to a particular deployment. The syndication formats have a colorful history, which is worthwhile reviewing to see how the present state of affairs has come to be.

A Little History

Web syndication arguably began in the mid-1990s, with the development of the *Meta Content Framework* (MCF) at Apple, essentially a table of contents for a website. This was a significant precursor of the Resource Description Framework (RDF). Not long after, Microsoft entered the fray with its *Content Definition Format* (CDF). This was specifically targeted to be a comprehensive syndication format that would appeal to traditional broadcasters, and support for it was built into Internet Explorer (since discontinued).

The CDF model of a feed and its items is essentially the same model in use today in all syndication formats, and it contains features that found their way into RSS and have stayed there ever since — channel (feed), item, title, and so on.

RSS first got its initials with *RDF Site Summary* (RSS) 0.9 from Netscape in early 1999. However, Netscape soon backed away from its original RDF-oriented approach to RSS, and its RSS 0.91 was more conventional XML. Out went RDF and namespaces and in came a DTD and a new name: *Rich Site Summary*. Not long after this, Netscape dropped RSS altogether. Dave Winer of the pioneering content-management system company Userland then adopted RSS and made it his own, releasing a slightly different version of RSS 0.91.

However, around the same time Winer was working on the RSS 0.91 line, an informal mailing list sprang up, *RSS-DEV*, with a general consensus that the RDF-based approach of RSS 0.9 (and Netscape's original planned future direction for RSS) was the best; and the result was the RSS 1.0 specification.

This proposal clashed head-on with the RDF/namespace-free 0.91 approach followed by Winer. Agreement wasn't forthcoming on a way forward, and as a result, RSS forked. One thread carried the banner of simplicity, the other of interoperability. Winer rebranded his version of RSS to *Really Simple Syndication*.

Then in 2002 Winer delivered something of a marketing coup: he released an RSS 2.0 specification and declared it frozen. This followed the RSS 0.91 side of the fork, with syntax completely incompatible with RSS 1.0. Namespace support was reintroduced, but only for extensions. While people continued to publish (and still do) RSS 1.0 feeds, the RSS 2.0 version gained a significant amount of new adoption, due in no small part to the evangelism of the specification's author.

The Self-Contained Feed

A lot of the development of RSS was driven by developments in web content management and publishing, notably the emergence of the *blog* (from "web log"). Similar to today, some early blogs were little more than lists of links, whereas others were more like online journals or magazines. This distinction is quite important in the context of syndication formats. The original RSS model contained a URL, title, and description, which all referred to the linked material, with its (remote) content. But increasingly the items in a feed corresponded with entries in a blog, to the extent that the feed became essentially another representation of the blog. The URL became the link to a (HTML) post sharing the same title, and the description became the actual content of that post, or a condensed version of it.

The demand for content in feeds highlighted a significant problem with the RSS 2.0 specification: It says that the `<description>` element may contain HTML, and that's all it says. There is no way for applications to distinguish HTML from plaintext, so how do you tell what content is markup and what content is just talking about markup?

This and other perceived problems with RSS 2.0 led to another open community initiative that launched in the summer of 2003, with the aim of fixing the problems of RSS 2.0 and unifying the syndication world (including the RSS 1.0 developers). Accepting the roadmap for RSS presented in the RSS 2.0 specification meant the name RSS couldn't be used, and after lengthy discussion the new project got a name: *Atom*. Before moving on to descriptions of what feed XML actually looks like, you should first know its purpose.

Syndication Systems

Like most other web systems, *syndication systems* are generally based around the client-server model. At one end you have a web server delivering data using the HyperText Transfer Protocol (HTTP), and at the other end is a client application receiving it. On the web, the server uses a piece of software such as Apache or IIS, and the client uses a browser such as Internet Explorer (IE) or Firefox. HTML-oriented web systems tend to have a clear distinction between the roles and location of the applications: the server is usually part of a remote system, and the client appears on the user's desktop. HTML data is primarily intended for immediate rendering and display for users to read on their home computer. Data for syndication takes a slightly different approach.

The defining characteristic of web syndication systems is that they follow a *publish-subscribe* pattern. This is a form of communication where senders of messages, called publishers, create the messages without knowledge of what, if any, subscribers there may be. Subscribers express interest in the messages of particular types or from particular sources, and receive only messages that correspond to those choices.

In the case of web syndication, the publisher generates a structured document (the feed) at a given URL. Subscribers use a dedicated tool, known as a newsreader, feed reader, or *aggregator*, to subscribe to the URL. Typically the subscriber's tool will periodically read (or *poll*) the document at the URL. The tool does this automatically; say once an hour or once a day. Over time the publisher will add new items to the feed (removing older ones), so that next time subscribers poll the feed, they receive the new material.

This isn't unlike visiting a site periodically with a browser to find out what's new. However, syndication material is designed to support automation and, hence, needs to be *machine-readable*. This means there is at least one extra stage of processing before the content appears on the user's screen. The *machine-readability* means that it is possible to pass around and process the data relatively easily, allotting for a huge amount of versatility in systems. The net result is that applications that produce material for syndication purposes can appear either server side or client side (desktop), as can applications that consume this material.

Key to understanding the differences between syndication and typical web pages is the aspect of time. A syndicated resource (an item in a feed) is generally available only for a short period of time at a given point in the network, at which stage it disappears from the feed, although an archived version of the information is likely archived on the publisher's site.

The different kinds of syndication software components can roughly be split into four categories: server-producer, client-consumer, client-producer, and server-consumer. In practice, software products may combine these different pieces of functionality, but it helps to look at these parts in isolation.

The following sections provide an overview of each, with the more familiar systems first.

Server-Producer

A server-producer, also known as a *server-side* system for publishing syndication material, is in essence no different from any typical web system used to publish regular HTML web pages. At minimum, this would be a static XML file in one of the syndication formats placed on a web server. More usefully, the XML data will be produced from some kind of content management system. The stereotypical content management systems in this context are blog tools. The main page of the (HTML) website features a series of diary-like entries, with the most recent entry appearing first. Behind the scenes is some kind of database containing the entry material, and the system presents this in reverse chronological order on a nicely formatted web page. In parallel with the HTML-generating subsystems of the application are syndication feed format (RSS and/or Atom) producing subsystems. These two subsystems are likely to be very similar, because the feed material is usually a bare-bones version of the HTML content. Many blogging systems include a common templating system, which may be used to produce either HTML or syndication-format XML.

Client-Consumer

Although it is possible to view certain kinds of syndicated feeds in a web browser, one of the major benefits of syndication comes into play with so-called newsreaders or aggregator tools. The reader application enables users to subscribe to a large number of different feeds, and present the material from these feeds in an integrated fashion. There are two common styles of a feed-reader user interface:

- *Single pane* styles present items from the feeds in sequence, as they might appear on a web log.
- *Multipane* styles are often modeled on e-mail applications, and present a selectable list of feeds in one panel and the content of the selected feed in another.

The techniques used to process and display this material vary considerably. Many pass the data directly to display, whereas others incorporate searching and filtering, usually with data storage behind the scenes; and occasionally, Semantic Web technologies are used to provide integration with other kinds of data.

Some newsreaders use a small web server running on the client machine to render content in a standard browser. Wide variations also exist in the sophistication of these tools. Some provide presentation of each feed as a whole; others do it item-by-item by date, through user-defined categories or any combination of these and other alternatives. You'll see the code for a very simple aggregator later in this chapter.

There's a useful page on Wikipedia containing lists of feed readers and comparing their characteristics at `http://en.wikipedia.org/wiki/Comparison_of_feed_aggregators`.

Client-Producer

Now you know that the server-producer puts content on a web server and the client-consumer processes and displays this content, but where does the content come from in the first place? Again, blogging tools are the stereotype. Suppose an author of a blog uses a tool to compose posts containing his thoughts for the day plus various cat photos. Clicking a button submits this data to a content management system that will typically load the content into its database for subsequent display, as in the preceding server-producer. The client-producer category covers desktop blogging clients such as BlogEd, Ecto, and Microsoft Windows Live Writer, which run as conventional applications. (Note that availability of tools like these is changing all the time; a web search for "desktop blogging tools" should yield up-to-date information.) Several existing desktop authoring tools incorporate post-to-blog facilities (for example, you can find plug-ins for MS Word and OpenOffice). When the user clicks Submit (or similar), the material is sent over the web to the content management system. However, the four categories presented here break down a little at this point, because many blogging tools provide authoring tools from the web server as well, with users being presented a web form in which they can enter their content.

A technical issue should be mentioned at this point. When it comes to communications, the server-producer and client-consumer systems generally operate in exactly the same way as HTML-oriented web servers and clients using the HTTP protocol directly. The feed material is delivered in one of the syndication formats: RSS or Atom.

However, when it comes to posting material to a management system, other strategies are commonly used. In particular, developers of the Blogger blogging service designed a specification for transmitting blog material from the author's client to the online service. Although the specification was intended only as a prototype; the "Blogger API" became the de facto standard for posting to blogging and similar content management systems. The Blogger API defines a small set of XML-RPC (remote procedure calling) elements to encode the material and pass it to the server. There were certain limitations of this specification, which led to the MetaWeblog API that extends the elements in a way that makes it possible to send all the most common pieces of data that might be required. There was a partial recognition in the MetaWeblog API that a degree of redundancy existed in the specifications. The data that is passed from an authoring tool is essentially the same, in structure and content, as the material passed from the server to newsreaders, so the MetaWeblog API uses some of the vocabulary of RSS 2.0 to describe the structural elements.

Since the XML-RPC blogging APIs came out, there has been a growing realization in the developer community that not only is there redundancy at the level of naming parts of the messages being passed around, but also in the fundamental techniques used to pass them around. To transfer syndicated material from a server to a client, the client sends an HTTP `GET` message to the server, and the server responds with a bunch of RSS/Atom-formatted data. On the other hand, when transferring material from the client to the server, the blogging APIs wrap the content in XML-RPC messages and use an HTTP `POST` to send that. The question is, why use the XML-RPC format when there is already a perfectly good RSS or Atom format? Recent developments have led to a gradual shift from XML-RPC to the passing of XML (or even JSON) data directly over HTTP, and more use of the less familiar HTTP verbs, such as `PUT` (to replace an XML document on the web) and `DELETE` (to remove a resource). Most established in the field is the Atom Publication Protocol (`http://tools.ietf.org/html/rfc5023`), a specification from the same group that produced the Atom format.

Server-Consumer

The notion of a server-consumer component covers several different kinds of functionality, such as the functionality needed to receive material sent from a client-producer, blog posts, and the like. This in itself isn't particularly interesting; typically, it's not much different than authoring directly on the server except the material is posted via HTML forms.

But it's also possible to take material from other syndication servers and either render it directly, acting as an online equivalent of the desktop newsreader, or process the aggregated data further. This approach is increasingly common, and online newsreaders such as Google Reader are very popular. The fact that feed data is suitable for subsequent processing and integration means it offers considerable potential for the future. Various online services have used syndicated data to provide enhanced search capabilities, however two of the pioneers, PubSub and Tailrank, are no longer in operation. It's interesting to note how similar functionality has found its way into systems like Twitter and Google Plus.

TechMeme (`www.techmeme.com`) is an example of a smarter aggregator, in that it uses heuristics (rules of thumb) on the data found on blogs to determine the most significant stories, treating an incoming link as a sign of importance for an entry. Plenty of fairly centralized, mass-appeal services are available, but there's also been a lot of development in the open source world of tools that can offer similar services for special-interest groups, organizations, or even individuals. It's relatively straightforward to set up your own "Planet" aggregations of topic-specific feeds by downloading and installing the Planet (`www.planetplanet.org`) or Chumpalogica (`http://www.hackdiary.com/projects/chumpologica/`) online aggregation applications. The Planet Venus aggregator (`http://intertwingly.net/code/venus/docs/`), an offshoot of Planet, includes various pieces of additional functionality, such as a personalized "meme-tracker" similar to TechMeme. An example of how such systems can be customized is Planète Web Sémantique (`http://planete.websemantique.org/`). This site uses Planet Venus to aggregate French-language posts on the topic of the Semantic Web. Because many of the bloggers on its subscription list also regularly post on other topics and in English, such material is filtered out (actually hidden by JavaScript).

Format Anatomy

Having heard how the mechanisms of syndication work, now it's time to look at the formats themselves. To avoid getting lost in the markup, you may find it useful to refer back to the diagram in Figure 13-1 to keep a picture in your mind of the overall feed structure.

RSS 2.0

You can find the specification for RSS 2.0 at `http://cyber.law.harvard.edu/rss/rss.html`. It's a fairly readable, informal document (which unfortunately has been a recurring criticism due to ambiguities in its language).

The format style of RSS 2.0 is hierarchical. The syntax structure looks like this:

```
rss
        channel
        (elements containing meta data about the feed)
            item
            (item content and meta data)
            item
            (item content and meta data)
...
```

In practice, most of the elements are optional; as long as the overall structure follows the preceding pattern, a reader should be able to make some sense of it.

The following is an extract from an RSS 2.0 feed. The original (taken from `http://www.fromoldbooks.org/rss.xml`) contained 20 items, but in the interests of space here all but one have been removed:

```
<?xml version="1.0" encoding="utf-8"?>

<rss version="2.0">

    <channel>

        <title>Words and Pictures From Old Books</title>

        <link>http://www.fromoldbooks.org/</link>

        <description>Recently added pictures scanned from old books</description>

        <pubDate>Tue, 14 Feb 2012 08:28:00 GMT</pubDate>

        <lastBuildDate>Tue, 14 Feb 2012 08:28:00 GMT</lastBuildDate>

        <ttl>180</ttl>

        <image>

       <url>http://www.holoweb.net/~liam/presspics/Liam10-70x100-amazon.jpg</url>

            <title>Words and Pictures From Old Books</title>

            <link>http://www.fromoldbooks.org/</link>

        </image>

        <item>

            <title>Winged Mermaid from p. 199 recto, from Buch der Natur
```

```
[Book of Nature] (1481), added on 14th Feb 2012</title>

            <link>http://www.fromoldbooks.org/Megenberg-
BookderNatur/pages/0199r-detail-mermaid/</link>

            <description>

&lt;p&gt;A fifteenth-century drawing of a mermaid with wings (and breast)
 taken from &lt;a href="0199r-strange-creatures"&gt;fol. 199r&lt;/a&gt; of a
(somewhat dubious) textbook
 on natural history.&lt;/p&gt; &lt;p&gt;The mermaid has the trunk and head of
a woman, the tail of a fish, and wings, or possibly large fins.&lt;/p&gt;</
description>

            <pubDate>Tue, 14 Feb 2012 08:19:00 GMT</pubDate>

            <author>liam&#64;holoweb.net (Liam Quin)</author>

            <guid isPermaLink="true">http://www.fromoldbooks.org/Megenberg-
BookderNatur/pages/0199r-detail-mermaid/</guid>

        </item>

...

    </channel>

</rss>
```

The document begins with the XML declaration followed by the outer <rss> element. Inside this is the <channel> element where the data begins:

```
<?xml version="1.0" encoding="utf-8"?>

<rss version="2.0">

    <channel>

        <title>Words and Pictures From Old Books</title>

        <link>http://www.fromoldbooks.org/</link>

        <description>Recently added pictures scanned from old books</description>

        <pubDate>Tue, 14 Feb 2012 08:28:00 GMT</pubDate>

        <lastBuildDate>Tue, 14 Feb 2012 08:28:00 GMT</lastBuildDate>

        <ttl>180</ttl>
```

These elements nested directly inside the <channel> element describe the feed itself. The preceding code contains the self-explanatory <title> and <description> along with a link. Note that the link refers to the website corresponding to the feed; this will typically be the homepage. The official publication date for the feed is expressed in the `<pubDate>` element using the human-readable format defined in RFC 822 (this specification is actually obsolete; if in doubt it's probably safest to refer to the more recent RFC 5322: `http://tools.ietf.org/html/rfc5322#section-3.3`).

The `<lastBuildDate>` refers to the last time the content of the feed changed (the purpose being to make it easy for consumers to check for changes, although best practice is to use the HTTP headers for this purpose).

The `<ttl>` element refers to "time to live." It's effectively a hint to any clients as to how frequently the feed changes, hence how often they should update.

The channel-level `<image>` element that follows enables a client to associate a picture or icon with the feed. As well as the URL of the image to be displayed, it also contains some meta data, which is usually identical to the corresponding elements referring to the feed:

```
<image>

    <url>http://www.holoweb.net/~liam/presspics/Liam10-70x100-amazon.jpg</url>

    <title>Words and Pictures From Old Books</title>

    <link>http://www.fromoldbooks.org/</link>

</image>
```

Next, still nested inside `<channel>`, the syndication items appear as content and meta data. The order of the elements inside `<item>` doesn't matter; they are rearranged a little here from the original for clarity:

```
<item>

     <description>
&lt;p&gt;A fifteenth-century drawing of a mermaid with wings (and breast)
taken from &lt;a href="0199r-strange-creatures"&gt;fol. 199r&lt;/a&gt; of a
(somewhat dubious) textbook on natural history.&lt;/p&gt; &lt;p&gt;The mermaid has
the trunk and head of a woman, the tail of a fish, and wings, or possibly large
fins.&lt;/p&gt;</description>
```

The RSS 2.0 specification says of the `<description>` element that it's "the item synopsis." Though it may be a shortened version of a longer piece, publishers often include the whole piece of content they want to syndicate. The specification is silent on the format of the content, but in practice most aggregators will assume that it is HTML and render it accordingly. But because this is XML, the markup has to be escaped, so `<p>` becomes `<p>` and so on.

There then follows the meta data associated with this piece of content:

```
    <title>Winged Mermaid from p. 199 recto, from Buch der Natur
```

```
[Book of Nature] (1481), added on 14th Feb 2012</title>

         <pubDate>Tue, 14 Feb 2012 08:19:00 GMT</pubDate>

         <author>liam&#64;holoweb.net (Liam Quin)</author>

         <link>http://www.fromoldbooks.org/Megenberg-
BookderNatur/pages/0199r-detail-mermaid/</link>

         <guid isPermaLink="true">http://www.fromoldbooks.org/Megenberg-
BookderNatur/pages/0199r-detail-mermaid/</guid>

     </item>
```

The `<title>` and `<pubDate>` are those of the content, which typically is also found (as HTML) at the URL specified in the `<link>` element. The author is specified as the e-mail address and (optionally) the name of the person who wrote the content.

The `<guid>` is specified as a string that is the "globally unique identifier" of the item. Although this can be arbitrary, most of the time the item will appear elsewhere (as HTML) so that URL can be used. In RSS 2.0, such a URL is indicated by using the `isPermaLink` attribute with the value `true`.

Usually there will be a series of around 10–20 items, before the channel-level and outer elements are closed off like so:

```
    </channel>

</rss>
```

Atom

Atom was developed as an open project using the processes of the Internet Engineering Task Force (IETF). The initial aim might have been to fix the problems of RSS, but it was realized early on that any sane solution would not only look at the format, but also take into account the protocols used in authoring, editing, and publication. So the Atom Publishing Format and Protocol was formed in June 2004. The first deliverable of the group, the Atom Syndication Format (RFC 4287, `www.ietf.org/rfc/rfc4287.txt`) was published in December 2005 followed by the Atom Publishing Protocol (`http://tools.ietf.org/html/rfc5023`) in October 2007.

These specifications are written a lot more formally than that of RSS 2.0, but are still quite approachable.

The Atom format is structurally and conceptually very much like its RSS predecessors, and its practical design lies somewhere between the RSS 1.0 and 2.0 versions. The syntax isn't RDF/XML, but it does have a namespace itself and includes flexible extension mechanisms. Most of the elements are direct descendants of those found in RSS, although considerable work has given it robust support for inline content, using a new `<content>` element.

Most of the elements of Atom are self-explanatory, although the naming of parts differs from RSS, so an Atom `feed` corresponds to an RSS `channel`, an Atom `entry` corresponds to an RSS `item`, and so on. Here's an example:

```
<feed xmlns="http://www.w3.org/2005/Atom">
   <link rel="self" href="http://example.org/blog/index.atom"/>
   <id>http://example.org/blog/index.atom</id>
   <icon>../favicon.ico</icon>
   <title>An Atom Sampler</title>
   <subtitle>No Splitting</subtitle>
   <author>
      <name>Ernie Rutherford </name>
      <email>ernie@example.org</email>
      <uri>.</uri>
   </author>
   <updated>2006-10-25T03:38:08-04:00</updated>
   <link href="."/>
   <entry>
      <id>tag:example.org,2004:2417</id>
      <link href="2006/10/23/moonshine"/>
      <title>Moonshine</title>
      <content type="text">
           Anyone who expects a source of power from the transformation of the atom
is talking moonshine.
      </content>
      <published>2006-10-23T15:33:00-04:00</published>
      <updated>2006-10-23T15:47:31-04:00</updated>
   </entry>
   <entry>
      <id>>tag:example.org,2004:2416</id>
      <link href="2006/10/21/think"/>
      <title type="html">&lt;strong&gt;Think!&lt;/strong&gt;</title>
      <content type="xhtml">
         <div xmlns="http://www.w3.org/1999/xhtml">
            <p>We haven't got the money, so we've got to think!</p>
         </div>
      </content>
      <updated>2006-10-21T06:02:39-04:00</updated>
   </entry>
</feed>
```

The first real enhancement is the `<id>` element, which roughly corresponds to the `<guid>` of RSS 2.0 and the `rdf:about` attribute found in RSS 1.0 (discussed in the net section) to identify entities. Rather than leave it to chance that this will be a unique string, the specification makes this a URI, which by definition is unique (to be more precise, it's defined as an Internationalized Resource Identifier or IRI — for typical usage there's no difference). Note the use of a `tag:` scheme URI in the example; these are not retrievable like `http:` scheme URIs. In effect, the identifiers (URIs) and locators (URLs) of entities within the format have been separated. This was a slightly controversial move, because many would argue that the two should be interchangeable. Time will tell whether or not this is a good idea. It is acceptable to use an `http: URI` in the `<id>` element, though in practice it's probably better to follow the spirit of the Atom specification. Whereas the `<id>` element identifies, the `<link>` element locates. The Atom `<link>` element is modeled on its namesake in HTML, to provide a link and information about related resources.

Whereas the <id> makes it considerably easier and more reliable to determine whether two entries are the same, the <content> element offers a significant enhancement in the description of the material being published. It's designed to allow virtually anything that can be passed over XML. In the first entry in the preceding example, the <entry> element has the attribute type="text". This explicitly states that the material within the element should not be treated as markup (and must not contain any child elements). The common case of HTML content is taken care of by making the attribute type="html". Again, there should be no child elements, and any HTML in the content should be escaped according to XML rules, so it would be <h1> (or one of the equivalent alternatives), rather than <h1>. However, although HTML content may be common, it's not the most useful. Atom is an XML format, and namespaces make it possible for it to carry data in other XML formats, which can be addressed using standard XML tools. The third kind of content support built into Atom is type="xhtml". To use XHTML in Atom, it has to be wrapped in a (namespace-qualified) <div> element. The <div> itself should be ignored by any rendering or processing tool that consumes the feed; it's only there for demarcation purposes.

Additionally, it's possible to include other kinds of content by specifying the type attribute as the media type. For XML-based formats this is straightforward; for example, the Description of a Project (DOAP) format (https://github.com/edumbill/doap/wiki) uses RDF/XML, which has a media type of "application/rdf+xml", and the DOAP vocabulary has the namespace "http://usefulinc.com/ns/doap#". For example, a project description payload in Atom would look something like the following:

```
<content type="application/rdf+xml">
     <doap:Project xmlns:doap="http://usefulinc.com/ns/doap#">
     <doap:name>My Blogging Tool</doap:name>
...
    </doap:Project>
</content>
```

Of course, not all data is found in XML formats. Text-based formats (that is, those with a type that begins "text/") can be included as content directly, as long as only legal XML characters are used and the usual escaping is applied to reserved characters. Other data formats can be represented in Atom using Base 64 encoding. (This is a mapping from arbitrary sequences of binary data into a 65-character subset of US-ASCII.)

RSS 1.0

You can find the specification for RSS 1.0 at http://web.resource.org/rss/1.0/spec. The following code is an example of RSS 1.0 format :

```
<?xml version="1.0" encoding="UTF-8"?>

<rdf:RDF xmlns="http://purl.org/rss/1.0/"

      xmlns:rdf="http://www.w3.org/1999/02/22-rdf-syntax-ns#"

      xmlns:dc="http://purl.org/dc/elements/1.1/"

      xmlns:sy="http://purl.org/rss/1.0/modules/syndication/"
```

```
    xmlns:content="http://purl.org/rss/1.0/modules/content/">

<channel rdf:about="http://journal.dajobe.org/journal">

     <title>Dave Beckett - Journalblog</title>

     <link>http://journal.dajobe.org/journal</link>

     <description>Hacking the semantic linked data web</description>

     <dc:date>2011-08-15T20:15:08Z</dc:date>

     <items>

          <rdf:Seq>

                         <rdf:li
rdf:resource="http://journal.dajobe.org/journal/posts/2010/06/28/happy-
10th-birthday-redland/"/>

                         <rdf:li
rdf:resource="http://journal.dajobe.org/journal/posts/2010/03/20/command-line-
semantic-web-with-redland/"/>



          </rdf:Seq>

     </items>

</channel>

<item rdf:about="http://journal.dajobe.org/journal/posts/2010/06/28/happy-
10th-birthday-redland/">

     <title>Happy 10th Birthday Redland</title>

     <link>http://journal.dajobe.org/journal/posts/2010/06/28/happy-10th-
birthday-redland/</link>

      <dc:date>2010-06-28T16:03:54Z</dc:date>

     <dc:creator>Dave Beckett</dc:creator>

     <description>Redland&#8216;s 10th year source code commit birthday is
today 28th Jun at 9:05am PST &#8211; the first commit was Wed Jun 28 17:04:57 2000
UTC. Happy 10th Birthday! Please celebrate with tea and
cake.</description>

     <content:encoded><![CDATA[<p><a
```

```
href="http://librdf.org/">Redland</a>&#8216;s 10th year source code commit birthday
is today 28th Jun at 9:05am PST &#8211; the <a
href="http://git.librdf.org/view?p=librdf.git;a=commit;h=8df358fb2bc1f4a69de08bc3fb
4ae7d784395521">first commit</a> was Wed Jun 28 17:04:57 2000 UTC.</p>

<p>Happy 10th Birthday!  Please celebrate with tea and cake.</p>

]]></content:encoded>

     </item>

</rdf:RDF>
```

To a human with a text editor, this format appears considerably more complex than RSS 2.0 or Atom. That's because it's RDF/XML, a syntax notorious for its complex nature. But despite the ugliness, it does have several advantages over RSS 2.0 and even Atom. These benefits all stem from the fact that a valid RSS 1.0 document is also a valid RDF document (and, not coincidentally, a valid XML document). Whatever a human might think, to a computer (for example, either a namespace-aware XML parser or an RDF tool), it contains the same kind of information as "simple" RSS but expressed in a less ambiguous and more interoperable form.

The XML has an outer `<rdf:RDF>` element (which incidentally is no longer a requirement of RDF/XML in general). Following the namespace declarations is a channel block, which first describes the channel feed itself and then lists the individual items found in the feed. The channel resource is identified with a URI, which makes the information portable. There's no doubt what the title, description, and so on refer to. Title, link, description, and language are all defined in the core RSS 1.0 specification. XML namespaces (with the RDF interpretation) are employed to provide properties defined in the Dublin Core (`dc:date`) and Syndication (`sy:updatePeriod`, `sy:updateFrequency`) modules.

Take a look at the following snippet from the RSS 1.0 code example:

```
     <items>

          <rdf:Seq>

                         <rdf:li
rdf:resource="http://journal.dajobe.org/journal/posts/2010/06/28/happy-10th-
birthday-redland/"/>

                         <rdf:li
rdf:resource="http://journal.dajobe.org/journal/posts/2010/03/20/command-line-
semantic-web-with-redland/"/>



          </rdf:Seq>

     </items>
```

The channel here has an `items` property, which has the `rdf:Seq` type. The RSS 1.0 specification describes this as a sequence used to contain all the items, and to denote item order for rendering and reconstruction. After this statement, the items contained in the feed are listed, each identified with a URI. Therefore, the channel block describes this feed, specifying which items it contains.

The items themselves are listed separately: each is identified by a URI, and the channel block associates these resources with the channel, so there's no need for XML element nesting to group them together. Each item has its own set of properties, a title, and a description, as shown in the preceding RSS formats, along with a link that is defined as the item's URL. Usually, this is the same as the URI specified by the item's own `rdf:about` attribute.

Now recall the following code from the source:

```
<item rdf:about="http://journal.dajobe.org/journal/posts/2010/06/28/happy-
10th-birthday-redland/">

     <title>Happy 10th Birthday Redland</title>

     <link>http://journal.dajobe.org/journal/posts/2010/06/28/happy-10th-
birthday-redland/</link>
```

Again, terms from Dublin Core are used for the subject, creator (author), and date. This makes it much better suited for broad-scale syndication, because Dublin Core has become the de facto standard for dealing with document-descriptive content. The properties look like this:

```
      <dc:date>2010-06-28T16:03:54Z</dc:date>

     <dc:creator>Dave Beckett</dc:creator>
```

The example given here includes both a `<description>` and a `<content:encoded>` element, each with a slightly different version of the content text (plain text and escaped-XML, respectively). This is fairly redundant, but does improve the chances of particular feed readers being able to use the data. There are no hard-and-fast rules for which elements should be included in an RSS 1.0 feed, as long as they follow the general structural rules of RDF/XML. RDF generally follows a principal of "missing isn't broken," and according to that you can leave out any elements for which you don't have suitable values. By the same token, if you have extra data that may be relevant (for example links to the homepages of contributing authors) it may be useful to include that (see Chapter 14, "Web Services" for more information). Although a feed reader may not understand the elements in the RSS feed, a more generic RDF consumer may be able to use the data.

Looking again from an RDF perspective, note that the object of the statements that list the `item` URIs become the subject of the statements that describe the items themselves. In most XML languages, this kind of connection is made through element nesting, and it's clear that tree structures can be built this way. However, using identifiers for the points of interest (the resource URIs) in RDF also makes it possible for any resource to be related to any other resource, allowing arbitrary node and arc graph structures. Loops and self-references can occur. This versatility is an important feature of RDF, and is very similar to the arbitrary hyperlinking of the web. The downside is that there isn't any elegant way to represent graph structures in a tree-oriented syntax like XML, which is a major reason why RDF/XML syntax can be hard on the eye.

WORKING WITH NEWS FEEDS

To get a handle on the practicalities of how syndication works, it's worth looking at the technology from both the perspective of the publisher and that of the consumer of feeds. The rest of the chapter is devoted to practical code, so you will see in practice most of the key issues encountered when developing in this field. It is *really simple* to set up a syndication feed, but that phrase can be misleading. Without a little care, the result can be *really bad*. Because of this, first you see development from a consumer's point of view. It's the harder part of the equation (after all, you could simply write an RSS feed manually and call it done), but the best way of seeing where potential problems lie.

Newsreaders

Tools are available so that anyone can set up their own personal "newspaper," with content selected from the millions of syndicated feeds published on the web.

These aggregators are usually known as *newsreaders*, applications that enable you to both add and otherwise manage RSS feeds into a single "newspaper" of articles. Although public awareness of feed reading probably isn't very sophisticated, the technology is becoming ubiquitous and many web users are almost certainly reading material that has passed through RSS/Atom syndication without realizing it.

Data Quality

Whenever you work with material on the web, keep in mind that not all data purporting to be XML actually *is* XML. It's relatively common to find RSS feeds that are not well formed. One of the most common failings is that the characters in the XML document aren't from the declared encoding (UTF-8, ISO-8859-1, or something similar). Another likely corruption is that characters within the textual content of the feed are incorrectly escaped. A stray < instead of a `<` is enough to trip up a standard XML processor. Unfortunately, many of the popular blogging tools make it extremely easy to produce an ill-formed feed, a factor not really taken into account by the "simple" philosophy of syndication.

There was considerable discussion by the Atom developers on this issue, and responses ranged from the creation of an "ultra-liberal" parser that does its best to read *anything*, to the suggestion that aggregation tools simply reject ill-formed feeds to discourage their production. For pragmatic reasons, current newsreaders tend very much toward the liberal, though for applications where data fidelity is a priority, strict XML (and the clear rules of Atom) is always an option.

> ***NOTE** There is a simple way of checking the quality of RSS and Atom feeds — the Feed Validator at `http://feedvalidator.org` (or the W3C's installation at `http://validator.w3.org/feed/`). You can use it online or download it. It's backed by a huge array of test cases, providing reliable results and explanations of any errors or warnings.*

A SIMPLE AGGREGATOR

This section describes how you can build a simple newsreader application in the Python language that will aggregate news items from several channels. The program uses a configuration file that contains a list of feed addresses and, when run, presents the most recent five items from those feeds. To keep things simple, the reader has only a command-line user interface and won't remember what it has read from the feeds previously.

NOTE *All the code for news feed application is available in the code download for this chapter. How to set up your Python development environment is discussed in the "Implementation" section.*

Modeling Feeds

The programmer has many options for dealing with XML data, and the choice of approach often depends on the complexity of the data structures. In many circumstances the data can be read directly into a DOM model and processed from there, but there is a complication with syndicated material — the source data can be in one of three completely different syntaxes: RSS 1.0, RSS 2.0 (and its predecessors), and Atom. Because the application is only a simple newsreader, the sophistication offered by the RDF model behind RSS 1.0 isn't needed, but a simple model is implicit in news feeds: a feed comprises a number of items, and each of those items has a set of properties (refer to Figure 13-1).

Therefore, at the heart of the aggregator you will be building is an object-oriented version of that model. A feed is represented by a `Feed` object, and items are represented by `Item` objects. Each `Item` object has member variables to represent the various properties of that item. To keep things simple, the feed `Item` has only three properties: title, date, and content. The `Item` itself and these three properties can be mapped to an XML element in each of the three main syntaxes, as shown in Table 13-1.

TABLE 13-1: Core Item Terms in the Major Feed Syntaxes

MODEL	RSS 1.0	RSS X.X	ATOM
Item	`rss:item`	`item`	`atom:entry`
Title	`dc:title`	`title`	`atom:title`
Date	`dc:date`	`pubDate`	`atom:updated`
Content	`dc:description, content:encoded`	`description, xhtml:body`	`atom:content`

The namespaces of the elements are identified by their usual prefixes as follows (note that the "simple" RSS dialects don't have a namespace):

- `rss` is RSS 1.0 (`http://purl.org/rss/1.0/`)
- `dc` is Dublin Core (`http://purl.org/dc/elements/1.1/`)
- `xhtml` is XHTML (`www.w3.org/1999/xhtml`)
- `content` is the content module for RSS 1.0 (`http://purl.org/rss/1.0/modules/content/`)
- `atom` is, you guessed it, Atom (`www.w3.org/2005/Atom`)

The correspondence between the different syntaxes is only approximate. Each version has its own definitions, and although they don't coincide exactly, they are close enough in practice to be used in a basic newsreader.

Syntax Isn't Model

Though there's a reasonable alignment between the different elements listed in Table 13-1, this doesn't hold for the overall structure of the different syndication syntaxes. In particular, both plain XML RSS and Atom use element nesting to associate the items with the feed. If you look back at the sample of RSS 1.0, it's clear that something different is going on. RSS 1.0 uses the interpretation of RDF in XML to indicate that the `channel` resource has a property called `items`, which points to a `Seq` (sequence) of `item` instances. The `item` instances in the `Seq` are identified with URIs, as are the individual `item` entries themselves, which enables an RDF processor to know that the same resources are being referred to. In short, the structural interpretation is completely different.

Two pieces of information, implicit in the XML structure of simple RSS, are made explicit in RSS 1.0. In addition to the association between the feed and its component items, there is also the order of the items. The use of a `Seq` in RSS 1.0 and the document order of the XML elements in the "simple" RSS dialects provide an ordering, though there isn't any common agreement on what this ordering signifies. Atom explicitly states that the order of entries shouldn't be considered significant.

To keep the code simple in the aggregator presented here, two assumptions are made about the material represented in the various syntaxes:

- The items in the file obtained from a particular location are all part of the same conceptual feed. This may seem obvious; in fact, it has to be the case in plain XML RSS, which can have only one root `<rss>` element, but in RDF/XML (on which RSS 1.0 is based), it is possible to represent practically anything in an individual file. In practice, though, it's a relatively safe assumption.
- The second assumption is that in a news-reading application, the end user won't be interested in the order of the items in the feed (element or `Seq` order), but instead will want to know the dates on which the items were published.

The first assumption means there is no need to check where in the document structure individual items appear, and the second means there is no need to interpret the `Seq` or remember the element order. There is little or no cost to these assumptions in practice, yet it enables considerable code simplification. The only thing that needs to occur is to recognize when an element corresponding to an item (`rss:item`, `item`, or `atom:entry`) occurs within a feed, and to start recording its properties. In all the syntaxes the main properties are provided in child elements of the `<item>` element, so only a very simple structure has to be managed.

In other words, although there are three different syntaxes, a part of the structure is common to all of them despite differences in element naming. An object model can be constructed from a simple one-to-one mapping from each set of elements. On encountering a particular element in the XML, a corresponding action needs to be carried out on the objects. An XML programming tool is ideally suited to this situation: SAX.

SAX to the Rescue!

SAX (the Simple API for XML) works by responding to method calls generated when various entities within the XML document are encountered. The Python language supports SAX out of the box (in the modules `xml.sax`). Given that, the main tasks for feed parsing are to decide which elements should be recognized, and what actions should be applied when encountering them.

The entities of interest for this simple application are the following:

- The elements corresponding to items
- The elements corresponding to the properties of the items and the values of those properties

Three SAX methods can provide all the information the application needs about these elements:

- `startElement`
- `characters`
- `endElement`

The `startElement` method signals which element has been encountered, providing its name and namespace (if it has one). It's easy enough to tell if that element corresponds to an item. Refer to Table 13-1, and you know its name will either be `item` or `entry`. Similarly, each of the three kinds of properties of elements can be identified. The data sent to characters is the text content of the elements, which are the values of the properties. A call to the `endElement` method signals that the element's closing tag has been encountered, so the program can deal with whatever is inside it.

Again, using Table 13-1, you can derive the following simple rules that determine the nature of the elements encountered:

- `rss:item` | `item` | `atom:entry` = item
- `dc:title` | `title` | `atom:title` = title
- `dc:date` | `pubDate` | `atom:updated` = date
- `dc:description` | `content:encoded` | `description` | `xhtml:body` | `atom:content` = content

If `startElement` has been called, any subsequent calls matching the last three elements will pass on the values of that particular property of that element, until the `endElement` method is called. There may be calls to the elements describing properties outside of an item block, and you can reasonably assume that those properties apply to the feed as a whole. This makes it straightforward to extract the title of the feed.

NOTE *You may notice that the element names are pretty well separated between each meaning — there is little likelihood of the title data being purposefully published in an element called* `<date>`*, for example. This makes coding these rules somewhat easier, although in general it is good practice to make it possible to get at the namespace of elements to avoid naming clashes.*

Program Flow

When your application is run, the list of feeds is picked up from the text file. Each of the addresses, in turn, is passed to an XML parser. The aggregator then reads the data found on the web at that address. In more sophisticated aggregators, you will find a considerable amount of code devoted to the reading of data over HTTP in a way that both respects the feed publisher, and makes the system as efficient as possible. The XML parsers in Python however, are capable of reading data directly from a web address. Therefore, to keep things simple, a Python XML parser is shown in Figure 13-2. Python XML is discussed in the following section.

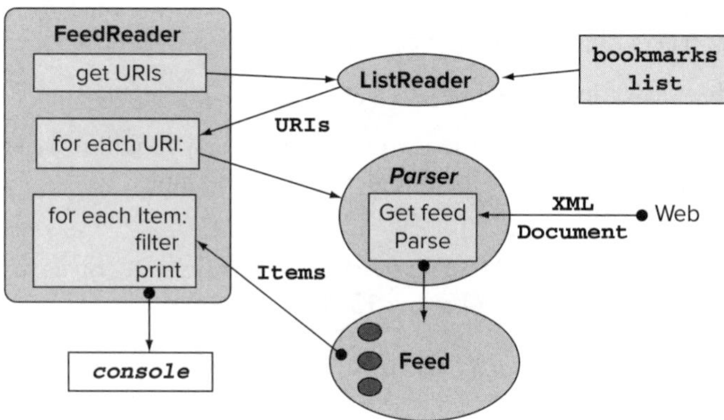

FIGURE 13-2

Implementation

Your feed reader is written in Python, a language that has reasonably sophisticated XML support. Everything you need to run it is available in the code downloads for this chapter, or as a free download from `www.python.org`. If you're not familiar with Python, don't worry — it's a very simple language, and the code is largely self-explanatory. All you really need to know is that it uses indentation to separate functional blocks (whitespace *is* significant), rather than braces `{}`. In addition, the `#` character means that the rest of the line is a comment. Python is explained in greater detail shortly in the next Try It Out, but before you begin using Python to run your feed reader, you need to take a few preparatory steps.

NOTE *It would be very straightforward to port this feed reader application to any other language with good XML support, such as Java or C#.*

1. Visit `www.python.org` and click the link to Download Python Now. Python comes in a complete package as a free download, available for most platforms — as its enthusiasts say, batteries are included. Installation is very straightforward; just follow the instructions on the website (you may have to add it to your system PATH; see the documentation for details). A Windows installer is included as part of the download. The standard package provides the Python interpreter, which can be run interactively or from a command line or even a web server. There's also a basic Integrated Development Environment tool called IDLE and plenty of documentation. Download and install Python now.
2. You will use Python to run the code for your feed reader. This code is contained in the following four files, which are all available in the code downloads for this chapter:

- `feed_reader.py` controls the operation.
- `feed.py` models the feed and items.
- `feed_handler.py` constructs objects from the content of the feed.
- `list_reader.py` reads a list of feed addresses.

Download these code files now, unless you want to create them yourself, because you will use them for the rest of the examples in the chapter. Save them to a local folder; for the example `C:\FeedReader` is used.

3. You also need the addresses of the feeds you'd like to aggregate. At its simplest, you can create a text file containing the URIs, as shown in Listing 13 -1:

LISTING 13-1: feeds.txt

```
http://www.fromoldbooks.org/rss.xml

http://www.25hoursaday.com/weblog/SyndicationService.asmx/GetRss

http://journal.dajobe.org/journal/index.rdf

http://planetrdf.com/index.rdf
```

An aggregator should be able to deal with all the major formats. In Listing 13-1 you have a selection: the first feed is in RSS 2.0 format, the second is Atom, and the third and fourth are in RSS 1.0. A text list is the simplest format in which the URIs can be supplied. For convenience, a little string manipulation makes it possible to use an IE, Chrome, or Firefox bookmarks file to supply the list of URIs. The addresses of the syndication feeds should be added to a regular bookmark folder in the browser. With IE, it's possible to export a single bookmark folder to use as the URI list, but with Chrome or Firefox, all the bookmarks are exported in one go.

The first code file you'll use is shown in Listing 13-2, and is set up to only read the links in the first folder in the aforementioned bookmark file. This source file contains a single class, `ListReader`, with a single method, `get_uris`:

LISTING 13-2: list_reader.py

```
import re

class ListReader:
    """ Reads URIs from file """

    def get_uris(self, filename):
        """ Returns a list of the URIs contained in the named file """
        file = open(filename, 'r')
        text = file.read()
        file.close()

        # get the first block of a Netscape file
        text = text.split('</DL>')[0]

        # get the uris
        pattern = 'http://\S*\w'
        return re.findall(pattern,text)
```

You can now begin your adventures with Python by using a simple utility class to load a list of feed URIs into the application.

TRY IT OUT Using Python to Read a List of URIs

The purpose here is just to confirm that your Python installation is working correctly. If you're not familiar with Python, this also demonstrates how useful command-line interaction with the interpreter can be.

1. Make sure that `feeds.txt` from Listing 13-1 is in the `C:\FeedReader` folder with the other `.py` files.
2. Open a command prompt and change directory to the folder containing these files.
3. Type in the command python and press Enter. You should see something like this:

   ```
   $ python

   Python 2.7.2+ (default, Oct  4 2011, 20:03:08)

   [GCC 4.6.1] on linux2

   Type "help", "copyright", "credits" or "license" for more information.

   >>>
   ```

   You are now in the Python interpreter.

4. Type in the following lines and press Enter after each line (the interpreter will display the >>> prompt):

```
>>> from list_reader import ListReader
>>> reader = ListReader()
>>> print reader.get_uris("feeds.txt")
```

After the last line, the interpreter should respond with the following:

```
['http://www.fromoldbooks.org/rss.xml',
'http://www.25hoursaday.com/weblog/SyndicationService.asmx/GetRss',
'http://journal.dajobe.org/journal/index.rdf', 'http://planetrdf.com/index.rdf']

>>>
```

How It Works

The first line you gave the interpreter was as follows:

```
from list_reader import ListReader
```

This makes the class `ListReader` in the package `list_reader` available to the interpreter (the package is contained in the file `list_reader.py`). This line creates a new instance of the `ListReader` class and assigns it to the variable `reader`:

```
reader = ListReader()
```

The next line you asked to be interpreted was as follows:

```
print reader.get_uris("feeds.txt")
```

This calls the `get_uris` method of the `reader` object, passing it a string, which corresponds to the filename of interest. The `print` method was used to display the object (on the command line) returned by the `get_uris` method. The object returned was displayed as follows:

```
['http://www.fromoldbooks.org/rss.xml',
'http://www.25hoursaday.com/weblog/SyndicationService.asmx/GetRss',
'http://journal.dajobe.org/journal/index.rdf', 'http://planetrdf.com/index.rdf']
```

This is the syntax for a standard Python list, here containing three items, which are the three URIs extracted from `feeds.txt`.

For an explanation of how `list_reader.py` worked internally, here's the source again:

```
import re

class ListReader:
    """ Reads URIs from file """

    def get_uris(self, filename):
        """ Returns a list of the URIs contained in the named file """
```

```
        file = open(filename, 'r')
        text = file.read()
        file.close()

        # get the first block of a Netscape file
        text = text.split('</DL>')[0]

        # get the uris
        pattern = 'http://\S*\w'
        return re.findall(pattern,text)
```

The get_uris method is called with a single parameter. This is the name of the file containing the list of URIs (the self parameter is an artifact of Python's approach to methods and functions, and refers to the method object). The file opens as read-only (r), and its contents are read into a string called text and then closed. To trim a Netscape bookmark file, the built-in split string method divides the string into a list, with everything before the first occurrence of the </DL> tag going into the first part of the list, which is accessed with the index [0]. The text variable will then contain this trimmed block, or the whole of the text if there aren't any </DL> tags in the file. A regular expression finds all the occurrences within the string of the characters http:// followed by any number of non-whitespace characters (signified by \S*) and terminated by an alphanumeric character. It's crude, but it works well enough for text and bookmark files. The URIs are returned from this method as another list.

Application Controller: FeedReader

The list of URIs is the starting point for the main control block of the program, which is the FeedReader class contained in feed_reader.py. If you refer to Figure 13-2, you should be able to see how the functional parts of the application are tied together. Here are the first few lines of feed_reader.py, which acts as the overall controller of the application:

Available for download on Wrox.com

```
import urllib2
import xml.sax
import list_reader
import feed_handler
import feed

feedlist_filename = 'feeds.txt'
def main():
    """ Runs the application """
    FeedReader().read(feedlist_filename)
```

feed_reader.py

The code starts with the library imports. urllib2 and xml.sax are used here only to provide error messages if something goes wrong with HTTP reading or parsing. list_reader is the previous URI list reader code (in list_reader.py), feed_handler contains the custom SAX handler (which you see shortly), and feed contains the class that models the feeds.

The name of the file containing the URI list is given as a constant. You can either save your list with this filename or change it here. Because Python is an interpreted language, any change takes effect the next time you run the program. The main() function runs the application by creating a new instance of the `FeedReader` class and telling it to read the named file. When the new instance of `FeedReader` is created, the `init` method is called automatically, which is used here to initialize a list that will contain all the items obtained from the feeds:

```
class FeedReader:
    """ Controls the reading of feeds """
    def __init__(self):
        """ Initializes the list of items """
        self.all_items = []
```

The `read` method looks after the primary operations of the aggregator and begins by obtaining a parser from a local helper method, `create_parser`, and then getting the list of URIs contained in the supplied file, as shown in the following code:

```
def read(self, feedlist_filename):
        """ Reads each of the feeds listed in the file """
        parser = self.create_parser()

        feed_uris = self.get_feed_uris(feedlist_filename)
```

The next block of code selects each URI in turn and does what is necessary to get the items out of that feed, which is to create a SAX handler and attach it to the parser to be called as the parser reads through the feed's XML. The magic of the SAX handler code will appear shortly, but reading data from the web and parsing it is a risky business, so the single command that initiates these actions, `parser.parse(uri)`, is wrapped in a `try...except` block to catch any errors. Once the reading and parsing occur, the `feed_handler` instance contains a `feed` object, which in turn contains the items found in the feed (you see the source to these classes in a moment). To indicate the success of the reading/parsing, the number of items contained in the feed is then printed. The items are available as a list of `handler.feed.items`, the length of this list (`len`) is the number of items, and the standard `str` function is used to convert this number to a string for printing to the console:

```
for uri in feed_uris:
            print 'Reading '+uri,
            handler = feed_handler.FeedHandler()
            parser.setContentHandler(handler)
            try:
                parser.parse(uri)
                print ' : ' + str(len(handler.feed.items)) + ' items'
                self.all_items.extend(handler.feed.items)

            except xml.sax.SAXParseException:
                print '\n XML error reading feed : '+uri
                parser = self.create_parser()
            except urllib2.HTTPError:
                print '\n HTTP error reading feed : '+uri
                parser = self.create_parser()
        self.print_items()
```

If an error occurs while either reading from the web or parsing, a corresponding exception is raised, and a simple error message is printed to the console. The parser is likely to have been trashed by the error, so a new instance is created. Whether or not the reading/parsing was successful, the program now loops back and starts work on the next URI on the list. Once all the URIs have been read, a helper method, `print_items` (shown in an upcoming code example), is called to show the required items on the console. The following methods in `FeedReader` are all helpers used by the `read` method in the previous listing.

The `get_feed_uris` method creates an instance of the `ListReader` class shown earlier, and its `get_uris` method returns a list of the URIs found in the file, like so:

```
def get_feed_uris(self, filename):
        """ Use the list reader to obtain feed addresses """
        lr = list_reader.ListReader()
        return lr.get_uris(filename)
```

The `create_parser` method makes standard calls to Python's SAX library to create a fully namespace-aware parser as follows:

```
def create_parser(self):
        """ Creates a namespace-aware SAX parser """
        parser = xml.sax.make_parser()
        parser.setFeature(xml.sax.handler.feature_namespaces, 1)
        return parser
```

The next method is used in the item sorting process, using the built-in `cmp` function to compare two values — in this case, the `date` properties of two items. Given the two values x and y, the return value is a number less than zero if $x < y$, zero if $x = y$, and greater than zero if $x > y$. The `date` properties are represented as the number of seconds since a preset date (usually January 1, 1970), so a newer item here will actually have a larger numeric date value. Here is the code that does the comparison:

```
def newer_than(self, itemA, itemB):
        """ Compares the two items """
        return cmp(itemB.date, itemA.date)
```

The `get_newest_items` method uses the `sort` method built into Python lists to reorganize the contents of the `all_items` list. The comparison used in the sort is the `newer_than` method from earlier, and a Python "slice" (`[:5]`) is used to obtain the last five items in the list. Putting this together, you have the following:

```
def get_newest_items(self):
        """ Sorts items using the newer_than comparison """
        self.all_items.sort(self.newer_than)
        return self.all_items[:5]
```

***NOTE** The slice is a very convenient piece of Python syntax and selects a range of items in a* `sequenceobject`*. For example,* `z = my_list[x:y]` *would copy the contents of* `my_list` *from index* `x` *to index* `y` *into list* `z`*.*

The print_items method applies the sorting and slicing previously mentioned and then prints the resultant five items to the console, as illustrated in the following code:

```
def print_items(self):
        """ Prints the filtered items to console """
        print '\n*** Newest 5 Items ***\n'
        for item in self.get_newest_items():
            print item
```

The final part of feed_reader.py is a Python idiom used to call the initial main() function when this file is executed:

```
if __name__ == '__main__':
    """ Program entry point """
    main()
```

Model: Feed and Item

The preceding FeedReader class uses a SAX handler to create representations of feeds and their items. Before looking at the handler code, following is the feed.py file, which contains the code that defines those representations. It contains two classes: Feed and Item. The plain XML RSS dialects generally use the older RFC 2822 date format used in e-mails, whereas RSS 1.0 and Atom use a specific version of the ISO 8601 format used in many XML systems, known as W3CDTF. As mentioned earlier, the dates are represented within the application as the number of seconds since a specific date, so libraries that include methods for conversion of the e-mail and ISO 8601 formats to this number are included in the imports. To simplify coding around the ISO 8601, a utility library will be used (dateutil).

The significance of BAD_TIME_HANDICAP is explained next, but first take a look at the following code:

Available for download on Wrox.com

```
import email.Utils
import dateutil.parser
import time

BAD_TIME_HANDICAP = 43200
```

feed.py

The Feed class in the following code is initialized with a list called items to hold individual items found in a feed, and a string called title to hold the title of the feed (with the title initialized to an empty string):

```
class Feed:
    """ Simple model of a syndication feed data file """
    def __init__(self):
""" Initialize storage """
        self.items = []
        self.title = ''
```

Although items are free-standing entities in a sense, they are initially derived from a specific feed, which is reflected in the code by having the `Item` instances created by the `Feed` class. The `create_item` method creates an `Item` object and then passes the title of the feed to the `Item` object's `source` property. Once initialized in this way, the `Item` is added to the list of items maintained by the `Feed` object like so:

```
def create_item(self):
        """ Returns a new Item object """
        item = Item()
        item.source = self.title
        self.items.append(item)
        return item
```

To make testing easier, the `Feed` object overrides the standard Python `__str__` method to provide a useful string representation of itself. All the method here does is run through each of the items in its list and add the string representation of them to a combined string:

```
def __str__(self):
        """ Custom 'toString()' method to pretty-print """
        string =''
        for item in self.items:
            string.append(item.__str__())
        return string
```

The `item` class essentially wraps four properties that will be extracted from the XML: `title`, `content`, `source` (the title of the feed it came from), and `date`. Each of these is maintained as an instance variable, the values of the first three being initialized to an empty string. It's common to encounter `date` values in feeds that aren't well formatted, so it's possible to initialize the `date` value to the current time (given by `time.time()`). The only problem with this approach is that any items with bad `date` values appear newer than all the others. As a little hack to prevent this without excluding the items altogether, a `handicap` value is subtracted from the current time. At the start, the constant `BAD_TIME_HANDICAP` was set to 43,200, represented here in seconds, which corresponds to 12 hours, so any item with a bad date is considered 12 hours old, as shown here:

```
class Item:
    """ Simple model of a single item within a syndication feed """
    def __init__(self):
        """ Initialize properties to defaults """
        self.title = ''
        self.content = ''
        self.source = ''
        self.date = time.time() - BAD_TIME_HANDICAP # seconds from the Epoch
```

The next two methods make up the setter for the value of the date. The first, `set_rfc2822_time`, uses methods from the e-mail utility library to convert a string (like `Sat, 10 Apr 2004 21:13:28 PDT`) to the number of seconds since 01/01/1970 (`1081656808`). Similarly, the `set_w3cdtf_time` method converts an ISO 8601–compliant string (for example, `2004-04-10T21:13:28-00:00`) into seconds. The method call is a little convoluted, but it works! If either conversion fails, an error message is printed, and the value of `date` remains at its initial (handicapped) value, as illustrated in the following code:

```
    def set_rfc2822_time(self, old_date):
            """ Set email-format time """
            try:
                temp = email.Utils.parsedate_tz(old_date)
                self.date = email.Utils.mktime_tz(temp)
            except ValueError:
                print "Bad date : \%s" \% (old_date)

        def set_w3cdtf_time(self, new_date):
            """ Set web-format time """
            try:
                self.date =  time.mktime(dateutil.parser.parse(new_date).timetuple())

            except ValueError:
                print "Bad date : \%s" \% (new_date)
```

The `get_formatted_date` method uses the e-mail library again to convert the number of seconds into a human-friendly form — for example, `Sat, 10 Apr 2004 23:13:28 +0200` — as follows:

```
    def get_formatted_date(self):
            """ Returns human-readable date string """
            return email.Utils.formatdate(self.date, True)
        # RFC 822 date, adjusted to local time
```

Like the `Feed` class, `Item` also has a custom — `str` — method to provide a nice representation of the object. This is simply the title of the feed it came from and the title of the item itself, followed by the content of the item and finally the date, as shown in the following code:

```
    def __str__(self):
            """ Custom 'toString()' method to pretty-print """
            return (self.source + ' : '
                + self.title +'\n'
                + self.content + '\n'
                + self.get_formatted_date() + '\n')
```

That's how feeds and items are represented, and you will soon see the tastiest part of the code, the SAX handler that builds `Feed` and `Item` objects based on what appears in the feed XML document. This file (`feed_handler.py`) contains a single class, `FeedHandler`, which is a subclass of `xlm.sax.ContentHandler`. An instance of this class is passed to the parser every time a feed document is to be read; and as the parser encounters appropriate entities in the feed, three specific methods are called automatically: `startElementNS`, `characters`, and `endElementNS`. The namespace-enhanced versions of these methods are used because the elements in feeds can come from different namespaces.

XML Markup Handler: FeedHandler

As a SAX parser runs through an XML document, events are triggered as different parts of the markup are encountered. A set of methods are used to respond to (handle) these events. For your feed reader, all the necessary methods will be contained in a single class, `FeedHandler`.

As discussed earlier, there isn't much data structure in a feed to deal with — just the feed and contained items — but there is a complication not mentioned earlier. The `<title>` and `<content>`

elements of items may contain markup. This shouldn't happen with RSS 1.0; the value of `content:encoded` is enclosed in a CDATA section or the individual characters escaped as needed. However, the parent RDF/XML specification does describe XML Literals, and material found in the wild often varies from the spec. In any case, the rich content model of Atom is designed to allow XML, and the RSS 2.0 specification is unclear on the issue, so markup should be expected. If the markup is, for example, HTML 3.2 and isn't escaped, the whole document won't be well formed and by definition won't be XML — a different kettle of fish. However, if the markup is well-formed XML (for example, XHTML), there will be a call to the SAX start and end element methods for each element within the content.

The code in `feed_handler.py` will have an instance variable, `state`, to keep track of where the parser is within an XML document's structure. This variable can take the value of one of the three constants. If its value is `IN_ITEM`, the parser is reading somewhere inside an element that corresponds to an item. If its value is `IN_CONTENT`, the parser is somewhere inside an element that contains the body content of the item. If neither of these is the case, the variable will have the value `IN_NONE`.

The code itself begins with imports from several libraries, including the SAX material you might have expected as well as the regular expression library `re` and the `codecs` library, which contain tools that are used for cleaning up the content data. The constant `TRIM_LENGTH` determines the maximum amount of content text to include for each item. For demonstration purposes and to save paper, this is set to a very low 100 characters. This constant is followed by the three alternative state constants, as shown in the following code:

Available for download on Wrox.com

```
import xml.sax
import xml.sax.saxutils
import feed
import re
import codecs

# Maximum length of item content
TRIM_LENGTH = 100

# Parser state
IN_NONE = 0
IN_ITEM = 1
IN_CONTENT = 2
```

feed_handler.py

The content is stripped of markup, and a regular expression is provided to match any XML-like tag (for example, `<this>`). However, if the content is HTML, it's desirable to retain a little of the original formatting, so another regular expression is used to recognize `<br>` and `<p>` tags, which are replaced with newline characters, as shown in the following code:

```
# Regular expressions for cleaning data
TAG_PATTERN = re.compile("<(.rt \n)+?>")
NEWLINE_PATTERN = re.compile("(<br.*>)rt(<p.*>)")
```

The `FeedHandler` class itself begins by creating a new instance of the `Feed` class to hold whatever data is extracted from the feed being parsed. The `state` variable begins with a value of `IN_NONE`, and an instance variable, `text`, is initialized to the empty string. The `text` variable is used to accumulate text encountered between the element tags, as shown here:

```
# Subclass from ContentHandler in order to gain default behaviors
class FeedHandler(xml.sax.ContentHandler):
    """ Extracts data from feeds, in response to SAX events """
def __init__(self):
        "Initialize feed object, interpreter state and content"
        self.feed = feed.Feed()
        self.state = IN_NONE
        self.text = ''
        return
```

The next method, `startElementNS`, is called by the parser whenever an opening element tag is encountered and receives values for the element name — the prefix-qualified name of the element along with an object containing the element's attributes. The name variable actually contains two values (it's a Python tuple): the namespace of the element and its local name. These values are extracted into the separate `namespace`, `localname` strings. If the feed being read were RSS 1.0, a `<title>` element would cause the method to be called with the values `name = ('http://purl.org/rss/1.0/', 'title'), qname = 'title'`. (If the element uses a namespace prefix, like `<dc:title>`, the `qname` string includes that prefix, such as `dc:title` in this case.) In this simple application the attributes aren't used, but SAX makes them available as an `NSAttributes` object.

NOTE *A tuple is an ordered set of values. A pair of geographic coordinates is one example, an RDF triple is another. In Python, a tuple can be expressed as a comma-separated list of values, usually surrounded by parentheses — for example,* `(1, 2, 3, "go")`. *In general, the values within tuples don't have to be of the same type. It's common to talk of* n-tuples, *where* n *is the number of values:* `(1, 2, 3, "go")` *contains four values so it is a 4-tuple.*

The `startElementNS` method determines whether the parser is inside content by checking whether the state is `IN_CONTENT`. If this isn't the case, the content accumulator `text` is emptied by setting it to an empty string. If the name of the element is one of those that corresponds to an item in the simple model (`item` or `entry`), a new item is created, and the state changes to reflect the parser's position within an item block. The last check here tests whether the parser is already inside an item block, and if it is, whether the element is one that corresponds to the content. The actual string comparison is done by a separate method to keep the code tidy, because several alternatives exist. If the element name matches, the state is switched into `IN_CONTENT`, as shown in the following code:

```
def startElementNS(self, name, qname, attributes):
        "Identifies nature of element in feed (called by SAX parser)"
        (namespace, localname) = name

        if self.state != IN_CONTENT:
            self.text = '' # new element, not in content
```

```
        if localname == 'item' or localname == "entry": # RSS or Atom
            self.current_item = self.feed.create_item()
            self.state = IN_ITEM
            return

        if self.state == IN_ITEM:
            if self.is_content_element(localname):
            self.state = IN_CONTENT
        return
```

The characters method merely adds any text encountered within the elements to the text accumulator like so:

```
    def characters(self, text):
        "Accumulates text (called by SAX parser)"
        self.text = self.text + text
```

The endElementNS method is called when the parser encounters a closing tag, such as </this>. It receives the values of the element's name and qname, and once again the name tuple is split into its component namespace, localname parts. What follows are a lot of statements, which are conditional based on the name of the element and/or the current state (which corresponds to the parser's position in the XML). This essentially carries out the matching rules between the different kinds of elements that may be encountered in RSS 1.0, 2.0, or Atom, and the Item properties in the application's representation. You may want to refer to the table of near equivalents shown earlier, and the examples of feed data to see why the choices are made where they are. Here is the endElementNS method:

```
    def endElementNS(self, name, qname):
        "Collects element content, switches state as appropriate
        (called by SAX parser)"
        (namespace, localname) = name
```

Now it is time to ask some questions:

1. First, has the parser come to the end of an item? If so, revert to the IN_NONE state (otherwise continue in the current state):

```
    if localname == 'item' or localname == 'entry': # end of item
                self.state = IN_NONE
                return
```

2. Next, are you in content? If so, is the tag the parser just encountered one of those classed as the end of content? If both answers are yes, the content accumulated from characters in text is cleaned up and passed to the current item object. Because it's the end of content, the state also needs shifting back down to IN_ITEM. Regardless of the answer to the second question, if the first answer is yes, you're done here, as shown in the following code:

```
    if self.state == IN_CONTENT:
                if self.is_content_element(localname): # end of content
                    self.current_item.content = self.cleanup_text(self.text)
                    self.state = IN_ITEM
                return
```

If you aren't in content, the flow continues.

Now that the content is out of the way, with its possible nested elements, the rest of the text that makes it this far represents the simple content of an element. You can clean it up, as outlined in the following code:

```
# cleanup text - we probably want it
        text = self.cleanup_text(self.text)
```

At this point, if the parser isn't within an `item` block and the element name is `title`, what you have here is the title of the feed. Pass it on as follows:

```
if self.state != IN_ITEM: # feed title
            if localname == "title":
                self.feed.title = self.text
            return
```

The parser must now be within an `item` block thanks to the last choice, so if there's a `title` element here, it must refer to the item. Pass that on too:

```
        if localname == "title":
               self.current_item.title = text
               return
```

Now you get to the tricky issue of dates. If the parser finds an RSS 1.0 date (`dc:date`) or an Atom date (`atom:updated`), it will be in ISO 8601 format, so you need to pass it to the item through the appropriate converter:

```
        if localname == "date" or localname == "updated":
               self.current_item.set_w3cdtf_time(text)
               return
```

RSS 2.0 and most of its relatives use a `pubDate` element in RFC 2822 e-mail format, so pass that through the appropriate converter as shown here:

```
           if localname == "pubDate":
               self.current_item.set_rfc2822_time(text)
               return
```

These last few snippets of code have been checking the SAX parser's position within the feed document structure, and depending on that position applying different processes to the content it finds.

Helper Methods

The rest of `feed_handler.py` is devoted to little utility or helper methods that wrap up blocks of functionality, separating some of the processing from the flow logic found in the preceding code. The first helper method, `is_content_element`, which checks the alternatives to determine whether the local name of the element corresponds to that of an item like so:

```
def is_content_element(self, localname):
        "Checks if element may contain item/entry content"
        return (localname == "description" or # most RSS x.x
```

```
            localname == "encoded" or # RSS 1.0 content:encoded
            localname == "body" or # RSS 2.0 xhtml:body
            localname == "content") # Atom
```

feed_handler.py

The next three methods are related to tidying up text nodes (which may include escaped markup) found within the content. Cleaning up the text begins by stripping whitespace from each end. This is more important than it might seem, because depending on the layout of the feed data there may be a host of newlines and tabs to make the feed look nice, but which only get in the way of the content. These unnecessary newlines should be replaced by a single space.

Next, a utility method, `unescape`, in the SAX library is used to unescape characters such as `<this>` to `<this>`. This is followed by a class to another helper method, `process_tags`, to do a little more stripping. If this application used a browser to view the content, this step wouldn't be needed (or even desirable), but markup displayed to the console just looks bad, and `<a href="...">` `hyperlinks` `<a>` won't work.

The next piece of cleaning is a little controversial. The content delivered in feeds can be Unicode, with characters from any international character set, but most consoles are ill prepared to display such material. The standard string encode method is used to flatten everything down to plain old ASCII. This is rather drastic, and there may well be characters that don't fit in this small character set. The second value determines what should happen in this case — possible values are `strict` (default), `ignore`, or `replace`. The `replace` alternative swaps the character for a question mark, hardly improving legibility. The `strict` option throws an error whenever a character won't fit, and it's not really appropriate here either. The third option, `ignore`, simply leaves out any characters that can't be correctly represented in the chosen ASCII encoding. The following code shows the sequence of method calls used to make the text more presentable:

```
    def cleanup_text(self, text):
        "Strips material that won't look good in plain text"
        text = text.strip()
        text = text.replace('\n', ' ')
        text = xml.sax.saxutils.unescape(text)
        text = self.process_tags(text)
        text = text.encode('ascii','ignore')
        text = self.trim(text)
        return text
```

The `process_tags` method (called from `cleanup_text`) uses regular expressions to first replace any <br> or <p> tags in the content with newline characters, and then to replace any remaining tags with a single space character:

```
    def process_tags(self, string):
        """ Turns <br/> into \n then removes all <tags> """
        re.sub(NEWLINE_PATTERN, '\n', string)
        return re.sub(TAG_PATTERN, ' ', string)
```

The cleaning done by the last method in the `FeedHandler` class is really a matter of taste. The amount of text found in each post varies greatly between different sources. You may not want to read whole essays through your newsreader, so the `trim` method cuts the string length down to a preset size determined by the TRIM_LENGTH constant. However, just counting characters and chopping when the desired length has been reached results in some words being cut in half, so this method looks for the first space character in the text after the TRIM_LENGTH index and cuts there. If there aren't any spaces in between that index and the end of the text, the method chops anyway. Other strategies are possible, such as looking for paragraph breaks and cutting there. Although it's fairly crude, the result is quite effective. The code that does the trimming is as follows:

```
    def trim(self, text):
        "Trim string length neatly"
        end_space = text.find(' ', TRIM_LENGTH)
        if end_space != -1:
text = text[:end_space] + " ..."
        else:
            text = text[:TRIM_LENGTH] # hard cut
        return text
```

That's it, the whole of the aggregator application. There isn't a lot of code, largely thanks to libraries taking care of the details. Now, with your code in place you can try it out.

TRY IT OUT Running the Aggregator

To run the code, you need to have Python installed (see the steps at the beginning of the Implementation section previously) and be connected to the Internet. There is one additional dependency, the dateutil library. Download this from http://pypi.python.org/pypi/python-dateutil and followed the installation instructions for your particular operating system. (The easiest, though not the most elegant way of installing this, is to copy the whole dateutil directory from the download into your code directory).

1. Open a command prompt window, and change directory to the folder containing the source files.
2. Type the following:

   ```
   python feed_reader.py
   ```

3. An alternative way to run the code is to use IDLE, a very simple IDE with a syntax-coloring editor and various debugging aids. Start IDLE by double-clicking its icon and then using its File menu, opening the feed_reader.py file in a new window. Pressing the F5 key when the code is in the editor window runs the application.
4. Run the application in you preferred manner. Whichever way you choose, you should see something like this:

```
        $ python feed_reader.py

        Reading http://www.fromoldbooks.org/rss.xml  : 20 items

        Reading
http://www.25hoursaday.com/weblog/SyndicationService.asmx/GetRss  : 10 items

        Reading http://journal.dajobe.org/journal/index.rdf  : 10 items

        Reading http://planetrdf.com/index.rdf  : 27 items
```

```
        *** Newest 5 Items ***
        Words and Pictures From Old Books : Strange and Fantastical
        Creatures, from Buch der Natur [Book of Nature] (1481), added on 13th Feb 20

               I cannot read the text (it&#x2019;s in medieval German), so
        these descriptions are arbitrary; I&#x2019;d ...

        liam@holoweb.net (Liam Quin)

Mon, 13 Feb 2012 10:15:00 +0100



        Dare Obasanjo aka Carnage4Life : Some Thoughts on Address Book
        Privacy and Hashing as an Alternative to Gathering Raw Email Addresses

          If you hang around technology blogs and news sites, you may have seen the
        recent dust up after it was ...

        Sun, 12 Feb 2012 21:29:28 +0100
```

... plus another three items.

How It Works

You've already seen the details of how this works, but here are the main points:

- A list of feed addresses is loaded from a text file.
- Each of the addresses is visited in turn, and the data is passed to a SAX handler.
- The handler creates objects corresponding to the feed and items within the feed.
- The individual items from all feeds are combined into a single list and sorted.
- The items are printed in the command window.

Extending the Aggregator

You could do a thousand and one things to improve this application, but whatever enhancement is made to the processing or user interface, you are still dependent on the material pumped out to feeds. XML is defined by its acronym as *extensible*, which means that elements outside of the core language can be included with the aid of XML namespaces. According to the underlying XML namespaces specification, producers can potentially put material from other namespaces pretty much where they like, but this isn't as simple as it sounds because consumers have to know what to do with them. So far, two approaches have been taken toward extensibility in syndication:

- RSS 2.0 leaves the specification of extensions entirely up to developers. This sounds desirable but has significant drawbacks because nothing within the specification indicates how an element from an extension relates to other elements in a feed. One drawback is that each extension appears like a completely custom application, needing all-new code at both the producer and consumer ends. Another drawback is that without full cooperation between developers, there's no way of guaranteeing that the two extensions will work together.

- The RSS 1.0 approach is to fall back on RDF, specifically the structural interpretation of RDF/XML. The structure in which elements and attributes appear within an RDF/XML document gives an unambiguous interpretation according to the RDF model, irrespective of the namespaces. You can tell that certain elements/attributes correspond to resources, and that others correspond to relationships between those resources. The advantage here is that much of the lower-level code for dealing with feed data can be reused across extensions, because the basic interpretation will be the same. It also means that independently developed extensions for RSS 1.0 are automatically compatible with each other.

Atom takes a compromise approach to extensions, through the specification of two constructs: Simple Extension Elements and Structured Extension Elements. The *Structured Extension Element* provides something similar to the extensibility of RSS 2.0, in that a block of XML that is in a foreign (that is, not Atom) namespace relies on the definition of the extension for interpretation (or to be ignored). Unlike RSS 2.0, some restrictions exist on where such a block of markup may appear in the feed, but otherwise it's open-ended. The *Simple Extension Element* provides something similar to the extensibility of RSS 1.0 in that it is interpreted as a property of its enclosing element, as shown here:

```
<feed xmlns="http://www.w3.org/2005/Atom"
      xmlns:im="http://example.org/im/">
...
     <author>
       <name>John Smith</name>
       <im:nickname>smiffy</im:nickname>
     </author>
...
</feed>
```

The Simple Extension Element, `<im:nickname>` here, must be in a foreign namespace. The namespace (`http://example.org/im/` with prefix `im:`) is given in this example on the root `<feed>` element, although following XML conventions it could be specified in any of the ancestor elements of the extension element, or even on the extension element itself. A Simple Extension Element can't have any child nodes, except for a mandatory text node that provides the value of the property, so this example indicates that the author has a property called `im:nickname` with the value `"smiffy"`.

To give you an idea of how you might incorporate support for extensions in the tools you build, here is a simple practical example for the demo application. As mentioned at the start of this chapter, a growing class of tools takes material from one feed (or site) and quotes it directly in another feed (or site). Of particular relevance here are online aggregators, such as the "Planet" sites: Planet Gnome, Planet Debian, Planet RDF, and so on. These are blog–like sites, the posts of which come directly from the syndication feeds of existing blogs or news sites. They each have syndication feeds of their own. You may want to take a moment to look at Planet RDF: the human-readable site is at `http://planetrdf.com`, and it has an RSS 1.0 feed at `http://planetrdf.com/index.rdf`. The main page contains a list of the source feeds from which the system aggregates. The RSS is very much like regular feeds, except the developers behind it played nice and included a reference back to the original site from which the material came. This appears in the feed as a per-item element from the Dublin Core vocabulary, as shown in the following:

```
...
<dc:source>Lost Boy by Leigh Dodds</dc:source>
...
```

The text inside this element is the title of the feed from which the item was extracted. It's pretty easy to capture this in the aggregator described here. To include the material from this element in the aggregated display, two things are needed: a way to extract the data from the feed and a suitable place to put it in the display.

Like the other elements the application uses, the local name of the element is enough to recognize it. It is certainly possible to have a naming clash on "source," though it's unlikely. This element is used to describe an item, and the code already has a way to handle this kind of information. Additionally, the code picks out the immediate source of the item (the title of the feed from whence it came) and uses this in the title line of the displayed results. All that is needed is another conditional, inserted at the appropriate point, and the source information can be added to the title line of the results.

In the following activity you see how such an extension can be supported by your feed reader application with a minor addition to the code.

TRY IT OUT Extending Aggregator Element Handling

This is a very simple example, but it demonstrates how straightforward it can be to make aggregator behavior more interesting:

1. Open the file `feed_handler.py` in a text editor.
2. At the end of the `endElementNS` method, insert the following code:

```
        ...
                if localname == "pubDate":
                    self.current_item.set_rfc2822_time(text)
                    return
if localname == "source":

                    self.current_item.source = '('+self.current_item.source+') '+text
                    return
            def is_content_element(self, localname):
                "Checks if element may contain item/entry content"
        ...
```

3. Run the application again (see the previous Try It Out).

How It Works

Among the items that the aggregator shows you, you should see something like this:

```
 (Planet RDF) Tim Berners-Lee : Reinventing HTML
     Making standards is hard work. It's hard because it involves listening
to other people and figuring ...
Tim Berners-Lee
Fri, 27 Oct 2006 23:14:10 +0200
```

The name of the aggregated feed from which the item has been extracted is in parentheses (Planet RDF), followed by the title of the original feed from which it came.

TRANSFORMING RSS WITH XSLT

Because syndicated feeds are usually XML, you can process them using XSLT directly (turn to Chapter 8, "XSLT" for more on XSLT). Here are three common situations in which you might want to do this:

- Generating a feed from existing data
- Processing feed data for display
- Browser Processing
- Preprocessing feed data for other purposes

The first situation assumes you have some XML available for transformation, although because this could be XHTML from cleaned-up HTML, it isn't a major assumption. The other two situations are similar to each other, taking syndication feed XML as input. The difference is that the desired output of the second is likely to be something suitable for immediate rendering, whereas the third situation translates data into a format appropriate for subsequent processing.

Generating a Feed from Existing Data

One additional application worth mentioning is that an XSLT transformation can be used to generate other feed formats when only one is available. If your blogging software produces only RSS 1.0, a standard transformation can provide your site with feeds for Atom and RSS 2.0. A web search will provide you with several examples (names like `rss2rdf.xsl` are popular!).

Be warned that the different formats may carry different amounts of information. For example, in RSS 2.0 most elements are optional, in Atom most elements are mandatory, virtually anything can appear in RSS 1.0, and there isn't one-to-one correspondence of many elements. Therefore, a conversion from one to the other may be lossy, or may demand that you artificially create values for elements. For demonstration purposes, the examples here use only RSS 2.0, a particularly undemanding specification for the publisher.

Listing 13-3 XSLT transformation generates RSS from an XHTML document (`xhtml2rss.xsl`):

Available for download on Wrox.com

LISTING 13-3: xhtml2rss.xsl

```
<xsl:stylesheet version="1.0"
    xmlns:xsl="http://www.w3.org/1999/XSL/Transform"
    xmlns:xhtml="http://www.w3.org/1999/xhtml">

<xsl:output method="xml" indent="yes"/>

<xsl:template match="/xhtml:html">
  <rss version="2.0">
    <channel>
    <description>This will not change</description>
    <link>http://example.org</link>
    <xsl:apply-templates />
```

```
      </channel>
    </rss>
  </xsl:template>

  <xsl:template match="xhtml:title">
    <title>
      <xsl:value-of select="." />
    </title>
  </xsl:template>

  <xsl:template match="xhtml:body/xhtml:h1">
    <item>
      <title>
        <xsl:value-of select="." />
      </title>
      <description>
        <xsl:value-of select="following-sibling::xhtml:p" />
      </description>
    </item>
  </xsl:template>

  <xsl:template match="text()" />

  </xsl:stylesheet>
```

This code can now be applied to your XHTML documents, as you will now see.

TRY IT OUT Generating RSS from XHTML

Chapter 8 contains more detailed information about how to apply an XSLT transformation to an XML document, but for convenience the main steps are as follows:

1. Open a text editor and type in Listing 13-3.
2. Save the file as `xhtml2rss.xsl`.
3. Type the following into the text editor:

Available for download on Wrox.com

```
<?xml version="1.0" encoding="UTF-8"?>
<!DOCTYPE html PUBLIC "-//W3C//DTD XHTML 1.0 Strict//EN"
        "http://www.w3.org/TR/xhtml1/DTD/xhtml1-strict.dtd">
<html xmlns="http://www.w3.org/1999/xhtml">
    <head>
        <title>My Example Document</title>
    </head>
    <body>
 <h1>A first discussion point</h1>
        <p>Something related to the first point.</p>
 <h1>A second discussion point</h1>
        <p>Something related to the second point.</p>
    </body>
</html>
```

document.html

4. Save the preceding code as `document.html` in the same folder as `xhtml2rss.xsl`.

5. Use an XSLT processor to apply the transformation to the document. Refer to Chapter 8 for details describing how to do this. A suitable processor is Saxon, available from `http://saxon.sourceforge.net/`.

   The command line for Saxon with `saxon9he.jar` and the data and XSLT file in the same folder is as follows:

```
java -jar saxon9he.jar -s:document.html -xsl:xhtml2rss.xsl -o:document.rss
```

   You will see a warning about "Running an XSLT 1 stylesheet with an XSLT 2 processor" — this can be ignored.

6. Open the newly created `document.rss` in the text editor. You should see the following RSS 2.0 document:

```
<?xml version="1.0" encoding="UTF-8"?>
<rss version="2.0" xmlns:xhtml="http://www.w3.org/1999/xhtml">
   <channel>
      <description>This will not change</description>
      <link>http://example.org</link>
      <title>My Example Document</title>
      <item>
         <title>A first discussion point</title>
         <description>Something related to the first point.</description>
      </item>
      <item>
         <title>A second discussion point</title>
         <description>Something related to the second point.</description>
      </item>
   </channel>
</rss>
```

How It Works

The root element of the style sheet declares the prefixes for the required namespaces, `xsl:` and `xhtml:`. The output element is set to deliver indented XML:

```
<xsl:stylesheet version="1.0"
    xmlns:xsl="http://www.w3.org/1999/XSL/Transform"
    xmlns:xhtml="http://www.w3.org/1999/xhtml">

<xsl:output method="xml" indent="yes"/>
```

The first template in the XSLT is designed to match the root `html` element of the XHTML document. In that document, the XHTML namespace is declared as the default, but in the style sheet it's necessary to refer explicitly to the elements using the `xhtml:` prefix to avoid conflicts with the no-namespace RSS. The template looks like this:

```
<xsl:template match="/xhtml:html">
  <rss version="2.0">
    <channel>
```

```
      <description>This will not change</description>
      <link>http://example.org</link>
      <xsl:apply-templates />
      </channel>
    </rss>
  </xsl:template>
```

This will output the `rss` and `channel` start tags followed by preset `description` and `link` elements, and then it applies the rest of the templates to whatever is inside the root `xhtml:html` element. The template then closes the `channel` and `rss` elements.

The next template is set up to match any `xhtml:title` elements like so:

```
<xsl:template match="xhtml:title">
  <title>
    <xsl:value-of select="." />
  </title>
</xsl:template>
```

There is just one matching element in the XHTML document, which contains the text `My example document`. This is selected and placed in a `title` element. Note that the input element is in the XHTML namespace, and the output has no namespace, to correspond to the RSS 2.0 specification.

The next template is a little more complicated. The material in the source XHTML document is considered to correspond to an item of the form:

```
<h1>Item Title</h1>
       <p>Item Description</p>
```

To pick these blocks out, the style sheet matches on `xhtml:h1` elements contained in an `xhtml:body`, as shown here:

```
<xsl:template match="xhtml:body/xhtml:h1">
  <item>
    <title>
      <xsl:value-of select="." />
    </title>
    <description>
      <xsl:value-of select="following-sibling::xhtml:p" />
    </description>
  </item>
</xsl:template>
```

An outer no-namespace `<item>` element wraps everything produced in this template. It contains a `<title>` element, which is given the content of whatever's in the context node, which is the `xhtml:h1` element. Therefore, the header text is passed into the item's `title` element. Next, the content for the RSS `<description>` element is extracted by using the `following-sibling::xhtml:p` selector. This addresses the next `xhtml:p` element after the `xhtml:h1`.

The final template is needed to mop up any text not directly covered by the other elements, which would otherwise appear in the output:

```
<xsl:template match="text()" />
</xsl:stylesheet>
```

NOTE *The style sheet presented in the preceding Try It Out assumes the source document will be well-formed XHTML, with a heading/paragraph structure following that of the example. In practice, the XSLT must be modified to suit the document structure. If the original document isn't XHTML (it's regular HTML 4, for example), you can use a tool such as HTML Tidy (*`http://tidy.sourceforge.net/`*) to convert it before applying the transformation.*

If the authoring of the original XHTML is under your control, you can take more control over the conversion process. You can add markers to the document to indicate which parts correspond to items, descriptions, and so on. This is the approach taken in the Atom microformat (`http://microformats.org/wiki/hatom`) — for example, `<div class="hentry">`. This enables an Atom feed to be generated from the XHTML and is likely to be convenient for CSS styling.

One final point: although this general technique for generating a feed has a lot in common with *screen scraping* techniques (which generally break when the page author makes a minor change to the layout), it's most useful when the authors of the original document *are* involved. The fact that the source document is XML greatly expands the possibilities. Research is ongoing into methods of embedding more general metadata in XHTML and other XML documents, with recent proposals available at the following sites:

- `http://microformats.org` (microformats)
- `www.w3.org/2004/01/rdxh/spec` (Gleaning Resource Descriptions from Dialects of Languages, or GRDDL)

Processing Feed Data for Display

What better way to follow a demonstration of XHTML-to-RSS conversion than an RSS-to-XHTML style sheet? This isn't quite as perverse as it may sound — it's useful to be able to render your own feed for browser viewing, and this conversion offers a simple way to view other people's feeds. Though it is relatively straightforward to display material from someone else's syndication feed on your own site this way, it certainly isn't a good idea without obtaining permission first. Aside from copyright issues, every time your page is loaded it will call the remote site, adding to its bandwidth load. You have ways around this — basically, caching the data locally — but that's beyond the scope of this chapter (see for example `http://stackoverflow.com/questions/ 3463383/php-rss-caching`).

Generating XHTML from RSS isn't very different from the other way around, as you can see in Listing 13-4:

Available for download on Wrox.com

LISTING 13-4: rss2xhtml.xsl

```
<xsl:stylesheet version="1.0"
    xmlns:xsl="http://www.w3.org/1999/XSL/Transform"
    xmlns="http://www.w3.org/1999/xhtml">
```

```
<xsl:output method="html" indent="yes"/>
<xsl:template match="rss">
  <xsl:text disable-output-escaping="yes">
    \&lt;!DOCTYPE html PUBLIC "-//W3C//DTD XHTML 1.0 Strict//EN"
    "http://www.w3.org/TR/xhtml1/DTD/xhtml1-strict.dtd"\&gt;
  </xsl:text>
  <html>
    <xsl:apply-templates />
  </html>
</xsl:template>

<xsl:template match="channel">
  <head>
    <title>
      <xsl:value-of select="title" />
    </title>
  </head>
  <body>
    <xsl:apply-templates />
  </body>
</xsl:template>

<xsl:template match="item">
  <h1><xsl:value-of select="title" /></h1>
  <p><xsl:value-of select="description" /></p>
</xsl:template>

<xsl:template match="text()" />

</xsl:stylesheet>
```

As you will now see, the same process can be used to make XHTML out of RSS that is used for making RSS out of XHTML.

TRY IT OUT Generating XHTML from an RSS Feed

Once again for more details of using XSLT see Chapter 8, but this activity gives you the basic steps for creating XHTML using an RSS Feed:

1. Enter Listing 13-4 into a text editor (or download it from the book's website).
2. Save it as `rss2xhtml.xsl` in the same folder as `document.rss`.
3. Apply the style sheet to `document.rss`. The command line for Saxon with `saxon9he.jar` and the data and XSLT file in the same folder is as follows:

```
java -jar saxon9he.jar -s:document.rss -xsl:rss2xhtml.xsl -o:document.html
```

4. Open the newly created `document.html` in the text editor. You should see the following XHTML document:

```
<!DOCTYPE html PUBLIC "-//W3C//DTD XHTML 1.0 Strict//EN"
 "http://www.w3.org/TR/xhtml1/DTD/xhtml1-strict.dtd">
<html xmlns="http://www.w3.org/1999/xhtml">
 <head>
```

```
        <title>My Example Document</title>
    </head>
    <body>
<h1>A first discussion point</h1>
        <p>Something related to the first point.</p>
        <h1>A second discussion point</h1>
        <p>Something related to the second point.</p>
    </body>
</html>
```

As you can see, it closely resembles the XHTML original (`document.html`) used to create the RSS data.

How It Works

As in the previous style sheet, the namespaces in use are those of XSLT and XHTML. This time, however, the output method is `html`. The `xml` output method can be used to produce equally valid data because XHTML is XML, but the syntax is a little tidier as shown in the following example (this is likely to vary between XSLT processors):

```
<xsl:stylesheet version="1.0"
    xmlns:xsl="http://www.w3.org/1999/XSL/Transform"
    xmlns="http://www.w3.org/1999/xhtml">

<xsl:output method="html" indent="yes"/>
```

The first template here matches the root `<rss>` element of the RSS 2.0 document. The template puts in place an appropriate `DOCTYPE` declaration, which is wrapped in an `xsl:text` element with escaping disabled to allow the end `<...>` characters to appear in the output without breaking this XML's well-formedness. The root element of the XHTML document is put in position, and the other templates are applied to the rest of the feed data. Here is the first template:

```
<xsl:template match="rss">
    <xsl:text disable-output-escaping="yes">
    &lt;!DOCTYPE html PUBLIC "-//W3C//DTD XHTML 1.0 Strict//EN"
    "http://www.w3.org/TR/xhtml1/DTD/xhtml1-strict.dtd"&gt;
  </xsl:text>
  <html>
    <xsl:apply-templates />
  </html>
</xsl:template>
```

The next template matches the `<channel>` element. This actually corresponds to two separate sections in the desired XHTML: the `head` and the `body`. All that's needed in the `head` is the content of the `title` element, which appears as an immediate child of `channel`. The material that must appear in the body of the XHTML document is a little more complicated, so other templates are applied to sort that out. Here, then, is the `channel` template:

```
<xsl:template match="channel">
  <head>
    <title>
      <xsl:value-of select="title" />
    </title>
```

```
    </head>
    <body>
      <xsl:apply-templates />
    </body>
  </xsl:template>
```

For each item element that appears in the feed, a pair of `<h1>` and `<p>` elements are created, corresponding to the RSS `<title>` and `<description>`. Here is the template, and you can see how the content is transferred from the RSS kinds of elements to their XHTML mappings:

```
<xsl:template match="item">
  <h1><xsl:value-of select="title" /></h1>
  <p><xsl:value-of select="description" /></p>
</xsl:template>
```

Once more a utility template is included to mop up any stray text, before the closing `xsl:stylesheet` element closes this document:

```
<xsl:template match="text()" />

</xsl:stylesheet>
```

Browser Processing

A bonus feature of modern web browsers, such as Mozilla and IE, is that they have XSLT engines built in. This means it's possible to style a feed format document in the browser. All that's needed is an XML Processing Instruction that points toward the style sheet. This is very straightforward, as shown here, modifying `document.rss`:

```
<?xml version="1.0"?>
<?xml-stylesheet type="text/xsl" href="rss2xhtml.xsl"?>
<rss version="2.0">
   <channel>
...
```

If you save this modified version as `document.xml` and open it with your browser, you'll see a rendering that's exactly the same as what you see with the XHTML version listed earlier.

NOTE *Browsers aren't that smart at figuring out what kind of document they're being presented with, so when saved and loaded locally, the filename extension has to be something the browser recognizes. If you try to load a file* `document.rss` *into a browser, chances are good it will ask you where you want to save it.*

When it comes to displaying XML (such as RSS and Atom) in a browser, the world's your oyster — you can generate XHTML using a style sheet, and the resulting document can be additionally styled using CSS. There's no real need for anyone to see raw XML in his or her browser. This is one reason the Atom group has created the `<info>` element, which can be used along with client-side styling to present an informative message about the feed alongside a human-readable rendering of the XML.

Preprocessing Feed Data

Another reason you might want to process feed data with XSLT is to interface easily with existing systems. For example, if you wanted to store the feed items in a database, you can set up a transformation to extract the content from a feed and format it as SQL statements, as follows:

```
INSERT INTO feed-table
   VALUES (item-id, "This is the title", "This is the item description");
```

One particularly useful application of XSLT is to use *transformation* to "normalize" the data from the various formats into a common representation, which can then be passed on to subsequent processing. This is, in effect, the same technique used in the aggregator application just shown, except there the normalization is to the application's internal representation of a feed model.

A quick web search should yield something suitable for most requirements like this, or at least something that you can modify to fit your specific needs. Two examples of existing work are Morten Frederiksen's anything-to-RSS 1.0 converter (`http://purl.org/net/syndication/subscribe/feed-rss1.0.xsl`) and Aaron Straup Cope's Atom-to-RSS 1.0 and 2.0 style sheets (`www.aaronland.info/xsl/atom/0.3/`).

Reviewing the Different Formats

A feed consumer must deal with at least three different syndication formats, and you may want to build different subsystems to deal with each individually. Even when XSLT is available this can be desirable, because no single feed model can really do justice to all the variations. How do you tell what format a feed is? Following are the addresses of some syndication feeds:

```
http://news.bbc.co.uk/rss/newsonline_world_edition/front_page/rss091.xml
http://blogs.it/0100198/rss.xml
http://purl.org/net/morten/blog/feed/rdf/
http://swordfish.rdfweb.org/people/libby/rdfweb/webwho.xrdf
http://icite.net/blog/?flavor=atom\&smm=y
```

You might suppose a rough rule of thumb is to examine the filename; however, this is pretty unreliable for *any* format on the web. A marginally more reliable approach (and one that counts as good practice against the web specifications) is to examine the MIME type of the data. A convenient way of doing this is to use the `wget` command-line application to download the files (this is a standard UNIX utility; a Windows version is available from `http://unxutils.sourceforge.net/`).

In use, `wget` looks like this:

```
D:\rss-samples>wget http://blogs.it/0100198/rss.xml
-16:23:35-  http://blogs.it/0100198/rss.xml
           => 'rss.xml'
Resolving blogs.it... 213.92.76.66
Connecting to blogs.it[213.92.76.66]:80... connected.
HTTP request sent, awaiting response... 200 OK
```

```
Length: 87,810 [text/xml]

100%[====================================>] 87,810        7.51K/s    ETA 00:00

16:23:48 (7.91 KB/s) - 'rss.xml' saved [87810/87810]
```

It provides a lot of useful information: the IP address of the host called, the HTTP response (`200 OK`), the length of the file in bytes (87,810), and then the part of interest, `[text/xml]`. If you run `wget` with each of the previous addresses, you can see the MIME types are as follows:

```
[application/atom+xml ] http://news.bbc.co.uk/rss/
                newsonline_world_edition/front_page/rss091.xml
 [text/xml] http://blogs.it/0100198/rss.xml
[application/rdf+xml] http://purl.org/net/morten/blog/feed/rdf/
[text/plain] http://swordfish.rdfweb.org/people/libby/rdfweb/webwho.xrdf
[application/atom+xml] http://icite.net/blog/?flavor=atom\&smm=y
```

In addition to the preceding MIME types, it's not uncommon to see `application/rss+xml` used, although that has no official standing.

However, this has still not helped determine what formats these are. The only reliable way to find out is to look inside the files and see what it says there (and even then it can be tricky). To do this you run `wget` to get the previous files, and have a look inside with a text editor. Snipping off the XML prolog (and irrelevant namespaces), the data files begin like this (this one is from `http://news.bbc.co.uk/rss/newsonline_world_edition/front_page/rss091.xml`):

```
<rss version="0.91">
   <channel>
   <title>BBC News  News Front Page  World Edition</title>
...
```

This example is clearly RSS, flagged by the root element. It even tells you that it's version 0.91. Here's another from `http://blogs.it/0100198/rss.xml`:

```
<rss version="2.0">
<channel>
   <title>Marc's Voice</title>
...
```

Again, a helpful root tells you this is RSS 2.0. Now here's one from `http://purl.org/net/morten/blog/feed/rdf/`:

```
<rdf:RDF xmlns="
http://purl.org/rss/1.0/" xmlns:rdf="http://www.w3.org/1999/02/22-rdf-syntax-ns#">

<channel rdf:about="http://purl.org/net/morten/blog/rdf">
 <title>Binary Relations</title>
...
```

The `rdf:RDF` root suggests, and the `rss:channel` element confirms, that this is RSS 1.0. However, the following from `http://swordfish.rdfweb.org/people/libby/rdfweb/webwho.xrdf` is a bit vaguer:

```
<rdf:RDF
    xmlns:rdf="http://www.w3.org/1999/02/22-rdf-syntax-ns#"
    xmlns:foaf="http://xmlns.com/foaf/0.1/">
...>

<rdf:Description rdf:about="">
  <foaf:maker>
    <foaf:Person>
      <foaf:name>Libby Miller</foaf:name>
...
```

The `rdf:RDF` root and a lot of namespaces could indicate that this is RSS 1.0 using a bunch of extension modules. You might have to go a long way through this file to be sure. The interchangeability of RDF vocabularies means that RSS 1.0 terms can crop up almost anywhere; whether or not you want to count any document as a whole as a syndication feed is another matter. As it happens, there aren't any RSS elements in this particular file; it's a *FOAF* (Friend-of-a-Friend) Personal Profile Document. It's perfectly valid data; it's just simply not a syndication feed as such.

Now for a last example from `http://icite.net/blog/?flavor=atom\&smm=y`:

```
<feed version="0.3"
    xmlns="http://purl.org/atom/ns#"
    xmlns:dc="http://purl.org/dc/elements/1.1/"
    xml:lang="en">

    <title>the iCite net development blog</title>
...
```

The `<feed>` gives this away from the start: this is Atom. The version is only 0.3, but chances are good it will make it to version 1.0 without changing that root element.

These examples were chosen because they are all *good* examples — that is to say, they conform to their individual specifications. In the wild, things might get messy, but at least the preceding checks give you a place to start.

USEFUL RESOURCES

Here's a selection of some additional resources for further information on the topics discussed in this chapter. The following sites are good specifications resources:

- **RSS 1.0:** `http://purl.org/rss/1.0/spec`
- **RSS 2.0:** `http://blogs.law.harvard.edu/tech/rss`
- **Atom:** `www.ietf.org/rfc/rfc4287.txt`
- **Atom Wiki:** `www.intertwingly.net/wiki/pie/FrontPage`
- **RDF:** `www.w3.org/RDF/`

These sites offer tutorials:

- **rdf:about:** `www.rdfabout.com`
- **Atom Enabled:** `www.atomenabled.org`
- **Syndication Best Practices:** `www.ariadne.ac.uk/issue35/miller/`
- **The Absolute Minimum Every Software Developer Absolutely, Positively Must Know About Unicode and Character Sets (No Excuses!), by Joel Spolsky:** `www.joelonsoftware.com/articles/Unicode.html`

Some miscellaneous resources include the following:

- `http://code.google.com/p/feedparser/`
- **Feed Validator:** `http://feedvalidator.org`
- **RDF Validator:** `www.w3.org/RDF/Validator/`
- **Dave Beckett's RDF Resource Guide:** `www.ilrt.bris.ac.uk/discovery/rdf/resources/`
- **RSS-DEV Mailing List:** `http://groups.yahoo.com/group/rss-dev/`

SUMMARY

- Current ideas of content syndication grew out of "push" technologies and early meta data efforts, the foundations laid by CDF and MCF followed by Netscape's RSS 0.9 and Scripting News format.
- The components of syndication systems carry out different roles: server-producer, client-consumer, client-producer, and server-consumer.
- RSS 1.0 is based on RDF using the RDF/XML syntax.
- RSS 2.0 is now more prevalent and uses a simpler XML model.
- Atom is the most recent XML feed format and is designed according to known best practices on the Web.
- Building an aggregator is straightforward using a standard programming language (Python).
- XSLT transformations can be used to convert between RSS and another format (XHTML).

EXERCISES

You can find suggested solutions to these questions in Appendix A.

1. At the end of the description of the simple Python aggregator, it was demonstrated how relatively simple it is to extend the range of the elements covered, by adding support for `dc: source`. Your first challenge is to extend the application so that it also displays the author of a feed entry, if that information is available.

2. You saw toward the end of the chapter how the most common syndication formats show themselves, and earlier in the chapter you saw how it is possible to run an XSLT style sheet over RSS feeds to produce an XHTML rendering. The exercise here is to apply the second technique to the first task. Try to write an XSLT transformation that indicates the format of the feed, together with its title.

▶ WHAT YOU LEARNED IN THIS CHAPTER

TOPIC	KEY POINTS
Syndication	Syndication of web feeds is similar to syndication in traditional publishing where a new item is added to the publication/feed.
XML feed formats	For historical reasons, three different formats are in common use: RSS 1.0, RSS 2.0, and Atom. Although the philosophy, style, and syntax of each approach is different, the data they carry is essentially the same.
RSS 1.0 characteristics	RSS 1.0 is based on the RDF data model, with names for the elements coming from different vocabularies. It's extremely versatile but at the cost of complexity in its syntax.
RSS 2.0 characteristics	RSS 2.0 is the simplest feed format and probably the most widely deployed. However, its specification is rather loose and somewhat antiquated.
Atom characteristics	Atom is a straightforward XML format but it has a very solid, modern specification.
Data quality	There is considerable variation in the quality of feed data on the Web. Software built to consume feeds should take this into consideration.
Syndication systems	Syndication is, like the Web on which it operates, a client-server system. However, individual components may act as publishers or consumers of feed data. For example, an online aggregator will operate server-side, but consume data from remote feeds.
Aggregation	A common component of feed systems is the aggregator, which polls different feeds and merges the entries it finds into a single display (and/or feed). Aggregators are relatively straightforward to build using regular programming languages.
Transformation	As the common feed formats are XML, standard XML tools such as XSLT can be put to good use. (Although RSS 1.0 uses the RDF model, the actual XML for feeds is simple enough that this still applies).

14 Web Services

WHAT YOU WILL LEARN IN THIS CHAPTER:

- What a Remote Procedure Call (RPC) is
- Which RPC protocols exist
- Why web services provides more flexibility than previous RPC Protocols
- How XML-RPC works
- Why most web services implementations should use HTTP as a transport protocol
- How HTTP works under the hood
- How the specifications that surround web services fit together

So far, you've learned what XML is, how to create well-formed and valid XML documents, and you've even seen ways of programatically interfacing with XML documents. You also learned that XML isn't really a language on its own; it's a meta language, to be used when creating other languages.

This chapter takes a slightly different turn. Rather than discuss XML itself, it covers an application of XML: *web services*, which enable objects on one computer to call and make use of objects on other computers. In other words, web services are a means of performing distributed computing.

WHAT IS AN RPC?

It is often necessary to design *distributed systems*, whereby the code to run an application is spread across multiple computers. For example, to create a large transaction processing system, you might have a separate server for business logic objects, one for presentation logic objects, a database server, and so on, all of which need to talk to each other (see Figure 14-1).

For a model like this to work, code on one computer needs to call code on another computer. For example, the code in the web server might need a list of orders for display on a web page, in which case it would call code on the business objects server to provide that list of orders. That code, in turn, might need to talk to the database. When code on one computer calls code on another computer, this is called a *remote procedure call (RPC)*.

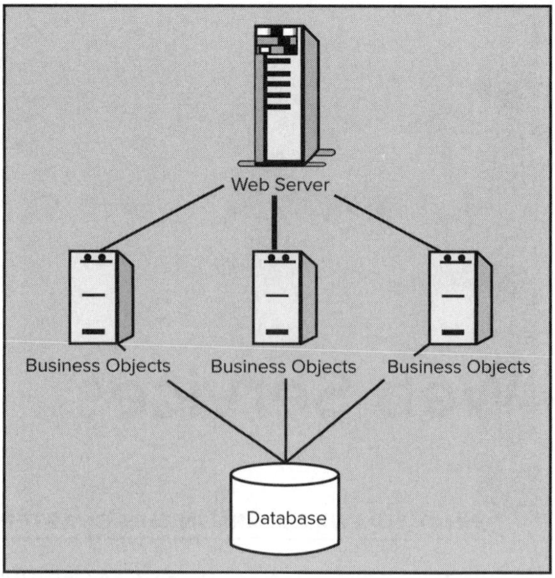

FIGURE 14-1

To make an RPC, you need to know the answer to the following questions:

- Where does the code you want to call reside? If you want to execute a particular piece of code, you need to know where that code is!
- Does the code need any parameters? If so, what type? For example, if you want to call a remote procedure to add two numbers, that procedure needs to know what numbers to add.
- Will the procedure return any data? If so, in what format? For example, a procedure to add two numbers would return a third number, which would be the result of the calculation, but some methods have no need to return a value.

In addition, you need to deal with networking issues, packaging any data for transport from computer to computer, and a number of other issues. For this reason, a number of RPC *protocols* have been developed.

NOTE *A* protocol *is a set of rules that enables different applications, or even different computers, to communicate. For example, TCP (Transmission Control Protocol) and IP (Internet Protocol) are protocols that enable computers on the Internet to talk to each other, because they specify rules regarding how data should be passed, how computers are addressed, and so on.*

These protocols specify how to provide an address for the remote computer, how to package data to be sent to the remote procedures, how to retrieve a response, how to initiate the call, how to deal with errors, and all of the other details that need to be addressed to enable multiple computers to communicate with each other. (Such RPC protocols often piggyback on other protocols; for example, an RPC protocol might specify that TCP/IP must be used as its network transport.)

RPC PROTOCOLS

Several protocols exist for performing remote procedure calls, but the most common are *Distributed Component Object Model* (DCOM), *Internet Inter-ORB Protocol* (IIOP) and *Java RMI* (you will learn more about these in the following sections). DCOM and IIOP are themselves extensions of earlier technologies, namely COM and CORBA respectively. Each of these protocols provides the functionality needed to perform remote procedure calls, although each has its drawbacks. The following sections discuss these protocols and those drawbacks, without providing too many technical details.

COM and DCOM

Microsoft developed a technology called the *Component Object Model*, or *COM* (see `http://www.microsoft.com/com/default.mspx`), to help facilitate *component-based software*, which is software that can be broken down into smaller, separate components that can then be shared across an application, or even across multiple applications. COM provides a standard way of writing objects so they can be discovered at run time and used by any application running on the computer. In addition, COM objects are language independent. That means you can write a COM object in virtually any programming language — C, C++, Visual Basic, and so on — and that object can talk to any other COM object, even if it was written in a different language.

A good example of COM in action is Microsoft Office. Because much of Office's functionality is provided through COM objects, it is easy for one Office application to make use of another. For example, because Excel's functionality is exposed through COM objects, you might create a Word document that contains an embedded Excel spreadsheet.

However, this functionality is not limited to Office applications; you could also write your own application that makes use of Excel's functionality to perform complex calculations, or that uses Word's spell-checking component. This enables you to write your applications faster, because you don't have to write the functionality for a spell-checking component or a complex math component yourself. By extension, you could also write your own shareable components for use in others' applications.

COM is a handy technology to use when creating reusable components, but it doesn't tackle the problem of distributed applications. For your application to make use of a COM object, that object must reside on the same computer as your application. For this reason, Microsoft developed a technology called *Distributed COM*, or *DCOM*. DCOM extends the COM programming model, enabling applications to call COM objects that reside on remote computers. To an application, calling a remote object from a server using DCOM is just as easy as calling a local object on the same PC using COM — as long as the necessary configuration has been done ahead of time.

DCOM therefore enables you to manipulate COM objects on one machine from another. A common use of this is seen when querying data sources that reside on different computers using SQL Server's distributed query mechanism. If you wish to make an update on one machine (only if you have first updated data on a second machine) then DCOM enables you to wrap both operations in a transaction which can be either rolled back if any step of the operation fails or committed if all steps are successful.

Nonetheless, as handy as COM and DCOM are for writing component-based software and distributed applications, they have one major drawback: both of these technologies are Microsoft-specific. The COM objects you write, or that you want to use, will work only on computers running Microsoft Windows; and even though you can call remote objects over DCOM, those objects also must be running on computers using Microsoft Windows.

NOTE *DCOM implementations have been written for non-Microsoft operating systems, but they haven't been widely accepted. In practice, when someone wants to develop a distributed application on non-Microsoft platforms, they use one of the other RPC protocols.*

For some people, this may not be a problem. For example, if you are developing an application for your company and you have already standardized on Microsoft Windows for your employees, using a Microsoft-specific technology might be fine. For others, however, this limitation means that DCOM is not an option.

CORBA and IIOP

Prior even to Microsoft's work on COM, the *Object Management Group*, or *OMG* (see `www.omg.org`), developed a technology to solve the same problems that COM and DCOM try to solve, but in a platform-neutral way. They called this technology the *Common Object Request Broker Architecture*, or *CORBA* (see `www.corba.org`). As with COM, CORBA objects can be written in virtually any programming language, and any CORBA object can talk to any other, even if it was written in a different language. CORBA works similarly to COM, the main difference being who supplies the underlying architecture for the technology.

For COM objects, the underlying COM functionality is provided by the operating system (Windows), whereas with CORBA, an *Object Request Broker* (ORB) provides the underlying functionality (see Figure 14-2). In fact, the processes for instantiating COM and CORBA objects are similar.

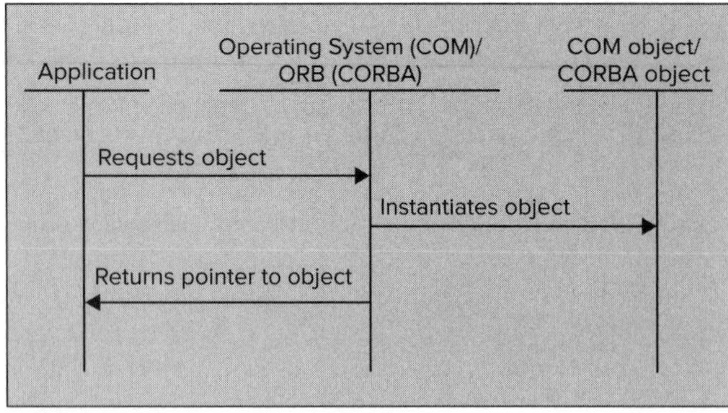

FIGURE 14-2

Although the concepts are the same, using an ORB instead of the operating system to provide the base object services offers one important advantage: it makes the CORBA platform independent. Any vendor that creates an ORB can create versions for Windows, UNIX, Linux, Mac, and so on.

Furthermore, the OMG created the *Internet Inter-ORB Protocol* (*IIOP*), which enables communication between different ORBs. This means that you not only have platform independence, but you also have ORB independence. You can combine ORBs from different vendors and have remote objects talking to each other over IIOP (as long as you avoid any vendor-specific extensions to IIOP).

Neither COM nor CORBA are easy to work with, which dramatically reduced their acceptance and take-up. Although COM classes are reasonably easy to use, and were the basis of thousands of applications including Microsoft Office, they are difficult to design and create. CORBA suffered similar problems, and these difficulties, as well as such scenarios as *DLL hell* in COM (mismatched incompatible versions of libraries of a machine) led to the design of other techniques.

Java RMI

Both DCOM and IIOP provide similar functionality: a language-independent way to call objects that reside on remote computers. IIOP goes a step further than DCOM, enabling components to run on different platforms. However, a language already exists that is specifically designed to enable you *to write once, run anywhere*: Java. (That was the theory; in practice it wasn't that smooth and many people complained that it was more like *write once, debug everywhere*.)

Java provides the *Remote Method Invocation*, or *RMI*, system (see `http://www.oracle.com/technetwork/java/javase/tech/index-jsp-136424.html`) for distributed computing. Because Java objects can be run from any platform, the idea behind RMI is to just write everything in Java and then have those objects communicate with each other.

Although Java can be used to write CORBA objects that can be called over IIOP, or even to write COM objects using certain nonstandard Java language extensions, using RMI for distributed computing can provide a shorter learning curve because the programmer isn't required to learn about CORBA and IIOP. All of the objects involved use the same programming language, so any data types are simply the built-in Java data types, and Java exceptions can be used for error handling. Finally, Java RMI can do one thing DCOM and IIOP can't: it can transfer code with every call. That is, even when the remote computer you're calling doesn't have the code it needs, you can send it and still have the remote computer perform the processing.

The obvious drawback to Java RMI is that it ties the programmer to one programming language, Java, for all of the objects in the distributed system.

THE NEW RPC PROTOCOL: WEB SERVICES

Because the Internet has become the platform on which the majority of applications run, or at least partially run, it's no surprise that a truly language- and platform-independent way of creating distributed applications would become the goal of software development. This aim has made itself known in the form of *web services*.

> ***NOTE*** *The exact definition of a web service is one of those never-ending discussions. Some would describe even a simple request for a standard web page as an example. In this book, a web service is a service that accepts a request and returns data or carries out a processing task. The data returned is normally formatted in a machine-readable form, without a focus on the content and the presentation, as you would expect in a standard web page. Another distinction is that made between a service and an XML web service. The latter means that at least one aspect, the request or the response, consists of XML. This chapter mostly covers services that utilize XML to some extent while pointing out where alternatives, such as JSON, could be adopted.*

Web services are a means for requesting information or carrying out a processing task over the Internet, but, as stated, they often involve the encoding of both the request and the response in XML. Along with using standard Internet protocols for transport, this encoding makes messages universally available. That means that a Perl program running on Linux can call a .NET program running on Windows.NET, and nobody will be the wiser.

Of course, nothing's ever quite that simple, especially when so many vendors, operating systems, and programming languages exist. To make these web services available, there must be standards so that everyone knows what information can be requested, how to request it, and what form the response will take.

XML web services have two main designs that differ in their approach to how the request is made. The first technique, known as *XML-RPC*, mimics how traditional function calls are made because the name of the method and individual parameters are wrapped in an XML format. The second version uses a *document* approach. This simply specifies that the service expects an XML document as its input, the format of which is predefined, usually by an XML Schema. The service then processes the document and carries out the necessary tasks.

The following sections look at XML-RPC, a simple form of web services. The discussion is then extended to look at the more heavy-duty protocols and how they fit together. The next chapter takes a closer look at two of the most commonly used protocols: SOAP and WSDL.

One topic that needs to be discussed before either method though is what's known as the *Same Origin policy.*

The Same Origin Policy

One of the problems you may face when you want to use a web service from a browser arises because, by default, a browser will not be able to access a web service that resides on a different domain. For example, if your web page is accessed via `http://www.myServer.com/customers.aspx`, it will not be allowed to make a web call to `http://www.AnotherDomain.com`. Ostensibly, this means that you won't be able to use the vast amount of web services that others have produced, many of which are free, from your own pages. Fortunately, you have a number of ways to work around the Same Origin policy.

Using a Server-Side Proxy

The restriction on calling services from a different domain applies only to code running in the client's browser. This means that you can overcome the limitation by wrapping the service you want with one of your own that runs on the same domain as the page you want to use it. Then, when you call a method from your browser the request is passed to the service on your domain. This is, in turn, passed to the original service, which returns the response to your proxy, which finally returns the data to the web browser. It's even often possible to create a generic proxy that can wrap many services with minimal configuration.

A secondary benefit of this sort of implementation is that you can often simplify the interface exposed by the original service. For example, to use Google's search service directly you need to include a secret key with each request. With a proxy, this key can be stored in the proxy's config file and the web browser doesn't need to know it. Additionally, the response from the service can be massaged to make it easier to use from a browser; some services might return a lot of extra data that is of no use, and this can be filtered out by the proxy.

In general, a server-side proxy gives you the most power, but it can be overkill in some cases. There are a few other workarounds that may be preferable in other situations.

Using Script Blocks

Another way around the Same Origin policy is to take advantage of the fact that script blocks themselves are allowed to be pulled from a different domain. For example, to embed Google Analytics code in your page you need to include a JavaScript block that has its `src` attribute pointing to Google's domain. You can use this facility to call simple web services that only need a `GET` request, that is, they rely on the URL carrying any additional data in the querystring. For example, follow these steps to get a service you may want to use to return the conversion rate for two currencies:

1. Create a request that contains the two denominations, such as:

    ```
    http://www.Currency.com/converter.asmx?from=USD&to=GBP
    ```

2. This returns the conversion factor to change U.S. dollars to British pounds. Instead of just a number being returned, the following JavaScript snippet is sent back:

    ```
    var conversionFactor = 0.638;
    ```

3. Take advantage of this service by dynamically creating a `<script>` block like the following:

    ```
    <script "type=text/javascript"
     src="http://www.Currency.com/converter.asmx?from=USD&to=GBP">
    </script>
    ```

4. The web service then effectively adds the code shown earlier so that now, in your page, is a block like this:

    ```
    <script type= "text/javascript"
     src="http://www.Currency.com/converter.asmx?from=USD&to=GBP">
    var conversionFactor = 0.638;
    </script>
    ```

You can now use the variable `conversionFactor` to turn any amount of dollars into pounds.

This process has been formalized and is known as JSONP. The technique is virtually identical, except that in JSONP the results are accessed via a function rather than a variable — for example, `getConversionFactor()` — and the data is in a JSON format. Helper methods are available to simplify the whole process in many client-side libraries; jQuery, for instance, makes the whole process very simple.

NOTE *JSON and JSONP are outside the scope of this chapter. If you want to learn more, there is simple introduction at the W3C's site:* `http://www.w3resource.com/JSON/JSONP.php`.

Allowing Different Domain Requests from the Server

You can call a service on a different domain in a few other ways that all have one thing in common: the server must be configured to allow such connections. Internet Explorer, from version 8 onward, has a native object called `XDomainRequest` that works in a similar manner to the more familiar `XMLHttpRequest` that is available in all modern browsers. The difference is that it enables cross-domain requests if the server that hosts the service includes a special heading, named `Access-Control-Allow-Origin`, to the browser's initial request that contains the domain name of the request. There are various ways to configure this header; you can find more information on usage at `http://msdn.microsoft.com/en-us/library/dd573303(v=vs.85).aspx`.

Another alternative to any of these workarounds in the Same Origin policy is to use Adobe's Flash component to make the request. Again, this plug-in can make cross-domain requests if the server is configured with a cross-domain policy file. The full details are available at `http://www.adobe.com/devnet/articles/crossdomain_policy_file_spec.html`.

Finally, Microsoft's IIS web server enables you to add a cross-domain policy file similar to Adobe's version, but with more options that lets you service calls from other domains. This is primarily intended to be used from Silverlight, a browser plug-in similar to Flash. You can find the details here: `http://msdn.microsoft.com/en-us/scriptjunkie/gg624360`.

Now that you've seen some of the hurdles in calling services on other domains, the next section returns to the XML-RPC scenario.

Understanding XML-RPC

One of the easiest ways to see web services in action is to look at the XML-RPC protocol. Designed to be simple, it provides a means for calling a remote procedure by specifying the procedure to call and the parameters to pass. The client sends a command, encoded as XML, to the server, which performs the remote procedure call and returns a response, also encoded as XML.

The protocol is simple, but the process — sending an XML request over the Web and getting back an XML response — is the foundation of web services, so understanding how it works will help you understand more complex protocols such as SOAP.

To practice eliminating the need for cross-domain workarounds, you'll use a service hosted on the same domain as the client in the following activity. The service is a simple math one; two numbers can be passed in, and an arithmetic operation performed on them. The service exposes two methods, which are identified as `MathService.Add` and `MathService.Subtract`.

TRY IT OUT Using a Basic RPC Service

This Try It Out won't go into the full details of creating the service, but it's basically a web page that accepts the request XML and parses it to extract the name of the method called and the two operands. It then performs the relevant operation and returns the result as an XML document.

1. An XML-RPC call simply wraps the required parameters in a standard form. The XML the service needs looks like the following:

Available for download on Wrox.com

```
<methodCall>
  <methodName>MathService.Add</methodName>
  <params>
    <param>
      <value>
        <double>17</double>
      </value>
    </param>
    <param>
      <value>
        <double>29</double>
      </value>
    </param>
  </params>
</methodCall>
```

XML-RPC Demo

2. Call the `MathService.Add` method and pass in two operands, 17 and 29. The function looks like this:

```
double result = Add(double operand1, double operand2)
```

3. Alternatively, had the service been designed that way, you could pass the request using a structure containing the operands like so:

```
<methodCall>
  <methodName>MathService.Add</methodName>
  <params>
    <param>
      <value>
        <struct>
          <member>
            <name>Operand1</name>
            <value>
              <double>17</double>
            </value>
```

```
              </member>
              <member>
                <name>Operand2</name>
                <value>
                  <double>29</double>
                </value>
              </member>
            </struct>
          </value>
        </param>
      </params>
    </methodCall>
```

For this example that method would have been over-complicated, but in some cases it is easier than having a function with a large number of arguments.

How It Works

The structure of a response in XML-RPC is similar to the request. You can return one value using a simple `<param>` element or a set of values using a `<structure>` element. The response from the `MathService.Add` method looks like this:

```
<methodResponse>
  <params>
    <param>
      <value>
        <double>46</double>
      </value>
    </param>
  </params>
</methodResponse>
```

Before you use this information to create a client that uses an XML-RPC service, take a closer look at what happens behind the scenes when you make a request and receive the response. The first thing to consider is *how do you deliver the request?*

Choosing a Network Transport

Generally, web services specifications enable you to use any network transport to send and receive messages. For example, you could use IBM MQSeries or Microsoft Message Queue (MSMQ) to send XML messages asynchronously over a queue, or even use SMTP to send messages via e-mail. However, the most common protocol used is probably HTTP. In fact, the XML-RPC specification requires it, so that is what you concentrate on in this section.

HTTP

Many readers may already be somewhat familiar with the HTTP protocol, because it is used almost every time you request a web page in your browser. Most web services implementations use HTTP as their underlying protocol, so take a look at how it works under the hood.

The *Hypertext Transfer Protocol (HTTP)* is a request/response protocol. This means that when you make an HTTP request, at its most basic, the following steps occur:

1. The client (in most cases, the browser) opens a connection to the HTTP server.
2. The client sends a request to the server.
3. The server performs some processing.
4. The server sends back a response.
5. The connection is closed.

An HTTP message contains two parts: a set of *headers*, followed by an optional *body*. The headers are simply text, with each header separated from the next by a newline character, whereas the body might be text or binary information. The body is separated from the headers by two newline characters.

For example, suppose you attempt to load an HTML page, located at `http://www.wiley.com/WileyCDA/Section/index.html` (Wiley's homepage) into your browser, which in this case is Internet Explorer 9.0. The browser sends a request similar to the following to the `www.wiley.com` server:

```
GET /WileyCDA/Section/index.html HTTP/1.1
Accept: */*
Accept-Language: en-us
Accept-Encoding: gzip, deflate
User-Agent: Mozilla/4.0 (compatible; MSIE 7.0; Win32)
Host: www.wiley.com
```

***NOTE** Wiley uses your IP address to ascertain which country you are browsing from, so, depending on your region, you may get different results than those shown here. The principles of HTTP are what matter here.*

The first line of your request specifies the method to be performed by the HTTP server. HTTP defines a few types of requests, but this code has specified `GET`, indicating to the server that you want the resource specified, which in this case is `/WileyCDA/Section/index.html`. (Another common method is `POST`, covered in a moment.) This line also specifies that you're using the HTTP/1.1 version of the protocol. Several other headers are there as well, which specify to the web server a few pieces of information about the browser, such as what types of information it can receive. Those are as follows:

- `Accept` tells the server what MIME types this browser accepts — in this case, `*/*`, meaning any MIME types.
- `Accept-Language` tells the server what language this browser is using. Servers can potentially use this information to customize the content returned. In this case, the browser is specifying that it is the United States (`us`) dialect of the English (`en`) language.

- `Accept-Encoding` specifies to the server whether the content can be encoded before being sent to the browser. In this case, the browser has specified that it can accept documents that are encoded using `gzip` or `deflate`. These technologies are used to compress the data, which is then decompressed on the client.

For a `GET` request, there is no body in the HTTP message. In response, the server sends something similar to the following:

```
HTTP/1.1 200 OK
Server: Microsoft-IIS/5.0
Date: Fri, 09 Dec 2011 14:30:52 GMT
Content-Type: text/html
Last-Modified: Thu, 08 Dec 2011 16:19:57 GMT
Content-Length: 98

<html>
<head><title>Hello world</title></head>
<body>
<p>Hello world</p>
</body>
</html>
```

Again, there is a set of HTTP headers, this time followed by the body. Obviously, the real Wiley homepage is a little more complicated than this, but in this case, some of the headers sent by the HTTP server were as follows:

- A status code, `200`, indicating that the request was successful. The HTTP specification defines a number of valid status codes that can be sent in an HTTP response, such as the famous (or infamous) 404 code, which means that the resource being requested could not be found. You can find a full list of status codes at `http://www.w3.org/Protocols/rfc2616/rfc2616-sec6.html#sec6`.
- A `Content-Type` header, indicating what type of content is contained in the body of the message. A client application (such as a web browser) uses this header to decide what to do with the item; for example, if the content type were a `.wav` file, the browser might load an external sound program to play it, or give the user the option of saving it to the hard drive instead.
- A `Content-Length` header, which indicates the length of the body of the message.

There are many other possible headers but these three will always be included in the response. To make the initial request you have a choice of methods (or *verbs* as they are often called). These verbs offer ways to request content, send data, and delete resources from the web server.

The `GET` method is the most common HTTP method used in regular everyday surfing. The second most common is the `POST` method. When you do a `POST`, information is sent to the HTTP server in the body of the message. For example, when you fill out a form on a web page and click the Submit button, the web browser will usually `POST` that information to the web server, which processes it before sending back the results. Suppose you create an HTML page that includes a form like this:

```
<html>
<head>
<title>Test form</title>
</head>
<body>
<form action="acceptform.aspx" method="POST">
  Enter your first name: <input name="txtFirstName" /><br />
  Enter your last name: <input name="txtLastName" /><br />
  <input type="submit" />
</form>
</body>
</html>
```

This form will `POST` any information to a page called `acceptform.aspx`, in the same location as this HTML file, similar to the following:

```
POST /acceptform.aspx HTTP/1.1
Accept: */*
Referer: http://www.wiley.com/myform.htm
Accept-Language: en-us
Content-Type: application/x-www-form-urlencoded
Accept-Encoding: gzip, deflate
User-Agent: Mozilla/4.0 (compatible; MSIE 7.0; Win32)
Host: www.wiley.com
Content-Length: 36

txtFirstName=Joe&txtLastName=Fawcett
```

Whereas the `GET` method provides for basic surfing the Internet, it's the `POST` method that enables things like e-commerce, because information can be passed back and forth.

NOTE *As you see later in the chapter, the* `GET` *method can also send information by appending it to the URL, but in general,* `POST` *is used wherever possible.*

Why Use HTTP for Web Services?

It was mentioned earlier that most web services implementations probably use HTTP as their transport. Here are a few reasons why:

- HTTP is already a widely implemented, and well understood, protocol.
- The request/response paradigm lends itself well to RPC.
- Most firewalls are already configured to work with HTTP.
- HTTP makes it easy to build in security by using Secure Sockets Layer (SSL).

HTTP is Widely Implemented

One of the primary reasons for the explosive growth of the Internet was the availability of the World Wide Web, which runs over the HTTP protocol. Millions of web servers are in existence, serving up HTML and other content over HTTP, and many, many companies use HTTP for e-commerce.

HTTP is a relatively easy protocol to implement, which is one of the reasons why the Web works as smoothly as it does. If HTTP had been hard to implement, a number of implementers would have probably gotten it wrong, meaning some web browsers wouldn't have worked with some web servers.

Using HTTP for web services implementations is therefore easier than other network protocols would have been. This is especially true because web services implementations can piggyback on existing web servers — in other words, use their HTTP implementation. This means you don't have to worry about the HTTP implementation at all.

Request/Response Works with RPC

Typically, when a client makes an RPC call, it needs to receive some kind of response. For example, if you make a call to the `MathService.Add` method, you need to get a result back or it wouldn't be a very useful procedure to call. In other instances, such as submitting a new blog post, you may not need data returned from the RPC call, but you may still need confirmation that the procedure executed successfully. As a common example, an order to a back-end database may not require data to be returned, but you should know whether the submission failed or succeeded.

HTTP's request/response paradigm lends itself easily to this type of situation. For your `MathService.Add` remote procedure, you must do the following:

1. Open a connection to the server providing the XML-RPC service.
2. Send the information, such as the operands and the arithmetic function needed.
3. Process the data.
4. Get back the result, including an error code if it didn't work, or a result identifier if it did.
5. Close the connection.

In some cases, such as in the SOAP specification, messages are one-way instead of two-way. This means two separate messages must be sent: one from the client to the server with, say, numbers to add, and one from the server back to the client with the result of the calculation. In most cases, however, when a specification requires the use of two one-way messages, it also specifies that when a request/response protocol such as HTTP is used, these two messages can be combined in the request/response of the protocol.

HTTP is Firewall-Ready

Most companies protect themselves from outside hackers by placing a *firewall* between their internal systems and the external Internet. Firewalls are designed to protect a network by blocking certain types of network traffic. Most firewalls allow HTTP traffic (the type of network traffic that would be generated by browsing the Web) but disallow other types of traffic.

These firewalls protect the company's data, but they make it more difficult to provide web-based services to the outside world. For example, consider a company selling goods over the Web. This web-based service would need certain information, such as which items are available in stock, which it would have to get from the company's internal systems. To provide this service, the company probably needs to create an environment such as the one shown in Figure 14-3.

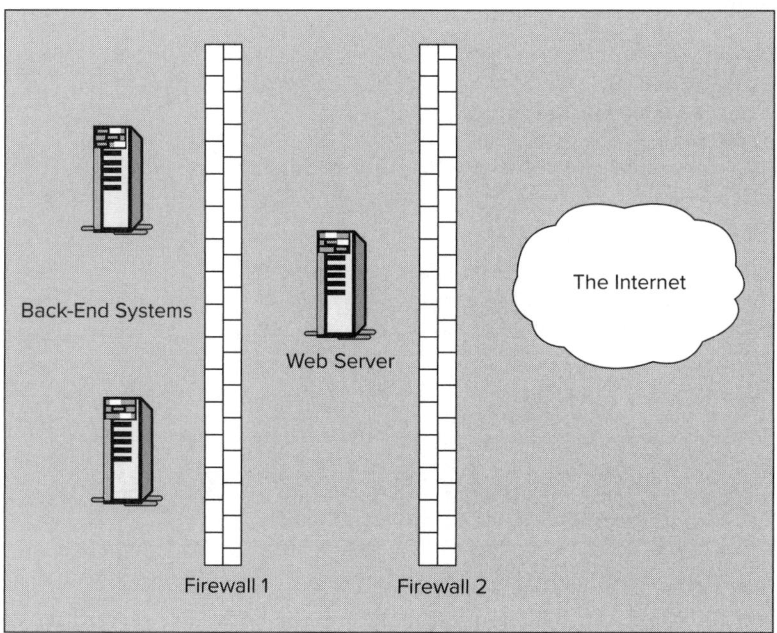

FIGURE 14-3

This is a very common configuration, in which the web server is placed between two firewalls. (This section, between the two firewalls, is often called a *demilitarized zone*, or *DMZ*.) Firewall 1 protects the company's internal systems and must be carefully configured to allow the proper communication between the web server and the internal systems, without letting any other traffic get through. Firewall 2 is configured to let traffic through between the web server and the Internet, but no other traffic.

This arrangement protects the company's internal systems, but because of the complexity added by these firewalls — especially for the communication between the web server and the back-end servers — it makes it a bit more difficult for the developers creating this web-based service. However, because firewalls are configured to let HTTP traffic go through, it's much easier to provide the necessary functionality if all of the communication between the web server and the other servers uses this protocol.

HTTP Security

Because there is already an existing security model for HTTP, the Secure Sockets Layer (SSL), it is very easy to make transactions over HTTP secure. SSL encrypts traffic as it passes over the Web to protect it from prying eyes, so it's perfect for web transactions, such as credit card orders. In fact, SSL is so common that hardware accelerators are available to speed up SSL transactions.

Using HTTP for XML-RPC

Using HTTP for XML-RPC messages is very easy. You need to do only two things with the client:

- For the HTTP method, use `POST`.
- For the body of the message, include an XML document comprising the XML-RPC request.

For example, consider the following:

```
POST /RPC2 HTTP/1.1
Accept: */* Accept-Language: en-us
Content-Type: application/x-www-form-urlencoded
Accept-Encoding: gzip, deflate
User-Agent: Mozilla/4.0 (compatible; MSIE 5.5; Windows NT 5.0)
Host: www.wiley.com
Content-Length: 180

<methodCall><methodName>MathService.Add</methodName><params>
<param><value><double>17</double></value></param>
<param><value><double>29</double></value></param>
</params></methodCall>
```

NOTE *The request is broken across lines here for readability. In a real request the body of the post is all on one line.*

The headers define the request, and the XML-RPC request makes up the body. The server knows how to retrieve that body and process it. In the next chapter, you look at processing the actual request, but for now you just send an XML-RPC request and process the response.

The following Try It Out shows how an XML-RPC service can be called from a simple web page using HTTP's POST method.

TRY IT OUT Using HTTP POST to Call Your RPC

This Try It Out concentrates on creating a web page that can be used to call an XML-RPC-style service. The actual service is included in the code download and can be run under IIS, IIS Express, or the built-in Visual Studio web server. The simplest option is to run the site using Visual Studio's built-in web server, which is the default option. This example doesn't go into much detail about the service itself, but it parses the incoming XML, executes the required method, and returns the result in an XML format. The code download contains all the files you will need for this Try It Out, or you can create the main page yourself as detailed in steps 1 to 3.

1. Create a new web page and add the following code to give a form that can accept two numbers and provides a button for each method that the service exposes, namely `MathService.Add` and `MathService.Subtract`:

```
<!DOCTYPE html PUBLIC "-//W3C//DTD XHTML 1.0 Transitional//EN"
 "http://www.w3.org/TR/xhtml1/DTD/xhtml1-transitional.dtd">
<html xmlns="http://www.w3.org/1999/xhtml">
<head>
  <title>XML-RPC Client</title>
  <!-- script will go here -->
</head>
<body>
<label for="txtOperand1">Operand 1:</label>
<input type="text" id="txtOperand1" /><br />
<label for="txtOperand2">Operand 2:</label>
<input type="text" id="txtOperand2" /><br />
<label for="txtResult">Result:</label>
<input type="text" id="txtResult" readonly="readonly" /><br />
<input type="button" value="Add" onclick="doAdd();" /><br />
<input type="button" value="Subtract" onclick="doSubtract();" /><br />
</body>
</html>
```

XML-RPC-Client.html

2. You'll be using jQuery to enable simplified cross-browser posting capabilities. This also means that you won't refresh the whole page each time, but will make the calls as a background request and just add the response to the `txtResult` box. Add the following line just after the document's `<title>` element to incorporate the jQuery library:

```
<head>
  <title>XML-RPC Client</title>
  <script type="text/javascript"
    src="http://code.jquery.com/jquery-1.6.4.js"></script>
  <!-- rest of script will go here -->
</head>
```

XML-RPC-Client.html

3. Add the following code just beneath the jQuery library block that is called whenever one of the two function buttons is pressed:

```
<script type="text/javascript">

  function doAdd()
  {
    var response = callService("MathService.Add");
  }

  function doSubtract()
  {
    var response = callService("MathService.Subtract");
  }
```

```
    function callService(methodName)
    {
      $("#txtResult").val("");
      var operand1 = $("#txtOperand1").val();
      var operand2 = $("#txtOperand2").val();
      var request = getRequest(methodName, operand1, operand2);
      //alert(request);
      $.ajax({ url: "Service.aspx",
               type: "post",
               data: request,
               processData: false,
               contentType: "text/xml",
               success: handleServiceResponse });
    }

    function getRequest(methodName, operand1, operand2)
    {
      var sRequest = "<methodCall>"
                   + "<methodName>" + methodName + "</methodName>"
                   + "<params>"
                   + "<param><value><double>"
                   + operand1
                   + "</double></value></param>"
                   + "<param><value><double>"
                   + operand2
                   + "</double></value></param>"
                   + "</params>"
                   + "</methodCall>";
      return sRequest;
    }

    function handleServiceResponse(data, textStatus, jqXHR)
    {
      if (textStatus == "success")
      {
        alert(jqXHR.responseText)
        var result = $("[nodeName=double]", jqXHR.responseXML).text();
        $("#txtResult").val(result);
      }
      else
      {
        alert("Error retrieving web service response");
      }
    }
  </script>
```

XML-RPC-Client.html

4. Add the completed page to the `MathService` project folder inside the `XML-RPC Demo` solution. Then, using Visual Studio, use File ➪ Open ➪ Web site... and browse to the `MathService` folder and click OK. Set `XML-RPC-Client.html` as the start page (to do this right-click the page and choose Set as start page). Press F5 to start the site.
5. Test the form by entering two numbers and trying the Add or Subtract functions.

How It Works

Once one of the two function buttons, Add or Subtract, has been clicked, `callService()` is invoked and passed the name of the server-side function required. The `callService()` method is shown in the following snippet:

```
function callService(methodName)
{
  $("#txtResult").val("");
  var operand1 = $("#txtOperand1").val();
  var operand2 = $("#txtOperand2").val();
  var request = getRequest(methodName, operand1, operand2);
  //alert(request);
  $.ajax({ url: "Service.aspx",
           type: "post",
           data: request,
           processData: false,
           contentType: "text/xml",
           success: handleServiceResponse });
}
```

Within `callService()` the `txtResult` element is cleared of any previous values, and then the two operands are retrieved from their respective textboxes. Because this is a demo, there's no code to make sure that the values are actually numbers rather than alphabetic, something you'd need in a production system.

Once the operands are known, a call is made to `getRequest()`, shown in the following snippet, which uses a string template to create the XML document needed for the request:

```
function getRequest(methodName, operand1, operand2)
{
  var sRequest = "<methodCall>"
               + "<methodName>" + methodName + "</methodName>"
               + "<params>"
               + "<param><value><double>"
               + operand1
               + "</double></value></param>"
               + "<param><value><double>"
               + operand2
               + "</double></value></param>"
               + "</params>"
               + "</methodCall>";
  return sRequest;
}
```

Once the XML is created, the jQuery function `ajax()` is used to post this XML to the web service:

```
  $.ajax({ url: "Service.aspx",
           type: "post",
           data: request,
           processData: false,
           contentType: "text/xml",
           success: handleServiceResponse });
}
```

The different parameters passed are as follows:

- `url`: Contains the URL of the web service being called.
- `type`: Contains the type of HTML request, usually `GET` or `POST`.
- `data`: Contains the actual XML message.
- `processData`: Says whether the data needs conversion from the format it is in. In this case that's false, otherwise the XML would be escaped using `<` for <, and so on.
- `contentType`: The content type of the data being posted.
- `success`: Defines which function to use if the web call is successful. As stated before, the possibility of an error is ignored in this simplified demo.

The web call is made asynchronously, and on returning the response is passed to the `handleServiceResponse()` method:

```
function handleServiceResponse(data, textStatus, jqXHR)
{
  if (textStatus == "success")
  {
    alert(jqXHR.responseText)
    var result = $("[nodeName=double]", jqXHR.responseXML).text();
    $("#txtResult").val(result);
  }
  else
  {
    alert("Error retrieving web service response");
  }
}
```

The `textStatus` is checked and, if it's equal to success, the raw response is shown as an aid to development (this wouldn't be included in a live application). Then jQuery is used to extract the value of the result, and the value is inserted into the `txtResult` textbox.

The full sequence is shown in Figures 14-4, 14-5, and 14-6.

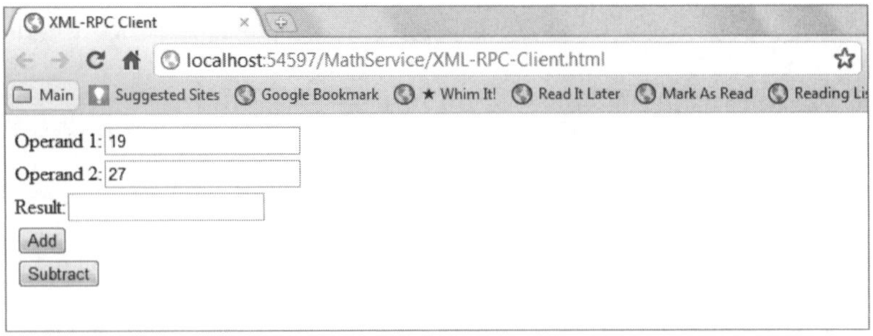

FIGURE 14-4

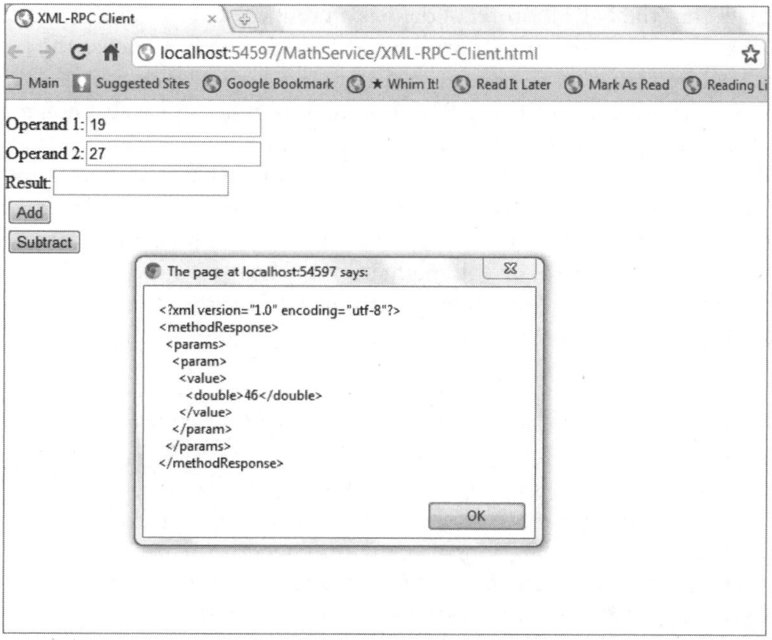

FIGURE 14-5

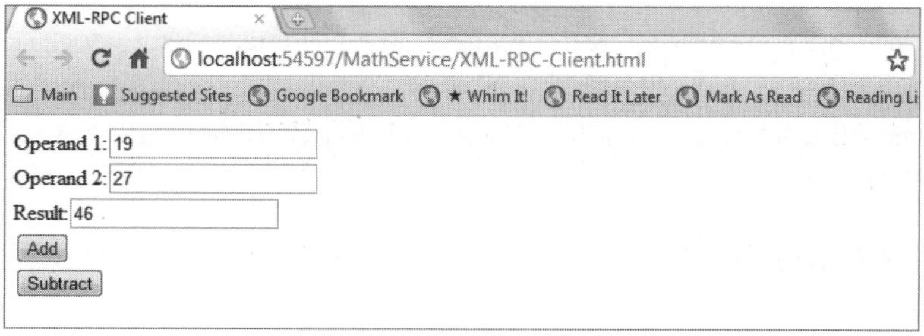

FIGURE 14-6

The next section describes a different way of using web services than XML-RPC: *REST*.

Understanding REST Services

REST stands for *Re*presentational *S*tate *T*ransfer and is a framework for creating web services that can, but do not have to, use XML. Following are two important principles of REST:

1. Resources to be acted on are represented by a URL.
2. The type of action to be carried out is dictated using the appropriate HTTP verb.

The first principle is easy to understand. If I want to retrieve a customer's details, I might use a URL such as `http://myServer.com/customers/123`, where 123 is the customer's unique identifier. The second principle relies on the fact that the HTTP protocol defines a number of verbs, or commands, indicating how a resource is treated. The most common verb is `GET`, which simply retrieves the resource based entirely on the URL requested. The next most common is `POST`, which passes a block of data, as seen in the preceding section, to a specified URL. A number of other less well-known verbs exist, such as `PUT`, which creates a resource, `DELETE`, which removes a resource, and `HEAD`, which asks for information about a resource without actually fetching it. REST uses these verbs along with the specified URL to fetch, create, and delete online resources. For example, to create a new customer you might `POST` the relevant data to a URL and the server would process the request and create a new customer in your sales database, or you might `PUT` the details instead. To delete an existing customer you might issue a `DELETE` request along with the URL of the customer to be removed, such as the customer already mentioned, `http://myServer.com/customers/123`.

NOTE *If you're wondering what the difference is between using* `POST` *and* `PUT`*, don't worry, you're not alone. In theory, a* `POST` *is used when you don't know all of the new customer's details; perhaps the system creates a new ID for the customer, which it passes back to you as a response.* `PUT` *is used when you already know the ID and are simply transferring the data to the server. In practice, there is often debate about which to use, and many web servers don't accept* `PUT` *requests anyway, so* `POST` *is used instead.*

You can find the original article on REST, written by its architect, Roy Fielding, at `http://www.ics.uci.edu/~fielding/pubs/dissertation/rest_arch_style.htm`.

The following Try It Out demonstrates how to call a REST style web service using Fiddler, a free web development and debugging tool.

TRY IT OUT Calling a REST Web Service

To demonstrate how to use a REST service, in this Try It Out you use a tool, Fiddler, to create a web request that calls the Google search engine.

1. To get started, register with Google to get hold of an API key. This key is passed with each request so that Google can identify the originator and make sure that, among other things, they are sticking to the pre-agreed limits for the free service. Go to `https://code.google.com/apis/console/` and, if you're not already registered, create an account; otherwise, sign in. You don't have to set up a new Gmail address if you don't want to. Once logged in, click Create Project.
2. In the list of available APIs, click the button next to Search API for Shopping and accept the terms and conditions.
3. Use the menu on the left to navigate to API Access. There you will see your API key. Copy it for use later in the exercise.
4. Now install the client you're going to use to create web requests. Go to `http://www.fiddler2.com/fiddler2/` and download the latest version of Fiddler. Fiddler is mainly used as a proxy,

sitting between your browser and a web server, and enabling you to see and modify requests and responses. In this case, however, you'll use it to create requests and examine the response. (In this demonstration you could probably just use the browser directly, but Fiddler is a great tool when working with web requests on a Windows platform and should definitely be a part of your arsenal. It makes debugging so much easier.)

5. Install Fiddler and start it up. You should see a screen similar to Figure 14-7.

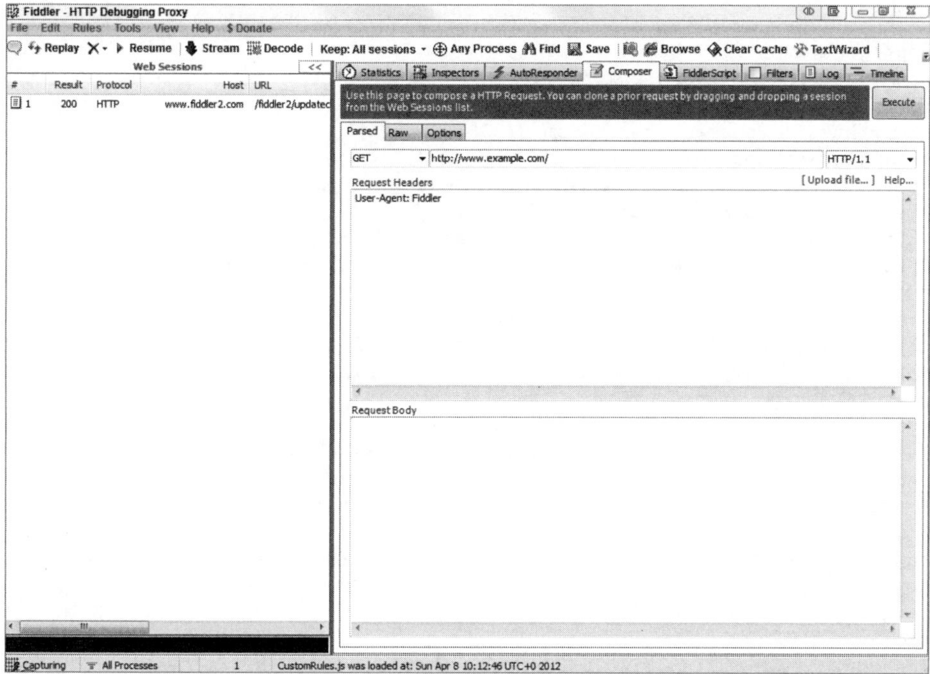

FIGURE 14-7

6. On the right-hand side of the Fiddler interface, choose the Composer tab from the upper section.

7. Paste in the following URL, which searches U.S. websites for digital cameras for sale, after inserting your own API key: https://www.googleapis.com/shopping/search/v1/public/products?key=<your API key here>&country=US&q=digital+camera&alt=atom.

8. Click the Execute button in the top right of Fiddler.

9. You should see the call listed in the left-hand screen, hopefully with a status code of 200.

10. You can now examine the response received by using the Inspectors tab and choosing Raw View. On the right-hand side of the word "GET," click the URL that you entered in step 8. The response will be composed of a number of headers followed by the results in an XML format, a shortened version of which is shown here:

```
<?xml version="1.0" encoding="UTF-8"?>
<feed gd:kind="shopping#products"
gd:etag="&quot;czKOfew9E3svi7vOBQ3vsAgGZzo/9wsxV-m1LokeaXtPG67Dj-pgCUI&quot;"
xmlns="http://www.w3.org/2005/Atom" xmlns:gd="http://schemas.google.com/g/2005"
xmlns:openSearch="http://a9.com/-/spec/opensearchrss/1.0/"
xmlns:s="http://www.google.com/shopping/api/schemas/2010">
 <id>tag:google.com,2010:shopping/products</id>
 <updated>2011-12-12T17:02:55.909Z</updated>
 <title>Shopping Products</title>
 <generator version="v1"
   uri="https://www.googleapis.com/shopping/search/">Search API for
 Shopping</generator>
 <link rel="alternate" type="text/html"
   href="https://www.googleapis.com/shopping/search/"/>
 <link rel="http://schemas.google.com/g/2005#feed"
   type="application/atom+xml"
 href="https://www.googleapis.com/shopping/search/v1/public/products?alt=atom"/>
 <link rel="self" type="application/atom+xml"
 href="https://www.googleapis.com/shopping/search/v1/
public/products?country=US&amp;q=digital+camera&amp;alt=atom&amp;
startIndex=1&amp;maxResults=25"/>
 <link rel="next" type="application/atom+xml"
 href="https://www.googleapis.com/shopping/search/v1/
public/products?country=US&amp;q=digital+camera&amp;alt=atom&amp;
startIndex=26&amp;maxResults=25"/>
 <link rel="previous" type="application/atom+xml"/>
 <openSearch:totalResults>745713</openSearch:totalResults>
 <openSearch:startIndex>1</openSearch:startIndex>
 <openSearch:itemsPerPage>25</openSearch:itemsPerPage>
 <entry gd:kind="shopping#product">
  <id>tag:google.com,2010:shopping/products/1172711/6875108646978882</id>
  <author>
   <name>B&amp;H Photo-Video-Audio</name>
  </author>
  <published>2011-10-12T14:56:40.000Z</published>
  <updated>2011-12-12T04:48:51.000Z</updated>
  <title>Canon EOS 5D Mark II Digital Camera (Body Only)</title>
  <content type="text">The Canon EOS 5D Mark II (Body Only) improves upon the EOS
 5D by increasing the resolution by about 40% to 21.1 megapixels and adds a Live
 View feature that allows users to preview shots on the camera&apos;s high
resolution 3.0 LCD display. It even incorporates the ability to record full motion
HD Video with sound so you can capture the action as well as superb images </
content>
  <link rel="alternate" type="text/html"
href="http://www.bhphotovideo.com/c/product/583953-REG/Canon_2764B003_EOS_5D_Mark_
II.html/BI/1239/kw/CAE5D2"/>
  <link rel="self" type="application/atom+xml"
href="https://www.googleapis.com/shopping/search/v1/public/products/1172711/gid/
6875108646978882?alt=atom"/>
  <s:product>
   <s:googleId>6875108646978882</s:googleId>
   <s:author>
    <s:name>B&amp;H Photo-Video-Audio</s:name>
    <s:accountId>1172711</s:accountId>
   </s:author>
```

```
    <s:creationTime>2011-10-12T14:56:40.000Z</s:creationTime>
    <s:modificationTime>2011-12-12T04:48:51.000Z</s:modificationTime>
    <s:country>US</s:country>
    <s:language>en</s:language>
    <s:title>Canon EOS 5D Mark II Digital Camera (Body Only)</s:title>
    <s:description>The Canon EOS 5D Mark II (Body Only) improves upon the EOS 5D by
increasing the resolution by about 40% to 21.1 megapixels and adds a Live View
feature that allows users to preview shots on the camera&apos;s high resolution
3.0 LCD display </s:description>
    <s:link>http://www.bhphotovideo.com/c/product/
583953-REG/Canon_2764B003_EOS_5D_Mark_II.html/BI/1239/kw/CAE5D2</s:link>
    <s:brand>Canon</s:brand>
    <s:condition>new</s:condition>
    <s:gtin>00013803105384</s:gtin>
    <s:gtins>
     <s:gtin>00013803105384</s:gtin>
    </s:gtins>
    <s:inventories>
     <s:inventory channel="online" availability="inStock">
      <s:price shipping="0.0" currency="USD">2209.95</s:price>
     </s:inventory>
    </s:inventories>
    <s:images>
     <s:image link="http://www.bhphotovideo.com/images/nowm/583953.jpg"/>
    </s:images>
   </s:product>
  </entry>
  <entry gd:kind="shopping#product">
   <id>tag:google.com,2010:shopping/products/1113342/13850367466326274615</id>
   <author>
    <name>Walmart</name>
   </author>
   <published>2011-07-04T19:48:28.000Z</published>
   <updated>2011-12-10T05:11:44.000Z</updated>
   <title>Canon Powershot Sx130-is Black 12.1mp Digital Camera W/ 12x Optical</title>
   <content type="text">Canon PowerShot SX130-IS 12.1MP Digital Camera:12.1-
megapixel </content>
   <link rel="alternate" type="text/html"
href="http://www.walmart.com/catalog/product.do?product_id=14972582&amp;sourceid=15000000
00000003142050&amp;ci_src=14110944&amp;ci_sku=14972582"/>
   <link rel="self" type="application/atom+xml"
 href="https://www.googleapis.com/shopping/search/v1/
public/products/1113342/gid/13850367466326274615?alt=atom"/>
   <s:product>
    <s:googleId>13850367466326274615</s:googleId>
    <s:author>
     <s:name>Walmart</s:name>
     <s:accountId>1113342</s:accountId>
    </s:author>
    <s:creationTime>2011-07-04T19:48:28.000Z</s:creationTime>
    <s:modificationTime>2011-12-10T05:11:44.000Z</s:modificationTime>
    <s:country>US</s:country>
    <s:language>en</s:language>
    <s:title>Canon Powershot Sx130-is Black
12.1mp Digital Camera W/ 12x Optical</s:title>
```

```
    <s:description>Canon PowerShot SX130-IS 12.1MP Digital Camera:
12.1-megapixel resolutionDelivers excellent picture </s:description>
<s:link>http://www.walmart.com/catalog/product.do?
product_id=14972582&amp;
sourceid=1500000000000003142050&amp;ci_src=14110944&amp;ci_sku=14972582</s:link>
    <s:brand>Canon</s:brand>
    <s:condition>new</s:condition>
    <s:gtin>00013803127386</s:gtin>
    <s:gtins>
     <s:gtin>00013803127386</s:gtin>
    </s:gtins>
    <s:inventories>
     <s:inventory channel="online" availability="inStock">
      <s:price shipping="0.0" currency="USD">169.0</s:price>
     </s:inventory>
    </s:inventories>
    <s:images>
     <s:image
 link="http://i.walmartimages.com/i/p/00/01/38/03/12/0001380312738_500X500.jpg"/>
    </s:images>
   </s:product>
 </entry>
 <s:requestId>0CIjh9NiB_awCFUcEtAod6jsAAA</s:requestId>
</feed>
```

How It Works

Fiddler takes the request and sends it to the web server in question, in this case Google's API server at `www.googleapis.com`. The request is executed and the results are returned in the format requested, in this case Atom, as expressed by the `alt` parameter in the querystring. (If you want to see the JSON format, replace the word *atom* at the end of the URL with the word *json*.)

Now that you've seen examples of both XML-RPC and REST-style services, it's time to look at other specifications related to the web services stack.

THE WEB SERVICES STACK

If you've been having trouble keeping track of all of the web services–related specifications out there and just how they all fit together, don't feel bad, it's not just you. In fact, literally dozens of specs exist, with a considerable amount of duplication as companies jockey for position in this field. Lately it's gotten so bad that even Don Box, one of the creators of the major web services protocol, SOAP, commented at a conference that the proliferation in standards has led to a "cacophony" in the field and that developers should write fewer specs and more applications. It's also led to a profusion of frameworks that try to make things easier for you by hiding much of the plumbing and letting you concentrate on the business logic. Many succeed, but often the frameworks themselves are so difficult to learn that they only end up making the tasks harder.

Not that some standardization isn't necessary, of course. That's the whole purpose of the evolution of web services as an area of work — to find a way to standardize communications between systems. This section discusses the major standards you must know in order to implement most web services systems, and then addresses some of the emerging standards and how they all fit together.

SOAP

If you learn only one web services–related protocol, *SOAP* is probably your best bet. Originally conceived as the Simple Object Access Protocol, SOAP has now been adapted for so many different uses that its acronym is no longer applicable.

SOAP is an XML-based language that provides a way for two different systems to exchange information relating to a remote procedure call or other operation. SOAP messages consist of a `Header`, which contains information about the request, and a `Body`, which contains the request itself. Both the `Header` and `Body` are contained within an `Envelope`.

SOAP calls are more robust than, say, XML-RPC calls, because you can use arbitrary XML. This enables you to structure the call in a way that's best for your application. For example, say your application ultimately needs an XML node such as the following:

```
<totals>
  <dept id="2332">
    <gross>433229.03</gross>
    <net>23272.39</net>
  </dept>
  <dept id="4001">
    <gross>993882.98</gross>
    <net>388209.27</net>
  </dept>
</totals>
```

Rather than try to squeeze your data into an arbitrary format such as XML-RPC, you can create a SOAP message such as the following:

```
<?xml version="1.0" encoding="UTF-8"?>
<SOAP:Envelope xmlns:SOAP="http://www.w3.org/2003/05/soap-envelope">

  <SOAP:Header></SOAP:Header>
  <SOAP:Body>
    <totals xmlns="http://www.wiley.com/SOAP/accounting">
      <dept id="2332">
        <gross>433229.03</gross>
        <net>23272.39</net>
      </dept>
      <dept id="4001">
        <gross>993882.98</gross>
        <net>388209.27</net>
      </dept>
    </totals>
   </SOAP:Body>
</SOAP:Envelope>
```

SOAP also has the capability to take advantage of technologies such as XML-Signature for security. You can also use attachments with SOAP, so a request could conceivably return, say, a document or other information. In Chapter 15, "SOAP and WSDL" you create a complete SOAP server and client, and look at the syntax of a SOAP message.

Of course, this suggests another problem: How do you know what a SOAP request should look like, and what it will return as a result? As you'll see next, WSDL solves that problem.

WSDL

The *Web Services Description Language* (WSDL) is an XML-based language that provides a contract between a web service and the outside world. To understand this better, recall the discussion of COM and CORBA. The reason why COM and CORBA objects can be so readily shared is that they have defined contracts with the outside world. This contract defines the methods an object provides, as well as the parameters to those methods and their return values. Interfaces for both COM and CORBA are written in variants of the *Interface Definition Language* (IDL). Code can then be written to look at an object's interface to determine what functions are provided. In practice, this dynamic investigation of an object's interface often happens at design time, as a programmer is writing the code that calls another object. A programmer would find out what interface an object supports and then write code that properly calls that interface.

Web services have a similar contract with the outside world, except that the contract is written in WSDL instead of IDL. This WSDL document outlines what messages the SOAP server expects in order to provide services, as well as what messages it returns. Again, in practice, WSDL is likely used at design time. A programmer would use WSDL to figure out what procedures are available from the SOAP server and what format of XML is expected by that procedure, and then write the code to call it.

To take things a step further, programmers might never have to look at WSDL directly or even deal with the underlying SOAP protocol. Already available are several SOAP toolkits that can hide the complexities of SOAP. If you point one of these toolkits at a WSDL document, it can automatically generate code to make the SOAP call for you! At that point, working with SOAP is as easy as calling any other local object on your machine. Chapter 15 of this book looks at the syntax for a WSDL document. After you've built it, how do you let others know that it's out there? Enter UDDI.

UDDI

The *Universal Discovery, Description, and Integration* (UDDI) protocol enables web services to be registered so that they can be discovered by programmers and other web services. For example, if you're going to create a web service that serves a particular function, such as providing up-to-the-minute traffic reports by GPS coordinates, you can register that service with a UDDI registry. The global UDDI registry system consists of several different servers that all mirror each other, so by registering your company with one, you add it to all the others.

The advantage of registering with the UDDI registry is twofold. First, your company's contact information is available, so when another company wants to do business with you, it can use the *white pages* type of lookup to get the necessary contact information. A company's listing not only includes the usual name, phone number, and address type of information, but also information on the services available. For example, it might include a link to a WSDL file describing the traffic reporting system.

The UDDI registry system also enables companies to find each other based on the types of web services they offer. This is called a *green pages* type of listing. For example, you could use the green pages to find a company that uses web services to take orders for widgets. Listings would also include information on what the widget order request should look like and the structure of the order confirmation, or, at the very least, a link to that information.

Many of the SOAP toolkits available, such as IBM's Web Services Toolkit, provide tools to work with UDDI. UDDI seems to be another of those *seemed like a good idea at the time* specifications. Most real-world developers naturally prefer to build their applications knowing that the web services they will consume are available, and are unwilling to risk having to discover them dynamically. This is one of the reasons why UDDI has never really taken off.

Surrounding Specifications

So far this chapter has described a landscape in which you can use a UDDI registry to discover a web service for which a WSDL file describes the SOAP messages used by the service. For all practical purposes, you could stop right there, because you have all of the pieces that are absolutely necessary, but as you start building your applications, you will discover that other issues need to be addressed.

For example, just because a web service is built using such specifications as SOAP and WSDL doesn't mean that your client is going to flawlessly interact with it. Interoperability continues to be a challenge between systems, from locating the appropriate resource to making sure types are correctly implemented. Numerous specifications have emerged in an attempt to choreograph the increasingly complex dance between web service providers and consumers. Moreover, any activity that involves business eventually needs security.

This section looks at some of the many specifications that have been working their way into the marketplace. Only time will tell which will survive and which will ultimately wither, but it helps to understand what's out there and how it all fits together.

Interoperability

At the time of this writing, the big name in interoperability is the Web Services Interoperability Organization, or WS-I (`www.ws-i.org`). This industry group includes companies such as IBM, Microsoft, and Sun Microsystems, and the purpose of the organization is to define specific "profiles" for web services and provide testing tools so that companies can be certain that their implementations don't contain any hidden "gotchas." WS-I has released a Basic Profile as well as a number of use cases and sample implementations.

Some other interoperability-related specifications include the following:

- WS-Addressing (`www.w3.org/Submission/ws-addressing/`) provides a way to specify the location of a web service. Remember this doesn't necessarily refer to HTTP. WS-Addressing defines an XML document that indicates how to find a service, no matter how many firewalls, proxies, or other devices and gateways lie between you and that service.

- WS-Eventing (`www.w3.org/Submission/WS-Eventing/`) describes protocols that involve a publish/subscribe pattern, in which web services subscribe to or provide event notifications.

Coordination

For a while, it looked like the winner in coordination and choreography was going to be ebXML (`www.ebxml.org`), a web services version of Electronic Data Interchange (EDI), in which companies become "trading partners" and define their interactions individually. ebXML consists of a number of different modules specifying the ways in which businesses can define not only what information they're looking for and the form it should take, but the types of messages that should be sent from a multiple-step process. Although ebXML is very specific and seems to work well in the arena for which it was designed, it doesn't necessarily generalize well in order to cover web services outside the EDI realm.

As such, Business Process Execution Language for Web Services (BPEL4WS) (`http://msdn2.microsoft.com/en-us/library/aa479359.aspx`) has been proposed by a coalition of companies, including Microsoft and IBM. BPEL4WS defines a notation for specifying a business process ultimately implemented as web services. Business processes fall into two categories: *executable business processes* and *business protocols*. Executable business processes are actual actions performed in an interaction, whereas business protocols describe the effects (for example, orders placed) without specifying how they're actually accomplished. When BPEL4WS was introduced in 2002, it wasn't under the watchful eye of any standards body, which was a concern for many developers, so work is currently ongoing within the Web Services Business Process Execution Language (WS-BPEL) (`www.oasis-open.org/committees/tc_home.php?wg_abbrev=wsbpel`) group at the OASIS standards body.

Not to be outdone, the World Wide Web Consortium has opened the WS-Choreography (`www.w3.org/2002/ws/chor/`) activity, which is developing a way for companies to describe their interactions with trading partners. In other words, they're not actually defining how data is exchanged, but rather the language to describe how data is exchanged. In fact, Choreography Definition Language is one of the group's deliverables. However, the group hasn't produced much since it started and the last main publication was 2004.

In the meantime, Microsoft, IBM, and BEA are also proposing WS-Coordination (`http://www.ibm.com/developerworks/library/specification/ws-tx/`), which is also intended to provide a way to describe these interactions. This specification involves the WS-AtomicTransaction specification for describing individual components of a transaction.

Security

Given its importance, perhaps it should come as no surprise that security is currently another hotly contested area. In addition to the basic specifications set out by the World Wide Web Consortium, such as XML Encryption (`www.w3.org/Encryption/2001/`) and XML Signature (`www.w3.org/Signature/`), the industry is currently working on standards for identity recognition, reliable messaging, and overall security policies.

All the major players such as IBM and Microsoft are working to simplify and standardize identity management for such tasks as provisioning users and authentication. A number of non-commercial organizations such as Kantara (`http://kantarainitiative.org/`) are also looking at the problem.

Perhaps the most confusing competition is between WS Reliable Messaging (`www.oasis-open.org/committees/tc_home.php?wg_abbrev=wsrm`) and WS-ReliableMessaging (`http://www.ibm.com/developerworks/library/specification/ws-rm/`). In essence, both specifications are trying to describe a protocol for reliably delivering messages between distributed applications within a particular tolerance, or Quality of Service. These specifications deal with message order, retransmission, and ensuring that both parties to a transaction are aware of whether a message has been successfully received.

Two other specifications to consider are WS-Security and WS-Policy:

- WS-Security (`http://www.ibm.com/developerworks/library/specification/ws-secpol/`) is designed to provide enhancements to SOAP that make it easier to control issues such as message integrity, message confidentiality, and authentication, no matter what security model or encryption method you use.
- WS-Policy (`http://www.ibm.com/developerworks/library/specification/ws-polfram/`) is a specification meant to help people writing other specifications, and it provides a way to specify the "requirements, preferences, and capabilities" of a web service.

SUMMARY

- Web services arose from a need for a cross-platform way for one machine to be able to invoke processes on a separate machine.
- The Same Origin policy means that under normal circumstances only pages residing in the same domain as the web service, can use that service.
- XML remote procedure calls were the original web services; they enable methods to be called across a network by wrapping parameters and returned values in a standard XML format.
- With REST services, when the URL of the service defines a specific resource, the HTTP verb used defines the action required, and the body of the request can contain any supplementary data.
- It is relatively simple to utilize web services, especially from a web page. There are many libraries, such as jQuery, that hide the underlying protocols and formats and just let you specify the service and any parameters.

EXERCISES

You can find suggested solutions to these questions in the Appendix A.

1. Imagine you are trying to contact an XML-RPC-based web service to submit a classified ad for a lost dog. The required information includes your name, phone number, and the body of the ad. What might the XML request look like?

2. You are trying to call a REST-based web service to check on the status of a service order. The service needs the following information:

```
cust_id: 3263827
order_id: THX1138
```

What might the request look like?

▶ WHAT YOU LEARNED IN THIS CHAPTER

TOPIC	KEY POINTS
Before web services	Many technologies such as DCOM and IIOP existed to enable cross-network method requests. However, they were not cross-platform.
Same origin policy	This policy means that a web service can only be consumed by a page in the same domain. There are ways to get around this restriction such as server-side proxies and client-access policies.
XML-RPC	XML remote procedure calls were an early attempt to solve the cross-platform issue. They wrap method calls and return values in a standard XML format.
REST services	REST services use a web URL as a resource identifier and the `HTTP` verb to specify what sort of action is required. They are generally the easiest type of service to use.
Consuming services	With the many libraries around, both script and code, it's relatively easy to create clients that can utilize remote services.

15

SOAP and WSDL

WHAT YOU WILL LEARN IN THIS CHAPTER:

- Why SOAP can provide more flexibility than previous RPC protocols
- How to format SOAP messages
- When to use GET versus POST in an HTTP request
- What SOAP intermediaries are
- How to describe a service using WSDL
- The difference between SOAP styles

In Chapter 14 you learned about web services and how they work toward enabling disparate systems to communicate. You can now see that if everyone just chose their own formats in which to send messages back and forth, interoperability would be quite difficult, so a standard format is a must. XML-RPC is good for remote procedure calls, but otherwise limited. SOAP overcomes that problem by enabling rich XML documents to be transferred easily between systems, even allowing for the possibility of attachments. Of course, this flexibility means that you need a way to describe your SOAP messages, and that's where Web Services Description Language (WSDL) comes in. WSDL provides a standard way to describe where and how to make requests to a SOAP-based service.

In this chapter you take your knowledge of web services a step further by creating a simple web service using a method called REST (covered in the previous chapter). You'll expand your horizons by creating a SOAP service and accessing it via SOAP messages, describing it using WSDL so that other developers can make use of it if desired.

LAYING THE GROUNDWORK

Any web services project requires planning, so before you jump into installing software and creating files, take a moment to look at what you're trying to accomplish. Ultimately, you want to send and receive SOAP messages, and describe them using WSDL. To do that, you need the following in place:

- **The client:** In the previous chapter, you created an XML-RPC client in Internet Explorer. This chapter uses a lot of the same techniques to create a SOAP client.
- **The server:** You create two kinds of SOAP services in this chapter, and they both use ASP.NET. Both use standard `.aspx` pages, rather than .NET's specialized `.asmx` page or the more modern Windows Communication Foundation (WCF). There are two reasons for not using the built-in web services tools. First, coding by hand ensures that you see how it works, and more importantly, you learn how to diagnose problems in real-life situations. Second, if you want to use these techniques in other languages, it's easier to port the code when it's not hidden by .NET's web service abstraction layer.

The examples in this chapter are all developed with Visual Studio. If you don't have the full version you can use Visual Studio Express Web Edition, which you can download free from `http://www.microsoft.com/visualstudio/en-us/products/2010-editions/visual-web-developer-express`. See the Introduction of this book for more details on downloading Visual Studio.

RUNNING THE EXAMPLE IN WINDOWS

Many of the examples in this chapter require a basic web server. The link in the preceding section, in addition to being used to download Visual Studio Express, actually leads to the Web Platform Installer, which you can also use to install a wide variety of software concerned with web development. One item is IIS Express, a slimmed-down version of Microsoft's Internet Information Server, which integrates nicely with Visual Studio. If you are not running a web server from your machine already, the easiest way to run the examples is to download this as well and, when you create a web service, right-click the project and choose the Use IIS Express option.

THE NEW RPC PROTOCOL: SOAP

According to the W3C SOAP specification at `http://www.w3.org/TR/2000/NOTE-SOAP-20000508/`, SOAP is "a lightweight protocol for exchange of information in a decentralized, distributed environment." Although many would argue about the *lightweight* part of that statement, SOAP is a standard way to send information from one computer to another using XML to represent the information.

SOAP originally stood for Simple Object Access Protocol, but because most people found it anything but simple, and it's not limited to object access, it is now officially a name rather than an acronym, so it doesn't stand for anything. You can find information on the current version of SOAP (SOAP 1.2 at the time of this writing) at `www.w3.org/2000/xp/Group/`.

In a nutshell, the SOAP recommendation defines a protocol whereby all information sent from computer to computer is marked up in XML, with the information transmitted, in most cases, via HTTP or HTTPS.

***NOTE** Technically, SOAP messages don't have to be sent via HTTP. Any networking protocol, such as SMTP or FTP, could be used, but for the reasons discussed in the previous chapter, in practice HTTP(S) has remained the only way that SOAP messages are transmitted in practical applications.*

Following is a list of advantages that SOAP has over other protocols such as DCOM or Java RMI:

***NOTE** DCOM and Java RMI are forerunners of SOAP and were both designed to solve the same problem: how to call methods of a class that resides on a remote machine and make the results available to the local machine. You can find a good tutorial about these techniques at* `http://my.execpc.com/~gopalan/misc/compare.html`.

- **It's platform-, language-, and vendor-neutral:** Because SOAP is implemented using XML and (usually) HTTP, it is easy to process and send SOAP requests in any language, on any platform, without having to depend on tools from a particular vendor.
- **It's easy to implement:** SOAP was designed to be less complex than the other protocols. Even if it has moved away from simplicity in recent years, a SOAP server can still be implemented using nothing more than a web server and an ASP page or a CGI script.
- **It's firewall-safe:** Assuming that you use HTTP as your network protocol, you can pass SOAP messages across a firewall without having to perform extensive configuration.

SOAP also has a few disadvantages that have led people to search for other methods. The three main disadvantages are as follows:

- SOAP and traditional web services have become more and more complicated as time has progressed.
- The size of the messages is quite large in many cases compared to the actual payload.
- Although it is supposed to be a standard, you will still find interoperability issues between SOAP-based services implemented in, for example, Java and those written in .NET.

It's these sorts of problems that have led to the adoption of such techniques as JSON, which are discussed in Chapters 16 and 17.

Even though SOAP is not without its faults, it is still has the advantages of working across platforms and can be used from a large number of clients. It also has the flexibility to represent complex messages, and can cope with situations where the processing of these messages requires them to pass along a chain of computers, rather than just a simple client to server journey. None of the other services that are in common use, such as REST or JSON, can compete on all these features. For this reason, SOAP is likely to be around for quite some time and is definitely a technology worth learning if you want to develop distributed systems.

Before you start creating SOAP messages though, you need to look at the process of creating an RPC server that receives a request and sends back a response. The following example begins with a fairly simple procedure to write: one that takes a unit price and quantity and returns the appropriate discount along with the total price.

TRY IT OUT Creating an RPC Server with ASP.NET

To begin, you create a simple ASP.NET page that accepts two numbers, evaluates them, and returns the results in XML. It won't be a fully-fledged SOAP service for reasons discussed later, but it contains a similar architecture. Later, you convert it to a full SOAP XML service.

1. Open Visual Studio and choose File ➢ New ➢ Website. Choose an ASP.NET Empty Website from the C# section and open the `BasicOrderService` folder. The empty website uses a file-based site to begin with, which you can convert to use IIS Express later if desired.
2. Right-click the project and choose Add New Item. Add a new Web Form named `GetTotal.aspx` and make sure the Place Code In A Separate File checkbox is checked. If the new page doesn't open automatically, open it in the editor.
3. Remove all the content from the page except the declaration at the top and add a new attribute, `ContentType`, with a value of `text/xml`. The page should now look like the following, although the code will all be on one line:

```
<%@ Page Language="C#" AutoEventWireup="true"
    CodeFile="GetTotal.aspx.cs" Inherits="GetTotal" ContentType="text/xml" %>
```

4. Save the page, right-click it in the Solution Explorer, and choose Set as Start Page.
5. Right-click in the body of the page and choose View Code. Replace the code you see with the code in Listing 15-1.

Available for download on Wrox.com

LISTING 15-1: GetTotal.aspx.cs

```
using System;
using System.Xml.Linq;

public partial class GetTotal : System.Web.UI.Page
{
  protected void Page_Load(object sender, EventArgs e)
  {
    string clientXml = string.Empty;
    try
    {
      double unitPrice = Convert.ToDouble(Request.QueryString["unitPrice"]);
      int quantity = Convert.ToInt16(Request.QueryString["quantity"]);
      double discount = GetQuantityDiscount(quantity);
```

```
        double basicTotal = GetBasicTotal(unitPrice, quantity);
        double finalTotal = basicTotal * (1 - discount);
        clientXml = GetSuccessXml(finalTotal, discount * 100);
      }
      catch (Exception ex)
      {
        clientXml = GetErrorXml(ex);
      }
      XElement doc = XElement.Parse(clientXml);
      doc.Save(Response.OutputStream);
    }


    private double GetBasicTotal(double unitPrice, int quantity)
    {
      return unitPrice * quantity;
    }

    private double GetQuantityDiscount(int quantity)
    {
      if (quantity < 6) return 0;
      if (quantity < 11) return 0.05;
      if (quantity < 51) return 0.1;
      return 0.2;
    }

    private string GetSuccessXml(double totalPrice, double discount)
    {
      string clientXml = "<GetTotalResponse><Discount>{0}</Discount>"
                       + "<TotalPrice>{1}</TotalPrice></GetTotalResponse>";
      return string.Format(clientXml, Convert.ToString(discount),
                           Convert.ToString(totalPrice));
    }

    private string GetErrorXml(Exception ex)
    {
      string clientXml = "<Error><Reason>{0}</Reason></Error>";
      return string.Format(clientXml, ex.Message);
    }

  }
```

The page is called with two values in the query string: `unitPrice` and `quantity`. The total price is calculated by multiplying the two values, and then a discount is applied. The discount depends on the quantity, and applies when the user requests more than five items. The results are returned in XML.

6. Test the page by right-clicking the project in the Solution Explorer and choosing View in Browser. When your browser appears, it should show a listing of the project files. Click on the link for `GetTotal.aspx` and then modify the URL in the browser address bar so it is: `GetTotal.aspx?unitprice=20&quantity=6` and press Enter. You should see XML similar to that shown in Figure 15-1. If invalid values are entered, such as a quantity of *q*, you should see the result shown in Figure 15-2.

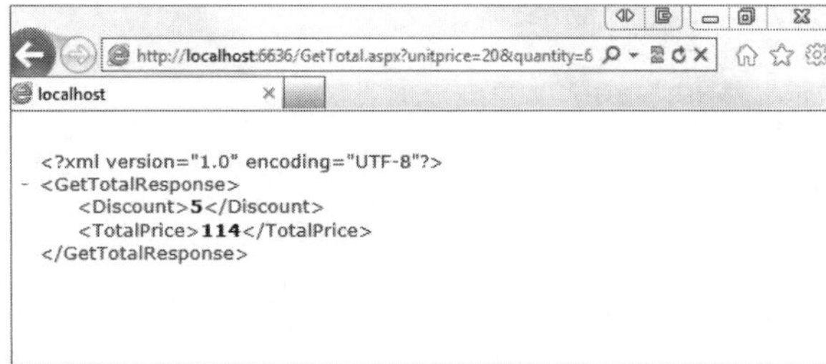

FIGURE 15-1

http://localhost:6636/GetTotal.aspx?unitprice=20&quantity=q

localhost

```
<?xml version="1.0" encoding="UTF-8"?>
- <Error>
    <Reason>Input string was not in a correct format.</Reason>
  </Error>
```

FIGURE 15-2

How It Works

This page pulls two values from the query string, converts them to numbers, and performs two actions. First, it requests a quantity discount using `GetQuantityDiscount()`, and then the page multiplies the two original numbers using `GetBasicTotal()`. Next, it returns the results as XML by loading a string of XML into an `XmlDocument` and saving to the `Response.OutputStream`. If either of the two values isn't numeric, meaning they can't be multiplied together, a different XML document is returned to the client, indicating a problem. This method of saving to the output stream is better than alternatives such as using `Response.Write`, because it preserves the character encoding that may be used in the document, whereas `Response.Write` always treats the content as `UTF-16`.

Note that this ASP.NET page isn't limited to being called from a browser. For example, you could load the XML directly and then retrieve the numbers from it, as in this VB.NET example:

```
Sub Main()
  Dim doc = new XDocument.Load
    ("http://localhost/BasicOrderService/gettotal.aspx?unitprice=20&quantity=6")

    If doc.Root.Name = "Error" Then
        MsgBox ("Unable to perform calculation")
    Else
        MsgBox(XDocument...<TotalPrice>.Value)
    End If
End Sub
```

You pass a URL, including the query string, to the `Load()` method, and then check the results. If the root element is named `Error`, you know something went wrong. Otherwise, you can get the results using an LINQ to XML expression. (See the last section in Chapter 12 for more on how these work.)

Comparing SOAP to REST

Technically speaking, what you just did in the preceding activity isn't actually a SOAP transaction, but maybe not for the reasons you might think. The issue isn't that you sent a URL rather than a SOAP message to make the request; SOAP actually defines just such a transaction. The problem is that the response wasn't actually a SOAP message.

Take a look at the output:

```
<GetTotalResponse>
  <Discount>0.95</Discount>
  <TotalPrice>44.46</TotalPrice>
</GetTotalResponse>
```

This doesn't conform to the structure of a SOAP message (as you'll see in the following section), but it is still a well-formed XML message and a perfectly valid way of creating a web service.

One of the main objections to SOAP is its complexity, and because of this many have looked for alternatives. One of the main contenders is known as REST which stands for *REpresentational State Transfer*. REST is based on the idea that any piece of information on the World Wide Web should be addressable via a URL. In this case, that URL included a query string with parameter information. REST also dictates that operations other than straightforward retrieval of information (deleting an item, for example) should ideally be instigated via the corresponding HTTP verb. So to delete a resource you send an HTTP `DELETE` request and pass the relevant URL rather than the use the normal HTTP `GET`.

REST is growing in popularity as people discover that it is, in many ways, much easier to use than SOAP. After all, you don't have to create an outgoing XML message, and you don't have to figure out how to `POST` it, as demonstrated in the previous chapter.

All of this begs the question: If REST is so much easier, why use SOAP at all? Aside from the fact that in some cases the request data is difficult or impossible to provide as a URL, the answer lies in the fundamental architecture of the Web. You submitted this request as a `GET`, which means that any parameters were part of the URL and not the body of the message. If you were to remain true to the way the Web is supposed to be constructed, `GET` requests are only for actions that have no side effects, such as making changes to a database. That means you could use this method for getting information, but you couldn't use it for, say, placing an order, because the act of making that request changes something on the server.

When SOAP was still growing in popularity, some developers insisted that REST was better because it was simpler. SOAP 1.2 ends the controversy by adopting a somewhat RESTful stance, making it possible to use an HTTP `GET` request to send information and parameters and in turn receive a SOAP response. You'll see this combination in action later, but first you should look at how SOAP itself works.

Basic SOAP Messages

As mentioned before, SOAP messages are basically XML documents, usually sent across HTTP. Following are the specifications that SOAP requires:

- **Rules regarding how the message should be sent:** Although the SOAP specification says that any network protocol can be used, specific rules are included in the specification for HTTP because that's the protocol most people use.

- **The overall structure of the XML that is sent:** This is called the *envelope*. Any information to be sent back and forth over SOAP is contained within this envelope, and is known as the *payload*.
- **Rules regarding how data is represented in this XML:** These are called the *encoding rules*.

When you send data to a SOAP server, the data must be represented in a particular way so that the server can understand it. The SOAP 1.2 specification outlines a simple XML document type, which is used for all SOAP messages. The basic structure of that document is as follows:

```
<soap:Envelope xmlns:soap="http://www.w3.org/2003/05/soap-envelope">
  <soap:Header>
    <head-ns:someHeaderElem xmlns:head-ns="some URI"
                            env:mustUnderstand="true OR false"
                            env:relay="true OR false"
                            env:role="some URI"/>
  </soap:Header>
  <soap:Body encodingStyle="http://www.w3.org/2003/05/soap-encoding">
    <some-ns:someElem xmlns:some-ns="some URI"/>
    <!-- OR -->
    <soap:Fault>
     <soap:Code>
       <soap:Value>Specified values</soap:Value>
       <soap:Subcode>
         <soap:Value>Specified values</soap:Value>
       </soap:Subcode>
     </soap:Code>
     <soap:Reason>
       <soap:Text xml:lang="en-US">English text</soap:Text>
       <v:Text xml:lang="fr">Texte francais</soap:Text>
     </soap:Reason>
     <soap:Detail>
       <!-- Application specific information -->
     </soap:Detail>
    </soap:Fault>
  </soap:Body>
</soap:Envelope>
```

Only three main elements are involved in a SOAP message itself (unless something goes wrong): `<Envelope>`, `<Header>`, and `<Body>`, and starting in version 1.2 of SOAP, a number of error-related elements. Of these elements, only `<Envelope>` and `<Body>` are mandatory; `<Header>` is optional, and `<Fault>` and its child elements are required only when an error occurs. In addition, all of the attributes (`encodingStyle`, `mustUnderstand`, and so on) are optional. The following sections take a closer look at these elements and the various attributes.

<Envelope>

Other than the fact that it resides in SOAP's envelope namespace (`http://www.w3.org/2003/05/soap-envelope`), the `<Envelope>` element doesn't really need any explanation. It simply provides the root element for the XML document and is usually used to include any namespace declarations.

<Body>

The `<Body>` element contains the main body of the SOAP message. The actual RPC calls are made using direct children of the `<Body>` element (which are called *body blocks*). For example, consider the following:

```
<soap:Envelope xmlns:env="http://www.w3.org/2003/05/soap-envelope">
    <soap:Body>
       <o:AddToCart xmlns:o="http://www.wiley.com/soap/ordersystem">
          <o:CartId>THX1138</o:CartId>
          <o:Item>ZIBKA</o:Item>
          <o:Quantity>3</o:Quantity>
          <o:TotalPrice>34.97</o:TotalPrice>
       </o:AddToCart>
    </soap:Body>
</soap:Envelope>
```

In this case, you're making one RPC call, to a procedure called `AddToCart`, in the `http://www.wiley.com/soap/ordersystem` namespace. (You can add multiple calls to a single message, if necessary.) The `AddToCart` procedure takes four parameters: `CartId`, `Item`, `Quantity`, and `TotalPrice`. Direct child elements of the `<soap:Body>` element must reside in a namespace other than the SOAP namespace. This namespace is what the SOAP server uses to uniquely identify this procedure so that it knows what code to run. When the procedure is done running, the server uses the HTTP response to send back a SOAP message. The `<soap:Body>` of that message might look similar to this:

```
<soap:Envelope xmlns:soap="http://www.w3.org/2003/05/soap-envelope">
  <soap:Body>
    <o:AddToCartResponse xmlns:o="http://www.wiley.com/soap/ordersystem">
      <o:CartId>THX1138</o:CartId>
      <o:Status>OK</o:Status>
      <o:Quantity>3</o:Quantity>
      <o:ItemId>ZIBKA</o:ItemId>
      </so:AddToCartResponse>
    </soap:Body>
</soap:Envelope>
```

The response is just another SOAP message, using an XML structure similar to the request, in that it has a `Body` in an `Envelope`, with the relevant information included as the payload.

Encoding Style

Usually, in the realm of XML, when you talk about encoding, you're talking about esoteric aspects of passing text around, but in the SOAP world, encoding is pretty straightforward. It simply refers to the way in which you represent the data. These examples use SOAP-style encoding, which means you're using plain-old elements and text, with maybe an attribute or two thrown in. You can let an application know that's what you're doing by adding the optional `encodingStyle` attribute, as shown here:

```
<soap:Envelope xmlns:soap="http://www.w3.org/2003/05/soap-envelope">
  <soap:Body soap:encodingStyle="http://www.w3.org/2003/05/soap-encoding">
    <o:AddToCartResponse xmlns:o="http://www.wiley.com/soap/ordersystem">
      <o:CartId>THX1138</o:CartId>
      <o:Status>OK</o:Status>
```

```
        <o:Quantity>3</o:Quantity>
        <o:ItemId>ZIBKA</o:ItemId>
      </o:AddToCartResponse>
    </soap:Body>
  </soap:Envelope>
```

This distinguishes it from other encodings, such as RDF, shown in the following code:

NOTE *RDF stands for Resource Description Framework, a protocol used to represent information on the Web. It is a W3C Recommendation, and the full details are available at* `www.w3.org/RDF/`.

```
<soap:Envelope xmlns: soap="http://www.w3.org/2003/05/soap-envelope">
  <soap:Body>
    <rdf:RDF xmlns:rdf="http://www.w3.org/1999/02/22-rdf-syntax-ns#"
          xmlns:o="http://www.wiley.com/soap/ordersystem"
      env:encodingStyle="http://www.w3.org/1999/02/22-rdf-syntax-ns#">
      <o:AddToCartResponse
         rdf:About=
         "http://www.wiley.com/soap/ordersystem/addtocart.asp?cartid
          =THX1138">
        <o:CartId>THX1138</o:CartId>
        <o:Status>OK</o:Status>
        <o:qQuantity>3</o:Quantity>
        <o:ItemId>ZIBKA</o:ItemId>
      </o:AddToCartResponse>
    </rdf:RDF>
  </soap:Body>
</soap:Envelope>
```

The information is the same, but it's represented, or encoded, differently. You can also create your own encoding, but of course if your goal is interoperability, you need to use a standard encoding style. In the preceding example `env:encodingStyle` is an attribute of the `<rdf:RDF>` element, but it could equally well have appeared on the `<soap:Body>`. In general, the attribute can appear anywhere and applies to all descendants of the element on which it appears, as well as the element itself. This means that different parts of the same SOAP message can use different encodings if needed.

You've now seen the core components of SOAP and how they fit together. It's now time to put this into practice and see how a SOAP web service uses the elements, such as `<soap:Envelope>` and `<soap:Body>`, to wrap the request and response messages. This turns a web service into a SOAP web service.

The previous Try It Out presented almost all of the benefits of SOAP. It works easily with a firewall, and all the information is passed over HTTP in XML, meaning you could implement your remote procedure using any language, on any platform, and you can call it from any language, on any platform. However, the solution is still a little proprietary. To make the procedure more universal, you need to go one step further and use a SOAP envelope for your XML.

TRY IT OUT GETting a SOAP Message

This example still uses a GET request, but rather than return the raw XML, it is enclosed in a SOAP envelope, like so:

```
<soap:Envelope xmlns:soap="http://www.w3.org/2003/05/soap-envelope">
  <soap:Body>
    <GetTotalResponse xmlns="http://www.wiley.com/soap/ordersystem">
      <Discount>10</Discount>
      <TotalPrice>243</TotalPrice>
    </GetTotalResponse>
  </soap:Body>
</soap:Envelope>
```

In this case, you'll also send the request and receive the response through an HTML form:

1. Create an HTML file in the text editor and save it as soaptester.html in a virtual folder. If you tried the previous example, just store the file in the same directory, BasicOrderService.
2. Add the HTML in Listing 15-2 to SoapTester.html.

Available for download on Wrox.com

LISTING 15-2: SoapTester.html

```
<html>
<head>
  <title>SOAP Tester</title>
  <!-- script will go here -->
</head>
<body onload="init();">
  <h3>
    Soap Pricing Tool</h3>
  <form name="orderForm">
  <select name="lstItems" id="lstItems" style="width: 350px"
    onchange="setPriceAndQuantity();">
    <option value="10.50" id="item1" selected>
      Cool Britannia, by The Bonzo Dog Doo-Dah Band</option>
    <option value="12.95" id="item2">
      Zibka Smiles, by The Polka Dot Zither Band</option>
    <option value="20.00" id="item3">
      Dr Frankenstein's Disco Party, by Jonny Wakelin</option>
  </select>
  <p>
    Unit price:<input type="text"
                 name="txtUnitPrice" id="txtUnitPrice"
                 size="6" readonly><br>
    Quantity:
    <input type="text"
      name="txtQuantity" id="txtQuantity"
      size="2">
  </p>
```

```
    <input type="button" value="Get Price" onclick="doGet()"><br>
    Discount (%):<input type="text" id="txtDiscount"
                    name="txtDiscount" size="4" readonly><br>
    Total price:<input type="text" id="txtTotalPrice"
                   name="txtTotalPrice" size="6" readonly>
    </form>
  </body>
  </html>
```

The form has a drop-down box to pick an item; this sets the price in the first textbox. The user then chooses the quantity and clicks the button. You have two read-only textboxes for the output: `txtDiscount` and `txtTotalPrice` (see Figure 15-3).

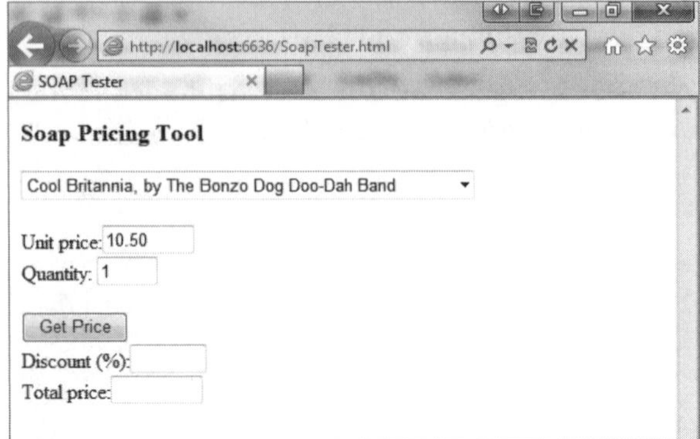

FIGURE 15-3

3. Add the script that's going to make the call to the SOAP server to the `SoapTester.html` file:

```
<head>
  <title>SOAP Tester</title>
  <script type="text/javascript"
          src="http://code.jquery.com/jquery-1.6.4.js"></script>
  <script type="text/javascript">
    function doGet()
    {
      var dUnitPrice = $("#txtUnitPrice").val();
      var iQuantity = $("#txtQuantity").val();
      var sBaseUrl = "GetTotal2.aspx";
      var sQuery = "?unitprice=" + dUnitPrice + "&quantity=" + iQuantity;
      var sRequest = sBaseUrl + sQuery;
      $.get(sRequest, null, handleGetTotalResponse, "xml");
    }

    function handleGetTotalResponse(data, textStatus, jqXHR)
    {
      if (textStatus == "success")
      {
        alert(jqXHR.responseText);
        var oBody = $("[nodeName=soap\\:Body]", jqXHR.responseXML);
        var dDiscount = oBody.find("[nodeName=Discount]").text();
        var dTotalPrice = oBody.find("[nodeName=TotalPrice]").text();
```

```
        if (!dDiscount)
        {
          var oError = $("[nodeName=Error]", jqXHR.responseXML);
          if (oError)
          {
            var sErrorMessage = oError.find("[nodeName=Reason]").text();
            alert(sErrorMessage);
          }
          else
          {
            alert("Unreadable error message.");
          }
        }
        showResults(dDiscount, dTotalPrice);
      }
      else
        alert("Error accessing web service.");
    }

    function showResults(discount, totalPrice)
    {
      $("#txtDiscount").val(discount);
      $("#txtTotalPrice").val(totalPrice);
    }

    function setPriceAndQuantity()
    {
      $("#txtUnitPrice").val($("#lstItems").val());
      $("#txtQuantity").val(1);
    }

    function init()
    {
      setPriceAndQuantity();
    }

  </script>
</head>
```

SoapTester.html

The first script is the jQuery library that is used to make getting the values of elements easier, and to make a background request to the web service to retrieve the discounted price. This code is in the `doGet()` function. The `handleGetTotalResponse()` function uses jQuery's XML parsing features to load the received request and look for a `<soap:Body>` element, and from there, the `<Discount>` and `<TotalPrice>` elements. If it can't find these, it treats the response as an error and shows the value of the `<Reason>` element. The script contains two other functions. `setPriceAndQuantity()` populates `txtUnitPrice` with the price of the selected item and resets the quantity to 1. `init()` sets the initial values of these boxes when the page loads.

The jQuery file is being hosted on jQuery's own content delivery network (CDN). If you'd rather have a local copy, download it and alter the `src` attribute accordingly. In a production environment you'd probably use the minified (compact) version, but here you use the full one because it's easier to debug if things go wrong.

4. Create the `aspx` page to serve the content. Save a copy of `GetTotal.aspx` and call it `GetTotal2.aspx`. Modify the content so that the `CodeFile` attribute points to `GetTotal2.aspx.cs` like so:

```
<%@ Page Language="C#" AutoEventWireup="true" CodeFile="GetTotal2.aspx.cs"
         Inherits="GetTotal" ContentType="text/xml" %>
```

GetTotal2.aspx

5. Copy the code file, `GetTotal.aspx.cs`, and name the new version `GetTotal2.aspx.cs`. Modify the `GetSuccessXml` to produce a SOAP-style message like so:

```
private string GetSuccessXml(double totalPrice, double discount)
{
  string clientXml = "<soap:Envelope xmlns:soap=\
"http://www.w3.org/2003/05/soap-envelope\"><soap:Body>"
 + "<GetTotalResponse"
 + " xmlns=\"http://www.wiley.com/soap/ordersystem\"><Discount>{0}</Discount>"
 + "<TotalPrice>{1}</TotalPrice>"
 + "</GetTotalResponse></soap:Body></soap:Envelope>";
  return string.Format(clientXml,
                       Convert.ToString(discount),
                       Convert.ToString(totalPrice));
}
```

GetTotal2.aspx

6. Reload the `soaptester.html` page in the browser, change the quantity, and click the Get Price button. The raw XML returned by the service is displayed in an alert box, as shown in Figure 15-4. The results are then extracted from this message and displayed in the bottom two textboxes. If you try an invalid quantity, you'll get an alert of the error message, as shown previously.

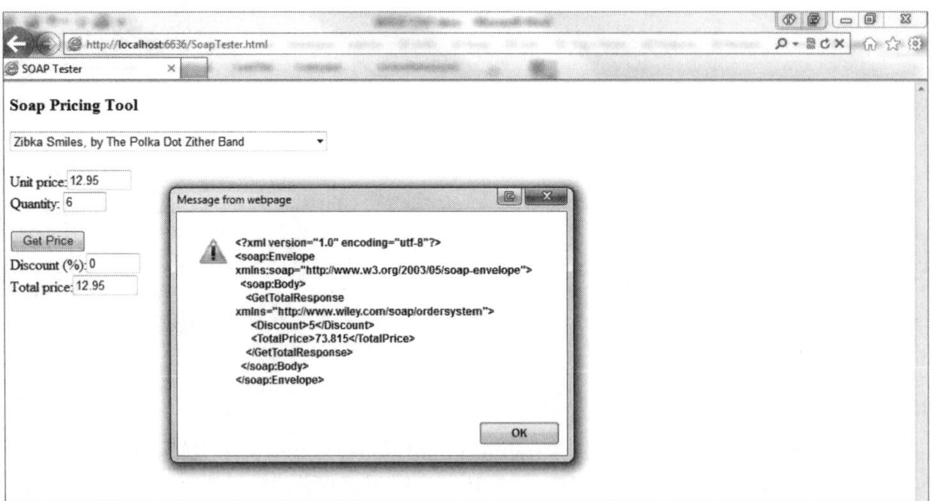

FIGURE 15-4

How It Works

This Try It Out illustrates a practical (if a bit contrived) example of working with a SOAP server. Using the browser, you created a simple SOAP client that retrieved information from the user interface (the quantity and unit price), sent a request to a SOAP server (the `GET` request), and displayed the results (the discount and extended price).

Because you created a client using the browser, you had to use a MIME type that the browser understands: `text/xml`. Under other circumstances, you'd want to use the actual SOAP MIME type, `application/soap+xml`. In other words, the ASP page would begin with the following:

```
Response.ContentType = "application/soap+xml"
```

This way, administrators can configure their firewalls to allow packets with this MIME type to pass through, even if they are blocking other types of content. Unfortunately, far too few clients understand this version, so the less accurate `text/xml` is still more common.

There's one final step before this service is fully SOAP compliant, and that's the error handling. At the moment, it still returns the error message in a proprietary format. You'll return to this after you've covered SOAP errors in more detail.

So far you've only scratched the surface of what SOAP can do. The following section looks at some more detailed uses.

More Complex SOAP Interactions

Now that you know the basics of how SOAP works, it's time to delve a little more deeply. SOAP messages can consist of not just a `Body`, which contains the payload or data to be processed, but also a `Header` element that contains information about the payload. The `Header` also gives you a good deal of control over how its information is processed.

Additionally SOAP messages also use `<Fault>` elements to return fault code errors, and can substitute the use of the `GET` operation with the `POST` operation in some circumstances. The following sections explain these more complex elements of SOAP.

<Header>

The `<Header>` element comes into play when you need to add additional information to your SOAP message. For example, suppose you created a system whereby orders can be placed into your database using SOAP messages, and you have defined a standard SOAP message format that anyone communicating with your system must use. You might use a SOAP header for authentication information, so that only authorized persons or systems can use your system. These elements, called *header blocks*, are specifically designed for *meta information*, or information about the information contained in the body.

When a `<Header>` element is used, it must be the first element child of the `<Envelope>` element. Functionally, the `<Header>` element works very much like the `<Body>` element; it is simply a placeholder for other elements in namespaces other than the SOAP envelope namespace. The `<Header>` element contains instructions, such as routing information; or meta data, such as user credentials, which need to be taken into account when processing the main SOAP message in the <Body>. In general, however, the <Header> doesn't contain information to be processed.

The SOAP 1.2 Recommendation also defines three optional attributes you can include on those header entries: mustUnderstand, role, and relay.

The mustUnderstand Attribute

The mustUnderstand attribute specifies whether it is absolutely necessary for the SOAP server to process a particular header block. A value of true indicates that the header entry is mandatory, and the server must either process it or indicate an error. For example, consider the following:

```
<soap:Envelope xmlns:soap="http://www.w3.org/2003/05/soap-envelope">
  <soap:Header xmlns:some-ns="http://www.wiley.com/soap/headers/">

    <some-ns:authentication mustUnderstand="true">
      <UserID>User ID goes here...</UserID>
      <Password>Password goes here...</Password>
    </some-ns:authentication>

    <some-ns:log mustUnderstand="false">
      <additional-info>Info goes here...</additional-info>
    </some-ns:log>
    <some-ns:log>
      <additional-info>Info goes here...</additional-info>
    </some-ns:log>
  </soap:Header>
  <soap:Body xmlns:body-ns="http://www.wiley.com/soap/rpc">
    <body-ns:mainRPC>
      <additional-info/>
    </body-ns:mainRPC>
  </soap:Body>
</soap:Envelope>
```

This SOAP message contains three header entries: one for authentication and two for logging purposes.

For the <authentication> header entry, a value of true was specified for mustUnderstand. (In SOAP 1.1, you would have specified it as 1.) This means that the SOAP server must process the header block. If the SOAP server doesn't understand this header entry, it rejects the entire SOAP message — the server is not allowed to process the entries in the SOAP body. This forces the server to use proper authentication.

The second header entry specified a value of false for mustUnderstand, which makes this header entry optional. This means that when the SOAP server doesn't understand this particular header entry, it can still go ahead and process the SOAP body anyway.

Finally, in the third header entry the mustUnderstand attribute was omitted. In this case, the header entry is optional, just as if you had specified the mustUnderstand attribute with a value of false.

The role Attribute

In some cases a SOAP message may pass through a number of applications on a number of computers before it arrives at its final destination. You might send a SOAP message to computer A, which might then send that message on to computer B. Computer A would be called a *SOAP intermediary*.

In these cases, you can use the `role` attribute to specify that some SOAP headers must be processed by a specific intermediary. The value of the attribute is a URI, which uniquely identifies each intermediary. The SOAP specification also defines the following three roles:

- `http://www.w3.org/2003/05/soap-envelope/role/next` applies to the next intermediary in line, wherever it is.
- `http://www.w3.org/2003/05/soap-envelope/role/ultimateReceiver` applies only to the very last stop.
- `http://www.w3.org/2003/05/soap-envelope/role/none` effectively "turns off" the header block so that it is ignored at this stage of the process.

When an intermediary processes a header entry, it must remove that header from the message before passing it on. Conversely, the SOAP specification also says that a similar header entry can be inserted in its place, so you can process the SOAP header entry and then add another identical header block.

The relay Attribute

The SOAP specification also requires a SOAP intermediary to remove any headers it doesn't process, which presents a problem. What if you want to add a new feature and target it at any intermediary that might understand it? The solution to this is the `relay` attribute. By setting the `relay` attribute to `true`, you can instruct any intermediary that encounters it to either process it or leave it alone. (If the intermediary does process the header, the intermediary still must remove it.) The default value for the relay attribute is `false`.

<Fault>

Whenever computers are involved, things can go wrong, and there may be times when a SOAP server is unable to process a SOAP message, for whatever reason. Perhaps a resource needed to perform the operation isn't available, invalid parameters were passed, or the server doesn't understand the SOAP request in the first place. In these cases, the server returns *fault codes* to the client to indicate errors.

Fault codes are sent using the same format as other SOAP messages. However, in this case, the `<Body>` element has only one child, a `<Fault>` element. Children of the `<Fault>` element contain details of the error. A SOAP message indicating a fault might look similar to this:

```
<soap:Envelope xmlns:soap="http://www.w3.org/2003/05/soap-envelope"
              xmlns:rpc="http://www.w3.org/2003/05/soap-rpc">
  <soap:Body>
   <soap:Fault>
     <soap:Code>
       <soap:Value>soap:Sender</soap:Value>
       <soap:Subcode>
         <soap:Value>rpc:BadArguments</soap:Value>
       </soap:Subcode>
     </soap:Code>
     <soap:Reason>
       <soap:Text xml:lang="en-US">Processing error</soap:Text>
       <soap:Text xml:lang="fr">Erreur de traitement</soap:Text>
     </soap:Reason>
     <soap:Detail>
       <o:orderFaultInfo xmlns:o="http://www.wiley.com/soap/ordersystem">
         <o:errorCode>WA872</o:errorCode>
         <o:message>Cart doesn't exist</o:message>
```

```
          </o:OrderFaultInfo>
        </soap:Detail>
      </soap:Fault>
    </soap:Body>
  </soap:Envelope>
```

The `<Code>` element contains a `<Value>` consisting of a unique identifier that identifies this particular type of error. The SOAP specification defines five such identifiers, described in the Table 15-1:

TABLE 15-1: Fault Code Values in SOAP

FAULT CODE	DESCRIPTION
VersionMismatch	A SOAP message was received that specified a version of the SOAP protocol that this server doesn't understand. (This would happen, for example, if you sent a SOAP 1.2 message to a SOAP 1.1 server.)
MustUnderstand	The SOAP message contained a mandatory header that the SOAP server doesn't understand.
Sender	The message was not properly formatted. That is, the client made a mistake when creating the SOAP message. This identifier also applies if the message itself is well formed, but doesn't contain the correct information. For example, if authentication information were missing, this identifier would apply.
Receiver	The server had problems processing the message, even though the contents of the message were formatted properly. For example, perhaps a database was down.
DataEncodingUnknown	The data in the SOAP message is organized, or encoded, in a way the server doesn't understand.

NOTE *Keep in mind that the identifier is actually namespace-qualified, using the* `http://www.w3.org/2003/05/soap-envelope` *namespace.*

You also have the option to add information in different languages, as shown in the previous example's `<Text>` elements, as well as application-specific information as part of the `<Detail>` element. Note that application-specific information in the `<Detail>` element must have its own namespace.

The previous two Try It Outs were devoted to simply getting information from the SOAP server. Because you weren't actually changing anything on the server, you could use the `GET` method and simply pass all of the information as part of the URL. (Remember that you're supposed to use `GET` only when there are no side effects from calling the URL.)

Now you examine a situation where that isn't the case. In this Try It Out, you look at a SOAP procedure that adds an item to a hypothetical shopping cart. Because this is not an "idempotent" process—it causes side effects, in that it adds an item to the order—you have to submit the information via the `POST` method, which means creating a SOAP message within the client.

TRY IT OUT POSTing a SOAP Message

In this activity you will call the `AddToCart` procedure using the following SOAP message (placeholders are shown in italics):

```
<soap:Envelope xmlns:soap="http://www.w3.org/2003/05/soap-envelope">
<soap:Body>
  <o:AddToCart xmlns:o="http://www.wiley.com/soap/ordersystem">
    <o:CartId>CARTID</o:CartId>
    <o:Item itemId="ITEMID">
      <o:Quantity>QUANTITY</o:Quantity>
      <o:TotalPrice>PRICE</o:TotalPrice>
    </o:Item>
  </o:AddToCart>
</soap:Body>
</soap:Envelope>
```

For the response, send the following XML back to the client:

```
<soap:Envelope xmlns:soap="http://www.w3.org/2003/05/soap-envelope">
  <soap:Body>
    <o:AddToCartResponse xmlns:o="http://www.wiley.com/soap/ordersystem">
      <o:CartId>CARTID</o:CartId>
      <o:Status>STATUS</o:Status>
      <o:Quantity>QUANTITY</o:Quantity>
      <o:ItemId>ITEMID</o:ItemId>
    </o:AddToCartResponse>
  </soap:Body>
</soap:Envelope>
```

You also need to handle the errors using a SOAP envelope. Use the following format for errors:

```
<soap:Envelope xmlns:soap="http://www.w3.org/2003/05/soap-envelope"
              xmlns:rpc="http://www.w3.org/2003/05/soap-rpc">
  <soap:Body>
   <soap:Fault>
     <soap:Code>
       <soap:Value>soap:FAULTCODE</soap:Value>
       <soap:Subcode>
         <soap:Value>SUBVALUE</soap:Value>
       </soap:Subcode>
     </soap:Code>
     <soap:Reason>
       <soap:Text>ERROR DESCRIPTION</soap:Text>
     </soap:Reason>
     <soap:Detail>
       <o:OrderFaultInfo xmlns:o="http://www.wiley.com/soap/ordersystem">
         <o:ErrorCode>APPLICATION-SPECIFIC ERROR CODE</o:ErrorCode>
         <o:Message>APPLICATION-SPECIFIC ERROR MESSAGE</o:Message>
       </o:OrderFaultInfo>
     </soap:Detail>
   </soap:Fault>
  </soap:Body>
</soap:Envelope>
```

This Try It Out will build on the Visual Studio project used in the previous one. You'll add the functionality of adding a product to your shopping basket, and all the messages passed between the client and the service will be in a SOAP format.

1. Add a new web form to the example project named `AddToCart.aspx`. Similar to the previous `aspx` pages, it indicates that the returned content is XML. It also has a `ValidateRequest` attribute set to `false`; otherwise, the `aspx` handler rejects the request as malformed.

Available for download on Wrox.com

```
<%@ Page Language="C#" AutoEventWireup="true" CodeFile="AddToCart.aspx.cs"
         Inherits="AddToCart" ContentType="text/xml" ValidateRequest="false" %>
```

AddToCart.aspx

2. Go to `AddToCart.aspx.cs` to create the basic page that retrieves the submitted SOAP message and extracts the appropriate information. The first part of the page (as shown in the following code) declares the namespaces of the libraries used in the service. These are the familiar `System.Web` as well as two namespaces for parsing and producing XML, `System.Linq` and `System.Xml.Linq`:

Available for download on Wrox.com

```
using System;
using System.Linq;
using System.Xml.Linq;

public partial class AddToCart : System.Web.UI.Page
{

  private readonly XNamespace cartNS = "http://www.wiley.com/soap/ordersystem";
  private readonly XNamespace soapNS = "http://www.w3.org/2003/05/soap-envelope";

  protected void Page_Load(object sender, EventArgs e)
  {
    try
    {
      XElement message = XElement.Load(Request.InputStream);
      // More code here to read incoming message
    }
    catch (Exception ex)
    {
      SendSoapFault("soap:Sender",
                    "rpc:BadArguments",
                    ex.Message,
                    "1",
                    ex.Message);
    }
  }
```

AddToCart.aspx.cs

3. Declare two `XNamespaces` to hold the two namespace URIs you'll need to read and create the SOAP messages, then load the incoming stream into an `XElement` named `message`. You do this in a `try/catch` block. If the `Load()` method fails because the input is invalid, the `catch` block returns a SOAP fault to the client using the `SendSoapFault()` method which is discussed later in this activity.

4. The relevant parts of the incoming XML are read using the techniques described in Chapter 12, "LINQ to XML":

Available for download on Wrox.com

```
    try
    {
      XElement message = XElement.Load(Request.InputStream);
      string cartId = message.Descendants(cartNS + "CartId").First().Value;
      string itemId =
```

```
      message.Descendants(cartNS + "Item").First().Attribute("itemId").Value;
    string quantity =
      message.Descendants(cartNS + "Quantity").First().Value;
    string totalPrice =
      message.Descendants(cartNS + "TotalPrice").First().Value;
    string status = ProcessData(cartId, itemId, quantity, totalPrice);
    SendSoapResponse(status, cartId, itemId, quantity);
  }
  catch (Exception ex)
```

AddToCart.aspx.cs

5. Once the four values are extracted, they are passed to the `ProcessData()` method like so:

```
private string ProcessData(string cartId,
                           string itemid,
                           string quantity,
                           string totalPrice)
{
  // do something with data
  return "OK";
}
```

AddToCart.aspx.cs

In a full application this method would validate the values and use `SendSoapFault()` if there was a problem such as a missing or illegal entry. If everything was okay, the data would be added to some sort of store, such as a database or the user's session. Here, you just return a status message of OK. (In a production system you wouldn't trust the `totalPrice` to be valid either, because it came from the client. You'd check the discount against the web service created earlier.)

6. Finally, a SOAP response is generated and saved to the `Response.OutputStream`. This method uses a template of the outgoing message and then fills it in using LINQ to XML. This is one area where VB.NET's XML Literals, discussed in Chapter 12, would make things much easier:

```
private void SendSoapResponse(string status,
                              string cartId,
                              string itemid,
                              string quantity)
{
  string template =
    "<soap:Envelope xmlns:soap=\"http://www.w3.org/2003/05/soap-envelope\">"
                + "<soap:Body>"
                + "<o:AddToCartResponse"
                + "xmlns:o=\"http://www.wiley.com/soap/ordersystem\">"
                + "<o:CartId></o:CartId>"
                + "<o:Status></o:Status>"
                + "<o:Quantity></o:Quantity>"
                + "<o:ItemId></o:ItemId>"
                + "</o:AddToCartResponse>"
                + "</soap:Body>"
                + "</soap:Envelope>";
  XElement soapResponse = XElement.Parse(template);
```

```
    XElement addToCartResponse =
            soapResponse.Descendants(cartNS + "AddToCartResponse").First();
    addToCartResponse.SetElementValue(cartNS + "CartId", cartId);
    addToCartResponse.SetElementValue(cartNS + "Status", status);
    addToCartResponse.SetElementValue(cartNS + "Quantity", quantity);
    addToCartResponse.SetElementValue(cartNS + "ItemId", cartId);
    soapResponse.Save(Response.OutputStream);
  }
```

AddToCart.aspx.cs

7. The method that creates a SOAP fault is similar; it uses a template and passes back the official SOAP fault details along with a user-friendly message derived from the `Exception` that was thrown:

```
  private void SendSoapFault(string faultCode,
                             string subvalue,
                             string description,
                             string appCode,
                             string appMessage)
  {
    string template =
      "<soap:Envelope xmlns:soap=\"http://www.w3.org/2003/05/soap-envelope\""
                  + " xmlns:rpc=\"http://www.w3.org/2003/05/soap-rpc\">"
                  + "<soap:Body>"
                  + "<soap:Fault>"
                  + "<soap:Code>"
                  + "<soap:Value></soap:Value>"
                  + "<soap:Subcode>"
                  + "<soap:Value></soap:Value>"
                  + "</soap:Subcode>"
                  + "</soap:Code>"
                  + "<soap:Reason>"
                  + "<soap:Text></soap:Text>"
                  + "</soap:Reason>"
                  + "<soap:Detail>"
                  + "<o:OrderFaultInfo"
                  + " xmlns:o=\"http://www.wiley.com/soap/ordersystem\">"
                  + "<o:ErrorCode></o:ErrorCode>"
                  + "<o:Message></o:Message>"
                  + "</o:OrderFaultInfo>"
                  + "</soap:Detail>"
                  + "</soap:Fault>"
                  + "</soap:Body>"
                  + "</soap:Envelope>";
    XElement soapResponse = XElement.Parse(template);
    XElement soapFault = soapResponse.Descendants(soapNS + "Fault").First();
    soapFault.Element(soapNS + "Code").
              SetElementValue(soapNS + "Value", faultCode);
    soapFault.Element(soapNS + "Code").
        Element(soapNS + "Subcode").SetElementValue(soapNS + "Value", subvalue);
    soapFault.Element(soapNS + "Reason").
       SetElementValue(soapNS + "Text", description);
    XElement orderFaultInfo =
```

```
            soapResponse.Descendants(cartNS + "OrderFaultInfo").First();
        orderFaultInfo.SetElementValue(cartNS + "ErrorCode", appCode);
        orderFaultInfo.SetElementValue(cartNS + "Message", appMessage);
        soapResponse.Save(Response.OutputStream);
    }
}
```

AddToCart.aspx.cs

8. Now the client needs to be amended. Once the total price has been retrieved, the user can add the items to the cart. You must make two changes to the HTML. First, you need to store the item's ID with each `select` option so it can be sent with the SOAP request:

```
<select name="lstItems" id="lstItems" style="width: 350px"
   onchange="setPriceAndQuantity();">
  <option value="10.50" id="item1"
   selected>Cool Britannia, by The Bonzo Dog Doo-Dah Band</option>
  <option value="12.95"
     id="item2">Zibka Smiles, by The Polka Dot Zither Band</option>
  <option value="20.00"
    id="item3">Dr Frankenstein's Disco Party, by Jonny Wakelin</option>
</select>
```

9. Now add a new function to create the request, `doPost()`, and one to handle the return, `handleAddToCartResponse()`. Both work similarly to the previous Try It Out, but create a `POST` request instead of a `GET`. The full listing of `SoapTester-Post.html` is shown in Listing 15-3, and Figure 15-5 shows it in action.

LISTING 15-3: SoapTester-Post.html

Available for download on Wrox.com

```
<html>
<head>
  <title>SOAP Tester</title>
  <script type="text/javascript"
     src="http://code.jquery.com/jquery-1.6.4.js"></script>
  <script type="text/javascript">
    function doGet()
    {
      var dUnitPrice = $("#txtUnitPrice").val();
      var iQuantity = $("#txtQuantity").val();
      var sBaseUrl = "GetTotal2.aspx";
      var sQuery = "?unitprice=" + dUnitPrice + "&quantity=" + iQuantity;
      var sRequest = sBaseUrl + sQuery;
      $.get(sRequest, null, handleGetTotalResponse, "xml");
    }

    function handleGetTotalResponse(data, textStatus, jqXHR)
    {
      if (textStatus == "success")
      {
        alert(jqXHR.responseText);
```

```
      var oBody = $("[nodeName=soap\\:Body]", jqXHR.responseXML);
      var dDiscount = oBody.find("[nodeName=Discount]").text();
      var dTotalPrice = oBody.find("[nodeName=TotalPrice]").text();
      if (!dDiscount)
      {
        var oError = $("[nodeName=Error]", jqXHR.responseXML);
        if (oError)
        {
          var sErrorMessage = oError.find("[nodeName=Reason]").text();
          alert(sErrorMessage);
        }
        else
        {
          alert("Unreadable error message.");
        }
      }
      showResults(dDiscount, dTotalPrice);
    }
    else
      alert("Error accessing web service.");
  }

  function showResults(discount, totalPrice)
  {
    $("#txtDiscount").val(discount);
    $("#txtTotalPrice").val(totalPrice);
  }

  function setPriceAndQuantity()
  {
    $("#txtUnitPrice").val($("#lstItems").val());
    $("#txtQuantity").val(1);
  }

  function doPost()
  {
    var oLst = document.getElementById("lstItems");
    var sItemId = oLst.options[oLst.selectedIndex].id;
    var sCartId = $("#hdCartId").val();
    var iQuantity = $("#txtQuantity").val();
    var dTotalPrice = $("#txtTotalPrice").val();
    var sSoapRequest =
      "<soap:Envelope xmlns:soap=\"http://www.w3.org/2003/05/soap-envelope\">"
                    + "<soap:Body>"
           + "<o:AddToCart xmlns:o=\"http://www.wiley.com/soap/ordersystem\">"
                    + "<o:CartId>" + sCartId + "</o:CartId>"
                    + "<o:Item itemId=\"" + sItemId + "\">"
                    + "<o:Quantity>" + iQuantity + "</o:Quantity>"
                    + "<o:TotalPrice>" + dTotalPrice + "</o:TotalPrice>"
                    + "</o:Item>"
```

```
                  + "</o:AddToCart>"
                  + "</soap:Body>"
                  + "</soap:Envelope>";
      alert(sSoapRequest);
      $.ajax({ url: "AddToCart.aspx",
               type: "post",
               data: sSoapRequest,
               processData: false,
               contentType: "text/xml",
               success: handleAddToCartResponse});
    }

    function handleAddToCartResponse(data, textStatus, jqXHR)
    {
      if (textStatus == "success")
      {
        alert(jqXHR.responseText);
        var oBody = $("[nodeName=soap\\:Body]", jqXHR.responseXML);
        var sStatus = oBody.find("[nodeName=o\\:Status]").text();
        if (!sStatus)
        {
          var sMessage = oBody.find("[nodeName=o\\:Message]").text();
          alert("Unable to add item to cart.\n" + sMessage);
        }
        else
        {
          if (sStatus == "OK")
          {
            alert("Item added to cart");
          }
          else
          {
            alert("Unable to add item to cart.");
          }
        }
      }
      else
      {
        alert("Unable to add item to cart.");
      }
    }


    function init()
    {
      setPriceAndQuantity();
    }

  </script>
</head>
<body onload="init();">
```

```
    <h3>
      Soap Pricing Tool</h3>
    <form name="orderForm">
    <select name="lstItems"
      id="lstItems" style="width: 350px" onchange="setPriceAndQuantity();">
      <option value="10.50"
      id="item1" selected>Cool Britannia, by The Bonzo Dog Doo-Dah Band</option>
      <option value="12.95"
      id="item2">Zibka Smiles, by The Polka Dot Zither Band</option>
      <option value="20.00"
      id="item3">Dr Frankenstein's Disco Party, by Jonny Wakelin</option>
    </select>
    <p>
      Unit price:<input type="text" name="txtUnitPrice"
       id="txtUnitPrice" size="6" readonly><br>
      Quantity:
      <input type="text" name="txtQuantity" id="txtQuantity" size="2">
    </p>
    <input type="button" value="Get Price" onclick="doGet()"><br>
    Discount (%):
      <input type="text" id="txtDiscount" name="txtDiscount" size="4" readonly><br>
    Total price:
     <input type="text" id="txtTotalPrice"
       name="txtTotalPrice" size="6" readonly><br>

    <input type="hidden" readonly name="hdCartId"
     id="hdCartId" value="cart123"><br>
    <input type="button" value="Add to Cart" onclick="doPost();">

    </form>
  </body>
  </html>
```

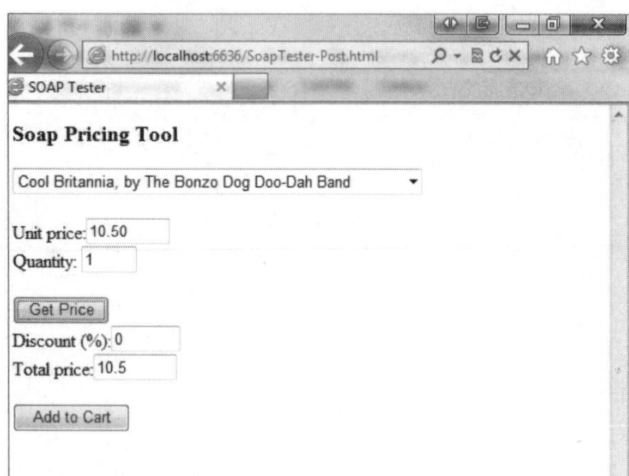

FIGURE 15-5

Figure 15-6 shows the raw XML response received after the Add to Cart button is clicked. If an error occurs (and you can test this by modifying the SOAP template by changing the `AddToCart` start tag to `AddToCar`), a SOAP fault is returned, as shown in Figure 15-7.

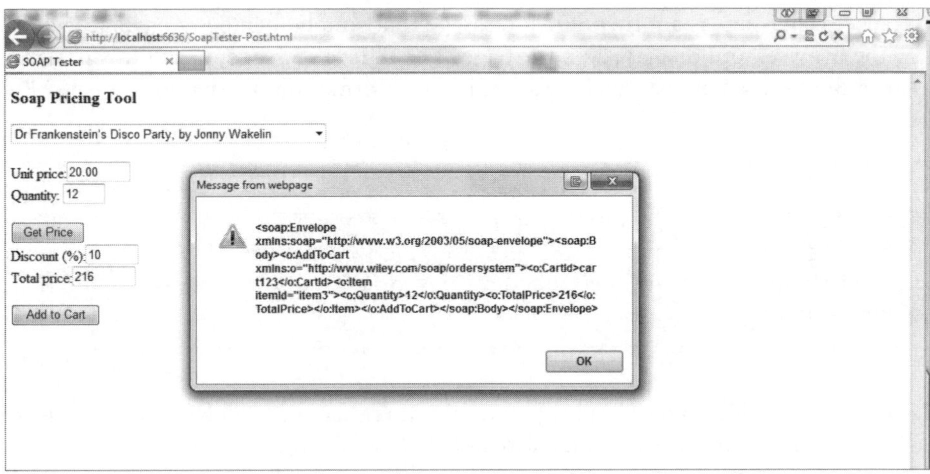

FIGURE 15-6

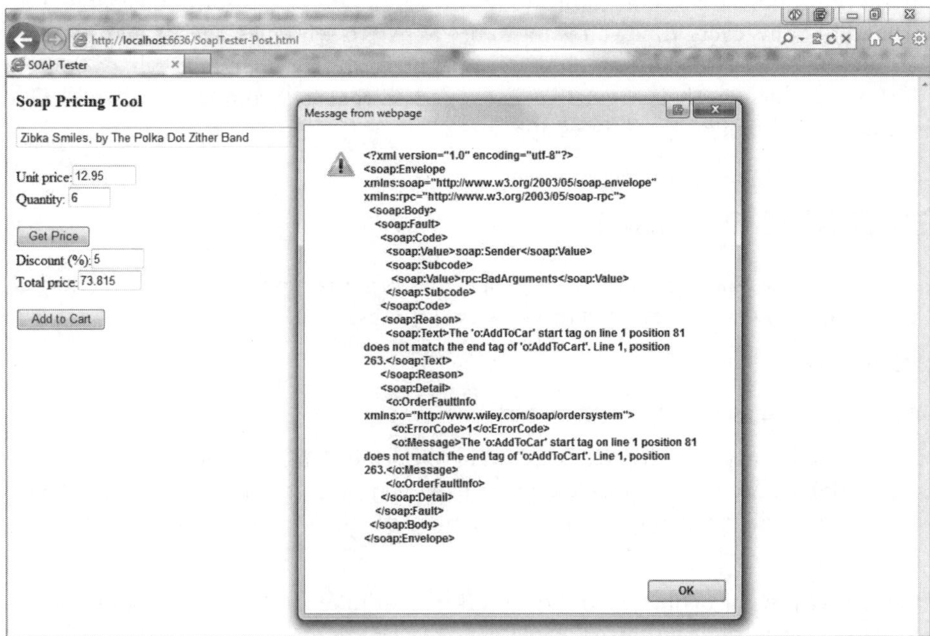

FIGURE 15-7

How It Works

Here you used the same techniques you used for raw XML messages to put together valid SOAP messages on both the incoming and the outgoing streams. You used data entered by the user on a form to create a SOAP message that was sent to a server. The server extracted information from that SOAP message using typical XML tactics, evaluated the data, and then determined whether to send a success or failure message. The success message is another SOAP message that simply includes a payload, which was then interpreted by the browser and displayed on the page. The failure message, or fault, was also analyzed by the browser. A SOAP 1.2 fault can include a wealth of information, related to both SOAP and the application itself.

NOTE *Some of the client-side script used in this example was deliberately glossed over, particularly the AJAX calls, because this topic is dealt with more fully in the next chapter.*

This may seem like a lot of work for a very simple operation, but realize that you have created, from scratch, all of the plumbing necessary to create an entire SOAP service. Implementing a more difficult SOAP service, such as some type of order-processing system, would require the same level of plumbing, even though the functionality being provided would be much more difficult.

In addition, several SOAP toolkits are available, meaning you won't necessarily have to generate the SOAP messages by hand like this every time you want to use SOAP to send messages from one computer to another. In any case, when you use those toolkits now, you'll understand what's going on under the hood. Until vendors get their respective acts together, that will come in handy when the inevitable inconsistencies and incompatibilities appear.

DEFINING WEB SERVICES: WSDL

You've built a web service. Now you hope that other people and organizations start using the service you've built. To do that, however, they need to know two things:

- How to call the service
- What to expect as a response from the service

Fortunately, there's a relatively easy way to provide answers to both questions: Web Services Description Language (WSDL). WSDL provides a standardized way to describe a web service. That means you can create a WSDL file describing your service, make the file available, and then sit back as people use it.

Of course, a WSDL file isn't just for people. Recall the toolkits that take most of the work out of creating SOAP messages. They're built on the principle that they can automatically generate a client for your web service just by analyzing the WSDL file. In this way, WSDL helps to make web services truly platform- and language-independent.

How's that, you ask? It's simple. A WSDL file is written in XML, describing the data to be passed and the method for passing it, but it doesn't lean toward any particular language. That means a web-services client generator can use the WSDL information to generate a client in any language. For example, a code generator for Java could create a client to access your ASP-based service, and the best part is that the client is pure Java. A developer writing an application around it doesn't have to know the details of the service, just the methods of the proxy class that actually accesses the service. The proxy sits between the client and the actual service, translating messages back and forth.

> ***NOTE*** *The latest version of WSDL, version 2.0, reached Candidate Recommendation in March 2006, but still seems to have had little impact so far. Most services still use the earlier version. The major differences between the two versions are highlighted when the various parts of the WSDL schema are discussed later in this chapter. You can read the specification for WSDL 1.1, the most common version, at* `www.w3.org/TR/wsdl`.

This chapter uses WSDL to describe a service that sends SOAP messages over HTTP, but in actuality WSDL is designed to be much more general. First, you define the data that will be sent, and then you define the way it will be sent. In this way, a single WSDL file can describe a service that's implemented as SOAP over HTTP as well as, say, SOAP over e-mail or even a completely different means. This chapter sticks with SOAP over HTTP because that's by far the most common usage right now.

The following sections discuss the various XML elements and attributes that make up a WSDL file and how they are mapped to a SOAP message.

<definitions>

A WSDL file starts with a `<definitions>` element like so:

```
<?xml version="1.0"?>
<definitions name="temperature"
    targetNamespace="http://www.example.com/temperature"
    xmlns:typens="http://www.example.com/temperature"
    xmlns:xsd="http://www.w3.org/2000/10/XMLSchema"
    xmlns:soap="http://schemas.xmlsoap.org/wsdl/soap/"
    xmlns="http://schemas.xmlsoap.org/wsdl/">
</definitions>
```

The first task in a WSDL file is to define the information that will be sent to and from the service. A WSDL file builds up the service in levels. First, it defines the data to be sent and received, and then it uses that data to define messages.

<types>

Remember that there's no way to know for sure that the web service being described will use SOAP, or even that the information passed in the request will be XML, but WSDL enables you to define the *information set*—in other words, the information itself, regardless of how it's ultimately represented—using XML Schemas (discussed in Chapter 5). For example, consider a simple service that takes a postal code and date and returns an average temperature. The service would have two types of data to deal with, as shown in the following code:

```
<types>
   <xsd:schema xmlns=""
        xmlns:xsd="http://www.w3.org/2000/10/XMLSchema"
        targetNamespace="http://www.example.com/temperature">
      <xsd:complexType name="temperatureRequestType">
         <xsd:sequence>
```

```
                <xsd:element name="where" type="xsd:string" />
                <xsd:element name="when" type="xsd:date"/>
            </xsd:sequence>
        </xsd:complexType>
        <xsd:complexType name="temperatureResponseType">
            <xsd:sequence>
                <xsd:element name="temperature" type="xsd:integer"/>
            </xsd:sequence>
        </xsd:complexType>
    </xsd:schema>
</types>
```

Just as in a normal schema document, you define two types: `temperatureRequestType` and `temperatureResponseType`. You can use them to define messages.

<messages>

When you define a message in a WSDL file, you're defining the content, rather than the representation. Sure, when you send SOAP messages, you are sending XML in a SOAP envelope, but that doesn't matter when you define the messages in the WSDL file. All you care about is what the message is, what it's called, and what kind of data it holds. Take the following example:

```
<message name="TemperatureRequestMsg">
    <part name="getTemperature" type="typens:temperatureRequestType"/>
</message>
<message name="TemperatureResponseMsg">
    <part name="temperatureResponse" type="typens:temperatureResponseType"/>
</message>
```

The preceding code defines a message that consists of an element called `getTemperature` of the type `temperatureRequestType`. This translates into the following SOAP message:

```
<env:Envelope xmlns:env="http://www.w3.org/2003/05/soap-envelope">
  <env:Body>
    <getTemperature>
      <where>POSTAL CODE</where>
      <when>DATE</when>
    </getTemperature>
  </env:Body>
</env:Envelope>
```

Notice that the namespace for the payload is still missing. You take care of that later in the WSDL file. In WSDL 2.0, messages are described within the `types` element and rely on XML Schemas.

<portTypes>

The `<portTypes>` element contains a number of `<portType>` elements that describe the individual operation provided by the service. These operations come in two varieties, input and output, and are made up of the messages you defined earlier. Consider the following example:

```
<portType name="TemperatureServicePortType">
    <operation name="GetTemperature">
        <input message="typens:TemperatureRequestMsg"/>
```

```
        <output message="typens:TemperatureResponseMsg"/>
    </operation>
</portType>
```

This portType shows that you're dealing with a request-response pattern; the user sends an input message, the structure of which is defined as a TemperatureRequestMsg, and the service returns an output message in the form of a TemperatureResponseMsg.

One of the major improvements coming in WSDL 2.0 is the change of the <portTypes> element to the <interfaces> element. Although portType seems to make sense from a structural point of view — later, you reference it when you define an actual port — it really is more of an interface, because it defines the various operations you can carry out with the service. The <interfaces> element can also be extended using the extends attribute, which allows inheritance and greater reuse of already successful code.

Next, you have to define how those messages are sent.

<binding>

Up until now, this section actually hasn't described anything related to SOAP. You've defined messages and put them together into operations, but you haven't learned anything about the protocol you use to send them. The <binding> element sets up the first part of this process. In this case, you bind the operations to SOAP as follows:

```
<binding name="TemperatureBinding" type="typens:TemperatureServicePortType">
   <soap:binding style="rpc" transport="http://schemas.xmlsoap.org/soap/http"/>
   <operation name="GetTemperature">
      <soap:operation />
      <input>
         <soap:body use="encoded"
                    encodingStyle="http://www.w3.org/2003/05/soap-encoding"
                    namespace="http://www.example.com/temperature" />
      </input>
      <output>
         <soap:body use="encoded"
                    encodingStyle="http://www.w3.org/2003/05/soap-encoding"
                    namespace="http://www.example.com/temperature" />
      </output>
   </operation>
</binding>
```

Notice that the soap: namespace finally comes into play at this point. There are two elements in this namespace: <soap:binding> and <soap:operation>. The following sections describe each one in detail.

<soap:binding>

The <soap:binding> element specifies that you are, in fact, dealing with a SOAP message, but it does more than that. The transport attribute is easy; it simply specifies that you're sending the message via HTTP. The style attribute is a little more complex (but just a little).

Both this chapter and the previous one concentrate on using web services as another means of performing remote procedure calls, but that's not their only use. In fact, in many cases information is simply passed to the service, which acts upon the data, rather than the data determining what should be done.

The `style` attribute has two possible values: `rpc` and `document`. The `rpc` value is a message in which you simply have a method name and parameters. For example, in this message, the payload represents a call to the `getTemperature` method with the parameters `34652` and `2004-5-23`, as shown in the following code:

```
<env:Envelope xmlns:env="http://www.w3.org/2003/05/soap-envelope">
  <env:Body>
    <getTemperature>
      <where>34652</where>
      <when>2004-05-23</when>
    </getTemperature>
  </env:Body>
</env:Envelope>
```

The data is contained in an outer element (`getTemperature`), which is itself contained within the `<env:Body>` element.

When you use the `document` style, however, the situation is slightly different. In that case, the entire contents of the `<env:Body>` element are considered to be the data in question. For example, you might have created a SOAP message of the following:

```
<env:Envelope xmlns:env="http://www.w3.org/2003/05/soap-envelope">
  <env:Body>
    <where>34652</where>
    <when>2004-05-23</when>
  </env:Body>
</env:Envelope>
```

The `document` style also enables you to send more complex documents that might not fit into the RPC mold. Note that neither of these examples shows the namespaces for the payload. That is set in the `soap:body` element, which you learn about shortly.

<soap:operation>

The `<soap:operation>` element is part of the `<binding>` section. If the `<soap:operation>` element looks out of place just sitting there with no attributes; that's because in many ways it is out of place. The SOAP 1.1 specification required all services to use a `SOAPAction` header defining the application that was supposed to execute it. This was an HTTP header, so you'd see something like this:

```
POST /soap.asp HTTP/1.1
Accept: image/gif, image/x-xbitmap, image/jpeg, image/pjpeg, */*
Accept-Language: en-us
Content-Type: application/x-www-form-urlencoded
Accept-Encoding: gzip, deflate
User-Agent: Mozilla/4.0 (compatible; MSIE 5.5; Windows NT 5.0)
Host: www.example.com
Content-Length: 242
SOAPAction: "http://www.example.org/soap/TemperatureService.asp"

<env:Envelope xmlns:env="http://www.w3.org/2003/05/soap-envelope">
  <env:Body>
    <getTemperature>
```

```
      <where>34652</where>
      <when>2004-05-23</when>
    </getTemperature>
  </env:Body>
</env:Envelope>
```

The SOAP 1.2 specification did away with the `SOAPAction` header, but it's still necessary to specify that this is a SOAP message — hence, the `soap:operation` element.

<soap:body>

The binding element references an operation, which in this case, is already defined as having an input and an output message. Within the binding element, you define how those messages are to be presented using the `soap:body` element. For example, you specify the following:

```
<soap:body use="encoded"
  encodingStyle="http://www.w3.org/2003/05/soap-encoding"
    namespace="http://www.example.com/temperature" />
```

For the input message, you're specifying that it's a SOAP message. Like the `style` attribute, the `use` attribute has two possible values: `literal` and `encoded`. When the `use` attribute is specified as `literal`, it means that the server is not to assume any particular meaning in the XML, but to take it as a whole. Normally, you use `literal` with the document style. If you specify the `use` attribute as `encoded`, you have to specify the `encodingStyle`. In this case, you specify the SOAP style, but you could use other encodings, such as RDF or even an entirely new encoding style. Finally, you specify the namespace of the payload, so you wind up with a complete message as follows:

```
<env:Envelope xmlns:env="http://www.w3.org/2003/05/soap-envelope">
  <env:Body>
    <t:getTemperature xmlns:t="http://www.example.com/temperature">
      <t:where>34652</t:where>
      <t:when>2004-05-23</t:when>
    </t:getTemperature>
  </env:Body>
</env:Envelope>
```

Now you just need to know where to send it.

<service>

The final step in creating a WSDL file is to specify the service that you're creating by putting all of these pieces together, as shown in the following code:

```
<service name="TemperatureService">
   <port name="TemperaturePort" binding="typens:TemperatureBinding">
      <soap:address location="http://www.example.com/temp/getTemp.asp"/>
   </port>
</service>
```

When you create a service, you're specifying where and how to send the information. In fact, the `<port>` element shown here will likely be renamed to `endpoint` in WSDL 2.0 because that's what it is: the endpoint for the connection between the server and a client. First, you reference the binding you just created, and then you send it as a SOAP message to the address specified by the `location` attribute. That's it. Now let's try this out in the following activity.

TRY IT OUT Specifying the Order Service via WSDL

In this Try It Out you create a WSDL file that describes the service you created earlier in the chapter:

1. Open a new text file and name it `WileyShopping.wsdl`.
2. Start by creating the overall structure for the file:

```
<?xml version="1.0"?>
<definitions name="WileyShopping"
    targetNamespace="http://www.wiley.com/soap/ordersystem"
    xmlns:typens="http://www.wiley.com/soap/ordersystem"
    xmlns:xsd="http://www.w3.org/2000/10/XMLSchema"
    xmlns:soap="http://schemas.xmlsoap.org/wsdl/soap/"
    xmlns:soapenc="http://schemas.xmlsoap.org/soap/encoding/"
    xmlns:wsdl="http://schemas.xmlsoap.org/wsdl/"
    xmlns="http://schemas.xmlsoap.org/wsdl/">
  <!-- more WSDL will go here -->
</definitions>
```

3. Add `types` for the XML in the messages to be passed as children of the `definitions` element:

```
<types>
  <xsd:schema xmlns=""
     xmlns:xsd="http://www.w3.org/2000/10/XMLSchema"
     targetNamespace="http://www.wiley.com/soap/ordersystem">
    <xsd:complexType name="AddToCartType">
      <xsd:sequence>
        <xsd:element name="CartId" type="xsd:string" />
        <xsd:element name="Item">
          <xsd:complexType>
            <xsd:sequence>
              <xsd:element name="Quantity"
                                type="xsd:string"/>
              <xsd:element name="TotalPrice"
                                type="xsd:string"/>
            </xsd:sequence>
            <xsd:attribute name="ItemId"
                                 type="xsd:string" />
          </xsd:complexType>
        </xsd:element>
      </xsd:sequence>
    </xsd:complexType>
    <xsd:complexType name="AddToCartResponseType">
      <xsd:sequence>
        <xsd:element name="CartId" type="xsd:string"/>
        <xsd:element name="Status" type="xsd:string"/>
        <xsd:element name="Quantity" type="xsd:string"/>
        <xsd:element name="ItemId" type="xsd:string"/>
      </xsd:sequence>
    </xsd:complexType>
  </xsd:schema>
</types>
```

4. Define the messages to be sent to and from the service:

```
<message name="AddToCartRequestMsg">
   <part name="AddToCart" type="typens:AddToCartType"/>
</message>
<message name="AddToCartResponseMsg">
   <part name="AddToCartResponse" type="typens:AddToCartResponseType"/>
</message>
```

5. Now define the `portType`, or interface, that will use the messages:

```
<portType name="WileyPort">
  <operation name="AddToCart">
    <input message="typens:AddToCartRequestMsg"/>
    <output message="typens:AddToCartResponseMsg"/>
  </operation>
</portType>
```

6. Bind the `portType` to a particular protocol, in this case, SOAP:

```
<binding name="WileyBinding"
                         type="typens:WileyPort">
  <soap:binding style="rpc"
     transport="http://schemas.xmlsoap.org/soap/http"/>
  <operation name="AddToCart">
    <soap:operation />
    <input>
      <soap:body use="encoded"
            namespace="http://www.wiley.com/soap/ordersystem"
            encodingStyle="http://schemas.xmlsoap.org/soap/encoding/"/>
    </input>
    <output>
      <soap:body use="encoded"
            namespace="http://www.wiley.com/soap/ordersystem"
            encodingStyle="http://schemas.xmlsoap.org/soap/encoding/"/>
    </output>
  </operation>
</binding>
```

7. Finally, define the actual service by associating the binding with an endpoint. This results in the following final file, Listing 15-4.

LISTING 15-4: WileyShopping.wsdl

```
<?xml version="1.0"?>
<definitions name="WileyShopping"
    targetNamespace="http://www.wiley.com/soap/ordersystem"
    xmlns:typens="http://www.wiley.com/soap/ordersystem"
    xmlns:xsd="http://www.w3.org/2000/10/XMLSchema"
    xmlns:soap="http://schemas.xmlsoap.org/wsdl/soap/"
    xmlns:soapenc="http://schemas.xmlsoap.org/soap/encoding/"
    xmlns:wsdl="http://schemas.xmlsoap.org/wsdl/"
    xmlns="http://schemas.xmlsoap.org/wsdl/">

  <types>
```

```
  <xsd:schema xmlns=""
     xmlns:xsd="http://www.w3.org/2000/10/XMLSchema"
     targetNamespace="http://www.wiley.com/soap/ordersystem">
    <xsd:complexType name="AddToCartType">
      <xsd:sequence>
        <xsd:element name="CartId" type="xsd:string" />
        <xsd:element name="item">
          <xsd:complexType>
            <xsd:sequence>
              <xsd:element name="Quantity"
                                type="xsd:string"/>
              <xsd:element name="TotalPrice"
                                type="xsd:string"/>
            </xsd:sequence>
            <xsd:attribute name="ItemId"
                                 type="xsd:string" />
          </xsd:complexType>
        </xsd:element>
      </xsd:sequence>
    </xsd:complexType>
    <xsd:complexType name="addToCartResponseType">
      <xsd:sequence>
        <xsd:element name="CartId" type="xsd:string"/>
        <xsd:element name="Status" type="xsd:string"/>
        <xsd:element name="Quantity" type="xsd:string"/>
        <xsd:element name="ItemId" type="xsd:string"/>
      </xsd:sequence>
    </xsd:complexType>
  </xsd:schema>
</types>

<message name="AddToCartRequestMsg">
  <part name="AddToCart" type="typens:AddToCartType"/>
</message>
<message name="AddToCartResponseMsg">
  <part name="AddToCartResponse" type="typens:AddToCartResponseType"/>
</message>

<portType name="WileyPort">
  <operation name="AddToCart">
    <input message="typens:AddToCartRequestMsg"/>
    <output message="typens:AddToCartResponseMsg"/>
  </operation>
</portType>
<binding name="WileyBinding"
                     type="typens:WileyPort">
  <soap:binding style="rpc"
        transport="http://schemas.xmlsoap.org/soap/http"/>
  <operation name="AddToCart">
    <soap:operation/>
    <input>
      <soap:body use="encoded"
namespace="http://www.wiley.com/soap/ordersystem"
encodingStyle="http://schemas.xmlsoap.org/soap/encoding/"/>
```

```
      </input>
      <output>
        <soap:body use="encoded"
  namespace="http://www.wiley.com/soap/ordersystem"
  encodingStyle="http://schemas.xmlsoap.org/soap/encoding/"/>
      </output>
    </operation>
  </binding>
  <service name="WileyService">
    <port name="WileyPort" binding="typens:WileyBinding">
      <soap:address
  location="http://localhost/BasicOrderService/AddToCart.aspx"/>
    </port>
  </service>
</definitions>
```

How It Works

Here you created a simple WSDL file describing the SOAP messages sent to and from the hypothetical Wiley Shopping Service. First, you created the data types for the messages to be sent. Next, you combined them into messages, created operations out of the messages, and finally, bound them to a protocol and a service.

Other Bindings

It's important to understand that WSDL doesn't necessarily describe a SOAP service. Earlier in this chapter, you looked at a situation in which messages were passed by HTTP without the benefit of a SOAP wrapper. These `REST` messages can also be defined via WSDL by adding the `HTTP` binding.

The basic process is the same as it was for SOAP:

1. Define the data types
2. Group them into messages
3. Create operations from the messages and `portTypes` from the operations
4. Create a binding that ties them all in to a particular protocol, as shown in Listing 15-5, `WileyShopping-Rest.wsdl`.

Available for download on Wrox.com

LISTING 15-5: WileyShopping-Rest.wsdl

```
<?xml version="1.0"?>
<definitions name="WileyShopping"
    targetNamespace="http://www.wiley.com/soap/ordersystem"
    xmlns:typens="http://www.wiley.com/soap/ordersystem"
    xmlns:xsd="http://www.w3.org/2000/10/XMLSchema"
    xmlns:soap="http://schemas.xmlsoap.org/wsdl/soap/"
    xmlns:soapenc="http://schemas.xmlsoap.org/soap/encoding/"
```

```
  xmlns:wsdl="http://schemas.xmlsoap.org/wsdl/"

  xmlns:http="http://schemas.xmlsoap.org/wsdl/http/"
  xmlns:mime="http://schemas.xmlsoap.org/wsdl/mime/"
  xmlns="http://schemas.xmlsoap.org/wsdl/">

<types>
  <xsd:schema xmlns=""
     xmlns:xsd="http://www.w3.org/2000/10/XMLSchema"
     targetNamespace="http://www.wiley.com/soap/ordersystem">
    <xsd:complexType name="AddToCartType">
      <xsd:sequence>
        <xsd:element name="CartId" type="xsd:string" />
        <xsd:element name="ItemId" type="xsd:string"/>
        <xsd:element name="Quantity" type="xsd:string"/>
        <xsd:element name="TotalPrice" type="xsd:string"/>
      </xsd:sequence>
    </xsd:complexType>
    <xsd:complexType name="AddToCartResponseType">
      <xsd:sequence>
        <xsd:element name="CartId" type="xsd:string"/>
        <xsd:element name="Status" type="xsd:string"/>
        <xsd:element name="Quantity" type="xsd:string"/>
        <xsd:element name="ItemId" type="xsd:string"/>
      </xsd:sequence>
    </xsd:complexType>

    <xsd:complexType name="GetTotalResponseType">
      <xsd:sequence>
        <xsd:element name="Discount" type="xsd:string" />
        <xsd:element name="TotalPrice"
type="xsd:string"/>
      </xsd:sequence>
    </xsd:complexType>
  </xsd:schema>
</types>
<message name="AddToCartRequestMsg">
  <part name="AddToCart" type="typens:AddToCartType"/>
</message>
<message name="AddToCartResponseMsg">
  <part name="AddToCartResponse" type="typens:AddToCartResponseType"/>
</message>


<message name="UpdateTotalsRequestMsg">
  <part name="Quantity" type="xsd:number"/>
  <part name="UnitPrice" type="xsd:number"/>
</message>
<message name="GetTotalResponseMsg">
  <part name="GetTotalResponse" type="typens:
       GetTotalResponseType"/>
</message>
<portType name="WileyPort">
  <operation name="AddToCart">
    <input message="typens:AddToCartRequestMsg"/>
    <output message="typens:AddToCartResponseMsg"/>
  </operation>
```

```
    </portType>
    <portType name="WileyRESTPort">

      <operation name="GetTotal2.aspx">
        <input message="typens:UpdateTotalsRequestMsg"/>
        <output message="typens:UpdateTotalsResponseMsg"/>
      </operation>
    </portType>

    <binding name="WileyBinding"
                              type="typens:WileyPort">
      <soap:binding style="rpc"
            transport="http://schemas.xmlsoap.org/soap/http"/>
      <operation name="AddToCart">
        <soap:operation/>
        <input>
          <soap:body use="encoded"
    namespace="http://www.wiley.com/soap/ordersystem"
    encodingStyle="http://schemas.xmlsoap.org/soap/encoding/"/>
        </input>
        <output>
          <soap:body use="encoded"
    namespace="http://www.wiley.com/soap/ordersystem"
    encodingStyle="http://schemas.xmlsoap.org/soap/encoding/"/>
        </output>
      </operation>
    </binding>
    <binding name="WileyRESTBinding"
                              type="typens:WileyRESTPort">
      <http:binding verb="GET"/>
      <operation name="GetTotal2.aspx">
        <http:operation location="GetTotal.aspx"/>
        <input>
          <http:urlEncoded/>
        </input>
        <output>
          <mime:content type="text/xml"/>
        </output>
      </operation>
    </binding>
    <service name="WileyService">
      <port name="WileyPort" binding="typens:WileyBinding">
        <soap:address
    location="http://localhost/BasicOrderService/GetTotal.aspx"/>
      </port>

      <port name="WileyRESTPort" binding="typens:WileyRESTBinding">
        <http:address location="http://localhost/BasicOrderService/"/>
      </port>

    </service>
  </definitions>
```

In this way, you can define a service that uses any protocol using WSDL.

NOTE *In real life, WSDL is created by the SOAP tool you use. Occasionally, a tweak or two might be needed — for example, the port or binding sections may need to be amended when you switch from development to live. In ASP.NET, for instance, if you build a service using* `asmx` *pages, the WSDL is created automatically.*

SUMMARY

This chapter covered the following areas:

- The advantages of SOAP include interoperability for web services; there is no tie-in between the client platform and the server one.
- SOAP is backed by many top name companies including Microsoft, Sun, IBM, and Google so the familiar proprietary wrangles are less prevalent.
- SOAP is flexible: You can choose to follow the XML-RPC style of message or just use the `<soap:Body>` to contain a system specific message that is processed on the server. You can also add any number of extra items to the `<soap:Header>` to implement security, message chaining, and any other instructions you may need.
- SOAP is not the only choice when it comes to web services. REST is a very popular standard that makes use of the underlying HTTP protocol to implement remote procedure calls. Although it lacks some of the lesser-used features of SOAP, REST is a good choice for simple services especially when they need to be made public and security is not a major consideration.
- WSDL is an XML format used to describe web services.
- With just a WSDL file you can create a web services client that produces messages in the correct format, can understand the responses and knows where the service is based.

In the next chapter you look at AJAX and how it uses XML.

EXERCISES

You can find suggested solutions to these questions in Appendix A.

1. Create a SOAP message that fulfills the following requirements:
    - It corresponds to an RPC called `GetStockPrice()`.
    - It takes one parameter, a `string` holding the recognized stock exchange code of the company whose stock price you require. For example Microsoft's code is MSFT.
    - The server responds with a `decimal` that is the latest stock price for the requested company.
2. Create a WSDL file that describes the document in Question 1.

▶ WHAT YOU LEARNED IN THIS CHAPTER

TOPIC	KEY POINTS
SOAP basics	A way to implement web services that is flexible yet standards based and platform independent.
Message format	Messages can be simple RPC style or just an abstraction of the data you need to send and receive.
SOAP header	The header contains any meta data and instructions that the service needs. These can include such things as credentials and routing information.
Other web service options	REST is another popular choice of web service implementation. It lacks the more sophisticated features of SOAP but is simpler to implement and client design is easier.
WSDL	WSDL is the web service description language. It is an XML format that provides a complete description of a service's location, message structure and available methods.
WSDL uses	All major software frameworks, such as Java and .NET, enable you to automatically construct a web services client by passing the WSDL to an appropriate application.

WHAT YOU LEARNED IN THIS CHAPTER

16

AJAX

WHAT YOU WILL LEARN IN THIS CHAPTER:

- What AJAX is used for
- How to use AJAX
- When to use JSON, HTML, or XML with AJAX
- How to generate JSON on the web server
- Web architecture, REST, and best practices

AJAX stands for Asynchronous JavaScript And XML, but the term refers to a way of writing web-based applications that are responsive and give a fast, positive user experience by leveraging the fact that the web server can be working at the same time as the client computer running the web browser. The trick that AJAX enables is to update parts of the current web page without having to reload the entire page. The extra interactivity this allows, combined with big shiny buttons and a particularly fashionable sort of color scheme, is known as Web 2.0. The biggest challenge, as you'll learn, is to create web applications that are accessible to people regardless of their needs and abilities, and that fit in with the web architecture of links and bookmarks. In this chapter you'll learn how AJAX works (including the JavaScript part) and you'll make a working AJAX-based web page so you can see how AJAX and XML fit together.

AJAX OVERVIEW

The AJAX pattern has several uses. This section first describes the situations in which you use AJAX, and then goes into detail about what it really is and how it works. The short description is that AJAX is a way for a web page to use the JavaScript language to fetch data quietly in the background without any need for the web page to reload in the browser.

The "X" in AJAX stands for XML, although as you learn in this chapter, AJAX is more commonly used with other data formats.

AJAX Provides Feedback

Consider a search page on a website, such as that shown in Figure 16-1. You enter a person's name, click Submit, and a second or two later you get a message saying that the person wasn't found, or, in a more favorable circumstance, you get a page giving information about the person.

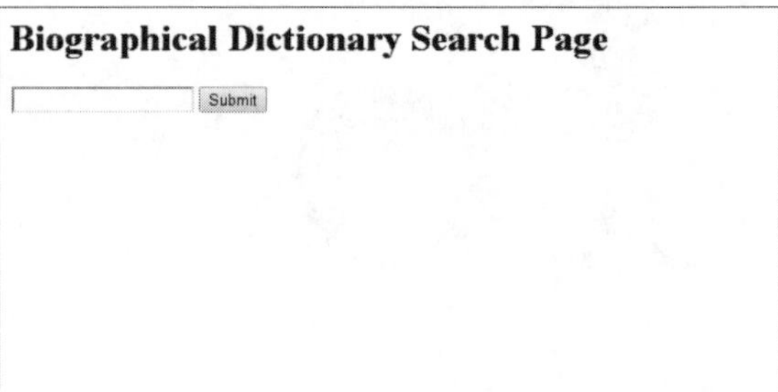

FIGURE 16-1

A Web 2.0 version of the same screen might look more like Figure 16-2. It's got more style, but that's not really the interesting part for this chapter. Instead, notice that now when you start typing a name, you get instant feedback of possible search terms. And when you click Submit, the resulting list of matches appears right under the Search box, without any flicker.

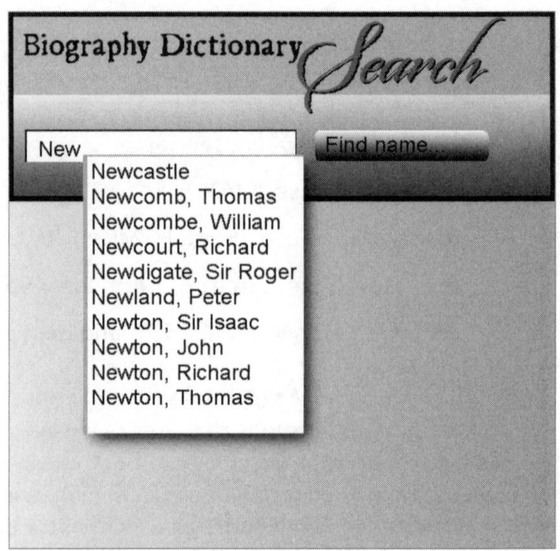

FIGURE 16-2

Loading Incomplete Data With AJAX

The complete XML file for the biographical dictionary from Chapter 9, "XQuery" is more than 50 megabytes in size. It's too large to load into a web browser and still have good network performance. If you want to be able to search the text of the dictionary, the traditional approach is the one shown in Figure 16-1: you have a search engine on the server and you click Search and wait for the results.

With AJAX, you can start typing your search, and even before you click Search, you can start to see results. This is possible only because the JavaScript code has updated the contents of the web page with the search box without disrupting the search box.

One difference between this pattern and the feedback pattern is that the search can indeed fall back to a remote server and still work, but feedback is not possible after you click a Submit button: the enter web page goes away and is replaced with the results. Another difference is data set size. The list of possible search terms in the feedback example could have been loaded along with the page (although it's large enough in this example that it also falls into the incomplete data pattern). Very often such completion lists are indeed loaded as part of the web page. But you couldn't load the entire 32-volume dictionary for a full text search.

AJAX Performs Asynchronous Operations

A web page might display a news feed, or recently added photographs on a popular site, and might update the display in real time without disrupting the reader by refreshing the page. The JavaScript updating the page again runs in the background using AJAX as opposed to relying on the user to refresh the page, or using the older style HTTP refresh which reloads the entire page every few seconds, annoyingly losing the user's scroll position along with any data entered into text boxes.

The obvious thing the AJAX use cases all have in common is that the Web page is fetching stuff quietly in the background, without stopping to wait for it. That's the meaning of the "A" in AJAX: *asynchronous*. As opposed to *synchronous*, asynchronous in computing means something that happens without the main programming stopping to wait for it. The "J" means JavaScript, the programming language for web applications. The next section introduces a little JavaScript, and then looks at a real code example.

INTRODUCTION TO JAVASCRIPT

In this section, you learn only enough JavaScript to make it through the examples and decide if you want to learn more. This is, after all, an XML book and not a JavaScript book. A good *thin* book on JavaScript is Douglas Crockford's *JavaScript: The Good Parts*.

NOTE *If you are already familiar with JavaScript (or ECMAScript, its official name), you can safely skip this section and go to the section "The XMLHttpRequest Function."*

NOTE *If you're not at all familiar with HTML and CSS, you may want to skip ahead to Chapter 17 and then come back to this chapter. This chapter and the next one depend on each other rather heavily because JavaScript is most often used from inside HTML web pages.*

JavaScript is a programming language used primarily in conjunction with web browsers. There is also at least one web server (`node.js`) that uses JavaScript as its main extension language, and the open source GNOME desktop uses JavaScript extensively; but for the purpose of this chapter you just need to know enough JavaScript to make sense of the AJAX examples, and perhaps to write some code yourself.

JavaScript should not be confused with Java: both languages were heavily influenced by the C programming language, but only in syntax.

The Web Browser Console

Before you try to learn any JavaScript, you should find a web browser with a console that lets you type simple expressions and shows their values. In Firefox, you can press Ctrl+Shift+K at the same time to bring up a console (see Figure 16-3), or you can use the Tools ➪ Web Developer ➪ Web Console menu item. In the Chrome (see Figure 16-4) browser, Midori, Epiphany, Safari, and other Webkit browsers, there's a picture of a spanner or wrench to the right of the location bar, and if you click that, you can choose JavaScript Console from the Tools submenu. Alternatively, you can right-click in the document window and choose Inspect Element.

There is also a JavaScript console in Internet Explorer, but the exact method to get to it may depend greatly on the version of Internet Explorer you are using; in IE 7 you have to go to Internet Options and uncheck the Browsing option Disable Script Debugging; after that, if your web page contains an error, Internet Explorer may ask you if you want to run the Microsoft Script Debugger. You could add a line like this to get an error:

```
var j = 1/0;
```

Inside the Microsoft Script Debugger, if you click Break, you can choose Window from the Debug menu, and enable the Immediate Window, which is Microsoft's name for the JavaScript Console.

All of these instructions to get to the JavaScript console change fairly often as the web browsers are updated, but the principle is always that, in the end, you get a window that lets you type JavaScript expressions and see the results, and, more importantly, displays error messages, syntax errors, and warnings. Without this, you are programming blind, and a faintly unpleasant but ultimately highly rewarding experience becomes a nightmare.

Figure 16-3 shows a JavaScript console in the Mozilla Firefox web browser, where it is connected to a web page, and Figure 16-4 shows the Google Chrome version, where it is a separate window. Both consoles have some example expressions: `3 + 3`, which turned out to equal 6 in both browsers, and `document`, which gave a slightly different representation of the HTML document in the corresponding document window in each browser.

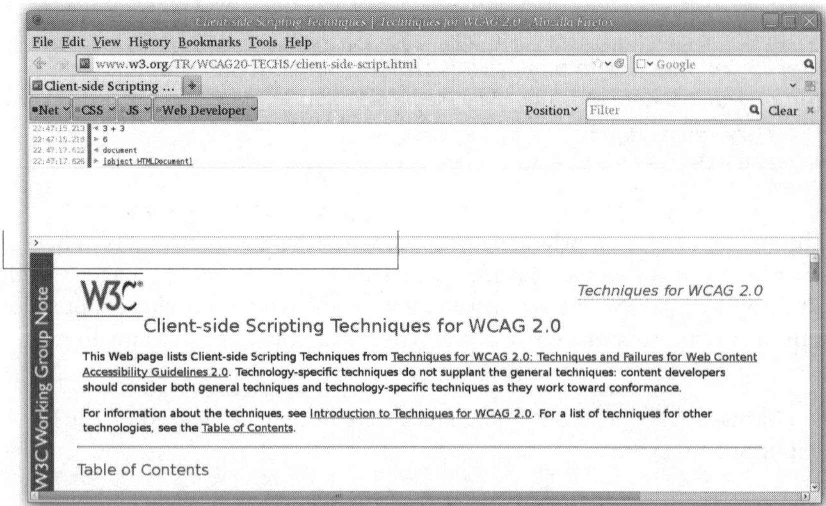

FIGURE 16-3

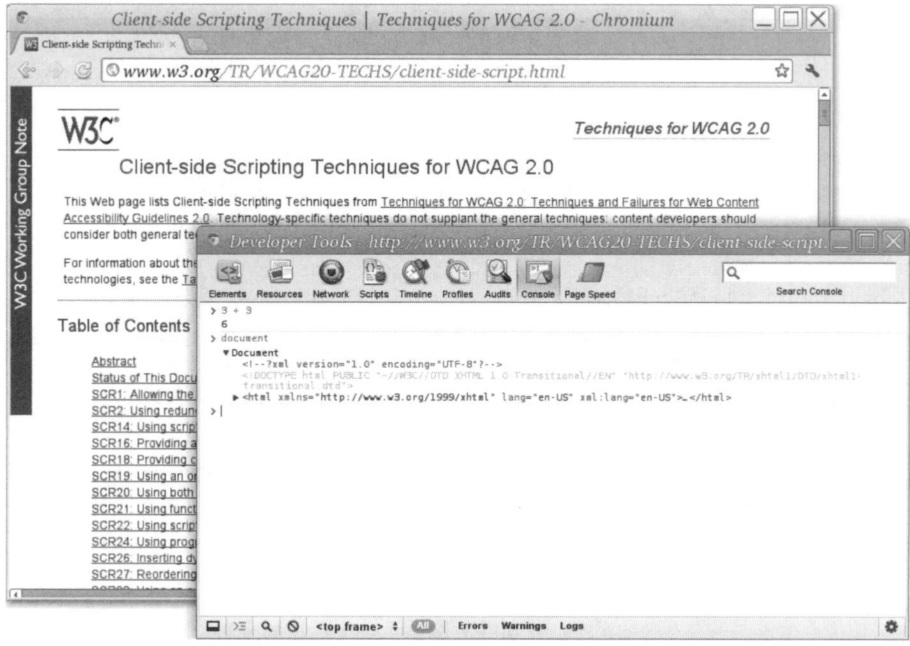

FIGURE 16-4

Values, Expressions, and Variables

It's time to dive in to JavaScript, if not at the deep end, at least in the paddling pool, so take off your shoes and socks and get started. In JavaScript, the result of evaluating an expression is a value, and (as in many other languages) you can store values in variables. Since almost everything in JavaScript boils down to values and expressions, that's where you'll start.

Simple Values

The simplest values are numbers, like 3, 0.5, and scientific, or exponential notation, 2.3e4, meaning 2.3×10^4, or 23000.

Next come strings, like `"Henry's argyle socks"` or `'don\'t look back'`. You can use the usual C-like escapes in strings: `\n` for newline, `\t` for tab, `\"` and `\'` for quotes, `\\` for `\` itself, and, as an addition, `\uDDDD`, where `DDDD` is exactly four hexadecimal digits, and represents the corresponding 16-bit Unicode codepoint. JavaScript can't handle Unicode characters above 65535 easily; it uses a mechanism called *surrogate pairs* for others.

JavaScript also has booleans, which can be true or false; these are even simpler than numbers, but the rules to decide equality are confusing. Take the following example:

```
"1" == true
```

This is true, because true is first converted to a number, and the string is converted to a number. However, the object identity test, ===, does not perform conversions. Therefore, the following example is false:

```
"1" === true
```

Always use `===` to test whether two values are the same, and `!==` to test if two values are not the same.

Expressions

An expression is a combination of values and operators; anywhere you can put a value, you can put an expression that computes a value. You can use simple arithmetical expressions, like `2 + 2`, and of course more complex ones with various operators. The most important operators are listed in Table 16-1.

TABLE 16-1: The Most Important JavaScript Operators

OPERATOR	MEANING	EXAMPLE
`.`	property access	`document.all`
`[]`	array subscript	`lines[3]`
`( )`	grouping	`3 * (2 + 6)`
`++, --`	increment, decrement	`++i`
`!`	logical not	`!false` is true
`*, /, %`	multiply, divide, modulo (remainder)	
`+, -`	normal addition and subtraction; + also joins strings	`var str = "hello" + " " + "world"`
<, ≤	less than, less than or equal to	
>, ≥	greater than, greater than or equal to	
`===`	equality, identity (three = signs in a row)	`if (a === b) {...}`
`!==`	not identical to (! and two = signs)	`if (a !== b) {...}`
`&&`	logical and	`if (a && (b > 6)) { … }`
`||`	logical or	`if (a == 0 || a > 42) { … }`

Now that you have seen values and operators, you can put them together in expressions like the following:

```
3 + 3
5 * 7
7 * (3 + 5)
```

Figure 16-5 shows the result of evaluating these expressions in the JavaScript console. You can put multiple expressions on a line if you separate them with a semicolon.

Variables

A variable is a named value; you can modify variables in JavaScript, unlike in XQuery or XSLT. Declare variables before you use them: the value can be any expression. Here are some examples of variables:

```
var pi = 3; // some people say it should be 4
var c = pi * r; // problem, r undeclared
var j = ++pi; // now pi is indeed 4, and j is also 4
```

```
> 3 + 3
6
> 5 * 7
35
> 7 * (3 + 5)
56
> !true
false
> !false
true
> !6
false
> !!6
true
> 7 / 2
3.5
>
```

FIGURE 16-5

Control Flow Statements

Normally the computer executes the statements in your program from beginning to end, one at a time, in order. You can use *control flow* statements to change this — to make the computer execute some statements repeatedly in a loop, or to make it skip some statements, or to make it choose to execute one group or statements or another.

JavaScript has quite a few control flow statements. For the examples in this chapter, and for using jQuery, it's enough to know `if`, `while`, and `for`. The following example shows a JavaScript *if* expression that will make the computer interpret either one set of statements (called a *block*) or another set depending on the value of an expression:

```
if (expression) {
    block used when the expression is true;
} else {
    block used when the expression is false;
}
```

The `while` loop tests its condition and, if it is true, executes the block just like an `if`, but then, after running through once, starts over, testing the condition again. The code in the block had better affect the condition, like so:

```
var sunshine = 6;
while (sunshine--) {
    make_hay();
    make_hay();
    rest();
}
```

The `for` statement is actually just the same as a `while` loop with a couple of extra parts. For example:

```
for (firstpart; test; secondpart) {
    block;
}
```

is the same as:

```
firstpart;
while (test) {
```

```
        block;
        secondpart;
    }
```

You often see `for` used to loop over an array or a fixed number of values like so:

```
    for (var i = 0; i < array.length; i++) {
        process(array[i];
    }
```

A variant of `for` iterates over all items in an array, or all properties of an object as shown here:

```
    for (person in peopleList) {
        process(person)
    }
```

A number of other control structures exist, including `try`/`catch`/`throw` and `switch`. Additionally, the `break` statement jumps out of the nearest enclosing loop, and there is a `return` statement that is discussed in the "Functions" section in a moment.

Properties, Objects, Functions and Classes

JavaScript is a very dynamic language, and has a much stronger relationship between objects, object properties, functions, and classes than most other languages. The following sections explain this in a little more detail.

Objects and Properties

An object in JavaScript is a set of name/value pairs called *properties*:

```
    var socks = {
      "size" : 44,
      "pattern" : "argyle",
      "are clean" : true,
    };
```

You get at the properties with the dot operator. In this example, `socks.pattern` has the value `argyle`. You can't use the dot operator to find out if your sock is clean, though, because of the space in the name, so you have to use `socks["are clean"]` instead. The two notations are equivalent when the property names are simple words.

The values can actually be objects, or arrays, as well as simple expressions.

Functions

Another kind of object is a *function*. Functions are declared like this:

```
    var triangle = function(width, height) {
        return width * height / 2;
    }
```

This example makes a new function that is shorthand for calculating an expression, similar to the named templates and functions you saw in Chapter 8, "XSLT," and Chapter 9, "XQuery." This particular function works out the area of a right-angled triangle given the lengths of the two shorter sides.

Now you can use your new function to find the area of a particular triangle:

```
var area = triangle(12, 7);
```

When an object has a function as the value of one of its properties, the property is said to be a *method*:

```
socks.wash = function() {
    this["are clean"] = 1;
}
```

The variable called `this` is the object, `socks` in this case. And now you can wash your socks:

```
socks.wash();
```

Calling the `wash()` method on an object — here, `socks.wash()` — will set its "`are clean`" member to true.

Classes

A *class* is a way to represent common properties and methods of a whole family of objects. For example, all `String` objects share a `length()` method. Defining your own classes is much more JavaScript that you need to know for this book, but you should know that, behind the scenes, there is a class mechanism in JavaScript, because documentation for libraries such as jQuery may mention it.

THE XMLHTTPREQUEST FUNCTION

The central part of AJAX is a single JavaScript function called `XMLHttpRequest`. It was originally introduced by Microsoft in Internet Explorer, was copied by other web browsers, and was later adopted by W3C.

The idea of `XMLHttpRequest` is that, when you build your web page, you arrange for this function to be called with a URL and a JavaScript function. The web browser will automatically call that JavaScript function when the resource at the requested URL has been downloaded by the Browser.

The call might look like this:

```
var client = new XMLHttpRequest();
client.onreadystatechange = handler;
client.open("GET", theURL);
client.send();
```

In this example, you create a new JavaScript object of class `XHTMLHttpRequest` and save a reference to it in the variable `client` so you can use it later. Then you set its `onreadystatechange` property to the name of a function you will define, `handler` in this example. You then tell the object that you are going to use the HTTP `GET` method to fetch the resource located at `theURL`. Finally, after setting everything up, `client.send()` sends the actual HTTP request off into space.

At some time later, the HTTP `GET` request will connect, and, if all goes well, will result in a document being loaded into memory. Once that has happened, your `handler` function will automatically be called. The function will also be called if there was an error when trying to fetch the document.

The handler looks like this:

```
function handler() {
  if (this.readyState == this.DONE) {
    if (this.status == 200 && this.responseXML != null) {
      for (var i = 0; i < this.responseXML.childNodes.length; i++) {
        document.getElementById("replaceme").appendChild(
          this.responseXML.childNodes[i]
        );
      }
    } else {
      alert("something went wrong");
    }
  }
}
```

NOTE *In a real application you'd call another function rather than having the* `for` *loop and the document manipulation right there in the handler. It's also not really a good idea to use an* `alert()` *to pop up a dialog box on errors: users hate them, and even for development they can be a nuisance, especially if one ends up inside a loop! But it's done this way in the example so that you will get an error if you make a mistake copying the program.*

The first thing your handler function does is to see if the HTTP transaction is finished. The `DONE` constant is defined by the browser just to make the code more readable; older web browsers need a number there, and `DONE` was always equal to four, so in older code you will see a test to see if `readyState === 4`. The handler will be called whenever the `readyState` property changes; it can be any of the values shown in Table 16-2.

TABLE 16-2: readyState Values, Constants, and Meanings

VALUES	CONSTANTS	MEANINGS
0	`UNSENT`	The object has been constructed (this one is not normally very useful).
1	`OPENED`	This happens after you've called `open()` on the object and before you have called `send()`, so that you can set HTTP headers.
2	`HEADERS_RECEIVED`	The HTTP response has started to arrive: all redirects have been followed, the browser is connected to the HTTP server at the final address, and the server has sent the HTTP headers to you.
3	`LOADING`	The data is coming in!
4	`DONE`	The data has all arrived, or there was a problem. You can check the object's error flag to see if there was an error.

Now that you have seen just enough JavaScript and have read about `XMLHttpRequest`, you should try it out for yourself and see how easy it is. In the upcoming activity you'll make an HTML page to contain the AJAX example, and you should start to see how all the parts fit together.

TRY IT OUT Simple AJAX Example

In this exercise you'll make a simple web page and experience AJAX in action. However, because of browser security restrictions, you will need to upload the files to a web server, or be running a web server such as Apache or Abyss on your computer. The example will not work in most web browsers if you just try directly opening a local file.

1. First, create the HTML file; call it `ajax.html`.

```
<!DOCTYPE html
  PUBLIC "-//W3C//DTD XHTML 1.1//EN"
         "http://www.w3.org/TR/xhtml11/DTD/xhtml11.dtd">
<html xmlns="http://www.w3.org/1999/xhtml" xml:lang="en">
  <head>
    <title>ajax example</title>
    <meta http-equiv="Content-Type" content="text/html; charset=utf-8" />
    <script type="text/javascript"><!--
      function handler() {
        if (this.readyState == this.DONE) {
          if (this.status == 200 && this.responseXML != null) {
```

```
            for (var i = 0; i < this.responseXML.childNodes.length; i++) {
              document.getElementById("replaceme").appendChild(
                  this.responseXML.childNodes[i]
                  );
            }
          } else {
            alert("something went wrong");
          }
        }
      }

      function getXML() {
        var client = new XMLHttpRequest();
        client.onreadystatechange = handler;
        client.open("GET", "hello.xml");
        client.send();
        alert("getXML done.");
      }
      //-->
    </script>
  </head>
  <body>
    <form onsubmit="return false;" action="">
      <p><input type="button" onclick="getXML();" value="Get XML"/></p>
    </form>
    <div id="replaceme"></div>
  </body>
</html>
```

2. Next, create the XML file. Call it `hello.xml` and place it in the same directory as the HTML file you just made:

```
<ajax>
  <p id="p">hello world</p>
</ajax>
```

3. Upload the two files to a web server; if you don't have a web server, you might want to consider installing one on your computer such as Aprelium's Abyss Web Server (`www.aprelium.com`), Apache (`www.apache.org`) or Microsoft Personal Web Server, so that you can test HTML and JavaScript.

4. Open `ajax.html` in your web browser and click the Get XML button. You should see a pop-up box when the call to `send()` has returned; then, when the data has been fetched, you will see "hello world" in the browser. If you are using a personal web server such as Abyss, which runs on port 8000 by default (with an administration interface on port 9999), you'll need to copy the files into the Abyss `htdocs` folder and then use a URL like `http://127.0.0.1:8000/ajax.html` to get to them.

5. If you are running the Google Chrome browser, Safari, or any other "Webkit" browser, right-click the words "hello world" and choose Inspect Element to see the developer window. In Firefox, you can use an extension, "add-on" called Web Developer to see a DOM tree window; another Firefox add-on called Firebug has a similar feature.

Whichever browser you use, if there are problems you should open the JavaScript Error Console window; in Chrome or Safari, click the Console icon at the top of the element inspector window. In Firefox, press Control+Shift+K to bring up a console, or in some versions, to bring up a menu item. Reloading the page with the console open will usually show any error messages.

Figure 16-6 shows the Google Chromium browser's element inspector on the working page, after clicking on the button to invoke the AJAX JavaScript code.

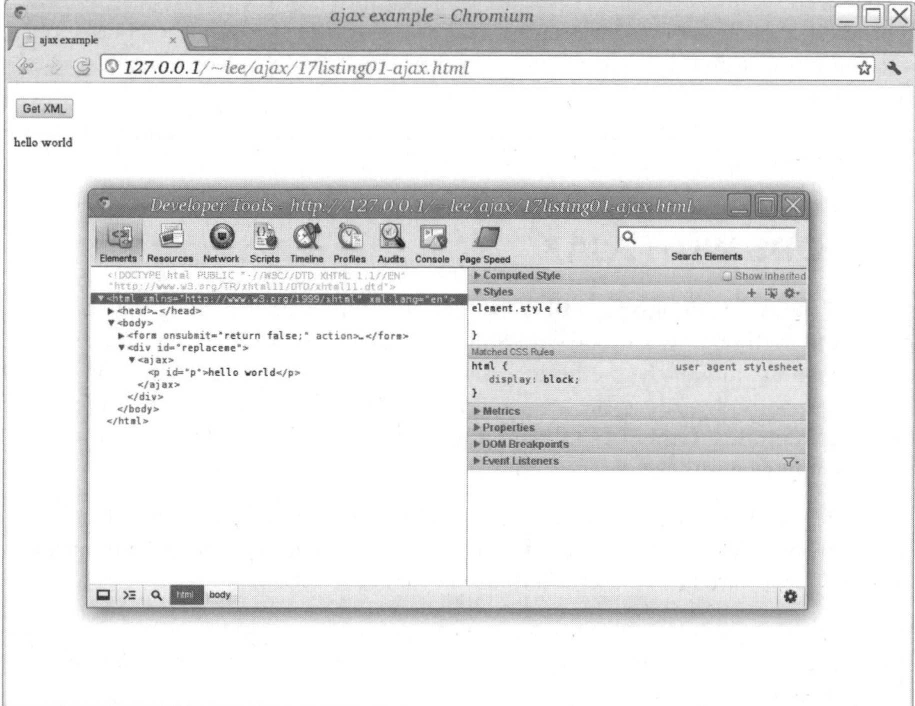

FIGURE 16-6

How It Works

When the web page loads into the browser, the JavaScript defines some functions. The HTML arranges that when you click the Get XML button, the `getXML()` function is called, by setting the `onclick` attribute on the `input` element (line 35, near the end of the file).

When you click the button, the browser calls `GetXML()`, and this in turn creates an `XMLHttpRequest` object, sets it to call `handler()` whenever the object's `readystate` property changes, sets its destination to `hello.xml`, and launches the request into space. `GetXML()` does not wait for the rocket to come back to earth; it draws a dialog box (`alert`) and then returns. While the dialog box is showing, though, the browser is busy loading `hello.xml`. During this process the handler function is called several times; eventually, it gets called with `readystate` set to 4, meaning done, or finished.

When the `handler()` function gets called, it is called as a method of the `XMLHttpRequest` object, so its `this` member is available as the object itself. The handler checks that the `readystate` is done, otherwise it just returns silently. If the HTTP status was 200 (OK) and there is an XML document available, its children get inserted using JavaScript DOM methods as new children underneath the `<div id="replaceme">` element in the HTML document.

If you click the button on the web page again, the document will again be loaded and the children appended, so that you will see "hello world hello world."

If it didn't work, check your web server's error logs carefully to make sure that the `hello.xml` file was loaded. Check the web browser console for error messages. Make sure you are loading the HTML document from a web server and not just double-clicking on it or opening it locally: the browser's location bar should show a web address.

USING HTTP METHODS WITH AJAX

The *asynchronous* part of the AJAX design pattern is the idea that the JavaScript code in your web page uses HTTP to ask your web server for some data and, sometime later, receives a response. AJAX-based applications can use any of the methods defined by the HTTP specification. You may have noticed the HTTP `GET` method used for the previous Try It Out exercise. It's also possible to use HTTP `POST` or `HEAD` methods. Other HTTP methods exist, but they are not so widely supported. How do you know when to use which method?

For the Try it Out example, no changes on the server were made. The client (the web browser) is affected, but not the server. No files are written, no database fields are updated, and no purchases are made. Therefore, the appropriate HTTP method to use in that case is `GET`.

For the other methods, the short answer is this: use `POST` when you are changing state on the remote server, use `GET` when you are fetching something without changing anything. Use other methods only if you know exactly what you are doing.

One of the results of loading a web page with `POST` is that when you refresh, the web browser may warn you that, for example, if you just bought a yacht, refreshing the page might buy a second yacht. When you use HTTP `POST` with `XMLHttpRequest` there's no way for the browser to warn the user, so you need to be careful when you write AJAX-based applications.

When you write the back-end part of an AJAX implementation, then, make sure your program does not require the use of `POST` if there is no state change. For example, logging in to a site is a state change, because you get back something different from pages before and after you log in, and the set of actions available to the user will probably change.

On the other hand, fetching a railway timetable would not change the railway company's server, and you'd expect to use HTTP `GET` for that; similarly, the first steps in reserving a train ticket can probably be repeated without problems and would use HTTP `GET`, even if moments later you used HTTP `POST` to buy a ticket.

Note also that users can only bookmark `GET` pages, not `POST` ones. It wouldn't make sense to bookmark the page to pay for a train ticket on a particular date, because you can generally do it only once. A well-designed application would include a transaction number to make sure that, if you did somehow reload the page, you didn't buy an extra set of tickets by mistake.

This begs the question, for an AJAX application, how do you represent state when parts of the page have been loaded separately? In older-style Web 1.0 applications, the URL changes whenever the user does anything, so it's easy to bookmark a state or to know where you are. With AJAX, any part of the page can change at any time!

One convention that is gaining traction is to change the displayed URL of the current web page when state changes. However, you can't actually change the URL itself from JavaScript, for obvious security reasons, but only the *fragment identifier*, the part starting with a `#`, for example, in `http://www.example.org/telephones.html#rotary`. It's important not to overdo this: when it makes sense, don't be afraid to move the user to a new web page.

For example, one of the authors of this book (Liam Quin) uses this `#` technique on his own website. The URL `http://www.fromoldbooks.org/Tymms-Illuminating/pages/43-letterR/`is a picture of a pretty medieval letter "R" in red; controls on the page let the user change the colors in the picture, and this is encoded in the URL like this: `http://www.fromoldbooks.org/Tymms-Illuminating/pages/43-letterR/#fg=%235f00bf_bg=%23ffff56`.

Here the `fg` and `bg` codes after the # encode the colors — this example is a purple "R" on a yellow background. This way people can share the link, bookmark it, and even experiment with editing the hexadecimal color codes. It's not perfect, however. If you change the color codes in the location bar of the web browser, the colors are not updated. Note also that the fragment identifier (the part after the first #) is not sent by the web browser to the web server, so the interaction must all be written using JavaScript.

The JavaScript to manage this has three parts:

1. When the page is loaded, check for a fragment identifier, and, if present, set the page state appropriately (in this case, color the image).
2. When the user chooses new colors, update the fragment identifier.
3. The code to color the image should be kept separate, of course, from the code that displays the state.

The code on that page actually avoids using `XMLHttpRequest`; instead, the JavaScript changes the URL in the HTML `<img>` element that shows the image. `XMLHttpRequest` is, however, used elsewhere on the same page for the list of similar images. In that case, HTTP `GET` is used with `XMLHTTPRequest` to fetch a list of images.

A rule of thumb is that if you are writing data back to the server, or changing state, you will use HTTP `PUT`, and if fetching the same page over HTTP multiple times will give the same result, use HTTP `GET`.

ACCESSIBILITY CONSIDERATIONS

It is easy to use JavaScript to make web pages that sing, dance, and move about. But you can also easily make web pages that are inaccessible by large numbers of people, or that are needlessly unpleasant or difficult to use.

It's sometimes tempting to ignore the needs of other people and to say your web page doesn't have to be accessible. However, there's generally no upper limit to civil liability for accessibility issues, and in increasing numbers of areas there's legislation requiring that pages be accessible. Even where there is no specific legislation about accessibility, there may be laws against discriminating against minorities.

If these reasons are not compelling enough (and they should be), remember that "Google is Blind" — the search engines tend to rank accessible pages more highly, leading to large increases in traffic — and also that a web page that is pleasant to use leaves a much more positive impression than one that is difficult.

Following is a list of pointers that address common accessibility issues:

- When you are manipulating the contents of the page, use `createElement()` with `appendChild()`, `removeChild()`, `insertBefore()`, and `replaceChild()`, and avoid `innerHTML`, `innerText`, and `document.write()`.
- Avoid using small text sizes, particularly in user interface controls.
- Remember that a significant proportion of the population may see colors differently than you do (color blindness).
- Inserting or removing controls dynamically can affect the tab order of the page; do not use the `tabindex` property on new controls, and remember that some people are using keyboards to interact with your page, not mice or fingers.
- Do not make things blink or flash.
- Do not put a time limit on completing an interaction. It's very frustrating if you are using a keyboard in which you have to wait for the right letter to be highlighted and then press a pedal, for example, if you are only given five or ten minutes to complete a transaction! Because users can wander off from the computer at any time, there is no amount of time that will provide complete security against a person leaving and another person wandering in and making financial transactions. Instead of "your session timed out," ask the user to re-enter a password *and then continue the session without loss of data.*
- Some users will have JavaScript disabled. You may want to provide an alternative web page in that case, but at the very least test for it. For example, if you rely on JavaScript to show information that starts out hidden, some users will never see it.
- Try to keep it obvious when something is happening, and what you expect from the user. A common convention is to use text with a yellow background saying "loading" when your JavaScript code sends off an AJAX request to fetch something that will be displayed to the user.

You learn more about accessibility in Chapter 17.

THE JQUERY LIBRARY

Although it's possible to use JavaScript directly, most modern web pages use a framework or library together with JavaScript. There are three main reasons for this:

- The libraries can hide differences between browsers, making programming more reliable, less error-prone, and more portable.
- The libraries are high level, with one line of jQuery (for example) often replacing dozens of lines of JavaScript manipulating the DOM directly.
- The libraries are popular, so lots of widgets and plug-ins are written for them, further speeding up development.

In this section you learn a little about jQuery, one of the more popular JavaScript libraries and (not by coincidence) one of the easiest to learn and use. You can get more information at `http://www.jquery.com/`, where you can also find hundreds of plug-ins, most freely available.

Learning jQuery

The jQuery JavaScript library introduces some top-level (global) objects and functions, and also introduces a new way of using JavaScript.

If you are not familiar with cascading style sheets (CSS) or HTML, see Chapter 17, "XHTML and HTML 5."

If you are not familiar with the idea of the document object model (DOM), you should review Chapter 7, "Extracting Data from XML," which contains a brief introduction; because jQuery shields you from using the DOM API, in most cases you only need the basic ideas to start.

The Domain-Specific Language (DSL) Approach

As you might have guessed, jQuery uses CSS selectors to locate and process nodes in the web browser's HTML DOM tree. The following jQuery JavaScript code turns all `<span>` elements in the document that have a class attribute of `born` a bright yellow color:

```
$("span.born").css("background-color", "yellow");
```

Notice how the oddly named `$()` function in jQuery actually returns an object with a `css` method; that `css` method is in turn a jQuery function that returns another jQuery object, which of course also has a `css` method, so you can chain the calls like so:

```
$("span.born").css("background-color", "yellow").css("color", "blue");
```

This approach lets the programmer think more in terms of the actual problem she's trying to solve and less in terms of the mechanics of how to solve it. It's higher level. This style, with function names that correspond to the problem domain and with chained calls, is sometimes called a *domain-specific language.*

You can use pretty much any CSS selectors with jQuery, and you don't have to worry about whether the particular selector works in any given web browser: jQuery emulates them where they are not available natively.

There is, of course, a lot more to jQuery than this, but you have probably now seen enough to know whether you want to know more, and to make some sense of the example that follows in the next Try It Out exercise.

jQuery Plug-ins and Add-On Libraries

Much of the power and popularity of jQuery comes from its clean and simple design, but there is also a huge array of add-ons. These come in two forms: plug-ins and libraries.

jQuery Plug-ins

Plug-ins usually provide a single feature. A widely used example is FancyBox, which produces a border around an HTML element to make it behave almost like a pop-up dialog box. An example of this is shown in Figure 16-7: the white pop-up box has a cross in a circle at its upper right to close it, and triangular arrows to move forward to the next image.

You can find literally hundreds of plug-ins, each with documentation and demos and examples; most are in the master index on `www.jquery.com`, which has both categories and a rudimentary search function. There is even an XPath plug-in, although it implements only a subset of XPath 1, unfortunately.

You'll see how to use a sample plug-in shortly.

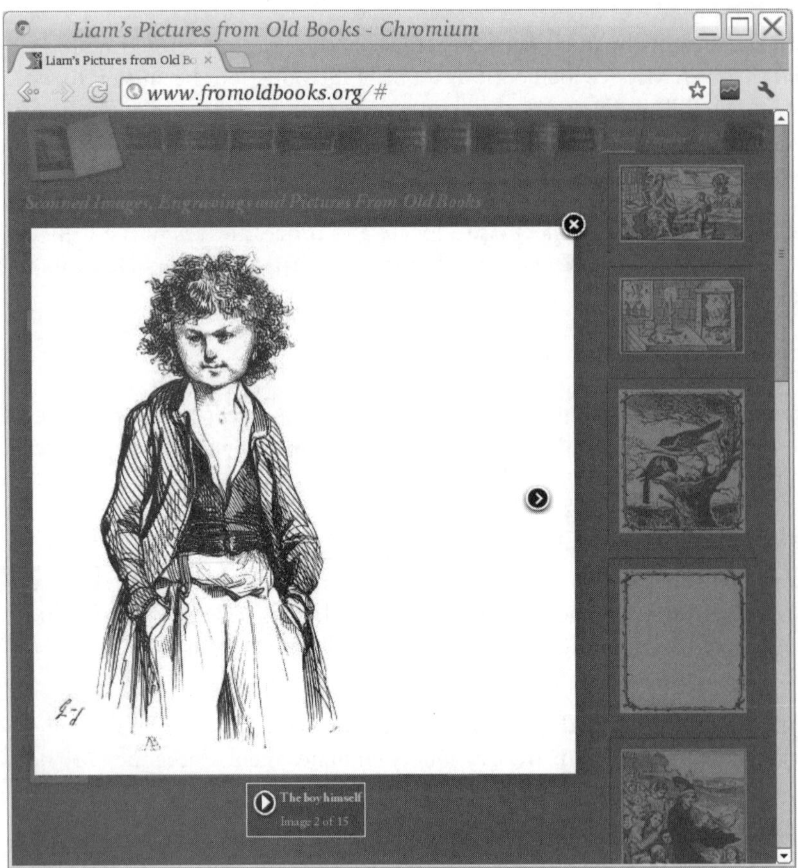

FIGURE 16-7

Add-on Libraries

Add-on libraries typically extend jQuery in multiple ways, rather than just providing a single feature, as a plug-in might. The most common add-on library is called jQueryUI and adds a lot of user-interface features such as notebook tabs and widgets; because those aren't needed for learning AJAX, this chapter won't cover jQueryUI, but if you start using jQuery yourself, you will want to read about it on the Web.

JQuery and AJAX

The jQuery library includes support for a lot of things that are often done on web pages, and it should be no surprise that it has direct support for AJAX using `XMLHttpRequest`. In the following activity you'll learn how to use jQuery to make a web page that is updated asynchronously (in the background) without being reloaded.

TRY IT OUT AJAX in jQuery

In this exercise you take the earlier Try It Out and load the same XML document with jQuery instead of raw JavaScript. You'll see jQuery in action, learn how to load the library, and compare the size of the code.

1. Make a new HTML document called `jqajax.html`. As in the previous activity, for security reasons you will need to upload it to a web server, or have a web server running on your own computer and access the document through that web server.

```
<!DOCTYPE html
  PUBLIC "-//W3C//DTD XHTML 1.1//EN"
         "http://www.w3.org/TR/xhtml11/DTD/xhtml11.dtd">
<html xmlns="http://www.w3.org/1999/xhtml" xml:lang="en">
  <head>
    <title>jQuery ajax example</title>
    <meta http-equiv="Content-Type" content="text/html; charset=utf-8" />
    <script type="text/javascript"
      src="https://ajax.googleapis.com/ajax/libs/jquery/1.7.1/jquery.min.js"></script>
  </head>
  <body>
    <form onsubmit="return false;" action="">
      <p><input type="button" onclick="getXML();" value="Get XML"/></p>
    </form>
    <div id="replaceme"></div>
    <script type="text/javascript">
      function handler(theData, theStatus, jqXHR) {
          $("div").append(theData.firstChild);
      }

      function getXML() {
        $.ajax({
          type: "GET",
          url: "hello.xml",
          dataType: "xml",
          success: handler
        });
```

```
      }
    </script>
  </body>
</html>
```

2. Make the XML file using the same XML file as before, `hello.xml`, like this:

```
<ajax>
  <p id="p">hello world</p>
</ajax>
```

3. Upload the two files to a web server (or put them where the web server on your computer can find them) and open the HTML file in a web browser.

4. Click the Get XML button as before to see the message. There's no `alert()` in this version, so "hello world" should just appear under the button.

How It Works

Line 12 sets the button's `onclick` attribute to call the `getXML()` function as in the previous example:

```
<p><input type="button" onclick="getXML();" value="Get XML"/></p>
```

Most of the HTML in the example is the same as before, but there are a couple of new parts. First, line 8 (shown in the following code) loads the jQuery library from the Google Content Delivery Network. Google provides this service because if lots of websites use the same library there's no point having it copied everywhere. It helps Google's web crawlers to know everyone is using the same library, too.

```
<script type="text/javascript"
  src="https://ajax.googleapis.com/ajax/libs/jquery/1.7.1/jquery.min.js"></script>
```

The second new part, of course, is the `<script>` element at the end of the document.

In the script, a function called `handler` is defined; this function adds the XML `<ajax>` element after the last child (if any) of every `<div>` element in the document. To add the content only to a particular element, you would use a more specific selector, such as `div#replaceme` in this case. (See the next chapter for more information on the CSS selectors used by XPath.)

Just defining a function called `handler` doesn't make it get called. When the user clicks the Get XML button, it's the `getXML` function that gets called. This is the meat, and it's both smaller and much easier to understand than in the previous Try It Out. The `$.ajax()` function in jQuery handles `XMLHttpRequest` for you. You tell it that you are going to use the HTTP `GET` method to fetch `hello.xml`, that you want XML back, and that when it has all arrived you want your function, `handler`, to be called.

Wow. To put the differences between the previous activity and this activity in perspective, it took an hour or so to get the first example to work on multiple web browsers, and five minutes to get the jQuery version to work.

JSON AND AJAX

Although the "X" in AJAX stands for XML (itself, in turn, not an exact acronym, of course!), people these days are more likely to use other formats with `XMLHttpRequest`. The main reason for this is that the XML DOM is too unpleasant to use, and now that you've seen some jQuery you can see why people think that way. Of course, XQuery is just as easy as using jQuery, but it's not supported in today's browsers.

The most common format for interchange of JavaScript objects between a web browser and a server was designed by Douglas Crockford, and is called JSON. In fact, a JSON stream is itself a JavaScript expression that, when evaluated, constructs the objects it represents.

WARNING *Because a JSON stream is an expression, in theory you could load it using* `eval()`*, a JavaScript function that takes a string and interprets it as JavaScript. This is a really, really bad thing to do, because you are trusting the data coming over the network. A person-in-the-middle could insert arbitrary JavaScript into your application! It could also mean someone compromising your server could use your application as a vector for a cross-site scripting attack (XSS) against another site. Use a library to parse JSON, or test the stream with the regular expression given in the JSON specification.*

JSON Example

The JSON format is defined by IETF RFC 4627, available at `http://www.ietf.org/rfc/rfc4627`.

A JSON text represents *either* a single JavaScript object or a single array. This object or array can, in turn, contain other arrays and objects. Arrays (with square brackets) contain simple values, and objects (with curly braces) contain member-lists. Here is a simple example:

```
{
    "students" : [
      {
        "name" : "Caitlin",
        "id" : 6
      },
      {
        "name" : "David",
        "eyes" : "blue",
        "age" : 26
      },
      {
        "id" : 12,
        "name" : "Leslie",
        "car" : {
          "make" : "Jeep",
```

```
                "color" : "green"
            }
        }
    ]
}
```

If you use this example in a JavaScript console, perhaps with:

```
var a = { "students" : [ ... } ;
a.students[2]name;
```

you will get "Leslie" printed back at you. That is the beauty of JSON: not only is it simple, but you can use it immediately. You can find JSON libraries for most programming languages, but it really shines with JavaScript on the web.

JSON Syntax

More formally, the syntax rules that define JSON are as follows:

- A JSON text is a single object or a single array.
- An *object* is a list of members (a *member-list*) enclosed in curly braces:

  ```
  { member-list }
  ```

- An *array* is a list of simple values enclosed in square brackets:

  ```
  [ value-list ]
  ```

- A *member-list* is a list, possibly empty, of pairs:

  ```
  "string" : value
  ```

- A *value-list* is just a list, again possibly empty, of values separated by commas.
- A *value* is a string, a number, an object, an array, `true`, `false`, or `null`. Strings must use double quotes, but you can use `\"` inside a string, as for JavaScript strings. You can also use the other JavaScript `\-` escapes described earlier in this chapter in the section on JavaScript strings.

JSON and jQuery

If you have a JSON text as a string you can use the following to turn the string into a JavaScript object:

```
var myJson = jQuery.parseJSON(theString);
```

You can use `$.getJSON` as a wrapper around `$.ajax()`, or you can use `$.ajax()` directly as in the following example, but with `dataType` set to JSON:

```
$.ajax({
  url: url,
  dataType: 'json',
  data: data,
  success: callback
});
```

Note that if your JSON stream has a syntax error in it, the call to `$.ajax()` will generally just fail silently.

JSONP and CORS

In most modern web browsers the `XMLHttpRequest` function implements a *Same Origin policy*, or *Same Origin restriction*. This means that you can only fetch data from the same domain as the caller; that is, the server that served the HTML document or the JavaScript code doing the fetching.

Sometimes you need to fetch data from another web server. JSONP and CORS are two mechanisms for doing this. Of these, JSONP (JSON with Padding) is supported by jQuery directly, but is very insecure because it is evaluated directly as raw JavaScript, and it is not recommended by experts. CORS is a newer, mechanism that lets you use `XMLHttpRequest` to fetch data from other sites as long as the remote web server is configured correctly. At the time of writing, CORS is not widely deployed, and the best way to fetch data from another server is often to write a proxy on your own server and fetch the data through that, rather than risk the insecure nature of JSONP.

THE WEB SEVER BACK END

Web architects sometimes speak of web applications as being divided into a *front end*, the web browser part that the user sees, and a *back end*, the part that's running on a server somewhere. Sometimes everything is running on the same machine, but the web server and the application code behind it still form the back end. This section takes a closer look at this back end.

So far in the examples, when the web browser sent an AJAX request to the server, it was to fetch a file. In real applications it's more often a request to a database server or some other application, and the glue that connects the web server to the database or application is part of the back end. The most common languages used to write the back end of a small web application are first PHP, then Microsoft C# or Visual Basic with Active Server Pages (ASP), and finally Java (not JavaScript so often) with a "servlet" API. But you also see XSLT and XQuery used.

Chapter 19, "Case Study: XML in Publishing" revisits the use of XQuery and XSLT, and later in this chapter you use the PHP language to generate data for an AJAX script. You could as easily use XSLT or XQuery, of course, as long as you arrange for those to be called appropriately on the server.

Just as you can use different languages on the back end, on the web server, you can send different formats to communicate with the browser, not just JSON. Although JSON is probably the format most often used with `XMLHttpRequest`, plaintext and HTML are the next most often used. The jQuery plug-in you'll see shortly uses plaintext in a simple line-based format the plug-in author devised. HTML is often used when you are sending HTML content back to the client to insert into the document, such as search results.

BACK END SECURITY

The important things to remember when writing the code on the server that responds to an AJAX request are similar to those for any web application, and for any API including Servlets, CGI, PHP, content management systems, and more. The summary is very simple: *Never trust the network.*

Remember that people can always view the source of your application. Because the web browser has to be able to run it, there's not much you can do about that. People can also watch the network traffic and see exactly what parameters you are sending back. They can then write their own program that sends the same parameters, perhaps slightly modified.

One reason why people would forge requests is to fool your application into showing their data mixed in with yours. Suppose you write an application that lets people add comments to other people's articles on your site. You use JavaScript to make sure they enter only plaintext, and not HTML tags. But someone figures out how to submit data to your site without going through the JavaScript, and manages to get HTML elements onto your website. At that point she could include an HTML `<script>` element that browsers would trust (because it came from your site), or she could add links to other sites, perhaps sites selling illegally imported hosiery!

Therefore, in the back end, you can never assume the request is actually coming from your trusted application. Even if you use a secure socket (`https`) or encryption, because someone else could read the source code to your program, they could probably break the encryption.

Sending Images and Other Non-Textual Data

Because the web browser is expecting XML or JSON, your back end should not try to send binary data. Instead, send an HTML or XHTML fragment with a link to the image or other data, and insert the link into the document, perhaps with `appendChild()`.

Performance

If your back end is too slow, things can go wrong silently. You can supply the jQuery `$.ajax()` function with a timeout parameter to counteract this; if you don't, there is generally a browser-specific default. Some programs and servers also buffer up the data until there's a certain amount of it, and you can often turn that off (for example, setting `$|` to 0 in Perl; see the *perldoc perlvar* command in a console or terminal, if you have Perl documentation available) so that the web browser will see the *start* of the data sooner.

If you know the data will take a long time to arrive, your JavaScript client can arrange for a function to be called each time data is available, instead of only at the end. An alternative is to send a short message saying "working..." every so often and have the client make a new request for the next part, but you have to make sure that if the user gets bored and wanders off, your server isn't still working hard!

The Server Logs Are Your Friend

One of the most useful things to do when you're writing the back end server part of web applications is to watch the error messages, and these usually go into files called *server error logs*.

Make sure you know where the web server's error logs are (`/var/log/httpd/error_log` or `/var/log/apache/error_log` are common locations); some Web hosting companies give you a log directory under your account somewhere instead.

You can also have a window running `tail -f /var/log/httpd/access_log` or some similar command to see each HTTP request logged as it completes. This will show you whether your Web browser sent out the AJAX request.

A LARGER EXAMPLE

It's time for an example to glue all the parts together. The example uses a jQuery plug-in that can handle the autocompletion suggestions, as you saw for the search page at the start of this chapter.

You may already have an extract from the biographical dictionary that was mentioned in Chapter 9; now you will make a web search form that takes the user to a chosen entry. Because the complete list of entries for the 32-volume dictionary is more than 350 kilobytes of text, it makes sense to design the interaction to do the searching on the server, even though the extract for this book is smaller. You can find the complete XML file at `http://words.fromoldbooks.org/xml` if you want to experiment with it.

> **NOTE** *When you are working with a web server, URLs and files are generally case sensitive: it must be* `people.php`*, and not* `PEOPLE.PHP` *or* `people.PHP`*, or it won't work.*

TRY IT OUT AJAX and jQuery Autocompletion Example

For this Try It Out you need to download the autocomplete plug-in; or you can look for it at `http://www.pengoworks.com/workshop/jquery/autocomplete.htm`.

The goal of the exercise is for you to see how easy it is to use a jQuery plug-in, and also to make a form with search suggestions.

Like most of the examples in this chapter, you need a web server: the examples will not run directly off the hard drive, because of the security restrictions built in to modern web browsers and JavaScript.

1. First make an HTML file called `people.html`, as shown here:

Available for download on Wrox.com

```
<!DOCTYPE html
  PUBLIC "-//W3C//DTD XHTML 1.1//EN"
         "http://www.w3.org/TR/xhtml11/DTD/xhtml11.dtd">
<html xmlns="http://www.w3.org/1999/xhtml" xml:lang="en">
  <head>
    <title>People Finder</title>
    <meta http-equiv="Content-Type" content="text/html; charset=utf-8" />
    <script type="text/javascript" src="js/jquery.js"></script>
    <script type="text/javascript" src="js/jquery.autocomplete.js"></script>
    <link rel="stylesheet" href="css/jquery.autocomplete.css" type="text/css" />
  </head>
  <body>
    <form method="GET" action="go.php">
      <p>People Finder: try <i>ala</i> for a start</p>
      <p>
        <input type="text" tabindex="10" style="width: 400px;" value=""
                                            id="Person" class="ac_input"/>
        <input type="submit" tabindex="20" id="gobutton" value="Go"/>
      </p>
    </form>

    <script type="text/javascript">//<![CDATA
      function findhref(row) {
          return row.extra[0];
      }

      function selectItem(row) {
        // set the form to go to the page on a select
        $("form").get(0).setAttribute('action', findhref(row));
      }

      $("#Person").autocomplete("people.php", {
          delay: 40, // in milliseconds
          minChars: 2,
          matchContains: 1,
          cacheLength: 10, // for better performance, see docs
          onItemSelect: selectItem,
          onFindValue: findhref,
          autoFill: true // put the value in the text box
        }
      );
    // ]]></script>
  </body>
</html>
```

people.html

2. Next you will need a way to search the list of biography entries on the server and return the matches. You only need to search the titles, and those are in a file called `entries.txt`, which makes it easier. Make a file called `people.php` like this:

```
<?php
$q = strtolower($_GET["q"]);
if (!$q) $q = "ama"; # silly default for testing more easily

$items = file("entries.txt", FILE_IGNORE_NEW_LINES);
if (!$items) return; # file not found
if (!$items[0]) return; # file was empty

$maxitems = 30; # too many completions...
$n_found = 0; # number found so far

# look for titles starting with $q
foreach ($items as $key => $value) {
    $where = strpos(strtolower($value), $q);
    if ($where !== false && $where == 0) {
        echo "$value\n";
        if (++$n_found > $maxitems) {
            return;
        }
    }
}
?>
```

people.php

3. Unpack the plug-in you downloaded, rename the `javascript` directory to `js`, and put `people.html` and `people.php` in the same directory as `autocomplete.php`, `css`, and `js`.

4. The `entries.txt` file that is searched by `people.php` is included with the files for this chapter, or, if you have the XML for the biographical dictionary (or the excerpt) you can make it with the following XQuery:

```
xfn:string-join(
        for $e in doc("chalmers-biography-extract.xml")//entry
        return
            concat(
                normalize-space(data($e/title)),
                "|",
                substring($e/@id, 1, 1), "/", $e/@id,
                ".html&#xa;"
            )
    ,
    ""
    )
```

5. Run this with Saxon as:

```
saxon -query make-entries.xq \!method=text > entries.txt
```

(The `\` is needed for *bash* on Linux or you will get a strange-sounding error about history; on MS-DOS you can use `!` instead of `\!`.)

If you prefer, you can make up your own data file. The format (dictated by the plug-in you are using) is

```
title|id
```

so that the first dozen lines look like this:

```
Aa, Christian Charles Henry Vander|a/aa-christian-charles-henry-vander.html
Aagard, Christian|a/aagard-christian.html
Aarsens, Francis|a/aarsens-francis.html
Abeille, Gaspar|a/abeille-gaspar.html
Abeille, Louis Paul|a/abeille-louis-paul.html
Abel, Gaspar|a/abel-gaspar.html
Abel, Frederick Gottfried|a/abel-frederick-gottfried.html
Abelli, Louis|a/abelli-louis.html
Aben-Ezra|a/aben-ezra.html
Abercromby, Patrick|a/abercromby-patrick.html
Abraham, Nicholas|a/abraham-nicholas.html
Abu-Nowas|a/abu-nowas.html
```

The idea is that the biography entry for Gaspar Abeille would be found in `a/abeille-gaspar.html`, with the "a" folder being alongside the `people.html` file.

6. With everything in place, open the `people.html` file in a web browser, either using a web server on your computer or by uploading everything (preserving the directory structure) onto a computer somewhere else running a web server.

7. Type a few letters into the search box: an "a" followed by an "l" gives the result shown in Figure 16-8. If you click one of the highlighted suggestions you can then click the Go button to be taken to an error message saying the biography entry isn't there. But that's OK, it means the part you just did is working properly!

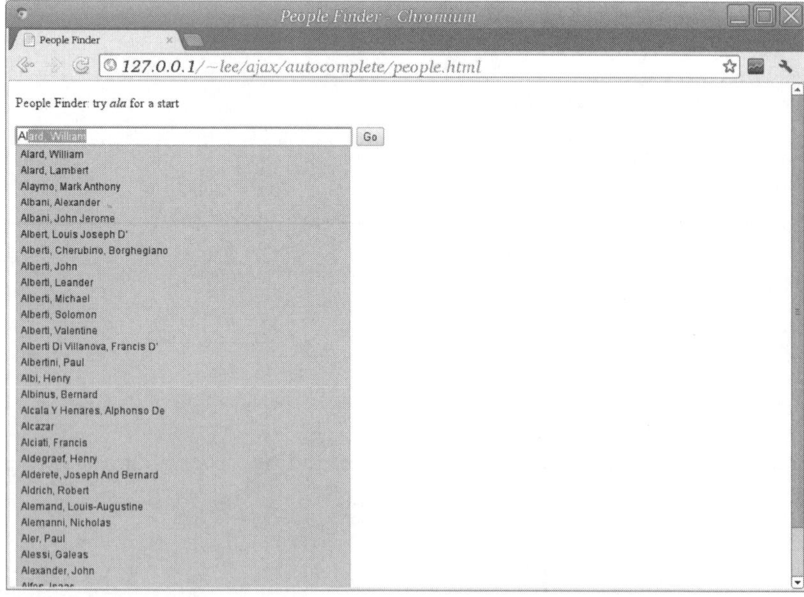

FIGURE 16-8

How It Works

There are quite a few pieces to this puzzle.

The HTML File

In the HTML file, you load the a copy of the jQuery library from the `js` folder; it would be better to load it from Google's Content Delivery Network, as you did for the previous example in this chapter, but this way you can include a version of jQuery and the plug-in on the website for this book and be confident that they work together.

After loading the jQuery library, you loaded the plug-in, again from the `js` directory.

There is also a cascading style sheet, `css/jquery.autocomplete.css`, which controls the appearance of the autocompletion list. Without the CSS, the autocomplete suggestions appear as a rather unexpected bulleted list, although everything else will still work. You learn more about CSS in Chapter 17.

After the JavaScript and style sheets the HTML file contains a `<form>` element and a `<script>` element. The form has a 400-pixel-wide input field for people to enter the name of a person to find, and a Submit button to make the browser go there.

The JavaScript in the `<script>` element defines two small functions and then does some plumbing.

To understand the JavaScript you need to recall that the data file, `entries.txt`, has one entry per line, and each line contains two items, a title and a URL, separated by a vertical bar character. When the jQuery autocomplete plug-in processes this data, it splits the lines into arrays, each of two fields.

The `findhref()` function then, is called with a "row" object that is really an HTML `<li>` DOM element node, with an extra property that holds any additional fields after the first one. Item zero is the second (and last) field on the data line, the URL. This is a rather complicated way of doing things, and an XML element or a JSON structure would be a better fit, but it's a good example of an *ad hoc* data format in real life. The `findhref` function, as you might guess, returns the URI for the biography entry in question.

The `selectItem()` function is called when the user clicks one of the suggestions. It sets the `action` attribute of the `<form>` element so that if you click the Go button, you go to the URI from the second field in the data entry.

Note that if users have disabled JavaScript, they won't get any suggestions, but they can enter a name into the box, click the Go button, and go to the original place, `go.php`, which could be a page that did a search.

The "plumbing" part is the call to a jQuery function:

```
$("#Person").autocomplete("people.php", { … } );
```

The first part selects an element with an ID of "Person" — that's the textbox inside the form.

Then the autocomplete method from your jQuery plug-in is called on the object found, on the textbox.

That autocomplete method is given two arguments: the base URL to fetch (`people.php`) and a list of options enclosed in braces. Notice how the option syntax is very similar to JSON; if you put the names on the left in quotes it would still work, and would also be valid JSON.

The options are documented in the `autocomplete_docs.txt` file included with the plug-in; the important ones here are `onItemSelect` and `onFindValue`, which arrange for the plug-in to call your two handler functions when needed.

Now that you can see what the HTML document is doing, you should look at the PHP back end a little.

The PHP Back-End Script

The PHP script named `people.php` is not really central to this example, and you could actually just have the jQuery fetch `entries.txt` instead of going to the search script, but of course that would always return the same autocompletions.

The script checks its `q` parameter, which is the user's search term from the textbox, sent to you by jQuery. Then it tries to read the `entries.txt` file. If the script fails to find `entries.txt`, it returns silently; a better approach might have been to have had it do this instead:

```
echo "Entries.txt not found|oops\n"; return;
```

That way the error would pop up on the screen. If your code does not work, you might want to try that change.

After loading the file into the `$items` array, the script sets a `$maxitems` variable to limit the number of results returned to 30, and `$n_found` to the number found so far (zero at the start, of course).

Then there's a loop over each line in the file, looking to see if the given prefix (`$q`) is at the start of one of the lines, and, if so, to print (`echo`) the line. If `$maxitems` items have been printed, the script finishes.

Making the Data File

The XQuery script is given as an example; if you have read Chapter 7 it should be reasonably clear. The only tricky part is that it calls `string-join()` on a sequence of strings generated by the inner `for...return` expression. The reason for this is that otherwise the XQuery engine separates the strings with a space between them when it prints the results, and that messes up the format.

SUMMARY

- AJAX is an acronym for Asynchronous JavaScript And XML, and is the name of a common design pattern in web development.
- AJAX is used in HTML or XHTML web pages to fetch data from a remote web server without having to wait for a network connection and response.
- The data fetched in the AJAX pattern does not need to be in XML; plain text, structured text, HTML, JSON, and XML are all widely used.

- JSON is an acronym for JavaScript Object Notation and is a useful text-based format for exchanging objects; it is not so useful for document fragments, since it does not handle XML's mixed content.
- You can easily generate XML or JSON on your web server using XQuery, XSLT, or almost any programming or scripting language.
- Use the AJAX pattern to make web pages that seem fast and responsive, updating without the user having to wait for a new page to load.
- Use the REST (Representational State Transfer) HTTP design pattern, making sure the user can bookmark a page in its current state whenever that makes sense.

EXERCISES

You can find solutions to these exercises in Appendix A.

1. Modify the PHP script to find strings at the start of words and in the middle of the names; return all the strings at the start *before* strings at the middle, because they are more likely to be wanted.
2. Modify the PHP script to find strings anywhere in the words.
3. Combine the XML Query fragment with the PHP script, to call XQuery on the fly; you could use the BaseX or Zorba XQuery implementations.

▸ WHAT YOU LEARNED IN THIS CHAPTER

TOPIC	KEY POINTS
What is AJAX	AJAX is an asynchronous programming technique used in web browsers. AJAX is often used with XML, JSON, HTML, or *ad hoc* text formats. To make the most out of AJAX, you need server-side programs as well as client-side JavaScript.
What is JSON	JSON is a text format for transmitting JavaScript data objects.
JavaScript syntax	JavaScript is a C-like interpreted language. It is not directly related to Java. Use the web browser console to help debug JavaScript programs.

PART VII
Display

17

XHTML and HTML 5

WHAT YOU WILL LEARN IN THIS CHAPTER:

- The relationships between XML, HTML, XHTML, and XHTML 5
- The structure of XHTML documents
- Creating XHTML with XSLT and XQuery
- Styling XHTML and XML with CSS
- The HTML 5 Open Web Platform
- Differences between HTML 5 and XHTML
- When to use which sort of HTML

The *HyperText Markup Language* (HTML) was introduced in 1989 as the way to create documents on the World Wide Web (WWW). The World Wide Web (Web for short) combined several ideas at the same time: it is *decentralized*, meaning that anyone can put up a web server without needing permission from a central authority. This decentralization allowed the Web to scale. The Web scales because it is *unreliable*: you can encounter broken links. Previous attempts at large-scale HyperText systems had required a single, central link database. Despite being unreliable and decentralized, the Web also gives every reachable resource a *name*. These names, Uniform Resource Identifiers, are commonly known as URIs, URLs, or web addresses. Any web client, such as a browser, can fetch any resource given its URI. The resources are usually fetched using the *HyperText Transfer Protocol* (HTTP); HTTP takes a list of formats and languages, and returns the requested resource in the best format available in the requested language. Most often, that format is HTML.

There was actually nothing special about any of the ideas in the World Wide Web, but the *combination of ideas* was new. For many early users, also new was the ability to mix links and text in the same document. Competing systems, such as Gopher, could not do this. Other systems could do this, but they were not freely available, or were not decentralized, or tried to be reliable and as a result did not scale.

In this chapter you learn how HTML works, how to style HTML with CSS, how to link JavaScript to HTML, and about the various dialects of HTML, including HTML 5. The short historical perspective in this introduction and the start of this chapter will help you to understand the relationship between the various parts.

BACKGROUND OF SGML

HTML and XML were both derived from an older international standard, ISO 8879, the Standard Generalized Markup Language (SGML). Like XML, SGML is a system for specifying your own markup languages. HTML was one such language. Up until HTML 4 there was an SGML document type definition (DTD) published for HTML.

NOTE *HTML, then, as you already know from earlier chapters in this book, supports hyperlinks in the middle of text. It's worth emphasizing this because most other formats used on the Web, including JSON and RDF, cannot easily do this.*

HTML and SGML

The most obvious feature of SGML that HTML used, and that is not available in XML, is called *minimization*. This feature lets you omit tags that the parser can imply. The following two HTML fragments are equivalent:

```
<P>This is a paragraph
<P>And this is another one.
```

and:

```
<P>This is a paragraph</P>
<P>And this is another one.</P>
```

The HTML parser knows you can't have one `<P>` element inside another, so it closes the current one automatically. This led some people to imagine that `<P>` was some sort of command to start a new line and that paragraphs did not contain content — a misconception one still encounters!

SGML also allows quotes to be left off attribute values in some cases; in others you can omit the attribute name and just put a value.

Elements declared as `EMPTY` in XML, as you know, use the self-closing tag, `<br/>`, or a close tag immediately after the open tag, `<br></br>`. But SGML uses the form `<br>`, and the SGML parser, after reading the DTD for HTML, would know that `<br>` was declared `EMPTY`, and would not even allow an end tag for it, but would just want `<br>` by itself.

HTML elements are also case insensitive, so you can close `<p>` with `</P>` if you like, or use `<Br>`.

XML and SGML

The syntactic flexibility of SGML also makes it complicated, and the truth is that most people writing web pages just guessed the syntax, saw what worked in their web browser, and used that. Because the early web browsers were often buggy, it was common for web pages to work in only one web browser. Soon, web browsers had to start copying each other's bugs.

By 1995, web development was already difficult because of browser differences. At the same time, a number of people and organizations who had been using SGML heavily wanted the web browsers to display *their* markup languages, and not only HTML.

They lost that battle, but the next best thing was to have browser plug-ins that displayed SGML directly. The plug-ins, though, did not support the full range of SGML minimization that HTML uses.

Work at the World Wide Web Consortium (W3C) on standardizing this subset of SGML without minimization led, as you know, to XML. Meanwhile, HTML and Web browsers continued to develop, and today's Web browsers provide a rich environment that mixes both XML and HTML.

THE OPEN WEB PLATFORM

Today's web has evolved into a powerful and thriving ecosystem in which the central parts are all defined by open, freely available, and freely implementable standards. The World Wide Web is not just a collection of documents; websites can be entire applications: word processors, spreadsheets, mapping tools, banking, music, painting, and much more. And the Web no longer needs an expensive workstation; most mobile phones can browse and interact with the Web. Tablets, multi-touch surfaces, spectacles, and even shoes are all connected as well.

The Web has become an operating environment, one step up from an operating system: it is the Web Platform. It is also called the Open Web Platform because the APIs, the formats, and the protocols are all freely available.

NOTE *The Web can also be scripted, or programmed, using the JavaScript language. You will have already seen some JavaScript if you have worked through Chapter 16, "AJAX." Web pages can be styled using cascading style sheets (CSS), and you learn more about CSS later in this chapter.*

This new flexibility and power demanded that Web browsers all behave the same, so that applications could be reliable. To do this, a new version of HTML (HTML 5) was produced that specifies exactly how browsers are to handle syntax errors, as well as introducing some new features.

Figure 17-1 is a screenshot of a modern web browser displaying `http://platform.html5.org/` with a list of some of the technologies that are part of the Open Web Platform. Many of those technologies are large enough and complex enough (or important enough, or at least self-important enough) to have had entire books written about them. This chapter focuses on HTML 5 and on two flavors of XHTML — 1.x and its successor, XHTML 5 — plus a few other technologies are mentioned as they arise.

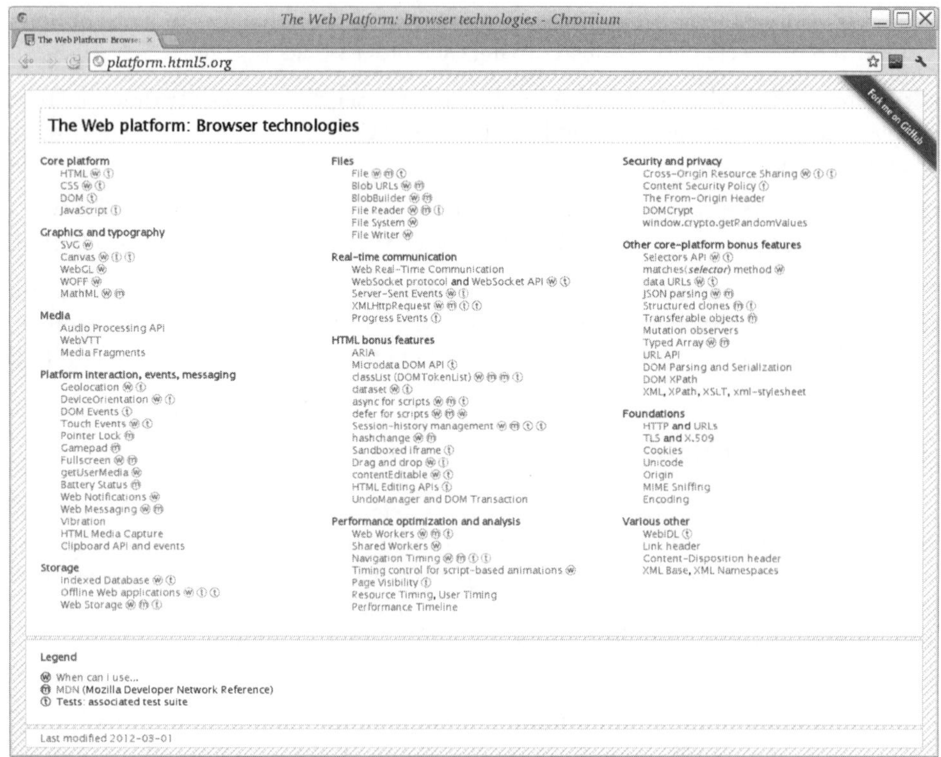

FIGURE 17-1

INTRODUCTION TO XHTML

The original creators of XML had no intention of replacing HTML; they just wanted to be able to use their SGML documents on the web so as not to have to worry about HTML.

However, there was such immediate popularity of XML (many would say *over*-popularity) that the idea arose to try to redefine HTML in terms of XML.

The result of this endeavor was XHTML, which has its benefits: XHTML documents can be processed by regular XML tools, edited in XML-aware software, and can also contain little islands of "non-HTML," including XML vocabularies such as MathML or Scalable Vector Graphics (SVG). However, XHTML does not attempt to *replace* HTML. It sits *alongside* HTML. It is compatible: if you are careful how you create it (explained later), you can feed XHTML to a regular HTML web browser and have everything work.

In this section you see the structure of an XHTML document, and also learn the main differences between XHTML and regular XML.

The section first describes XHTML 1.1, and then covers the differences between that and HTML 5, together with its XML representation that is sometimes called XHTML 5.

WARNING *Because XHTML is really XML, element names are case sensitive, and must be in lowercase instead of capital letters. Use* `<div>` *and not* `<DIV>`*, for example.*

The XHTML <html> Element

An XHTML 1.x document always begins with a reference to the XHTML DTD like so:

```
<!DOCTYPE html
    PUBLIC "-//W3C//DTD XHTML 1.0 Transitional//EN"
           "http://www.w3.org/TR/xhtml1/DTD/xhtml1-transitional.dtd"
>
```

You can actually use several different XHTML DTDs including *strict*, *transitional*, *loose*, and *frameset* (for documents using the Netscape `<frame>` element; the frameset DTD is now relatively rarely used).

See `http://www.w3.org/QA/2002/04/valid-dtd-list.html` for the full list. In general, you should use the *strict* versions if you are generating XHTML documents, but you may need to use the *transitional* DTDs if you have external content, such as advertising that's included on your server, or for a few compatibility features.

WARNING *Many XML programs will try to download these DTD files from* `www.w3.org`*; they will fail, because W3C does not allow this. Unfortunately, W3C's web servers get tens of millions of requests for these files a day (sometimes in a single hour), and so W3C now slows down (throttles) requests for the files.*

The solution is that you should set up an XML Catalog file to point to local copies of these files. The same is true of XML Schema files. Consult the documentation for the XML software you are using to see how to set up an XML Catalog.

After the XML declaration and the DOCTYPE declaration you get to the start of the XHTML document, which looks like this:

```
<html xmlns="http://www.w3.org/1999/xhtml" lang="en" xml:lang="en">
```

It is unfortunate that the designers of XHTML chose to use an XML namespace, but they did. You must get it *exactly* right. Worse, to match XHTML elements in XPath, whether from XQuery, XSLT, or some other environment, you will generally need to bind a namespace prefix to that URI (h perhaps) and use XPath expressions like this:

```
/h:html/h:body/h:div//h:span[contains(concat(" ", @class, " "), " date ")]
```

It's all too easy to forget the prefix and fail to get a match! Refer to Chapter 7, "Extracting Data from XML," for more detail. If you call XPath from JavaScript, or use the jQuery XPath plug-in, you may find you do not need to worry about namespaces in XPath expressions.

The lang and xml:lang elements in the <html> tag repeat the same value, and should indicate the primary language of the document.

If your document is using SVG, MathML, or other vocabularies that use a namespace, you should normally declare them on the <html> element. It's not uncommon to see XHTML documents start with a dozen or more namespace declarations.

The <html> element normally has exactly two children: <head> and <body>. These are discussed in the following sections. The exception is for documents using frames, which have a <frameset> element instead of <body>.

The XHTML <head> Element

The <head> element in all versions of HTML is a place to store information about the document: it's not generally rendered, although it does contain the document title, which is used on many platforms for bookmarks and window titles. Any unknown element ends the <head> regardless of your tagging structure.

The following sections describe the elements that are most commonly used inside the document's head. After reading about the head, you get to the body and try some examples.

Information about the Document: The <meta> Element

You use the <meta> element to describe the document. Some of this information is used by web servers, proxies, and clients (browsers); some is used by search engines such as Google; and some may be used by other applications, or for your own purposes. This section examines some examples. Following is the first:

```
<meta http-equiv="Content-Type" content="text/html; charset=utf-8" />
```

This example, using http-equiv, is used by some web servers and by web browsers to override the default character encoding for HTTP, which is Latin 1 (ISO 8859-1). The http-equiv attribute contains the name of the HTTP header, and the content attribute contains the requested value.

Early web servers supported using `http-equiv` to override any of the HTTP headers that would be sent back before the document; today most servers (including Apache) ignore this, and you have to use external configuration to have a document served in UTF-8. Even so, including this header tells a web browser that the encoding is UTF-8 even when the file is read from a local disk, and this is a good idea. To send HTML documents as UTF-8 with Apache, add the following to an `.htaccess` file in the same directory as the files:

```
<Files ~ "*\.html">
ForceType 'text/html; charset=UTF-8'
</Files>
```

Notice the trailing space inside the empty element tag, just before the `/>`. This is needed so that web browsers can read the document as HTML, which does not use the XML empty-element syntax.

If you generate XHTML with XSLT, use the `xhtml` output method and the XSLT processor will add the space automatically. This isn't needed with XSLT inside the web browser, because the elements are never actually written out in that case. Web browser XSLT processors do a direct tree transform. But it *is* needed if you generate web pages on the server to be sent over the network, or if the files are to be opened directly.

Now take a look at some informational examples. The first, `generator`, is really a sort of vanity header; some programs add it so that you can tell which application was used to create or edit the file:

```
<meta name="generator" content="/usr/bin/vi" />
```

The next two headers, `description` and `keywords`, are used by search engines. The description should be a short sentence or two describing the purpose of the web page, and the keywords are a list of up to ten words or phrases relevant to the content.

```
<meta name="keywords" content="isaac newton,gravity,biography,biographies,people" />
<meta name="description"
  content="An account of the life and works of Sir Isaac Newton, written in 1814" />
```

The description is sometimes shown alongside search results or in directories.

The idea of keywords is that when someone searches for one of the words or phrases you give, they will find your web page, even if the keywords do not appear elsewhere in the document.

Unfortunately, these two headers are widely abused. Therefore, if you use more than ten keywords, your page will probably be downgraded in search results on the grounds that it's likely to be a fake web page with ads on it. However, there's some evidence that current search engines *do* take note of the `description` and `keywords` headers.

Finally, here's an example of a proprietary header: Pinterest is a website that enables people to upload pictures that are of interest to them. Because of copyright and terms-of-use concerns, web publishers can opt out of Pinterest using the following header on every page:

```
<meta name="pinterest" content="nopin" />
```

If you use Google AdSense or Yahoo ads, you will be asked to add a meta header to your homepage to show the page is yours. If you look at the source of homepages of large commercial websites, you will probably see quite a lot more examples of meta headers.

The Document Title: The <title> Element

The document title is used in bookmarks, browser history, window title bars or tab labels, and other places where a web page has to be named. It is a plain string: it cannot contain any elements, which limits its usefulness for mathematical documents (no formulas!) and for Japanese or Chinese (no ruby annotations).

Although the items in the document head can appear in any order, the character set and the title should normally be the first two, and in that order so that the title can be interpreted correctly, like so:

```
<title>Isaac Newton - his life and works (1814)</title>
```

The title is often truncated in user interfaces — for example, if a browser tab is too narrow — so it's a good idea to put the most important information at the beginning. If you want to identify your website in the title, do so at the end, because otherwise all the web pages from your website will have the same prefix, which may be all that the user sees!

Every XHTML document should have a title, even if the document does not contain any headings or is an intermediate page.

Linking to External Resources: The <link> Element

Use the XHTML <link> element to connect your web page to other files and documents. This is not a hyperlink: users don't get to see any of the document head directly, and that includes link elements, so they won't be clicking these links. Instead, these are links to style sheets, scripts, icons, and other supporting resources that make up the web page.

Using JavaScript and CSS: The <script> and <style> Elements

See Chapter 16 for details of JavaScript; you learn more about the <style> element later in this chapter.

The XHTML <body> Element

The <body> element contains the actual text of the document. This section looks at some of the most important elements you can use in an XHTML document, and then shows you how to control the appearance of the document using cascading style sheets (CSS). After you've tried it out, you go through more of the elements with some of the more commonly used techniques for styling them.

WARNING *The HTML specification is several hundred pages long; CSS is also very large. The goal of this chapter is to show you how XML, XHTML, and HTML fit together, and to you teach enough to get started and be able to learn from other resources. A complete description of HTML, CSS, JavaScript, and how to use them requires an entire bookshelf! Most people learn just enough HTML, CSS, and JavaScript to do what they need and search the web when they need more, perhaps keeping some reference books by their side. But after working through this chapter, you'll have started the journey!*

Listing 17-1 shows a complete, if not very interesting, XHTML 1.1 document.

LISTING 17-1: Isaac Newton in XHTML.html

Available for download on Wrox.com

```
<!DOCTYPE html PUBLIC "-//W3C//DTD XHTML 1.0 Strict//EN"
    "http://www.w3.org/TR/xhtml1/DTD/xhtml1-strict.dtd">
<html xmlns="http://www.w3.org/1999/xhtml" lang="en-UK" xml:lang="en-UK">
 <head>
  <meta http-equiv="Content-Type" content="text/html; charset=utf-8" />
  <title>Newton, Isaac: Life and Works</title>
 </head>
 <body>
   <h1>Sir Isaac Newton</h1>
   <p>Isaac Newton was born at a very young age,
   had a brief but unsuccessful career as an apple picker,
   and later died.</p>
 </body>
</html>
```

Figure 17-2 shows the result of loading this XHTML file in three different web browsers: Google Chrome (Chromium), Dillo (a very simple and fast web browser), and Lynx (a text-only web browser running in a terminal emulator). In the two graphical browsers (rear left and right) the contents of the HTML `<title>` element was used for the window title, along with the browser name. Lynx (lower front left) does not use windows directly, and did not attempt to set the terminal's window title. Similarly, the fonts and text sizes differ between the browsers. However, the document is recognizably the same in all three cases.

NOTE *If you download any of the HTML files in this chapter, you may need to use your web browser's View Source feature (it's usually in the File or View menu), or open the file in a text editor, to see the actual HTML markup.*

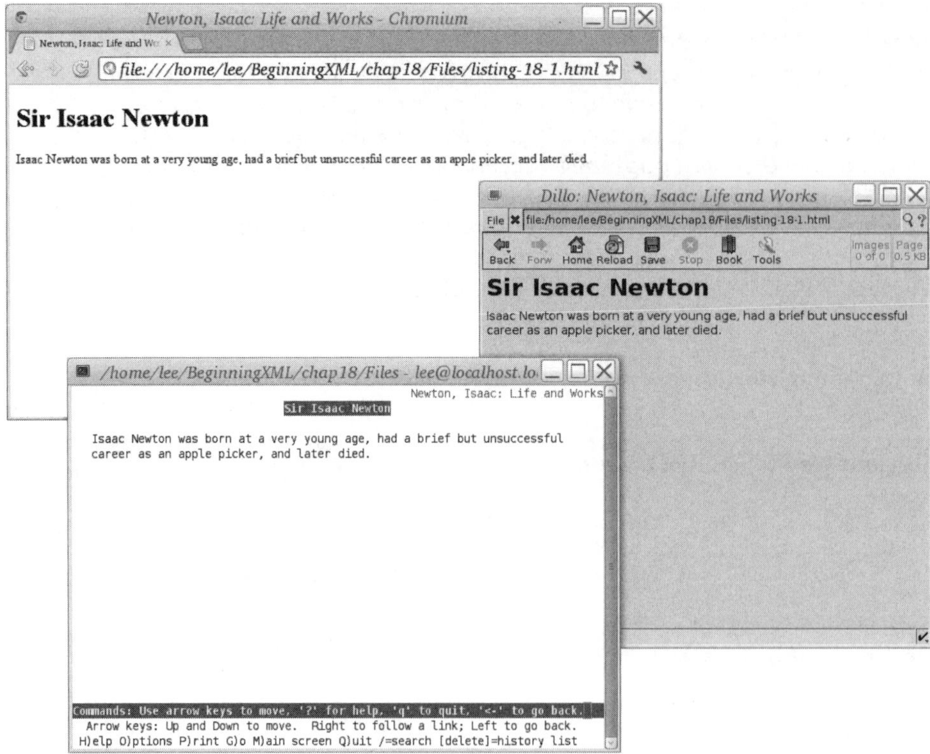

FIGURE 17-2

Your goal in making web pages should not be to get the page to look identical in every browser, but rather to make a page that will convey the right information.

In the following sections you learn about the things you can put inside the HTML `<body>` element (such as the `<h1>` and `<p>` elements shown in Listing 17-1), but first, you need to validate your XML document against its DTD, and to do that you need an XML Catalog file.

Using an XML Catalog File for Local Validation

One of the first problems you'll run into if you try to work with XHTML documents using XML tools is that you can't validate your documents against the DTD files from the W3C website, `http://www.w3.org`, W3C restricts DTD traffic because so many programs try to download the files.

The solution to this is to make a local copy of the DTD files and to use an XML Catalog to tell XML software to use your local copies instead of going to `www.w3.org` for them.

Listing 17-2 shows a complete XML Catalog file for this purpose; it assumes that the DTD files are in a subfolder called `dtds`. Note that the forward slash (`/`) is used in the filenames, even on Windows, because they are really URLs. You can use any name you like for the file, but `catalog.xml` or `xhtml-catalog.xml` might be good choices.

Available for download on Wrox.com

LISTING 17-2: samplexmlcatalog.xml

```
<catalog prefer="public" xmlns="urn:oasis:names:tc:entity:xmlns:xml:catalog">
  <system systemId="http://www.w3.org/TR/xhtml1/DTD/xhtml1-strict.dtd "
          uri="dtds/xhtml1-strict.dtd"/>

  <public publicId="-//W3C//DTD XHTML 1.0 Strict//EN"
          uri="dtds/xhtml1-strict.dtd"/>

  <public publicId="-//W3C//DTD XHTML 1.0 Transitional//EN"
          uri="dtds/xhtml1-transitional.dtd"/>

  <public publicId="-//W3C//DTD XHTML 1.0 Frameset//EN"
          uri="dtds/xhtml1-frameset.dtd"/>

  <public publicId="-//W3C//ENTITIES Latin 1 for XHTML//EN"
          uri="dtds/xhtml-lat1.ent"/>

  <public publicId="-//W3C//ENTITIES Symbols for XHTML//EN"
          uri="dtds/xhtml-symbol.ent"/>

  <public publicId="-//W3C//ENTITIES Special for XHTML//EN"
          uri="dtds/xhtml-special.ent"/>
</catalog>
```

You can use an XML Catalog with most XML tools; here is an example of using the catalog with the `xmllint` program in a Linux shell:

```
$ export SGML_CATALOG_FILES=$HOME/lib/xmlcatalog/catalog.xml
$ xmllint --noout --valid --loaddtd --catalogs listing-17-1.html
$
```

The first line sets the shell variable `$GML_CATALOG_FILES` to the name of the XML Catalog file; you will have to use the actual filename you created, of course.

The second line runs the `xmllint` program with no output (except error messages, if any exist), telling it to check validity, to load the DTD files, and to use the XML Catalog file named by the `$SGML_CATALOG_FILES` variable.

***NOTE** The `xmllint` command is very useful because most web servers run the GNU/Linux operating system, Solaris, FreeBSD, or another Unix or Unix-like operating system on which the `xmllint` program is likely to be preinstalled. You can also configure Saxon, oXygen, and other programs to use catalogs.*

You can also check your HTML file online at `http://validator.w3.org/`, but you will still want the XML Catalog for use with XSLT or other XML tools.

Paragraphs, Block Quotes, and Headings

Paragraphs, block quotes, and headings are all *block-level* elements: they are rendered by web browsers starting on a new line and with blank space above and below them.

The `<p>` element is used to contain a logical paragraph; a browser might display the first line indented, or put a blank line between paragraphs.

The `<blockquote>` element is intended to contain a long quotation, and is normally rendered indented, with a left margin; it contains block-level elements such as paragraphs, lists, and even block quotes.

Do not use paragraphs or block quotes just for formatting: if you want an indented block of text (that's not really a logical paragraph), use a `<div>` element as described later in this chapter. If you want a paragraph that's formatted slightly differently from other paragraphs, give it a class attribute and use CSS, as described in the "Cascading Style Sheets (CSS)" section later in this chapter.

Paragraphs can only contain phrase-level markup and text; block quotes can contain block-level elements.

For headings you use `<h1>` for the most important heading in the document. This is often the same as the `<title>` element but doesn't need to be; `<h1>` can contain phrase-level markup, whereas `<title>` is a plain string. There's usually only one `<h1>` element in an HTML document.

For the next most important heading you use `<h2>`, and there can be any number of these. Then there's `<h3>`, `<h4>`, and so on. If you find yourself wanting anything over `<h5>` or `<h6>`, you should ask yourself how the reader will keep track, and maybe split the document into multiple web pages, the body of each starting with an `<h1>` element.

If you're used to more traditional XML vocabularies such as DocBook or the Text Encoding Initiative, you may be wondering whether there's a container around each section. No container is required. HTML 5 supplies a `<section>` element for this purpose, but older versions of HTML and XHTML do not have such a thing. The headings are interspersed between paragraphs and it's a flat structure. You can have an `<h3>` directly followed by an `<h6>` if you like.

If this sounds too chaotic, you can use `<div>` elements as if they were sections as shown in the following snippet. The `<div>` element is explained in more detail in the "Generic <div> and <span> Elements" section later in this chapter.

```
<div class="section">
  <h2>His Life As An Apple Picker</h2>
  <p>After leaving school, young Isaac was very poor,
  and had no mobile 'phone or shoes, so he picked apples.</p>
</div>
```

Using `<div>` elements in this way can make processing your XHTML documents with XQuery or XHTML much easier, and can also help with styling, as you learn in the section "Cascading Style Sheets."

Lists

A *list* is a sequence of related items, perhaps numbered, or perhaps with a bullet at the start of each item. You can use CSS to turn numbering on or off, or to change the shape of the bullet. You can also turn off list-like rendering with CSS; this is most commonly used when you're making a drop-down menu effect. You mark up the data as a list so that a non-CSS-aware browser will still show something reasonable, but then you use CSS to turn off the list bullets and indents, and to add borders, making something that looks like a user-interface component.

Use `<ol>` for an ordered (that is, numbered) list, and `<ul>` for an unordered bulleted list. Of course, the web browser always presents the list items in the order they were found in the document; ordered/unordered is just an obscure way to say whether the items are numbered. Lists of either sort contain zero or more list items, marked up with `<li>` elements.

You can also have *definition lists* — showing the origin of HTML as a language for computer documentation! A definition list uses `<dl>` as the container, `<dt>` for terms to be defined, and `<dd>` for the definitions.

List items can only contain block-level elements such as `<p>`, `<blockquote>`, and `<ol>`, and not text or `<li>` elements. The only exception is that you can have `<li>` elements inside an `<ol>` or `<ul>` that's inside an `<li>` element.

If you wanted to format the preceding paragraphs in this section as a bulleted list, you would mark it up like this:

```
<ul>
  <li>
    <p>A <i>list</i> is . . . </p>
  </li>
  <li>
    <p>Use &lt;ol&gt; for . . .</p>
  </li>
  . . .
</ul>
```

NOTE *To help you remember, notice that* `ol` *stands for ordered list,* `ul` *stands for unordered list, and* `dl` *stands for definition list.*

Hypertext Links

The best-known HTML element is probably the `<a>` element; "a" is short for *anchor*, a term in HyperText meaning one end or another of a link. In its simplest form a link is just an `<a>` element around some text like so:

```
<a href="http://www.fromoldbooks.org/">my web site</a>
```

The `href` attribute contains a *URI reference*; that is, a web address. A web browser will follow this link when you click (or activate) the link.

The URI reference part means you can put a *fragment identifier* after the URL, separated from it by a hash (`#`), and the browser will search for an element in the target document having that identifier (without the `#`), and scroll to that location. See the following code snippet:

```
<a href="http://www.example.org/staff.html#daniel">More about Daniel</a>
```

When you click this link, your browser will load the `staff.html` document and search for a `name="daniel"` or `id="daniel"` attribute; if it finds one, it will scroll the view to make that visible.

NOTE *Most web browsers will highlight links, usually by coloring them blue and underlining them (because that is what an early web browser from NCSA called "Mosaic" used to do). Browsers show links differently if you have visited the destination recently and also sometimes when the link is* active, *meaning, for example, you clicked it but the browser hasn't yet gone there.*

An `<a>` element with a `name` attribute is a potential target for a link. An example is shown here as it might appear in the `staff.html` file mentioned in the previous example:

```
<a name="daniel">Daniel is the grand vizier of Shemyaza.</a>
```

WARNING *Although XHTML uses the* `id` *attribute name on various elements, and browsers will indeed find them, many users will put values in them that are not, in fact, legal XML (or SGML) ID values. An SGML or XML ID value must start with a (Unicode) letter and then contain only name characters: letters, digits, hyphens, dots, and underscores. If you are generating XHTML for use with XML tools, you should make sure that your ID attribute values are legal.*

Here's a slightly longer example:

```
<a href="liam.html" title="Author of this chapter" rel="author">About Liam</a>
```

The content of the `title` attribute here will usually be used to make a *tooltip* when a mouse pointer hovers over the link; this is a poor design because you can't put element markup inside attribute values, but this is the way it is.

You can also indicate the relationship between the web page containing the link and the link destination, using the `rel` attribute; this is not often done in practice, but some specialist applications use it.

One common use of the `rel` attribute is to add `rel="nofollow"` to your links. This is a proprietary value for the `rel` attribute introduced by Google, and it indicates that you do not endorse the target page. What does that mean? When Google's search engine displays search results, it tends to favor web pages that have a lot of links pointing to them. This is called Google's *pagerank* algorithm, and although these days it is only one of more than 200 factors Google takes into account when generating search results, the advantage of being linked to is still high enough that people are willing to pay for links to their websites selling somewhat dubious services (the sleazy side of the Web). If Google finds that you link to such a site, it will downgrade *your* web page, or even remove you from its search results altogether. Adding `rel="nofollow"` to a link indicates that you don't want it to affect search result placement, perhaps because the link came from user-supplied content such as a forum posting on your website.

Additionally, you can include any mixture of text and phrase-level markup inside an <a> element. *Phrase-level markup*, unlike block-level markup, does not begin and end on a new line, but just affects part of a sentence or paragraph. Some examples of phrase-level markup include emphasis, inline images, formatting, and of course the <a> element, as in the following example:

```
<p>All about <a href="liam.html">Liam <em>and</em> his nice clean socks</a>.
```

The `href` value here, `liam.html`, is a *relative URI reference*: it does not begin with a URI scheme such as `http:` or `file:` and does not start with a `/`. The web browser will look for the resource in the same place it got the resource containing the link, and will use the same method (for example, HTTP, FTP) to fetch it. This lets you move whole trees of documents around without changing them, or publish a website from your own computer to a server, perhaps using a remote file copy program such as *ftp* or (more securely) *rsync* or *scp* over the secure shell, *ssh*.

Images

The ability to mix text, images, and links in one document is one of the things that helped the World Wide Web succeed in its early days. Soon after, images of a particularly intimate nature were, for a while, the driving force of Web commerce. We are past that today: the Web has matured considerably, but images are still very important.

An image can be the subject of a web page or an image can be part of the *page background*, perhaps providing texture like old paper or a canvas, so that the contents of the page overwrite the image. Images are also used for page components such as borders, buttons, and decoration. Finally, images can be used as part of corporate branding or marketing, including organizational logos.

You have three main ways to include images in your web pages:

- Using the HTML <img> element. This is described shortly.
- Using cascading style sheets (CSS); see the section on CSS later in this chapter.
- Using SVG markup in the document; see Chapter 18, "Scalable Vector Graphics (SVG)."

To include an image in your web page using the HTML <img> element you write something like this:

```
<p>Daniel's socks: <img src="argyle.jpg" alt="picture of blue and yellow argyle
socks" /></a>.
```

The `src` attribute (pronounced *source*) indicates where the image comes from; as with the <a> element, it can be a relative URI, although the fragment identifier is not currently used.

The `alt` attribute contains a short textual description of the image.

WARNING *When you are including images you must remember that not everyone can see them in the same way. Some people will have difficulty seeing fine details in images; others will see colors differently than you, and some won't be able to see at all. Laws exist about making web pages accessible, and about not discriminating against people based on their abilities, so even if it were not a moral imperative to be as inclusive as possible, it can become a legal imperative.*

When an image is an important part of a web page, you must include a short piece of text to be used as an alternative to the image. If necessary you can also link to a longer description, either using a `longdesc` attribute containing a URI, or, more commonly, with a letter `D` linked to the description, and perhaps hidden by default using CSS.

NOTE *The `<img>` element is empty: it does not have any content. In XML the tag needs to end with `/>`, but this is a syntax error in HTML. To get around this, put a space before the `/>` — it's still technically an error, but it works in all browsers.*

Loading Images More Quickly

Images will appear to load much faster if you include `width` and `height` attributes on your `<img>` elements; the result is also less disruptive to the user. This is because the browser will leave space for the image. In the following example the picture is presumably a JPEG image 700 pixels wide and 900 pixels high:

```
<img src="argyle.jpg" alt="picture of blue and yellow argyle socks" width="700"
height="900" />
```

WARNING *Make sure you use the* actual *pixel width and height for images. If you give a different size the browser will scale the image to fit, but this can look very bad. If you try to make a thumbnail-sized picture of a large image this way, users still have to wait for the whole image to download before they can see the thumbnail. Image sizes mentioned in `height` and `width` attributes must always be measured in pixels, not in other units such as inches.*

Because XSLT and XQuery do not give access to image sizes, XML-based content management systems have to provide some way to communicate the information. Some systems do this with calls to external functions; some simply encode the image size in the filename (`argyle-socks-700x900.jpg`); and others store image meta data in a separate database.

You can find out the size of the image using the `identify` command (part of the ImageMagick package) on many systems, including most Linux servers.

If your images files are particularly large and slow to download, you can include an alternate image by putting its URI in the `lowsrc` attribute; some browsers will load this first and display it while the larger image is loading.

Images and Links

The obvious way to make an image link to another web page is this:

```
<p>
  <a href="newton-sir-isaac.html">Read more:
    <img src="isaac-newton-300x310.jpg"
         alt="Sir Isaac Newton" width="300" height="310" />
  </a>
</p>
```

Although this is technically correct, the result of adding this to the Isaac Newton biography from Listing 17-1 is shown in in Figure 17-3. Notice the underlined space after the "Read more:" — that comes from the spaces between the text and the `<img>` tag. With some older browsers you'll also see an irritating blue border around the image. You can get rid of this border in HTML using the `border="0"` attribute, but the approved way is to use CSS; you learn about that later in this chapter, but for now you could add a CSS `style` attribute to the `<img>` element to get rid of the blue border. That still leaves the underlined space; you could get rid of that by changing the markup so that the space isn't inside an `<a>` element like so:

```
<p>
  <a href="newton-sir-isaac.html">Read more:</a>
  <a href="newton-sir-isaac.html"><img src="isaac-newton-300x310.jpg"
         style="border: 0;"
         alt="Sir Isaac Newton" width="300" height="310" /></a>
</p>
```

FIGURE 17-3

NOTE *Notice that the bottom of the image in Figure 17-3 is lined up with the baseline of the text saying "Read more." You will see how to change this using CSS in the section on cascading style sheets later in this chapter.*

Image Formats

The most common image formats used on the Web are shown in Table 17-1.

TABLE 17-1: Common Image Formats Supported by Web Browsers

FORMAT	DESCRIPTION
GIF (8-bit)	Can be animated, but as implemented generally supports only a limited "web-safe" palette of 256 colors, one of which can be used for transparency. For most uses of GIF today, except animation, PNG is preferred.
PNG	Open format defined by the IETF and W3C; has lossless compression and supports 256 levels of transparency. Internet Explorer 6 needs an add-on such as CSS3 PIE to handle transparent PNG images properly, but despite this PNG is very commonly used.
JPEG	This format is *lossy*: if you convert an image from PNG to JPEG, you will lose some detail, and the colors may change slightly. If you convert back to PNG the lost detail is not restored. Excessive levels of JPEG compression tend to introduce visible fringes so you need to check image files carefully, and always keep a copy of your images in some other format. If you *start* with a JPEG image, for example from a digital camera, save your work in PNG as well as in JPEG at the end, because there is a loss in quality every time you open a JPEG file and save it again.

People use JPEG images more on the Web because they are typically much smaller in file size than PNG for a given image size in pixels, and this means they get downloaded more quickly.
See Chapter 18 for more on SVG.

You may encounter some other image formats, including TIFF (mostly on the Mac) or BMP (mostly on Windows), as well as proprietary or application-specific formats such as Adobe Photoshop files (PSD) or The GIMP's save files (XCF), but most web browsers can only be relied upon to display JPEG, PNG, and GIF.

Inline Emphasis and Formatting Elements

So far all of the text you have seen has been pretty plain; links were underlined, but that's as far as it went.

HTML supports a number of *inline elements*, also called *phrase-level elements*, both to add meaning and for stylistic purposes. You've already read about some of these in this chapter. You should use the semantic elements where they are available rather than the formatting elements: for example, it's better to use <em> for emphasis rather than <i> for italics, because then a text reader can use different inflection in its auto-generated voice. However, you should not use <em> if the italics are for some purpose *other* than emphasis. The word *other* in the previous sentence is an example of emphasis; the italics used for *inline elements* and *phrase-level elements* at the start of this paragraph signify a keyword, and are not emphasis. For those you might use this: <i class="keyword">inline elements</i>.

NOTE *If you are transcribing a document you didn't write, and the author is not available to answer questions, you should not normally try to add semantics; if you don't know why a particular word is in italics, just use* <i> *rather than guessing.*

Table 17-2 shows most of the more common phrase-level elements in HTML that are used for formatting. Note that not all elements are available in all versions of the HTML DTDs.

TABLE 17-2: Some Inline HTML Elements Associated with Formatting

ELEMENT	DESCRIPTION	EXAMPLE
abbr	An abbreviation; also used for acronyms	<abbr title="adjective">adj.</abbr>
b	Bold (other than strong emphasis or headings)	Vol <b>3</b> No. 6.
big	Bigger text	I want to say <big>I love you</big>
dfn	A single word or phrase being defined	A <dfn>sock</dfn> is a covering for the foot, often made of milk custard.
em	Emphasis, usually italicized	He was <em>very</em> nervous
i	Italics, other than emphasis	She was an <i lang="la">ex post facto</i> standard!
q	A quote; use CSS to add quote marks	She said <q>Take off your boots</q>
small	Smaller text; use CSS instead	<small>By reading this text you agree...</small>
strike, s	Strikethrough, crossed-out text	This is <s>wrong</s>.
strong	Strong emphasis, shouting, often displayed in bold	The sock was <strong>extremely</strong> dangerous.
sub	Subscript	<i>x</i>_j (x_j)
sup	Superscript	e = mc² ($e = mc^2$)
tt	Typewriter text	<tt>dear archie, I am typing this letter...</tt>
u	Underline, but not a link	See <u>The Journal Of Ankle Coverings</u> for July 1895

Generic <div> and <span> Elements

When you need to produce a particular formatting effect with HTML, but it's not about semantics, or if there is no built-in semantics close to what you want, you can use the `<div>` and `<span>` elements. The `<div>` element can contain any mix of text, phrase-level elements, and block-level elements, including more `<div>` elements. The `<span>` element is a phrase-level element and can contain text and other phrase-level elements (including, of course, more `<span>` elements).

You can use the class attribute to attempt to impart meaning to your HTML source code; this will generally be of more use to you in maintaining the markup than to anyone else, but as you see soon, the class attributes are also used by CSS. If you have read Chapter 16, "AJAX" already you'll also recall that jQuery uses class attributes in constructs like this:

```
$("div.sock-weaving-pattern").css("background-color: grey;");
```

to match:

```
<div class="sock-weaving-pattern">. . .</div>
```

The `<div>` and `<span>` elements are used extensively in almost every modern web page, partly because they are free from the baggage of history and are not weighed down with existing style rules that might vary from browser to browser, and partly because they're the closest HTML ever got to user-defined elements.

More Advanced HTML Topics

Because this book is really about XML and not HTML, it's time to move on a little faster. The following sections provide you with just enough of an idea about some other HTML tools to pique your interest so that you can learn more.

HTML Forms

Use the HTML `<form>` element along with its children to generate buttons, controls, and areas where users can enter text or upload files. See Chapter 16 for a simple example of an HTML form.

HTML and JavaScript

Refer back to Chapter 16 for an introduction to the JavaScript language, jQuery, and AJAX.

HTML and Accessibility

If you become involved with professional web development you will need to dive into accessibility feet first, perhaps with one of the many books on the topic.

The high-level view is that anyone, regardless of physical abilities, must be able to use your web pages. If you design your pages using the semantic elements like `<h1>`, `<p>`, `<em>`, and `<strong>`, there's a good chance they will be easy to make very accessible indeed. Visit `http://www.w3.org/WAI/` for lots of helpful articles, resources, tutorials, and testing tools for web accessibility.

Of course, the devil is in the details. Make sure your `<img>` elements have `alt` attributes (if the image is decorative, give it `alt=""` rather than leave off the `alt` attribute: this reassures readers that they aren't missing something). Don't use HTML tables for layout when you could use CSS. Try to use flexible layouts, not fixed-width layouts, and make sure people can do everything on your web page from the keyboard.

XHTML AND HTML: PROBLEMS AND WORKAROUNDS

Most HTML on the web is not even close to being syntactically correct, so there was never any hope of replacing HTML with XML or XHTML, as some people thought was the intent.

One difficulty is that the XML specification forbids applications from claiming that a data stream was a well-formed XML document if it contains errors. The web browser makers interpret this as meaning the web browser should not display the document at all if it contained errors. In fact, a fix-up is perfectly fine in this situation and allowed *as long as you let the user know*. An error message in the browser's developer console would be enough. In practice, this situation means that XHTML, unlike HTML, is very unforgiving of errors.

Another difficulty is that if you serve XHTML documents with the correct Internet media type (MIME Content Type) of `application/html+xml`, older versions of Internet Explorer will not display the document but instead will prompt the user to save it to a file! As a result, it's best to serve XHTML documents as `text/html`.

Some people use "browser sniffing" to serve different documents to IE users; others use a simple trick with client-side XSLT in the browser to fix the problem, but this turns out to have other difficulties, not least of which is that it makes the resulting web pages hard to debug.

Because the syntax of HTML and of XML is slightly different, you have to do some special tricks to get the XHTML to work properly. You can find more details on these at `http://www.w3.org/TR/xhtml1/#guidelines` on the W3C website, but a few of the most important ones are listed here:

- Avoid using the XML declaration or processing instructions; this means you must use UTF-8 or UTF-16 for your files and make sure they are served correctly.
- Put a space at the end of empty element tags: `<br />` rather than `<br/>`.
- Do not use close tags for empty elements, even though XML allows this; `<br><br/>` in HTML does not do what you might expect.
- Avoid inline style sheets or JavaScript; refer to external files instead.
- Do not rely on being able to include newlines in attribute values.
- Use both `xml:lang` and `lang` attributes to specify language.
- The `'` XML entity does not work reliably in HTML; use `'` instead.

If you are using XSLT or XQuery to generate XHTML, you will need to make sure you enable the appropriate serialization options to make this work. You may need to check the documentation of the XQuery or XSLT system you use in order to learn how to set the serialization options.

The XHTML Working Group at W3C went on to define a much more sophisticated version of XHTML, XHTML 2, but it did not get the necessary support in web browsers.

As a result, work on XHTML at W3C ended, and the XML representation of HTML 5 took over. XHTML 1 is still widely useful in its own right, and, as you see later in this chapter, HTML 5 keeps most of the same ideas. First, though, you need to look at cascading style sheets, and also at Unobtrusive JavaScript, so that you have more of the background you'll need.

CASCADING STYLE SHEETS (CSS)

Cascading style sheets are a mechanism to associate formatting with HTML or XML markup. A *style sheet* is simply a name for a set of rules for formatting a document; the *cascading* part is that several such style sheets get combined to format an HTML document, and the cascading rules determine how the styles are merged. Most modern web browsers let authors have their own style sheet, which is merged with that of the document author.

As you read in the first part of this chapter, most HTML elements already have styles associated with them. The `<em>` element is usually rendered in italics, and `<h1>` headings usually appear in larger text, possibly a different font, and in bold. Unfortunately, the default styles were created by computer programmers with no experience in graphic design or typography, and, as a result, they are not very appropriate. Luckily, you can override them with CSS.

CSS Levels and Versions

CSS has four "levels": CSS 1, CSS 2.1, CSS 3, and CSS 4. CSS Level 2 second edition is the odd ball that is (confusingly) called CSS 2.1, but it has the best support. CSS 3 introduces many new features but is less widely supported. CSS 4 is new and not yet defined, and because CSS 3 is not yet finished, CSS 4 won't be available for a while, but now at least if someone mentions it you can guess what they're talking about. You can find out more about the different levels at `http://www.w3.org/Style/`. This chapter mostly talks about CSS 2.1, with occasional mention of CSS 3 features.

Individual web browsers also support features of their own, and sometimes support features that have been proposed for CSS but that are not yet standardized. Such features are given a *vendor prefix* so you know you've left the safety of the boardwalk, and are well into walking-on-broken-glass territory. Mozilla Firefox uses `-mozilla-` as a prefix, Apple Safari and Google Chrome (both based on a browser toolkit called WebKit) use `-webkit-`, Opera uses `-o-`, and Internet Explorer tends to stick to standards.

WARNING *CSS is evolving rapidly, and support for some of the more advanced features of CSS is not available in all web browsers. Internet Explorer Version 6 is the best-known browser that has incomplete support for CSS 2.1 selectors; for CSS 3 you have to be using IE 9 or later, and Opera doesn't work in all cases (as of June 2012). See* `http://www.quirksmode.org/css/contents.html` *or* `http://www.caniuse.com` *for more information.*

CSS at a Glance

Cascading style sheets are collections of *rules*, and each rule is made of a *selector* and a *declaration*. Here is a rule with a CSS selector to match any `<h1>` element in the document; it sets the color of text inside the heading to blue and also adds a margin at the top of the heading:

```
h1 {
    color: blue;
    margin-top: 300px;
}
```

The selector in the example is `h1` and the declaration is inside the curly braces. Inside the declaration are two *properties*, `color` and `margin-top`, together with values for them. The semicolon separates the individual property-value pairs, but it turns out to be easier to remember and edit if you always put a semicolon after every value.

You can put the style rules into the document or into a separate file. If you put them in the document some very old browsers will display the styles rather than using them, so it's usually best just to put them in a separate file. If you have more than one web page using the same CSS file, your site will work faster if the CSS is in a separate file, too.

In the following activity you use some basic CSS to work through an example.

TRY IT OUT Some Simple CSS

In this exercise you expand on the example from Listing 17-1 earlier in this chapter, edit it very slightly, and add some styles in a separate file. Remember to keep the web browser's console window open as you work so that you can see if you make mistakes; see Chapter 16 for more information about the browser console.

1. Make a new text file called `NewtonWithCSS.html` containing the following HTML markup:

```
<!DOCTYPE html PUBLIC "-//W3C//DTD XHTML 1.0 Strict//EN"
    "http://www.w3.org/TR/xhtml1/DTD/xhtml1-strict.dtd">
<html xmlns="http://www.w3.org/1999/xhtml" lang="en-UK" xml:lang="en-UK">
  <head>
    <meta http-equiv="Content-Type" content="text/html; charset=utf-8" />
    <title>Newton, Isaac: Life and Works</title>
    <link rel="stylesheet" type="text/css" href="newton.css" />
  </head>
  <body>
    <h1>Sir Isaac Newton</h1>
    <p class="intro"><img src="isaac-newton-150x155.jpg"
    alt="Sir Isaac Newton" width="150" height="155"
    style="float: left;" />Newton, Sir Isaac, the most splendid genius that has
    yet adorned human nature, and by universal consent placed at the head of
    mathematics and of science, was born on Christmas-day, O. S. 1642, at
    Woolsthorpe, in the parish of Colsterworth, in the county of Lincoln.  When
    born he was so little that his mother used to say he might have been put
    into a quart mug, and so unlikely to live that two women who were sent to
    lady Pakenham's, at North Witham, for something for him, did not expect to
    find him alive at their return.</p>
```

```
    <p>He was born near three months after the death of his father,
    who was descended from the eldest branch of the family of sir
    John Newton, bart. and was lord of the manor of Woolsthorpe.  The
    family came originally from Newton, in the county of Lancaster, from which,
    probably, they took their name.  His mother was Hannah Ayscough, of an
    ancient and honourable family in the county of Lincoln. She was married a
    second time to the rev. Barnabas Smith, rector of North Witham, a rich old
    bachelor, and had by him a son and two daughters.</p>
  </body>
</html>
```

NewtonWithCSS.html

Be careful to note the added line that links to `newton.css` for the styles.

2. Type the following file, and call it `newton.css` (you can use a different name as long as you change the HTML file accordingly). Make sure you save it as a plaintext (UTF-8) file.

```
body {
    background: #fff;
    color: #000;
    margin-left: 1em;
}

h1 {
    font-family: "Origins", "Palatino", "Book Antiqua",serif;
    font-weight: normal;
    font-size: 64pt;
    margin-top: 24pt;
    line-height: 120%;
    margin-bottom: -24pt;
}

p.intro {
    color: #666;
}

p.intro:first-line {
    font-variant: small-caps;
}

p {
    max-width: 25em;
    margin-left: 100px;
    margin-right: auto;
}

p img {
    display: block;
    float: left;
    margin-left: -73px;
    margin-right: 3px;
}
```

newton.css

(Be careful to use a space in `p img`, and to have a dot in `p.intro`, and to use American spelling for `color`.)

3. Navigate to the HTML file and load it; unlike the examples in Chapter 16 you can load this file directly from your computer's hard drive. The result should look more or less like Figure 17-4. You probably won't have the same font for the heading, but you should see the other formatting.

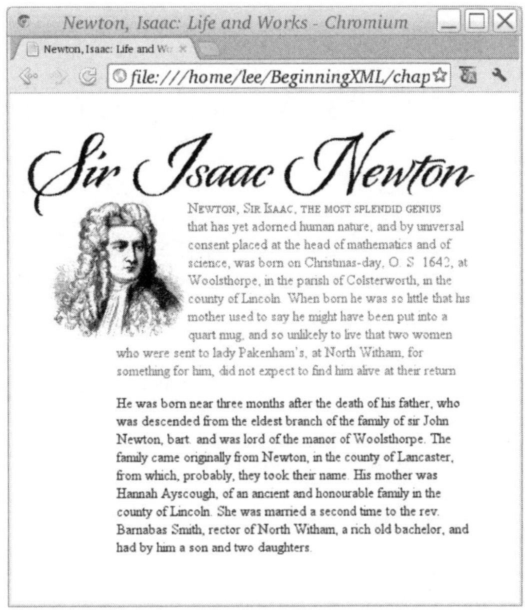

FIGURE 17-4

How It Works

The first CSS rule is for the HTML `<body>` element. It sets the background color to `#fff`. CSS color values refer to red, green, and blue levels, respectively. They usually have either three hexadecimal digits (as here) or six. `#abc` is the same as `#aabbcc` in CSS, so `#fff` is the same as `#ffffff`, and means that red, green, and blue all have the maximum value of `ff` in hexadecimal (255 in decimal notation). When red, green, and blue are all the same, you get a grey. When they are all zero you get black, and when they are all `ff` you get white, so `#fff` or `#ffffff` sets the background to white. If you prefer you could type **`white`** or maybe **`yellow`** instead, like this:

```
background: yellow;
```

After setting the background, the rule for `<body>` sets the text color to `#000`, which of course is `#000000` or black. Although this is a common default users can change it, and so if you set either the text or background color you need to set both colors, to avoid users with (say) a black default browser background from seeing black text on a black background. Remember to choose colors that contrast well so that older people (or people with less-then-perfect vision) can still read your page.

The final part of the `<body>` style sets a left margin of one `em`: that is, one unit equal to the font size in effect, which here will be the browser's default.

The remaining rules are explained in the rest of this chapter, but for now you should notice how a relatively sophisticated style can be achieved fairly easily.

CSS Selectors

You've seen some examples of CSS selectors in the previous section and in the Try It Out. Selectors are patterns that identify one or more elements in a document. They are like a quirky and less powerful version of XPath, and were developed independently, but they do have a lot in common.

Recall that CSS rules have a selector and then a set of property-value pairs in braces; the properties are set to the values you give on every element that matches the selector.

NOTE *HTML element names are not case sensitive, so you can use either uppercase or lowercase for them in selectors;* `H1 { color: blue; }` *and* `h1 { color: blue; }` *do the same thing. You should leave the property names in lowercase, however.*

XML names are case sensitive, so the selector must match the document. For XHTML the element names must be in lowercase, so it's best to use lowercase element names in CSS too.

Table 17-3 shows the different CSS selectors you can use.

TABLE 17-3: CSS Selectors

CSS SELECTOR	DESCRIPTION	EXAMPLES
element type	The name of an HTML element	`p`
`*`	Any single element	`*`
`B > A`	Any A element that is a direct child if a B element (like the XPath expression B/A)	`p > span > a`
`B + A`	Any A elements when immediately preceded by a B element	`blockquote + p` matches a `<p>` element immediately after a `<blockquote>` element
`[attr]`	Matches on attribute *presence*	`a[name]`
`A[attr="value"]`	Matches any A elements having an attribute called `attr` whose value is exactly equal to *value*	`img[alt="argyle socks"]`
`A[attr~="value"]`	Matches any A elements whose `attr` attribute contains a word equal to *value*, where words are separated by spaces	`div[class~="navigation"]`
`A[lang|="lang"]`	Language-specific matching	`div[lang|="en"]`
`A.word`	Matches any A element whose class attribute contains the given word	`div.navigation` would match `<div class="navigation redbg">...`
`A#id`	Matches the first A element (or all A elements) having the given id value	`div#topbar` to match `<div id="topbar">...`

CSS SELECTOR	DESCRIPTION	EXAMPLES
`A:first-child`	Any A elements that are the first child (not counting whitespace) of their parents	`li:first-child`
`A:link, A:visited, A:active, A:hover, A:focus`	Matches an unvisited link, a visited one, an active link, an element when the mouse pointer is over it, and an element ready to accept keyboard input	`a:visited { color: purple; }` `img:hover`
`A:lang(lang)`	Any A elements in language *lang*	`a:lang(en)`
`A:first-line`	A *pseudo-element* matching the first formatted line of content	`p:first-line`
`A:first-letter`	A *pseudo-element* matching the first letter of content, if it is at the very start of the element	`p:first-letter`
`A:before, A:after`	*Pseudo-elements* considered to occur immediately before, or after, the A element's content	`div.caption:before`
`A, B, C`	Matches any of A, B, or C elements (a shorthand)	`h1, h2, h3, h4 { font-weight: bold; }`
`ns|A`	Matches A with the namespace URI bound to prefix "ns" using @namespace (see CSS and XML)	`svg|text`

CSS 3 adds more selectors, including `:nth-child()`, `:nth-of-type()`, `:nth-last-of-type()`, and more bizarre variations, but these are not all available today. If you find yourself needing them, for example with jQuery, ask yourself if the XPath jQuery plug-in wouldn't be a little saner.

CSS Properties

Once you've identified your HTML elements with CSS selectors, you can assign values to their formatting properties. Again, since this is an XML book, only a few are listed in this section; you can go to `http://www.w3.org/TR/CSS21/` for a longer list, and also see `www.quirksmode.org` for information on which properties are actually supported by browsers.

Figure 17-5 shows the WebKit Developer Tools (found in Epiphany, Midori, Safari, Chrome, and other WebKit-based browsers); for Firefox there is the Web Developer extension and also FireBug with roughly similar functionality. You can see the Computed Style and Matched CSS Rules windows for the selected element (a `<div>` element with `class="footer"` in this case). If you double-click the CSS property values, you can change them and see the results right away. If you click the Console icon in the list of icons on the top of the window, you can see any syntax errors in the CSS, which is obviously also important. See Chapter 16, "AJAX" for instructions on how to find the Console in various different Web browsers.

You look at some of the more important CSS properties later, but first you need to understand the CSS Box Model.

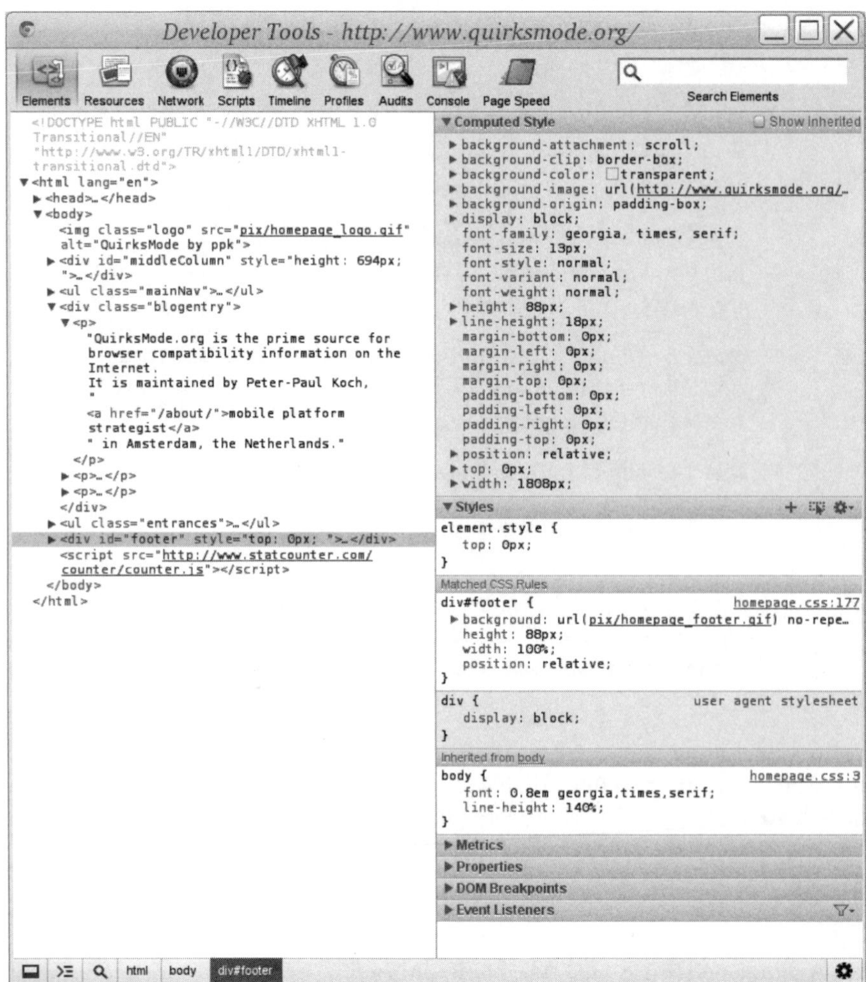

FIGURE 17-5

The CSS Box Model

In the CSS Box Model every `block` element, like a paragraph, has an invisible margin all round it, and then a border, and then *padding*, and then the actual content. The vertical margin between two blocks is actually the larger of the margins of the two boxes, not the result of adding up the margins. This process of using the larger value is called *collapsing*. Horizontal margins do not collapse.

NOTE *For vertical text, such as is common with Japanese or Chinese writing, browsers presumably would collapse the horizontal margins instead; CSS 2.1 appears not to account for this case though.*

You can refer to the individual margin, border, and padding properties as `padding-top`, `padding-right`, `padding-bottom`, `padding-left` (the values go clockwise), `margin-top`, `border-top`, and so on.

You can also use shorthand properties to set top, right, bottom, and left all in one go. For example:

```
p img.button {
    padding: 0.5em 12px 0.5em 12px;
}
```

is the same as:

```
p img.button {
    padding-top: 0.5em;
    padding-right: 012px;
    padding-bottom: 0.5em;
    padding-left: 12px;
}
```

You control the box size with the width and height properties. If you set the size too small, you will get overflow and you can use the `overflow` property to tell the browser whether to "clip" (throw away whatever does not fit) or add a scroll bar. The default width and height are `100%` (relative to the available space in the containing element) and `auto`, respectively. You can also constrain the box size with `min-width`, `max-width`, `min-height`, and `max-height`.

You can draw the border and give it thickness with the `border` property; this is shorthand for setting `border-width`, `border-style`, and `border-color` individually. You can also have rounded corners; the following example makes a bright-red dotted (rather than solid) border 4 pixels (actually 4/96ths of an inch) wide with rounded corners having a corner radius of 12 pixels. You would have to use CSS3 PIE or some other add-on to get border radius working in Internet Explorer 6, however, and vendor prefixes for other browsers.

```
p {
    border: 4px dotted red;
    border-radius: 12px;
}
```

If you set the border radius you normally need to make sure that your element's padding is at least as large as the radius, to stop text from getting chopped off at the corners.

You can set the individual border widths with `border-top`, `border-right`, `border-bottom`, and `border-left`, and these are, in turn, shorthand properties for `border-top-width`, `border-top-style`, `border-top-color`, and so on.

NOTE *CSS 3 also proposes image borders, using repeated images to make borders.*

You can use the display property of any inline element to make it into a block. One reason to do that is so that you can position it: `display` can be set to `inline` or `block`. You can use other values of `display` for special-purpose formatting, including `list-item`, `inline-block`, `inline-table`, and more. In CSS 2 each element is either entirely inline or a block; CSS 3 adds a display value of `run-in` for elements that cause a break at one end and not the other.

If you need to have a border around more than one element, you must put a wrapper element there; most people use `<div>` elements for this purpose.

CSS Units

CSS property values can be given units of `em` (the current font size), `px` (there are officially 96 CSS pixels per inch), `pt` (there are officially 72 CSS points per inch), `pc` (picas, equal to 12 points), and you can also try for `in`, `mm`, and `cm` (inches, millimeters, and centimeters), although that depends on the user having set the screen resolution correctly, an event with vanishingly small probability. There is also `ex`, for the "*x*-height" of the font, a unit both obscure and unreliable. You can also use percentages or the keyword `inherit` in most cases; a percentage is usually relative to the value of the same property in the parent element. However, CSS is irregular: for example, a percentage value for the `line-height` property is taken as a percentage of the `font-size` property.

Some More CSS Properties

Following are some of the more widely used CSS properties:

- `font-family`: Fonts matching the given family names will be searched in order for characters. Note that depending on the characters in the fonts and the text in your document you could end up with an E from Palatino and an É from Palatino Linotype even in the same word. See the following code for an example of a `font-family` property:

```
body {
font-family: "Palatino", "Palatino Linotype", "Book Antiqua", "Sistina", serif;
}
```

- `font-weight`: Values are `bold` or `normal`; you can also use `bolder`, `lighter`, or a multiple of 100 between 100 and 900 inclusive, where 900 is very dark and 100 is very light.
- `font-variant`: You can use this to turn on FAKE SMALL CAPS. Uppercase letters in the input remain uppercase and lowercase letters become small caps. A professional typographer would want to do this only if the font had real small caps, and to do that you have to use

the OpenType font property access that's been proposed for CSS 3; it's still an early draft, though, so not included in this book, unfortunately.

- `font-size`: This sets the size for text. Remember that most people have configured their browsers to make the default font size be readable comfortably for them, so you should not normally make it smaller. There was a fashion for a while to start with `font-size: 80%` to make a more professional look, but for most people all this does is cause irritation and a reach for the zoom button, which in turn will make the images on your site look bad.
- `line-height`: When you set the text size you should also set the distance apart for lines of text. A good value is 120 percent for headings and 130 percent for text, to give space between the lines. The percentage is relative to the font size.
- `background`: This is a shorthand for setting `background-color`, `background-image`, `background-repeat`, `background-attachment`, and `background-position`; see `http://www.w3.org/TR/CSS21/colors.html#propdef-background` for the full details. If you set the background color you also need to set colors for the foreground (that is, the text) for links in all states (default/unvisited, visited, active, and hover) so that users don't end up getting (for example) white text on a white background. Do not assume that users have the same browser defaults as you: browsers have been "theme-able" for more than a decade, and some people have light-colored text on a dark background for accessibility or aesthetic reasons. The `newton1.css` example does not set link colors because the sample HTML document contains no links.

  If you use a background image, for example a texture of paper or canvas, it's a good idea to set the background color to be the same as the predominant color of the image so that if the image loads slowly, or doesn't load at all, the page still more or less works. You could change the style for the `<body>` element in the `newton1.css` file to be like this and reload the HTML document:

```
body {
  background: url('000-paper-tile-256x256.jpg') #faf1de repeat scroll;
  margin-left: 1em;
}
```

The color in this example, `#faf1de`, was chosen using the color picker in an image editor with the `000-paper-tile` image open. The values `repeat` (for `background-repeat`) and `scroll` (for `background-attachment`) are likely defaults; `repeat` means the background is tiled, and `scroll` means that as you scroll the document the background moves along with the text.

NOTE *Some image editing programs include a filter that will make any image tile without obvious joins; in The GIMP this is under Filters ➪ Map Make Seamless, for example. You can also find lots of tutorials for how to do this with The GIMP and other programs.*

- `color`: This property sets the color of text, borders (unless overridden), and text decorations like strikethrough and underline.
- `float`: Normally, the renderer in the web browser shows the block-level elements in the document one after the other when they're loaded. You can use the `float` property to make the text wrap around an object such as a `<div>` element or an image. This property was used on the image in `NewtonWithCSS.html` to put the image on the left and have the text of the document flow around it, with the result shown in Figure 17-4. Usually, you'd also set a margin on the floated element to keep it from bumping into the text. You also need to give a width for the object so that the browser knows where to put the text that flows around it. Values for `float` are `left`, `right`, `inherit` or `none`. The float property is also commonly used to make a multi-column web page design, by floating an entire column to one side of the page. The floated column must appear in the HTML before anything you want to float around it.
- `clear`: Sometimes you want to make sure an element appears after any floated content. If you use `clear: left;` on an element, and the element started part-way down a floated object to its left, the element is moved down beneath the floated object, leaving a gap. Values are `left`, `right`, `both`, `none`, and `inherit`.

CSS Special Rules

CSS defines a number of rules starting with an at sign (`@`); these rules affect the behavior of the style sheet in some way. The most important of these are defined in the following list and include `@charset`, `@font-face`, `@import`, `@media`, and `@page`. `@font-face` is defined in a separate specification.

- `@charset`: Use this if your CSS file is not in Unicode UTF-8. In practice you should always use UTF-8 these days.
- `@import`: You can use this to include other style sheets; it can also be conditional on media type like so:

```
#import url("print.css") print;
```

- `@media`: You can use this for rules that are specific to a particular context in which the style sheet is used. Media can be any of `all`, `braille`, `embossed` (a variant of `braille`), `handheld`, `print`, `projection`, `screen`, `speech`, `tty` (fixed-width printers), and `tv`. In the following example, footnotes are shown in print but not on the screen:

```
@media print {
  body {
    font-size: 11pt;
    line-height: 12pt;
  }
  div.footnote {
    font-size: 9pt;
    line-height: 11pt;
  }
}
```

```
@screen {
  div.footnote {
    visibility: hidden
  }
}
```

- `@font-face`: It's impossible to know what fonts users will have available on their computer when they view a web page; with `@font-face` you can arrange for a web browser to download fonts on the fly. Fonts are often fairly large files, so doing this can cause a delay, or can cause the page to be redrawn once the font is available, but if your users typically visit several pages on your site that all use the same font, they will experience the delay only the first time they encounter each font.

Support for downloaded fonts is changing rapidly, but the following example works well at the time of writing. It assumes you have a font called biography in the subdirectory `f` in multiple font formats: EOT for Microsoft Explorer 3.5 and later, WOFF (a W3C format) for most recent browsers, raw TrueType for a couple of older browsers, and SVG as a fallback.

```
@font-face {
  font-family: 'biography';
  src: url('f/biography.eot?#iefix') format('embedded-optntype'),
          url('f/biography.woff') format('woff'),
          url('f/biography.ttf') format('truetype'),
          url('f/biography.svg#svgFontName') format('svg');
  style: normal;
  weight: 400;
}
```

You would then use this example with `font-family: biography;` elsewhere in the same CSS file. You can get both free and paid fonts at Typekit, Google Fonts, MyFonts.com, `OpenFontLibrary.org`, Adobe, Linotype, Scriptorium, and elsewhere. Check the end-user license agreement (EULA, often in a file called README) to make certain that web use is permitted.

CSS and XML

You can use CSS with arbitrary XML documents, although it can be tricky. In September 2011, more than a decade after the release of XML, the CSS namespaces module became a W3C Recommendation. You declare a namespace and use it like this:

```
@namespace svg "http://www.w3.org/2000/svg";

svg|text {
  color: red;
}
```

Now, you may be wondering what good this is when XML doesn't define a `<style>` element or a `<link>` element to point to your CSS file. It means that to refer to the file you must use a processing instruction like so:

```
<?xml-stylesheet type="text/css" href="mydoc.css" title="My Nice Styles"?>
```

This must appear *after* the XML declaration and before any content. The style rules must be in an external file, and cannot appear inline in the XML document.

WARNING *Web browsers do* not *load external DTDs, and generally do not process entity declarations in the internal subset, so it's best to avoid a* `DOCTYPE` *declaration.*

In addition to web browsers, a number of commercial XML editors, including XMetaL, Oxygen XML, and Serna, support styling documents with CSS in this way.

Web search engines however, such as Bing, Yahoo, and Google, won't know how to display result fragments from your XML documents, and may not be able to index them very well. CSS is primarily useful for the author, not for web publication of arbitrary XML documents.

Separating Style and Markup: Unobtrusive CSS

In XHTML and HTML any element can have a `style` attribute containing CSS property/value pairs. For a while this was widely used, then widely misused. It is now better in most cases to use HTML class attributes and to use CSS selectors to associate those elements with styles. The class attribute takes a space-separated list of words, so you can write the following:

```
<span class="person blue linktobio">Isaac Newton</span>
```

and have a CSS rule for the separate classes like so:

```
span.blue { color: blue; }
span.person:before {
    content: "[person] ";
    color: #AAA;
}
```

This example colors Isaac Newton blue and puts the text `[person]` just before his name. You see the `linktobio` word in use in the next section.

UNOBTRUSIVE JAVASCRIPT

Taking the JavaScript out of the document and into a separate file is called Unobtrusive JavaScript. As with CSS, the class attribute is used to decouple the markup from the behavior, and to make web pages that degrade gracefully in the face of errors or if JavaScript is not available. You can refer to Chapter 16 to see examples using jQuery with CSS selectors like `span.linktobio` to make the span clickable like so:

```
$("span.linktobio").click(function(){
  // go to the biography
  document.location = this.innerText + ".html";
});
```

See also `http://en.wikipedia.org/wiki/Unobtrusive_JavaScript` for more information on good practice and Unobtrusive JavaScript.

HTML 5

As you recall, HTML 5 is the latest version of HTML, after HTML 4. It came about when a group of browser implementers were unhappy with slow progress since HTML 4 and didn't want to move to XHTML. HTML 5 has lots of new elements and ideas that are discussed here. Many of these new features are beneficial, but they also have their caveats. This section explains both the pros and cons of HTML 5 so you can make an informed decision of when to use it for yourself.

Benefits of HTML 5

The HTML 5 specification introduces several new ideas to HTML. The first is that it specifies exactly how web browsers and other programs are to read HTML documents. This is intended to mean that documents will be handled the same way in all browsers even if they contain syntax errors.

HTML 5 and the renewed interest in web browser features is driving renewed interest in CSS; HTML and CSS are being used for electronic books, and publishers are also demanding more sophisticated styling. XML-based workflows are very widespread in book publishing, so XML's promise of "write once, publish many" is being fulfilled.

This is also the first HTML specification that includes both the older SGML-influenced HTML syntax and an XML syntax. People often refer to the XML syntax for HTML 5 as XHTML 5, but, unlike the HTML syntax, the XML syntax must not contain syntax errors.

SVG and MathML are included in HTML 5 and are scriptable. You return to SVG in the next chapter, and look very briefly at MathML in Chapter 19, "Case Study: XML in Publishing."

Internationalization is also greatly improved with the downloadable fonts you saw earlier in this chapter, and with better OpenType support. At the time of writing, support for Graphite fonts from the Summer Institute of Linguistics (SIL) is also being considered, which will improve support for some more complex scripts, including the Devanagari writing system used for the Hindi language.

But above all, HTML 5 is the foundation for the Open Web Platform, and today is as much about writing sophisticated web applications with a rich "user experience" as it is about marking up documents. Earlier in this chapter Figure 17-1 showed you `http://platform.html5.org/`, a page listing the specifications that are part of the Open Web Platform. HTML 5 and the Open Web Platform is becoming the universal operating system of the future.

Caveats of HTML 5

New technology always comes with a mixture of benefits and drawbacks, and the hype and enthusiasm must be tempered with cautions; this is as true for HTML 5 as it was for XML in the early days. HTML 5 is not yet mature, and people are still learning how best to use it, but already it has brought huge changes to the Web.

The first two features that got people excited about HTML 5 were the ability to do dynamic, scripted graphics with `<canvas>` and the precise parsing algorithm that made browsers behave the same way in the face of errors in markup. But the caveats with these two features are that it can be difficult or impossible to create fully accessible applications using `<canvas>`, and that saying what the browser should do in the face of errors appears to legitimize invalid markup. HTML 5 is also still evolving, and if you're going to dive in to HTML 5 Web development you need to keep an active eye out for changes.

HTML 5 also plays fast and loose with namespaces, and the XML syntax, if deployed as the HTML 5 specification mandates, won't work in Internet Explorer 6, 7, or 8. It is planned that XSLT 3 and Query 3 processors will be able to read and write HTML 5 documents, but these specifications are not yet final at the time of writing this book.

So the HTML 5 Open Web Platform is not necessarily mature, but it's growing up fast.

New Elements in HTML 5

HTML 5 introduces more than two dozen new elements. The descriptions here are taken from `http://www.w3.org/TR/html5-diff/`, which is a useful document to read. There are other changes besides new elements too. For example the `HTML DOCTYPE` declaration has changed to:

```
<!DOCTYPE html>
```

This declaration has no `SYSTEM` or `PUBILC` identifiers: HTML 5 is no longer an SGML application. Other changes include new attributes, new input controls for forms, but, above all, entirely new elements; Table 17-4 lists the new elements.

TABLE 17-4: New Elements in HTML 5

ELEMENT	DESCRIPTION
`article`	Represents an independent piece of content of a document, such as a blog entry or newspaper article.
`aside`	Represents a piece of content that is only slightly related to the rest of the page.
`audio`	(see entry for "video")
`bdi`	Represents a span of text that is to be isolated from its surroundings for the purposes of bidirectional text formatting.
`canvas`	Used for rendering dynamic bitmap graphics on the fly, such as graphs or games.
`command`	Represents a command the user can invoke.
`datalist`	Together with a new `list` attribute for input can be used to make combo boxes.
`details`	Represents additional information or controls that the user can obtain on demand. The summary element provides its summary, legend, or caption.
`embed`	Used for plug-in content.

`figcaption`	Can be used as a caption in a figure.
`figure`	Represents a piece of self-contained flow content, typically referenced as a single unit from the main flow of the document.
`footer`	Represents a footer for a section and can contain information about the author, copyright information, and so on.
`header`	Represents a group of introductory or navigational aids.
`hgroup`	Represents the header of a section.
`keygen`	Represents control for key pair generation.
`mark`	Represents a run of text in one document marked or highlighted for reference purposes, due to its relevance in another context.
`meter`	Represents a measurement, such as disk usage.
`nav`	Represents a section of the document intended for navigation.
`output`	Represents some type of output, such as from a calculation done through scripting.
`progress`	Represents a completion of a task, such as downloading or when performing a series of expensive operations.
`ruby,`	`rt` and `rp` allow for marking up ruby annotations, for example for Japanese or Chinese text.
`section`	Represents a generic document or application section. It can be used together with the h1, h2, h3, h4, h5, and h6 elements to indicate the document structure.
`time`	Represents a date and/or time.
`track`	Provides timed tracks for the video element, such as subtitles or captions.
`video`	(Added along with "audio" for multimedia content.) Both provide an API so application authors can script their own user interface, but there is also a way to trigger a user interface provided by the user agent. `<source>` elements are used together with these elements if multiple streams of different types are available.
`wbr`	Represents a line break opportunity.

New types of HTML form input are also available. A number of elements and attributes are changed, and the HTML Working Group has removed some elements from the specification that were in previous versions of HTML. Browsers will still have to support these older elements, because otherwise users would complain that web pages had stopped working, so the desirability of removing them from the specification is questionable.

The new elements and the overall changes are incremental, and yet at the same time are part of a stunning revival in interest in web browser features. The main people to benefit are not the implementers of web browsers, but web developers and, ultimately, web users.

SUMMARY

In this chapter you learned:

- HTML is a very simple markup language, which is why it's so widely used.
- The Cascading Style Sheets (CSS) specification adds more sophisticated formatting.
- MathML and SVG are both included directly in HTML 5 and are supported by today's web browsers.
- HTML 5 introduces other new features and greatly increases the scriptability of the browser using JavaScript.
- The most important innovation of HTML 5 is that it is parsed in the same way by all web browsers, so that you can develop to a standard instead of working around differences between browsers.
- When you generate HTML using XQuery or XSLT, you must use the appropriate `html` or `xhtml` serialization option.
- As the Open Web Platform matures it is commoditizing the user interface, so that many applications that used to be standalone desktop programs are becoming web applications.

EXERCISES

You can find suggested solutions to these questions in Appendix A.

1. How would you change the `newton.css` file from the Try it Out activity so that the picture fits entirely in the left margin?
2. XHTML is defined with an XML DTD; in what language was the original DTD for HTML written?
3. Explain the differences between CSS margins and padding.
4. Why do all HTML 5 web browsers behave the same even on faulty input?
5. Use CSS to style the examples in this chapter and in Chapter 16. This is an open-ended exercise.

▶ WHAT YOU LEARNED IN THIS CHAPTER

TOPIC	KEY POINTS
SGML, XML, and HTML	HTML was originally defined using ISO 8879 SGML, the Standard Generalized Markup Language. XML, the Extensible Markup Language, was designed so people could put documents on the World Wide Web that were defined in their own SGML markup languages, not just HTML.
XHTML and HTML	XHTML is a version of HTML that uses XML syntax. It is useful for authors because of its stricter syntax.
Cascading Style Sheets (CSS)	CSS is a property-value system for specifying how HTML documents are to be formatted. CSS can also be used with XML.
HTML 5	HTML 5 was the first major new version of HTML in over a decade. It is no longer based on SGML, although it does have an alternative syntax defined in XML. HTML 5 defines behavior, so that web pages work the same across different browsers. HTML 5 introduces new elements and attributes. HTML 5 includes SVG and MathML as part of the language.
The Open Web Platform	HTML 5, JavaScript APIs and recent versions of CSS are collectively called the Open Web Platform. The Open Web Platform is used for building cross-platform Web apps, both for mobile and for desktop systems.

18

Scalable Vector Graphics (SVG)

WHAT YOU WILL LEARN IN THIS CHAPTER:

- The differences between bitmap and scalable graphics
- Where and why to use SVG
- How SVG works
- Basic SVG drawing: shapes, lines, colors
- Using text in SVG
- Using splines, gradients, and filters
- Generating SVG from XSLT or XQuery
- A high-level view of web apps, SVG animation and scripting, and SVG in the web browser

W3C Scalable Vector Graphics (SVG) is widely used to define pictures and animations and to represent them using XML. SVG pictures can be scaled — that is, you can enlarge them or reduce them to any size without losing quality. The text inside SVG pictures remains editable, so that images made with SVG can be accessible to people with special needs and can be translated to other languages. SVG is also now part of the Open Web Platform introduced with HTML 5, and can be displayed and animated in a web browser. It's easy to generate SVG with XML tools and easy to manipulate it with JavaScript libraries. SVG is just a bundle of awesome win!

SCALABLE VECTOR GRAPHICS AND BITMAPS

Computer graphics come in two main formats: *bitmap graphics* and *vector graphics*. Each of these two formats can work in a way that is either procedural or declarative.

Procedural Graphics

The oldest way to make a computer show a picture is to write a computer program that, when run, produces the desired result. This method is called *procedural graphics*, because you tell the computer what to do: first this then that, like a "procedure." You might write code like the following snippet:

```
1. Pick up the red pen.
2. Move the drawing arm to the middle of the page.
3. Lower the pen until it touches the paper.
4. Move the drawing arm right one inch.
5. Move the drawing arm up one inch.
6. Move the drawing arm left one inch.
7. Move the drawing arm down one inch.
8. Lift the drawing arm.
9. Put down the red pen.
```

Programs that run code like this are often in FORTRAN and can be very hard to read. If you wanted to take such a program and make it draw a three-inch square you'd need to change lines 4, 5, 6 and 7, and maybe also line 2. It's hard to see that it draws a square. Worse, by the time you've written a program like this in FORTRAN and initialized the device library, it will drive only a single printer (actually a pen-plotter) on a single computer operating system, which is not very portable.

Procedural graphics are still used today for plotting graphs, drawing visualizations of large data sets, and even for computer-generated art such as the popular Mandelbrot set pictures. On the Web, procedural graphics can be used by web browser plugins, or can be written in JavaScript.

When you send someone an image made in a procedural graphics format, you are sending them a computer program. Exchanging programs over an untrusted network provides a potential security risk of viruses, and that, combined with the difficulty of maintaining them, has made procedural graphics less common than they once were.

Declarative Graphics

Procedural graphics can be contrasted with declarative graphics. Where procedural graphics say *how* to draw something without ever having to say *what* is being drawn, declarative graphics say *what* to draw and leave the computer to work out how to draw it. In a declarative format you might make a picture with a square in it with something like this:

```
let s be a square 1 inch × 1 inch at position (1,1)
```

This is a much shorter description and is easier to understand. It would be easy in this format to write a program to find all the images that contain squares, although still difficult to find all the pictures of houses that were drawn using squares and triangles.

SVG, like most things in the XML world, is a declarative graphics format. As you'll learn in the "SVG Definitions and Metadata" section later in this chapter, it also has a way to say "this is a picture of a house" using RDF.

Why talk about procedural graphics at all then? Partly to show how much better SVG is, of course, but also so that you can see how this approach can be combined with SVG's declarative approach. Procedural graphics are also used with the HTML 5 <canvas> element, as mentioned in

Chapter 17, "XHTML and HTML 5." Let's put procedural graphics aside for a moment and look at the second way that computers work with pictures.

Bitmap Graphics

Bitmap graphics, also called *raster images*, are made up of an array of "picture elements," or *pixels*. Each pixel is actually just a color value at a particular location, and the whole image is a huge grid of values. Figure 18-1 shows a bitmap graphic that's a picture of a castle, along with an enlargement of part of the castle spire, and a further enlargement showing how the image is made up of rectangles.

> ***WARNING*** *Showing examples of images in a book such as this is complicated slightly by the way books are made. A printed copy of this book will usually have black ink on whitish paper; a pattern of dots is used to simulate gray ink. This is called a "dot screen" and is not the same as the pixels in the image. The printer might use hundreds of dots for each pixel in the image; if you take a magnifying glass to the printed page, or have strong vision, you will be able to see them. The dot screen process (properly called* halftoning*) is used to simulate colors or grays of differing degrees of darkness, regardless of how the image is being produced.*
>
> *An electronic book will usually not have halftone dot screens in it because most book reader displays can show the different tonal values directly.*

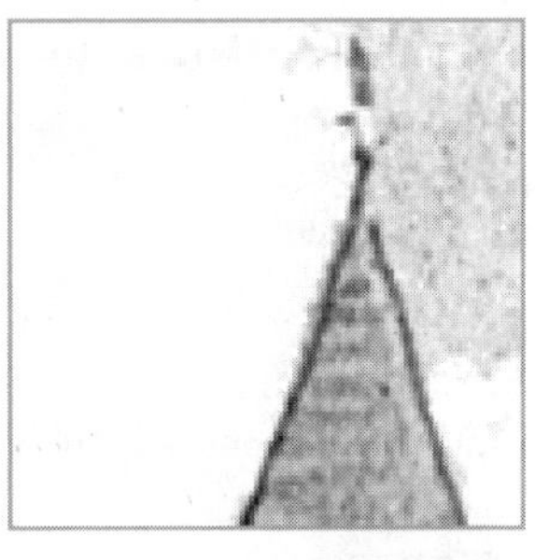

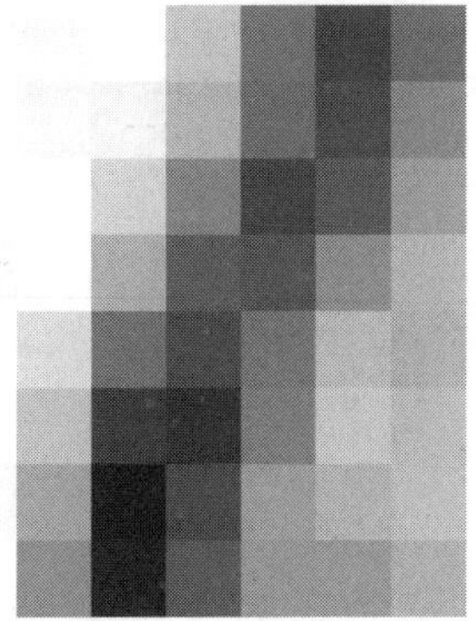

FIGURE 18-1

When a bitmap image is enlarged, it becomes *pixelated*, meaning that you can see the individual pixels. This is because the computer can't invent more detail to fill in the gaps between the centers of the pixels, and as the pixels are moved wider apart to make the image larger, that space eventually becomes large enough to be visible.

The computer can do much better than the example in Figure 18-1: it can guess values between the pixels of the original image, a process known as *interpolation*. However, even this process doesn't really add detail. You could include the additional detail in the image, but then the image files quickly get large; a modern digital camera makes bitmap images that are 30 to 100 megabytes in size, and images from a flatbed scanner can easily be more than a gigabyte.

The advantages of bitmap images are the photographic image quality and detail possible at the intended size, the simple data format that is not normally a host to viruses, near-universal portability for the most common bitmap image formats, and widespread availability of tools to process the images.

The obvious disadvantages of bitmap images are the size of the files and the fact you can't enlarge them very well. A less obvious disadvantage is that bitmap image formats usually do not allow the image to contain text, but only pictures of text. If you photograph a road sign, you capture the words on the sign, but extracting those words involves using optical character recognition, which is an unreliable process. Worse, someone blind obviously cannot see the image, and therefore cannot read the text. In the next section you'll find out how vector-based images can help with that problem too.

Vector Images

The third of the most common ways to represent images in a computer is using vectors. A *vector* is a mathematical name for a straight line, but modern vector images are made up not only of straight lines but also of curves and text. Vector images can be scaled to any size. A diagonal line will be drawn as a diagonal line however you look at it. Although the image still doesn't invent more detail as you zoom in, the quality of what's there doesn't degrade. File sizes are also usually very small.

Vector images are best suited for diagrams, logos, buttons, and other user-interface controls, and any other application where the overall effect is *designed* rather than *photographed*. Bitmaps are still better for photographs or other highly detailed and irregular images such as scans of oil paintings.

Most modern font formats, including OpenType, TrueType, PostScript Type 1, and Graphite, are also vector-based, which is why you can change font sizes in a word processor and still have good-looking text.

Text in most vector-image formats generally remains as text, and can be extracted and even replaced. This also means that a text reader being used by someone blind could read out the text contained in the image, something not possible with a bitmap image.

SVG Images

With W3C's SVG format you can have the best of all three worlds. SVG is a vector-based scalable format, as the name "Scalable Vector Graphics" implies; SVG images can also include bitmap images. You can create SVG easily, either in XML or using the document object model (the DOM) that you read about in Chapter 7, “Extracting Data from XML,” and you learn more about that in this chapter. SVG is a declarative, not procedural, image format: instead of saying “next draw a circle” you say “there’s a circle here.” This makes it possible to process SVG images with XSLT, for example to replace text or to move objects around.

In the following activity you first look at a simple SVG image and then move on to learn about how SVG works in more detail.

TRY IT OUT A Simple SVG Image

In this exercise you create a very simple SVG file and see the resulting image in a web browser. You will need a web browser that supports SVG such as Mozilla Firefox, Google Chrome (Chromium), Apple Safari, Gnome Epiphany, or Internet Explorer 9 or later. If you don’t have that, see the next Try It Out in this chapter for instructions on how to download Inkscape, an SVG editor and viewer.

1. Type the following simple SVG document into a file called `simple.svg`; make sure to save it as plaintext. You can use an XML editor such as oXygen XML or a text editor. Make sure you save the file in UTF-8, not UTF-16 (or change the first line appropriately).

```
<?xml version="1.0" encoding="UTF-8" ?>
<svg version="1.0" xmlns="http://www.w3.org/2000/svg">
   <circle cx="100" cy="100" r="75"
     fill="#b0b0b0" stroke="#FF0000" stroke-width="1pt" />
</svg>
```

simple.svg

2. Open the SVG file in a web browser. You can open it directly from your computer with no need for a web server. Figure 18-2 shows the expected result: a gray (`#b0b0b0`) circle with a red (`#FF0000`) outline.

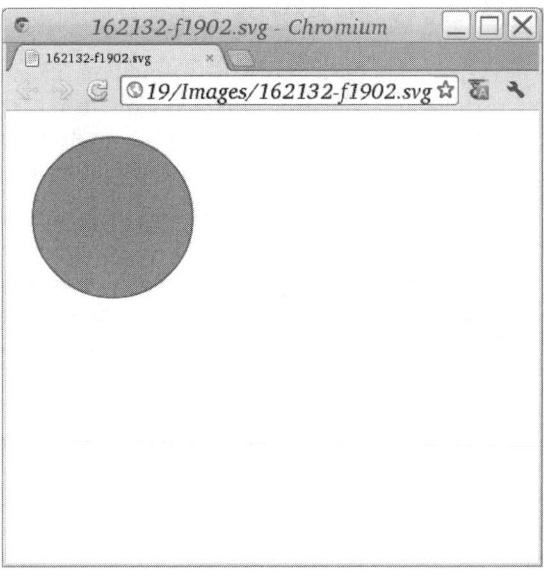

FIGURE 18-2

How It Works

Line 1 of the SVG file is just the familiar XML declaration. It reminds you that SVG files are indeed XML.

Line 2 opens the `<svg>` element, indicates that the document conforms to SVG version 1, and also declares the SVG namespace. Often you’ll also see the namespace associated with an `svg` prefix, in which case elements in the document will be `<svg:svg>`, `<svg:circle>`, and so on, instead of just `<svg>` or `<circle>`.

Line 3 has a `<circle>` element inside the `<svg>` element; the circle will be centered 100 units from the left and 100 units down from the top of the drawing, and will have a radius of 75 units. The circle element also has some styling attributes: `b0b0b0` sets the fill color of the circle to gray, `#FF0000` sets the border to red, and `stroke-width="1pt"` sets the width of the line that draws the circle to 1 point (recall from Chapter 17 that 72 points equals an inch).

If the example didn't work for you, check the syntax of your SVG file carefully: make sure you have put straight quotes, not "typewriter quotes," around the attributes, and that you closed the empty elements with `/>` and not just `>`. If you are using Windows Notepad or WordPad, make sure you saved the file as plaintext in the UTF-8 encoding.

If you have installed the `xmllint` command you can check the syntax of your SVG with the following command:

```
xmllint --noout yourfile.svg
```

(If there is no output, your file is OK.)

You can install `xmllint` from `www.libxml.org` if you are on Windows; on OS X and Linux `xmllint` is either already installed or available as a system package. You could also use the oXygen XML editor to edit the SVG file, since it is XML.

If that's not the problem, and you got all of the numbers right, try a different web browser, or download Inkscape as described in the next exercise. You need a sufficiently recent browser such as (April 2012) Internet Explorer 9, Firefox 9, Chrome 17, Safari 5, or Opera 11.6.

THE SVG GRAPHICS MODEL

SVG graphics are said to be painted onto a canvas. The "paint," like the "canvas," is usually opaque, but can also be partially or entirely transparent. However, there's no way to remove things that have been drawn. You can draw over things and hide them, but you can't scratch a hole through something you have drawn and see what was underneath.

An apparent exception is that you can use SVG animation to change the opacity of objects *after* they've been drawn, making them transparent, and the drawing changes as if those objects were always transparent. Figure 18-3 shows a double-path spiral with a gray rectangle painted on top of it and then a white circle added; the spiral had already been painted over and cannot be seen through the white circle. If you paint a hole in a wall it can look good but you can't crawl through it! If you use scripting, such as JavaScript within a web browser, you can also set `<clipPath>` on an object to cause only parts of it to be visible, and whatever was painted underneath the newly-invisible parts of the object will then be shown. But if you are using scripting you could also change the object's shape, and build a wall with an arched gateway in it.

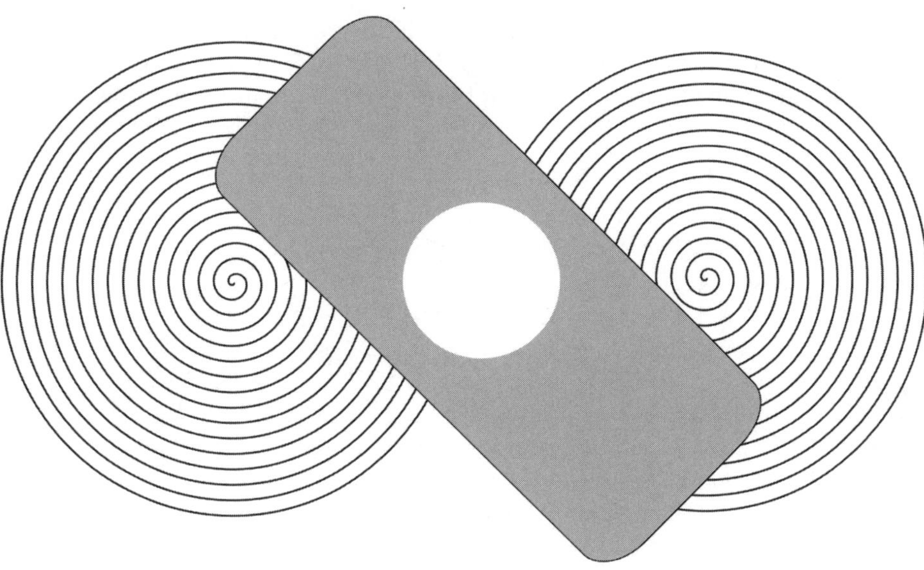

FIGURE 18-3

If you did want to see the spiral through a hole in the rectangle you'd need to plan for it, for example by making a single combined shape of a rectangle with a circular hole in it; Figure 18-4 shows the result.

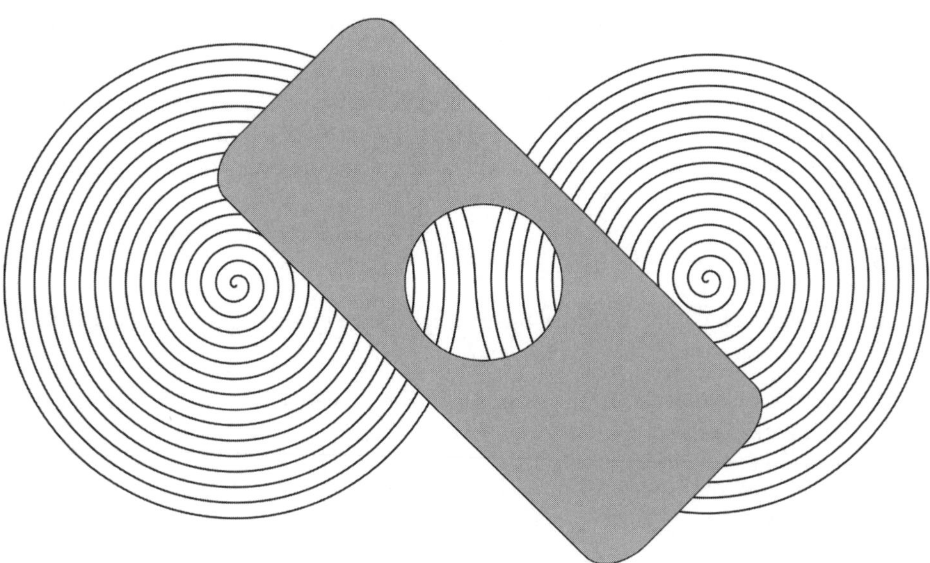

FIGURE 18-4

You could also go back and change the opacity of the rectangle; Figure 18-5 shows what this might look like, even if the change was made after the rectangle had already been painted as opaque. You might just make this change in an editor, or you might be using JavaScript in a web browser.

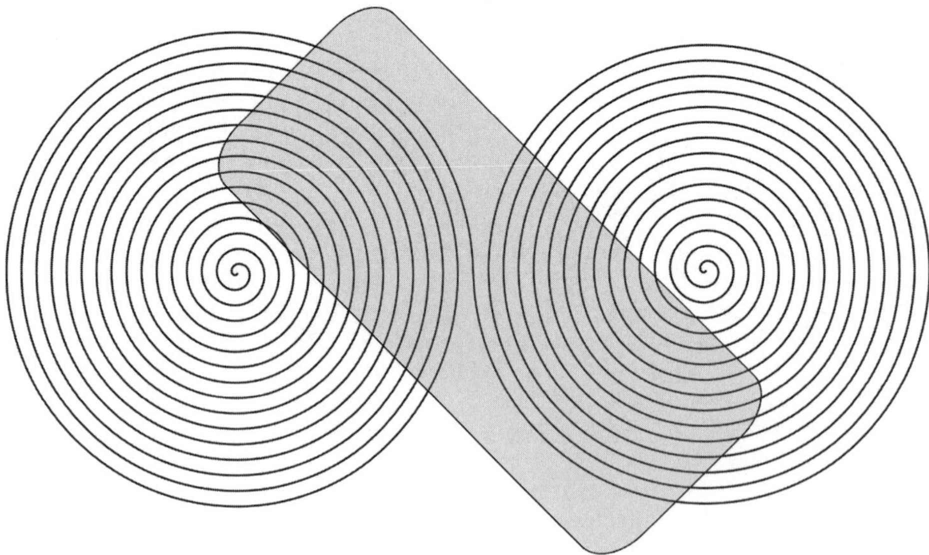

FIGURE 18-5

The SVG model is very close to the older Adobe PostScript graphics model, except that PostScript did not have opacity and was procedural.

You can already see that making complex drawings with SVG can require careful thought. If that's not your style, don't panic: after reviewing the way SVG works with CSS, you learn about some tools that handle a lot of the SVG for you automatically and reduce the need for careful planning.

SVG AND CSS

If you worked your way through Chapter 17 you have already seen cascading style sheets (CSS). If you don't know about CSS you should review that chapter now.

SVG uses CSS properties to style objects. In the example in the previous Try It Out, you saw the following `<circle>` element:

```
<circle cx="100" cy="100" r="75"
  fill="#b0b0b0" stroke="#FF0000" stroke-width="1pt" />
```

The `fill`, `stroke`, and `stroke-width` attributes are names of CSS-like properties defined by SVG. You can also use them with a `style` attribute like so:

```
<circle cx="100" cy="100" r="75"
   style="fill: #b0b0b0; stroke: #FF0000; stroke-width: 1pt;" />
```

The two forms are interchangeable *except* when it comes to animation. It is not a good idea to use both the CSS `style` attribute and individual XML attributes for the same property. The SVG renderer might know what to do with it, since the CSS properties always take precedence over the attributes, but it's all too easy to change one and not the other.

You can use the `class` attribute in SVG just as you can in HTML, and even style your SVG with an external style sheet.

Table 18-1 lists some of the CSS properties that apply to most SVG objects. You can use many other CSS properties with SVG; they are defined both in the SVG specification (`http://www.w3.org/TR/SVG11/`) and the CSS specification (`http://www.w3.org/TR/CSS21/`).

TABLE 18-1: Some CSS Properties Commonly used with SVG Objects

PROPERTY	DESCRIPTION
`color`	SVG interprets this CSS property to apply to fill, stroke, and other properties if you don't override it.
`fill`	The value of this property determines the color of the inside of an object. Use `none` if you don't want the object filled at all.
`fill-opacity`	Determines whether the fill color is solid or transparent. Use 1 for opaque, 0 for transparent, 0.5 for halfway, or any number between.
`font`	A shortcut property for `font-style`, `font-variant`, `font-weight`, `font-size`, `line-height`, `font-family`, for example: `font="italic small-caps bold 16pt/18pt Caslon"`. See the section "SVG Text and Fonts" later in this chapter.
`kerning`	A value of `auto` enables pair kerning, and a length disables pair kerning and enables letter spacing. To get both you can use `kerning` and `letter-spacing` together. The `kerning` property is a CSS3 feature.
`letter-spacing`	Takes a length, such as `1px`, `0.04em`, or `1cm`, and adds that much space between letters; if pair kerning is enabled the actual space is also affected by the font's built-in kern pairs.
`opacity`	A value of zero means totally transparent and a value of one means that the object is opaque and completely covers up whatever was previously drawn. Use `fill-opacity` and `stroke-opacity` to specify them separately.
`stroke`	Specifies the color used to draw along a given path, such as the outline of a circle or rectangle; overrides the `color` property.

continues

TABLE 18-1 *(continued)*

PROPERTY	DESCRIPTION
`stroke-dasharray`	Contains a space-separated list of numbers for making dashed lines. The first number is the length of a dash, the next the length of a gap, then the length of the next dash, and so on. Always supply an even number of values. The SVG renderer starts again at the beginning of the array if it runs out of values.
`stroke-opacity`	Like `fill-opacity` except for the outline of the shape or path rather than the inside.
`stroke-width`	The width of the line when a path is drawn (stroked); a value of zero turns off the stroking of the outline.
`transform`	See the section "SVG Transforms and Groups" later in this chapter.
`word-spacing`	Can be normal or a length to be added to the default; a negative value reduces the space between words.

SVG TOOLS

SVG is widely used today. Web browsers display SVG natively, and SVG is now part of HTML 5. Many desktop and mobile environments, and even camera menu user interfaces, are defined using SVG. Displaying SVG documents is easy, but you still need to know how to make them and edit them. In this section you look at one of the most widely used SVG editors, Inkscape. Later in this chapter you'll see various ways to create SVG graphics using programs and scripts.

Some widely used commercial vector graphics editors support import and export of SVG, including Adobe Illustrator and Corel Draw. This activity looks at Inkscape, an open source editor and viewer whose primary format is SVG-based. Even if you use other programs for most of your work, knowledge of Inkscape can help you to test for portability and can help with development; it's also cross-platform.

TRY IT OUT The Inkscape SVG Editor

In this exercise you install Inkscape and use it to open a sample file and to create a sample image.

1. Install Inkscape. If you are using the GNU/Linux operating environment, or a BSD or Solaris system, you should install Inkscape using the regular packaging system to get any system-specific patches.

   If you are using Microsoft Windows or Apple Macintosh OS X environments, you can download binary packages for Inkscape (directly or indirectly) from the `http://inkscape.org/` download page.

2. Start Inkscape; it comes up with a blank document. Click the "create circles, ellipses and arcs" icon on the toolbar; the mouse pointer (in most environments) will change to an ellipse with a plus sign.

3. Click the canvas inside the box representing the page, and drag out a shape. If you hold the Ctrl key down, Inkscape will constrain the aspect ratio to keep the shape close to a circle; drag out a circle and let go.

4. Choose Fill and Stroke from the Object menu. Depending on the version of Inkscape you have, this may open a dialog box or a "dock" inside the main Inkscape window.

   The status bar at the foot of the Inkscape window should say something like "Ellipse in layer 1" and the circle should have double arrows around it; if not, use the Inkscape "select and transform tool" (top left on the default toolbar) and click the circle once to select it.

5. Click the Fill tab in the Fill and Stroke window and you can play with Hue, Saturation, Lightness, and Alpha (H, S, L and A); notice the "RGBA" hexadecimal value change as you do so. Choose a gray or brown for the fill.

6. Click the Stroke tab in the Fill and Stroke window and choose a bright red for the border. In older versions of Inkscape you may need to click an OK or Apply button to see the changes.

How It Works

The Inkscape program is *free* software that runs on your computer; it's a graphical editor in which you can manipulate objects, such as squares and circles, directly with a mouse pointer or a tablet. People use Inkscape for professional technical illustration as well as for art and drawing. What makes Inkscape special is that it is entirely based on SVG graphics.

You could use other image editors, such as Adobe Illustrator or Corel Draw, but these do not use SVG as a native format, so there is always conversion. There are also some web-based SVG editors such as svg-edit available at `http://code.google.com/p/svg-edit/` but you need network access to run them.

In this Activity, then, you downloaded and installed a useful program and created a simple SVG diagram. You can also try editing the XML directly in Inkscape by choosing XML Editor from the Edit menu, or save the file and edit it in oXygen XML or another text or XML editor to see what happens.

If you have problems creating the sample file, see Listing 18-1 at the start of the next section in this chapter. The SVG created by Inkscape looks somewhat different, and you learn about some of these differences in the rest of this chapter.

Figure 18-6 shows Inkscape with the sample file after adding three more circles and some straight lines. (It's a cubist flower in a pot.) Notice that you can move objects to the back or front with the page up/page down keys on the keyboard, or using the Layer menu, so that the ends of the lines are hidden behind the circles.

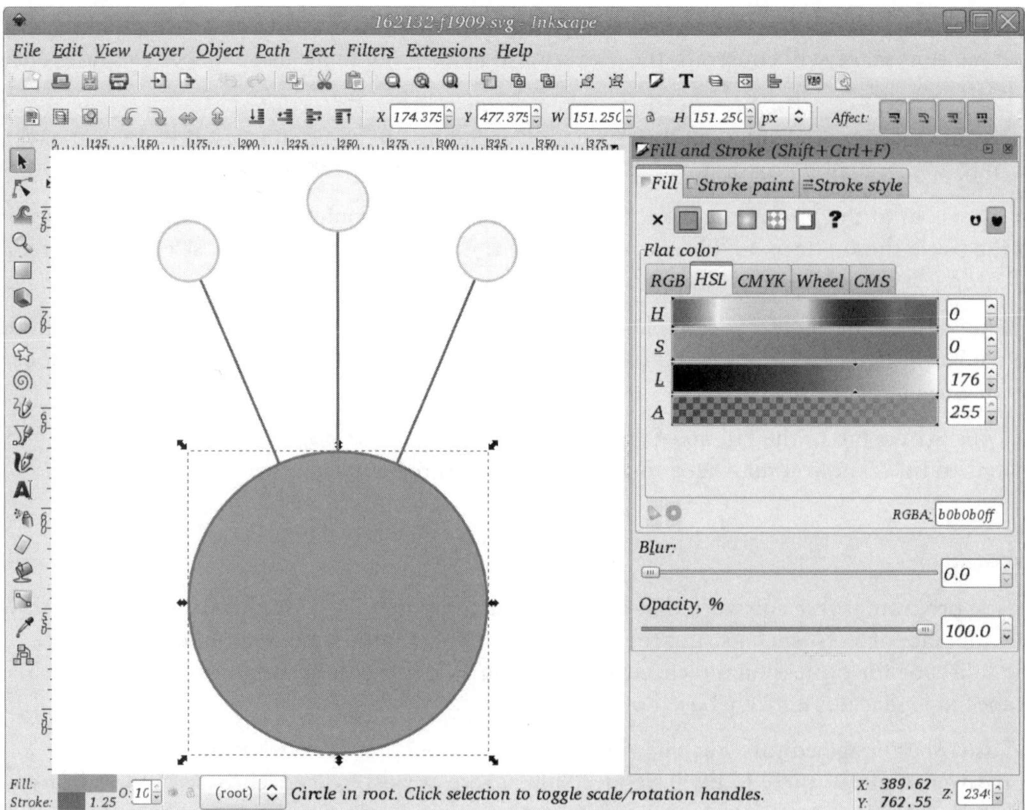

FIGURE 18-6

SVG BASIC BUILT-IN SHAPES

SVG defines a number of basic shapes and then provides a more general path facility so you can make shapes of your own.

The different predefined shapes are described in the following sections, along with the more general construction, SVG paths, and Listing 18-1 shows you some examples:

LISTING 18-1: shapes.svg

Available for download on Wrox.com

```
<?xml version="1.0" encoding="UTF-8" ?>
<svg version="1.0" width="745" height="1053"
   xmlns="http://www.w3.org/2000/svg">
    <path d="m 250,500 -75,-175"
       stroke="green" stroke-width="1pt" />
```

```
    <path d="m 250,500 75,-175"
       stroke="green" stroke-width="1pt" />
    <path d="m 250,500 0,-200"
       stroke="green" stroke-width="1pt" />
   <!--* the plant pot *-->
   <circle cx="250" cy="500" r="75"
     fill="#b0b0b0" stroke="#FF0000" stroke-width="1pt" />
   <circle cx="175" cy="325" r="15"
     fill="yellow" stroke="#CCCCCC" stroke-width="1pt" />
   <circle cx="250" cy="300" r="15"
     fill="yellow" stroke="#CCCCCC" stroke-width="1pt" />
   <circle cx="325" cy="325" r="15"
     fill="yellow" stroke="#CCCCCC" stroke-width="1pt" />
</svg>
```

NOTE *Inkscape, like Microsoft Visio and many other vector editors, comes with other predefined shapes not listed in this chapter, such as spirals and stars. When you create these shapes, the resulting SVG just contains an SVG path, possibly with an extension attribute in a program-specific namespace so that if you load the file again the program remembers it was a built-in shape.*

Rectangles

The SVG `<rect>` element defines a rectangle; the specific attributes are:

- `x`, `y`: Defines the top-left corner of the rectangle.
- `width`, `height`: Defines the size of the rectangle.
- `rx`, `ry`: Radius of corners (default is zero, giving sharp corners).

NOTE *Although the element is called* `rect`*, you can make a square if width and height are the same and, if you use a transformation to rotate the square, you can have a diamond.*

The standard attributes such as `stroke-width`, `stroke`, and `fill` all apply, of course, both to the `<rect>` element and to all the other shapes. Listing 18-2 shows some example of rectangles, including one that has been rotated. The result is shown in Figure 18-7.

LISTING 18-2: shapes-rect.svg

```
<?xml version="1.0" encoding="UTF-8" ?>
<svg version="1.0" width="745" height="1053"
   xmlns="http://www.w3.org/2000/svg">

   <rect x="10" y="10" width="30" height="100"
     fill="#BBBBFF" stroke="#CC0000" stroke-width="1pt" />
   <rect x="60" y="10" width="100" height="100"
     fill="#9999CC" stroke="#CC0000" stroke-width="1pt" />

   <rect x="167" y="-155" width="73" height="73"
     transform="rotate(45)"
     fill="#666699" stroke="#CC0000" stroke-width="1pt"
     stroke-dasharray="5 3" />
</svg>
```

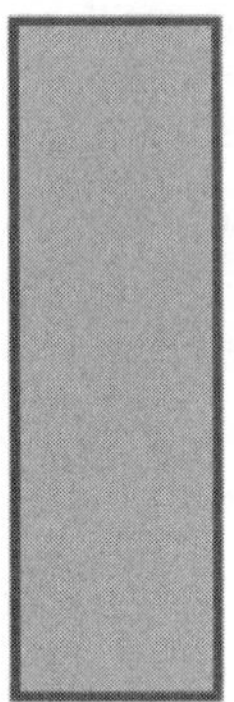

FIGURE 18-7

Circles

The <circle> element uses a center and a radius; if you want to make a circle that touches a line you'll need to use trigonometry, or use a visual program like Inkscape and zoom in a lot! The attributes for circles are:

- cx, c: Defines the center of the circle.
- r: The radius of the circle (the distance from the middle to the outside).

Ellipses

Ellipses are squashed circles. You can use the <ellipse> element to make both ellipses and circles, but <circle> is more convenient for circles and also gets across the higher-level idea that you want a circle.

Ellipses get the following extra attributes:

- cx, cy: Defines the center of the ellipse.
- rx, ry: The x-axis and y-axis radius of the ellipse; an ellipse here is modeled as having a center rather than having two focal points.

Listing 18-3 shows some circles and ellipses, and Figure 18-8 shows the result.

LISTING 18-3: shapes-circles.svg

```
<?xml version="1.0" encoding="UTF-8" ?>
<svg version="1.0" width="745" height="1053"
   xmlns="http://www.w3.org/2000/svg">

   <circle cx="60" cy="60" r="50"
     fill="#BBBBFF" stroke="#CC0000" stroke-width="1pt" />

   <ellipse cx="145" cy="60" rx="15" ry="50"
     fill="#9999CC" stroke="#CC0000" stroke-width="1pt" />

   <ellipse cx="215" cy="-55" rx="20" ry="55"
     transform="rotate(30)"
     fill="#666699"
     stroke="#CC0000" stroke-width="1pt"
     stroke-dasharray="5 3" />

   <circle cx="900" cy="60" r="50"
     fill="#333366" stroke="#CC0000" stroke-width="1pt"
     transform="scale(0.3, 1)"
     />
</svg>
```

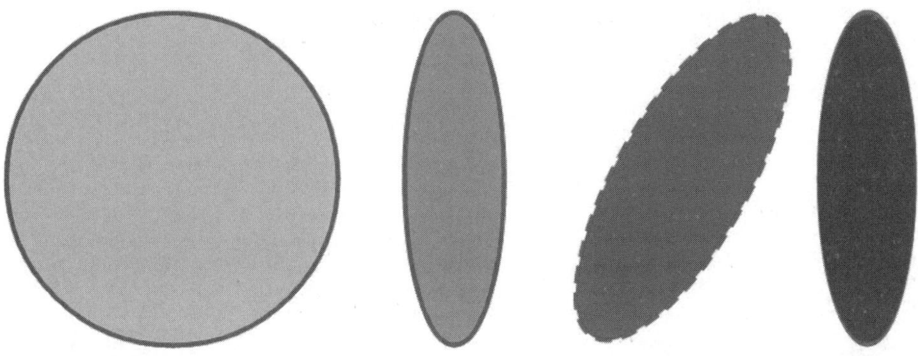

FIGURE 18-8

Straight Lines

Use the `<line>` element to draw a single straight line in any direction. Its attributes are:

- `x1`, `y1`: The first end of the line.
- `x2`, `y2`: The second end of the line.

Lines don't have an inside, so you can't fill them. You can't make filled shapes with <line> either — use <polygon> instead.

Polylines and Polygons

Use the SVG <polyline> and <polygon> elements to make shapes out of straight lines; the only difference between the two is that the <polygon> element quietly adds an extra line segment joining the first and last point you give it.

These two elements take the extra attribute `points`, which is a list of *x*, *y* pairs making up the points on the line. The pairs are separated by spaces: `points="100,100 100,200 200,200 200,100"` draws three lines with <polyline> and a complete square with <polygon>, because the polygon has an extra line from the start point to the end point.

A <polyline> with two points is the same as a <line>. Listing 18-4 shows a polyline, a filled polygon and a straight line that's dashed and wide, and Figure 18-9 shows the result. Notice how it's much harder to work out that the polygon is a pink triangle than it was to understand the shape of a `rect` or `circle` element. It's almost always easier to use the specific elements for shapes when they are available.

Available for download on Wrox.com

LISTING 18-4: shapes-polylines.svg

```
<?xml version="1.0" encoding="UTF-8" ?>
<svg version="1.0" width="1925" height="70"
   xmlns="http://www.w3.org/2000/svg">

   <polyline points="10,10 30,50 50,50 15,45 60,30"
     fill="none" stroke="#000000" stroke-width="1pt" />

   <polygon points="70,10 90,50 110,10"
     stroke="#000000" stroke-width="1pt" fill="#FFCCCC" />

   <line x1="120" y1="17" x2="170" y2="43"
     stroke="#666666" stroke-width="20"
     stroke-dasharray="7 3" />
</svg>
```

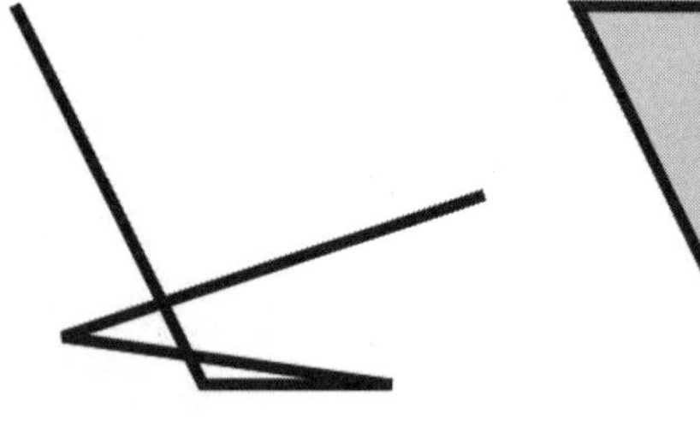

FIGURE 18-9

SVG Paths

A *path* in SVG (as in the older PostScript language) is the most general shape: you can make all the other shapes from paths, and all the other shapes are defined in terms of paths. A path is a sequence of *nodes* with connecting lines between them. The connecting lines can be curved or straight.

At the beginning of this chapter you read about procedural graphics using a pen-plotter as an example; SVG paths are a bit like using a pen-plotter with a simple set of commands. In the case of SVG paths the commands are each one character long, and are shown in Table 18-2, along with longer names to help you remember the letters. In the table only the uppercase version of each command is given; the corresponding lowercase letter gives a "relative" version of the command. For example, if the current point is (30, 30), `L 45 20` is the same as `l 15 -10`. In most cases you can supply additional points; for `moveto` or `lineto` the extra points draw straight line segments, and for Bézier curves the extra points add more curves.

TABLE 18-2: SVG Path Commands

LETTER	MNEMONIC	DESCRIPTION	EXAMPLE
M	moveto	Moves the pen to the given coordinates.	`M 23 117`
L	lineto	Draws a line from the current point to the given location.	`L 300 312`
H	horizontal lineto	Draws a horizontal line to the given `x` coordinate.	`H 312`
V	vertical lineto	Draws a vertical line to the given `y` coordinate.	`Y 23`
Z	closepath	Draws a straight line to the start of the current path and ends the current path.	`Z`
C	curveto	Draws a cubic Bézier curve; takes two control points and an end point (see next section).	`C 20 -17  30 -8 40 40`
S	smooth curveto	An advanced version of C with only one explicit control point.	`S 30 -8 40 40`
Q	quadratic	Draws a quadratic Bézier curve (a spline) using a control point and an end point (see next section).	`Q 20 -17 40 40`
T	smooth spline	An advanced version of Q.	`T 30 45`
A	arcto	Draws an elliptical arc to the given location. Takes x radius, y radius, rotation, two flags, x and y. The flags are large-arc-flag and sweep-flag.	`A 150,150 0 1 1 40 40`

The SVG `<path>` element has a `d` attribute that takes a space-separated list of the one-letter drawing commands listed in Table 18-2. This terse syntax was used for efficiency. Listing 18-5 shows two examples, one unclosed (open) and one closed (with a `z` to close the path). The rectangle in the listing is there so that you can see the single path is actually made up of two subpaths, making a hole in the middle so the filled rectangle shows through. If you look carefully you can find the `z` that ends the first path followed by the `m` that starts the next one. The command letters have been highlighted to make them easier to find in the listing. The result is shown in Figure 18-10.

Available for download on Wrox.com

LISTING 18-5: shapes-curves.svg

```
<?xml version="1.0" encoding="UTF-8"?>
<svg xmlns="http://www.w3.org/2000/svg" version="1.0" width="165" height="75">
  <rect width="154" height="62" x="5" y="5" fill="#6588b1" />

  <path
    d="M 10,10 C 10,27 48,60 58,60 68,60 70,44 45.5,27 45,10 87,10 87,10"
    style="fill:none;stroke:#000000;stroke-width:1pt" />

  <path
    d="m 129.5,9.2
    c -3.4,0.1 -5.1,0.9 -6.2,6.1 -1.3,5.8 3.9,17.0 3.9,17.0 0,0 -6.2,0.6 -9.5,0
    C 114.3,31.8 114.3,31.5 114.3,31.5 l 1.9,5.2 -2.2,3.2 c 0,0 5.9,-0.6
    6.8,-0.6 0.9,0 3.5,0.0 6.3,0.1 0,5.4 -1.7,22.1 -1.7,22.1 0,0 2.8,-2.4
    5.5,-2.4 2.7,0 5.5,2.4 5.5,2.4 0,0 -1.7,-16.7 -1.7,-22.1 2.7,-0.1 5.3,-0.1
    6.3,-0.1 0.9,0 6.8,0.6 6.8,0.6 l -2.2,-3.2 1.9,-5.2 c 0,0 -0.0,0.3 -3.2,0.9
    -3.2,0.6 -9.5,0 -9.5,0 0,0 5.2,-11.1 3.9,-17.0 -1.3,-5.8 -3.2,-6.1
    -7.8,-6.1 -0.5,0 -1.0,-0.0 -1.5,0 z m 1.5,2.8 c 1.4,0.0 2.4,0.3 3.8,1.3
    2.1,4.7 0.5,9.4 -1.9,13.5 -0.6,0.9 -1.2,1.8 -1.9,2.7 -0.6,-0.9 -1.3,-1.8
    -1.9,-2.7 -2.4,-4.0 -4.0,-8.7 -1.9,-13.5 0.6,-0.7 2.8,-1.3 3.8,-1.3
    z"
    fill="#b5b5b5" stroke="#000000" stroke-width="1" />
</svg>
```

FIGURE 18-10

Path Segments: Splines

Splines are smooth curves that go through nodes and have *control points*. The control points determine the shape of the curve. An example is shown in Figure 18-11. The nodes are the dots on the curve; the thinner straight lines join up the nodes with the control points so you can see where the control points are.

You could think of splines as a way to control a racing car; the car must drive through each of the nodes, and its speed and direction when it enters or leaves each node is determined by the direction and length of the "handles" drawn from the nodes to the two control points.

SVG uses Bézier curves for its splines. An important property of Bézier curves is that the curve always goes through the end points (the nodes) on the curve, which makes them easy to work with.

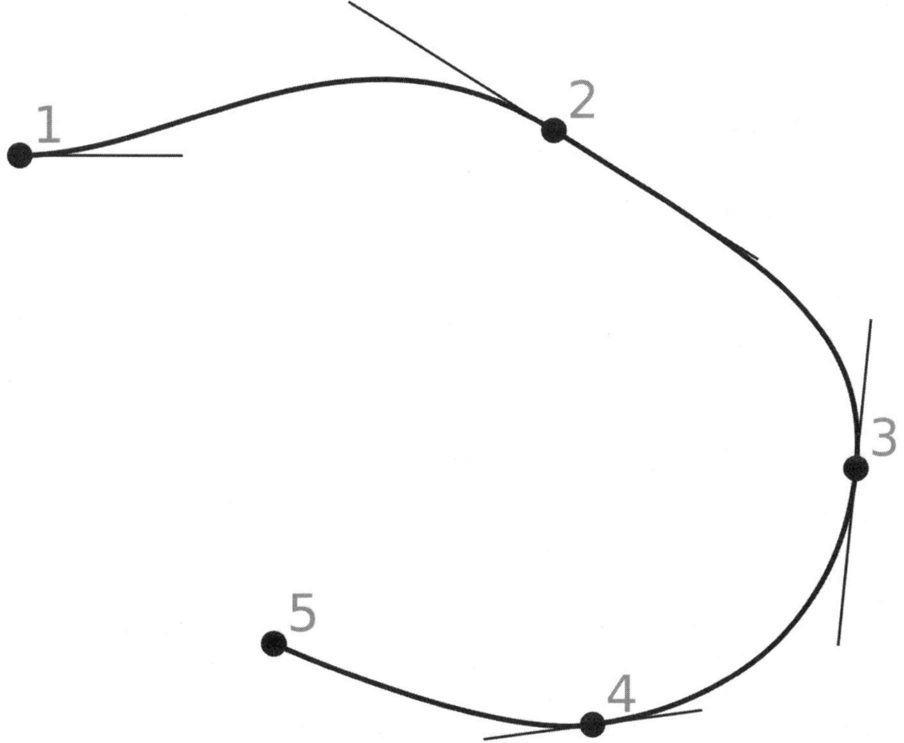

FIGURE 18-11

Path Segments: Arcs

The SVG path's `A` (`arcto`) command takes a bewildering number of parameters. The arc starts at the current point in the path and ends at the `x`, `y` coordinates you supply. Because it's actually an arc of an ellipse, not just of a circle, it takes two numbers for radius (`rx` and `ry`). The ellipse from which the arc is taken could be horizontal or it could be rotated, so there's an angle parameter, `x-axis-rotation`. It then has two "flags" that can each have the value 0 or 1 for false and true, respectively. Figure 18-12, taken from the SVG specification at `http://www.w3.org/TR/`, shows the effect of the two flags, given the following path:

```
<path d="M 125,75 a100,50 0 ?,? 100,50"
      style="fill:none; stroke:red; stroke-width:6"/>
```

Here the `?,?` is replaced by `0,0`, `0,1`, `1,0`, and `1,1` in turn, to generate the four possible cases.

As you can see, SVG provides a number of built-in shapes, including lines, circles, ellipses, squares and rectangles, polygons and polylines; these are defined in terms of SVG paths. It's usually easier for programs to work with paths everywhere, but it's easier for us humans to use the higher-level shapes.

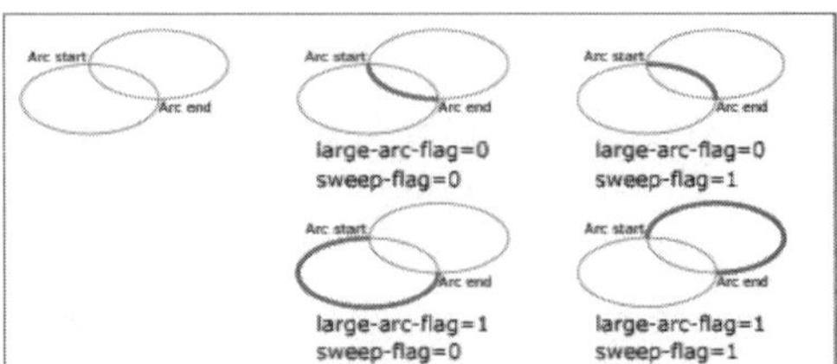

FIGURE 18-12

SVG TRANSFORMS AND GROUPS

Transforms provide a way to take a shape or path and move it, squeeze it, rotate it, change its size, or even flip it over. Under the hood, transforms use a piece of mathematics called a *transformation matrix* to do this.

Groups are a way of combining several smaller objects into one larger one; you can then apply a transformation to a whole group and affect all the objects inside it at once.

Transforms

In SVG (as in PostScript and PDF) every object is affected by at least one transformation matrix. If your mathematics skills never reached the dizzying heights of matrix multiplication and the very mention of a matrix makes you think of a movie, don't panic — it's actually very easy once you get past the jargon and the weird notation. Every number, such as a width or a point on a line, is multiplied by the transformation matrix to get a new number that's actually used.

Because computer graphics like SVG are often both generated and manipulated by computer programs, the people who created SVG wanted the language to be as regular as possible. Transformations apply to any object or (as you'll soon see) any group of objects in exactly the same way. More precisely, it's not the object itself that's transformed but the whole *coordinate system*. It's as if the object were drawn on a separate sheet of paper, and that entire sheet of paper were first moved, then pinned to the drawing at one corner and rotated, stretched, and maybe skewed.

Figure 18-7 earlier in this chapter included an example of a diamond shape made by rotating a rectangle:

```
<rect x="167" y="-155" width="73" height="73" transform="rotate(45)"  />
```

Most SVG elements have a transform attribute. You can put any of the following transform functions into the attribute; if you want to use more than one, separate them with a space, like this:

```
<rect x="167" y="-155" width="73" height="73" transform="rotate(45) scale(0.5, 0.5)"  />
```

- **`translate(tx [ty])`:** Move the whole sheet of paper.
- **`scale(sx sy)`:** Make the paper (and everything drawn on it) larger or smaller.
- **`rotate(angle [cx cy])`:** Turn (rotate) the paper using its top-left corner as the center.
- **`skewX(angle), skewY(angle)`:** You can't actually do this one to paper; every analogy has its limits! Skewing is when you push just the top of a rectangle to one side to make it into a lozenge shape.
- **`matrix(a b c d e f)`:** Set the transformation matrix. See `http://www.w3.org/TR/2011/REC-SVG11-20110816/coords.html#TransformAttribute`.

***WARNING** When you rotate objects, you should imagine that the object is printed on a sheet of paper whose top-left corner is at the origin, the point where x = 0 and y = 0. If your object is then in the middle of the piece of paper and you rotate it, it will move. A common mistake is to forget this and then wonder where the object went! Either take it into account or give an explicit center for rotation.*

Groups

Very often you want to transform several objects together; to do this you group them in a `<g>` element. This element takes `transform` and `style` attributes. Groups can contain any mixture of `<g>` elements and SVG shapes and paths.

Groups are also used with an `id` attribute so that you can animate them or make an entire group visible or invisible.

SVG DEFINITIONS AND METADATA

So far the SVG examples in this chapter have been very minimal, but in practice you'll very quickly need to know more about how SVG files work, especially if you look at images that other people have made, or at files that Inkscape or other programs create. In this section you learn about the structure of an SVG document, including the various XML elements beyond the shapes you have already seen, and you'll also learn a little about the way that definitions and metadata interact.

The SVG <title> and <desc> Elements

SVG documents, like the HTML documents that you saw in Chapter 17, usually use `<title>` and `<desc>` elements. There is also a `<metadata>` element that conventionally contains RDF information about the document, the document's author, and/or whatever might be depicted.

The <title> element can go at the start of the document as well as inside any "container" element such as <circle>. It must always be the first child of its parent, though. A user agent such as a web browser may well show tooltip messages when the mouse pointer hovers over elements containing a <title>, just as HTML browsers do for a title attribute. The use of an element rather than an attribute is appropriate for new vocabularies: the designers of HTML were forced to use attributes because of HTML's poor extensibility design, but the SVG designers built the <title> element in early on.

Because <title> is an element, it can have an xml:lang attribute to indicate the natural language of its content. However, although this may imply that you could have multiple <title> elements with different languages, the SVG specification mandates that user agents use only the first <title> element. The outermost <title> element should describe the whole document, and should stand alone, rather like the <title> element of an HTML document. Titles within the SVG document obviously can assume the reader has more context, and can be terser.

The <desc> element is similar to <title> in that you would use it to give a description of the document or any subelement, but <desc> is meant for longer descriptions and is not usually rendered. It might be used to provide a description of an image to someone who can't see a screen, or by a web search engine. Listing 18-6 has a title for the overall drawing and also a title and <desc> element for the "roundabout." Hovering the mouse pointer over the circle makes (for example) the Chrome Web browser display a tooltip saying "This is where Dougal was seen."

Available for download on Wrox.com

LISTING 18-6: dougal.svg

```
<?xml version="1.0" encoding="UTF-8" ?>
<svg version="1.0" xmlns="http://www.w3.org/2000/svg">
  <title xml:lang="en">Diagram of the M25 roundabout at St Alban's</title>
   <circle cx="100" cy="100" r="75" fill="#b0b0b0" stroke="#FF0000"
        stroke-width="1pt">
     <title>This is where Dougal was seen.</title>
     <desc>The roundabout is just shown as a circle.
       Mr. McHenry said he saw Dougal here with the missing sugar,
       but the picture just shows a grey circle with a red border.
     </desc>
   </circle>
</svg>
```

The SVG <metadata> Element

You use the <metadata> element to give extra information about a drawing. Unlike the human-readable content of the <title> and <desc> elements, however, <metadata> is intended for machine-readable information. It is often used with RDF to try to indicate the subject matter of the image, and also to identify the author using Dublin Core meta data. Listing 18-7 helps you relate this to what you learned in that chapter:

Available for download on Wrox.com

LISTING 18-7: rdf-inside.svg

```
<?xml version="1.0" encoding="UTF-8" ?>
<svg version="1.1" xmlns="http://www.w3.org/2000/svg"
    xmlns:rdf = "http://www.w3.org/1999/02/22-rdf-syntax-ns#"
```

```
    xmlns:rdfs = "http://www.w3.org/2000/01/rdf-schema#"
    xmlns:dc = "http://purl.org/dc/elements/1.1/" >
  >
  <title xml:lang="en">Diagram of the M25 roundabout at St Alban's</title>
  <metadata>
    <rdf:RDF>
      <rdf:Description about="http://example.org/dougal.svg"
        dc:title="Diagram of the M25 roundabout at St Alban's"
        dc:date="2014-04-11"
        dc:description="Evidence for a criminal investigation of Dougal"
        dc:publisher="Hoy Books Ltd."
        dc:format="image/svg+xml"
        dc:language="en" >
        <dc:creator>
          <rdf:Bag>
            <rdf:li>Liam Quin</rdf:li>
            <rdf:li>Dougal</rdf:li>
          </rdf:Bag>
        </dc:creator>
      </rdf:Description>
    </rdf:RDF>
  </metadata>
  <circle cx="100" cy="100" r="75" fill="#b0b0b0" stroke="#FF0000" stroke-width="1pt">
    <title>This is where Dougal was seen.</title>
  </circle>
</svg>
```

WARNING *Be careful that if you make an SVG version of a painting of (say) Isaac Newton, the creator of the SVG, the painter, and the subject (Newton) are all different people; Isaac Newton is not the same as the painted representation, and should not have the same URI. This is a common error people make when creating RDF about images.*

The SVG <defs> Element and Reusable Content

SVG documents can contain a `<defs>` element near the start, right after the optional `<title>`, `<desc>`, and `<metadata>` elements. Things you put inside the `<defs>` element won't be rendered, but you can refer to them as many times you like with a `<use>` element in the body of your SVG document, and then of course they do get shown. The `<defs>` element is also the way that you use SVG fonts and gradients. Listing 18-8 shows an example. The `<circle>` element is defined in the definitions section (the `<defs>` element) and is later used by a `<use>` element. Notice how the `<use>` element also defines the stroke width and adds a title. You can't override attributes using `<use>`, so if the `<circle>` already had a `stroke-width` attribute, that would take precedence.

You can also put a `<defs>` element inside a group (the `<g>` element), again after any `<title>` and `<desc>` elements.

LISTING 18-8: defs-and-use.svg

Available for download on Wrox.com

```
<?xml version="1.0" encoding="UTF-8" ?>
<svg version="1.0" xmlns="http://www.w3.org/2000/svg"
  width="200" height="200"
  xmlns:xlink="http://www.w3.org/1999/xlink">
  <title xml:lang="en">Diagram of the M25 roundabout at St Alban's</title>
  <defs>
    <circle id="magic" cx="100" cy="100" r="75" fill="#b0b0b0" stroke="#FF0000" />
  </defs>
  <use xlink:href="#magic" stroke-width="12pt">
    <title>This is where Dougal was seen.</title>
  </use>
</svg>
```

VIEWPORTS AND COORDINATES

SVG graphics are rendered onto a virtual piece of paper called a *canvas*. Although the size of this canvas has no fixed limits, there is also a rectangular viewing area called the *viewport*. You can use `width` and `height` attributes on the `<svg>` element to define the size of the initial viewport; these are CSS values so you can use units like `in` for inches or `px` for pixels.

Because you give `x` and `y` locations for SVG objects like rectangles, there has to be a definition for where `(0, 0)` lies; it's at the top-left corner of the viewport, unless you have transformed the coordinate system to move it. The bottom-right corner of the viewport corresponds to the position defined by the width and height attributes on the SVG element, or on the viewport. The SVG renderer might well scale the image to fit inside a user's window, or on a sheet of physical paper, so a rectangle with a width of `3in` in the SVG will end up sized proportionally. If you said your image was six inches wide, the rectangle would be half as wide as the viewport, even if the viewport was only five inches wide on a user's screen, or was ten meters wide on a billboard. This goes back to the *scalable* part of Scalable Vector Graphics!

You can establish a new coordinate system, relative to the one in effect at the time, using a `<g>` element with a `transform` attribute. Then all the objects inside the `<g>` element are drawn relative to that new coordinate system. For example, the following code generates the image shown in Figure 18-13:

```
<?xml version="1.0" encoding="UTF-8" ?>
<svg version="1.0" xmlns="http://www.w3.org/2000/svg"
  xmlns:xlink="http://www.w3.org/1999/xlink"
  width="200px" height="300px">
  <title>Demonstration of SVG coordinates</title>
  <rect x="10" y="10" width="100" height="50"
    stroke="#000000" stroke-width="2pt" fill="none" />
  <g transform="scale(2.5)">
    <rect x="10" y="10" width="100" height="50"
      stroke="#000000" stroke-width="2pt" fill="none" />
  </g>
</svg>
```

Notice how the larger rectangle is not all visible because it goes outside the viewport. Notice also how the *same* rectangle definition is rendered larger inside the <g> element because of the transformation.

It doesn't really matter whether you think in terms of coordinate systems and transformations or whether you look at groups as being able to transform what's inside them, but it's useful to understand both ways of looking at it so you can work with other descriptions of SVG and with tools that might favor one approach over the other.

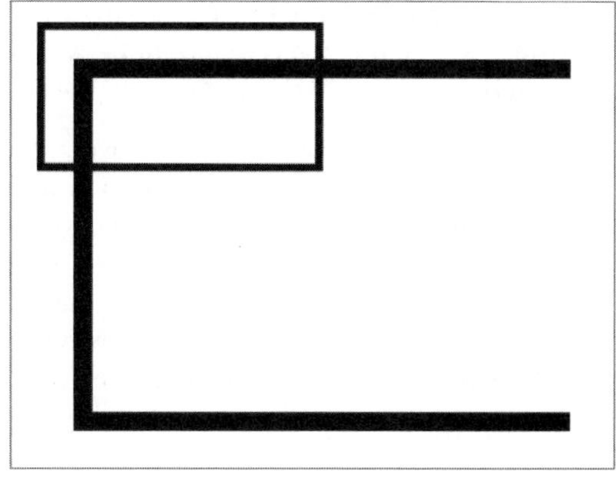

FIGURE 18-13

The <svg>, <symbol>, <image> and <foreignObject> SVG elements can be included within your graphics — including <svg> elements inside <svg> elements — and they each establish new viewports. The <symbol> element is just here for completeness; you use <image> to include bitmap images (see the section Including Bitmap Images), and you can use <foreignObject> to include other markup such as HTML 5 or MathML inside your images, as described in the section SVG and HTML 5.

SVG COLORS AND GRADIENTS

If you are reading the print version of this book you'll probably find that all the examples in this chapter are in black and white. Even the gray parts, as you've already learned, are made up of tiny black dots.

Color in graphics, whether for fine art, graphic design, or commercial job-printing, is a very complex subject with many more facets than one might expect. Color perception also varies greatly between individuals: biological factors can affect the way our eyes and brains perceive colors; and instinctual, cultural, and emotional associations can give different meanings to color, such as blue for distant objects (instinctual) and red for happiness and good fortune (cultural, emotional). Technical factors, such as limitations on the total amount of ink a commercial printing machine can place at any one point on a page, can also affect how colors appear in print.

NOTE *SVG uses the sRGB color space by default; it's also possible to specify a color space such as AdobeRGB for print work, using an ICC color profile. ICC color profiles are a way to describe how a device handles colors, and are defined by the International Color Consortium. They are well beyond the scope of this book, but if you are designing for print you should read the Color section of the latest SVG specification at* `http://www.w3.org/TR/` *and use the ICC color profile provided by your printer.*

SVG colors, then, are like CSS colors that you learned about in Chapter 17. You specify them as three two-digit hexadecimal numbers squished together into a single string, such as `#1122CC`, where `11` indicates the red component, `CC` the green, and 33 the blue.

A *gradient* is a variation of color over distance, such as a rectangle painted dark at one end and light at the other. SVG has two kinds of gradients built in: linear and radial. Figure 18-14 shows first a linear and then a radial gradient, made with the following SVG code. Notice that the gradients are defined inside a `<defs>` element and are given `id` attributes, which are then used with the `url()` syntax in the `fill` attribute. You can define any number of stops as long as the positions increase each way: you can't go backward and define a stop color at 100 percent of the way along and then have one at 75 percent of the way or it won't work. Listing 18-9 shows how to mark up gradients in SVG, and Figure 18-14 shows the result.

Available for download on Wrox.com

LISTING 18-9: gradients.svg

```
<?xml version="1.0" encoding="UTF-8" ?>
<svg version="1.0" xmlns="http://www.w3.org/2000/svg"
  xmlns:xlink="http://www.w3.org/1999/xlink"
  width="120px" height="140px">
  <title>SVG Gradients</title>
  <defs>
    <linearGradient id="leonard">
      <stop offset="5%" stop-color="#000000" />
      <stop offset="95%" stop-color="#FFFFFF" />
    </linearGradient>
    <radialGradient id="rasputin">
      <stop offset="0%" stop-color="#000000" />
      <stop offset="100%" stop-color="#FFFFFF" />
    </radialGradient>
  </defs>
  <!--* linear *-->
  <rect x="10" y="10" width="100" height="50"
    stroke="#000000" stroke-width="2pt" fill="url(#leonard)" />
  <!--* radial *-->
  <rect x="10" y="70" width="100" height="50"
    stroke="#000000" stroke-width="2pt" fill="url(#rasputin)" />
</svg>
```

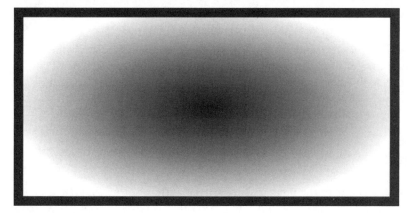

FIGURE 18-14

SVG also supports patterns that you can use to fill shapes. See `http://www.w3.org/TR/2011/REC-SVG11-20110816/pservers.html#Patterns` for the details.

INCLUDING BITMAP IMAGES IN SVG

The start of this chapter mentioned that SVG gives you the best of both worlds — bitmap and vector — because you could include bitmap (raster) images in SVG diagrams. Here's how. Listing, 18-10 uses the Isaac Newton picture from Chapter 17, but uses SVG to give Sir Isaac a red nose:

Available for download on Wrox.com

LISTING 18-10: isaac-nose.svg

```
<?xml version="1.0" encoding="UTF-8" ?>
<svg version="1.0" xmlns="http://www.w3.org/2000/svg"
  xmlns:xlink="http://www.w3.org/1999/xlink">
```

continues

LISTING 18-10 *(continued)*

```
    <title xml:lang="en">Isaac Newton Picture With SVG</title>
    <image x="10" y="10" width="300px" height="310px"
        xlink:href="isaac-newton-300x310.jpg">
      <title>Sir Isaac Newton</title>
    </image>
    <!--* the red nose: *-->
    <circle cx="190px" cy="140px" r="10px"
        stroke="#000000" stroke-width="2px" fill="#FF6666" />
</svg>
```

NOTE *When images have transparent regions, supported in formats such as PNG and GIF, the transparency is also imported into SVG.*

You can add a `preserveAspectRatio` attribute to the `<image>` element, and give it a value of `xMinYMin` to make it fit (be careful with the mixture of lowercase and uppercase letters) or `xMaxYMax` to make it fill the available height and width even if some of the image is lost. Other values for `preserveAspectRatio` are listed in the SVG specification, and have to do with where to place the image in the viewport if it does not all fit.

SVG TEXT AND FONTS

So far there hasn't been any text in any of the images. Because the author of this chapter has a background in digital typography, we can't go without text! SVG text is fairly unsophisticated compared to (say) Quark Passport or Adobe InDesign, but it is *more* sophisticated than most other image formats, including PostScript.

You can design your own SVG fonts, embed existing fonts into SVG documents (assuming the license allows it), or refer to external fonts. In this regard SVG is rather like HTML 5 and CSS web fonts described in Chapter 17.

To include text in an SVG image, use the `<text>` element. You can style it with CSS, and you can include `<tspan>` elements inside `<text>` to format spans of text, rather like `<span>` in HTML.

NOTE *If you want text to flow and maybe be hyphenated, like an HTML paragraph, and if your SVG is being used in HTML 5 (as described later in this chapter), you can use a* `foreignObject` *element and put HTML inside it instead of using the SVG* `text` *element.*

The example in Listing 18-11 uses several concepts from earlier parts of this chapter to illustrate text. There's Isaac Newton's picture, there's a `<defs>` element with a group containing the text, and then the actual text is placed twice, once in light yellow, almost white (`#FFFF99`) moved down and to the right by 2 pixels, and once in dark green (`#003300`) on top. The lighter text makes the words more legible against the texture of the image.

The font used, IM FELL English PRO, is a TrueType font made by Igino Marini and available freely from `http://iginomarini.com/fell/`. If you don't have the font installed, the SVG renderer will substitute some other font.

LISTING 18-11 gravity.svg

```
<?xml version="1.0" encoding="UTF-8" ?>
<svg version="1.0" xmlns="http://www.w3.org/2000/svg"
  xmlns:xlink="http://www.w3.org/1999/xlink">
  <title xml:lang="en">Isaac Newton Picture With text</title>
  <defs>
    <g id="thetext">
      <text width="300px" height="60px" x="20" y="60"
          font-family="IM FELL English PRO" font-size="32pt"
           >Sir Isaac Newton</text>
      <text width="300px" height="60px" x="20" y="120"
          font-family="IM FELL English PRO" font-size="24pt"
           >was the
        <tspan font-size="48">inventor</tspan></text>
      <text width="300px" height="60px" x="20" y="170"
          font-family="IM FELL English PRO" font-size="32pt"
           font-style="italic">of</text>
      <text width="300px" height="60px" x="20" y="250"
          font-family="IM FELL English PRO" font-size="48pt"
          >gravity.</text>
    </g>
  </defs>
  <image x="10" y="10" width="300px" height="310px"
      xlink:href="isaac-newton-300x310.jpg">
    <title>Sir Isaac Newton</title>
  </image>
  <g transform="translate(2, 2)">
    <use xlink:href="#thetext" fill="#FFFF99"/>
  </g>
  <use xlink:href="#thetext" fill="#003300"/>
</svg>
```

You can see how each line of text has to be a separate `<text>` element in SVG. This quickly gets tedious for humans editing SVG by hand, and it makes it difficult to create images that can reflow or change the text as they are resized, but you could use scripted animation for that, as described in the next section.

SVG ANIMATION FOUR WAYS

There are several ways to introduce interactivity and motion into SVG images. In this section you read a little about the four main ways to do so and when to use each of them. These four methods are Synchronized Multimedia Integration Language (SMIL, pronounced *smile*), scripted animation, CSS animation, and external libraries.

WARNING *As of April 2012, Internet Explorer's support for SVG was far behind that of the other browsers when it comes to animation. However, JavaScript libraries are available to make SMIL-based animation work in Internet Explorer.*

Synchronized Multimedia Integration Language (SMIL)

W3C SMIL is a specification for animating XML languages, and SVG incorporates a number of SMIL features. Native implementations of SMIL are also available, such as RealPlayer.

In most cases, SMIL is the best way to animate SVG images. SVG includes the `<animate>`, `<set>`, `<animateMotion>`, `<animateColor>`, and `<animateTransform>` elements. You can use these to make an SVG graphic element change over time or in response to user events, such as hovering over an object with the mouse pointer or touching a circle with a fingertip.

The restriction on these SMIL-based elements is that you can only use them to change SVG attributes or CSS properties. Additionally, although the SVG Recommendation says you can have, for example, a rectangle change size when the mouse hovers over a circle, that doesn't work in web browsers, and in practice you can only have SMIL animation elements affect the object that includes them.

Within these limitations SMIL animation is still very powerful, and because it is declarative, it is usually easier to write, debug, and maintain than the other animation methods. It is also the most widely supported. Listing 18-12 shows an SVG document that describes a circle and an ellipse. If you hover the mouse pointer over the circle, the `<animate>` element inside the circle fills it with red. When the mouse pointer leaves the circle, its original gray fill is restored. Similarly, if you hover the mouse over the ellipse, it moves to the right and gets thinner.

Available for download on Wrox.com

LISTING 18-12: SMIL-animation.svg

```
<?xml version="1.0" encoding="UTF-8" ?>
<svg version="1.0" xmlns="http://www.w3.org/2000/svg">
  <g>
    <circle cx="60" cy="60" r="50"
      fill="#BBBBFF" stroke="#CC0000" stroke-width="1pt">
      <set attributeType="XML" attributeName="fill"
        from="#9999CC" to="#CC0000"
        begin="mouseover" end="mouseout"
        />
    </circle>
  </g>

  <ellipse id="wink" cx="145" cy="60" rx="15" ry="50"
    fill="#9999CC" stroke="#CC0000" stroke-width="1pt">
      <animate attributeName="cx" attributeType="XML"
        from="145" to="300"
        begin="mouseover" dur="2s"
        />
```

```
      <animate attributeName="rx" attributeType="XML"
        from="10" to="0"
        begin="mouseover" dur="2s"
        />
  </ellipse>
</svg>
```

Scripted Animation

If your SVG images are intended for use in a web browser, or some other environment with JavaScript and DOM-based scripting, you can use DOM events in SVG for animation. The DOM was described briefly in Chapter 7, "Extracting Data from XML," and the JavaScript language was introduced in Chapter 16, "AJAX."

To use this method you should be familiar with JavaScript, the JavaScript error console, DOM events, and cross-browser portability. However, because native support for SVG in web browsers (other than Firefox and Opera) didn't really happen until 2011, support for older browsers isn't an issue: the issue becomes one of fallback instead, of providing an alternative. Even if you are familiar with JavaScript, it may still be simpler to use an External Library.

Listing 18-13 shows some simple JavaScript animation used to show or hide the ellipse when you hover the mouse over the circle by adding the `onmouseover` and `onmouseout` attributes. Note that making the ellipse move smoothly is much harder with this approach.

Available for download on Wrox.com

LISTING 18-13: js-animation.svg

```
<?xml version="1.0" encoding="UTF-8" ?>
<svg version="1.0" xmlns="http://www.w3.org/2000/svg">
  <circle cx="60" cy="60" r="50"
    fill="#BBBBFF" stroke="#CC0000" stroke-width="1pt"
    onmouseover="document.getElementById('wink').style.visibility = 'visible';"
    onmouseout="document.getElementById('wink').style.visibility = 'hidden';"
    >
  </circle>

  <ellipse id="wink" cx="145" cy="60" rx="15" ry="50" visibility="hidden"
    fill="#9999CC" stroke="#CC0000" stroke-width="1pt"/>
</svg>
```

A new JavaScript technique called Web Animation was proposed in May 2012; it is not available yet (as of this writing) but may be in the future.

CSS Animation

This technique is new at the time of writing (Spring 2012) and not yet standardized. It is mentioned here partly because by the time you read this book it might be more popular. At least one company (Microsoft) has suggested that it plans to support CSS animation rather than SMIL animation in its web browser, although the market may well have voted for a mixture of SMIL and JavaScript already.

External Libraries

Sometimes the easiest approach is to let others do the hard work. In Chapters 16 and 17 you read about the jQuery library; jQuery plug-ins are available to show SVG documents that can fall back to other methods in versions of Internet Explorer without SVG support. Libraries are also available for doing visualizations of data in SVG, for charts and graphs that move, and much more.

Rather than learn about a single library in this book you should think about your needs, your environment, and the skills of people who will have to maintain what you write, and then look at drawing libraries. Most programming languages contain libraries for creating SVG, as well as frameworks for handling animation.

The question then becomes one of choosing a project. Most of the best libraries for web-based work are open source and free, and, most important of all, you can get the full source code, so that if necessary, you could fix bugs (or pay someone to fix bugs). Make sure the project is widely used and active and you can be pretty sure that it will still be maintained for years to come.

See the "Resources" section later in this chapter for some popular libraries.

SVG AND HTML 5

HTML 5 includes SVG and MathML as if they were part of HTML. It doesn't even need the SVG namespace to be declared. This has a number of implications for people working with XML. One is that you'll start to see HTML documents containing SVG fragments with syntax errors in them. Fortunately, standalone SVG documents are still parsed as XML, so authors have to fix the errors to make them work. Another implication is that SVG has gone mainstream, so there will be better tool support. And another is that you can mix SVG with HTML, including HTML fragments inside a `foreignObject` element. Listing 18-14 (`isaac-again.html`) shows an example, and Figure 18-15 shows what it looks like in the Firefox web browser.

LISTING 18-14: isaac-again.html

Available for download on Wrox.com

```
<!DOCTYPE html>
<html>
  <head>
    <title>HTML 5 and SVG</title>
  </head>
  <body>
    <h1>Isaac Again</h1>
      <svg version="1.0" xmlns="http://www.w3.org/2000/svg"
        xmlns:xlink="http://www.w3.org/1999/xlink" width="300" height="310">
      <title xml:lang="en">Isaac Newton Picture With text</title>
      <defs>
        <g id="thetext">
          <foreignObject x="10" y="15" width="290" height="300">
          <body xmlns="http://www.w3.org/1999/xhtml">
            <div style="font-size: 32pt; line-height:36pt;">Sir Isaac Newton
              <i>was the</i> <big>inventor</big> of
```

```
          <big>gravity</big>.</div></body></foreignObject></g>
    </defs>
    <image x="10" y="10" width="300px" height="310px"
        xlink:href="isaac-newton-300x310.jpg">
      <title>Sir Isaac Newton</title>
    </image>
    <g transform="translate(2, 2)">
      <use xlink:href="#thetext" color="#ffffff" />
    </g>
    <use xlink:href="#thetext" color="#666666" />
  </svg>
</body>
```

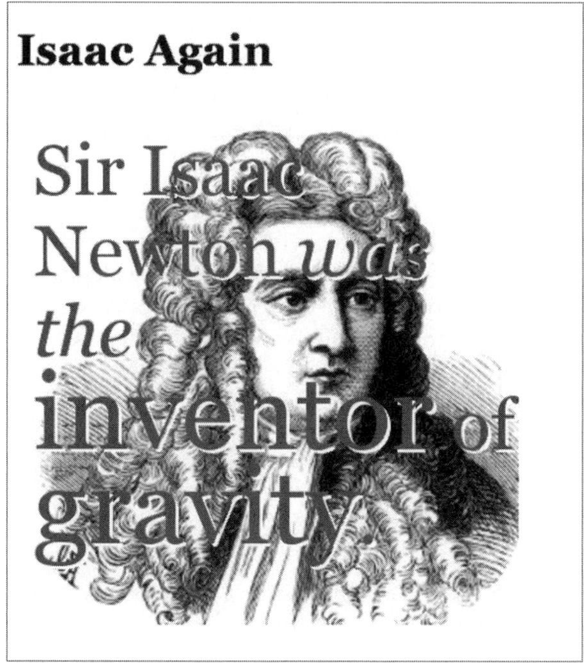

FIGURE 18-15

SVG AND WEB APPS

In Chapter 17, you read about the Open Web Platform and HTML 5. There's a whole host of APIs and languages you can use to make web applications, and one of several driving forces in creating these has been the increased use of mobile computing devices with Internet and web access. The idea of a web application, or app, is that it's a self-contained web page that interacts with a server as little as possible, keeping you on the same page using AJAX (see Chapter 16 for an introduction to AJAX). But a web application is really just any application you access through a web browser.

Web apps tend to draw themselves as if they have dialog boxes and controls just like a desktop application, and they generally use a mixture of SVG and CSS to do this, usually via a library such as jQuery.

In many cases with web app development the SVG will actually be hidden from the developer by the library, but, because SVG is XML-based, you can generate it with XQuery and XSLT on your web server, or even using the XSLT engine that's built in to many web browsers. This turns XSLT and XQuery into potential user-interface generation systems, and you look at that next.

MAKING SVG WITH XQUERY OR XSLT

It's easy to create SVG graphics using XQuery queries or XSLT stylesheets. SVG is an XML-based format and XQuery and XSLT are excellent languages for creating XML documents. There are only a few things to watch out for when doing this and they are described in this section.

The first consideration is that you need to set your serialization options to XML. With XQuery 3 and XSLT 3 you'll also be able to use HTML 5 as an output method if you are creating HTML with embedded SVG.

The next area of concern is that if you are creating CSS, you must decide whether to style SVG or HTML or even XML. You will want to put the CSS in a separate file with the output method set to text. The same applies to JavaScript. If you include inline CSS in the files that you generate with XQuery you'll go insane because of all the curly braces. JavaScript is even harder because of the dollar signs and curly braces. It's also hard to get the serialization options right to include CSS in XHTML: you have to use `<xsl:comment>` to contain the inline CSS. But if you keep the JavaScript and CSS in separate, external files rather than creating them with XQuery or with XSLT, you won't have any problems.

Having said all that, there are lots of uses for SVG in the web browser, and the idea of combining SVG with AJAX can make for exciting effects. You can also generate SVG and use jQuery to surround an HTML element with an SVG border, for example, by "reparenting" the HTML element.

XQuery in the browser (see `http://xqib.org`) and Saxonica's Client Edition of Saxon for XSLT 3 in the browser are also exciting developments at blurring the distinction between client and server.

With many of the world's book publishers using XML, XQuery, XHTML, and XSL-FO (see next chapter), having SVG in electronic books will for sure be the next exciting development in this area. It's also fabulously easy to make charts and business graphics in SVG from XQuery. In Chapter 19, Case Study: XML in Publishing, you'll get a chance to try it out!

RESOURCES

It would be easy to expand this chapter into a whole book because there's so much that can be said about SVG. You have seen enough to know if you're interested; if you are, some of the extra resources in this section will help you.

- **Introduction to SVG:** The W3C homepage for SVG at `http://www.w3.org/Graphics/SVG/`.
- **Learning SVG:** `http://www.learnsvg.com/` and `http://svgelves.com/`.

- **Popular Visualization Libraries:** `http://mbostock.github.com/d3/` and `http://raphaeljs.com/`

SUMMARY

- Scalable Vector Graphics (SVG) is an XML-based format for declarative vector graphics.
- SVG is widely supported, with desktop icons, camera menus, photocopier controls, and web browsers all using it.
- SVG includes XML elements for describing simple shapes such as rectangles. More complex shapes are described using SVG paths.
- The Inkscape program is an open source graphics editor you can use to create and edit SVG graphics.
- HTML 5 includes SVG, so you can put SVG graphics directly into web pages.

EXERCISES

You can find possible solutions to these exercises in Appendix A.

1. What is the difference between an `<ellipse>` and a `<circle>` element in SVG?
2. Name two different methods of animating an SVG image so that a shape changes when the user clicks on it.
3. Why is it important to provide text descriptions of the different parts of a diagram using `<desc>`?
4. What is the difference between uppercase and lowercase commands in SVG path data?

▶ WHAT YOU LEARNED IN THIS CHAPTER

TOPIC	KEY POINTS
The different kinds of images	Image drawing can be procedural or declarative; SVG is declarative, and tells you what, not how. Images can be bitmap or vector; SVG images are vector-based, but can also contain bitmap (raster) images.
Basic shapes in SVG	Circles, ellipses, rectangles, lines, polylines, and polygons are all defined in terms of SVG paths.
SVG is XML	SVG is an XML-based format. SVG images can be generated by and manipulated with XML tools.
SVG is also part of HTML 5	You can include SVG diagrams directly in HTML documents.
SVG and fonts	SVG supports web fonts, CSS font descriptions, platform-native fonts, as well as its own format, SVG fonts.
Viewports and coordinates	SVG images are seen through scalable, stretchy viewports; subelements like <g> can establish new viewports and also new coordinate systems for their contents.

PART VIII
Case Study

19

Case Study: XML in Publishing

WHAT YOU WILL LEARN IN THIS CHAPTER:

- How XML fits into a publisher's workflow
- How XSLT, XQuery, SVG, HTML and XML might be used together in practice
- How to generate SVG images with XSLT
- The purpose of XProc, XSL-FO and MathML
- How to generate PDF from XML with XSL-FO and XSLT
- How XML technologies are used together

This chapter is about a fictional publishing company making a move to an XML-based workflow. Although the company is fictional, the scenario is typical of an actual XML project and shows you how the various topics that you have studied in this book can be used together. You also encounter some new XML vocabularies and projects, such as the Text Encoding Initiative (TEI), MathML, the Darwin Information Typing Architecture (DITA), and DocBook, and learn a little about their strengths and how to discover more vocabularies yourself. This is the last chapter in this book, but it could also be the first chapter of a book about using XML in practice.

BACKGROUND

Hoy Books is a (fictional) reference book publisher operating out of the city of Lyness in Orkney, UK. It has recently purchased another publishing company, Halfdan Books, based in North Ronaldsay. The two companies have combined into a single office in nearby Kirkwall, and are in the process of trying to sort out who does what and what happened to the tea bags that were by the water cooler.

Halfdan Books has published a popular series of books on heraldry. Hoy Books, the larger company, publishes a series of *Who's Who* reference books and a larger biographical dictionary, *Hoy's Who.*

The chief technology officer of the amalgamated company has decided that the biographical books should incorporate heraldic information where available, and the business development officer has determined that, to keep the biographies more current and to reduce costs, a new production system should be installed.

The new system must enable remote writers on the various islands of Orkney to update articles, and must support creation of electronic books as well as the existing print publications.

PROJECT INTRODUCTION: CURRENT WORKFLOW

In the distant past, the editorial team in Lyness would determine the list of people, both living and historical, to include in a new edition of Hoy's Who, and would send out letters to biographers. The biographers would research histories — sometimes transcribing old manuscripts or books and sometimes writing articles, all on neatly typed pages — and then send back what they had written to Lyness. The pages would be edited in-house and then typeset and printed as "galley proofs," which would be sent back to the authors for corrections.

Currently, the authors send files using Microsoft Word and a template with named styles, but the process is essentially the same. The in-house editors at Hoy Books have to make sure that the styles have been used correctly, as well as making the same editorial corrections and suggestions that they did in the paper-based system.

Once the Word files are final they are imported to a page layout program (Adobe InDesign) and assembled into files, each representing 64 complete pages. These are then printed as PDF files, checked one last time, and sent to the company that does the printing. The printer must have even multiples of 64 pages to make "signatures" for the folding and binding machines.

Each time all the files are ready for a new edition to be made, the staff focus all their time on the editing, on sorting out conversion problems, and on getting everything ready; they are unable to accept new articles during this time, and the authors have had to learn that there's a month in which there's no new work for them. This situation proved to be less than ideal, therefore a New System Task Force (NSTF) was created at Hoy Books and tasked with finding and implementing a solution.

INTRODUCING A NEW XML-BASED WORKFLOW

To remain competitive, Hoy Books needed a more streamlined workflow. They had to reduce the time it took to make a new edition of their book, and also produce electronic books (e-books) and a searchable website.

To publish faster, the editorial staff needed to be able to edit incoming articles all the time without having to drop everything to become production managers; this would also help them to retain the external writers they hired. The new workflow also needed to incorporate the Halfden Books heraldry database publishing business.

The best technology for gluing together all of these components is XML, and because of this, Hoy Books decided to attempt a move to an XML-based workflow. In doing so, they chose to equip their external authors with a customized XML editor so that they would no longer need to convert the articles from the word processing format, as that process was error-prone and expensive.

The following sections describe some of the process that Hoy Books went through along their journey to an XML-based workflow. Similar processes are followed by many organizations when they adopt XML: identifying the people who would be affected, consulting with them to learn their needs and also to make them feel part of the project, building prototypes and testing, training staff as needed, documenting the work, and gradually adding functionality as the system grows.

Consultations

At Hoy Books a previous attempt to move to an expensive content management system failed because it relied on the authors having a fast Internet connection, something not always possible on the islands. The island-dwelling authors weren't consulted in this matter before the new system was implemented, and as a result it was unsuccessful.

The single most important aspect to the success of a major new project is to get buy-in from everyone who will be affected. Because it's often impossible to determine exactly who will be affected, it's also essential to communicate clearly. Therefore, meetings to determine who should be involved, and why, must always be part of any XML project.

This time the New System Task Force (NSTF) consulted the authors as well as the printers, external editors, and all of the staff.

People were consulted at every stage, representatives were interviewed, and careful notes were taken.

Documenting the Project

A traditional way of approaching a new project is to make a Requirements document and a Specification document, then implement the specifications and check that the requirements were met. In practice, as soon as people start to see the new system, the requirements will change. The Hoy Books team learned about a newer methodology called *agile development*, in which the requirements and design evolve continuously as the people on the project start to understand what they really need. The team thought this was a good idea, and kept both a Requirements document for tracking the needs they knew they had to meet, and a Current Issues document for tracking issues they needed to resolve.

Prototyping

Having sessions in which people who will use a new system walk through a mock-up, even if it's just based on sketches on paper, can serve several goals. It can turn the new users into enthusiastic evangelists, telling their co-workers how good the new system will be, and it can lead to immediate and essential feedback for the designers. It's important not to oversell a system at this stage, because the most ardent evangelist, when disappointed, can quickly become the most hardened opponent. The Hoy Books task force explained to employees and clients that they really valued the users' opinions and experience, and that it was a learning experience for everyone, so no one should be worried if there were problems at early stages.

After the design mock-ups, the team built some web-based prototypes. However, at this point they had a major setback: the new chief technology officer had heard that XML was slow and unreliable and dropped by to insist that everyone use HTML 5. The task force spokeswoman explained that they had ruled out that approach for cost reasons, and she explained why they needed to use custom schema-based validation for the articles from the authors. She showed the chief technology officer the prototype and the workflow diagrams the task force had prepared, and he grudgingly admitted they had some good ideas. However, he then bet twelve bottles of 25-year-old Highland Park single malt that they would not have a working system within a year!

CREATING A NEW PROCESS

Once the Hoy Books New System Task Force introduced their plan to their employees, created the necessary documents to facilitate the transformation, and started getting employees to test out the new concepts in simulated environments, it was time to start creating the real thing. The NSTF started by deciding what they wanted their XML system to look like and how they wanted the new work flow system to function. They considered the available technologies, preferring a standards-based approach where possible, performed a cost-benefit analysis and estimated the amount of work needed, built and tested small-scale prototypes, and finally deployed the system. This model is a great one to follow if you too are introducing and creating a new XML-based system in your company.

Challenging Criteria

The NSTF identified several difficult criteria the new system would have to include:

- The new system had to be easy for the authors. It had been difficult to get the authors to use styles in Microsoft Word, and a constant problem was articles arriving with ad-hoc styles in them, or with unusual formatting such as a poem in the middle of a place name. Such articles would sometimes be sent off to pieceworkers to be fixed by hand rather than trying to deal with the authors, so they wanted to keep using Microsoft Word, or use something that sounded as easy but that had stricter control over formatting.
- With more than 20,000 articles, each of which could be in any of a number of production states, the system had to provide tracking and summaries.
- Being able to check consistency between articles, especially for things like the spelling of proper names in cross references and titles, would not only improve quality but also save work and money. At least one duplicate article was written every year because of a difference in spelling.
- The system needed a full-text search that was aware of the different sorts of information in the articles, especially place names, people, and dates.

- The new system needed to be able to include diagrams and some simple mathematics.
- The new system would need to expand its production from print books to e-books in a variety of formats.
- A subscription-based website, something that had been too difficult for them to do with their older workflow, would be another great improvement to the system.
- The new amalgamation also meant incorporating heraldic information into the biographies, connecting different publications together.

The development team wrote this up in a document that they circulated not only to their management, but also to everyone who had been involved in the consultation process. They included a short summary as well as notes about how the interviews with outside writers and selected customers were taken into account, so that no-one would feel left out and become a potential barrier in the future. Based on all their needs and on the information they had discovered so far, the team proposed a new workflow, described next.

The New Workflow

The team selected an XML-based content management system this time round, so that they could get the benefits of validated markup, which include the following:

- Better quality control on the input
- Semantic markup that supports the searches and integrity checks they need
- Multiple output formats
- A website that could support a search function
- Formatting for print based on the validated markup, so there would be no need to develop unneeded styles
- Standard and open scripting and programming languages such as XSLT, XQuery, JavaScript, and PHP
- Editorial comment system based on W3C XForms
- Reports generated by XQuery and using SVG for charts

They even found an open source program to format heraldic crests as SVG so that they could be included in web pages and for e-books! Their experts in heraldry were also able to contribute graphics to the open source program for some of the more obscure items.

Document Conversion and Technologies

After the initial checklists were made and workflow determined, at Hoy Books, the next question was, "What should the XML look like?"

The team looked at existing standards and at inventing their own markup. In the end they decided on a hybrid: they would use markup from the Text Encoding Initiative (TEI) for the articles, because it already had the features they needed for transcriptions of old manuscripts for the more scholarly articles. They looked at DocBook, an industry standard maintained by the Oasis standards body, for the technical documentation. They also considered Oasis DITA, a more complex standard for documentation that comes with an information architecture methodology. In the end they settled on a subset of DocBook called Mallard, partly for simplicity and partly because it was used by the content-management system they chose.

After deciding what the XML should look like, Hoy Books needed to figure out how to deal with the twenty thousand main articles and many additional smaller articles, including how to categorize them, what format they needed to be in, and how to convert them into the desired format. When your core business asset is information, keeping your documents current sounds like a pretty important thing to do, but it's often seen as an unwanted expense. You find publishers using decades-old word processors running on emulators of old operating systems to avoid training and conversion costs. Sometimes it's because the profit margin is too low and sometimes it seems to be fear of the unknown! Hoy didn't want to make this mistake with their articles.

The team did end up inventing their own RDF ontology to describe the various states of articles: requested from author, in process, received draft and awaiting edit, being copyedited, and so forth. Because their content management system used XQuery, they used an RDF XQuery module to produce editorial reports at first, but later moved to using SPARQL implemented in XQuery. The team was also able to use SPARQL to search the heraldry database that Hoy Books had bought, and to associate heraldic coats of arms and family crests with people in the *Hoy's Who* books.

Once they had chosen the formats, the team was able to send data to a company in India that owned technology to convert Word files to XML. Because the Word files followed a rigid use of styles, the conversion ended up with very few problems and was inexpensive. An alternative suggested, made by a visiting consultant from Dublin they had, was to run XSLT on the Microsoft Word Office Open XML files, but most of the documents were in the proprietary binary format from older Word versions. It turned out that a few files would no longer open in recent versions of Word, but the conversion people in India had libraries that could recover the text and most of the styles.

The mathematics in the articles was another matter, and had to be re-keyed, but, luckily, that cost could be spread over several years, as and when the relatively few articles containing equations were needed.

Costs and Benefits Analysis

Most modern publishers need to produce electronic books in order to survive, and the market is no longer willing to accept just PDF images of printed pages: the pages must fit the width of the book reader. So the right question for the publisher (Hoy or any) is not "What's the cheapest way to continue what we have been doing?" but rather, "How do we adapt to new technology without losing our reputation in the marketplace?"

With this view, the XML-based system is a sound investment. It supports the new technologies and is also adaptable to future technologies. In addition, publishing is a core strength of XML. The capability to pick data out of mixed content, such as fetching titles and dates of books that the biography subjects had written, and linking them to online copies of the books, is something that would likely have been considerably more expensive in a relational database system.

Deployment

When the NSTF was completely ready, they started implementing the new system with their entire company and the external authors. Most of the authors happily switched to using an XML editor; it was actually easier for them to concentrate on the content rather than the formatting. The team had expected one older writer in his late eighties, to whom they had given the nickname "the Old Man of Hoy," to have problems, but, in fact, he loved the new system. They did lose one writer who took an early retirement rather than learn something new.

The formatter that Hoy Books chose was able to handle both SVG and MathML, and could produce high-quality PDF from XML input using W3C's eXtensible Stylesheet Language Formatting Objects (XSL-FO) standard. Hoy Books hired a consultant for three months to set up the formatting, and although it was expensive because she came all the way from Dublin, the company actually saved more money than expected. The new system could produce PDF not only for print, but also for some of the older e-books.

The team spent a happy week in Oxford learning XSLT, and came back ready for the website challenge. They worked with their web design firm and soon had HTML 5 web pages. They used XQuery to generate XML summaries from their database, which were then formatted using XSLT for the Web.

The content management system used XProc, the XML Pipelining Language, to specify how the content for any given web page should be generated from the database, for example using XQuery to do a search or make an article summary, followed by running an XSLT transformation on the result of the query to turn it into HTML using the Hoy Books web template.

With the new production in place, Hoy Books could accept articles from the authors all the time, and because their new content-management system would keep track of the status of the articles for them, and because they didn't have to convert the articles to the page layout program format any more, the staff had time to check the articles and keep the external authors paid. The new website had all of the articles available, and an unexpected benefit was that they were able to offer custom e-books to their users.

The end result was that time between an external author finishing an article and the article being available to the customers went from several weeks down to a few days, and, being much more responsive, the company was able to make better use of its assets to increase revenue. Therefore, the project was a success.

This project was fictional, of course, but it is based on real projects. Many of the world's largest publishers (and some of the smallest) do use XML in the ways described in this chapter. Similar projects can also be found all over the world in documentation and engineering departments of large companies. In the next section of this chapter you read in more detail about some of the technologies that were mentioned here but that have not been covered in depth elsewhere in this book.

SOME TECHNICAL ASPECTS

The first part of this chapter mentioned a lot of technologies that were used in the example project at Hoy Books. The next part of this chapter is devoted to introducing you to some of those technologies in more detail, so that you can decide whether you need to learn more about them. Examples are included for some of the technologies but not for others — the decision on which to include was based on how much explanation you'd need for an example to make sense, not on the importance or usefulness of the technology. The tools that work in your situation are the most important for you, of course, and tens of thousands of XML vocabularies and tools are available! In some cases the technologies have been covered in more detail in earlier chapters, and are presented here to put them into a larger context of how they might be used.

XQuery and Modules

You learned about XQuery modules in Chapter 9. The team at Hoy Books used XQuery modules to make their own API; a set of XQuery functions for accessing both meta data and documents from the database. This enabled them to be flexible when they changed their RDF ontologies and XML Schemas from time to time, and kept the details hidden.

XInclude

XInclude is the W3C "XML Inclusions" specification. The Hoy Books XQuery module for reports generates XML elements with reference to some external XML documents that are included using an `XInclude` element like so:

```
<xi:include xmlns:xi="http://www.w3.org/2001/XInclude"
    href="management-structure.html" />
```

An XInclude processor will replace the `xi:include` element with the document to which it refers. Of course, the URI could use the HTTP protocol, perhaps referring to a document generated by the database on the fly.

Equations and MathML

MathML is W3C's XML vocabulary for representing equations. It has two subtypes: *content* and *presentational*. The content form uses markup that describes the meaning, whereas the presentational form describes the intended appearance. Because mathematics is open ended, and research mathematicians invent new symbols and notations constantly, you always have to use at least a little presentational markup. However, the content markup would suffice for school text books up to undergraduate level in most cases, and in some cases beyond that.

For Hoy Books, simple equations were usually enough: plenty of books and papers on science-related subjects have fragments of equations in their titles, and for historical notations the team at Hoy Books used a mixture of SVG and scanned images. Using MathML meant that they could generate e-books as well as print from the same source, and could also search on text included in the equations. Discovering that there was web browser support for MathML was the final piece in the puzzle that led them to move away from proprietary word-processing formats.

Although MathML is now incorporated into HTML 5, browser support has been slow to follow. Mozilla Firefox was first, and supports both content and presentational markup. You can use a JavaScript library from `www.mathjax.org` to support MathML on browsers such as Internet Explorer or Google Chrome, and XSLT style sheets are also available; see `http://www.w3.org/Math/` for more details.

MathML also introduces literally hundreds of named symbols that can be used in HTML or XML documents via entity references. You can define additional symbols using SVG (see Chapter 18, "Scalable Vector Graphics (SVG)"), or you could use downloadable web fonts as described in Chapter 17, "XHTML and HTML 5."

Listing 19-1 shows an example of an equation marked up in MathML, and Figure 19-1 shows the result in Firefox. The file shown in the browser also contains three additional equations whose markup is not included in the book, but the file on the accompanying website does include all four examples. The CSS in the example puts a dotted box around the equation.

Available for download on Wrox.com

LISTING 19-1: mathml-in-html5.html

```
<!DOCTYPE html>
<html>
  <head>
    <title>MathML Examples</title>
    <style type="text/css">
      body {
        color: #000;
        background-color: #fff;
      }
      div.m {
        float: left;
        padding: 3em;
        border: 1px dotted;
        margin: 1em;
      }
      h2 {
        text-size: 100%;
        clear: both;
      }
    </style>
  </head>
  <body>
    <h1>MathML Examples</h1>
    <h2>Quadratic and Integral</h2>
    <div class="m">
      <math display="block">
        <mrow>
          <mi>x</mi>
          <mo>=</mo>
          <mfrac>
            <mrow>
              <mo form="prefix">&minus;</mo>
              <mi>b</mi>
              <mo>&PlusMinus;</mo>
              <msqrt>
                <msup>
                  <mi>b</mi>
                  <mn>2</mn>
                </msup>
                <mo>&minus;</mo>
```

continues

LISTING 19-1 *(continued)*

```
                <mn>4</mn>
                <mo>&InvisibleTimes;</mo>
                <mi>a</mi>
                <mo>&InvisibleTimes;</mo>
                <mi>c</mi>
              </msqrt>
            </mrow>
            <mrow>
              <mn>2</mn>
              <mo>&InvisibleTimes;</mo>
              <mi>a</mi>
            </mrow>
          </mfrac>
        </mrow>
      </math>
    </div>
    [. . .]
  </body>
</html>
```

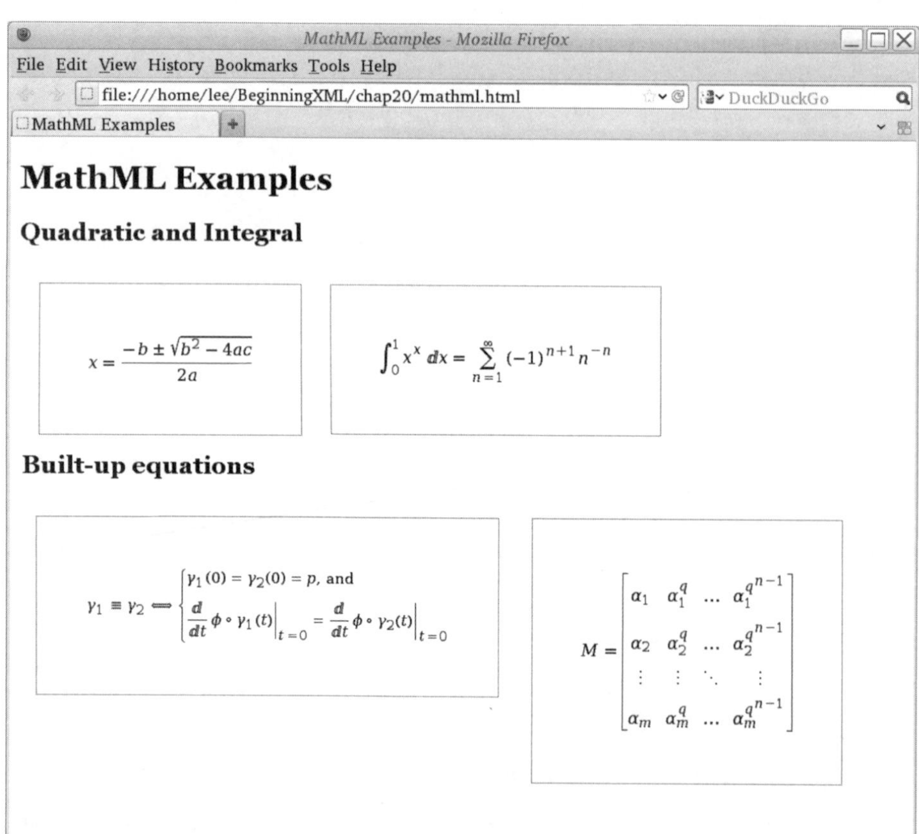

FIGURE 19-1

XProc: An XML Pipelining Language

The team at Hoy Books used a native XML database with XQuery to power their content-management system. To generate reports, they first extracted information from the database with XQuery and then ran XSLT to make a mixture of SVG and XHTML; in some cases this involved running more than one XSLT transformation. Remembering the steps for each report would be tedious. Utilities like *ant* or *make* could be used, or shell scripts or batch files, to automate the process, but XProc provides a clearer framework not tied to any one technology, and, being XML-based, was stored in the database, so it was a good fit for Hoy Books.

Listing 19-2 shows a sample pipeline that first extracts some data — perhaps a list of articles that are overdue from the authors, who of course are always late!

Available for download on Wrox.com

LISTING 19-2: xproc.xml

```
<p:pipeline xmlns:p="http://www.w3.org/ns/xproc" version="1.0">
  <!--* First run Query to get the data *-->
  <p:xquery>
    <p:input port="query">
      <p:data href="reports/editorial-status.xq" />
    </p:input>
  </p:xquery>

  <!--* The Query generates XML that can include some
      * boilerplate text, so run XInclude next:
      *-->
  <p:xinclude/>

  <!--* Validate the result to make sure that we didn't
      * make a mistake:
      *-->
  <p:validate-with-xml-schema>
    <p:input port="schema">
      <p:document href="reports/editorial-status.xsd"/>
    </p:input>
  </p:validate-with-xml-schema>

  <!--* Generate SVG graphs of the data *-->
  <p:xslt>
    <p:input port="stylesheet">
      <p:document href="reports/editorial-status-svg.xslt" />
    </p:input>
  </p:xslt>

 <!--* Generate a report that can be viewed in a Web browser: *-->
  <p:xslt>
    <p:input port="stylesheet">
      <p:document href="reports/editorial-html.xslt" />
    </p:input>
  </p:xslt>
</p:pipeline>
```

The XQuery (not shown) generates an XML document with the data, and also with `XInclude` elements that refer to some boilerplate documents for the reports. The pipeline explicitly includes an XProc `xinclude` step to handle this.

After the boilerplate text (the list of staff and their positions, in fact) is included, the resulting XML document is validated against a W3C XML Schema. This helps the developers know that everything worked as expected. The next step runs XSLT to turn the numeric data into SVG graphics, and then, finally, the XML document is turned into an HTML web page for viewing.

This modular approach can also be used for the printed books and for the website, of course, as well as for producing e-books.

See `www.w3.org/TR/xproc/` for the latest XProc specification.

XForms, REST, and XQuery

The W3C XForms language provides a way for users to interact with a web page. It separates data using the model-view-controller system, avoiding unnecessary round trips to the server and reducing the need for scripting.

Hoy Books used XForms embedded within XHTML for an editorial comment interface; the form sends XML back to the content management system, which, being based on a native XML database powered by XQuery, can use it directly. You can learn more about Xforms at `www.w3.org/MarkUp/Forms/`.

REST, or REpresentational State Transfer, is a term coined by Roy Fielding to describe a way of using the World Wide Web. It describes how to write web applications, and although a detailed explanation is outside the scope of this book, you are *strongly* encouraged to read more about REST and "XRX" if you write applications that use XForms and XQuery. REST is the "R" that connects XForms and XQuery.

Formatting to PDF with XSL-FO

The W3C eXtensible Stylesheet Language Formatting Objects specification is a vocabulary for document formatting. It uses the idea of pouring a stream of content, called the flow, into a sequence of page templates. The elements in the flow are styled with CSS (and with some additional properties more suited to print work than CSS 2), and are positioned within the page templates by the formatting engine.

The XSL-FO specification assumes that you're generating the input XML (in the FO vocabulary) using XSLT: you transform elements in your XML documents into formatting objects like `<fo:block>` and `<fo:inline>` with CSS style properties, and then run a formatter to make PDF or other output formats.

Listing 19-3 shows an XSLT style sheet that will convert either the tiny `armstrong.xml` file or the larger `chalmers-biography-extract.xml` file that you first saw in Chapter 9 into XSL-FO; you could then run a formatter such as the open source `xmlroff` or Apache FOP programs to make PDF. Hoy Books used a commercial XSL-FO formatter that also included MathML support. Figure 19-2 shows one page of a PDF document made by first running the XSLT stylesheet in Listing 19-3 on the `chalmers-biography-extract.xml` file and then taking the result of that and running it through the Apache FOP program.

Available for download on Wrox.com

LISTING 19-3: make-xsl-fo.xsl

```
<?xml version="1.0" encoding="utf-8" ?>
<xsl:stylesheet version="1.0"
    xmlns:xsl="http://www.w3.org/1999/XSL/Transform"
    xmlns:fo="http://www.w3.org/1999/XSL/Format">

 <xsl:strip-space elements="dictionary entry body" />

 <xsl:template match="/">
      <fo:root font-family="Times"
          font-size="10pt" line-height="12pt">
      <fo:layout-master-set>
        <fo:simple-page-master master-name="dictpage"
          page-width="8.5in" page-height="11in"
          margin-top="0.5in" margin-bottom="0in"
          margin-left="1in" margin-right="0.75in">
          <fo:region-body margin-bottom="0.75in"
              column-count="2" column-gap="0.5in" />
          <fo:region-after extent="0.5in" />
        </fo:simple-page-master>
      </fo:layout-master-set>
      <fo:page-sequence master-reference="dictpage">
        <fo:static-content flow-name="xsl-region-after">
          <fo:block text-align="center">Page <fo:page-number /></fo:block>
        </fo:static-content>
        <fo:flow flow-name="xsl-region-body">
          <!--* generate the content here *-->
          <xsl:apply-templates/>
        </fo:flow>
      </fo:page-sequence>
    </fo:root>
  </xsl:template>

  <xsl:template match="dictionary"><xsl:apply-templates/></xsl:template>

  <xsl:template match="entry">
    <fo:block text-indent="-2em" margin-bottom="12pt">
      <xsl:apply-templates/>
    </fo:block>
  </xsl:template>

  <xsl:template match="entry/title">
    <fo:inline font-style="italic">
      <xsl:apply-templates/>
    </fo:inline>
  </xsl:template>

  <xsl:template match="entry/body"><xsl:apply-templates/></xsl:template>

  <xsl:template match="p">
    <fo:block keep-together="auto" text-indent="1.5em">
      <xsl:apply-templates/>
    </fo:block>
  </xsl:template>
```

continues

LISTING 19-3 *(continued)*

```
    <xsl:template match="body/p[1]">
      <fo:inline><xsl:apply-templates/></fo:inline>
    </xsl:template>

    <!--* note: the Apache Fop renderer does not support small caps *-->
    <xsl:template match="entry/title/csc">
      <fo:inline font-variant="small-caps">
        <xsl:apply-templates/>
      </fo:inline>
    </xsl:template>

    <xsl:template match="i">
      <fo:inline font-style="italic">
        <xsl:apply-templates/>
      </fo:inline>
    </xsl:template>
  </xsl:stylesheet>
```

1676, published in 1710 the history of Prussia and Brandenburg, "Preussische und Brandisburgische Staats-Historie," Leipsic, 8vo; in 1714, some favourite satires; and, in 1715, a work of far more utility and importance, "Historia Monarchiarum orbis antiqui," Leipsic, 8vo; a Greek Archaeology, 1738; and a translation of Boileau. He died at Westdorf in 1763 .

Abel, Frederick Gottfried , a physician, assessor of the College of Physicians, and member of the Literary Society at Halberstadt, the son of the preceding Gaspar, was born July 8, 1714. In 1731, he commenced his theological studies at Halberstadt, under the celebrated Mosheim, and a year after removed to Halle, where he attended the lectures of Wolfe and Baumgarten, and often preached with much applause. In a few years, however, he gave up his theological pursuits, studied medicine, and in 1744 was admitted to the degree of doctor at Konigsberg. On his return to Halberstadt, he practised as a physician above half a century, and died Nov. 23, 1794. He is said to have been uncommonly successful in practice, yet had very little faith in medicine, and always prescribed such remedies as were cheap and common. Probity, modesty, and humanity, were the most striking features in his character. While studying medicine at Halle, he did not neglect polite literature. He made some poetical translations, particularly one of Juvenal into German, which he published in 1738 .

Abelli, Louis was born in the Vexin Francois, in 1603. He was promoted to be grand vicar of Bayonne, then curate of Paris, and lastly bishop of Rhodes, in 1664, which he resigned about three years afterwards, in order to live a retired life in the house of St. Lazare, at Paris. He died Oct. 4, 1691, aged 88 years. His principal works are: 1. "Medulla Theologica," 2 vols. 12mo, which gained him the title of Modleuz A belli (the marrowy) from Boileau. 2. A treatise "De la Hierarchic, et de l'autorité du Pape," 4to. 3. "La Tradition de l'Eglise, touchant la devotion a Sainte Vierge," 8vo, 1662, a work which the Protestants have often quoted against Bossuet. 4. "La Vie de M. Renard," 12mo. 5. "La Vie de St. Vincent de Paul," 4to, in which he openly declares himself against the Jansenists. 6. "Enchiridion sollicitudinis pastoralis," 4to. 7. "Meditation pour chaque jour de Tanne'e," 2 vols. 12mo. His Latin style is harsh, and his French writings are accounted by his countrymen flat and insipid. They allow him, however, to have excelled in every sacerdotal virtue, and to have been exemplary in his pastoral offices.

Aben-Ezra , Aven-Hezer, or Ben-Meir, (Abraham), a celebrated Rabbi, born at Toledo, in Spain, in 1099, called by the Jews, the wise, great, and admirable doctor, was a very able interpreter of the Holy Scriptures, and was well skilled in grammar, poetry, philosophy, astronomy, and in medicine. He was also a perfect master of the Arabic. His style is in general clear, elegant, concise, and much like that of the Holy Scriptures; he almost always adheres to the literal sense, and everywhere gives proofs of his genius and good sense: he however advances some erroneous sentiments, and his conciseness sometimes makes his style obscure. He travelled in most parts of Europe, visiting England, France, Italy, Greece, &c. for the purpose of acquiring knowledge, and far surpassed his brethren both in sacred and profane learning. He wrote theological, grammatical, and astronomical works, many of which remain in manuscript, but the following have been published: 1. "Perus a l'Altora," or a commentary on the Law, fol. Constantinople, 5262 (1552), a very rare edition. There is likewise another edition printed at Venice, 1576, fol. 2. "Jesod Mora," intended as an exhortation to the study of the Talmud, Constantinople, 8vo. 1530, by far the most scarce of all his works. 3. "Elegantiæ Grammaticæ," Venice, 1546, 8vo. 4. "De Luminaribus et Diebus criticis liber," Leyden, 1496, 4to. of which there have been three editions. 5. "De Nativitatibus," Venice, 1485, 4to, republished by John Dryander, Col. 1537, 4to. He died in 1174 at the island of Rhodes, in the 75th year of his age, but some have placed his death in 1165.

Abercromby, Patrick , a physician and historian, was the son of Alexander Abercromby, of Fetternear, in Aberdeenshire, and brother of Francis Abercromby, who was created lord Glasford in July 1685. He was born at Forfar, in the county of Angus, in 1656, and educated in the university of St. Andrew's, where he took the degree of doctor in medicine in 1685. Some accounts say that he spent Ims youth in foreign countries, was probably educated in the university of Paris, and that his family were all Roman Catholics, who partook of the misfortunes of James II.; others, that on his return to Scotland he renounced the Protestant religion, at the request of king James, and was by him appointed one of the physicians to trie court, which he was obliged to relinquish at the Revolution. Soon after he attached himself to the study of antiquities, and published, "The Martial Achievements of Scotland," 2 vols. fol. 1711 and 1715, to which he was encouraged by a large list of subscribers. The first volume abounds in the marvellous, but the second is valuable on account of its accurate information respecting the British history in the fourteenth and fifteenth centuries. He wrote also a treatise on Wit, 1686, which is now little known, and translated M. Beague's very rare book, "L'Histoire de la Guerre d'Escosse," 1556, under the title of "The History of the Campagnes 1548 and 1549: being an exact account of the martial expeditions performed in those days by the Scots and French on the one side, and the English and their foreign auxiliaries on the other: done in French by Mons. Beague, a French gentleman. Printed in Paris 1556, with an introductory preface by the translator," 1707, 8vo. The ancient alliance between

Page 2

FIGURE 19-2

XML Markup for Documentation

An undocumented project often becomes a problem when key people leave the company or change roles. The Hoy Books team knew this and documented not only the final system but also the decision process, so that people changing the system would understand not only *how* it worked but *why*.

They used Oasis DocBook as an XML format for their documentation, and some open source XSLT style sheets that converted DocBook documents into XHTML and PDF.

They could have used the same markup that was used for the dictionary entries, and although that was tempting, the needs were different. The biographical dictionary does not contain code listings or sequences of instructions, for example, but the documentation probably does.

Another format widely used for documentation is the Darwin Information Typing Architecture (DITA), also produced by Oasis. DITA is a framework for topic-based authoring, and is best suited for use when the end product is documentation. At the (fictional) Hoy Books company the end product is, of course, world-class biographical dictionaries, and the team felt that DITA was too much for them to take on to document their system.

Markup for the Humanities: TEI

The Text Encoding Initiative is a consortium that produces guidelines for markup of scholarly texts in XML. The Hoy Books team chose the TEI P5 guidelines because it met their needs for transcriptions of manuscripts, books, and articles, because work had already been done on biographical dictionaries, and because there was already support for the markup in existing tools and editors. The oXygen XML Editor you used in earlier chapters, for example, includes TEI support (as well as support for DocBook and DITA). The Text Encoding Initiative Guidelines (both P4 and P5) are by far the most widely used XML vocabularies in humanities computing.

You should choose markup that suits your own projects, so rather than read an example in this book you are referred to `www.tei-c.org` to learn more.

THE HOY BOOKS WEBSITE

For their website, the Hoy Books team used a copy of their XML database rather than the original, partly fearing that production might be affected in an attack, and partly so that the server could be located in nearby Scotland, where the Internet connections were stronger.

They used XSL-FO on the server so that users could download PDF versions of articles, and they used XQuery Full Text to provide searching. Their content management system could run XSLT using XProc, so the Hoy Books staff made some pipelines that added interactive SVG content to the dictionary entries.

They included heraldic shields using the open source “drawshield” program, SVG time lines showing when people in the articles were born and died, and marking other events such as publications of their woks. They also made a visualization showing clusters of people’s colleagues and likely acquaintances.

There was an RSS feed so people could see new or updated articles as they were published; this was made using XQuery to generate RDF on the fly, and the flexibility this gave them meant they could easily generate customized RSS feeds based on users' searches.

Connections between the RDF meta data in the biography articles and the RDF for the heraldry information in the Halfdan Books database enabled automatic links from biographies to genealogies and to entries for family members, which was an unexpected benefit.

Most of the concepts here have already been illustrated in this book. To understand them in context, the following activity demonstrates generating an SVG visualization from documents in the database using both XQuery and XSLT.

TRY IT OUT Making SVG Using XQuery and XSLT

This activity has three main parts. First, you use XQuery to generate a summary XML document containing just the data of interest. Second, you use XSLT to generate an SVG graphic based on that data. Third, you use an SVG viewer or web browser to see the result. The files are all included with this book, so you can compare them with the ones you generate yourself.

1. Type the query from Listing 19-4 into a file called `timelines.xq` and run Saxon in query mode:

```
java -cp saxon9he.jar net.sf.saxon.Query timelines.xq > timelines.xml
```

If you prefer, you can use the command-line query processor included in the BaseX database package you downloaded in Chapter 9:

```
basex/7.1/bin/basex -w timelines.xq > timelines.xml
```

The `-w` option to `basex` tells it to preserve whitespace; this is needed because the input document in the database has *mixed content*, which is a mixture of text and elements, in the article titles that the query extracts.

(See Chapter 9 for more details on XQuery.)

Available for download on Wrox.com

LISTING 19-4: timelines.xq

```
xquery version "1.0";
(: read dict. of biog. and extract timelines. :)

<timelines>{
  for $e in doc("chalmers-biography-extract.xml")//entry
  where $e[xs:integer(@born) gt 1250] and $e[@died]
  return
    <entry born="{$e/@born}" died="{$e/@died}" id="{$e/@id}">
      { normalize-space(string-join($e/title//text(), "") }
    </entry>
}</timelines>
```

The result of running the query is shown in part in the following code snippet; the actual file generates a lot more entries, but this activity will still work if you use the shorter version shown in the listing.

```
<timelines>
  <entry born="1616" died="1664" id="aagard-christian">Aagard, Christian</entry>
  <entry born="1572" died="1641" id="aarsens-francis">Aarsens, Francis</entry>
  <entry born="1648" died="1718" id="abeille-gaspar">Abeille, Gaspar</entry>
  <entry born="1676" died="1763" id="abel-gaspar">Abel, Gaspar</entry>
  <entry born="1603" died="1691" id="abelli-louis">Abelli, Louis</entry>
  <entry born="1589" died="1655" id="abraham-nicholas">Abraham, Nicholas</entry>
  <entry born="1428" died="1478" id="acciaioli-donato">Acciaioli, Donato</entry>
  <entry born="1418" died="1483" id="accolti-francis">Accolti, Francis</entry>
  <entry born="1455" died="1532" id="accolti-peter">Accolti, Peter</entry>
  <entry born="1696" died="1772" id="achard-anthony">Achard, Anthony</entry>
  <entry born="1556" died="1621" id="achen-john-van">Achen, John Van</entry>
</timelines>
```

timelines-short.xml

2. Now that you've made a compact file with just the data you need, it's easy to see how to process it with XSLT. Because XSLT processors traverse the entire input, they are much easier to work with if you have one small file rather than 100,000 separate articles. XQuery processors with a database, by contrast, are often excellent at fetching a small amount of data from many documents.

   The XSLT file for this stage is shown in Listing 19-5. Type it into a file called `timelines.xsl` (or use the version included with the book).

Available for download on Wrox.com

LISTING 19-5: timelines.xsl

```
<xsl:stylesheet version="2.0"
  xmlns:svg="http://www.w3.org/2000/svg"
  xmlns:xs="http://www.w3.org/2001/XMLSchema"
  xmlns:xsl="http://www.w3.org/1999/XSL/Transform">

  <xsl:variable name="itemwidth" select="10" as="xs:integer" />
  <xsl:variable name="height" select="600" as="xs:integer" />
  <xsl:variable name="labeloffset" select="200" as="xs:integer" />
  <xsl:variable name="lineoffset" select="230" as="xs:integer" />

  <xsl:variable name="earliest"
    select="min(for $y in //entry/@born return xs:integer($y))" />
  <xsl:variable name="latest"
    select="max(for $y in //entry/@died return xs:integer($y))" />
  <xsl:variable name="yscale"
    select="($height - 200) div ($latest - $earliest)" />

  <xsl:template match="timelines">
    <svg xmlns="http://www.w3.org/2000/svg"
      style="font-size:10pt;background-color:white;color:black;">
      <xsl:apply-templates />
    </svg>
```

continues

LISTING 19-5 *(continued)*

```
  </xsl:template>

  <xsl:template match="entry">
    <xsl:variable name="x" select="$itemwidth * position()" />
    <xsl:variable name="y1"
      select="$lineoffset + (@born - $earliest) * $yscale" />
    <xsl:variable name="y2"
      select="$lineoffset + (@died - $earliest) * $yscale" />

    <xsl:if test="position() mod 5 eq 0">
      <svg:line x1="{$x - $itemwidth div 2}" y1="{$lineoffset}"
        x2="{$x - $itemwidth div 2}" y2="{$height + 60}"
        style="stroke-width:1px;stroke:#CCCCCC;stroke-dasharray=2,2"/>
    </xsl:if>

    <svg:text x="0" y="0"
      transform="translate({$x}, {$labeloffset}) rotate(-60)">
      <xsl:apply-templates />
    </svg:text>

    <svg:line x1="{$x}" y1="{$y1}" x2="{$x}" y2="{$y2}"
      style="stroke-width:4pt;stroke:#CCCCCC" />

    <svg:circle cx="{$x}" cy="{$y1}" r="{$itemwidth idiv 3}"
      style="fill:#CCCCCC;stroke-width:1pt;stroke:#000"
      title="born {@born}" />

    <svg:circle cx="{$x}" cy="{$y2}"
      r="{$itemwidth idiv 3}"
      style="fill:#CCCCCC;stroke-width:1pt;stroke:#000"
      title="died {@died}" />
  </xsl:template>
</xsl:stylesheet>
```

3. Run the XSLT transformation on the `timelines.xml` file you created with XQuery to make an SVG file, `timelines.svg`, like this:

```
saxon timelines.xml timelines.xsl > timelines.svg
```

The resulting SVG should look like Listing 19-6, except that long lines were broken for the book.

Available for download on Wrox.com

LISTING 19-6: timelines.svg

```
<?xml version="1.0" encoding="UTF-8"?>

<svg xmlns:xs="http://www.w3.org/2001/XMLSchema"
  xmlns:svg="http://www.w3.org/2000/svg" xmlns="http://www.w3.org/2000/svg"
  style="font-size:10pt;background-color:white;color:black;">
  <svg:text x="0" y="0" transform="translate(20, 200) rotate(-60)">
    Aagard, Christian</svg:text>
  <svg:line x1="20" y1="453.728813559322" x2="20" y2="507.96610169491527"
```

```
      style="stroke-width:4pt;stroke:#CCCCCC"/>
    <svg:circle cx="20" cy="453.728813559322" r="3"
      style="fill:#CCCCCC;stroke-width:1pt;stroke:#000" title="born 1616"/>
    <svg:circle cx="20" cy="507.96610169491527" r="3"
      style="fill:#CCCCCC;stroke-width:1pt;stroke:#000" title="died 1664"/>

    <svg:text x="0" y="0" transform="translate(40, 200) rotate(-60)"> Aarsens,
      Francis</svg:text> <svg:line x1="40" y1="404.01129943502826" x2="40"
      y2="481.9774011299435" style="stroke-width:4pt;stroke:#CCCCCC"/>
    <svg:circle cx="40" cy="404.01129943502826" r="3"
      style="fill:#CCCCCC;stroke-width:1pt;stroke:#000" title="born 1572"/>
    <svg:circle cx="40" cy="481.9774011299435" r="3"
      style="fill:#CCCCCC;stroke-width:1pt;stroke:#000" title="died 1641"/>

    <svg:text x="0" y="0" transform="translate(60, 200) rotate(-60)"> Abeille,
      Gaspar</svg:text> <svg:line x1="60" y1="489.88700564971754" x2="60"
      y2="568.9830508474577" style="stroke-width:4pt;stroke:#CCCCCC"/>
    <svg:circle cx="60" cy="489.88700564971754" r="3"
      style="fill:#CCCCCC;stroke-width:1pt;stroke:#000" title="born 1648"/>
    <svg:circle cx="60" cy="568.9830508474577" r="3"
      style="fill:#CCCCCC;stroke-width:1pt;stroke:#000" title="died 1718"/>
  </svg>
```

4. Finally, look at the result in an SVG viewer such as Inkview (included with Inkscape) or with a web browser. The result is shown in Figure 19-3.

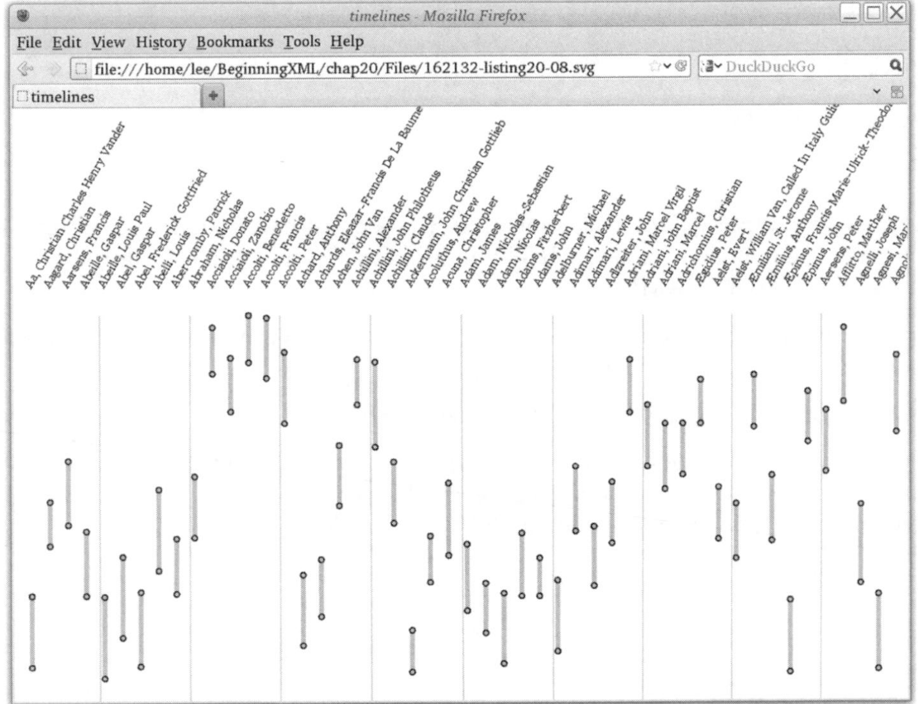

FIGURE 19-3

How It Works

First, the XQuery fragment searches `chalmers-biography-extract.xml` for all `<entry>` elements that have a `born` attribute whose integer value is larger than `1250` and that also has a `died` attribute.

For each such element `$e`, the query constructs an entirely new `<entry>` element having `born`, `died`, and `id` attributes taken from `$e`. The new element contains the value of an `{` *expression* `}`, made from building a sequence of all text nodes in the title, assembling them into one string with `string-join()`, and then converting newlines into spaces and squishing multiple blanks. (Because the XML file uses indenting, copying multiple blank lines to the output made the file take up lots of space in the book.)

Next, the XSLT style sheet has a template (starting on line 26, `match="entry"`) to match the freshly made `<entry>` elements. The template draws a vertical line and some text for the entry, so first it computes the horizontal position (`x`), then the start and end vertical positions of the line (`y1` and `y2`).

Every fifth entry (`position() mod 5 eq 0`) gets a thin, dashed vertical line to make the chart easier to read.

Then, the template makes a `<text>` element with the content of the `<entry>` element; this content is the name of the person the article is about.

The text is positioned at `(0, 0)` so that it can be rotated easily; the actual positioning is done with the `transform` on line 40.

After the text, the vertical line is drawn, followed by two circles. The line is drawn first so that the circles sit on top of it; if you move the `<svg:line>` element down in the style sheet after the circles, you'll see that the result looks very messy.

SUMMARY

- An organization can use XML technologies to reduce costs, have a faster turnaround, do its own typesetting in-house, produce e-books and a website from the same content, and generally became immersed in XML!
- A number of XML vocabularies and standards not covered in chapters of their own exist, including XSL-FO, XProc, and MathML.
- You can generate SVG by combining XQuery and XSLT.

Hoy Books has entered the Modern Era, and if some of its staff still keep sheep or sail out in fishing boats from time to time, it is a reminder that technology alone cannot replace people's interests and needs. It's time for you to go build, make and, on the way, enjoy XML.

EXERCISES

You can find possible solutions to these exercises in Appendix A.

1. The SVG file generated in the Try It Out included a definition for the XML Schema namespace and bound it to the prefix `xs`. Why was it included? How would you remove it?

2. The generated SVG did not use the `id` attribute in `timesheet.xml`; if you laboriously typed it in, you're probably cursing. Let's not waste it: change the XSLT to generate links from the article titles to the articles, using the `id` attributes.

3. The team at Hoy Books could have used a relational database and stuck with a proprietary word processor. What advantages did they get from an XML database?

4. You may have noticed that the XSLT style sheet in Listing 19-3 does not handle all of the elements in the longer dictionary sample. Add XSLT templates for the missing elements.

▶ WHAT YOU LEARNED IN THIS CHAPTER

TOPIC	KEY POINTS
XML content management	XML-native databases can offer a cost-effective solution. XQuery, XSLT, XForms, and XHTML make a powerful combination.
XQuery and XSLT	Use XQuery to extract data from collections. Use XSLT when entire documents will be processed.
Markup vocabularies	DocBook is primarily for technical documentation of systems, or for technical books. DITA is especially suitable when the documents are the primary product of a department or organization. The Text Encoding Initiative Guidelines are designed primarily for humanities computing, including transcriptions and critical editions.
XSL-FO	XSL-FO is a W3C XML vocabulary for formatting; it uses (and extends) CSS for print.

Answers to Exercises

CHAPTER 1 ANSWERS TO EXERCISES

Exercise 1 Solution

A sample document, now element-centric, is shown here:

```
<applicationUsers>
  <user>
    <firstName>Joe</firstName>
    <middleName>John</middleName>
    <lastName>Fawcett</lastName>
  </user>
  <user>
    <firstName>Danny</firstName>
    <middleName>John</middleName>
    <lastName>Ayers</lastName>
  </user>
  <user>
    <firstName>Catherine</firstName>
    <middleName>Elizabeth</middleName>
    <lastName>Middleton</lastName>
  </user>
</applicationUsers>
```

Exercise 2 Solution

The main disadvantage is that the size of the file is greatly increased. In general, each additional user needs an extra 72 bytes, compared to the original version. For a small number of users this probably won't matter, but with a large number, or if you are transmitting many of these files, this could mean much more network traffic, leading to higher costs and reduced efficiency. This is one reason that, when designing an XML format for your data, it is recommended to choose attributes unless you have good reason not to.

CHAPTER 2 ANSWERS TO EXERCISES

Exercise 1 Solution

There are four errors altogether:

- `<xmlLibrary>` is wrong as element names cannot begin with the letters XML whether uppercase or lowercase.
- `publicationYear=1898` is incorrect as all attribute values must be quoted, whether or not they contain spaces.
- `<title> Arms & The Man</title>` is using a forbidden character, `&`, which needs be replaced with a entity reference, `&`.
- `<play description>` is illegal as it contains a space in the element name.

A corrected version of the file could look like this:

```
<library>
  <play publicationYear="1898">
    <title>Arms &amp; The Man</title>
    <author>George Bernard Shaw</author>
    <playDescription>Comedy dealing with the futility of war
 and the hypocrisy of human nature.</playDescription>
  <play>
  <play publicationYear="1950">
    <title>The Mousetrap</title>
    <author>Agatha Christie</author>
    <playDescription>A traditional whodunnit
 with an extraordinary twist.</playDescription>
  <play>
</library>
```

Exercise 2 Solution

An example of declaring an entity reference for an e-mail address is shown in the following snippet which first declares the reference in a document type definition and then uses it by surrounding the name of it, `email`, with an ampersand (`&`) and a semi-colon (`;`):

```
<!DOCTYPE data [
  <!ENTITY email "notMyRealEmail@example.com">
]>
<data>Entity reference example to insert my email: &email;</data>
```

CHAPTER 3 ANSWERS TO EXERCISES

Exercise 1 Solution

The three mistakes are:

- The xmlData prefix is used on the <document> element before it is declared.
- Prefixes beginning with xml are not allowed.
- The ns prefix is used on the <details> element without being declared.

The corrected document is shown in the following snippet:

```
<data:document xmlns:ns="http://www.wrox.com/chapter3/exercise1/ns"
               xmlns:data="http://www.wrox.com/chapter3/exercise1/data">
  <data:item>
    <ns:details>There's nothing wrong with this document?</ns:details>
  </data:item>
</data:document>
```

Exercise1-answer.xml

Exercise 2 Solution

The three errors are:

- You presumably don't control the wrox.com domain; instead you should choose a domain you do control or have permission to use, for example the company that you work for.
- It is not good practice to have spaces in a namespace URI.
- Problems can arise when using escaped characters, in this instance %7e. This corresponds to the ~ character but namespaces are compared on the literal string. This means that often, due to the vagaries of software support for escaped characters, you'll see two namespace URIs which appear identical but aren't. Assuming you work for example.com a better URI would be:

  ```
  http://www.example.com/namespaces/HRapplication/~config
  ```

CHAPTER 4 ANSWERS TO EXERCISES

Exercise 1 Solution

Your solution should look very much like the examples already in the document, in following the form:

```
<contact person="Your Name" tags="whatever tags you chose">
...
</contact>
```

Exercise 2 Solution

In any document valid to your DTD, the contact element will now contain the extra gender attribute, like this:

```
  <contact person="Joe_Fawcett" tags="author xml poetry" gender="male">
...
</contact>
```

To support this, your DTD will now include the following new line:

```
<!ATTLIST contact gender (male | female) #REQUIRED>
```

Exercise 3 Solution

To specify that each contact has zero or more phone numbers, you need to provide a cardinality indicator. In Table 4-1 you can see that the * character is used for "zero or more." The phone numbers are given in the XML documents using the <phone> element, but the cardinality is specified in that element's parent, leading to the result:

```
<!ELEMENT contact (name, location, phone*, knows, description)>
```

Extending the DTD to include website and email elements is a matter of first of adding these to the declaration of their parent element, <contact>, like so:

```
<!ELEMENT contact (name, location, phone*, knows, description, website, email)>
```

Then you should have described what kind of content these elements should support.

```
<!ELEMENT website (#PCDATA)>
<!ELEMENT email (#PCDATA)>
```

These elements are probably good candidates for using cardinality constraints, so for example if you wanted to specify that each contact should have one or more e-mail addresses, but zero or more websites, the declaration for the <contact> element would now look like this:

```
<!ELEMENT contact (name, location, phone*, knows, description, website*, email+)>
```

CHAPTER 5 ANSWERS TO EXERCISES

Exercise 1 Solution

One possible approach to adding the gender attribute is to define the type separately in the document. After the line:

```
<attribute name="person" type="ID"/>
```

you can add:

```
<attribute name="gender" type="GenderType" use="required"/>
```

Note the use attribute, ensuring a value is provided. Then for the definition itself:

```
<simpleType name="GenderType">
          <restriction base="string">
            <enumeration value="male"/>
            <enumeration value="female"/>
          </restriction>
</simpleType>
```

Exercise 2 Solution

To support one or more phone numbers, it's enough to add appropriate cardinality attributes to the phone element:

```
<element name="phone" type="contacts:PhoneType" minOccurs="0"
maxOccurs="unbounded"/>
```

Exercise 3 Solution

The solution to this problem follows the requirements fairly literally, leading to this:

```
<complexType>

    <sequence maxOccurs="unbounded">

       <any processContents="lax"
               namespace="http://www.w3.org/1999/xhtml" />

    </sequence>

 </complexType>
```

Remember that <any> cannot be placed directly inside an <complexType>. You need a container like a sequence or choice.

CHAPTER 6 ANSWERS TO EXERCISES

Exercise 1 Solution

If you want to use the XML based syntax then you first need to add a reference to the XML Schema data type library on the <element> element like so:

```
<element xmlns="http://relaxng.org/ns/structure/1.0" name="library"
         datatypeLibrary="http://www.w3.org/2001/XMLSchema-datatypes">
```

You can then add the actual attribute with its data type, and wrap it in an <optional> element as follows:

```
<element xmlns="http://relaxng.org/ns/structure/1.0" name="library"
        datatypeLibrary="http://www.w3.org/2001/XMLSchema-datatypes">
    <oneOrMore>
        <element name="book">
            <attribute name="id"/>
            <attribute name="publishedDate"/>
            <attribute name="genre"/>
            <optional>
              <attribute name="url">
                <data type="anyURI" />
              </attribute>
            </optional>
            <element name="title">
                <text/>
            </element>
```

If you choose to use the compact syntax then you don't need to declare the data type library because XML Schema types are already bound to the xsd prefix. You just need to declare the attribute with its data type, and follow it with a question mark to make it optional, as shown here:

```
element library {
  element book {
    attribute id { text},
    attribute publishedDate { text },
    attribute genre { text },
    attribute url { xsd:anyURI }?,
    element title { text },
    element authors {
      attribute count { text },
      element author {
        attribute id { text },
        text
      }+
    },
    element characters {
      element character {
        attribute id { text },
        element name { text },
        element description { text }
      }*
    },
    element description { text }?
  }+
}
```

Exercise 2 Solution

Add an <xs:annotation> element containing an <xs:appinfo> element to hold the Schematron rule. The rule's context is set to character and then you can use XPath's string-length() function to compare the two values:

```
<xs:element name="characterDescriptionLength">
    <xs:annotation>
      <xs:appinfo>
        <sch:pattern id="character">
          <sch:rule context="character">
            <sch:assert test="string-length(description) &gt;
 string-length(name)">The character's description must be
 longer than their name.</sch:assert>
          </sch:rule>
        </sch:pattern>
      </xs:appinfo>
    </xs:annotation>
```

CHAPTER 7 ANSWERS TO EXERCISES

Exercise 1 Solution

```
//entry[.//born]
```

Recall that `//` is short for descendant (in effect), so that `.//born` evaluates to a list of all `<born>` elements anywhere under the current node and at the start of the expression `//` means the root element or any child or descendent of the root element.

Exercise 2 Solution

It returns all `<div>` elements that are the first child of their parent, anywhere inside the `<body>` element that's the child of the outermost element, `<html>` in this case.

It may return more than one node. An *incorrect* answer might be that it returns the first `<div>` element in the document; it doesn't do that.

Exercise 3 Solution

```
//div[not(@id)]
```

CHAPTER 8 ANSWERS TO EXERCISES

Exercise 1 Solution

Choose three from the following:

- `generate-id()`: Generates a unique ID for a node.
- `last()`: Gives the size of the context.
- `position()`: Gives a nodes position in the context.
- `system-property()`: Used to discover various system properties. For example: `system-property("xsl:version")` gives the version of XSLT the processor supports such as 2.0.

- `key()`: Returns a node based on a predefined key declared with the `<xsl:key>` element.
- `function-available()`: Tests whether a function, whose name is passed in as a string, is available to be used.

There are plenty more; see the XSLT specifications at www.w3.org/TR/xslt20 for full details.

Exercise 2 Solution

First you'll need an external document to represent the currency rates; this should be created via a web service but for this example it's just a hard-coded list of values like so:

Available for download on Wrox.com

```
<conversions>
 <conversion from="USD" to="GBP" rate="0.625195374"/>
 <conversion from="GBP" to="USD" rate="1.5995" />
 <conversion from="USD" to="EUR" rate="0.75001875" />
 <conversion from="EUR" to="USD" rate="1.3333" />
 <conversion from="GBP" to="EUR" rate="1.19965499" />
 <conversion from="EUR" to="GBP" rate="0.833572992" />
</conversions>
```

ConversionRates.xml

The actual stylesheet has three `<xsl:param>` elements to represent the currency that you are converting from, the currency you are converting to, and the amount to convert. These all have defaults specified as shown here.

Available for download on Wrox.com

```
<?xml version="1.0" encoding="utf-8"?>
<xsl:stylesheet version="2.0"
                xmlns:xsl="http://www.w3.org/1999/XSL/Transform"
                xmlns:xs="http://www.w3.org/2001/XMLSchema"
                exclude-result-prefixes="xs">

  <xsl:output indent="yes" />

  <xsl:param name="currencyFrom" select="'USD'" as="xs:string" />
  <xsl:param name="currencyTo" select="'GBP'" as="xs:string" />
  <xsl:param name="amountToConvert" select="1" as="xs:decimal"/>
  <xsl:variable name="conversionRates"
       select="document('conversionrates.xml')/*" />

  <xsl:template name="main">
    <xsl:variable name="rate" select=
"$conversionRates/conversion
[@from = $currencyFrom and @to = $currencyTo]/@rate" />
    <conversion>
      <from><xsl:value-of select="$currencyFrom" /></from>
      <to><xsl:value-of select="$currencyTo" /></to>
      <amountToConvert>
  <xsl:value-of select="$amountToConvert" /></amountToConvert>
      <rate><xsl:value-of select="$rate" /></rate>
      <convertedAmount>
  <xsl:value-of select="$amountToConvert * $rate" /></convertedAmount>
```

```
    </conversion>
  </xsl:template>
</xsl:stylesheet>
```

CurrencyConvertor.xslt

The `document()` function is used to access the conversion rates and then the individual `<conversion>` element is chosen by matching its `from` and `to` attributes. Finally the full details are output, including the converted amount that is found by multiplying the input amount by newly acquired `$rate`.

You can test this code by using one of the following command lines:

```
java net.sf.saxon.Transform -s:CurrencyConvertor.xslt -it:main
  currencyFrom=GBP currencyTo=EUR amountToConvert=100
```

or

```
Transform -s:CurrencyConvertor.xslt -it:main
  currencyFrom=GBP currencyTo=EUR amountToConvert=100
```

You should see the following output:

```
<?xml version="1.0" encoding="UTF-8"?>
<conversion>
   <from>GBP</from>
   <to>EUR</to>
   <amountToConvert>100</amountToConvert>
   <rate>1.19965499</rate>
   <convertedAmount>119.965499</convertedAmount>
</conversion>
```

CHAPTER 9 ANSWERS TO EXERCISES

Exercise 1 Solution

You can either list the input numbers (1, 2, 3...) or use (1 to 100) as here:

```
for $i in (1 to 100)
return $i * $i
```

Exercise 2 Solution

Here's one way to do it. You can use `normalize-space()` because some of the titles in the dictionary have newlines inside them, making the output hard to read.

```
for $e in //entry[@born and @died]
let $age := xs:integer($e/@died) - xs:integer($e/@born)
where $age gt 88
order by $age descending
return concat(normalize-space($e/title), " ", $age, "&#xa;")
```

Exercise 3 Solution

Please contact the authors directly with the solution ☺.

Exercise 4 Solution

There is actually only one matching entry, for John Alexander. Find it like this:

```
for $e in //entry[count(.//p) ge 5]
return concat(normalize-space($e/title),"&#xa;")
```

CHAPTER 10 ANSWERS TO EXERCISES

Exercise 1 Solution

The main reasons to choose a relational database with XML features over a pure XML database include the following:

- Unless all your data is XML, you'll need a traditional relational database for your tabular data, meaning one that uses two systems.
- It is easier to have these two forms of data stored in one system rather than two, as it makes writing queries that need elements from both formats simpler.
- Relational databases are well-established and highly efficient; XML databases are still somewhat rare and understood less.
- There are few features that XML databases have that can't be implemented in a relational one but there are many relational features that an XML database just won't have.

Exercise 2 Solution

The five methods of the `xml` data type are:

- `query()`: Use XQuery or XPath to retrieve and create XML.
- `value()`: Use XPath to extract an atomic value as a SQL Server data type.
- `exist()`: Check if a particular node exists in an XML document.
- `modify()`: Used to `replace`, `delete`, or `insert` nodes in an existing document.
- `nodes()`: Used to turn XML into a tabular format so it can be treated a traditional SQL table.

Exercise 3 Solution

There are many candidates to be included in future updates of MySQL's XML capabilities. Some suggestions include:

- A proper way to store XML rather than just as text.
- The ability to return XML fragments defined by XPath rather than just text.
- Proper namespace handling rather than just having to use the same prefix as defined in the XML.
- Full XQuery support to be able to create new documents based on ones held in the database.
- A way to treat XML data as relational similar to SQL Server's `nodes()` method.

CHAPTER 11 ANSWERS TO EXERCISES

Exercise 1 Solution

There are four changes to Listing 11-5, `SaxParser5.java`, which need to be made to receive comment notifications.

1. Add a reference to the `org.xml.sax.ext` package so that you can use the newer `DefaultHandler2` interface. This reference is included with those at the beginning of the file:

```
import org.xml.sax.*;
import org.xml.sax.helpers.*;
import org.xml.sax.ext.*;
import java.io.*;
```

2. Change the class to inherit from `DefaultHandler2`:

```
public class SaxParser6 extends DefaultHandler2 {
```

3. Use the `setProperty()` method to specify the handler that will deal with comments; this needs to be set to the `SaxParser6` class itself:

```
SaxParser6 parser = new SaxParser6();
reader.setContentHandler(parser);
reader.setErrorHandler(parser);
reader.setProperty("http://xml.org/sax/properties/lexical-handler", parser);
```

4. Add a `comment()` method to receive the event, this looks very similar to the `characters()` method:

```
public void comment(char[] ch,
       int start,
       int length)
       throws SAXException{
System.out.print( "SAX Event: COMMENT[ " );
  StringBuffer commentBuffer = new StringBuffer();
  try {
```

```
        commentBuffer.append(ch, start, length);
        System.out.println(commentBuffer.toString());
      } catch (Exception e) {
       e.printStackTrace();
      }
     System.out.println("]");
    }
```

The full code is shown in Listing A-1:

LISTING A-1: SaxParser6.java

Available for download on Wrox.com

```
import org.xml.sax.*;
import org.xml.sax.helpers.*;
import org.xml.sax.ext.*;
import java.io.*;

public class SaxParser6 extends DefaultHandler2 {

  private Locator docLocator = null;
  private StringBuffer charactersBuffer = new StringBuffer();

  public void setDocumentLocator(Locator locator)
  {
    docLocator = locator;
  }

  public void startDocument( ) throws SAXException {
    System.out.println( "SAX Event: START DOCUMENT" );
  }

  public void endDocument( ) throws SAXException {
    System.out.println( "SAX Event: END DOCUMENT" );
  }

  public void startElement(String namespaceURI,
                           String localName,
                           String qName,
                           Attributes attr ) throws SAXException {
    int lineNumber = 0;
    if (docLocator != null)
    {
      lineNumber = docLocator.getLineNumber();
    }
    System.out.println( "SAX Event: START ELEMENT[ " + localName + " ]");
    if (lineNumber != 0)
    {
      System.out.println("\t(Found at line number: " + lineNumber + ".)");
    }
    for ( int i = 0; i < attr.getLength(); i++ ){
    System.out.println( " ATTRIBUTE: " + attr.getLocalName(i) +
  " VALUE: " + attr.getValue(i) );
    }
```

```
    charactersBuffer.setLength(0);
  }

  public void endElement(String namespaceURI,
                         String localName,
                         String qName ) throws SAXException {
    System.out.print( "SAX Event: CHARACTERS[ " );
    System.out.println(charactersBuffer.toString());
    System.out.println( " ]" );
    System.out.println( "SAX Event: END ELEMENT[ " + localName + " ]" );
  }

  public void characters(char[] ch,
                         int start,
                         int length ) throws SAXException {
    try {
      charactersBuffer.append(ch, start, length);
    } catch (Exception e) {
     e.printStackTrace();
    }
  }

  public void warning (SAXParseException exception)
    throws SAXException {
    System.err.println("[Warning] " +
      exception.getMessage() + " at line " +
      exception.getLineNumber() + ", column " +
      exception.getColumnNumber() );
  }

  public void error (SAXParseException exception)
    throws SAXException {
    System.err.println("[Error] " +
      exception.getMessage() + " at line " +
      exception.getLineNumber() + ", column " +
      exception.getColumnNumber() );
  }

  public void fatalError (SAXParseException exception)
    throws SAXException {
    System.err.println("[Fatal Error] " +
      exception.getMessage() + " at line " +
      exception.getLineNumber() + ", column " +
      exception.getColumnNumber() );
    throw exception;
  }

  public void comment(char[] ch,
             int start,
             int length)
             throws SAXException{
   System.out.print( "SAX Event: COMMENT[ " );
     StringBuffer commentBuffer = new StringBuffer();
     try {
```

continues

LISTING A-1 *(continued)*

```
        commentBuffer.append(ch, start, length);
        System.out.println(commentBuffer.toString());
      } catch (Exception e) {
       e.printStackTrace();
      }
    System.out.println("]");
   }


  public static void main( String[] argv ){
    String inputFile = argv[0];
    System.out.println("Processing '" + inputFile + "'.");
    System.out.println( "SAX Events:" );
    try {
      XMLReader reader = XMLReaderFactory.createXMLReader();
      SaxParser6 parser = new SaxParser6();
      reader.setContentHandler(parser);
      reader.setErrorHandler(parser);
      reader.setProperty
 ("http://xml.org/sax/properties/lexical-handler", parser);
      try
      {
        reader.setFeature("http://xml.org/sax/features/validation", true);
      } catch (SAXException e) {
      System.err.println("Cannot activate validation");
      }

      reader.parse( new InputSource(
                  new FileReader( inputFile )));
    }catch ( Exception e ) {
       e.printStackTrace();
    }
  }
}
```

When this class is run against the `PeopleWithComment.xml` sample it reports two comments as expected.

Exercise 2 Solution

The way to restrict external file access to be limited to those residing locally, is very similar to the example in "Controlling External Resources" section of the chapter that let files only be retrieved from specific servers. In this case though you use a `FileIOPermission` rather than a `WebPermission` as shown in the following snippet:

```
var localFilesPermission = new FileIOPermission(PermissionState.None);
localFilesPermission.AllLocalFiles = FileIOPermissionAccess.Read;
var permissionSet = new PermissionSet(PermissionState.None);
permissionSet.AddPermission(localFilesPermission);
var reader = XmlReader.Create(@"myXmlFile.xml");
reader.XmlResolver = new XmlSecureResolver(new XmlUrlResolver(), permissionSet);
```

A `FileIOPermision` is created and its `AllLocalFiles` property set to `true`. This permission is then added to a new `PermissionSet` which is, in turn, used to construct an `XmlSecureResolver`.

CHAPTER 12: ANSWERS TO EXERCISES

Answer to Exercise 1

The code is similar to the element-centric version, the only changes being in the `CreateMusicLibrary()` function:

```
Private Function CreateMusicLibrary() As XElement
  Dim cdData = GetCDs()
  Dim musicLibrary =
    <musicLibrary>
      <%= From item In cdData
        Select <cd id=<%= item.ID %> year=<%= item.Year %> artist=<%= item.Artist
%> genre=<%= item.Genre %>>
                 <title><%= item.Title %></title>
               </cd> %>
    </musicLibrary>
  Return musicLibrary
End Function
```

The only difference is that the literals used to create the elements, other than that of `<title>` which remains, have been replaced with those to use attributes.

Module1.vb in AttributeCentricLibrary project

CHAPTER 13 ANSWERS TO EXERCISES

Exercise 1 Solution

You should check the specs and some real-world feeds yourself, but the elements used for identifying the author of an item are usually one of the following: `author`, `dc:creator`, `atom:name`, or `foaf:name`. The `author` element appears in the "simple" RSS versions (0.9x, 2.0) and has no namespace. However, note a slight complication: there is also an element in RSS 2.0 called `name`, which is used for the name of the text object in a text input area (the text input area elements are rarely encountered in practice, but it does make for a more interesting exercise).

The solution will involve adding a little more checking of element names towards the end of the `endElementNS` method, with code that looks something like this:

```
...
if localname == "author":
```

```
                self.current_item.author = text
                return
```

Exercise 2 Solution

To determine the format of a feed the obvious approach is to test the root element for its qualified name, with the following possible values:

- `rdf:RDF` — RSS 1.0
- `rss` — RSS 2.0 (or one of the other "simple" RSS variants)
- `atom:feed` — Atom

The title of the feed is in a different part of the document in each case, so here it is:

- `rdf:RDF/rss1:channel/rss1:title` — RSS 1.0
- `rss/channel/title` — RSS 2.0 (and variants)
- `atom:feed/atom:title` — Atom

There are many different ways of examining/accessing the parts of an XML document with XSLT. Here is a sample solution that demonstrates two approaches:

```
<xsl:stylesheet version="1.0"
    xmlns:xsl="http://www.w3.org/1999/XSL/Transform"
    xmlns:xhtml="http://www.w3.org/1999/xhtml"
    xmlns:atom="http://www.w3.org/2005/Atom"
    xmlns:rss1="http://purl.org/rss/1.0/"
    xmlns:rdf="http://www.w3.org/1999/02/22-rdf-syntax-ns#"
    xmlns:dc="http://purl.org/dc/elements/1.1/">

<xsl:output method="html" indent="yes"/>

<xsl:template match="/">
  <xsl:text disable-output-escaping="yes">
    &lt;!DOCTYPE html PUBLIC "-//W3C//DTD XHTML 1.0 Strict//EN"
"http://www.w3.org/TR/xhtml1/DTD/xhtml1-strict.dtd"&gt;
  </xsl:text>
  <html>
  <head>
    <title>Feed Info</title>
  </head>
  <body>
<dl>
  <dt>Format : </dt>
    <dd>
<xsl:if test="/rdf:RDF">RSS 1.0</xsl:if>
<xsl:if test="/rss">RSS 2.0</xsl:if>
<xsl:if test="/atom:feed">Atom</xsl:if>
</dd>
  <dt>Title : </dt>
    <dd><xsl:apply-templates /></dd>
</dl>
```

```
  </body>
  </html>
</xsl:template>

<xsl:template match="rdf:RDF">
    <xsl:value-of select="rss1:channel/rss1:title" />
</xsl:template>

<xsl:template match="rss">
    <xsl:value-of select="channel/title" />
</xsl:template>

<xsl:template match="atom:feed">
    <xsl:value-of select="atom:title" />
</xsl:template>

<xsl:template match="text()" />

</xsl:stylesheet>
```

Checking the root element to detect the format (and supplying a suitable display value) is achieved through a series of simple `xsl:if` expressions, e.g:

```
<xsl:if test="/rdf:RDF">RSS 1.0</xsl:if>
```

So here if the root element of the document has the name `RDF` and is in the appropriate namespace (declared as `http://www.w3.org/1999/02/22-rdf-syntax-ns#`), the value "RSS 1.0" will be passed to the output from the XSLT.

The titles are extracted using templates, for example:

```
<xsl:template match="atom:feed">
    <xsl:value-of select="atom:title" />
</xsl:template>
```

Here, if there's a match in the document to Atom's root element, this template will pull out the text content of the corresponding title element for the feed.

CHAPTER 14 ANSWERS TO EXERCISES

Exercise 1 Solution

There are three pieces of information to send so you have two choices: either send three parameters or wrap the three pieces of data in a structure and send the structure. The first of these options would look like the following:

```
<methodCall>
  <methodName>AdSevice.Add</methodName>
  <params>
    <param>
```

```
      <value>
        <string>Joe Fawcett</string>
      </value>
    </param>
    <param>
      <value>
        <string>555-1234</string>
      </value>
    </param>
    <param>
      <value>
        <string><![CDATA[ My dog, Fido, has gone missing
 from my home near... ]]></string>
      </value>
    </param>
  </params>
</methodCall>
```

The second option, using a structure would look like the following:

```
<methodCall>
  <methodName>AdService.Add</methodName>
  <params>
    <param>
      <value>
        <struct>
          <member>
            <name>Name</name>
            <value>
              <string>Joe Fawcett</string>
            </value>
          </member>
          <member>
            <name>PhoneNumber</name>
            <value>
              <string>555-1234</string>
            </value>
          </member>
          <member>
            <name>AdText</name>
            <value>
              <string><![CDATA[ My dog, Fido, has gone missing
 from my home near... ]]></string>
            </value>
          </member>
        </struct>
      </value>
    </param>
  </params>
</methodCall>
```

Exercise 2 Solution

In theory REST style requests don't have to have any bearing on what they are trying to achieve but in practice most people like to make them *guessable*, that is if you have seen one you can guess the format needed for similar ones. In addition to the request having an easy to understand format, most REST services shy away from using the querystring to pass data and prefer instead to use the different components of the URL. Bearing these two practices in mind, a typical request would look like one of the following:

```
http://services.wrox.com/customer/3263827/order/THX1138
```

```
http://services.wrox.com/orderinquiry/3263828/THX1138
```

CHAPTER 15 ANSWERS TO EXERCISES

Exercise 1 Solution

The SOAP document will look similar to the following:

```
<soap:Envelope
  xmlns:soap="http://schemas.xmlsoap.org/soap/envelope/"
  soap:encodingStyle="http://schemas.xmlsoap.org/soap/encoding/">
  <soap:Body>
    <q:StockPriceRequest xmlns:q="http://wrox.com/beginningXml/stockprice">
      <StockSymbol>MSFT</StockSymbol>
    </q:StockPriceRequest>
  </soap:Body>
</soap:Envelope>
```

StockPriceRequest.xml

Your answer may differ in the choice of namespace bound to the `q` prefix and, of course, you may have chosen a different prefix altogether.

Exercise 2 Solution

There can be quite a variety in how the WSDL looks but a sample is shown here:

```
<?xml version="1.0"?>
<definitions name="StockPrice"
             targetNamespace=
"http://wrox.com/beginningXml/stockprice"
             xmlns:tns="http://wrox.com/beginningXml/stockprice"
             xmlns:q="http://wrox.com/beginningXml/stockprice/"
             xmlns:soap="http://schemas.xmlsoap.org/wsdl/soap/"
             xmlns="http://schemas.xmlsoap.org/wsdl/">
```

```
<types>
  <schema targetNamespace="http://wrox.com/beginningXml/stockprice"
          xmlns="http://www.w3.org/2000/10/XMLSchema">
    <element name="StockPriceRequest">
      <complexType>
        <all>
          <element name="StockSymbol" type="string"/>
        </all>
      </complexType>
    </element>
    <element name="StockPriceResponse">
       <complexType>
         <all>
           <element name="price" type="decimal"/>
         </all>
       </complexType>
    </element>
  </schema>
</types>

<message name="GetStockPriceRequest">
  <part name="body" element="q:StockPriceRequest"/>
</message>

<message name="GetStockPriceResponse">
  <part name="body" element="q:StockPriceResponse"/>
</message>

<portType name="StockPricePortType">
  <operation name="GetStockPrice">
    <input message="tns:GetStockPriceRequest"/>
    <output message="tns:GetStockPriceResponse"/>
  </operation>
</portType>

<binding name="StockPriceSoapBinding"
type="tns:StockPricePortType">
  <soap:binding style="document"
transport="http://schemas.xmlsoap.org/soap/http"/>
  <operation name="GetStockPrice">
    <soap:operation soapAction=
"http://wrox.com/beginningXml/GetStockPrice"/>
    <input>
      <soap:body use="literal"/>
    </input>
    <output>
      <soap:body use="literal"/>
    </output>
  </operation>
</binding>

<service name="StockPriceService">
  <documentation>Example stock price service</documentation>
  <port name="StockPricePort"
binding="tns:StockPriceSoapBinding">
```

```
      <soap:address
 location="http://wrox.com/beginningXml/services/stock"/>
    </port>
  </service>

</definitions>
```

StockPrice.wsdl

The main point is that the namespace chosen in Exercise 1 is the same as the `targetNamespace` attribute on the `<schema>` element and that the element name specified in the `<message>` section and the names specified by `<element>` elements in the `<schema>` section also match.

CHAPTER 16 ANSWERS TO EXERCISES

Exercise 1 Solution

You could add a second loop, perhaps like this:

```
# match on start of an interior word
$wordstart = ' ' . $q;
foreach ($items as $key => $value) {
    $where = strpos(strtolower($value), $wordstart);
    if ($where !== false) {
        echo "$value\n";
        if (++$n_found > $maxitems) {
            return;
        }
    }
}
```

Exercise 2 Solution

Here's one way to do it. The regular expression handling in PHP is less central than in Perl, but is still very useful. You could use `strpos()` again instead, though, if you were careful not to match strings already returned.

```
# next, anywhere in the word *except* at the start
# of a word
$pattern = '/[^ \#]$q.*#/i';
foreach ($items as $key => $value) {
    $where = preg_match($pattern, $value);
    if ($where !== false && $where != 0) {
        echo "$value\n";
        if (++$n_found > $maxitems) {
            echo "\n";
            return;
        }
    }
}
```

Exercise 3 Solution

This question could be a project for an undergraduate class, or could be done in a day or two by someone fairly determined. The result is a very powerful architecture that is explored a little more in Chapter 19, "Case Study: XML in Publishing."

CHAPTER 17 ANSWERS TO EXERCISES

Exercise 1 Solution

Change the `margin-left` property of the `p` rule to be at least 150px, and change the margin-left of the `img` rule from –73 pixels to 150 pixels or more.

Exercise 2 Solution

HML was defined as an SGML application; the SGML is ISO 8879, the Standard Generalized Markup Language.

Exercise 3 Solution

CSS margins are *outside* the border, and padding is *inside* the border, between the border and the content. CSS top and bottom margins collapse when blocks are adjacent; padding never collapses. CSS margins are always transparent, whereas padding takes on the element's background.

Exercise 4 Solution

The HTML 5 specification defines the algorithm to be used to parse the input regardless of whether it conforms. All browsers use the same algorithm.

CHAPTER 18 ANSWERS TO EXERCISES

Exercise 1 Solution

A `<circle>` element has a single radius attribute, `r`; an `<ellipse>` element has two, `rx` and `ry`.

Exercise 2 Solution

Any two of SMIL animations, scripted animations, CSS animations, or using a library (which will in turn probably use one or more of the other three methods).

Exercise 3 Solution

It is important to provide text descriptions so that a web search engine crawler can index the text, making the diagram findable using a web search. It is also important to make web pages accessible to people who are blind, and the `<desc>` element enables those people to understand the diagram or picture based on textual descriptions of the various components.

Exercise 4 Solution

In the lowercase versions of the commands, the coordinates are relative to the starting point of the subpath, and in the uppercase version they are absolute.

CHAPTER 19 ANSWERS TO EXERCISES

Exercise 1 Solution

The XSD namespace was used in the style sheet; the XSLT processor has no way of knowing it's not needed, because you might be using QNames in content, for example `<type>xs:integer</type>`. To remove it, along with the XSLT namespace, add the following to the `<xsl:stylesheet>` element's start tag:

```
exclude-result-prefixes="xs xsl"
```

Exercise 2 Solution

Use something like this:

```
<xlink:a href="{@id}.html"><xsl:apply-templates/></xlink:a>
```

You'll have to declare the `xlink` namespace prefix properly of course; see Chapter 18 for examples.

Exercise 3 Solution

The team at Hoy Books used XQuery to extract information from inside documents. With a relational database they would have needed to extract the information on import (perhaps using a Visual Basic program) and store it in separate tables, risking integrity problems. They would also have had a greater mixture of technologies with their respective limitations and necessary skills, because they need to generate XHTML for e-book publishing. Perhaps you can come up with other advantages.

Exercise 4 Solution

[open-ended]

B

XPath Functions

This appendix includes a complete list (as of when this book was written) of functions that can be called by XPath expressions (including those from XQuery and XSLT) to process and manipulate values. The functions are marked as to the XPath version in which they were introduced: XPath 1 in 1999, XPath 2 in 2006, or XPath 3, still a draft for this edition of *Beginning XML* but considered close to final. The list does *not* include extensions to XPath by other languages such as Java or PHP or SQL, and does *not* include the XPath 1.1 draft since that was obsoleted by XPath 2.

***NOTE** If you are using an XPath 1 engine, such as those found in web browsers, PHP, Python, Perl, and many other languages, keep to the functions marked for 1.0.*

***NOTE** See* `www.expath.org` *for some extra functions that are fairly widely implemented, and also for some implementations of XSLT 2 and XPath 2 functions that work in XSLT 1.*

The tables in this appendix give an alphabetical list of functions roughly sorted into the following categories:

- Boolean functions
- Time and Data
- Files and the Environment

- Functions that Operate on Functions
- Functions that Operate on Items
- Numeric Functions
- Functions that Operate on Nodes
- Functions that Operate on QNames
- Functions that Operate on Sequences
- Functions that Operate on Strings and URIs
- Functions to Construct Objects by XSD Type

Each table gives three items for each function:

1. The function name, with its signature
2. The XPath version in which the function first appeared, in a table column headed V to save space
3. A short description

The functions are shown in the Functions and Operators namespace, which in XQuery is bound by default to the prefix `fn`. Because this is the default namespace, you can actually omit the `fn:` in most cases. In XSLT the prefix is not bound by default, and you should either bind it yourself or just omit the prefix entirely, because, again, it's the default. If you need to bind them, use the following URIs:

- `err: http://www.w3.org/2005/xqt-errors` (used for error codes)
- `fn: http://www.w3.org/2005/xpath-functions`
- `math: http://www.w3.org/2005/xpath-functions/math`
- `xs: http://www.w3.org/2001/XMLSchema`

The information about Schema types makes sense only for XPath 2 and later. XSLT 2 and XQuery 1.0 used XPath 2.0, but in XPath 1 everything was a string or numeric or simply untyped, and there were no XML Schema type names. For example, the first function in the first table, `fn:boolean()`, is declared as taking a single argument, `$arg`. The `$arg` argument must have a type that matches a sequence of zero or more (because of the `*`) things, each of which match `item()`. You'd call the function, for example, `boolean(/book/@isPaperback)` and it would return `xs:boolean`.

A full explanation of the XPath type notation is beyond the scope of a *Beginning* book, but if you need it you can refer the References section at the end of the XPath specification (`http://www.w3.org/TR/`), which is more readable than you might expect!

Some of the functions appear more than once in this appendix, with different numbers of arguments. This is sometimes called *function overloading*; the XPath engine decides which version of the function to call based on the number of arguments you give it. Often there is a zero-argument version that will default to using the context item, so you can use it in a predicate. For example, the following code finds all chapter titles that are more than 100 characters long.

```
/book/chapter/title[string-length() > 100]
```

A few functions were originally defined in XSLT, and were not available for use in XPath or XQuery. Later most of them were moved into the Functions and Operators document so that they could also be part of both XPath and XQuery as well as XSLT. They have been marked as such so you know whether you can use them in specific environments such as XPath 1.

Boolean Functions

Boolean functions operate on the values true and false, represented in XPath as `true()` and `false()`.

FUNCTION NAME AND SIGNATURE	V	DESCRIPTION
`fn:boolean($arg as item()*) as xs:boolean`	1.0	Computes the effective boolean value of the sequence `$arg`.
`fn:not($arg as item()*) as xs:boolean`	1.0	Returns true if the effective boolean value of `$arg` is false, or false if it is true.
`fn:true() as xs:boolean`	1.0	Returns the `xs:boolean` value true.

Time and Date Functions

Time and Date functions operate on values defined by XML Schema to represent times, dates, and durations.

FUNCTION NAME AND SIGNATURE	V	DESCRIPTION
`fn:adjust-dateTime-to-timezone ($arg as xs:dateTime?) as xs:dateTime`	2.0	Adjusts an `xs:dateTime` value to a specific time zone, or to no time zone at all.
`fn:adjust-dateTime-to-timezone ($arg as xs:dateTime?, $timezone as xs:dayTimeDuration?) as xs:dateTime`	2.0	
`fn:adjust-date-to-timezone ($arg as xs:date?) as xs:date?`	2.0	Adjusts an `xs:date` value to a specific time zone, or to no time zone at all; the result is the date in the target time zone that contains the starting instant of the supplied date.
`fn:adjust-date-to-timezone ($arg as xs:date?, $timezone as xs:dayTimeDuration?) as xs:date?`	2.0	

continues

(continued)

FUNCTION NAME AND SIGNATURE	V	DESCRIPTION
`fn:adjust-time-to-timezone ($arg as xs:time?) as xs:time?`	2.0	Adjusts an `xs:time` value to a specific time zone, or to no time zone at all.
`fn:adjust-time-to-timezone ($arg as xs:time?, $timezone as xs:dayTimeDuration?) as xs:time?`	2.0	
`fn:current-date() as xs:date`	2.0	Returns the current date; subsequent calls within the same program will usually return the same value.
`fn:current-dateTime() as xs:dateTimeStamp`	2.0	Returns the current date and time (with time zone); subsequent calls within the same program will usually return the same value.
`fn:current-time() as xs:time`	2.0	Returns the current time; subsequent calls within the same program will usually return the same value.
`fn:dateTime($arg1 as xs:date?, $arg2 as xs:time?) as xs:dateTime?`	2.0	Returns an `xs:dateTime` value created by combining an `xs:date` and an `xs:time`.
`fn:day-from-date($arg as xs:date?) as xs:integer?`	2.0	Returns the day component of an `xs:date`.
`fn:day-from-dateTime($arg as xs:dateTime?) as xs:integer?`	2.0	Returns the day component of an `xs:dateTime`.
`fn:days-from-duration($arg as xs:duration?) as xs:integer?`	2.0	Returns the number of days in a duration.
`fn:format-dateTime($value as xs:dateTime?, $picture as xs:string) as xs:string?`	3.0	Returns a string containing an `xs:dateTime` value formatted for display (formerly in XSLT only).
`fn:format-dateTime($value as xs:dateTime?, $picture as xs:string, $language as xs:string?, $calendar as xs:string?, $place as xs:string?) as xs:string?`	3.0	
`fn:format-date($value as xs:date?, $picture as xs:string) as xs:string?`	3.0	Returns a string containing an `xs:date` value formatted for display (formerly in XSLT only).

FUNCTION NAME AND SIGNATURE	V	DESCRIPTION
fn:format-date($value as xs:date?, $picture as xs:string, $language as xs:string?, $calendar as xs:string?, $place as xs:string?) as xs:string?	3.0	
fn:format-time($value as xs:time?, $picture as xs:string) as xs:string?	3.0	Returns a string containing an xs:time value formatted for display (formerly in XSLT only).
fn:format-time($value as xs:time?, $picture as xs:string, $language as xs:string?, $calendar as xs:string?, $place as xs:string?) as xs:string?	3.0	
fn:hours-from-dateTime ($arg as xs:dateTime?) as xs:integer?	2.0	Returns the hours component of an xs:dateTime.
fn:hours-from-duration ($arg as xs:duration?) as xs:integer?	2.0	Returns the number of hours in a duration.
fn:hours-from-time($arg as xs:time?) as xs:integer?	2.0	Returns the hours component of an xs:time.
fn:implicit-timezone() as xs:dayTimeDuration	2.0	Returns the value of the implicit time zone property from the dynamic context.
fn:minutes-from-dateTime ($arg as xs:dateTime?) as xs:integer?	2.0	Returns the minutes component of an xs:dateTime.
fn:minutes-from-duration ($arg as xs:duration?) as xs:integer?	2.0	Returns the number of minutes in a duration.
fn:minutes-from-time($arg as xs:time?) as xs:integer?	2.0	Returns the minutes component of an xs:time.
fn:month-from-date($arg as xs:date?) as xs:integer?	2.0	Returns the month component of an xs:date.
fn:month-from-dateTime ($arg as xs:dateTime?) as xs:integer?	2.0	Returns the month component of an xs:dateTime.
fn:months-from-duration ($arg as xs:duration?) as xs:integer?	2.0	Returns the number of months in a duration.
fn:seconds-from-dateTime ($arg as xs:dateTime?) as xs:decimal?	2.0	Returns the seconds component of an xs:dateTime.
fn:seconds-from-duration ($arg as xs:duration?) as xs:decimal?	2.0	Returns the number of seconds in a duration.

continues

(continued)

FUNCTION NAME AND SIGNATURE	V	DESCRIPTION
`fn:seconds-from-time($arg as xs:time?) as xs:decimal?`	2.0	Returns the seconds component of an `xs:time`.
`fn:timezone-from-date($arg as xs:date?) as xs:dayTimeDuration?`	2.0	Returns the time zone component of an `xs:date`.
`fn:timezone-from-dateTime($arg as xs:dateTime?) as xs:dayTimeDuration?`	2.0	Returns the time zone component of an `xs:dateTime`.
`fn:timezone-from-time($arg as xs:time?) as xs:dayTimeDuration?`	2.0	Returns the time zone component of an `xs:time`.
`fn:year-from-date($arg as xs:date?) as xs:integer?`	2.0	Returns the year component of an `xs:date`.
`fn:year-from-dateTime($arg as xs:dateTime?) as xs:integer?`	2.0	Returns the year component of an `xs:dateTime`.
`fn:years-from-duration($arg as xs:duration?) as xs:integer?`	2.0	Returns the number of years in a duration.

Files and the Environment

These functions interact with the system beyond the XPath engine itself, such as reading or creating files. Note that XQuery and XSLT do not allow you to read from a file in the same query or stylesheet in which you created the file.

FUNCTION NAME AND SIGNATURE	V	DESCRIPTION
`fn:available-environment-variables() as xs:string*`	2.0	Returns a list of environment variable names that are suitable for passing to `fn:environment-variable`, as a (possibly empty) sequence of strings.
`fn:collection($arg as xs:string?) as node()*`	2.0	Returns a sequence of nodes representing a collection of documents identified by a collection URI; or a default collection if no URI is supplied.
`fn:collection() as node()*`	2.0	
`fn:default-collation() as xs:string`	2.0	Returns the value of the default collation property from the static context.

FUNCTION NAME AND SIGNATURE	V	DESCRIPTION
`fn:doc-available($uri as xs:string?) as xs:boolean`	2.0	The function returns true if and only if the function call `fn:doc($uri)` would return a document node. This is useful because it's generally an error if `fn:doc()` fails to load a file.
`fn:doc($uri as xs:string?) as document-node()?`	2.0	Retrieves a document using a URI supplied as an `xs:string`, and returns the corresponding document node.
`fn:environment-variable ($name as xs:string) as xs:string?`	2.0	Returns the value of a system environment variable, if it exists.
`fn:error() as none`	2.0	Calling the `fn:error` function raises an application-defined error.
`fn:error($code as xs:QName) as none`	2.0	
`fn:error($code as xs:QName?, $description as xs:string) as none`	2.0	
`fn:error($code as xs:QName?, $description as xs:string, $error-object as item()*) as none`	2.0	
`fn:parse-xml($arg as xs:string?) as document-node(element (*, xs:untyped))`	3.0	This function takes as input an XML document represented as a string, and returns the document node at the root of an XDM tree representing the parsed document. It was experimental at the time of writing.
`fn:parse-xml-fragment ($arg as xs:string?) as document-node(element(*, xs:untyped))`	3.0	This function takes as input an XML fragment such as an external XML entity, represented as a string, and returns the document node at the root of an XDM tree representing the parsed document. It was experimental at the time of writing.
`fn:serialize($arg as item()*) as xs:string`	3.0	This function serializes the supplied input sequence `$arg` as described in "XSLT and XQuery Serialization 3.0," returning a string.
`fn:serialize($arg as item()*, $params as element(output:serialization-parameters)?) as xs:string`	2.0	

continues

(continued)

FUNCTION NAME AND SIGNATURE	V	DESCRIPTION
`fn:trace($value as item()*, $label as xs:string) as item()*`	2.0	Provides an execution trace intended to be used in debugging queries.
`fn:unparsed-text-available ($href as xs:string?) as xs:boolean`	3.0	Determines whether a call with particular arguments would succeed. Provided because errors in evaluating the `fn:unparsed-text` function are non-recoverable (formerly XSLT only).
`fn:unparsed-text-available ($href as xs:string?, $encoding as xs:string) as xs:boolean`	3.0	
`fn:unparsed-text($href as xs:string?) as xs:string?`	3.0	Reads an external resource (for example, a file) and returns its contents as a string (formerly in XSLT only).
`fn:unparsed-text($href as xs:string?, $encoding as xs:string) as xs:string?`	3.0	
`fn:unparsed-text-lines ($href as xs:string?) as xs:string*`	3.0	Reads an external resource (for example, a file) and returns its contents as a sequence of strings, one for each line of text in the file (formerly only in XSLT 2.1).
`fn:unparsed-text-lines ($href as xs:string?, $encoding as xs:string) as xs:string*`	3.0	
`fn:uri-collection($arg as xs:string?) as xs:anyURI*`	3.0	Returns a sequence of `xs:anyURI` values representing the document URIs of the documents in a collection.
`fn:uri-collection() as xs:anyURI*`	3.0	

Functions that Operate on Functions

XPath 3, XSLT 3, and XQuery 3 all introduce *higher order functions*: functions that operate on other functions.

FUNCTION NAME AND SIGNATURE	V	DESCRIPTION
`fn:filter($f as function(item()) as xs:boolean, $seq as item()*) as item()*`	3.0	Returns those items from the sequence `$seq` for which the supplied function `$f` returns true.
`fn:fold-left($f as function(item()*, item()) as item()*, $zero as item()*, $seq as item()*) as item()*`	3.0	Processes the supplied sequence from left to right, applying the supplied function repeatedly to each item in turn, together with an accumulated result value.
`fn:fold-right($f as function(item(), item()*) as item()*, $zero as item()*, $seq as item()*) as item()*`	3.0	Processes the supplied sequence from right to left, applying the supplied function repeatedly to each item in turn, together with an accumulated result value.
`fn:function-arity($func as function(*)) as xs:integer`	3.0	Returns the *arity* of the function identified by a function item. The arity is the number of arguments a function takes.
`fn:function-name($func as function(*)) as xs:QName?`	3.0	Returns the name of the function identified by a function item.
`fn:map($f as function(item()) as item()*, $seq as item()*) as item()*`	3.0	Applies the function item `$f` to every item from the sequence `$seq` in turn, returning the concatenation of the resulting sequences in order.

Functions that Operate on Items

These functions take one or more XDM values (items) as arguments.

FUNCTION NAME AND SIGNATURE	V	DESCRIPTION
`fn:deep-equal($parameter1 as item()*, $parameter2 as item()*) as xs:boolean`	2.0	Returns true if two sequences, treated as trees, have the same structure and values.
`fn:deep-equal($parameter1 as item()*, $parameter2 as item()*, $collation as xs:string) as xs:boolean`	2.0	
`fn:element-with-id($arg as xs:string*) as element()*`	2.0	Returns the sequence of element nodes that have an ID value matching the value of one or more of the IDREF values supplied in `$arg`.

continues

(continued)

FUNCTION NAME AND SIGNATURE	V	DESCRIPTION
`fn:element-with-id($arg as xs:string*, $node as node()) as element()*`	2.0	
`fn:empty($arg as item()*) as xs:boolean`	2.0	Returns true if the argument is the empty sequence.
`fn:exactly-one($arg as item()*) as item()`	2.0	Returns `$arg` if it contains exactly one item. Otherwise, raises an error.
`fn:exists($arg as item()*) as xs:boolean`	2.0	Returns true if the argument is a non-empty sequence.
`fn:index-of($seq as xs:anyAtomicType*, $search as xs:anyAtomicType) as xs:integer*`	2.0	Returns a sequence of positive integers giving the positions within the sequence `$seq` of items that are equal to `$search`.
`fn:index-of($seq as xs:anyAtomicType*, $search as xs:anyAtomicType, $collation as xs:string) as xs:integer*`	2.0	

Numeric Functions

These functions work with numbers; XPath 1 implementations had to convert numbers to and from strings when they were used, but in XPath 2, and especially XQuery and XSLT, you can declare variables and functions to have numeric types and often achieve improvements both in performance and in error reporting.

FUNCTION NAME AND SIGNATURE	V	DESCRIPTION
`fn:abs($arg as numeric?) as numeric?`	2.0	Returns the absolute value of `$arg`.
`fn:avg($arg as xs:anyAtomicType*) as xs:anyAtomicType?`	2.0	Returns the average of the values in the input sequence `$arg`, that is, the sum of the values divided by the number of values.
`fn:ceiling($arg as numeric?) as numeric?`	1.0	Rounds `$arg` up to a whole number.
`fn:floor($arg as numeric?) as numeric?`	1.0	Rounds `$arg` down to a whole number.
`fn:max($arg as xs:anyAtomicType*) as xs:anyAtomicType?`	2.0	Returns a value that is equal to the highest value appearing in the input sequence.

FUNCTION NAME AND SIGNATURE	V	DESCRIPTION
`fn:max($arg as xs:anyAtomicType*, $collation as xs:string) as xs:anyAtomicType?`	2.0	
`fn:min($arg as xs:anyAtomicType*) as xs:anyAtomicType?`	2.0	Returns a value that is equal to the lowest value appearing in the input sequence.
`fn:min($arg as xs:anyAtomicType*, $collation as xs:string) as xs:anyAtomicType?`	2.0	
`fn:number($arg as xs:anyAtomicType?) as xs:double`	1.0	Returns the value indicated by `$arg` or, if `$arg` is not specified, the context item after atomization, converted to an `xs:double`.
`fn:number() as xs:double`	1.0	
`fn:round($arg as numeric?) as numeric?`	1.0	Rounds a value to a specified number of decimal places, rounding up if two such values are equally near.
`fn:round($arg as numeric?, $precision as xs:integer) as numeric?`	3.0	
`fn:round-half-to-even ($arg as numeric?) as numeric?`	2.0	Rounds a value to a specified number of decimal places, rounding to make the last digit even if two such values are equally near.
`fn:round-half-to-even($arg as numeric?, $precision as xs:integer) as numeric?`	2.0	
`fn:sum($arg as xs:anyAtomicType*) as xs:anyAtomicType`	1.0	Returns a value obtained by adding together the values in `$arg`.
`fn:sum($arg as xs:anyAtomicType*, $zero as xs:anyAtomicType?) as xs: anyAtomicType?`	2.0	
`math:acos($arg as xs:double?) as xs:double?`	3.0	Returns the arc cosine of the argument, the result being in the range zero to +π radians.
`math:asin($arg as xs:double?) as xs:double?`	3.0	Returns the arc sine of the argument, the result being in the range -π/2 to +π/2 radians.

continues

(continued)

FUNCTION NAME AND SIGNATURE	V	DESCRIPTION
`math:atan2($y as xs:double, $x as xs:double) as xs:double`	3.0	Returns the angle in radians subtended at the origin between a line drawn to the point on a plane with coordinates (x, y) and the positive x-axis, the result being in the range -π to +π.
`math:atan($arg as xs:double?) as xs:double?`	3.0	Returns the arc tangent of the argument, the result being in the range -π/2 to +π/2 radians.
`math:cos($θ as xs:double?) as xs:double?`	3.0	Returns the cosine of the argument, expressed in radians.
`math:exp10($arg as xs:double?) as xs:double?`	3.0	Returns the value of 10 to the power of x.
`math:exp($arg as xs:double?) as xs:double?`	3.0	Returns the value of e to the power of x.
`math:log10($arg as xs:double?) as xs:double?`	3.0	Returns the base-ten logarithm of the argument.
`math:log($arg as xs:double?) as xs:double?`	3.0	Returns the natural logarithm (base e) of the argument.
`math:pi() as xs:double`	3.0	Returns an approximation to the mathematical constant π.
`math:pow($x as xs:double?, $y as numeric) as xs:double?`	3.0	Returns the result of raising the first argument to the power of the second.
`math:sin($θ as xs:double?) as xs:double?`	3.0	Returns the sine of the argument, expressed in radians.
`math:sqrt($arg as xs:double?) as xs:double?`	3.0	Returns the square root of the argument.
`math:tan($θ as xs:double?) as xs:double?`	3.0	Returns the tangent of the argument, expressed in radians.

Functions that Operate on Nodes

These functions operate on the various XDM node types such as elements, text nodes, and processing instructions, but not on atomic values such as a string or a number.

FUNCTION NAME AND SIGNATURE	V	DESCRIPTION
`document()`	1.0	This was replaced by `fn:doc()` in XPath 2.0.
`fn:base-uri($arg as node()?) as xs:anyURI?`	2.0	Returns the base URI used for resolving relative URI references; usually this will be the same for every node in a document, but çan be different if external XML entities were used.
`fn:base-uri() as xs:anyURI?`	3.0	
`fn:data($arg as item()*) as xs:anyAtomicType*`	2.0	Takes a sequence of items and returns a sequence of atomic values. The items can be any mix of atomic values and nodes.
`fn:data() as xs:anyAtomicType*`	3.0	
`fn:document-uri($arg as node()?) as xs:anyURI?`	2.0	Returns the URI of the document containing the given node, if it has one and is known.
`fn:document-uri() as xs:anyURI?`	3.0	
`fn:generate-id($arg as node()?) as xs:string`	2.0	This function returns a string that uniquely identifies a given node, suitable for use as an XML or HTML ID value (originally in XSLT 1.0 and 2.0 only, not XPath or XQuery).
`fn:generate-id() as xs:string`	3.0	
`fn:has-children($node as node()?) as xs:boolean`	2.0	True if the supplied node has one or more child nodes (of any kind).
`fn:id($arg as xs:string*) as element()*`	1.0	Returns the sequence of element nodes that have an ID value matching the value of one or more of the IDREF values supplied in `$arg`.
`fn:id($arg as xs:string*, $node as node()) as element()*`	1.0	
`fn:idref($arg as xs:string*) as node()*`	2.0	Returns the sequence of element or attribute nodes with an IDREF value matching the value of one or more of the ID values supplied in `$arg`.

continues

(continued)

FUNCTION NAME AND SIGNATURE	V	DESCRIPTION
`fn:idref($arg as xs:string*, $node as node()) as node()*`	2.0	
`fn:innermost($nodes as node()*) as node()*`	2.0	Returns every node within the input sequence that is not an ancestor of another member of the input sequence.
`fn:in-scope-prefixes($element as element()) as xs:string*`	2.0	Returns the prefixes of the in-scope namespaces for an element node.
`fn:lang($testlang as xs:string?) as xs:boolean`	2.0	Tests whether the language of `$node`, as specified by `xml:lang` attributes, is the same as, or is a sublanguage of, the language specified by `$testlang`.
`fn:lang($testlang as xs:string?, $node as node()) as xs:boolean`	1.0	
`fn:local-name($arg as node()?) as xs:string`	1.0	Returns the local part of the name of `$arg` as an `xs:string` that is either the zero-length string, or has the lexical form of an `xs:NCName`.
`fn:local-name() as xs:string`	1.0	
`fn:local-name-from-QName($arg as xs:QName?) as xs:NCName?`	2.0	Returns the local part of the supplied `QName`.
`fn:name($arg as node()?) as xs:string`	1.0	Returns the name of a node, as an `xs:string` that is either the zero-length string, or has the lexical form of an `xs:QName`.
`fn:name() as xs:string`	1.0	
`fn:namespace-uri($arg as node()?) as xs:anyURI`	1.0	Returns the namespace URI part of the name of `$arg`, as an `xs:anyURI` value.
`fn:namespace-uri() as xs:anyURI`	1.0	
`fn:namespace-uri-for-prefix ($prefix as xs:string?, $element as element()) as xs:anyURI?`	2.0	Returns the namespace URI of one of the in-scope namespaces for `$element`, identified by its namespace prefix.
`fn:namespace-uri-from-QName($arg as xs:QName?) as xs:anyURI?`	2.0	Returns the namespace URI part of the supplied QName.

FUNCTION NAME AND SIGNATURE	V	DESCRIPTION
`fn:nilled($arg as node()?) as xs:boolean?`	2.0	Returns true for an element that is *nilled*; that is, for an element with `xsi:nilled="true"`.
`fn:node-name($arg as node()?) as xs:QName?`	2.0	Returns the name of a node, as an `xs:QName`.
`fn:node-name() as xs:QName?`	3.0	
`fn:outermost($nodes as node()*) as node()*`	2.0	Returns every node within the input sequence that has no ancestor that is itself a member of the input sequence.
`fn:path($arg as node()?) as xs:string?`	3.0	Returns a path expression that can be used to select the supplied node relative to the root of its containing document.
`fn:path() as xs:string?`	3.0	
`fn:root($arg as node()?) as node()?`	2.0	Returns the root of the tree to which `$arg` belongs. This will usually, but not necessarily, be a document node.
`fn:root() as node()`	2.0	
`fn:static-base-uri() as xs:anyURI?`	2.0	Returns the value of the Base URI property from the static context.

Functions that Operate on QNames

A QName is a *qualified name*: a name that has an optional prefix associated with an XML namespace.

FUNCTION NAME AND SIGNATURE	V	DESCRIPTION
`fn:prefix-from-QName($arg as xs:QName?) as xs:NCName?`	2.0	Returns the prefix component of the supplied QName.
`fn:QName($paramURI as xs:string?, $paramQName as xs:string) as xs:QName`	2.0	Constructs an `xs:QName` value given a namespace URI and a lexical QName.
`fn:resolve-QName($qname as xs:string?, $element as element()) as xs:QName?`	2.0	Returns an `xs:QName` value (that is, an expanded-QName) by taking an `xs:string` that has the lexical form of an `xs:QName` (a string in the form “prefix:local-name” or “local-name”), and resolving it using the in-scope namespaces for a given element.

Functions on Sequences

FUNCTION NAME AND SIGNATURE	V	DESCRIPTION
`fn:count($arg as item()*) as xs:integer`	1.0	Returns the number of items in a sequence.
`fn:distinct-values($arg as xs:anyAtomicType*) as xs:anyAtomicType*`	2.0	Returns the values that appear in a sequence, with duplicates eliminated. Also available in some XPath 1.0 implementations.
`fn:distinct-values($arg as xs:anyAtomicType*, $collation as xs:string) as xs:anyAtomicType*`	2.0	
`fn:head($arg as item()*) as item()?`	3.0	Returns the first item in a sequence.
`fn:insert-before($target as item()*, $position as xs:integer, $inserts as item()*) as item()*`	2.0	Returns a new sequence made by inserting an item or a sequence of items at a given position within an existing sequence.
`fn:last() as xs:integer`	1.0	Returns the context size from the dynamic context.
`fn:map-pairs($f as function(item(), item()) as item()*, $seq1 as item()*, $seq2 as item()*) as item()*`	3.0	Applies the function item `$f` to successive pairs of items taken one from `$seq1` and one from `$seq2`, returning the concatenation of the resulting sequences in order.
`fn:one-or-more($arg as item()*) as item()+`	2.0	Returns `$arg` if it contains one or more items. Otherwise, raises an error.
`fn:position() as xs:integer`	1.0	Returns the context position from the dynamic context.
`fn:remove($target as item()*, $position as xs:integer) as item()*`	2.0	Returns a new sequence containing all the items of `$target`, except the item at position `$position`.
`fn:reverse($arg as item()*) as item()*`	2.0	Returns a new sequence with the items in the reverse order.
`fn:subsequence($sourceSeq as item()*, $startingLoc as xs:double) as item()*`	2.0	Returns the contiguous sequence of items in the value of `$sourceSeq` beginning at the position indicated by the value of `$startingLoc`, and continuing for the number of items indicated by the value of `$length`.

FUNCTION NAME AND SIGNATURE	V	DESCRIPTION
`fn:subsequence($sourceSeq as item()*, $startingLoc as xs:double, $length as xs:double) as item()*`	2.0	
`fn:tail($arg as item()*) as item()*`	3.0	Returns all but the first item in a sequence.
`fn:unordered($sourceSeq as item()*) as item()*`	2.0	Returns the items of `$sourceSeq` in an implementation-dependent order.
`fn:zero-or-one($arg as item()*) as item()?`	2.0	Returns `$arg` if it contains zero or one items. Otherwise, raises an error.

Functions that Operate on Strings and URIs

A *string* is just a sequence of zero or more characters. A *URI*, or *Uniform Resource Identifier*, is the more general name for URLs or web addresses. URIs and their more modern international counterparts, IRIs, are a separate type from strings, although you can convert between them.

Most string operations can also take a URI identifying a collation. A *collation* is a system-specific object that says how to sort characters: whether upper and lower case characters are considered different; whether accented characters like é or ø sort before, together with, or after their unaccented counterparts; and where letters like æ and œ fit into the alphabet, as all these details vary from culture to culture and in some cases depending on purpose.

FUNCTION NAME AND SIGNATURE	V	DESCRIPTION
`fn:analyze-string($input as xs:string?, $pattern as xs:string) as element(fn:analyze-string-result)`	3.0	Analyzes a string using a regular expression, returning an XML structure that identifies which parts of the input string matched or failed to match the regular expression. In the case of matched substrings, determines which substrings matched each capturing group in the regular expression.
`fn:analyze-string($input as xs:string?, $pattern as xs:string, $flags as xs:string) as element (fn:analyze-string-result)`	3.0	
`fn:codepoint-equal($comparand1 as xs:string?, $comparand2 as xs:string?) as xs:boolean?`	2.0	Returns true if two strings are equal, considered codepoint-by-codepoint.

continues

(continued)

FUNCTION NAME AND SIGNATURE	V	DESCRIPTION
fn:codepoints-to-string ($arg as xs:integer*) as xs:string	2.0	Creates an xs:string from a sequence of codepoints expressed as integers.
fn:compare($comparand1 as xs:string?, $comparand2 as xs:string?) as xs:integer?	2.0	Returns -1, 0, or 1, depending on whether $comparand1 collates before, equal to, or after $comparand2 according to the rules of a selected collation.
fn:compare($comparand1 as xs:string?, $comparand2 as xs:string?, $collation as xs:string) as xs:integer?	2.0	
fn:concat($arg1 as xs:anyAtomicType?, $arg2 as xs:anyAtomicType?, ...) as xs:string	1.0	Returns a new string made by joining together all the strings given as arguments. See also string-join().
fn:contains($arg1 as xs:string?, $arg2 as xs:string?) as xs:boolean	1.0	Returns true if the string $arg1 contains $arg2 as a substring, taking collations into account.
fn:contains($arg1 as xs:string?, $arg2 as xs:string?, $collation as xs:string) as xs:boolean	1.0	
fn:encode-for-uri($uri-part as xs:string?) as xs:string	2.0	Encodes reserved characters in a string that is intended to be used in the path segment of a URI.
fn:ends-with($arg1 as xs:string?, $arg2 as xs:string?) as xs:boolean	2.0	Returns true if the string $arg1 contains $arg2 as a trailing substring, taking collations into account.
fn:ends-with($arg1 as xs:string?, $arg2 as xs:string?, $collation as xs:string) as xs:boolean	2.0	
fn:escape-html-uri($uri as xs:string?) as xs:string	2.0	Escapes a URI in the same way that HTML user agents handle attribute values expected to contain URIs.
fn:format-integer($value as xs:integer?, $picture as xs:string) as xs:string	3.0	Converts an integer to a string representation according to a given picture string (that is, a format), using the conventions of a given natural language if specified.

FUNCTION NAME AND SIGNATURE	V	DESCRIPTION
`fn:format-integer($value as xs:integer?, $picture as xs:string, $language as xs:string) as xs:string`	3.0	
`fn:format-number($value as numeric?, $picture as xs:string) as xs:string`	2.0	Converts a number to a string representation according to a given picture string (that is, a format), using the conventions of a given natural language if specified (originally only in XSLT).
`fn:format-number($value as numeric?, $picture as xs:string, $decimal-format-name as xs:string) as xs:string`	3.0	
`fn:iri-to-uri($iri as xs:string?) as xs:string`	2.0	Converts a string containing an IRI into a URI according to the rules of IETF RFC 3987, the specification for Internationalized Resource Identifiers (IRIs). See `http://www.ietf.org/rfc/rfc3987.txt`
`fn:lower-case($arg as xs:string?) as xs:string`	2.0	Converts a string to lowercase.
`fn:matches($input as xs:string?, $pattern as xs:string) as xs:boolean`	2.0	True if the supplied string matches a given regular expression.
`fn:matches($input as xs:string?, $pattern as xs:string, $flags as xs:string) as xs:boolean`	2.0	
`fn:normalize-space($arg as xs:string?) as xs:string`	1.0	Returns the value of `$arg` with leading and trailing whitespace removed, and sequences of internal whitespace reduced to a single space character.
`fn:normalize-space() as xs:string`	1.0	
`fn:normalize-unicode($arg as xs:string?) as xs:string`	2.0	Returns the value of `$arg` after applying Unicode normalization.
`fn:normalize-unicode($arg as xs:string?, $normalizationForm as xs:string) as xs:string`	2.0	

continues

(continued)

FUNCTION NAME AND SIGNATURE	V	DESCRIPTION
`fn:replace($input as xs:string?, $pattern as xs:string, $replacement as xs:string) as xs:string`	2.0	Returns a string produced from the input string by replacing any substrings that match a given regular expression with a supplied replacement string.
`fn:replace($input as xs:string?, $pattern as xs:string, $replacement as xs:string, $flags as xs:string) as xs:string`	2.0	
`fn:resolve-uri($relative as xs:string?) as xs:anyURI?`	2.0	Resolves a relative IRI reference against an absolute IRI. An IRI is an Internationalized version of a URI; the function name has "`uri`" in it because it predates the IRI specification.
`fn:resolve-uri($relative as xs:string?, $base as xs:string) as xs:anyURI?`	2.0	
`fn:starts-with($arg1 as xs:string?, $arg2 as xs:string?) as xs:boolean`	1.0	Returns true if the string `$arg1` contains `$arg2` as a leading substring, taking collations into account.
`fn:starts-with($arg1 as xs:string?, $arg2 as xs:string?, $collation as xs:string) as xs:boolean`	1.0	
`fn:string($arg as item()?) as xs:string`	1.0	Constructs a new string.
`fn:string() as xs:string`	1.0	
`fn:string-join($arg1 as xs:string*, $arg2 as xs:string) as xs:string`	2.0	Returns a single new string made by joining the given strings together, but putting `$arg2` (if given) between the strings.
`fn:string-join($arg1 as xs:string*) as xs:string`	3.0	
`fn:string-length($arg as xs:string?) as xs:integer`	1.0	Returns the number of characters in a given string.
`fn:string-length() as xs:integer`	1.0	
`fn:string-to-codepoints($arg as xs:string?) as xs:integer*`	2.0	Returns the sequence of integer codepoints corresponding to each character in turn in the given string.

FUNCTION NAME AND SIGNATURE	V	DESCRIPTION
fn:substring-after($arg1 as xs:string?, $arg2 as xs:string?) as xs:string	1.0	Returns the part of $arg1 that follows the first occurrence of $arg2, taking collations into account.
fn:substring-after($arg1 as xs:string?, $arg2 as xs:string?, $collation as xs:string) as xs:string	2.0	
fn:substring-before($arg1 as xs:string?, $arg2 as xs:string?) as xs:string	1.0	Returns the part of $arg1 that precedes the first occurrence of $arg2, taking collations into account.
fn:substring-before($arg1 as xs:string?, $arg2 as xs:string?, $collation as xs:string) as xs:string	2.0	
fn:substring($sourceString as xs:string?, $start as xs:double) as xs:string	1.0	Returns the portion of the value of $sourceString, beginning at the position indicated by the value of $start and continuing for the number of characters indicated by the value of $length. The first character is numbered one, not zero.
fn:substring($sourceString as xs:string?, $start as xs:double, $length as xs:double) as xs:string	1.0	
fn:tokenize($input as xs:string?, $pattern as xs:string) as xs:string*	2.0	Returns a sequence of strings constructed by splitting the input wherever a separator is found; the separator is any substring that matches a given regular expression.
fn:tokenize($input as xs:string?, $pattern as xs:string, $flags as xs:string) as xs:string*	2.0	
fn:translate($arg as xs:string?, $mapString as xs:string, $transString as xs:string) as xs:string	1.0	Returns the value of $arg modified by replacing every character in $mapString with the corresponding character in $transString, or deleting the character if $mapString is longer than $transString.
fn:upper-case($arg as xs:string?) as xs:string	2.0	Converts a string to uppercase.

Functions to Construct Objects by XSD Type

These functions construct objects of the named types. You may need to bind the `xs` namespace prefix to the URI `http://www.w3.org/2001/XMLSchema` (this is already done for you in XQuery).

FUNCTION NAME AND SIGNATURE	V	DESCRIPTION
`xs:anyURI($arg as xs:anyAtomicType?) as xs:anyURI?`	2.0	Constructs a new object of XML Schema type `xs:anyURI`.
`xs:base64Binary($arg as xs:anyAtomicType?) as xs:base64Binary?`	2.0	Constructs a new object of XML Schema type `xs:base64Binary`.
`xs:boolean($arg as xs:anyAtomicType?) as xs:boolean?`	2.0	Constructs a new object of XML Schema type `xs:boolean`.
`xs:byte($arg as xs:anyAtomicType?) as xs:byte?`	2.0	Constructs a new object of XML Schema type `xs:byte`.
`xs:date($arg as xs:anyAtomicType?) as xs:date?`	2.0	Constructs a new object of XML Schema type `xs:date`.
`xs:dateTime($arg as xs:anyAtomicType?) as xs:dateTime?`	2.0	Constructs a new object of XML Schema type `xs:dateTime`.
`xs:dateTimeStamp($arg as xs:anyAtomicType?) as xs:dateTimeStamp?`	3.0	Constructs a new object of XML Schema type `xs:dateTimeStamp`.
`xs:dayTimeDuration($arg as xs:anyAtomicType?) as xs:dayTimeDuration?`	2.0	Constructs a new object of XML Schema type `xs:dayTimeDuration`.
`xs:decimal($arg as xs:anyAtomicType?) as xs:decimal?`	2.0	Constructs a new object of XML Schema type `xs:decimal`.
`xs:double($arg as xs:anyAtomicType?) as xs:double?`	2.0	Constructs a new object of XML Schema type `xs:double`.
`xs:duration($arg as xs:anyAtomicType?) as xs:duration?`	2.0	Constructs a new object of XML Schema type `xs:duration`.
`xs:ENTITY($arg as xs:anyAtomicType?) as xs:ENTITY?`	2.0	Constructs a new object of XML Schema type `xs:ENTITY`.
`xs:float($arg as xs:anyAtomicType?) as xs:float?`	2.0	Constructs a new object of XML Schema type `xs:float`.
`xs:gDay($arg as xs:anyAtomicType?) as xs:gDay?`	2.0	Constructs a new object of XML Schema type `xs:gDay`.
`xs:gMonth($arg as xs:anyAtomicType?) as xs:gMonth?`	2.0	Constructs a new object of XML Schema type `xs:gMonth`.

FUNCTION NAME AND SIGNATURE	V	DESCRIPTION
xs:gMonthDay($arg as xs:anyAtomicType?) as xs:gMonthDay?	2.0	Constructs a new object of XML Schema type xs:gMonthDay.
xs:gYear($arg as xs:anyAtomicType?) as xs:gYear?	2.0	Constructs a new object of XML Schema type xs:gYear.
xs:gYearMonth($arg as xs: anyAtomicType?) as xs:gYearMonth?	2.0	Constructs a new object of XML Schema type xs:gYearMonth.
xs:hexBinary($arg as xs:anyAtomicType?) as xs:hexBinary?	2.0	Constructs a new object of XML Schema type xs:hexBinary.
xs:ID($arg as xs:anyAtomicType?) as xs:ID?	2.0	Constructs a new object of XML Schema type xs:ID.
xs:IDREF($arg as xs:anyAtomicType?) as xs:IDREF?	2.0	Constructs a new object of XML Schema type xs:IDREF.
xs:int($arg as xs:anyAtomicType?) as xs:int?	2.0	Constructs a new object of XML Schema type xs:int.
xs:integer($arg as xs:anyAtomicType?) as xs:integer?	2.0	Constructs a new object of XML Schema type xs:integer.
xs:language($arg as xs:anyAtomicType?) as xs:language?	2.0	Constructs a new object of XML Schema type xs:language.
xs:long($arg as xs:anyAtomicType?) as xs:long?	2.0	Constructs a new object of XML Schema type xs:long.
xs:Name($arg as xs:anyAtomicType?) as xs:Name?	2.0	Constructs a new object of XML Schema type xs:Name.
xs:NCName($arg as xs:anyAtomicType?) as xs:NCName?	2.0	Constructs a new object of XML Schema type xs:NCName.
xs:negativeInteger($arg as xs: anyAtomicType?) as xs:negativeInteger?	2.0	Constructs a new object of XML Schema type xs:negativeInteger.
xs:NMTOKEN($arg as xs:anyAtomicType?) as xs:NMTOKEN?	2.0	Constructs a new object of XML Schema type xs:NMTOKEN.
xs:nonNegativeInteger ($arg as xs:anyAtomicType?) as xs:nonNegativeInteger?	2.0	Constructs a new object of XML Schema type xs:nonNegativeInteger.
xs:nonPositiveInteger ($arg as xs:anyAtomicType?) as xs:nonPositiveInteger?	2.0	Constructs a new object of XML Schema type xs:nonPositiveInteger.

continues

(continued)

FUNCTION NAME AND SIGNATURE	V	DESCRIPTION
`xs:normalizedString($arg as xs:anyAtomicType?) as xs:normalizedString?`	2.0	Constructs a new object of XML Schema type `xs:normalizedString`.
`xs:positiveInteger($arg as xs:anyAtomicType?) as xs:positiveInteger?`	2.0	Constructs a new object of XML Schema type `xs:positiveInteger`.
`xs:QName($arg as xs:anyAtomicType) as xs:QName?`	2.0	Constructs a new object of XML Schema type `xs:QName`.
`xs:short($arg as xs:anyAtomicType?) as xs:short?`	2.0	Constructs a new object of XML Schema type `xs:short`.
`xs:string($arg as xs:anyAtomicType?) as xs:string?`	2.0	Constructs a new object of XML Schema type `xs:string`.
`xs:time($arg as xs:anyAtomicType?) as xs:time?`	2.0	Constructs a new object of XML Schema type `xs:time`.
`xs:token($arg as xs:anyAtomicType?) as xs:token?`	2.0	Constructs a new object of XML Schema type `xs:token`.
`xs:unsignedByte($arg as xs:anyAtomicType?) as xs:unsignedByte?`	2.0	Constructs a new object of XML Schema type `xs:unsignedByte`.
`xs:unsignedInt($arg as xs:anyAtomicType?) as xs:unsignedInt?`	2.0	Constructs a new object of XML Schema type `xs:unsignedInt`.
`xs:unsignedLong($arg as xs:anyAtomicType?) as xs:unsignedLong?`	2.0	Constructs a new object of XML Schema type `xs:unsignedLong`.
`xs:unsignedShort($arg as xs:anyAtomicType?) as xs:unsignedShort?`	2.0	Constructs a new object of XML Schema type `xs:unsignedShort`.
`xs:untypedAtomic($arg as xs:anyAtomicType?) as xs:untypedAtomic?`	2.0	Constructs a new object of XML Schema type `xs:untypedAtomic`.
`xs:yearMonthDuration($arg as xs:anyAtomicType?) as xs:yearMonthDuration?`	2.0	Constructs a new object of XML Schema type `xs:yearMonthDuration`.

XML Schema Data Types

This appendix shows the data types available for use in W3C XML Schemas, which were covered in Chapter 5.

THE TREE OF TYPES

The types in XML Schema follow the traditional pattern of a tree found in many other software libraries. For example, in Java the basic type is `Object` from which all other classes ultimately derive. The inheritance tree for the XML Schema types is shown in Figure C-1.

As you can see, all W3C Schema types are based on `anyType`. From here come all the built-in types, or you can create a complex type using restriction and extension, as detailed in Chapter 5.

These types are all grouped under the namespace `http://www.w3.org/2001/XMLSchema`. It is common to use a prefix of `xs` or `xsd` to represent this namespace URI but, because all the types discussed in this appendix fall under this namespace, no prefix is used when specifying them.

Most of the types shown can be constrained, that is they can be limited to hold a narrower range of data than originally intended. This is because the types have a number of *facets*. Each facet allows you to specify a property of the type. For example, the `double` type has a facet called `minInclusive`. This means you can specify the minimum value that can be held by this type. If you specified `0` for this property, your type would not be able to contain any negative values. Another common facet is `pattern`. This allows you to specify a regular expression that the lexical representation (that is, how it's written) must follow. So you could start with a `string` type and specify a pattern of `[A-Z]` to restrict it to uppercase letters from the traditional Latin alphabet.

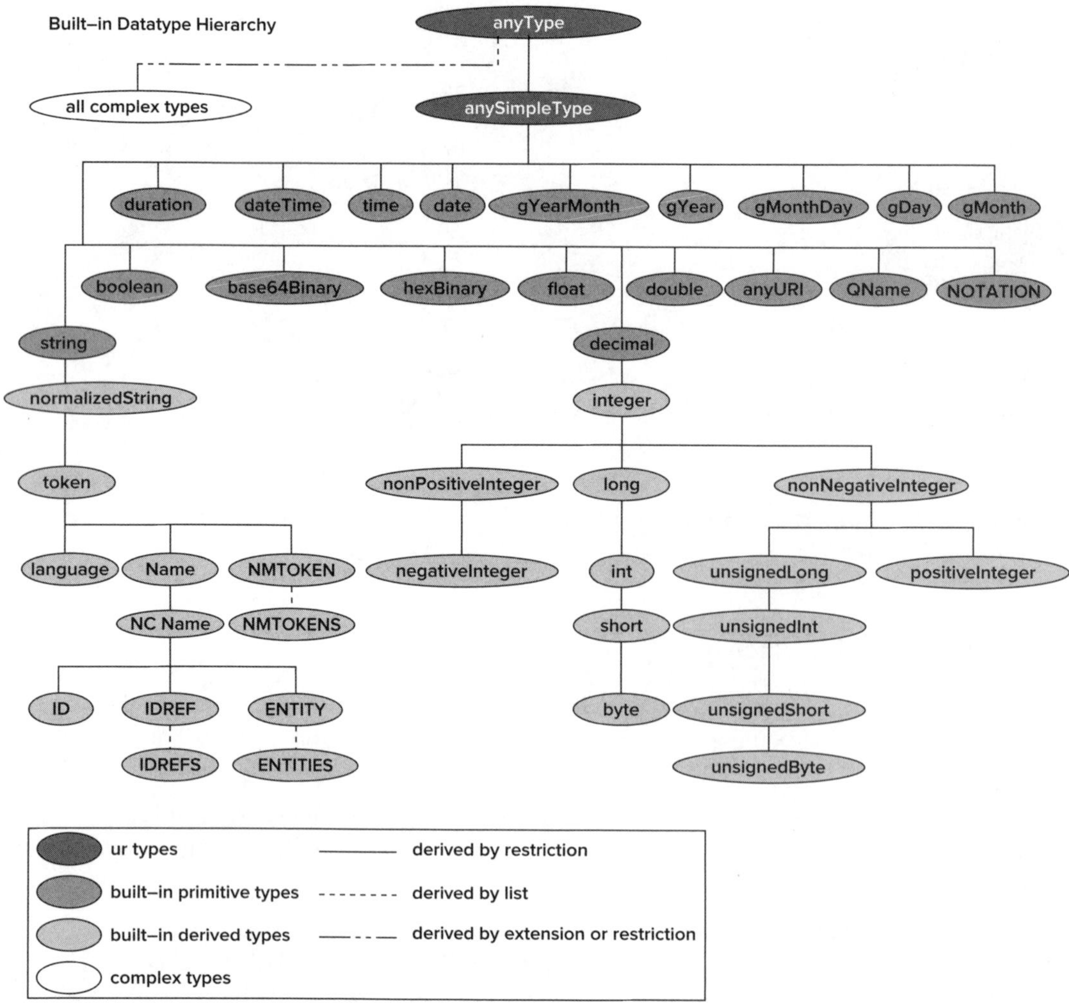

FIGURE C-1

STYLES OF TYPES

The built-in types can have three different styles. They can be *atomic* meaning they cannot be broken down into a simpler type, for example, `double`. They can also be *lists*, in which there are many values of one type. For instance, `NMTOKENS` is a list of `NMTOKEN`. Lastly, they can be *unions*, in which a single item can be of one or more of the simple types. For an example of a union type, take the `maxOccurs` attribute on the `<xs:element>` element in XML Schema. This is used to specify how many times the element may appear at most. It can be either a positive integer, such as 3, or the string `unbounded`. As such it is a union of two types, positive integer and string.

THE BUILT-IN TYPES

Table C-1 gives a summary of most of the built-in types along with any facets that they might have and an example usage.

TABLE C-1: The Primitive Built-In XML Schema Types

TYPE NAME	DESCRIPTION	EXAMPLES	FACETS

`string`	A sequence of Unicode characters. In XML 1.1 only the `null` character (0x0) is forbidden.	abcdefghijk
		αβγδεζηθικ
			`LengthminLength`
			`maxLength`
			`pattern`
			`enumeration`
			`whiteSpace`

`boolean`	Used to represent two-valued logic.	true false	`pattern` `whiteSpace`

`decimal`	A base-10 fixed-point number. There must be at least one digit before the decimal point and it can be positive or negative.	-1.23
		555
		879.657
			`totalDigits`
			`fractionDigits`
			`whiteSpace`
			`enumeration`
			`maxInclusive`
			`maxExclusive`
			`minInclusive`
			`minExclusive`

`float`	A 32-bit floating-point decimal number.	-1e3
		1234.56789E7
		-INF
		NaN
			`pattern`
			`whiteSpace`
			`enumeration`
			`maxInclusive`
			`maxExclusive`
			`minInclusive`
			`minExclusive`

`double`	A 64-bit floating-point decimal number.	-1E5
		1234.56789E11
		1.1e-3
		INF (representing infinity)
		-INF (representing negative infinity)
		NaN (representing Not a Number)
			`pattern`
			`whiteSpace`
			`enumeration`
			`maxInclusive`
			`maxExclusive`
			`minInclusive`
			`minExclusive`

continues

TABLE C-1 *(continued)*

TYPE NAME	DESCRIPTION	EXAMPLES	FACETS

`duration`	A duration of time. It can start with a - if negative. Then the letter `P`. Years, months, and days are specified by `Y`, `M`, and `D`, respectively, and follow the actual number. Similarly, if present, hours, minutes, and seconds are shown with `Y`, `M`, and `S` always preceded by a `T`.	P100Y3M4D represents 100 years, 3 months and 4 days
		-P2D represents a negative duration of 2 days
		P1Y2M3DT4H20M5S represents 1 year, 2 months, 3 days, 4 hours, 20 minutes and 5 seconds
		P1Y1D represents 1 year and 1 day
			`pattern`
			`whiteSpace`
			`enumeration`
			`maxInclusive`
			`maxExclusive`
			`minInclusive`
			`minExclusive`

`dateTime`	Represents a specific instance of time with an optional time zone.	1642-12-25T14:30:20
		1642-12-25T14:30:20.143
		1642-12-25T14:30:20+14:00
			`pattern`
			`whiteSpace`
			`enumeration`
			`maxInclusive`
			`maxExclusive`
			`minInclusive`
			`minExclusive`

`time`	An instant of time. The format is hh:mm:ss.sss with an optional time zone.	13:42:55
		13:42:55.001
		13:42:55.001-05:00
			`pattern`
			`whiteSpace`
			`enumeration`
			`maxInclusive`
			`maxExclusive`
			`minInclusive`
			`minExclusive`

`date`	Represents a specific date with an optional time zone.	1642-12-25
		1642-12-25+13:00
			`pattern`
			`whiteSpace`
			`enumeration`
			`maxInclusive`
			`maxExclusive`
			`minInclusive`
			`minExclusive`

`gYearMonth`	Represents a Gregorian year and month. Shown by YYYY-MM plus an optional time zone.	1962-11 represents November 1962.	`pattern`
			`whiteSpace`
			`enumeration`
			`maxInclusive`
			`maxExclusive`
			`minInclusive`
			`minExclusive`

TYPE NAME	DESCRIPTION	EXAMPLES	FACETS

`gYear`	Represents a Gregorian year. Shown by YYYY plus an optional time zone.	1643	`pattern`
			`whiteSpace`
			`enumeration`
			`maxInclusive`
			`maxExclusive`
			`minInclusive`
			`minExclusive`

`gMonthDay`	A Gregorian month and day. Shown by--MM-DD plus an optional time zone.	--07-04 represents the 4th of July.	`pattern`
			`whiteSpace`
			`enumeration`
			`maxInclusive`
			`maxExclusive`
			`minInclusive`
			`minExclusive`

`gDay`	A day of the month in the Gregorian calendar, such as the fifth of the month. Shown by--DD where DD is the actual day. A time zone can be added.	--25
		--25+12:00
			`pattern`
			`whiteSpace`
			`enumeration`
			`maxInclusive`
			`maxExclusive`
			`minInclusive`
			`minExclusive`

`gMonth`	A month of a Gregorian year. Shown by--MM where MM is the actual month. A time zone can be added.	--11 represents November	`pattern`
			`whiteSpace`
			`enumeration`
			`maxInclusive`
			`maxExclusive`
			`minInclusive`
			`minExclusive`

`hexBinary`	Hexadecimal encoded binary data where each byte needs two characters taken from 0–9 and A–F.	0FB8 represents the base ten integer 4024	`length`
			`minLength`
			`maxLength`
			`pattern`
			`enumeration`
			`whiteSpace`

continues

TABLE C-1 *(continued)*

TYPE NAME	DESCRIPTION	EXAMPLES	FACETS
base64Binary	A sequence of bytes encoded as detailed in RFC 2045 (`http://www.ietf.org/rfc/rfc2045.txt`). This is often used to represent the contents of a binary file within a document, because otherwise a null character would not be allowed.	VGhpcyBpcyBhIGdy ZWF0IGJvb2sh==	length minLength maxLength pattern enumeration whiteSpace
anyURI	Must conform to the URI standard as given in RFC 2396 (`http://www.ietf.org/rfc/rfc2396.txt`).	http://www.wrox.com/	length minLength maxLength pattern enumeration whiteSpace
QName	Represents a fully qualified XML name consisting of a namespace URI and a local name. `QNames` cannot be directly expressed; you need to use a namespace URI to prefix mapping first and then use the *prefix:local name* representation.	<root xmlns:myNS= "http://wrox.com/ ns/example"> <myNS:myElement /> </root>	length minLength maxLength pattern enumeration whiteSpace
NOTATION	`NOTATIONs` cannot be used in XML Schema directly, only their derived types. `NOTATIONs` need to be declared in a DTD and can be used only on attributes. Should be used only in schemas with no target namespace. They are represented as `QNames`. For more information, see Chapter 4.		length minLength maxLength pattern enumeration whiteSpace

Table C-2 shows the built-in data types that are derived from the primitive types in Table C-1.

TABLE C-2: The Derived Built-In XML Schema Types

TYPE NAME	DESCRIPTION	EXAMPLES	FACETS
normalized String	Derived from string. A normalizedString's whitespace will only be the space character (0x20).	Hello, World!	length minLength maxLength pattern enumeration whiteSpace
token	Derived from normalizedString. As well as the only whitespace being the space characters, multiple spaces are truncated into a single space and leading and trailing spaces are removed.	Hello, World!	length minLength maxLength pattern enumeration whiteSpace
language	Derived from token. A natural language identifier as specified by RFC 3066 (http://www.ietf.org/rfc/rfc3066.txt).		length minLength maxLength pattern enumeration whiteSpace
NMTOKEN	Derived from token. Used to represent a name and generally only found on attributes. Unlike the names used in elements and attributes, the NMTOKEN can start with a digit.	1Name	length minLength maxLength pattern enumeration whiteSpace
NMTOKENS	A list type containing a space-separated list of NMTOKENs.	1Name 2Name	length minLength maxLength pattern enumeration whiteSpace
Name	Derived from token. Represents a name in XML. A name can begin with a letter, underscore, or colon and then can contain letters, digits, and characters.	Name1 _Name2 :Name3	length minLength maxLength pattern enumeration whiteSpace

continues

TABLE C-2 *(continued)*

TYPE NAME	DESCRIPTION	EXAMPLES	FACETS
NCName	Derived from Name and short for non-colon name; a name not containing a colon.	Name1 _Name2	length minLength maxLength pattern enumeration whiteSpace
ID	Derived from NCName. An ID has the same format as an NCName but they are used only on attributes and must be unique within the XML document.	ID1 _ID2	length minLength maxLength pattern enumeration whiteSpace
IDREF	Derived from NCName. Takes the same form as ID but refers to an ID within a document so it can appear more than once. Used only on attributes.	ID1 _ID2	length minLength maxLength pattern enumeration whiteSpace
IDREFS	A list type derived from NCName. IDREFS is a space-separated list of IDREF.	ID1 _ID2	length minLength maxLength pattern enumeration whiteSpace
ENTITY	Derived from NCName. Represents an unparsed entity declared in a DTD. Used only on attributes.	nbsp	length minLength maxLength pattern enumeration whiteSpace
ENTITIES	A list type derived from NCName. A space-separated list of ENTITY.	nbsp eacute	length minLength maxLength pattern enumeration whiteSpace

TYPE NAME	DESCRIPTION	EXAMPLES	FACETS

`integer`	Derived from `decimal` but with a `fractionDigits` equal to zero.	`123456789`	`totalDigits`
			`fractionDigits`
			`pattern`
			`whiteSpace`
			`enumeration`
			`maxInclusive`
			`maxExclusive`
			`minInclusive`
			`minExclusive`

`nonPositive Integer`	Derived from `integer`. An integer that is negative or zero.	`0`
		`-1`
			`totalDigits`
			`fractionDigits`
			`pattern`
			`whiteSpace`
			`enumeration`
			`maxInclusive`
			`maxExclusive`
			`minInclusive`
			`minExclusive`

`negative Integer`	Derived from `nonPostiveInteger`. An integer that is less than zero.	`-1`	`totalDigits`
			`fractionDigits`
			`pattern`
			`whiteSpace`
			`enumeration`
			`maxInclusive`
			`maxExclusive`
			`minInclusive`
			`minExclusive`

`long`	Derived from `integer`. An integer between 9223372036854775807 and −9223372036854775808.	`-92233720368`
		`54775808`
			`totalDigits`
			`fractionDigits`
			`pattern`
			`whiteSpace`
			`enumeration`
			`maxInclusive`
			`maxExclusive`
			`minInclusive`
			`minExclusive`

continues

TABLE C-2 *(continued)*

TYPE NAME	DESCRIPTION	EXAMPLES	FACETS

`int`	Derived from `long`. An integer between 2147483647 and –2147483648.	`2147483647`	`totalDigits`
			`fractionDigits`
			`pattern`
			`whiteSpace`
			`enumeration`
			`maxInclusive`
			`maxExclusive`
			`minInclusive`
			`minExclusive`

`short`	Derived from `int`. An integer between 32767 and –32768. Cannot have a preceding plus sign or leading zeros.	`325`	`totalDigits`
			`fractionDigits`
			`pattern`
			`whiteSpace`
			`enumeration`
			`maxInclusive`
			`maxExclusive`
			`minInclusive`
			`minExclusive`

`byte`	A signed 8-bit integer between –128 and 127. Cannot have a preceding plus sign or leading zeros.	`-16`
		`23`
			`totalDigits`
			`fractionDigits`
			`pattern`
			`whiteSpace`
			`enumeration`
			`maxInclusive`
			`maxExclusive`
			`minInclusive`
			`minExclusive`

`nonNegative Integer`	Derived from `integer`. An integer greater or equal to zero.	`0`
		`123456789`
			`totalDigits`
			`fractionDigits`
			`pattern`
			`whiteSpace`
			`enumeration`
			`maxInclusive`
			`maxExclusive`
			`minInclusive`
			`minExclusive`

TYPE NAME	DESCRIPTION	EXAMPLES	FACETS
unsignedLong	Derived from nonNegativeInteger. An integer between 0 and 18446744073709551615 inclusive.	0 184467440737 09551615	totalDigits fractionDigits pattern whiteSpace enumeration maxInclusive maxExclusive minInclusive minExclusive
unsignedInt	Derived from unsignedLong. An integer between 0 and 4294967295 inclusive.	0 4294967295	totalDigits fractionDigits pattern whiteSpace enumeration maxInclusive maxExclusive minInclusive minExclusive
unsignedShort	Derived from unsigned int. An integer between 0 and 65535 inclusive. Leading zeros are prohibited.	0 65535	totalDigits fractionDigits pattern whiteSpace enumeration maxInclusive maxExclusive minInclusive minExclusive
unsignedByte	Derived from unsignedShort. An integer between 0 and 255 inclusive. Leading zeros are prohibited.	0 255	totalDigits fractionDigits pattern whiteSpace enumeration maxInclusive maxExclusive minInclusive minExclusive

continues

TABLE C-2 *(continued)*

TYPE NAME	DESCRIPTION	EXAMPLES	FACETS
positive Integer	Derived from nonNegativeInteger. An integer greater than zero.	1 +1000 001000	totalDigits fractionDigits pattern whiteSpace enumeration maxInclusive maxExclusive minInclusive minExclusive

FACETS

Table C-3 describes how each facet can be used to constrain a type.

TABLE C-3: XML Schema Type Facets

FACET NAME	DESCRIPTION	EXAMPLE
length	The exact number of characters, bytes, or items in a list.	<restriction base="string"><length value="6" /></restriction> means a string of exactly six characters.
minLength	The minimum number of characters, bytes, or items in a list.	<restriction base="anyURI"><minLength value="20" /></restriction> means http://www.wrox.com would fail but http://www.wrox.com/ would pass.
maxLength	The maximum number of characters, bytes, or items in a list.	<restriction base="anyURI"><maxLength value="19" /></restriction> means http://www.wrox.com/ would fail but http://www.wrox .com would pass.

FACET NAME	DESCRIPTION	EXAMPLE
pattern	A regular expression that limits what the value can hold.	<restiction base="string"><pattern value="[0-9]{5}(-[0-9]{4})?" /></restriction> limits a string to a representation of a U.S. postal code (ZIP). The expression means five digits followed by an optional group that starts with a hyphen and is followed by four digits.
enumeration	Restricts the value by specifying a limited number of specific values.	<restriction base="gMonthDay"> <enumeration value="--07–04"/><enumeration value="--12-25"/></restriction> limits a gMonthDay to one of July 4th or December 25th.
whiteSpace	How whitespace is treated. This can take one of three values. preserve: whitespace is left alone. replace: All instances of whitespace such as tab (#x9), linefeed (#xA), and carriage return (#xD) are replaced with a space (#x20). collapse: Like replace but then multiple contiguous spaces are replaced by a single space and any leading and trailing spaces are removed.	preserve replace collapse
maxExclusive	The exclusive upper bound of a numeric data type.	<restriction base="integer"> <maxExclusive value="101" /> </restriction> restricts an integer to 100 or less.
maxInclusive	The inclusive upper bound of a numeric data type.	<restriction base="integer"> <maxInclusive value="100" /> </restriction> restricts an integer to 100 or less.

continues

TABLE C-3 *(continued)*

FACET NAME	DESCRIPTION	EXAMPLE
`minExclusive`	The exclusive lower bound of a numeric data type.	`<restriction base="integer"> <minExclusive value="0" /> </restriction>` restricts an integer to 1 or more.
`minInclusive`	The inclusive lower bound of a numeric data type.	`<restriction base="integer"> <minInclusive value="1" /> </restriction>` restricts an integer to 1 or more.
`totalDigits`	A positive integer specifying the maximum number of total digits used to represent a data type derived from decimal.	`<restriction base="integer"> <totalDigits value="6" /> </restriction>` restricts an integer to between –999999 and 999999.
`fractionDigits`	A positive integer specifying the maximum number of digits that can appear after the decimal point in a type derived from decimal.	`<restriction base="decimal"> <fractionDigits value="2" /> </restriction>` means that 1.23 is allowed but not 1.234.

For the original specifications on XML Schema data types, which contain more information and where the definitions are more rigorous, see `http://www.w3.org/TR/xmlschema-1/` and `http://www.w3.org/TR/xmlschema-2/`.

INDEX

B

C

J

K

L

T

U

V

W

X-Z